LAW'S DOCUMENTS

LAW'S DOCUMENTS

AUTHORITY, MATERIALITY, AESTHETICS

Edited by Katherine Biber, Trish Luker and Priya Vaughan

Routledge
Taylor & Francis Group
LONDON AND NEW YORK

First published 2022
by Routledge
605 Third Avenue, New York, NY 10158

and by Routledge
4 Park Square, Milton Park, Abingdon, Oxon, OX14 4RN

A GlassHouse book

Routledge is an imprint of the Taylor & Francis Group, an informa business

Library of Congress Cataloging-in-Publication Data
A catalog record for this title has been requested

ISBN: 9780367441517 (hbk)
ISBN: 9781032162218 (pbk)
ISBN: 9781003247593 (ebk)

DOI: 10.4324/9781003247593

Typeset in Bembo
by Deanta Global Publishing Services, Chennai, India

Contents

Acknowledgements

The editors wish to acknowledge the Australian Research Council which supported the scholarship that has culminated in this book through a Discovery Project grant (DP 160100414).

One of the key events that gave rise to this collection was a symposium held at the University of Technology Sydney (UTS), and we acknowledge the contributors and participants for their rigorous scholarship and their commitment to interdisciplinary dialogue and listening: Alana Piper, Andy Kaladelfos, Anne Burdick, Bonnie Mak, Carolyn McKay, Charlotte Epstein, Daniel Joyce, Diane Kirkby, Donna West Brett, Hilary Yerbury, Isabella Alexander, Jacqueline Lorber-Kasunic, Jesse Adams Stein, Kate Sweetapple, Katherine Bode, Laila Ellmoos, Lars Rutz, Lauren Gray, Maryanne Dever, Mayee Warren, Nerida Campbell, Nicole Moore, Paul Turnbull, Rachel Bolton, Sara Dehm and Shaunnagh Dorsett.

At UTS Law, we have a collegial environment. In particular we wish to thank Lesley Hitchens, Isabel Karpin, Jenni Millbank, Nikki Lengkeek and Nic Connolly who, in different ways, supported this work.

During the project we received excellent research assistance from Divya Murthy, Jack Fogl and Priya Vaughan.

In the making of associated podcasts, we had expert guidance from UTS Impact Studios which produces HistoryLab, and in particular we thank Emma Lancaster, Tamson Pietsch and Olivia Rosenman.

We thank Magabala Books for permitting us to reproduce the powerful poetry of Alison Whittaker.

We acknowledge Carey Young and Paula Cooper Gallery for permitting us to reproduce a large body of artwork by Carey Young.

We are grateful to Colin Perrin at Routledge for supporting this collection.

Contributor biographies

Katherine Biber is a legal scholar, historian and criminologist. Her work explores evidence in various contexts: visual evidence, documentary evidence, criminal evidence, histories of evidence. Her most recent book is *In Crime's Archive: The Cultural Afterlife of Evidence* (2019, Routledge). She is currently writing a legal history of Australia's last outlaw, Jimmy Governor.

Donna West Brett is Associate Professor and Chair of Art History at the University of Sydney. She is author of *Photography and Place: Seeing and Not Seeing Germany after 1945* (Routledge, 2016) and co-editor with Natalya Lusty, *Photography and Ontology: Unsettling Images* (Routledge, 2019), which was awarded the 2020 Art Association of Australia and NZ Best Anthology Book Prize. Brett is a recipient of the 2017 Australian Academy of the Humanities, Ernst and Rosemarie Keller Award, Research Leader for the Photographic Cultures Research Group and Editorial Member for the Visual Culture and German Contexts Series, Bloomsbury.

Anne Burdick is a Professor of Visual Communication Design and Co-Director of the Knowledge Design Lab in the Faculty of Design, Architecture, and Building at the University of Technology Sydney.

Georgine Clarsen is an honorary Associate Professor of History at the University of Wollongong. Her research interests include race, gender and mobilities, and the ways that Indigenous peoples in Australia have shaped automobility according to their own needs and cultural imperatives.

Sara Dehm is a Senior Lecturer at the Faculty of Law, University of Technology Sydney. She researches and writes on the history and theory of international law's regulation of human mobility and the subjects of migration, with a focus on questions of international administration, knowledge production and changing state regimes of border controls. Her book, *Administering Migration: International Law and the Global Ordering of People*, is forthcoming with Cambridge University Press.

John Curtin Distinguished Professor **Anna Haebich** is a leading Australian historian known for her innovative research in Indigenous histories, performing and visual arts, crime and gender, assimilation, immigration, race and environmental studies. She has received numerous awards and honours. Judges commenting on her book, *Dancing in Shadows: Histories of Nyungar Performance*, shortlisted for the 2019 Prime Minister Literary Awards, wrote that she is 'one of our nation's great interpreters of our collective Indigenous and Australian settler histories. She personifies the spirit of reconciliation, ethical research, commitment, and generosity. *Dancing in Shadows* is a tour de force, as it presents a wonderfully nuanced history of Nyungar performative responses to European invasion, incursions, dispossession, and various other interactions'. Anna is project lead for the ARC-funded project, *Ancestors Words: Nyungar Letter Writing in the Archives 1860–1960*, at Curtin University (Western Australia).

Natalie Harkin is a Narungga woman and activist poet from South Australia. She is a Senior Research Fellow at Flinders University with an interest in decolonising state archives, currently engaging archival-poetic methods to research and document Aboriginal women's domestic service and labour histories in South Australia.

Jessie Hohmann is Associate Professor in the Faculty of Law, University of Technology Sydney (UTS). Her work encompasses the material culture, materiality and objects of international law, human rights and the rights of Indigenous Peoples. Her publications include the groundbreaking *International Law's Objects* (Hohmann and Joyce, eds, 2018). Before joining UTS, Jessie was a senior lecturer at Queen Mary, University of London. She holds degrees from the University of Cambridge, Sydney University, Osgoode Hall (York University) and the University of Guelph.

Joan Kee is Professor in the History of Art at the University of Michigan in Ann Arbor. The author of *Models of Integrity: Art and Law in Post Sixties America* (2019) and the editor of 'Art and Law', a special issue of *Law and Literature* (2022), she is a contributing editor to *Artforum* and an occasional practicing attorney in Detroit.

Anthony Kickett is a Noongar Nation man from south-western West Australia belonging to these clans—Whadjuk, Ballardong, Yuat and Wilman. He grew up at Dryandra Woodlands and Cuballing town, with his Wilman clan in his grandmother's country. Anthony has worked for Indigenous services in Western Australia and New South Wales and for the Queensland government in employment and education. He continued in health and cultural work with the Department of Rural Health, Sydney University, in Broken Hill and is now a Lecturer at Curtin University, Centre for Aboriginal Studies (CAS). He has also contributed to Stolen Generations work and alcohol and drug counselling with Aboriginal service organisations.

Darryl Kickett is a Nyungar-Bibbulmen Elder who grew up near Narrogin, Western Australia. He worked with Aboriginal services for years including in the Australian Parliament and as the head of Land Councils, Aboriginal Health and the Curtin Aboriginal Studies Centre. He was on the State Suicide Prevention Committee and the Telethon Kids Institute Aboriginal Research Committee. In 2013, Darryl was awarded the National NAIDOC Person of the Year Award. He has a BA degree in Social Science. His recent work at Curtin University (Western Australia) includes the Ancestors' Words archives project, returning letters written by ancestors to their descendants. As a Senior Research Fellow in the School of Media, Culture, Arts, and Social Inquiry (MCASI) at Curtin University, Darryl is the project lead for the ARC-funded *Healing Land, Healing People: Novel Nyungar Perspectives* research project.

Marion Kickett is a Noongar woman from the Ballardong language group of south-western Western Australia. She is a highly respected community leader and matriarch in her extended family. She has strong connections with local and national Aboriginal and Torres Strait Islander communities. Marion's background is in nursing. She lectured in Aboriginal Health and Culture for 28 years and completed her PhD on resilience from an Aboriginal perspective. Since 2014 Marion has been the Director of the Centre for Aboriginal Studies (CAS) at Curtin University where she leads a team of 40 academic and professional staff. She provided cultural leadership for Curtin's global flagship Massive Open Online Course (MOOC) on Noongar language and culture.

Jeanine Leane is a Wiradjuri writer, poet and academic from southwest New South Wales. She has published widely in the area of Aboriginal literature, writing otherness and creative non-fiction. Jeanine teaches Creative Writing and Aboriginal Literature at the University of Melbourne and is the recipient of an Australian Research Council (ARC) Fellowship for a project called *Aboriginal Writing: Shaping the Literary and Cultural History of Australia, since 1988* (2014–2018), and a second ARC grant that looks at *Indigenous Storytelling and the Archive* (2020–2024).

Jacqueline Lorber-Kasunic is Associate Professor, Director of Visual Communication as well as Co-Director of the Knowledge Design Lab in the Faculty of Design, Architecture and Building at the University of Technology Sydney.

Trish Luker is a legal scholar based at the Faculty of Law, University of Technology Sydney. Her research interests are located at the intersections of evidence law, legal decision-making and documentary theory and practice. She is an editor of *Australian Feminist Judgments: Writing and Re-Writing Law* (with Heather Douglas, Francesca Bartlett and Rosemary Hunter)

(Hart Publishing, 2014), *The Court as Archive* (with Ann Genovese and Kim Rubenstein) (ANU Press, 2019) and *Evidence and the Archive: Ethics, Aesthetics and Emotion* (with Katherine Biber) (Routledge, 2017).

Bonnie Mak is an associate professor in Information Sciences at the University of Illinois Urbana-Champaign and holds courtesy appointments in History and Medieval Studies. Her work explores information and its practices from antiquity to the twenty-first century. Mak's first book, *How the Page Matters* (2011), investigates the enduring role of the page in the transmission and production of knowledge. More recently, she has experimented with different approaches to the publication of her scholarship, including in the form of cabinets, journal articles, boxes and file cards.

Carolyn McKay is a Senior Lecturer at the University of Sydney Law School (teaching Criminal Law, Civil and Criminal Procedure and Digital Criminology) and Co-Director, Sydney Institute of Criminology. She has been awarded an Australian Research Council DECRA fellowship 2021–2024. One stream of her research focuses on technologies in justice, and she is author of *The Pixelated Prisoner: Prison Video Links, Court 'Appearance' and the Justice Matrix* (2018, Routledge). Her other stream of criminal law and visual criminological research intersects with her visual arts practice to explore a range of criminal justice issues.

Jeannie Morrison is an Elder of the Goreng language group of the Bibbulmen Nation, living in Wadjuk Country (Perth). She is from a well-known family in the Nyungar community. Jeannie has been employed for over 20 years at the Centre for Aboriginal Studies at Curtin University. She is currently a member of the Carrolup Elders Reference Group for the John Curtin Gallery Carrolup Children's Art Collection, representing her mother Maisie Weston (nee Loo). She was previously involved in the Curtin Reconciliation Action Plan. Jeannie has three adult daughters and six grandchildren. She is an emerging artist and writer.

Jesse Adams Stein is a Senior Lecturer and Chancellor's Postdoctoral Research Fellow at the School of Design, University of Technology Sydney. She is a design researcher and an oral historian, and the author of *Hot Metal: Material Culture and Tangible Labour* (Manchester University Press, 2016). In partnership with the National Library of Australia, she established the *Reshaping Australian Manufacturing Oral History Project* in 2017. Stein was recently awarded an Australian Research Council Discovery Early Career Research Fellowship (DECRA 2021) for the project: *Australian Design, Trades and Manufacturing 1945–2007: Connecting Histories.*

Kate Sweetapple is a Professor of Design, Head of School (Design) and Co-Director of the Knowledge Design Lab in the Faculty of Design, Architecture, and Building at the University of Technology Sydney.

Priya Vaughan uses visual art and material culture as a frame through which to explore Australian cultures, experiences, ideologies, identities and histories. Priya is a post-doctoral fellow at the Black Dog Institute, University of New South Wales and a lecturer at the National Art School (NAS).

Anthea Vogl is a Senior Lecturer in law at the University of Technology Sydney. Her research addresses refugee and migration law, focusing on the use of executive power to exclude refugees and noncitizens and intersections between law and narrative in the regulation of migration.

Alison Whittaker is a Gomeroi woman, poet and academic.

Shevaun Wright is an artist and former lawyer who is primarily engaged in an interdisciplinary practice that utilises the contractual medium and the notion of the 'social contract', as well as re-contextualised dialogues as a tool for engaging in institutional legal and artistic critique. Informed by her Aboriginal heritage, she aims to extrapolate feminist and post-colonial critiques of the law and art as a means to access and reveal similarities in their discursive practices.

Since 2002, **Carey Young**'s artistic work across varied media has addressed law as subject and as artistic medium. Recent works explore relations between jurisprudence, materiality, gender and fiction, most particularly with *Palais de Justice* (2017), a video in which Young surreptitiously filmed female judges at Belgium's main courthouse, which seems to portray a judicial system controlled by women. Young's solo exhibitions include Dallas Museum of Art, Migros Museum für Gegenwartskunst (Zurich), Contemporary Art Museum, St. Louis and The Power Plant (Toronto). Group exhibitions include Centre Pompidou, Tate Britain, Walker Art Center (Minneapolis), the New Museum (New York), MoMA/PS1 (New York) and the Venice, Moscow, Sharjah and Busan Biennials. Young's works are held in noted collections including Centre Pompidou and Tate, and she is Associate Professor in Fine Art at the Slade School of Fine Art, UCL.

Part I

What is a document?

Chapter 1

Law's documents

Authority, Materiality, Aesthetics

Katherine Biber, Trish Luker and Priya Vaughan

Introduction

> I am an archive. I am a chapter in a bigger archive. All the women I knew were archives. We are the first archives, before the many arms of the state constructed its fiction.
>
> (Jeanine Leane, Chapter 3)

In their fierce and lyrical dialogue, First Nations poets Natalie Harkin and Jeanine Leane denounce the trauma and pain perpetrated by law's documents. For Indigenous people, legal records and archives are 'time bombs', 'violent collisions of worlds' (Chapter 3). Leane, a Wiradjuri woman, finds a box of papers hidden in her grandmother's bedroom. This discovery unleashes a rage that sends her into the settler colonial archive, where she finds documents representing her loved ones and ancestors, but they are 'unrecognisable': 'I went back and seethed at these effigies; these violent representations are not the women I know'. Together with Harkin, a Narungga woman, she initiates a 'sovereign woman conversation', in which two poets, armed with words, family memories and a lifetime of deep listening, reimagine the meaning and purpose of legal documentation.

Law's Documents represents our effort to capture and re-think law's relationship with the documentary form. In this collection, we bring diverse approaches and methods into dialogue with each other, and with law. We focus on the authority, materiality and aesthetics of legal and other official documents, and examine their circulation, use and interpretation. We seek to challenge what can be understood as a legal document, and we explore the ways that legal documentation might generate harm, violence, pain, trauma and also sometimes acts of liberation and transformation. We trace the document across legal, social, historical and cultural disciplinary spheres globally, and locate moments of cooperation and rupture, intentional and inadvertent. This is not a complete or comprehensive survey of approaches to law's documents, but rather represents the debates and challenges of our current moment. In part, this is shaped by the transition from the analogue to the digital age, and

DOI: 10.4324/9781003247593-2

the disruptions wrought by new technologies. In a different way, this moment is also marked by the urgent need to attend to historical and contemporary injustices; for us, this is reflected in our commitment to examining the ongoing violence of settler colonialism, and the demand by First Nations peoples to be heard and prioritised.

As co-editors, we bring different perspectives, interests and knowledge to this collection, including law, history, anthropology, material culture research, information management, publishing and the visual arts. We have drawn together contributors from these fields, and also from others, including documentary theory, photography, design, artistic and curatorial practice and poetry. Whilst this collection represents a contribution to the field of documentary theory generally, it also makes important interventions in law and justice. *Law's Documents* illuminates the breadth and diversity of documents which proliferate, shape and record contemporary worlds. Some of the key themes that we canvas include the affective, aesthetic, creative and sensory attributes of legal documents; the materiality and immateriality of legal documents; the poetics of legal documents; legal documents and authority; embodiment and disembodiment through documentation; secrecy and destruction as documentary practices; and legal documents in the digital age. This collection challenges the distinctions between the core evidentiary categories—documents, witnesses, real evidence—and demonstrates that they are entangled and mutually reliant. Understood as textual sources of authority, documents are also material sites and aesthetic artefacts. Documents are created, filed and analysed; they record and direct; they command; they denote the passage of time, movement through space, the unfolding of a process; documents contain the residue of an event.

We have organised this collection around the three themes of authority, materiality and aesthetics because this furnishes the reader with a sense of the breadth of influence of documentary practices and ideas. It also points to the fact that documents can be at once powerful and slippery, and their significance and tenacity enable their power to radiate widely.

What is a document?

In law, a 'document' can be anything that includes writing, marks, figures, symbols and perforations; it can include maps, plans, drawings and photographs; and can contain sounds and images. In law, a document is a multimedia artefact. By comparison, a physical object becomes real evidence when its material properties are the focus of factual and legal examination and interpretation. The legal definition of a document is broadly drawn and focuses on the information that rests upon the surface of, or is embedded within, the object designated as a document. It is this information, rather than the material form of the document, that becomes the focus of judicial and other scrutiny.

At the same time, legal theory demonstrates that the history and development of law can be apprehended through acts of documentation and that law's material practices are produced in relationships between documents and other entities (Riles 2006; Vismann 2008; Motha and van Rijswijk 2016; Genovese, Luker, Rubenstein 2019). In her influential book *Files: Law and Media Technology* (2008), Cornelia Vismann demonstrated that the history of the law is written in the acts of documentary processes. Vismann examines in detail the media-technological conditions of files and recording devices in law to illustrate how they produce the separation of law into authority and administration. For Vismann, files contribute to the formation of the three major entities on which law is based: 'truth, state, and subject' (2008, xii).

While documents are conceptualised, and operate, in a distinct manner in law, in other disciplines they are approached differently. In 1951, Suzanne Briet, a librarian at the Bibliothèque Nationale in Paris, famously said that an antelope could be a document, thereby radically changing the way documents were analysed and understood. Her answer to the question 'What is a Document?' has been foundational to the contemporary field of documentary theory (as well as the project resulting in this collection).[1] For Briet, a distinction could be made between an antelope in the wild (being fauna) and one that was confined in a zoo, or taxidermal in a museum, captured audio-visually or described in an encyclopaedia (1951 [2006], 10-11). For Briet, what defined a document was its informational qualities, not its materiality; a document is not confined to writing implement and surface.

In equating a document with evidence, Briet was following an earlier documentary theorist, Paul Otlet (1934), who had also taken an object-oriented approach to documentation. Otlet suggested that it is the process of being informed through observation that defines documents, giving examples including natural objects, artifacts, objects bearing traces of human activity, explanatory models, educational games and works of art (1934, 217). Over 40 years later, on the cusp of the digital information revolution, documentary theorist Michael Buckland (1998) used this framework to address then-contemporary concerns about how to define digital documents. Buckland argued that all documents are objects and that while they must exist in some kind of material form, this need not be limited to printed texts; indeed, a document could be any kind of signifying object. The rapid transition from a knowledge economy based on the medium of paper to a contemporary digital information society has presented real challenges to all fields working with documentary forms. Digital documents are voluminous, ubiquitous, intangible, difficult to authenticate, easy to duplicate and modify, and they generate new questions about what they mean and what they can prove. What we understand as a 'document' now includes a potentially limitless range of digital forms and technological devices for the capture and storage of data.

The approach exemplified by Otlet and Briet has been influential in the humanities where understandings of documentation are not restricted to the textual medium, but rather are recognised as forms of material culture (Cramerotti 2009; Connarty and Lanyon 2006). In anthropology, sociology, cultural studies and information science, documents, and their use, medium, form, classification and circulation, have been examined and found to reveal, reflect and shape human systems of knowledge, political and other ideologies, and aesthetic regimes (see, for example, Manoff 2006; Mak 2011; Gitelman 2014). Here, documents, like other kinds of material culture, are not merely reflections of the socio-cultural sphere in which they are produced, but are also constitutive of this sphere (Miller 2010, 59; Ingold 2011, 6).

Documents are also investigated in relation to record-keeping practices, archivisation, media technology and bureaucratisation (see Gitelman 2014). For example, the legal scholar and anthropologist Annelise Riles writes, 'the ability to create and maintain files is the emblem of modern bureaucracy, part of what Thomas Osborne has called the establishment of the "ethical competence to rule"' (2006, 5). Cultural anthropologists argue that the form, placement and organisation of records produce meaning and value (Ash 1997; Steedman 2002; Ridener 2008; Stoler 2009; Latour 2010; Gupta 2012; Hull 2012; Farge 2013; Weld 2014). In this way, a document becomes an 'artefact', to be subjected to ethnographic analysis and description, bringing a distinctive epistemology, ethics, and aesthetics (Riles 2006). Sometimes the focus is upon the ethnographer scrutinising their own documentary practices; at other times, they examine the 'formal and aesthetic properties of documents', whereby the form of the document requires a rethinking of its informational purpose (Riles 2006, 19). Notably, historians and cultural scholars are exploring the effects of digitisation on the materiality of documents (Mak 2011; Eichhorn 2013; Dever and Morra 2014), and there is a burgeoning interest in the field of digital humanities, where new technologies are transforming research methodologies and communication of ideas.

There are a number of influential scholars who directly tackle questions about what documents *are* and what they *do*. The philosopher Barry Smith has advanced the concept of 'document acts' (2012, [6], [15]). For Smith, there are two categories of document acts. In the first, people use documents in a manner that makes clear they understand them as documents, as opposed to being objects, ephemera or mere paper. Signing a document, stamping it, showing it as a form of identification, displaying it as a licence or certificate or permit; each of these is a document act (2012, [11]). In the second category, and here Smith draws upon the scholarship of the economist Hernando de Soto, documents can inaugurate new states of affairs (Smith 2012, [15]). By doing things with documents, we can change the world (Smith 2012, [5]–[6].). This is both social reality and ontological magic (Smith 2012, [7]).

Documents create systems, institutions, processes, outcomes, lines of authority and of course jobs for the people who fulfil all of these documentary functions. For Smith, documents are 'objects' or 'continuants', and this means that they are more tangible than speech; they are material, and they materialise other phenomena. They survive over time, sometimes they survive their creators, sometimes they require the collaboration of numerous creators, sometimes they are conjoined with other documents; sometimes they 'float free' of their creators and 'enjoy an existence of their own' (Smith 2012, [10]). The economic system, the legal system: these are constructed from documents. Smith writes:

> *by doing things with documents* – whether made of paper and ink or of patterns of blips in computers – we are able to *change the world* by bringing into being new types of ownership relations, of legal accountability, of business organizations, and other creatures of modern economies, including mortgages, stocks, shares, insurance protection, and financial derivatives.
>
> (Smith 2012, [15], italics in original)

Jacques Derrida (1988) also engaged with documentary theory, arguing that most speech acts were inscribed acts, meaning that the speech act needs to be augmented by some form of documentation in order to achieve its transformative function. For example, a marriage, a graduation, a conference, each of these speech acts was able to endure and be socially transformative through associated acts of documentation. The philosopher Maurizio Ferraris (2013) took this approach a step further by arguing that all speech acts are inscribed acts, and that these include inscriptions in our brain. For Ferraris, documentality—the term he coined to refer to the ontology of documents—explains how acts of inscription bring about social objects, not all of which are captured by a narrow definition of 'documents' (Ferraris 2013).

The media scholar Lisa Gitelman (2014, 1) captures the difficulty of defining a document. Documents, for Gitelman, are a 'vernacular genre', 'sprawling and ubiquitous'. Any effort to define or delineate the document ends up being either circular or vague. Documents exist to document; documents are what we treat as documents; 'epistemic objects', 'evidential structures', 'the know-show function' (2014, 1). Following Suzanne Briet, Gitelman says that what makes a thing into a document depends upon context, or framing; here she reminds us of Briet's distinction between an antelope in the wild and one in a zoo (2014, 2–3). Gitelman notes that some items are both things and documents at the same time: a ticket or a receipt, for instance (2014, 3). She accepts that in the digital age, what counts as a thing, and what counts as a document, are harder to grasp, and that our interactions with the digital domain often rely on analogies with the paper age: *documents*, *files*, *folders*, *pages*. For Gitelman, perhaps the best starting point is to consider what makes documents important, namely the way they are 'integral to the ways people think and live' (2014, 4). This includes lives that may be 'undocumented' (2014, 5), and events that might be off-the-record. But it also needs to take account of documents which might be lost, destroyed, secret or fake, which is where the know-show function also starts to crumble.

Gitelman recounts that in the history of documentation, destruction is matched by radical acts of proliferation; she relates the episode of Daniel Ellsberg's copying and leaking of the Pentagon Papers, a massive report which undermined public statements made by US government officials about the true objectives of the Vietnam War. The *History of U.S. Decision-Making Process on Vietnam Policy* was a 47-volume report; Ellsberg took it home gradually, in sections, starting somewhere in the middle. He used the photocopier of a sympathetic friend, sometimes assisted by his young children, making two complete sets, which would ultimately be revealed and extracted in *The New York Times* in June 1971. Gitelman notes that the benign technique he deployed—xerography—was asymmetrically crushed by the legal armoury of charges on his indictment: theft, embezzlement, conspiracy, treason (2014, 88). Gitelman notes that in the legal response to Ellsberg's leaks, there was no reckoning with the Pentagon Papers *as* papers, as documents and as photocopies.

Our collection opens with a chapter from Bonnie Mak, scholar of the history and future of the book whose work, *How the Page Matters* (2011), made an important contribution to understanding how changing technology has affected the reception of visual and written information. In 'In Wood or Word, or, a Gloss on Documents and Documentation in the Humanities' (Chapter 2), Mak illustrates what documents are, and what they do, in the realm of academia, via an experiment in scholarly publishing. Offering a radical rethinking of conventions of humanities scholarship, she explores an alternative form for academic publishing, through the production of an object, specifically, a wooden cabinet. As an historically informed investigation of the rationalities of dissemination of humanities scholarship, Mak's inquiry speaks to the foundational work in the field of law's documents by Vismann (2008). Taking from Vismann's argument that files are a mode of creating legal identity, Mak argues that 'research publication is the act that produces and defines allegiance to a scholarly identity'. Mak starts from the premise that scholarly publication in the humanities need not be limited to a particular medium ('technological platform'). She challenges the dominant mode of knowledge production through the written word, arguing that the type of document that has come to stand in for scholarship is entirely amenable to particular disciplinary management (bureaucratic seeing and knowing), and defines what 'counts as knowledge and how to count it'. Indeed, in the field of academic publishing, the 'written document is used as documentable evidence of research activity and how it partakes in its own documentation'. In a refreshing critique of the contemporary obsession with the quantity, rather than the quality, of scholarship within academic institutions, Mak investigates knowledge production as performance and production of objects. *A cabinet of curiosity: the library's dead time* was an exhibition of sculptures and performance pieces, introduced by a wooden cabinet. It engages with sensorial knowledge and includes preservation of the sweat of the librarian and the tears of the researcher, resonant of the importance of dust in Carolyn Steedman's (2002) account of modern history writing as an experience in and of the archive. In subsequent iterations, the project took the form of a suitcase, facilitating its delivery at international conferences, another favoured documentary mode for academic scholarship. Mak's project aims to interrupt institutional academic practices by challenging the primacy and exclusivity of the medium of the published written word, and in this way, undermines the document's claim to authority.

Authority

The document is the exemplar *par excellence* of legal authority. Paperwork, file notes, briefs, reports and books: these, and more, provide evidence of law's work in progress. Documents also affirm the finality of law's decisions. With the creation, modification and transaction of documents, law's authority is displayed and enacted. For some scholars, an examination of the properties and features of the document enables us to come to some understanding of how legal authority becomes embedded within—and enforced through—documentation. This *paratextual* analysis looks to the elements of the document that, through convention and repetition, have come to signify its legal authority.

Writing in 1992, Collins and Skover noted that once, 'legal reality … [was] shaped largely by the printed word' (1992, 510). However, increasingly this reality had begun to shift. To acknowledge this, Collins and Skover deployed the term 'paratext' to capture all of those expressions that went *beyond* the text and which were reshaping legal processes. Here, the representative form of the paratext, embracing sounds and images, was the videotape. Collins and Skover identified all those areas of law that did—or could—use videotape, including torts, wills, copyright, contracts, insurance, evidence and procedure (1992, 510). They then noticed that, rather than merely replacing textual forms with audio-visual ones, the technological affordance of videotape actually re-shaped those areas of legal practice. Furthermore, the changing technology would go on to impact the architecture of courtrooms, the employment of new categories of legal professionals and the emergence of new industries seeking to monetise the increased legal reliance upon videotape (1992, 511–512).

The legal historian, Christopher Tomlins, takes paratextual analysis into the domain of literary structuralism. For Tomlins, documents are sources, and they generate evidence in one of three ways: through their contents, genre and paratexts (2014, 6). Each of these gives rise to evidentiary difficulties and interpretive strategies to which lawyers, historians and others bring their own tools. For Tomlins, the paratext relates to a document's *form* (2014, 7). Drawing upon the work of Gérard Genette, the literary theorist, Tomlins shows how paratextual elements—qualities of a document's form rather than its content—can be evidentiary. For Genette, the paratext can be divided into the *peritext*, *epitext* and *hypotext*. Peritext relates to the formal structures within a document which generate an understanding between the text and the reader, and which might include titles, sub-titles, author's name, copyright and publication details, design, font and layout. Tomlins describes peritext as 'the framework of conditions upon which the text is to be encountered' (2014, 13), and later as 'the cage of control' by which the author *authorises* or *authenticates* what is written (2014, 15). Epitext refers to processes beyond the text and which relate to its production and circulation; these might include distribution networks, advertisements of the text, reviews, commentaries, critiques and so on. In an evidentiary sense, these give the document its credibility. Hypotext relates to the sources of the text; Tomlins describes it as 'the text before the text' (2014, 7). The sources of the text are tethered to its reliability. Together, these qualities—authenticity, credibility and reliability—are evidentiary attributes, both for lawyers and historians, and paratextual analysis enables a document to be understood as evidence regardless of its contents. Through its paratextual elements, a document performs its own documenticity, becoming somehow vibrant and alive to its reader, even when the reader has not read it in the conventional way. For Tomlins, Genette's paratextual schema is most powerful when applied to legal and quasi-legal documents because they 'possess a hugely elaborated, grandly formulaic peritext of structural and compositional authority'; moving constantly 'within an epitextual penumbra of production, projection, reception, interpretation and reinterpretation' (2014, 27).

In *Law's Documents*, many contributions engage directly or indirectly with paratextual elements. One chapter to engage with the paratextual elements of legal documentation is by Jesse Adams Stein (Chapter 6). Stein is a scholar engaged in the histories of technology, work and material culture, and particularly the contributions of industrial and manufacturing workers. In 'The Historian as Document Producer', Stein recounts her employment as a writer of timed summaries of oral history interviews, which are, essentially, finding aids for scholars seeking to use these interviews in library and archive collections. Excavating the layers of documentation that are digitally embedded in what historians would regard as primary sources, Stein draws upon paratextual theories from Genette to digital media scholars (Benzon 2013; Birke and Christ 2013; McCracken 2013). In her chapter, she writes:

> digital library catalogues, library metadata, links, supplemental images, online media players, transcripts and timed summaries: these (and other elements) are what make up the paratextual layering surrounding the digital audio recording. None of these layers are entirely neutral, inevitable or natural.
>
> (Chapter 6)

Stein's work also invokes the important contribution to documentary scholarship of the anthropologist Don Brenneis, for whom mundane documents reveal important things about knowledge and power (in Riles 2006, 41–70). Stein explains the emergence of oral history as a mainstream method, championed by interventions from social and feminist historians. Resulting from this were practices of transcription which, in the digital age, are replaced with timed summaries. Each of these makes reading, not listening, the dominant form of scholarly engagement with oral history, which marks a sad irony for the method that sought to centre the voices of marginalised peoples into primary sources. Stein also notes that this layering of documentation generates new hierarchies, and creates a new class of low-wage labour for the makers of timed summaries.

Law's Documents is proud to include works of poetry by Alison Whittaker, selected from her collection *Blakwork* (2018), in 'Forty-Nine Most Common Phrases' (Chapter 7). A Gomeroi poet and legal scholar, one strand of Whittaker's poetry is made from legal documents. Three of the poems represented here—'of the', 'exhibit tab' and 'the skeleton of the common law'—are comprised of the 49 most common 3-word phrases that appear in legal documents, ranked in order of frequency. The first is taken from the judgment in the case of *Trevorrow v State of South Australia* (No. 5) [2007] SASC 285, in which Bruce Trevorrow, a member of the Stolen Generations, sued the state for his removal from his family by the Aborigines Protection Board (APB). The second is taken from the 2016 findings of the Western Australia Coroner following the inquest into the death in police custody of Ms Dhu, which was found to have been caused by inhumane police conduct and substandard medical care. The third is taken from the judgment in *Mabo v Queensland (No 2)* (1992) 175 CLR 1, in which the High Court of Australia recognised the fragile concept of native title. The fourth poem reproduced here, 'An Act', is Whittaker's imagined legislative instrument, combining First Nations language with legal language, and which describes itself as 'An Act for the regulation of visiting feet on Country'. Jeanine Leane, in her review of Alison Whittaker's *Blakwork*, describes it as a 'unique hybrid of poetry, memoir, reportage, legal documentation, fiction, non-fiction, satire, and social commentary' which also defies genre as a form of resistance to colonialism (2019, n.p.). Leane observes that

> Whittaker also joins a growing number of Aboriginal women poets, most notably Narungga poet and academic Natalie Harkin, who use poetry to critique and expose the duality of government documents, archival reports, files, letters, media reportage that intervene and affect almost all facets of Aboriginal life.
>
> (2019, n.p.)

In noting that Whittaker's reader needs to work hard, Leane writes: 'These poems are literary simulations of the daily lives of many Aboriginal communities caught in webs of bureaucratic government-speak' (2019, n.p.).

Harkin and Leane are both represented in *Law's Documents*, in a dialogue in which they pit poetry against the ongoing violence of the colonial archive and state bureaucracy. In 'When Records Speak We Listen' (Chapter 3), Harkin tells Leane:

> as poets and educators, I feel like we're in a unique position to flip the gaze so these 'ledgers' become our ultimate cabinets of curiosity; ripe for decolonising and critique so that beyond blood-memory recognition, our ancestors can exhale with ease towards a just future.

Elsewhere, Harkin has undertaken a counter-archival project in which she has taken letters from the Children's Welfare Board files of her grandmother and great-grandmother, and woven them into a basket, an undertaking that she acknowledges is at once metaphorical, literal, liberating and a labour of love (Harkin, 2020, 157). In the dialogue with Leane, Harkin recounts the visits to her family by Inspectors, who they called 'State Ladies', who would check that beds were made, that the contents of cupboards were in order, and peer into pots to see what was cooking: their intrusive surveillance generated records that, for Harkin, demand an Indigenous-led truth-telling. Leane recognises the same impulse: 'to read one's own record, or that of a loved one, can be to experience a violent collision of worlds, an internal shattering as one witnesses one's own life made unrecognisable by the logic of the state'.

Leane and Harkin condemn those collectors, anthropologists and historians who dispossessed First Nations people of their life stories, consigning them to archives where they are often shielded from the scrutiny of those who gave their stories, using bureaucratic and legal devices to obfuscate and frustrate Indigenous people searching for their ancestors in law's documents.

Chapters by legal scholars Sara Dehm and Anthea Vogl examine legal documentation that facilitates or impedes the global movement of people. Dehm's chapter, 'Passport Struggles' (Chapter 4), analyses the passport as a jurisdictional document. In her work, the passport is an instrument of state inclusion and recognition of identity; being without a passport, or carrying a passport that mis-describes one's identity, gives rise to the passport struggles that her chapter narrates. Dehm's chapter teaches us about the gendered and racialised histories of the passport. In one section, she recounts the legal struggles over the 'sex' category that appears on the passport page, and how gender non-conforming individuals have deployed legal strategies to demand alternatives to male/female in the 'sex' field, challenging what she terms 'bureaucratic forms of violence, mis-identification and exclusion'. In another section, Dehm explains how passports have been used as sites of First Nations declarations of sovereignty. In her account of the Iroquois nation's lacrosse team, who sought to travel with their Haudenosaunee passport whilst touring internationally, Dehm cites the team's executive director, Percy Abrams, who stated, 'We have the right of self-determination. We have the right to present our own passport'. Traditionally in migration studies, the passport is used to distinguish citizens from non-citizens, and to manage global mobility. In the digital age of machine-readability, new questions arise about the materiality of passports, their bearers and the biometric border. Ultimately, the document itself becomes redundant, albeit it remains compulsory to have and to carry, and the body of the passport-holder becomes the document subjected to border control and management.

In 'What Is a Bogus Document?' (Chapter 5), Anthea Vogl interrogates the sinister legal construct of the 'bogus' document, conjured by Australian migration legislation as a potentially limitless tool for the denial of refugee claims. Vogl interprets this as an incremental shift by bureaucrats and decision makers; whereas previously, they regarded refugee applicants as deceitful, now, the documents presented by applicants become sites of deception. These documents also become objects of new forms of 'expert' analysis and assessment, creating new methods by which applicants can be accused of clogging up systems with their undeserving claims. Vogl notes that bogus document claims are made in the knowledge that they occur in what is frequently a documentary void. People making refugee claims often do not have documentation that relates to their identity, their travel, their education and their residence. It is well known that they cannot provide documentation to counter the departmental allegation that the documents they have provided are bogus. She also makes the important point that, where people are claiming persecution by their home state, their production of authentic documents is frequently used to disprove their persecution claims. Further, as larger numbers of people begin to furnish documents that fulfil the requirements of the department, the probative value of these documents begins to diminish.

Vogl draws on the work of social anthropologist Susan Bibler Coutin on 'the quasi-magical power of papers and records to transform persons by regularizing or criminalizing their presence' whereby documents 'create opportunities and double binds: they are key to obtaining legal status, but they also can make legalization impossible' (2020, 133). For Vogl, the invocation of an unreliable and unverifiable scientific discourse around authenticity—undertaken upon the document, instead of the refugee claimant—marks a new shift in border control.

Each of these chapters, and others, helps to broaden our understanding of how we might look to documents to tell us something about legal authority. They may be sources of authority, evidence of authority, or they might illuminate the violence and trauma caused by legal authority.

Materiality

Our attention to the materiality of law's documents reflects a wider interest within humanities and social science scholarship in re-exploring materialist modes of analysis (see, for example, Coole and Frost 2013). Within documentary theory, new materialist approaches investigate the role of documents and documentary practices in actually constituting and materialising information.

Following the pioneering work of Otlet (1934), Briet (1951) and Buckland (1997), information philosopher Bernd Frohmann suggests that there are four properties of information practices that contribute to the informativeness of documents: 'their materiality; their institutional sites; the ways in which they are socially disciplined; and their historical contingency' (2004, 387). The particular characteristics of these properties when they concern law's documents are reflected in the contributions to this collection.

In legal scholarship, law's reliance on textual modes of expression has led to particular interest in legal forms of materiality through investigating 'legal media of inscription, their circulation and interpretation' (Kang 2018, 459). As Hyo Yoon Kang points out, in legal materialist analyses, 'texts, in various forms and genres, are taken as vital matters through which legality is materialised through inscription and speech and institute law as a system of knowledge' (2018, 459). This field has been inspired by the ground-breaking work of Vismann (2008), who engaged in a detailed historical genealogical investigation of the media of law's files to argue that legality is produced through their materiality and the acts that they perform. In Bruno Latour's ethnographic study of the Conseil d'État (2010), the author employs his actor-network theory in analysis of the production of French administrative law through the movement of people and objects, including close attention to the life of legal files (dossiers) (70–106). As Ron Levi and Marianne Valverde explain, for Latour, 'The relations among the documents and other entities constitute legality' (2008, 817).

Some investigations of the materiality of law's documents engage with archival theory and practice to examine the role of court records, including transcripts and evidentiary materials (Biber 2013; Biber and Luker 2014). Other work examines law's materiality through the legal institutions in which documents are created, deployed, stored, retrieved or destroyed (Genovese, Luker and Rubenstein 2019). In settler-colonial contexts such as Australia, research involving legal archives needs to take account of the power of state recordkeeping practices as a method of control and oppression of Indigenous people. Furthermore, when claims for reparative justice are made, archival records have been unreliable sources of evidence, resulting in Indigenous peoples' mistrust of state and institutional archives, demands for control of archives and legal actions for the destruction of records (Luker 2017).

There has been attention paid to the 'afterlife' of legal documents, where materials survive in non-legal settings after their legal life has lapsed, where they acquire new contexts and meanings (Biber 2019). In some types of afterlife, a non-legal document (say, personal letters, diary entries, private papers) acquires legal significance. In other contexts, legal documents (forensic reports, prisoner registers, transcripts of proceedings) acquire cultural significance, and might appear in museums, artworks, theatre and other creative contexts.

A number of the contributions in the collection attend to the materiality of law's documents, including international treaty documents, the signature, informal wills, state archives and surveillance photographs.

Jessie Hohmann investigates the material claim to authority of one of law's most prestigious documents, international agreements. In 'Treaty Documents: Materialising International Legal Agreement' (Chapter 9), Hohmann investigates the relationship between the legal agreement and its documented form, pointing out that treaty documents do not themselves constitute law, but rather, it is the legal relations and intentions that precede them that form the basis of the treaty. Nevertheless, as Hohmann demonstrates, international treaties are often valued for their material status and preserved as historical artefacts of law. From the requirements of the Sovereign's seal and signature in English treaties to the prescription of fonts and formats in United Nations paper documents, great care is taken in preserving the material form of treaty documents, as well as ensuring their secure location within repositories. However, the documentary form is a distinctly Western mode for recording treaty agreements, as Hohmann demonstrates in her discussion of treaties in Wampum, made by First Nations peoples from the north eastern parts of North America (Turtle Island). These treaties, made for over a thousand years, are in the form of belts made from small, coloured beads of shell arranged in precise forms, and are used in various ceremonies to record important events. As Hohmann and others have pointed out, Wampum is a binary, hypertextual information communication technology, incorporating storage and retrieval functions, not unlike the digitisation of information. However, as they are not written down, they have been excluded from states' archives and record keeping—literally, written out of the historical record.

Hohmann points to the way that, in their uniformity of form—complying with rules for layout, font, grammar and language—international treaties carry traces of law's requirement for universality. In colonial contexts, standard form treaties have been used by colonising powers in the wholesale theft of land from sovereign First Nations. These pro forma documents contain blank spaces so that later they can be filled in to record key information such as geographic region, the place of the treaty's 'conclusion', the names of parties and their signatures. As Aalberts (2018) highlights, the paradoxical function of signatures on treaties with First Nations leaders serves at the same time to recognise sovereign rights whilst disenfranchising First Nations as parties to the agreements.

In 'Law's Signature Acts' (Chapter 8), legal scholar Trish Luker shows how the signature draws a direct line between a document's materiality and its authority. Signed, sealed and delivered: each of these processes marks a legal event and produces a legal outcome. Luker's chapter examines these processes: the act of signing, in which presence and intention are implicated in authenticity and authority; and the signature itself, as a graphic sign that conveys legal force. Each of these processes has been challenged by the digital age, giving rise to theoretical and jurisprudential debates about form/function, and inscription/action. Luker's chapter brings into this collection an engagement with the scholarship of Béatrice Fraenkel, the French anthropologist whose book-length analysis of the signature is a key text of documentary theory. Fraenkel regards signatures as part of the 'family' of writing acts, wherein they are recognisable entities on their own—'micro-acts'—but derive new meanings and acquire new force when combined with other family members. Luker's chapter also examines the scant jurisprudence of the signature, where it has authorised financial transactions, the casting of ballots or the forced removal of First Nations children from their parents.

Documents as acts is a theme taken up by Katherine Biber in her account of informal wills and the challenges they present to courts attempting to elicit from them the testamentary intentions of the deceased. In 'Conjuring Documents: Informal Wills' (Chapter 10), Biber looks to examples where wills have not been recorded on conventional documents but where courts have nevertheless interpreted them as wills. Biber's chapter draws upon Smith's theory of document acts, which observes that documents are instruments of change; they perform acts that create new social and legal states of affairs. Biber argues that, in law, wills need to be a documentary object in order to achieve documentary effects: they need to *be* in order to *do*. However, in some circumstances, courts have had to conjure documents from performances; document acts sometimes give rise to documentary objects that would otherwise not exist. Drawing on a fascinating array of examples of material surfaces on which the testamentary wishes of people have been recorded—a scratched statement on a tractor fender, a nurse's petticoat, a tattoo, an eggshell, scratchings on a wall, and suicide notes—Biber reveals how informal wills have been conjured from artefacts. In the digital age, valid informal wills have been found in other unconventional forms, such as an unsent text message.

In 'Powerful Documents from the Archive: Nyungar Letters and the Ancestors' Words Project' (Chapter 11), Anna Haebich, Darryl Kickett, Marion Kickett, Anthony Kickett and Jeannie Morrison investigate situations where documents provide access to the past, specifically, the colonial past. In the Ancestors' Words project, letters written by Nyungar people during the first half of the twentieth century have been located in state archives and then returned to the Elders of the community from which they originated. The *Aborigines Act 1905* (WA) granted the state extraordinary levels of bureaucratic control over all aspects of Aboriginal people's lives, administered by the state through extreme levels of centralised record-keeping, resulting in extensive archival holdings of files relating to individual people. Over half of the files held by the Western Australian State Archives for the period 1926–1959 concerned Indigenous people, including personal correspondence by them to the authorities. The long-term Chief Protector, A.O. Neville (1915–1940), introduced the first centralised card system and register for the recording of Indigenous individuals' vital statistics that formed the basis of eugenicist classification based on perceived racial quantum. The project demonstrates a strategy that is part of the radical movement to decolonise colonial archives by destabilising the presumed authority of state archival documents and drawing on Indigenous knowledge based in oral history to inform understanding (Luker 2017; Thorpe 2019). By focussing on *letters* written by Nyungar people to state authorities, the project uses material artefacts to bring Elders into contact with the past through the words of their Ancestors. It also engages creative activism by facilitating the use of the letters by families in the creation of visual arts, performance, literature and story-telling. The chapter includes creative writing based on the letters and photos located by Nyungar Elders Darryl Kickett and Jeannie Morrison.

In 'Material Violence: Destruction, Mishaps, and Redaction of Stasi Photographs' (Chapter 12), Donna West Brett also engages with the violence of the archive in her investigation of covert surveillance photographs taken and kept as documentation of citizens' activities by the Stasi in the former German Democratic Republic. During the last moments of the regime's collapse in 1989, instructions were issued to destroy the vast archive of files and photographs. Brett argues that these photographic documents evidence a double destruction: first, through the violence of the act of surveillance, and second, through attempts to destroy them as evidence of the state surveillance. Having gained access to some remaining files, she engages in careful analysis of the material features of surviving photographs, including their haptic qualities, such as fragility, but also camera angle and framing, folds and tears, as evidence of destruction. She points to the distinctive material characteristics of the photos beyond their subject matter—poorly shot, badly exposed, marked by processing chemicals or water stains—as indicia of their signification. Furthermore, the files requested are inevitably marked by redaction or pixilation to conceal individual identities. In digitisation of the images, their materiality transforms from paper and chemical to pixel and code, and often omits distinctive qualities, such as handwritten marks or inscriptions.

Aesthetics

Law's documents operate within, and produce, a broad range of aesthetic norms and effects which, in turn, reflect the aesthetic modes generated by, and governing, systems of law. Legal aesthetics have long been subject to interrogation by legal theorists exploring various issues including the interrelationship between art (and images) and law (Douzinas and Nead 1999; Biber and San Roque 2006; Ben-Dor 2011; Kee 2019; Manderson 2000), legal arbitration of aesthetic value (Shapiro et al 2014), the law's use of images in the affirmation of authority (Dahlberg 2012a) and the role of aesthetics in the perception and enactment of law (Schlag 2002). While some posit a distinction between the law's aesthetic dimensions and its operation, such as maintaining a division between law's form and content (see, for example, Morgan 2007, 3), most conceptualise legal aesthetics as inextricably interspersed with legal action. In other words, here, legal aesthetics communicate, inform, serve and connect to legal ways of knowing and acting (see, for example, Dahlberg 2012b, 4). This holistic vision often relies on frustratingly broad (even vague) definitions of *aesthetics* and, as legal theorist Anne Barron notes, there is 'little by way of consensus among those who invoke the term' (2000, 301). However, this definitional imprecision is often strategically exploited by scholars to present an expansive analysis of the law and its dimensions.

Although narrower conceptions of legal aesthetics, as related to notions of beauty and art, are mooted (see discussion in Gearey 2001, 2–9; Schlag 2002, 10), often legal theorists conceptualise aesthetics as something akin to affect or ontology; a force that structures and informs feeling, action and sense (Manderson 2000, 23-24; Schlag 2002, 1050). Positioning law's documents within this broadly constituted aesthetic field reveals the way documents reflect and constitute legal aesthetics (and through this, legal operations) in visual, material and intellectual ways.

Annelise Riles argues that documents are 'artifacts of modern knowledge practices' (2006, 2) and, seeking to move beyond an instrumental view of documents, presents them instead as 'aesthetic objects with uses distinct from their qualities as "texts"' (1998, 378). Riles works with a more precise definition of aesthetics than those used by the legal scholars described above. For Riles aesthetics relate to the formal, visual and material elements connected to 'the production, use, and circulation of documents' (2006, 19). Here, particular legal and bureaucratic documents embody certain genres or 'aesthetic commitments' that direct ideas and actions (2006, 19). Focusing on documents co-authored by various parties at a UN-sponsored international conference, Riles contends that 'the document's principal aesthetic device involves an alternation between concreteness (the document as object) and abstraction (the document as pattern)' (1998, 388). During the writing process, the object status of documents (as entities to be collected, circulated or valued) fades, and the authoring delegates focus only on operating within, and maintain the rules of, the genre to which the document belongs (1998, 389). In these moments, the document dissolves into pattern; patterns of 'structure, organisational logic, language, format, typeface, layout, even substantive content' (1998, 386). In the service of maintaining this pattern, sometimes the representational quality of language becomes less significant than enacting the aesthetic of the document. Thus, under the auspices of the pattern, 'language [has] … a shape, a rhythm, a feel, not simply a meaning' (1998, 386). Here, the document's aesthetic shapes and produces action in ways that extend beyond the textual meaning of the words inscribed upon it.

Like Riles, Mak (2011), in her historical analysis of the *page*, considers the interaction between aesthetic modes and the production and communication of meaning. Mak shows that different types of pages (e.g. the scroll, webpage, leaf of a book) both act to convey information, and via their material, visual and textual characteristics, shape the communication and reception of this information (2011, 3). Importantly, Mak positions the page as a mediating, communicative technology that is intellectually (and aesthetically) formulated by authors and designers and received by readers. As Mak observes,

> readers interpret text, space, and image as they are inclined, but the meanings that they formulate are predicated upon the materiality of each

> carefully designed page. The page is thus an interface, standing at the centre of the complicated dynamic of intention and reception.
>
> (2011, 21)

The interpersonal, social implications of document aesthetics are also explored by Brenda Danet (1997) as she traces the aesthetic evolution of documents resulting from print culture's incorporation into the digital realm. Danet argues that the circulation (particularly gifting and exchange) of books, letters, cards and other documents is core to many social actions and activities. The aesthetic attributes of these objects (alongside the meanings written or inscribed onto them), *and* the aesthetic modes of the social situations in which they are circulated, are 'critical to the constitution of new social arrangements and relationships' (1997, 5). Thus, as print culture moves from the haptic and material to the optical and digital, new document aesthetics (with new attendant social aesthetics) are produced to maintain and enact relationships (1997).

Riles, Mak and Danet provide richly textured detail regarding various types of documents and their aesthetics by focusing particularly on specific visual, material and textual modes. Elsewhere, scholars contribute to our knowledge on document aesthetics through their analysis of the visual, material, affective, instrumental and historical qualities of documents. In particular, they consider the way these qualities act on, or are adapted or interrogated by, those using or producing documents. Here, authors focus on diverse topics including collections of documents, such as archives (see for example, Luker 2016, 2017; Biber 2018); documents produced in the course of legal and bureaucratic operations (see for example, Navaro-Yashin 2007; White 2014; Barrera 2008; Göpfert 2013); and the afterlife of documents, particularly images and materials resulting from violent crime and death (see for example, Young 1996; Biber, Doyle and Rossmanith 2013; Bray 2013, 2014 and 2017; Biber and Luker 2014; Biber 2017, 2019). These engagements reveal the multiplicity and importance of documents and show that their familiar, even ubiquitous, aesthetic qualities may mask their power to direct and shape legal activities, actions and ways of making meaning.

While theoretical and philosophical engagements with legal and document aesthetics are not the focus of this collection, the instrumental and affective impact of legal document aesthetics permeates and informs many of the chapters presented here. In her contribution to the collection, 'The Rape Contract' (Chapter 14) Shevaun Wright observes that feminist and critical race theorists have done much to enrich the field of legal aesthetics by 'giving a human form to the purportedly abstract, disembodied operations of the law'. Similarly, various chapters in this volume make tangible the socio-economic, gendered, racialised, ideologically driven dimensions and impacts of document aesthetics. In these chapters, the authors' gaze is trained specifically on art and design, particularly on imaginative, intellectual encounters with documents connected to, or reflecting, the law. For example, in 'Artists and Legal Documents'

(Chapter 13), Priya Vaughan explores a rich vein in contemporary art making: artistic engagement with legal documents. Vaughan analyses three dimensions of legal documents amplified by artists in their creative engagements: the *aesthetic of the form*, the *witnessing potential* of documents and the legal document's *affective power*. In exploiting these qualities, artists put legal documents to work as 'avatars for the legal institutions' that produced them, thus cultivating a creative space for interrogation, critique and exploration of the law's mechanisms, operations and ideologies.

The encounters between artists and law's documents tracked by contributors are all politically engaged and socially embedded, reflecting and directing attention to the real-world impacts and corollaries of law in action. For example, in 'The Aesthetic Archive' (Chapter 15), Carolyn McKay demonstrates the power of art to deliver a 'critique of justice' received by diverse audiences, including legal professionals. Building on theoretical approaches from visual criminology, McKay shows how *justiceINjustice*—an exhibition curated by the author—succeeded in producing affecting sensory encounters with true stories of legal injustice. Artworks made for the exhibition were created through artistic use of the legal archive in close consultation and collaboration with those individuals (and their families) documented in this archive. Here, ethical and equitable art making processes delivered a kind of remedial justice, which was, in itself, a critique of legal processes that culminate in injustice.

While artworks in *justiceINjustice* represent specific individual encounters with the law, elsewhere, authors focus on art created to address the wide-ranging effects and outcomes of the principles embedded in legal systems. Shevaun Wright (Chapter 14) reflects upon her own creative practice, through discussion of her work, *The Rape Contract*, a textual, document-based installation that manifests and interrogates the *social contract* between a cis-gendered women, who was a victim of rape, and her nation state. Here, Wright interprets, unsettles and cannibalises law's documents to explore the interconnections between art and law, and to lay bare systemic exclusion of 'Indigenous and female voices' within both spheres. Central here is an interest in things lost, obscured or omitted by legal systems and processes. Things which, nevertheless, cry out to be seen, heard and accommodated. Wright's works are conduits for just this kind of empathetic engagement with the hidden and marginalised. Wright's approach is informed both by her training as a lawyer, and ongoing engagement with feminist, critical race and other scholarship. Her work visualises and materialises abstracted theoretical and legal concepts for audiences for whom legal philosophies and apparatus are often intimidating and opaque.

Art's communicative power is also central to Georgine Clarsen's sophisticated analysis of Reko Rennie's immersive video work, *OA_RR*. In '*OA_RR*: Documenting Sovereignty' (Chapter 16), Clarsen creates an automobile-centred art history of Australian Indigenous contemporary art, to show how the car (once a colonising device) has operated as an important tool, and symbol, for Aboriginal peoples in the course of political action, cultural practice, and quotidian activity. In *OA_RR*, the car driven by the artist is literally a vehicle 'through which Rennie commands his viewers to live with and around the fact of Indigenous sovereignty'. In communicating and affirming this sovereignty, *OA_RR* operates as an art-document, presenting a counter-archival challenge to enshrined narratives about the colonial formation of the Australian nation, and the legacy of this formation in the present.

Authors engaged with document aesthetics are united by a belief in the power of creative products to not only represent and communicate vital issues, but importantly, to produce new understandings of these issues. In 'Historio-Graphic' (Chapter 17), Anne Burdick, Jacqueline Lorber-Kasunic and Kate Sweetapple reflect on two of their own design projects, each involving 'graphically configuring' historical documents, with the aim of generating 'new knowledge'. One of these projects culminated in the production of a suite of diagrams visualising the process of creating *The Declaration of Rights of Man and the Citizen* (1789). These creative and interpretative diagrams visually and spatially capture the difficult, intensely iterative and often 'chaotic' process of drafting this document. Here, designed diagrams reveal processual negotiations and conflicts otherwise masked by the formal and implacable aesthetic of the completed document. Thus, the authors reveal how their *deformance*-oriented design is not merely intended to visualise, or act as an adjunct to, textual meanings. Rather it is strongly generative, producing new meanings and casting extant ones in new light.

Beyond the production of new knowledge, contributors also reveal the power of art-objects and performances to act, disrupt, intervene and bring-into-being. The dialogue between Carey Young and Joan Kee in 'Artistic license' (Chapter 18) reveals how the law can be, in and of itself, an artistic medium. Young's extended artistic work in and through the law—including via the creation of 'bespoke legal instruments (which also take the form of video, photography, performance etc.)'—both critically analyses and enacts the law's mechanisms. Through these art-instruments, Young addresses a broad array of issues including the law's power and violence, law's aesthetic qualities, legal discrimination and inequity, art's contribution to legal processes, non-institutional legal practices and the law's malleability in the hands of the artist.

These chapters contribute to extant scholarship tracing artistic engagements with the law (see for example, Young 2013; Kee 2019), but, in foregrounding law's documents and the art-objects' agentic power, add further dimension and depth to knowledge about the law's aesthetic and affective parameters.

Documents—in manifold and multiple forms—perform, proliferate and perpetuate the law. The chapters in this collection each seek to describe, interrogate and make sense of this proliferation and its effects. Taken individually, the explorations of contributors provide rich critical analysis of diverse forms of legal documents and of their power, meanings and mediations across time and space. Taken together, they form a new branch of documentary scholarship, coalescing around themes of authority, materiality and aesthetics, which transforms how we might conceive of law's documents.

Note

1 This collection is the result of an ARC-funded Discovery research project entitled 'What Is a Document? Evidentiary Challenges in the Digital Age' (2016-18) (DP160100414).

References

Aalberts, Tanja, 2018. Sovereign Marks. *In*: Jessie Hohmann and Joyce Daniel, eds. *International Law's Objects*. Oxford: Oxford University Press, 453–62.

Barrera, Leticia, 2008. Files Circulation and the Forms of Legal Experts: Agency and Personhood in the Argentine Supreme Court. *Journal of Legal Anthropology*, 1, 3–24.

Barron, Anne, 2000. Spectacular Jurisprudence. *Oxford Journal of Legal Studies*, 20 (2), 301–15.

Ben-Dor, Oren, ed., 2011. *Law and Art: Justice, Ethics and Aesthetics*. Abingdon, Oxon, Canada and New York: Routledge.

Benzon, Paul, 2013. Bootleg Paratextuality and Digital Temporality: Towards an Alternate Present of the DVD. *Narrative*, 21 (1), 88–104.

Biber, Katherine, 2013. In Crime's Archive: The Cultural Afterlife of Criminal Evidence. *British Journal of Criminology*, 53 (6), 1033–49.

Biber, Katherine, and Luker, Trish, 2014. Evidence and the Archive: Ethics, Aesthetics, and Emotion. *Australian Feminist Law Journal*, 40 (1), 1–14.

Biber, Katherine, 2017. The Archival Turn in Law: The Papers of Lindy Chamberlain in the National Library of Australia. *Sydney Law Review*, 39 (3), 277–301.

Biber, Katherine, 2018. Evidence in the Museum: Curating a Miscarriage of Justice. *Theoretical Criminology*, 22 (4), 505–22.

Biber, Katherine, 2019. *In Crime's Archive: The Cultural Afterlife of Evidence*. Oxon and New York: Routledge.

Biber, Katherine, and San Roque, Mehera, 2006. The Trouble with Pictures. *Law Text Culture*, 10, 1–5.

Biber, Katherine, Doyle, Peter, and Rossmanith, Kate, 2013. Perving at Crime Scenes. *Griffith Law Review*, 22 (3), 804–14.

Bibler Coutin, Susan, 2020. Opportunities and Double Binds: Legal Craft in an Era of Uncertainty. *In*: Sarah B. Horton and Josiah Heyman, eds. *Paper Trails: Migrants, Documents, and Legal Insecurity*. Durham: Duke University Press, 130–152.

Birke, Dorothee and Christ, Birte, 2013. Paratext and Digitised Narrative: Mapping the Field. *Narrative*, 21 (1), 65–87.

Bray, Rebecca Scott, 2013. Uneasy Evidence: The Medico-Legal Portraits of Teresa Margolles and Libia Posada. *Griffith Law Review*, 22 (1), 28–62.

Bray, Rebecca Scott, 2014. Rotten Prettiness? The Forensic Aesthetic and Crime as Art. *Australian Feminist Law Journal*, 40 (1), 69–95.

Bray, Rebecca Scott, 2017. Images of Fatal Violence: Negotiating the Dark Heart of Death Research. *Mortality*, 22 (2), 136–54.

Briet, Suzanne, [1951] 2006. *What is Documentation? English Translation of the Classic French Text.* Translated and edited by Ronald E. Day, Laurent Martinet, and Hermina G. B. Anghelescu. Lanham, MD: Scarecrow Press.
Buckland, Michael, 1997. What is a "Document"? *Journal of the American Society for Information Science*, 48 (9), 804–9.
Buckland, Michael, 1998. What is a Digital Document? *Document Numérique (Paris)*, vol. 2 (2), 221–30.
Collins, Ronald K. L., and Skover, David M., 1992. Paratexts. *Stanford Law Review*, 44 (3), 509–52.
Connarty, Jane, and Lanyon, Joesphine, 2006. *Ghosting: The Role of the Archive within Contemporary Artists' Film and Video.* Brisol, UK: Picture This Moving Image.
Coole, Diana, and Frost Samantha, eds., 2013. *New Materialisms. Ontology, Agency, and Politics.* Durham, NC and London: Duke University Press.
Cramerotti, Alfredo, 2009. *Aesthetic Journalism: How to Inform without Informing.* Bristol, UK and Chicago, USA: Intellect.
Dahlberg, Lief, ed., 2012a. *Visualizing Law and Authority: Essays on Legal Aesthetics.* Berlin, Germany: De Gruyter.
Dahlberg, Lief, 2012b. Introduction. Visualising Law and Authority. *In*: Lief Dahlberg, ed. *Visualizing Law and Authority: Essays on Legal Aesthetics.* Germany: De Gruyter.
Danet, Brenda, 1997. Books, Letters, Documents: The Changing Aesthetics of Text in late Print Culture. *Journal of Material Culture*, 2 (1), 5–38.
Derrida, Jacques, 1988. *Limited Inc.* Evanston, IL: Northwestern University Press.
Dever, Maryanne, and Morra, Linda, 2014. Literary Archives, Materiality and the Digital. *Archives and Manuscripts*, 42 (3), 223–6.
Douzinas, Costas, and Nead, Lynda, eds., 1999. *Law and the Image: The Authority of Art and the Aesthetics of Law.* Chicago, IL: University of Chicago Press.
Eichhorn, Kate, 2013. *The Archival Turn in Feminism: Outrage in Order.* Philadelphia, PA: Temple University Press.
Farge, Arlette, 2013. *The Allure of the Archives.* Translated by Railton, Thomas Scott. New Haven and London: Yale University Press.
Ferraris, Maurizio, 2013. *Documentality: Why It is Necessary to Leave Traces.* Translated by Davies, Richard. New York: Fordham University Press.
Frohmann, Bernd, 2004. Documentation Redux: Prolegomenon to (Another) Philosophy of Information. *Library Trends*, 52 (3), 387–407.
Garton Ash, Timothy, 1997. *The File: A Personal History.* New York: Vintage Books.
Gearey, Adam, 2001. *Law and Aesthetics.* Oxford and Portland, OR: Hart Publishing.
Genovese, Ann, Luker, Trish, and Rubenstein, Kim, eds., 2019. *The Court as Archive.* Canberra: ANU Press.
Gitelman, Lisa, 2014. *Paper Knowledge: Toward a Media History of Documents.* Durham and London: Duke University Press.
Göpfert, Mirco, 2013. Bureaucratic Aesthetics: Report Writing in the Nigerien Gendarmerie. *American Ethnologist*, 40 (2), 324–34.
Gupta, Akhil, 2012. *Red Tape: Bureaucracy, Structural Violence, and Poverty in India.* Durham and London: Duke University Press.
Harkin, Natalie, 2020. Weaving the Colonial Archive: A Basket to Lighten the Load. *Journal of Australian Studies*, 44 (2), 154–66.
Hull, Matthew S., 2012. *Government of Paper: The Materiality of Bureaucracy in Urban Pakistan.* Berkeley, CA: University of California Press.

Ingold, Tim, 2011. *Being Alive: Essays on Movement, Knowledge and Description*. London and New York: Routledge.

Kang, Hyo Yoon, 2018. Law's Materiality: Between Concrete Matters and Abstract Forms, or How Matter Becomes Material. *In*: Andreas Philippopoulos-Mihalopoulos, ed. *Routledge Handbook of Law and Theory*. London: Routledge, 453–74.

Kee, Joan, 2019. *Models of Integrity: Art and Law in Post-Sixties America*. Oakland, CA: University of California.

Latour, Bruno, 2010. *The Making of Law: An Ethnography of the Consel d'Etat*. Translated by Brilman, Marina, and Pottage, Alain. Cambridge: Polity Press.

Leane, Jeanine, 2019. Ultima Thule: BlakWork by Alison Whittaker. *Sydney Review of Books*. Available from: https://sydneyreviewofbooks.com/review/ultima-thule-blakwork-by-alison-whittaker/ [Accessed 10 March 2021].

Levi, Ron, and Valverde, Marianne, 2008. Studying Law by Association: Bruno Latour Goes to the Conseil d'Etat. *Law & Social Inquiry*, 33 (3), 805–25.

Luker, Trish, 2016. Animating the Archive: Artefacts of Law. *In*: Stewart Motha and Honni van Rijswijk, eds. *Law, Memory, Violence: Uncovering the Counter-Archive*. Oxon and New York: Routledge.

Luker, Trish, 2017. Decolonising Archives: Indigenous Challenges to Record Keeping in 'Reconciling' Settler Colonial States. *Australian Feminist Studies*, 32 (91–92), 108–25.

McCracken, Ellen, 2013. Expanding Genette's Epitext/Peritext Model for Transitional Electronic Literature: Centrifugal and Centripetal Vectors on Kindles and iPads. *Narrative*, 21 (1), 105–24.

Mak, Bonnie, 2011. *How The Page Matters*. Toronto, ON; Buffalo, New York; London, England: University of Toronto Press.

Manderson, Desmond, 2000. *Songs without Music: Aesthetic Dimensions of Law and Justice*. Berkley, CA and Los Angeles, CA: University of California Press.

Manoff, Marlene, 2006. The Materiality of Digital Collections: Theoretical and Historical Perspectives'. *Portal*, 6 (3), 311–25.

Miller, Daniel, 2010. *Stuff*. Cambridge: Polity Books.

Morgan, Ed, 2007. *The Aesthetics of International Law*. Toronto, ON; Buffalo, New York; London, England: University of Toronto Press.

Motha, Stewart, and van Rijswijk, Honni, eds., 2016. *Law, Memory, Violence: Uncovering the Counter-Archive*. Oxon and New York: Routledge.

Navaro-Yashin, Yael, 2007. Make-Believe Papers, Legal Forms and the Counterfeit: Affective Interactions between Documents and People in Britain and Cyprus. *Anthropological Theory*, 7 (1), 79–98.

Otlet, Paul, [1934] 1990. *International Organization and Dissemination of Knowledge: Selected Essays*. Translated and edited by W. Boyd Rayward. Amsterdam: Elsevier.

Ridener, John, 2008. *From Polders to Postmodernism: A Concise History of Archival Theory*. Duluth Minnesota: Litwin Books.

Riles, Annelise, 1998. Infinity within the Brackets. *American Ethnologist*, 25 (3), 378–89.

Riles, Annelise, ed., 2006. *Documents: Artifacts of Modern Knowledge*. Ann Arbor, MI: University of Michigan Press.

Schlag, Pierre, 2002. The Aesthetics of American Law. *Harvard Law Review*, 115, 1047–2364.

Shapiro, Daniel, Cole, David, Heins, Marjorie, Lehv, Richard, Shiner, Roger A., Brian Soucek, and Pottage, Alain, 2014. Law and Art. *In*: Michael Kelly, ed. *Encyclopedia of Aesthetics* (2nd ed.) Oxford and New York: Oxford University Press.

Smith, Barry, 2012. How to Do Things with Documents. *Rivista di Estetica*, 50, 179–98.

Steedman, Carolyn, 2002. Dust: The Archive and Cultural History. Brunswick, NJ: Rutgers University Press.

Stoler, Ann Laura, 2009. *Along the Archival Grain: Epistemic Anxieties and Colonial Common Sense*. Princeton, NJ and Oxford: Princeton University Press.

Thorpe, Kirsten, 2019. Transformative Praxis—Building Spaces for Indigenous Self-Determination in Libraries and Archives. *In the Library with a Lead Pipe*. Available from: http://hdl.handle.net/10453/140810 [Accessed 10 March 2021].

Tomlins, Christopher, 2014. The Confessions of Nat Turner: A Paratextual Analysis. *Law & History*, 1 (1), 1–28.

Vismann, Cornelia, 2008. *Files: Law and Media Technology*. Stanford, CA: Stanford University Press.

Weld, Kirsten, 2014. *Paper Cadavers: The Archives of Dictatorship in Guatemala*. Durham and London: Duke University Press.

White, Melissa Autumn, 2014. Archives of Intimacy and Trauma: Queer Migration Documents as Technologies of Affect'. *Radical History Review*, 120 (Fall 2014), 75–93.

Whittaker, Alison, 2018. *Blakwork*. Broome: Magabala Books.

Young, Alison, 1996. *Imaging Crime: Textual Outlaws and Criminal Conversations*. London and California: Sage.

Young, Alison, 2013. *Judging the Image Art, Value, Law: Representations, Technologies, Critique*. London and New York: Taylor and Francis.

Chapter 2

In wood and word, or, a gloss on documents and documentation in the humanities

Bonnie Mak

Attention in the humanities has lately turned to the re-thinking of established modes and means of publishing. Yet contests about publication in the academy, digital or not, monograph or not, collaborative or not, can distract from the more challenging question of the intellectual quality of the scholarship (Liu 2013). If the major hallmarks of the humanities include critical inquiry, careful hermeneutics and clear argumentation, then all research in humanistic disciplines should be appraised accordingly—whether in handwritten, printed, digital or yet another form. That is, scholarly publication in the humanities need not be limited to a particular technological platform; rather, it perdures across platforms. But is the academy prepared to assess work that deviates from the recognised forms and formats associated with 'digging down and standing back' (Felski 2015, 52)? How are meticulous analysis and lucid reasoning to be performed, communicated and adjudicated, if not with the written word?

Knowledge was understood in the Middle Ages 'as a realm of sensorial delight', which consequently positioned books as objects that could be touched, kissed, chewed over and digested as a way to grapple with ideas (Camille 1998, 40). In the modern academic world, however, such embodied and sensory performance is not the dominant model of knowledge-transmission. Quite the opposite, ideas are to be conveyed primarily through the eye, in a written document. The format of these documents is furthermore delimited by conventions around the accepted mode of sharing scholarship. In the same way that Vismann (2008) observes that files can be understood as a mode of creating a legal identity, the research publication is an act that produces and demonstrates allegiance to a scholarly identity. 'Naturalised through the social relations established by people working together' (Poovey 1995, 9) and codified as part of disciplinary practice, the regimentations of the page have come to determine the look of knowledge in the academy.

There is nothing miraculous about the form of the written document. It is manufactured through a 'convergence of social, intellectual, economic, and political forces' (Nussdorfer 2009, 230). A particular kind of document has been produced in the academy that enables the management of activity at a distance, the favoured mode of bureaucratic seeing and knowing.

DOI: 10.4324/9781003247593-3

In this disciplinary system, the written document is configured to generate documentation that, in turn, propagates more documentation: titles to aid abstracting, abstracting to aid indexing, bibliographic references to aid citation analysis, citation analysis to aid performance assessment and so on. The cascade of ever more documentary inscriptions is mobilised in 'a giant "optical device"' (Latour 1986, 19), contriving new phenomena to see and legitimising a different way to see. Thus integrated into the management of academic life, the scholarly document defines what 'counts' as knowledge and how to count it. But if reconsidered a site for the exercise of administrative power, the document makes visible the politics of the infrastructures in which it is enmeshed.

What will become evident in the following discussion is how the scholarly document has been organised to aid in its own oversight—how the written document is used as documentable evidence of research activity and how it partakes in its own documentation. In many fields, a 'publication' can be as narrowly defined as a peer-reviewed book from an academic press or an article in a particular sort of journal (Biagioli and Lippman 2020, 4). Because the book and peer-reviewed article have been so naturalised as to be imperceptible, the written publication will be weighed against two alternatives in the present discussion: a cabinet and a box. This chapter introduces the possibility that humanistic research might be expressed in word or wood and investigates the consequences of such a provocation. Whereas journal articles and books profit from long-standing customs in academic milieux, their counterparts in other forms must strive to establish even the most basic scholarly warrant. Documentary forms signal a particular mode of reception for authors, readers and librarians. They can communicate a scholarly identity, set expectations, express their acknowledgement of and perform a docility to institutional infrastructures of knowledge. Meanwhile, because the cabinet and box are not generally associated with humanistic output, they offer few clues as to their intellectual tradition or proper interpretation. But by wresting the notion of academic publication from the written document, this chapter offers a way to consider how the 'gradual articulation of a set of practices (publishing, labeling, traveling, referencing, compiling)' (Daston 2004, 157) inaugurated a scholarly identity that has been taken up as universal. Scholarly identity and practice have, of course, never been free of influence. Indeed, disciplinary communities, universities and their libraries and academic publishers have long shaped how knowledge is to be expressed and disseminated—for example, helping establish numerical representation as a plausible discursive strategy (Porter 1996; Poovey 1998) or the journal article as a legitimate form of scholarly communication (Bazerman 1988; Csiszar 2018; Dawson et al. 2020). But a historically informed perspective can help show that such developments are contingent and have come to be accepted over time through concerted effort. As universities continue to forge partnerships with private interests to facilitate the management of academic life, it is of the utmost importance to apprehend the dynamics that are establishing the bounds of what will be recognised as knowledge in the future.

This discussion offers a promontory view on an initiative that devised scholarly publications in the three forms of a cabinet, box and journal article. Such a prospect will bring into relief many of the practices in the academy related to its documents and documentation. The chapter concerns itself with select dimensions of scholarly publication that are especially apparent from a perspective across wood and word—among them, peer review, assessment, dissemination, citation and ownership. In an analogous context, Smith explicates the value of inspecting translation for evidence of changes in the practices of knowledge: 'What we read in, what we leave out, may become visible or at least open to study, once what we have grasped of an expression appears and is fixed in quite another vocabulary'. Such work, particularly when rendered in 'a different language from the original, may function as rich and firm documentation for even quite subtle shifts in conceptual and perceptual habits' (1984, 27). The particular examples of the *Cabinet*, *Box* and *Article* examined in this study might therefore be read for evidence of 'subtle shifts in conceptual and perceptual habits' in academic life. The making of scholarship in the forms of a cabinet, box and journal article investigated how the physical manifestation of an argument contributes to its persuasive force; descriptions of those efforts may be found elsewhere (Mak and Pollack 2013a, 2013b, 2020). The present chapter uses the specificity of the practice-based project to adumbrate the relationship between forms of publication and the expectations of the academy. In so doing, it reveals how the scholarly document is implicated in institutional and institutionalised ways of knowing.

This consideration draws upon histories of textual transmission that explore the communication of ideas through time (Wilson and Reynolds 2014). Although emerging from the humanistic traditions of philology and palaeography, the study also shares points of contact with efforts in visual poetics that examine the material expression of letterforms (Drucker 1998), media archaeology that explore the agencies and temporalities of the digital through a framework of new and 'obsolete' technologies of recent centuries (Parikka 2012), platform studies that investigate the computer systems that undergird digital games (Bogost and Montfort 2009; Montfort and Bogost 2009) and trans-text and -media studies that are concerned with narrative, writing, performance and participation across contemporary media (Richards 2017). In an early investigation of new media, Bolter and Grusin (1998) identify a 'remediation' that occurs in photography, film, television and virtual reality, in which technologies seek to erase their own presence according to an aesthetic of transparency. It is in the disappearing act of mediation that this project situates itself. The apparent efficiency of the word as a mode of expression conceals the fact that written documents benefit from customised networks of circulation. Such documents are able to be assessed, described, classified and moved expeditiously because the system in which they function was developed with and around them. As the 'same' argument unfolds across the forms of a cabinet, box and peer-reviewed article, we will discover to what extent the scholarly document has been cultivated for academic service.

The first publication—a making public—of the research was staged in a community gallery. *A cabinet of curiosity: the library's dead time* was an exhibition of sculptures and performance pieces, introduced by a wooden cabinet of two metres in height (Figure 2.1). All elements, including the cabinet, were built custom for the event to highlight different aspects of the complex relations between material form and meaning. By conveying scholarship in a register other than that of the typical peer-reviewed article or book, the *Cabinet* exhibition gave cause to examine how certain forms of academic publication are related to disciplinary identity. However, the *Cabinet* first had to establish that it was indeed scholarship, and, furthermore, in the humanities. There is no tradition of academic publishing in the form of joinery that helps locate the *Cabinet* in the landscape of humanistic scholarship. Moreover, the use of sculptures and performance worked outside the disciplinary expectations related to the word. Indeed, the *Cabinet* lacked an important feature of academic publications, that is, a scholarly apparatus. Composed of bibliographical references or citations, this apparatus helps to signal the intellectual orientation of the work (Barney 1991; Rouse and Rouse 1991; Grafton 1999). It identifies the particular disciplinary discussions that are being engaged and indicates the context in which readers should understand the contribution. In journal articles and books, the device manifests as footnotes, endnotes or a list of bibliographical references documenting a relevant field of research. A wooden cabinet, by contrast, does

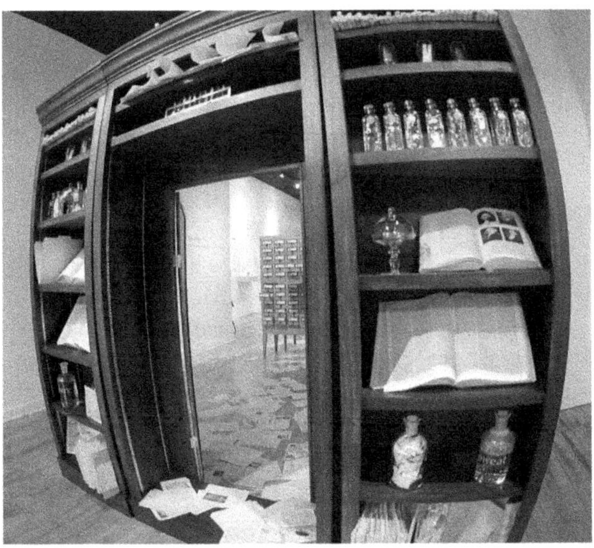

Figure 2.1 The cabinet in *A cabinet of curiosity: the library's dead time.*

not have an analogous infrastructure. In eschewing the customs and shorthand of academic communication that would make the work identifiable, the material form of the *Cabinet* had to be deployed in a different way to establish its scholarly *bona fides* and its humanistic orientation.

A cabinet had been selected as the material form for the publication because it not only indexed a particular kind of space and approach to meaning-making, but also embodied it. Rather than citing with words, the *Cabinet* cited with its material form. The cabinet and, indeed, the other pieces of the exhibition in *A cabinet of curiosity: the library's dead time*, were coordinated to make reference to the cabinets of curiosity of the early modern period. Such cabinets were spaces in which collectors experimented with different ways of ordering and understanding the world, especially as travellers began to return from foreign lands with extraordinary stories and objects that had to be reconciled with conventional knowledge. Not yet set into formalised systems of classification, disparate objects such as botanical oddities, books, religious relics and works of art were arranged in multiple ways; descriptions might emphasise their curiousness, rarity and beauty, offering a link between aesthetics and the production of knowledge (Findlen 1996; Stafford 2001). By recalling this tradition as a legitimate way of knowing, the form of the cabinet signalled a particular approach for the entire exhibition. Namely, the audience was given licence to incorporate sensation in the act of interpretation and transgress the disciplinary boundaries of knowledge-production that now divide the arts, sciences and humanities (Haskins 1957; Leclerq 1961; Kelley 1997; Forman 2012). The implied references of the *Cabinet* encouraged a re-appraisal of ways of seeing and knowing that have only recently been separated for codification in different disciplines.

Although the words of a footnote serve to negotiate scholarly credibility by parading intellectual kinships before the eye of the reader, the wood of the *Cabinet* worked differently. The *Cabinet* constituted a physical site in which other ways of observing and knowing could be sensed and experienced with the body. As Bowersock observes regarding the practice of citation, there are 'many other ways of telling the reader why he should believe what he reads' (1984, 54). For academic readers, the wooden cabinet indexed scholarship on early modern ways of knowing by historians Findlen (1996), Daston and Park (1998) and Smith (2004), among others. But the *Cabinet*'s life-sized reference to the history of cabinets of curiosity also situated and provided the grounds to practise sensation as a legitimate way of knowing. The *Cabinet* encouraged the audience to reflect on how bodily engagement influenced their interpretation of the publication. That is, did touching and smelling the argument add to its persuasiveness? The negotiation of credibility, then, was located not in the textual documentation of scholarly references but in the ability of the *Cabinet* to engender an experience that convincingly substantiated its argument—the *Cabinet* used instantiation to substantiate.

Now imbricated in the management of scholarly activity, the stakes of citing have been raised. Many universities assess academic performance based on a calculation of how often a publication has been mentioned—or cited—by others in recent scholarship, an approach known as citation analysis. Presently conceived, citation analysis compels a standardising of form, style and convention to facilitate the extraction of bibliographic references. Yet there are sources of inspiration that evade documentation or need no reference. The gifts of the Muses are eternal, and their impact is timeless. Influence may manifest as an allusion or imitation of form; it may be expressed in a veiled acknowledgement of debt that is not ratified with a citation in words. Although traditional bibliometric methods have been augmented by tallies of page views, bookmarks, downloads, tags and shares on social networks in an effort to secure a more comprehensive view of academic performance, these measures nevertheless require research to be arranged and accessed in particular ways (Cronin and Sugimoto 2014). Such metrics shift attention away from the internal characteristics of a publication, such as the quality of its argument or the originality of the contribution. They instead 'focus on those features of the publication that are external to its claims', harvesting elements that 'are literally at its *physical margins*: publication title and date, journal titles, citations, references, authors' names—everything but the content' (Biagioli 2018, 255). The measures suppose, moreover, that the effect of scholarship—its influence on and use by others—results in traces that are also documented and documentable. And it is these visible traces that are now constituted as interchangeable units of evidence in the final reckoning of scholarly performance.

Although bibliographic citations have been collected since at least the third century as research aids *for* scholars, it is in the last 50 years that such data have been deployed to assess the performance *of* scholars. Throughout the nineteenth century, judicial decisions in the United States were traced through time so that lawyers could quickly ascertain whether a particular case was authoritative in terms of establishing precedent (Shapiro 1992; Ogden 1993; Wouters 1999). In Frank Shepard's *Adhesive Annotations* of the last quarter of the nineteenth century, and his later *Citations*, cases were annotated with codes to signal whether a judgment had subsequently been affirmed, questioned, modified or overturned. Because the references were to case law, they could not be mistaken as an indicator of the performance of legal professionals—except, of course, when it emerged that someone had failed to conduct a comprehensive check of the authority of a ruling (Ogden 1993, 42). This tradition formed the basis of Eugene Garfield's initiative, the *Science Citation Index*, which amassed bibliographical information that tracked when a scientific journal article appeared in the notes or reference lists of other publications. Although developed as an 'association-of-ideas index' (Garfield 1955, 108) to aid a thorough search of related literature and thus discourage redundant publications, the *Science Citation Index* was quickly taken up to study the behaviour of scholarly communities—for example, examining the nature of scientific consensus or the emergence of new ideas (Wouters 2014; Csiszar 2020). That turn having been made, the path was cleared for deploying citation analysis to measure the performance of those same scholarly communities.

The involvement of the private sector has further intensified the use of citation metrics in the academy. Information traffickers have monetised the collection and analysis of bibliographic data and consequently saturated the field with market-driven rhetoric about the utility of their metrological products. One such company is Clarivate, a self-anointed 'global leader' that provides 'trusted insights and analytics to accelerate the pace of innovation' (Clarivate nda). Seeking to maximise return on its ownership of Garfield's *Science Citation Index* (now part of a collection called *Web of Science*), Clarivate uses its bibliometric data to compile an annual list of *Highly Cited Researchers* that recognises the 'world's most influential researchers of the past decades, demonstrated by the production of multiple highly-cited papers that rank in the top 1% by citations for field and year in *Web of science*' (Clarivate ndb). The characterisation makes explicit that a research paper that has been mentioned frequently by other publications should be assumed to be influential or even, it is insinuated, of some quality. Enamoured with the convenience of this proxy, many universities permit quality to be perceived as a function of quantity. The same citation metric from this perspective can therefore be extended to be interpreted as an indicator of the quality of not only the particular article, but also the researcher who produced it (Biagioli 2018; Wouters 2020).

One of Clarivate's major competitors in academic bibliometrics is Elsevier, a publisher of 2,500 scientific journals, which reported revenues of £2,637 million in 2019 (RELX nd, 12 and 15). Also among its assets are Scopus—described as 'the largest abstract and citation database of peer-reviewed literature'—and CiteScore, a citation metric that draws data from the Scopus database (Elsevier ndb, 2020b). Jockeying for market share, Elsevier takes pains to explicate the methodological differences between its citation tool and its more established rival, the Journal Impact Factor (JIF), owned by Clarivate (Elsevier 2020a). Although Elsevier had introduced other analytical indicators before the launch of CiteScore in 2016, such tools were never 'as popular as the JIF' (Van Noorden 2016, 325). Both CiteScore and the JIF track how many times a serial or journal has been mentioned by other publications within a specific timeframe. In other words, the 'impact factor' is derived from the number of times the title of a journal—not an article—is listed in the bibliographical references of another publication. Despite widespread cautions against using CiteScore or the JIF to perform granular assessments, 'researchers are judged by the impact factor of the journal in which their work appears, rather than by what they actually write' (Van Noorden 2016, 325). The impact of a forthcoming article is probably close to none, having been read and discussed by very few. But the article-to-be is nevertheless considered more valuable if it is to appear in a journal with a high impact factor because it is perceived to have a better chance of receiving a greater number of citations in that venue than if published elsewhere (Biagioli and Lippman 2020, 7).

Another of Elsevier's products is Pure, which offers modules customised for various national assessment schemes. These schemes include the Research Excellence Framework in the United Kingdom, as well as the Higher Education Research Data Collection and Excellence in Research for Australia (ERA). Pure consolidates bibliometric data from Elsevier's portfolio to help institutions 'improve their performance' by delivering reports on 'researchers' activities, areas of expertise and accomplishments' (Elsevier nda). When questioned about the company's relationship with academia, the chairman of Elsevier, Y.S. Chi—a former trustee of Princeton University and current trustee of Princeton University Press—bluntly stated, 'Our business is absolutely contingent on the competition among researchers and the assessment of their research' (Schonfeld 2018). As evidence of the traction gained in academic circles for performance evaluation, Elsevier was selected by the Australian Research Council as the sole provider for citation data for the ERA assessments of 2010, 2012 and 2015 (Elsevier 2014), and Clarivate was named for the assessment of 2018 (Australian Research Council 2018). In this configuration of the academic reward system, the leading desideratum is the potential to be highly cited and, indeed, in ways and venues that make such references visible to the instruments that dominate the market. The savvy scholar may then puzzle over whether to excoriate their adversaries in print (the explicit citations nevertheless improving the bibliometric scores of the opposing side) or to condemn with silence. Thus interlocked with commercial and institutional interests—and the performance assessments of colleagues, friends and rivals—citation has become an important political act.

The *Cabinet* engaged the ongoing debates around the measurement of scholarly performance by invoking the notion of 'dead time' in the title of the publication and in the sculptural argument of the *Cabinet* itself. In the context of cinema studies, Doane (2002) explains that dead time refers to events that are edited out of a film because they are considered unproductive to the final narrative. Biddick (2009) goes further, noting that dead time is not only about selective seeing, but also and more consequentially about selective archiving. Dead time, then, can refer to activities that are devalued and made imperceptible when systems favour other sorts of work. As instantiated in the *Cabinet*, a collection of the unseen and unregistered 'dead time' of scholarly work challenged the metrics that are currently used to assess performance in the academy (Figure 2.2). On display were paper forms from the University Library, dating from the early part of the twentieth century. These documents transmitted various measurements of work related to research that included counts of librarian-patron interactions, the duration of the exchanges and numerical representations of the effort expended. Next to these devices were other models of adjudicating the work of research, including laboratory glassware containing a 'good sum' of bitter tears that had been collected from a frustrated researcher and 'a noble accumulation' of sweat from the brow of a librarian (Figure 2.3).

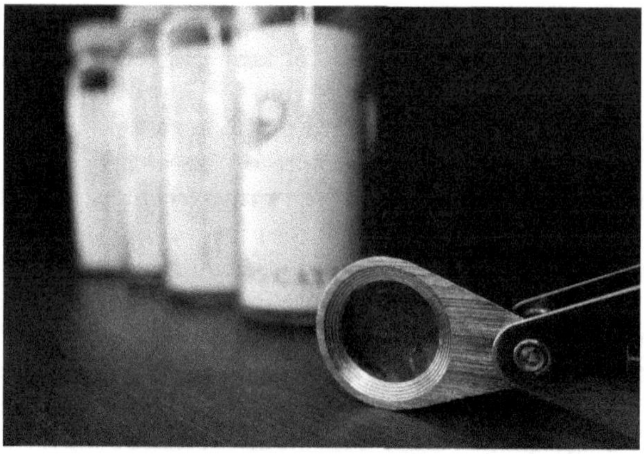

Figure 2.2 Seeing 'dead time' in the *Cabinet*.

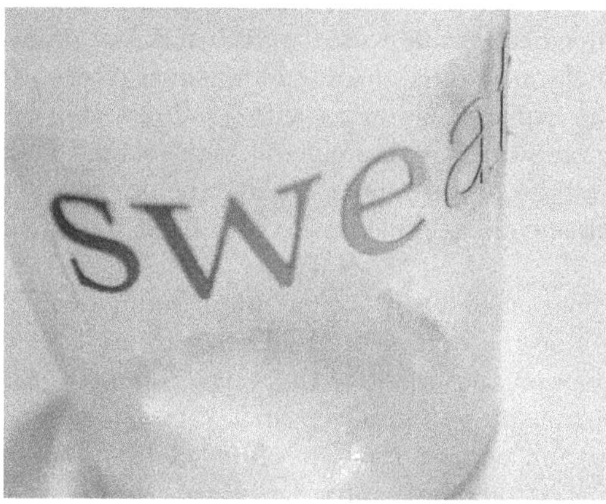

Figure 2.3 Sweat from the brow of a librarian in the *Cabinet*.

When a limited set of activities have been defined and validated as 'research work', other practices—specifically those that have been rendered difficult or impossible to measure according to those same gauges—are never entered into the archive of academia. Yet, as the *Cabinet* sought to remind the audience with its material form, this system of observation was not always the default mode of perceiving the world; it is instead the manifestation of a 'visual epistemology' that rationalises a particular way of seeing and representing the world (Daston and Lunbeck 2011; Bleichmar 2012, 45–45). The argument is not that scholarship cannot be quantified for measurement, but rather that anything can, if so nominated by administrative imperative (Joseph 2014, 140). To raise this point for discussion, modern scientific equipment was marshalled in the *Cabinet* to make visible the practices that are routinely passed over in contemporary valuations of research activity. For example, specimen jars borrowed from a laboratory bestowed a kind of authority upon samples of bodily effluvia in a resurrection of the dead time of scholarship. Fixed under glass, a scholar's tears of frustration were offered for scientific analysis. The *Cabinet* thus instantiated a new 'centre of calculation' (Latour 1986, 32) in which lachrymae could be presented as quantifiable, interchangeable and transportable. The juxtaposition of various approaches to evaluating scholarly performance suggested that the work of research could equally be adjudicated by the smell of perspiration as by the data analytics that are currently in favour. It furthermore suggested that things which appear commensurable have been made so by design and furthermore transmit their own logic of assessment. All measures 'construct a commensurability that did not exist before their own calibration. Nothing is, by itself, either reducible or irreducible to anything else' (Latour 1993, 113). The *Cabinet* made evident that other approaches of marking and classifying scholarly activity are no more or less credible than the prevailing method that has been institutionalised. Taking advantage of its material form, the *Cabinet* enacted this dynamic in its presentation of observing, understanding and acknowledging different aspects of scholarly activity.

Because the *Cabinet* could not be easily shared with people around the world, the second phase of the project engaged the issue of dissemination. A new publication was proposed in the form of a portable, suitcase-sized box (Figures 2.4 and 2.5). The *Box* was also composed of wood but operated on a different scale. Travel restrictions concerning carry-on luggage, liquids and hazardous materials, as well as the limitations of budget and feasibility, were taken into account in the construction of the *Box*. Despite its purposeful design, the material form of the *Box* remained a challenge to circulating

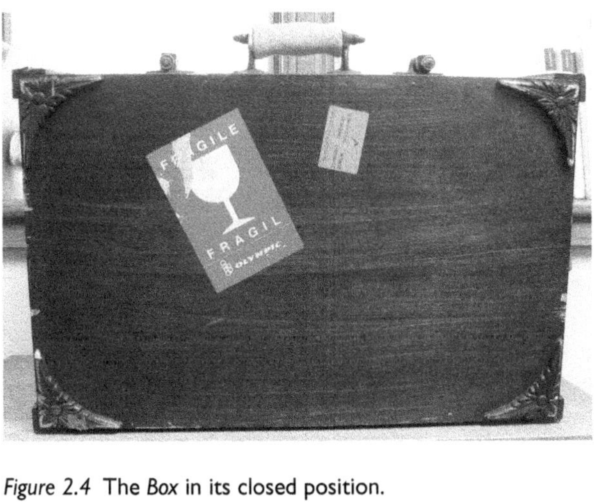

Figure 2.4 The *Box* in its closed position.

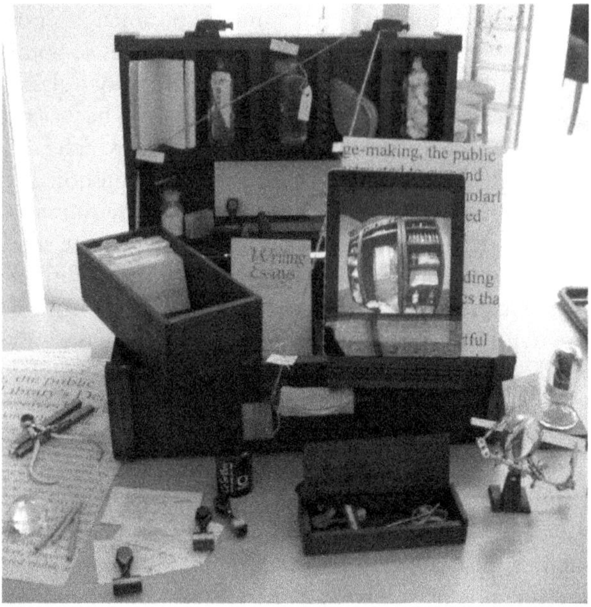

Figure 2.5 The *Box*, prepared for dissemination.

the research, a stark reminder of the extent to which the written document has been domesticated. The *Box* had to be hauled through one of Greece's record-breaking heat waves, trundled over cobbled streets in Copenhagen and navigated through traffic in Washington, DC, and London in support of dissemination. Its contents needed to be packed for transport, laid out on arrival at its publication venue, explicated and then packed up again. As the attempt to disseminate research in the form of the *Box* illustrates, what 'shareable' has come to mean and for what end has been strategically cultivated by the infrastructures that moderate the practice of scholarship.

The *Cabinet* and *Box* disseminate research beyond the walls of the academy in ways that the journal article or scholarly monograph do not. They circulate scholarship through site-specific performance, calling upon and responding to local expertise in their engagement of knowledge practices that extend beyond the written document. Aiming to exhilarate and invigorate, the *Cabinet* and the *Box* exert influence by inspiring reflective practices; they are not designed to prompt citation. The *Cabinet* and the *Box* are intended to stimulate thinking that might be shared with friends and family, and they encourage the rehearsal of other ways of knowing on whatever timeline might be appropriate. For instance, marking its departure from scholarly convention, the *Cabinet* dislocated academic readers from their usual spaces of knowledge-exchange. Installed in a community gallery, the *Cabinet* provided an opportunity for a heterogeneous audience of those who do not regularly participate in citation to experience scholarship with their academic counterparts who do. Multiple groups came together in time and space to 'read' the publication and practise diverse ways of knowing. Meanwhile, the *Box* was shared in different geographical regions with an international audience of students and scholars from various disciplines. The *Box* developed an ever-changing list of influences as its constituent parts were revised each time to index more apprehensible bodies of scholarship and knowledge practices. In addition, the *Box* was received by inquisitive taxi drivers and audio-visual technicians around the world who were 'readers' and partners in its publication, but not occupied with generating visible traces of their interest in documented form. Indeed, the reaction sought from the audience was not one of citation. The *Cabinet* and *Box* therefore test the bureaucratic eye: they do not cite with words, and they are themselves difficult to cite. They share research and produce effects, but not in ways that make the impact perceptible by current techniques of surveillance. Such contributions are therefore classified as 'bibliometrically unsuitable research achievements' (Ball 2017, 65). Whereas the scholarly paper has been refined to generate a fixed list of bibliographic references *to* other publications and solicit references to itself *in* other publications, the forms of a cabinet and box have not. 'Writing' with wood thus exposed assumptions about how documents of scholarship are expected to perform and, specifically, in relation to the documentation of scholarly activity.

Under the intensifying exigencies of documentation, components of the written document that were once provisional become obligatory and codified through practice. Indeed, certain features of documentary records from the sixth century onwards began to be enshrined as formal requirements—'formalities with legal force'—as authority shifted to the document itself and away from agents who could attest to its trustworthiness (Vismann 2008, 72). Once simply a sealant, the seal was granted the faculty and responsibility of being its own authenticating mechanism. The document consequently emerges as a 'training ground for administrative routine' (101) and its regimentation an important exercise of bureaucratic power. The prioritising of managerial efficiency in academia has similarly consecrated a particular form of the document. It is around a standardised conception of scholarship and its documents that the academy has configured grant competitions, categories that identify and assess contributions and library practices that help organise, circulate and preserve the research. From this perspective, the application of creativity risks producing non-conforming documents that do not 'do' what they need to do to support their own administration. In a framework that orients scholarly practice towards market-driven calculations of efficiency, several core priorities of the humanities will be rendered dead time or, worse, acknowledged but ascribed little or no value. For example, although it has been said that writing 'is the cheapest way to reach a big audience' (McCloskey 1985, 188), writing well emerges as a liability. Economist Jack C. High had already observed some 30 years ago that 'good writing has a lower economic value and a higher opportunity cost'. He explains, 'good writing requires long study, hard thought, and repeated edits ... If the goal is to publish, writing well misdirects time and labour' (1987, 543–544). Imbricated in the operations of management, the scholarly document—and thus practice—is policed closely by administrative procedure.

To permit a closer inspection of how writing may be a liability even within the confines of a document, the third publication of the project adopted the form of the journal article. The *Article*, having been composed with words, was more ostensibly a written document (Figure 2.6). It could be integrated into the existing infrastructures of academic publishing, and therefore offered the opportunity to scrutinise the system of peer review. In contrast to citation metrics that allow any observer to perform an audit by checking features that are external to the claims of a scholarly paper, peer review relies on specialist knowledge and focuses on the evidence, argument and quality of the contribution (Biagioli 2018, 255). Although peer review is sometimes preferred for its individualised and discipline-specific approach, Wouters observes that relying on the assessment of expert colleagues can nevertheless hinder radical advances in scholarship. Peer review may 'delay interdisciplinary innovation because this often entails not only a reconfiguration of substantive or methodological research areas, but may also mean a redefinition of the very criteria of what counts as high quality research' (2020, 72). Set within the current reward infrastructure, he notes that peer review can actively work against innovation because such contributions do not conform to standard expectations. Indeed, innovative scholarship is often deemed innovative precisely because it eludes the usual measures of time, space and influence.

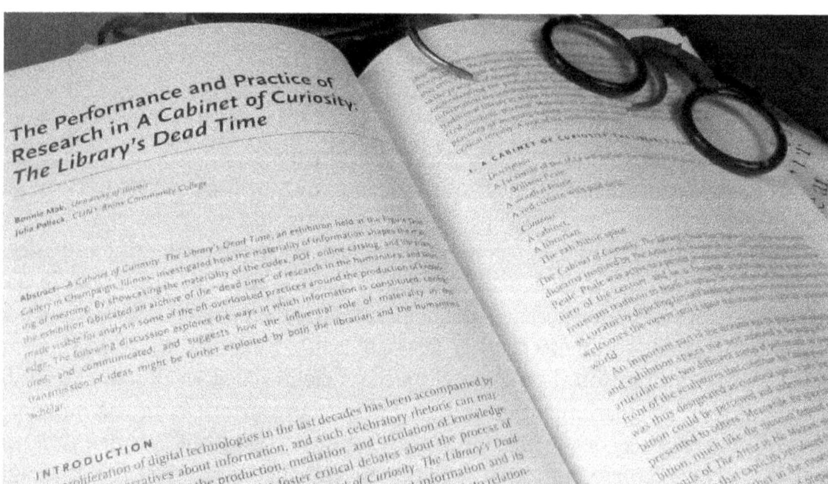

Figure 2.6 The *Article*.

In the same way that the *Cabinet* and the *Box* employed wood to stimulate an aesthetic response in support of their argument, the *Article* mobilised the printed word. The visual arrangement of the *Article* intimates its deviation from the typical journal submission. With a glance, readers might already surmise that they are to embark on another way of grappling with ideas. The words of the *Article* draw attention to themselves in an acutely visible way; they suggest that the activities of reception and interpretation are to be performed by the audience in the reading of the journal article (Auslander 2016, 6). The layout of the page was configured to suggest to readers that they are exploring a cabinet of curiosity. To that end, the text was divided into subsections that described each item in detail and offered an analysis. Also serving the performance of the argument was the prose itself. As the words on the page verbally explicate the role of material form in the shaping and mediation of knowledge, so too do they physically embody it. The shapely letterforms and layout invite the reader to experience—and then consider—how the materiality of the *Article* strengthens its own argument by participating in it. Working within the infrastructures of academic publishing, the *Article* performs research with words but nevertheless tests the limits of the scholarly document.

Scholarship in wood might have predictably been difficult to integrate into the infrastructures of academic publishing, but the *Article*—despite having been written with words—likewise proved a challenge. The process of peer review made evident that the *Article* did not match the expectations regarding genres of academic publication, which may be understood as 'social contracts between a writer and a specific public, whose function is to specify the proper use of a particular cultural artefact' (Jameson 1982, 106). The divergent peer reports indicated that some readers had struggled to understand the research or its project. Without explicit instruction to do otherwise, these reviewers had assumed that the *Article* was participating in the tradition of performance-documentation in the arts (Auslander 2016, 1). They expected a comprehensive description of the show: a reprise with words, accompanied by an extensive account of audience reaction, a floor plan and a full set of images that would provide witness to the event. The *Article*, they reasoned, should act archivally, functioning as a recording—as documentation—of a historical moment. One reader indicated that the article should furthermore provide enough information so that others might arrange a similar event. The overtly designed layout of the page, the organisational structure of the article and the analytical discussion were seen to be interfering with the depiction of the past spectacle as it had unfolded; these authorial choices were considered inappropriate interventions.

Caught between disciplinary genres and imperatives, the *Article* could be mistaken as an attempt to reproduce a work that had been performed and completed elsewhere, for and to a different audience. But the *Article* was not designed to provide a faithful recording of a past event—it does not reproduce; it produces. The notion of reproducibility has recently emerged as a fundamental concern in some areas of scientific research, often said to account for investment by validating results. Tendered as an important procedure of stabilisation for scientific knowledge, the successful repetition of the same experiment is by no means a metric of universal application if considered historically and across the disciplines. Reproducibility in the humanities is tantamount to plagiarism. As early as antiquity, imitation was recognised as a valuable educational technique. But Quintilian argues in his *Institutio oratoria* that although of some merit, the copying of models should give way to mature judgement towards the goal of progress, that is, improving upon past achievements: 'Nothing grows by imitation alone' (*Inst.* 10.2.9). Indeed, humanistic research is not usually formulated as a reproduction of an earlier achievement (Mak and Pollack 2016). The ambition, then, is not to replicate or repeat. Instead, each contribution proposes and is valued for its unique iteration of an idea.

But how is the quality of uniqueness to be assessed by standardised measures? The current metrics of the academy rely on a credible abstraction from scholarly practice from which an apparatus of normalisation can be developed. This abstraction must be based on particular examples in order to be defensible; the abstraction is also distanced far enough from the characteristics of any specific instance that it can acquire a moral neutrality. The grounds for measurement and its calibration have been cultivated by and for a particular perspective, but—under the cover of abstraction—the metric assumes an air of authoritativeness that permits it to be imposed as an objective and universal standard. Poovey explains:

> Modern abstraction … derives from the imposition of a conceptual grid that enables every phenomenon to be compared, differentiated, and measured by the same yardstick. Such comparisons and measurements, of course, produce some phenomena as normative—ostensibly because they are more numerous, because they represent an average, or because they constitute an ideal towards which all other phenomena move.
>
> (1995, 9)

With the assessment of academic performance yoked to this abstracted way of seeing, some scholarly practices are fixed as an ideal towards which all others should now tend. The normalising effect in the academy will be profound, likely to 'change the criteria for future scientific and scholarly performance' (Wouters 2014, 49). Cronin characterises the dynamic simply: 'The easier data capture is, the richer the picture of use and performance that can be produced' (2014, 6). A vivid example of the unresolved tensions between humanistic research and the needs related to its 'data capture' is described by Tibbo:

> Humanists frequently use vague or metaphorical titles for their writing, both fictional and nonfictional, which lend little evidence as to what the body of the text is about … Humanities scholars may also strive to make their writing 'dense' rather than 'readable.' While this may win them

> scholarly accolades, it can make comprehension of the text difficult for anyone, including indexers and abstractors, except a small cadre of subject experts. This may result in poorly written document surrogates.
>
> (1994, 609)

Scientific papers are amenable to the extraction of descriptive information by non-specialists because they are frequently organised into distinct sections that identify the purpose, methodology, results and conclusion of the contribution. Moreover, terminology may be tightly monitored by controlled vocabularies, which further aids the management of the documents. These customs that regulate the scholarly document in the sciences are rarely observed in the humanities. Similarly, legal scholarship follows different conventions and is therefore difficult for traditional bibliometrics to capture. Didactic articles, commentaries and hearings are considered important achievements in law, but 'completely fall through the bibliometric cracks' (Ball 2017, 64).

As Poovey (1995; 1998) and Porter (1996) have shown, some disciplines were configured for external assessment from the outset as part of negotiating their claims to authority and are therefore equipped to respond swiftly to the bureaucratised audits that are presently in favour. Meanwhile, disciplines that were not constituted with these mechanisms as an integral dimension of their practice struggle to rationalise their contributions according to the market-driven conceits of accounting and accountability (Newfield 2009, 279; Joseph 2014, 140–148; Biagioli 2018, 271–272). Having discovered that their documents are not optimally configured for the bureaucratic eye and its reward structure, many established fields are modifying their routines. For example, some scholars have embraced select English-language or international venues of publication to increase the visibility of their work in citation metrics. But studies in law, literature, history and archaeology frequently have regional or national foci; such work might have greater impact if published in a venue devoted to a specific time period or geographical context. In these areas, then, publishing in international journals may not be as desirable as it might be in the natural sciences—yet the metrics are still oriented towards this ideal (Ball 2017, 59). The gaming of the reward system may therefore result in a significant reduction of high-quality research of local, regional or national interest and furthermore raises the question of what 'sharing' means and with whom (Hicks et al. 2015, 430). Already made into dead time by bibliometric judgement, scholarship that does not receive the support of institutional recognition may languish. In that case, 'the notion of knowledge itself as an important aspect of human culture would no longer be an important *leitmotiv* of universities' (Wouters 2020, 67–68).

Despite the challenges posed by the *Cabinet*, *Box* and *Article* to the surveillance and management of scholarship, all three publications were readily handled by the institutional grip on intellectual property. The comprehensive documentation by the university on the topic of ownership reveals another way in which scholarly output has been constituted a site for the exercise of administrative control. Books, journal articles, educational software and 'works of artistic imagination' are considered by the university as 'traditional academic copyrightable works' (University of Illinois 2019, Art. III, Sec. 2.b). In general, the intellectual property rights over such materials remain with the creators. However, any work produced with 'funds under the control of or administered by the University' (Sec. 5) is owned by the institution. Accordingly, the rights over the *Cabinet* and the *Article* are both retained by the creators. The *Box*, in contrast, having been funded in part by a university grant, is classified as the property of the public institution—and, consequently, the state of Illinois. There were nevertheless benefits to having the *Box* placed in the same category as office furniture: expenses related to its dissemination were permitted to be reimbursed; these costs included local transportation involving the conveyance of the *Box* by taxi to a conference venue and postage to send its contents overseas. But human travel was not considered essential to the act of publication. As a result, other sources of funding had to be secured in order for the creators to accompany the *Box* and explicate its argument in support of dissemination. Although the publications of *Cabinet*, *Box* and *Article* offer alternative ways to think about classification and knowledge-production, the respective pieces themselves were entangled in institutional infrastructures that dictated what they were and how they should be managed. As the documentation regarding intellectual property shows, significant attention has been paid to formulating a conception of scholarly work that expedites normalisation and control. It seems that where considered an institutional priority, it is indeed possible to devise an expansive definition of scholarship that accommodates a range of practices and products.

One of the aims of the tripartite project was to create a momentary interruption during which some of the infrastructures that discipline academic practice were made visible for investigation. The infrastructures supporting scholarship have been carefully refined over centuries, and the tenets of classification continue to play a role in articulating the boundaries of knowledge, both within the university and without (Bowker and Star 1999; Clark 2000, 2006; Garberson 2006; Grafton 2006; Adler 2017). Such schemes can be read both as historical relics of the society that produced them and as disciplinary systems that configure how knowledge is—for the moment—understood. The forms of a cabinet and box were deliberately selected for the initiative because they do not 'conform to the abstract character of market value' (Kula 1986, 123) and are thus more able to expose the metrological fictions in question. The *Cabinet* and *Box* sought to frustrate the bureaucratic sleight that so easily converts research activities into discrete units in an accounting of academic performance—they do not cite in a conventional manner and were not designed to stimulate documentable effects; they lack the portability and interchangeability assigned to the written document. Meanwhile, composed with words, the *Article* that cites and is citable may still challenge the bounds of the scholarly document in the academy. The trajectories of the *Cabinet*, *Box* and *Article* reveal in what ways the research publication has already been shaped by administrative routine and to what extent administrative routine has already been written into scholarly practice. As an arena for the exercise of surveillance, measurement and management, the scholarly document now underwrites and authenticates a bureaucratic mode of seeing knowledge.

The foregoing discussion of a historically informed experiment in academic publishing raises for consideration how specific practices of knowledge have been legitimised over time. Making visible and grappling with the infrastructures that shape knowledge-production is key to understanding fundamental assumptions related to what counts as knowledge and how knowledge is counted. The moments of friction encountered by the *Cabinet*, *Box* and *Article* provide clues about how certain forms of knowledge gain traction over time. Conceiving publications as unique performances of meaning may stimulate alternative strategies of assessment, interpretation and dissemination that are cognisant of—and work in concert with—the diverse forms at issue. The project furthermore sheds light on new modes and technologies of publication which emerge from this study as less revolutionary when compared with cabinets or boxes that can present distinct and acute challenges to the long-standing activities of collection, curation, circulation and citation that have been organised around a particular form of the written document.

References

Adler, Melissa, 2017. *Cruising the Library: Perversities in the Organization of Knowledge*. New York: Fordham University Press.

Auslander, Philip, 2016. The Performativity of Performance Documentation. *PAJ: A Journal of Performance and Art*, 28 (3), 1–10.

Australian Research Council, 2018. Clarivate Selected as Citation Provider for ERA 2018. Available from: https://www.arc.gov.au/news-publications/media/media-releases/clarivate-selected-citation-provider-era-2018 [Accessed 16 October 2020].

Ball, Rafael, 2017. *Introduction to Bibliometrics: New Development and Trends*. Cambridge, MA: Chandos Publishing.

Barney, Stephen A., ed., 1991. *Annotation and Its Texts*. New York: Oxford University Press.

Bazerman, Charles, 1988. *Shaping Written Knowledge: The Genre and Activity of the Experimental Article in Science*. Madison, WI: University of Wisconsin Press.

Biagioli, Mario, 2018. Quality to Impact, Text to Metadata: Evaluation and Publication in the Age of Metrics. *KNOW: A Journal on the Formation of Knowledge*, 2 (2), 249–75.

Biagioli, Mario, and Lippman, Alexandra, 2020. Introduction: Metrics and the New Ecologies of Academic Misconduct. *In*: Mario Biagioli and Alexandra Lippman, eds. *Gaming the Metrics: Misconduct and Manipulation in Academic Research*. Cambridge, MA: MIT Press, Cambridge, 1–23.

Biddick, Kathleen A., 2009. Doing Dead Time for the Sovereign: Archive, Abandonment, Performance. *Rethinking History: The Journal of Theory and Practice*, 13 (2), 137–51.

Bleichmar, Daniela, 2012. *Visible Empire: Botanical Expeditions and Visual Culture in the Hispanic Enlightenment*. Chicago, IL: The University of Chicago Press.

Bolter, Jay D., and Grusin, Richard A., 1998. *Remediation: Understanding New Media*. Cambridge, MA: MIT Press.

Bogost, Ian, and Montfort, Nick, 2009. Platform Studies: Frequently Questioned Answered. *UC Irvine: Digital Arts and Culture*. Available from: https://escholarship.org/uc/item/01r0k9br [Accessed 16 October 2020].

Bowersock, Glen W., 1984. The art of the footnote. *The American Scholar*, 53 (1), 54–62.

Bowker, Geoffrey C., and Star, Susan Leigh, 1999. *Sorting Things Out: Classification and Its Consequence*. Cambridge, MA: MIT Press.

Camille, Michael, 1998. Sensations of the Page: Imaging Technologies and Medieval Illuminated Manuscripts. *In*: George Bornstein and Theresa Tinkle, eds. *The Iconic Page in Manuscript, Print, and Digital Culture*. Ann Arbor, MI: University of Michigan Press, 33–53.

Clark, William, 2000. On the Bureaucratic Plots of the Research Library. *In*: Marina Frasca-Spada and Nick Jardine, eds. *Books and the Sciences in History*. Cambridge: Cambridge University Press, 190–206.

Clark, William, 2006. *Academic Charisma and the Origins of the Research University*. Chicago, IL: The University of Chicago Press.

Clarivate, nda. About us. Available from: https://clarivate.com/about-us/ [Accessed 16 October 2020].

Clarivate, ndb. Researcher Recognition. Available from: https://clarivate.com/webofsciencegroup/solutions/researcher-recognition/ [Accessed 16 October 2020].

Cronin, Blaise, 2014. Scholars and Scripts, Spoors and Scores. *In*: Blaise Cronin and Cassidy R. Sugimoto, eds. *Beyond Bibliometrics: Harnessing Multidimensional Indicators of Scholarly Performance*. Cambridge, MA: MIT Press, 3–21.

Cronin, Blaise, and Sugimoto, Cassidy R., eds., 2014. *Beyond Bibliometrics: Harnessing Multidimensional Indicators of Scholarly Performance*. Cambridge, MA: MIT Press.

Csiszar, Alex, 2018. *The Scientific Journal: Authorship and the Politics of Knowledge in the Nineteenth Century*. Chicago, IL: The University of Chicago Press.

Csiszar, Alex, 2020. Gaming Metrics Before the Game: Citation and the Bureaucratic Virtuoso. *In*: Mario Biagioli and Alexandra Lippman, eds. *Gaming the Metrics: Misconduct and Manipulation in Academic Research*. Cambridge, MA: MIT Press, 31–42.

Daston, Lorraine, 2004. Type Specimens and Scientific Memory. *Critical Inquiry*, 31 (1), 153–82.

Daston, Lorraine, and Park, Katherine, 1998. *Wonders and the Order of Nature 1150–1750*. Cambridge, MA: MIT Press.

Daston, Lorraine, and Lunbeck, Elizabeth, eds., 2011. *Histories of Scientific Observation*. Chicago, IL: The University of Chicago Press.

Dawson, Gowan, Lightman, Bernard, Shuttleworth, Sally, and Topham, Jonathan R., eds., 2020. *Science Periodicals in Nineteenth-Century Britain: Constructing Scientific Communities*. Chicago, IL: The University of Chicago Press.

Doane, Mary Ann, 2002. *The Emergence of Cinematic Time: Modernity, Contingency, the Archive*. Cambridge, MA: Harvard University Press.

Drucker, Johanna, 1998. *Figuring the Word: Essays on Books, Writing, and Visual Poetics*. New York: Granary Books.

Elsevier, 2014. Australian Research Council Selects Elsevier's Scopus for ERA 2015 (Excellence in Research for Australia) Assessment. Available from: https://www

.elsevier.com/about/press-releases/science-and-technology/australian-research-council-selects-elseviers-scopus-for-era-2015-excellence-in-research-for-australia-assessment [Accessed 16 October 2020].

Elsevier, 2020a. CiteScore Journal Metric – FAQs. Available from: https://service.elsevier.com/app/answers/detail/a_id/30562/supporthub/scopus/kw/citescore/ [Accessed 16 October 2020].

Elsevier, 2020b. How are CiteScore Metrics Used in Scopus?. Available from: https://service.elsevier.com/app/answers/detail/a_id/14880/kw/citescore/supporthub/scopus/ [Accessed 16 October 2020].

Elsevier, nda. [Pure] Features. Available from: https://www.elsevier.com/solutions/pure/features [Accessed 16 October 2020].

Elsevier, ndb. Scopus. Available from: https://www.elsevier.com/en-in/solutions/scopus [Accessed 16 October 2020].

Felski, Rita, 2015. *The Limits of Critique*. Chicago, IL: The University of Chicago Press.

Findlen, Paula, 1996. *Possessing Nature: Museums, Collecting, and Scientific Culture in Early Modern Italy*. Berkeley, CA: University of California Press.

Forman, Paul, 2012. On the Historical Forms of Knowledge Production and Curation: Modernity Entailed Disciplinarity, Postmodernity Entails Antidisciplinarity. *Osiris*, 27 (1), 56–97.

Garberson, Eric, 2006. Libraries, Memory and the Space of Knowledge. *Journal of the History of Collections*, 18 (2), 105–136.

Garfield, Eugene, 1955. Citation Indexes for Science: A New Dimension in Documentation Through Association of Ideas. *Science*, 122 (3159), 108–11.

Grafton, Anthony, 1999. *The Footnote: A Curious History*. Cambridge, MA: Harvard University Press.

Grafton, Anthony, 2006. Libraries and Lecture Halls. *In*: Katharine Park and Lorraine Daston, eds. *The Cambridge History of Science, Vol.* 3, *Early Modern Science*. Cambridge: Cambridge University Press, 238–50.

Haskins, Charles Homer, 1957 [1923]. *The Rise of Universities*. Ithaca, NY: Cornell University Press.

Hicks, Diana, Wouters, Paul, Waltman, Ludo, de Rijcke, Sarah, and Rafols, Ismael, 2015. Bibliometrics: The Leiden Manifesto for Research Metrics. *Nature*, 520 (7548), 429–31.

High, Jack C., 1987. The Costs of Economical Writing. *Economic Inquiry*, 25, 543–5.

Jameson, Fredric, 1982. *The Political Unconscious: Narrative as a Socially Symbolic Act*. Ithaca, NY: Cornell University Press.

Joseph, Miranda, 2014. *Debt to Society: Accounting for Life under Capitalism*. Minneapolis, MN: University of Minnesota Press.

Kelley, Donald R., ed., 1997. *History and the Disciplines: The Reclassification of Knowledge in Early Modern Europe*. Rochester, NY: Rochester University Press.

Kula, Witold, 1986. *Measures and Men*. Translated by R. Szreter. Princeton, NJ: Princeton University Press.

Latour, Bruno, 1986. Visualization and Cognition: Thinking with Eyes and Hands. *Knowledge and Society: Studies in the Sociology of Culture Past and Present*, 6, 1–40.

Latour, Bruno, 1993. *We Have Never Been Modern*. Translated by Catherine Porter. Cambridge, MA: Harvard University Press.

Leclerq, Jean, 1961, *The Love of Learning and the Desire for God: A Study of Monastic Culture*. Translated by Catharine Misrahi. New York: Fordham University Press.

Liu, Alan, 2013. The Meaning of the Digital Humanities. *PMLA*, 128 (2), 409–23.

Mak, Bonnie, and Pollack, Julia, 2013a. Book Unbound: An Exploration of the Material Forms of the Codex and e-Book. *Book 2.0*, 3 (2), 137–147.

Mak, Bonnie, and Pollack, Julia, 2013b. The Performance and Practice of Research in "A Cabinet of Curiosity: The Library's Dead Time". *Art Documentation*, 32 (2), 202–21.

Mak, Bonnie, and Pollack, Julia, 2016. On the Design of the Humanities. *Interactions*, 23 (4), 76–9.

Mak, Bonnie, and Pollack, Julia, 2020. Research Box. *In*: Susanne Bauer, Martina Schlünder, and Maria Rentetzi, eds. *Boxes in Action: A Field Guide*. Manchester, UK: Mattering Press, 606–23.

McCloskey, Donald, 1985. Economical Writing. *Economic Inquiry*, 23, 187–222.

Montfort, Nick, and Bogost, Ian, 2009. *Racing the Beam: The Atari Video Computer System*. Cambridge, MA: MIT Press.

Newfield, Christopher, 2009. Ending the Budget Wars: Funding the Humanities during a Crisis in Higher Education. *Profession*, 270–84.

Nussdorfer, Laurie, 2009. *Brokers of Public Trust: Notaries in Early Modern Rome*. Baltimore, MD: The Johns Hopkins University Press.

Ogden, Patti J., 1993. "Mastering the Lawless Science of Our Law:" A Story of Legal Citation Indexes. *Law Library Journal*, 85 (1), 1–48.

Parikka, Jussi, 2012. *What is Media Archaeology?* London: Polity.

Poovey, Mary, 1995. *Making a Social Body: British Cultural Formation, 1830–1864*. Chicago, IL: The University of Chicago Press.

Poovey, Mary, 1998. *A History of the Modern Fact: Problems of Knowledge in the Sciences of Wealth and Society*. Chicago, IL: The University of Chicago Press.

Porter, Theodore M., 1996. *Trust in Numbers: The Pursuit of Objectivity in Science and Public Life*. Princeton, NJ: Princeton University Press.

RELX, nd. Annual Report and Financial Statements 2019. Available from: https://www.relx.com/investors/annual-reports/2019 [Accessed 16 October 2020].

Richards, Denzell, 2017. Historicizing Transtexts and Transmedia. *In*: Benjamin W. L. Derhy Kurtz and Mélanie Bourdaa, eds. *The Rise of Transtexts: Challenges and Opportunities*. New York: Routledge, 15–32.

Rouse, Mary A., and Rouse, Richard H., 1991. *Authentic Witnesses: Approaches to Medieval Texts and Manuscripts*. Notre Dame, IN: University of Notre Dame Press.

Schonfeld, Roger C., 2018. Elsevier Chairman YS Chi: An Interview. *The Scholarly Kitchen*. Available from: https://scholarlykitchen.sspnet.org/2018/12/10/elsevier-chairman-ys-chi-interview/ [Accessed 16 October 2020].

Shapiro, Fred R., 1992. Origins of Bibliometrics, Citation Indexing, and Citation Analysis: The Neglected Legal Literature. *Journal of the American Society of Information Science*, 43 (5), 337–9.

Smith, Wilfred Cantwell, 1984. On Mistranslated Booktitles. *Religious Studies*, 20 (1), 27–42.

Smith, Pamela H., 2004. *The Body of the Artisan: Art and Experience in the Scientific Revolution*. Chicago, IL: The University of Chicago Press.

Stafford, Barbara Maria, 2001. Revealing Technologies/Magical Domains. *In*: Barbara Maria Stafford and Frances Terpak, eds. *Devices of Wonder: From the World in a Box to Images on a Screen*. Los Angeles, CA: Getty Research Institute, 1–142.

Tibbo, Helen R., 1994. Indexing for the Humanities. *Journal of the American Society for Information Science*, 45 (8), 607–19.

University of Illinois Board of Trustees, 2019. The General Rules Concerning University Organization and Procedure. Available from: https://www.bot.uillinois.edu/governance/general_rules [Accessed 16 October 2020].

Van Noorden, Richard, 2016. Controversial Impact Factor Gets a Heavyweight Rival. *Nature*, 540 (7633), 325–6.

Vismann, Cornelia, 2008. *Files: Law and Media Technology*. Translated by Geoffrey Winthrop-Young. Stanford, CA: Stanford University Press.

Wilson, N. G., and Reynolds, L. D., 2014. *Scribes and Scholars: A Guide to the Transmission of Greek and Latin Literature* (4th ed.). Oxford: Oxford University Press.

Wouters, Paul, 1999. The Creation of the Science Citation Index. *In*: Mary Ellen Bowden, Trudi Bellardo Hahn, and Robert V. Williams, eds. *Proceedings of the 1998 Conference on the History and Heritage of Science Information Systems*. Medford, NJ: Information Today, 127–36.

Wouters, Paul, 2014. The Citation: From Culture to Infrastructure. *In*: Blaise Cronin and Cassidy R. Sugimoto, eds. *Beyond Bibliometrics: Harnessing Multidimensional Indicators of Scholarly Performance*. Cambridge, MA: MIT Press, 47–66.

Wouters, Paul, 2020. The Mismeasurement of Quality and Impact. *In:* Mario Biagioli and Alexandra Lippman, eds. *Gaming the Metrics: Misconduct and Manipulation in Academic Research*. Cambridge, MA: MIT Press, 67–75.

Part II

Authority

Chapter 3

When records speak we listen

Conversations with the archive

Jeanine Leane and Natalie Harkin

> I came back decades later to rooms she cleaned, in ruins of a homestead on the River of, my Country. Cast iron gates built on years of bumper crops, golden fleeces, free labour, swing open on rusty hinges like pages in an unfinished story.
>
> (Leane 2019)

This paper reflects a conversation between two Aboriginal women poets and scholars from unique Wiradjuri and Narungga standpoints, as we enter the colonial archive via those *cast iron gates swung open on rusty hinges*. We seek beginnings to stories from different places and points in history; un-ending stories that are embodied and lived, and also 'officially' traced via the state's legal archive. We consider what happens when the archive box is opened, when records speak and are heard for the first time. We consider what the archive means to us and how we define it, recognise it, live with it and use it. We share insights on the potential and possibility of poetry as an affective-tool and literary-intervention; our way to actively transform out from the archive-box and rupture the ongoing violence of the colonial archive. Our past methods and praxis are located on unique interventionist continuums that shape our current research: Aboriginal women's labour stories, the Queensland literary Unaipon Award stories and storytelling as a living archive. We recognise each other's stories here, despite our cultural, spatial and temporal differences. Our Grandmothers, from forever away and not so long ago, have invited themselves once again to join us. This is a sovereign-woman conversation, devoid of any colonial filter that might read us in ways we do not intend; a contemplation on history, poetry and our relationship with the state's gendered and racialised colonial archive. The gates will be open when we leave, *swinging on rusty hinges*, and we invite you to follow.

Natalie: intuitively, the 'archive' is everything; embodied, grounded and everywhere like a bottomless well or a map, deep and impossible to trace toward one specific origin or life-source. It is our blood memory (Momaday 1969; Allen 2002). Our corporeal connectedness. Our sense of belonging and 'relationality' centred through our ways of knowing, being and doing; learnt

DOI: 10.4324/9781003247593-5

through ‘reciprocity, obligation, shared experiences, coexistence, cooperation and social memory’; and grounded in holistic inter-connectedness between and among all living things (Moreton-Robinson 2000, 16; Moreton-Robinson 2017). This archive is the assemblage of feelings, objects and stories we gather, and all that is unknowingly gathered around us. It can be difficult to grasp or pin down, while at the same time being as constant and natural as the life-giving air we breathe; air that has been carried on winds with messages from generations and lifetimes ago, comprised from the concentrated elements of our ancestors' breaths that have returned for us to breathe in deep. We listen to it, wait for it and breathe it in. It is our re-memory; a triggering landscape that holds lessons, warnings, secrets and signs that lure us in, trip us up and guide our tomorrows to come. If we open up, we can feel it beneath our feet as we tread forward leaving traces upon traces on paths already well worn. Same air. Same path. Different time. I recognise this non-linear temporal-familiar archive as my imprinted-imprint; sentimental, known and safe.

Beyond this intuitive recognition, I have an entrenched default position that is hard to shake. The ‘archive’ is a dark room. A square box. A distant warehouse with a web of corridors and a revolving loading dock. It is an object. An artefact. A document. Something precious. It has been stolen, collected, recorded, categorised and contained. A fixed sacred process of consignment where provenance, objectivity and security are assured. This archive can be violent and difficult to approach. It has a history of preservation so painstakingly maintained, and a history of loss for all that is discarded and deemed abject, marginal, inferior and irrelevant to future memory. It is the paradox I love and hate.

> navigate this wretched ocean: Board of Anthropological Research expedition reports/ South Australian Museum data-card files and collections/ State Aboriginal Record files/ Aborigines Protection Board files/ Children's Welfare Board files/ and be transported with family at the hands of scientists being measured-bled photographed-labelled, objects of fascination standing before Inspectors/ ‘State-Ladies’/ Probation Officers/ Police Constables/anthropologists being charged/ file-noted/ watched/ shamed in the great Australian assimilation-experimentnavigate back through the wakeseek light-housesstay afloat and keep watchtry not to drown as you consider …

> *when they come*
> *to claim mename meframe me*
>
> *will they slice me half*
> *or quarters*
> *or one sixteenths?*
>
> (Harkin 2019, 26)

Jeanine: these places they call archives! They did my head in for years. What are these buildings? These structures, these bricks and mortar gods that hold and withhold; include and exclude. Create false images. Doppelgänger ghosts that haunt the soul of the self they were stolen from.

Archives are elusive, yet everywhere. They are everywhere in their surveillance of Aboriginal people. They are state record offices, government departments, colonial courts, they are police stations, schools, hospitals, employers, public buildings, amenities and even neighbours with an eye for otherness and a taste for the long-running national discourse that Aboriginality is everyone's business. Yet at the same time, these archives are both direct and elusive in what they take; notes, files, photos, medical reports, legal reports. What do they say? Where do they go? Who else reads them? Who keeps them? For how long? Where do you find these inventions of the fragmented 'other self' or 'selves', and loved ones that someone else has made and filed, owned and controlled? How do we *re*-member our *dis*-membered selves in these archives:

> The water under the bridge ripples over my memory now
>
> the river a deep archive…
>
> (Leane 2017, 25)

Let me tell you a story. Archives are bloodlines. I grew up in a house of women. There was my Grandmother, two Aunts, my mother and my sister for the most part of my childhood and early adulthood. The women who raised me were strong, determined and optimistic for a better future for my sister and me. But they were also guarded. Their former lives before I arrived in the 1960s were revealed to me only in snippets over time.

Once my cousin was visiting from a long way. We were friends. We liked different games to our other cousins. One day, when the big women were busy cooking a family dinner at the front of the house and our cousins were playing outside, we went snooping through an old wardrobe in my Grandmother's bedroom at the back of the house. We were looking for old hats, petticoats, stockings with garters and all sorts of other apparel that women wore in the 1920s and 1930s. We were just little. I was seven and my cousin was nine and we were searching for clothes to play a game we made up called 'Olden Days'. I found a metal box on the top shelf behind a stack of old hats.

I got it down. '*Let's open it!*' my cousin said. '*Maybe it's old jewels*'. But I knew it wasn't because it didn't rattle. It felt like silence. It was full of paper, most of it typed or printed. With the box between us on the floor we flicked through the first few layers: **Registrar of Births Deaths and Marriages, Protection Board. Ward.** Mostly words we didn't know. My fingers would have kept sifting through, but my cousin snapped the box shut. '*Put it away!*' she said, like she'd seen a ghost. We replaced the box in the back corner of the top shelf.

I didn't see my cousin again for a long time. I knew before the visit even ended that I was going back to that box. I went back time and time again every time I was alone over the years that I spent in my Grandmother's house. Found more words. Words that nobody said. Over the next decade or so, I found more boxes stashed away in the drawers and cupboards of the women I lived with. My head bulged with anger and confusion. Why keep such violent documents? Yet they did keep them like bits of themselves that needed to be stashed away. Did they keep them, knowing somehow that years later someone might find those other selves and put them to rest? Years later, I thought about it like going back for the ghosts that jumped at my cousin and I when we opened that first box.

> When I'm alone I search through boxes, wardrobes, sewing drawers and cabinets. All the places I shouldn't go. I touch all the things I shouldn't touch. Old letters. Papers with thick black words. *Quadroon, Ward of State, Illegitimate, Orphanage, Carnal Knowledge, Destitute, Rape, Octoroon.* I can read better than I should at age seven. I don't tell anyone. Secrets help me know what big people can't say. I put them back where I found them until they find me again.

Natalie: this archive, as papers, words and labels, is not just a product. It is also a process manifested by institutions that were conceived, created and ordered by law-makers with particular ways of knowing, surveying and capturing information 'about' us. This information effectively morphed from colonial-fantasy to grand-narrative and persuasive mythology, such as *The Aboriginal Problem, The Missing Link* and *The Dying Race*; rhetorical and sinister. Such representations and fantasy-impressions have endured to this day yet are often reduced or dismissed as being *a product of the time* or *the thinking of the day.* Ironically, such impressions can be countered via the very source that produced them due to conditions of intense state surveillance and record keeping. Contemporary scholars of archives and colonialism are increasingly working through an ethnographic lens to expose the racialised regimes that underpin the making of nation and empire. Here, the archive is revealed through its logic of consignation, order and exclusion, as 'a repository of codified beliefs' that cluster and bear witness to reveal connections between secrecy, the law and power (Stoler 2002, 1).

Despite a growing body of decolonising scholarship in this field (for example, Burton 2005; Lowe 2015; Shellam and Cruikshank 2019; Stoler 2009, 2013, 2016), I think the most potent counter-narratives are the embodied intergenerational stories we carry, individual and collective, that reveal how our families strategically navigated oppressive conditions of *Segregation, Protection* and *Assimilation*, from the moment of first contact.

> it is possible to stay afloat with others who tread carefully through archive and memory with dignity and purpose who refuse to be fixed in time

> and biologically determined who bear witness to colonising practices of dispersal and erasure who re-signify the colonial archive for a broader Indigenous cultural memory for hopeful and just futures.
>
> (Harkin 2019, 27)

As Julie Gough (2008) so fittingly reflects, 'our shared pasts linger, as accessibly amidst hills and along old roadways of this island, as in the texts of the library and archive. To read either well, the other is required'.

Jeanine: I left home angry, at 19, because the women gave me lots of things—stories, strength, determination, intergenerational knowledge that you can't learn in a system, but they had never talked about those other selves I found in the words of documents and reports stashed away. I lacked their generous spirits that forgave but didn't forget the past.

I wanted to rage at the past. Follow the paper trail of bits and pieces I found back to those bricks and mortar storehouses where false images are housed. I went back and seethed at these effigies; these violent representations are not the women I know.

> My memory is a steel trap where
> the release clasp is permanently jammed.
> Things go in but they can never go
> out again. They are lodged – permanently.
> Stuck forever in an inescapable maze
> of time, of place, of detail.
> Collective history captured projecting
> on a never-ending reel
> across the screen of my mind.

Natalie: we approach this archive tentatively, sometimes feverishly, and always with caution. We know these official records are not the source of an objective truth, but are, as Julie Gough states, 'ledgers leaking attitudes' that bring particular meaning to our work (2001, 64). As poets and educators, I feel like we're in a unique position to flip the gaze so these 'ledgers' become our ultimate cabinets of curiosity; ripe for decolonising and critique so that beyond blood-memory recognition, our ancestors can exhale with ease towards a just future. Such praxis contributes to a growing body of Indigenous-led research engaging with the violence of the colonial archive concerning issues of access and transparency; the state's archivisation processes; and questions of surveillance, representation, agency and truth-telling.

When you enter the archive, you have to really prepare yourself for the coloniser's madness. I have gathered thousands of documents since the early 1990s from multiple state repositories in order to make some sense of our colonisation story in South Australia. These files are predominantly from State Aboriginal Records, Children's Welfare Records, the South Australian Museum and the

National Archives of Australia and provide a chilling and intimate snapshot of lives lived under extraordinary surveillance and control. Collectively, they expose a culture of biopolitics underpinning the science-based social policy experimentation that all Indigenous families were subjected to across Australia during this time. An insurmountable collation of data has been gathered, dovetailing between the Aborigines Protection Board and the Children's Welfare Board, and their associated departments.

In one body of family records I obtained in 2000, every file featured the signature of those representatives of state responsible for observing, reporting and documenting my Nanna's life (Harkin 2014a). They determined what data was important, relevant and interesting for the record, which in turn influenced government mechanisms and policies designed to regulate and control our family's fate. Colonial regimes of authority are clearly on display here, revealing how power is executed through strategies of control, discipline and regulation over individual lives and societies (Stoler 2006a; Moreton-Robinson 2015). In my family's case, this included forced movements from lands, including between mission stations and communities; child removal; institutionalisation; and indentured work placements.

Aileen Moreton-Robinson's (2004) ground-breaking transformative work on the 'the possessive logic of white patriarchal sovereignty' makes perfect sense here. This 'possessive logic' operates to naturalise the nation as a white possession and is operationalised, deployed and affirmed via the archive. It is both a process and mode of rationalisation, where the state's regulatory mechanisms of control and order 'are extremely busy reaffirming and reproducing this possessiveness through a process of perpetual Indigenous dispossession, ranging from the refusal of Indigenous sovereignty to overregulated piecemeal concessions' (Moreton-Robinson 2015, xi).

Such overregulation and piecemeal concessions are clearly evidenced in my family's records where Inspectors, or 'State Ladies' as my family called them, regularly reported on items such as the contents of kitchen cupboards, what was cooking at the point of Inspector visits, what the children were wearing, where they slept, their physical appearance and whether the beds were made at the time of inspection.

In bearing witness to this surveillance, those inter-dependent systems of governance that wielded such power become transparent. We encounter colonial intimacies that engender 'precarious affections: awkward familiarities, unsolicited attention, uninvited caresses, and probings that cannot be easily refused' (Stoler 2006b, 15). 'Colonial intimacies' are understood to be implicated in the wielding of power via the 'expert and habituated benevolence of the state' (Stoler 2006b, 15); a power rationalised through blood-quantum and racial hierarchy that positions Aboriginal people as the problem to be solved.

Jeanine: the personal and the public archives are oppositional. When a person encounters themselves, or a loved one on a file, a record, a report, a photograph created and kept by the arms of the state, they are unable to recognise themselves or their loved ones. Even though that reign of terror may be over, the other self, the double self is still walking about. Haunting. For how much longer? I was too young for a while to see the real archive right under my nose that can write back to the other that the state created. The women I knew—their lives, things they loved, held and wore. The letters they wrote and received. The pictures they took.

A file is a text that lurks in a dusty archive like a time bomb. It is a text of violence, and it is a text of doubling: it presents itself—and sees itself—as one kind of text but is actually quite another. It is a text that straddles two worlds, and two realities. To be an outsider reading such texts affords a glimpse inside the mind of the state, a place of paranoia and suspicion; but to read one's own record, or that of a loved one, can be to experience a violent collision of worlds, an internal shattering as one witnesses one's own life made unrecognisable by the logic of the state.

As a young adult, in the 1980s, I did not yet have the beautiful words of First Nations poets, theorists, essayists and novelists such as Alexis Wright, Melissa Lucashenko, Romaine Moreton, Ali Cobby-Eckermann, Aileen Moreton-Robinson, Larissa Behrendt, Yvette Holt, Charmaine Papertalk Green (just to name a few), that I have today. The nation failed me for the words to describe what it has done to us. What it still does. I looked outside Australia to find the words.

It's not surprising that I first looked to Black women poets and thinkers in the United States. The women at home encouraged and taught me to love words, both spoken and written, and to listen to and respect other peoples' stories. With this in mind I turned to the beautiful words of Audre Lorde:

> As we learn to bear the intimacy of scrutiny and to flourish within it, as we learn to use the products of that scrutiny for power within our living, those fears which rule our lives and form our silences begin to lose their control over us.
>
> (Lorde 2007, 36)

My silences began to lose their control over me. I read further afield. I obsessed over archives, files and record keeping.

I found 'doppelgänger'. This German term, first used in the eighteenth century, means 'double walker'. The spectre of a person seen by the one it resembles while they still live. The 'other self' that someone else has made for their own liking that is still at large. Martin Heidegger said 'a boundary is not that at which something stops', but that 'which something begins its presencing' (Heidegger 1971, 152). I began to feel the doppelgänger-ghosts pressing in on me, crying out: *take back that other person the state created and captured.*

Jacques Derrida was the first western theorist I encountered who acknowledged the presence of ghosts and the importance of listening to them. Derrida gave me the words to describe the way I ached.

> It is to burn with a passion. It is never to rest, interminably, from searching for the archive, right where it slips away. It is to run after the archive, even if there's too much of it, right where something in it anarchives itself. It is to have a compulsive, repetitive, and nostalgic desire for the archive, *an irrepressible desire to return to the origin, a homesickness, a nostalgia for the return to the most archaic place of absolute commencement.*
>
> (Derrida 1995, 91, emphasis added)

I had to go back to the documents—the violent words I found in the boxes of my Grandmother and Aunties' lives. Confront the ghosts.

My Grandmother passed without ever talking about what I found in the box at the back of her closet. My Aunties were old women, and I'd had children of my own before they ever broached those 'other selves'; the hideous ghosts of the state-managed archives that kept them awake at night. These women, my blood, have lived different lives as sisters, daughters, mothers, aunties, grandmothers, friends and lovers. They are stalked by that slither of 'other self'; that piece of their lives that someone else stole. That shadow that left them in the half-light.

I read the *Police Gazette*, 1924:

> *Leslie Stanley to face court over the carnal knowledge of Beulah Lilian Smart, aged 14 years.*
>
> My son of twenty-one years finds this as he researches ninety-four years later.
>
> I feel fifty-seven years shifting. But I don't want to start there because I wasn't there.
>
> I want to start here, nearly a century later, where the ghosts still stalk me.
>
> Where the words in the box come back.

Natalie: we are now stalking the stalkers. My current research on Aboriginal domestic service labour stories in South Australia concerns how this white possessive logic plays out in domestic intimacies of the everyday mundane. It is clear that Aboriginal women were subjugated through state possession in particularly violent ways, and indeed continue to suffer from multiple inequalities and injustices that intersect race, class and gender directly resulting from historical colonialism (Watson and Venne 2010, 347). As Stoler states:

> Women may have been the boundary markers of empire. But it was the gendered and racialized intimacies of the everyday that women, men, and children were turned into subjects of particular kinds, as domination was routinized and rerouted in intimacies that the state sought to know but could never completely master or work out.
>
> (2006a, 57)

The majority of Aboriginal families I know in South Australia carry intimate histories of domestic service through living memory and intergenerational blood-memory passed on. Despite the significance of these stories in the collective memory of Aboriginal South Australians, government-orchestrated systems of indentured labour remain largely hidden and unacknowledged in the state's dominant and official public narratives of history. This research is an extension of my previous archival-poetic work based on a significant collection of state record files on my family, including a snapshot of the 'domestic years' of my Nanna's life at the height of *Assimilation* in the 1940s when her employment was managed by the Children's Welfare and Public Relief Board (Harkin 2016, 2019).

I acknowledge the great scope of existing national literature and research since the 1980s on the history and impact of Aboriginal domestic labour, particularly in Queensland, Victoria and New South Wales. This includes important work by Indigenous scholars, writers, poets, filmmakers and artists who have been telling these stories for a very long time; stories that are often reluctantly disclosed yet shape our identity and subjectivity to leave an indelible imprint on our future (for example, Jackie Huggins, r e a Saunders, Yhonnie Scarce, Inala Walden). Such research and blood-memory narratives, however, are limited on our official record in South Australia, with particular denial by the State Government on the topic of 'stolen wages' (Harkin 2020a).

Jeanine: I am an archive. I am a chapter in a bigger archive. All the women I knew were archives. We are the first archives, before the many arms of the state constructed its fiction.

I am Wiradjuri. I grew up next to a big river—the Murrumbidgee. My Aunty used to say the river was her church. The river is also an archive—its constant flow documents the lives of my people, and its flow is like memory that joins generations of women as a force to speak back to those boxes of violence.

Audre Lorde believed that when 'we view living in the european (sic) mode only as a problem to be solved' we are totally dependent on 'our ideas to make us free' because that's 'what the white fathers told us were precious'. Lorde spoke of the need for colonised and enslaved peoples to become more in

> touch with our own ancient, non-european (sic) consciousness of living as a situation to be experienced and interacted with, we learn more and more to cherish our feelings, and to respect those hidden sources of our power from where true knowledge and, therefore, lasting action comes.
>
> (Lorde 2007, 37)

Lorde believed that women carried the possibility within us for fusion of both these ways of thinking about the world and our position in it. And that we come closest to this combination of both critique and interrogation of western society that is grounded and nourished by a deeper, older archive of knowledge, beyond the colonial structure that seeks to confine us.

Audre Lorde says that for women poetry is not a luxury:

> It is a vital necessity of our existence. It forms the quality of the light within which we predicate our hopes and dreams toward survival and change, first made into language, then into idea, then into tangible action. Poetry is the way we help give name to the nameless so it can be thought. The farthest horizons of our hopes and fears are cobbled by our poems, carved from the rock of our experiences of our daily lives.
>
> (2007a, 37)

For me then, bringing the living and lived archive of the women I knew outside the box and off the record to the fore to overwrite the fictitious one created by the state, became not just my motivation but my responsibility. I want to acknowledge their resilience and their pain as strong Aboriginal women who *are* my archive first.

Derrida defined an archive as something much broader than, but including storehouses of, official paperwork and records, and that which evokes voices from the past that re-call and re-member trauma and resilience through memory and through the bodies of the Aboriginal women I belong to and am part of (Leane 2017). With Audre Lorde's words in my head and the women's memories, voices and stories in my heart, I turned to my archive of origin, my 'body&blood' memory (see Allen 2002 on Blood Narratives). Our bodies are archives where memories are etched, stored and anchored. I inherit this living archive of mind and body, and my mind and body become a repository of my family's Aboriginal history—even before it was told to me, and even now that some of it still remains untold and is still missing (Leane 2017).

My method in using poetry to reclaim the fragments of the women's lives stolen by state record keepers in their many guises was largely sensory, afferent, auditory, gustative; recalled and perceived through sight, sound, smell, taste and touch. This work is extra-sensory; I felt the *feel* of presences, the ghosts of those whose lives were being restored and reclaimed. Memory is transmitted not only through stories, but through ways of walking, talking, sitting, laughing, eating, thinking, holding someone and touching of objects. I came to see the brick-and-mortar storehouses as cardboard prisons. I write to juxtapose the violent snippets and fragments of peoples' lives incarcerated within these archival cells against a 'body&blood' memory of the lives lived outside it, to expose and interrogate its violent fictions. It is to confront the hideous effigies constructed by the colonial imagination that once captured us.

> That's my Grandmother on the cutting board
> prodded and poked, exposed and invaded
> being measured and studied.

And this is me
off the cutting board – and you under the microscope
the difference is I'm remembering – putting
back together, *you* sought to dismember.

(Leane 2018, 9)

I conjured in my writing the things the state never got its clutches on: voices, places, movement, mannerisms, special objects held time and time again, birthday cards, gifts and the letters they'd written me; the ways the women laughed, walked, sang, cooked; their anger, their frustrations, their fears, their hopes shared, their dreams for us and their memories.

As a grown woman in the twenty-first century, I draw on the words of my sisters-in-writing, strong Black women like Alexis Wright, Melissa Lucashenko, Charmaine Papertalk Green, Ellen van Neerven, Yvette Holt, Ali Cobby Eckermann, Evelyn Araluen. These women use words as weapons and tools to produce works that may appear in the same form as those of the coloniser and make use of their introduced language. But, as First Nations poets, their words and works take their power and meaning from a deeper, older reservoir of cultural knowledge; they use these words to bring our resilience, voices, her/histories to the fore and keep them there while at the same time doing the hard work of critiquing and interrogating the colonial structures that continue to misrepresent and silence us.

Natalie: the process to access our records is lengthy and frustrating and subject to convoluted and obstructionist bureaucratic vetting. It has become increasingly difficult to access State Aboriginal records in South Australia, since the success of the late Uncle Bruce Trevorrow's case in 2007 (*Trevorrow v State of South Australia No. 5* [2007] SASC 285; Raynes 2009). Bruce, a Ngarrindjeri Elder, was the first Aboriginal person to win a case against any government in Australia for his forced illegal removal from his family as a child. He was awarded a substantial compensation payment of $525,000 and a further $250,000 in lieu of interest, much more than any of the Stolen Generation compensation schemes have offered. In addition, the detailed indexing of the vast records of the Aborigines Protection Board and its associated government departments is incomplete, making it impossible to know what information is available to us. As a contemporary form of gatekeeping, records that have been indexed may now be deemed as 'too sensitive' and blocked for release under legal professional privilege by the state's Attorney General (Commonwealth of Australia 2006, 86; Raynes 2009).

The process to obtain access to the correspondence files of the Aboriginal Department, which date back to 1866, is quite involved. This is the repository that contains detailed personal information about our families and the oppressive policies that impacted them. When an applicant seeks information from State Records, a database search is conducted and a list of available and relevant files generated. The applicant then forwards this list to the Department for Aboriginal Affairs and Reconciliation (AAR) requesting access approval. An AAR Records

Officer must then seek legal advice through the Attorney General's Department to check for material subject to legal professional privilege (LPP), at which point access determinations are made. This advice to withhold, approve or redact information deemed of a personal sensitive nature is provided to AAR who then communicates the advice back to the applicant. The process to copy and release the files is administered back through State Records. The fact that Aboriginal Records are the only set of State Department files automatically subject to LPP is a significant issue regarding archive access and transparency. The state is not required to provide reasons why access to records may be been denied (Raynes 2009), and those unattainable files identified as 'missing' or 'Access Denied' are, as Judy Watson states, often the most revealing (Watson and Martin-Chew 2009, 84). The state increasingly fears the dead as well as the living, and of course these are the records I most want to get my hands on.

> first light   first breath   first cry
> born in the wake of immeasurable loss
> we rock   navigate   float
> we keep watch with the missing
> while you sleep
> through deep colonialisms
>
> (Harkin 2019, 9)

Despite these barriers, the largest number of public enquiries to State Records in South Australia is from members of the Aboriginal community, signalling a burgeoning interest in family history via the archive. Our late friend and writer, Fabienne Bayet-Charlton, documented her experience tracing her Bundjalung family story via the archive, including State Records, noting that the anthropologist and historian had more power and access to the archives than she did. Fabienne laments:

> Within the largest collection of Aboriginal-related material in the southern hemisphere, no, in the world, I am marooned. The white anthropologist who collected the material of my family, of my ancestors, has greater right of access than I do. It is his work. It is his information. I am dispossessed of it. Another gate has been locked. I wonder how many other people have come into this great institute, this wonderful cornucopia of information, and gone away empty-handed.
>
> (Bayet-Charlton 2002, 157)

Thankfully we find ourselves in the company of others who labour creatively as decolonising artists, poets and writers; those who refuse to accept an Australian culture of amnesia, or to once again be left out of history. For me, they are activists of the most important kind, who effectively disrupt this circular logic of misrepresentation, so the fantasy archive is no longer maintained to effectively rebreed what is silenced or forgotten (Mansour 2007). Their ideas and visions are compelling in their quest for sovereignty and justice, transformation and liberation. The affective dimensions of their work invite us to lean in close, so we too can witness intimate rupturings of a seething, colonial, hegemonic norm; so we too can bear witness to their love. Theirs is a work of mourning that generates new ideas and conversations as they pursue collective recognition, honouring and remembrance; as they maintain past lives in the present, and offer new ways to negotiate individual and collective cultural loss, and to effect social change. Memories and oral histories are gathered to assert and re-insert complex and layered Indigenous subjectivities; new offerings for the future archives are created, imbued with an affective-aesthetic concern for justice.

Such a reckoning, to confront and expose spectres of colonialism that continue to haunt, requires significant emotional labour. We inform each other's work in so many ways and offer new insights into intimate histories of colonialism. Despite coming from different places, and being born in different places and times, the recognition of each other's stories is uncanny: being cast as 'the Aboriginal problem' through government, scientific and popular culture discourse; being subjected to and threatened with child removal and institutionalisation under charges of 'destitute' and 'neglect'; obtaining 'Exemption Certificates' and being subjected to charges of 'consorting' and 'absconding' under the 'Act'; being subject to indentured domestic labour and servitude; being recorded and followed while living under an extreme culture of government surveillance; and being dehumanised, collected and observed as the object of scientific subjection through anthropological expeditions led by the South Australian Museum, and the Board of Anthropological Research.

Our sistergirl, Bundjalung author/poet/scholar, Melissa Lucashenko (2018) reminds us to choose our own reference points from where our stories are told; to interrogate colonial fantasies and be 'vigilant about what we allow into our consciousness and what we recognize as the very Big Lie of colonialism'. Michi Saagiig Nishnaabeg poet/artist/scholar Leanne Betasomasake Simpson also urges us to think big: to forge strategic alliances with others who refuse western patriarchal structures of colonialism; build movements with intellectual-warriors in Black communities and radical communities of colour; and seek inspiration from those creative, compassionate visionaries who are interested in building new worlds that affirm and reinsert our Indigenous presence (Simpson 2016; Simpson and Brand 2018). These kinds of conversations, framed by Black, queer, postcolonial and Indigenous feminisms, have been critical to my own thinking on poetry as decolonial praxis; to better understand those intersecting dynamics of power and oppression, and think through alternative systems of accountability for race, class and gender-based violence (Anzaldúa and Keating 2002; Green 2007; Lorde 2007; Moraga and Anzaldúa 2015; Simpson 2017; Suzack et al. 2010). As a community of Indigenous and 'people of colour' writers, we recognise each other's stories. We have a responsibility to remain alive on the page; to rise up and keep fighting and staying strong with our words; to counter the deficit gendered and racialised narratives, and demonstrate our survival, intelligence, beauty and pride.

Jeanine: my current research in Aboriginal literature and storytelling grew out of my own personal need and ache to make—to create through my writing and research a better story for my family and loved ones. It takes me beyond of the buildings and storehouses of the state to the archives of 'body&blood' memory through story that we create and leave as legacy.

In 1981, Toni Morrison addressed the Ohio Arts Council with the following words: 'writing to me is an advanced and slow form of reading. If you find a book you really want to read but it hasn't been written yet, then you must write it' (quoted in Brown 1981). Many First Nations people in Australian have taken up the pen as a tool of cultural transmission to do what I did and take the stories of our own families, Country, communities and loved ones into our own hands to record a story outside of the state archives.

This research takes what I've learnt from my own family's archive and the schism between the public and personal/family archive into the creative realm of First Nations Peoples' self-representation and creation of their own and their families her/histories through and with writing. How do we as First Nations Peoples armed now with the tools that once oppressed us—writing, reading, books, theory, etc.—create our own archives?

Alexis Wright's landmark essay *The Politics of Writing* speaks to the capacity of our writing to both liberate and repatriate the kidnapped memories hostage to the archives, state records and history books:

> Throughout my life I have learnt to piece the mysteries together with gathered facts from historical records that have been revealed through anthropological and family research. I can only now feel I can tell the story of our family revealing the voices of loved ones who never told a story that they felt too shameful to tell.
>
> (Wright 2002, 10)

With these words in mind I turn to the literary archive that we are now creating ourselves. My current research is an extensive study of our writings through the David Unaipon Award for an Unpublished Indigenous writer. The David Unaipon Award grew out of the intensification of ongoing Aboriginal activism in the lead-up to the bicentenary of the Invasion in 1988, and the shifting consciousness of a certain sector of settler society who increasing came to see the nation they reside in and on as an archive of crimes, dark secrets and hidden histories. The award was set up and administered through University of Queensland Press in 1989, and each year it recognises a new Aboriginal or Torres Strait Islander writer. Its creation and continuation as the only discrete writing and publishing award for an unpublished Indigenous writer were a radical intervention into what was previously a monocultural white-settler literary landscape. Since its instigation, it has been the longest running Indigenous writing award. It was the first space to open up where Aboriginal writers could write in language, in English, in combinations of both, in any form, style or genre on any topic or issue, story/stories important to the writer and their community. This research uses the award as a lens to read Aboriginal self-representation through writing, as it is through the accumulation of writing—telling our own stories—that we build our own archive.

This research brings to the fore the important work our writing does in a national landscape that has for 200 or more years written us out of the picture, misrepresented us when we were/are in the picture and used us like chess-pieces in the literary landscape to reflect white consciousness of and white fetishes and fears about us. How does our literature do what national history fails to, for us as First Nations Peoples? How does literature perform the hard work and carry out the essential role of cultural transmission necessary for our survival? For our children to know how they come to be where they are and who they belong to? I think of how my younger self once so craved the written words of Black women at home. How does our literature do the important and ongoing work of decolonisation? How does it connect us as First Nations Peoples nationally and transnationally across settler colonies?

Our literature is our living archive. It is the national barometer across time, space and place of what is on the minds and what is in the hearts of Aboriginal Peoples across the many Countries of this colonial nation. Aboriginal storytelling, in its many different forms, is our living archive. It recasts and reframes the archives as living, breathing entities to be entered into and into conversation with. It is my hope that this research will go some way towards addressing First Nations Peoples' alienation from collections, such as galleries, libraries, archives and museums (GLAM sector). Storytelling is a critical method of enquiry for supporting a community-based, collaborative participatory research methodology, that positions Indigenous worldviews as vital to achieving a dynamic, interactive and living archive.

Natalie: I am a product of layered histories and disruptions, intergenerational and collective memories and (re)connections to country. As a Narungga woman living on Kaurna Country, my sense of 'belonging' through relationship to place is necessarily woven into the fabric of the land on which I live and work, and knowing its colonial legacies (Justice 2013). Access to certain archival material has actually heightened this sense of belonging and has become central to reckoning with my personal histories, and in turn, the collective histories of community, state and nation.

My own research initially set out to follow ghosts and paper trails in search of answers to some missing links in my family story. My desire to go back to the origin of the archive manifested as a compelled searching, a restless gathering and a feverish hoarding of records, to the point of replicating the very thing I set out to interrogate and disrupt: the 'archive-box'. When I considered all that had been conjured via the archive the weight of it nearly stopped my heart. The only way for me to shift and transform from this archive-box was to write poetry and weave my way out; an active and embodied reckoning with history's record in an attempt to better understand my family's place in it all.

As a method, 'archival-poetics' developed as a slow, situated unfolding; a writing and creating into unexpected, uncanny moments where blood-memory, haunting and the potency of place collide (Harkin 2016; 2019). In these moments, the past comes alive as 'the lever for the work of the present' where space opens up for a new-telling through and beyond the colonial archive; the haunted and haunting writer examining repressed or hidden personal and collective histories, to project forward (Gordon 2008, 66). Archival-poetics felt like a natural and necessary embodied response to that collision of oral history, memory and colonial archive representations that take me back to places I've never been yet am compelled to enter. I was able to recognise that, despite our lives being historically controlled and archived by the colonisers to the point of erasure, our memories still exist, out there in the world as 're-memory' (Gordon 2008; Morrison 2019); deeply social, collective and waiting for us to bump into so we might read the signs and write at that point of struggle between remembering and forgetting.

Such intimate encounters with the colonial archive that collide with blood-memory inevitably contribute toward much larger decolonising stories of resistance, resilience and refusal. We trace our families' agency and complex subjectivities within these files. We find their hand-written letters or their signatures on petitions demanding justice, access to children, opposition to controlling policies and better living conditions. We find evidence of children and teenagers absconding from institutions or leaving indentured domestic work placements. We find their sass and their will; their defiance through refusal to comply with authorities despite the threat of punishment. We find photographs and we stare into their gaze in search of a message, or some recognition. In my own records, I recognise my Nanna's 'husky voice' they describe. I recognise her tone and find her resilience and strength. I touch her hand-writing and feel her fingertips in letters that reveal so much more than what is filed and recorded about her. As pieces of the jigsaw come together, we can see how our loved ones carefully and strategically negotiated a system that was designed to control and oppress them; and this is their lasting impression.

Nigerian artist, curator, writer and poet Okwui Enwezor identifies the archive as 'a site of lost origins where memory is dispossessed', while at the same time being a site for hopeful and just futures where 'acts of remembering and regeneration occur' (Enwezor 2008, 47). The material medium through which buried histories can work to affect include primary-source records such as file-note surveillance data, letters, correspondence files, inspector reports, genealogies and photos. There is so much potential to transform these violent records by creating something else with them, be it a poem or literally transforming them through the act of weaving archives; an archival-poetic turning of brutal representations into objects of beauty, but still with disrupting intent. My basket of letters has been exhibited in multiple ways, including digital media video with sound installation (Harkin 2014b; 2020b).

I think this is where it's at for many Indigenous writers and artists who labour creatively with the contested, racialised colonial archive as a dynamic site of potential strength and renewal (Judy Watson, Vernon Ah Kee, Yhonnie Scarce, Brenda Croft, Tony Birch, Bruce Pascoe and Julie Gough immediately come to mind). Regardless of the mode or creative intervention, working with material primary source archives has potential to disrupt and subvert those official recorded narratives of history that maintain currency as 'truth' in the present.

Archival-poetics is thus one small contribution to rethinking and reassessing the transparent possessive logic and political rationalities of imperial history; and a method to seek out and respond to critical minor histories that reveal gendered and racialised conditions of empire that play out in the mundane intimacies of every day (Stoler 2009). I find immense comfort in creatively honouring the strength and resilience of Old people who were controlled under the Aborigines Protection Act and its associated laws, whilst also honouring their pain. For me, writing 'against the grain' of the colonial archive, as Ann Stoler (2009) describes, will allow my kids and grandkids to find our truth, our voices and reflections of themselves on the future record; not those colonial interpretations that have defined and objectified us in powerful and damaging ways. Our stories can be woven and re-written into the world to affectively re-claim terrain via blood-memory, found objects and creaking gates.

Jeanine: *A Picture*: I am not told about the violence that happened to the Black women in my family. I am not told about the taunting and teasing. I am not told about the beatings. I am not told about the rapes. I am not told about what happened to my Nana in 1901. I am not told about what happened to my Aunty in 1924. Or my other Aunty in 1937. I am not told about what happened to my mother in 1961. It is thought that for me to know such things might stop me from getting on with it. Whatever *it* is. But I find all these secrets. There is a brain in that egghead of mine.

A picture tells a million lies. The family photographs. The weddings. The christenings. The funerals. Perhaps the women were right. To know I am a link in a bigger assault chain might have stopped me from getting on with *it*. *It* is success. Freedom. That they both craved and feared.

There's a picture of you. Looks like me. Or you as me as you. History lands on your face. On my face. Mine as yours as mine. You as me as you.

A final note

We approached the colonial archive with our senses heightened, each searching for missing narratives, following ghosts and paper-trails, and experiencing these potent documents and sites in particular ways. Although we arrived at different locations and points in time, we recognised the shape of each other's stories and memories, a recognition grounded in shared histories and our unique Wiradjuri and Narungga woman standpoints.

These colonial sites are not neutral. They do not represent the source of our truth. We know them as racialised and gendered; slippery, unending and incomplete. They were created and maintained by a powerful industry of people who could never fully know us, and the data they collected, contained and maintained about us is deeply affecting.

As the archive-box revealed itself, old wounds became visible. An archive-fever affliction compelled our attempts to comprehend the archive itself and its multiplicity of contexts, processes and origins: the governing bureaucracies that generated it; the agents that consigned and protected it; the discourse and mythology that fed and sustained it; and the circular 'white-patriarchal logic' (Moreton-Robinson 2015) of colonialism that rationalised, fortified and revered it. We were never alone; our ancestors guiding beside us.

Our poetic situated imaginings shine a literary spotlight, bright with intent, to expose the state's violence, and all that our families endured. This is what we carry with us. It is written on the body, and it pumps through our blood. Our family story investigations have become larger archival-poetic offerings; interventionist-continuums that are influenced by a legacy of Indigenous poets, writers and artists as activists who continue to inspire and inform our work. Growing into relationality, through and beyond the archive, is our reckoning and responsibility. We will bear witness for as long as it takes, honour our Grandmothers, all our stories and live our truths.

References

Allen, Chadwick, 2002. *Blood Narrative: Indigenous Identity in American Indian and Maori Literary and Activist Texts*. Durham: Duke University Press.

Anzaldúa, Gloria and Keating, AnaLouise, eds., 2002. *This Bridge We Call Home: Radical Visions for Transformation*. London: Routledge.

Bayet-Charlton, Fabienne, 2002. *Finding Ullagundahi Island*. Sydney: Allen & Unwin.

Brown, Ellen, 1981. Writing is Third Career for Morrison. *The Cincinnati Enquirer*, 27, 106.

Burton, Antoinette, ed., 2005. *Archive Stories: Facts, Fictions and the Writing of History*. Durham: Duke University Press.

Commonwealth of Australia, 2006, *Unfinished Business: Indigenous Stolen Wages*. Canberra: The Senate Standing Committee on Legal and Constitutional Affairs.

Derrida, Jacques, 1995. *Archive Fever: A Freudian Impression*. Chicago, IL: University of Chicago Press.

Enwezor, Okwui, 2008. *Archive Fever: Uses of the Document in Contemporary Art*. New York: International Centre of Photography.

Gordon, Avery, 2008. *Ghostly Matters: Haunting and Sociological Imagination* (2nd ed.). Minneapolis, MN: University of Minnesota Press.

Gough, Julie, 2001. *Transforming Histories: The Visual Disclosure of Contentious Pasts*. Thesis (Phd). University of Tasmania, Hobart. Available from: http://eprints.utas.edu.au/2644/ [Accessed 26 November 2020].

Gough, Julie, 2008. *The Haunted and the Bad [Exhibition Catalogue]*. Melbourne: Linden Contemporary Arts Centre.

Green, Joyce, ed., 2007. *Making Space for Indigenous Feminism*. Halifax: Fernwood Publishing.

Harkin, Natalie, 2014a. The Poetics of (Re)mapping Archives: Memory in the Blood. *Journal of the Association for the Study of Australian Literature*, 14 (3): 1–14.

Harkin, Natalie, 2014b. Archive Fever Paradox 2, Whitewash Brainwash, 2014 (Video Excerpt). Available from: https://www.youtube.com/watch?v=TLH6rlUdHmE [Accessed 26 November 2020].

Harkin, Natalie, 2016. *"I Weave Back to You": Archival-Poetics for the Record*. Thesis (PhD). University of South Australia, Adelaide.

Harkin, Natalie, 2019. *Archival-Poetics*. Melbourne: Vagabond Press.

Harkin, Natalie, 2020a. Intimate Encounters: Aboriginal Labour Stories and the Violence of the Colonial Archive. *In:* Brendan Hokowhitu, Alieen Moreton-Robinson, Linda Tuhiwai Smith, Chris Anderson, and Steve Larkin, eds. *The Routledge Handbook of Critical Indigenous Studies*. London: Routledge.

Harkin, Natalie, 2020b. Weaving the Colonial Archive: A Basket to Lighten the Load. *Journal of Australian Studies*, 44 (2): 154–66.

Heidegger, Martin, 1971. *Poetry, Language and Thought*. New York: Harper Row.

Justice, Daniel, 2013. Global Native Literary Studies—Panelist Daniel Justice Presents. *Words in the World: Literatures, Oratures, and New Meeting Grounds Symposium*. University of Hawaii. Available from: https://scholarspace.manoa.hawaii.edu/handle/10125/29708 [Accessed 26 November 2020].

Leane, Jeanine, 2017. Gathering: The Politics of Memory and Contemporary Aboriginal Women's Writing. *Antipodes: A Journal of Australian and New Zealand Literature*, 31 (2), 242–51.

Leane, Jeanine, 2018. *Walk Back Over*. Melbourne: Cordite Books.

Leane, Jeanine, 2019. Unfinished Business. *In:* Natalie Harkin, ed. *Cordite 89: Domestic*. Available from: http://cordite.org.au/poetry/domestic/unfinished-business/ [Accessed 26 November 2020].

Lorde, Audre, 2007. *Sister Outsider: Essays and Speeches* (Reprint ed.). Berkeley, CA: Crossing Press.

Lowe, Lisa, 2015. *The Intimacies of Four Continents*. Durham: Duke University Press.

Lucashenko, Melissa, 2018. Writing as a Sovereign Act. *Meanjin Quarterly*, Summer 2018. Available from: http://meanjin.com.au/essays/writing-as-a-sovereign-act/ [Accessed 26 November 2020].

Mansour, Wisam, 2007. The Violence of the Archive. *English Language Notes*, 45 (1), 41–4.

Momaday, N. Scott, 1969. *The Way to Rainy Mountain*. Albuquerque: University of New Mexico.

Moraga, Cherrie, and Anzaldúa, Gloria, eds., 2015. *This Bridge Called my Back: Writings by Radical Women of Colour* (4th ed.). New York: State University of New York.

Moreton-Robinson, Aileen, 2000. *Talkin' Up to the White Woman*. St Lucia: University of Queensland Press.

Moreton-Robinson, Aileen, 2004. The Possessive Logic of Patriarchal White Sovereignty: The High Court and the Yorta Yorta Decision. *Borderlands e-Journal*, 3(2). Available from:

http://www.borderlands.net.au/vol3no2_2004/moreton_possessive.htm [Accessed 26 November 2020].

Moreton-Robinson, Aileen, 2015. *The White Possessive: Property, Power, and Indigenous Sovereignty*. Minneapolis, MN: University of Minnesota Press.

Moreton-Robinson, Aileen, 2017. Relationality: A Key Presupposition of an Indigenous Social Research Paradigm. *In:* J. M. O'Brien and C Andersen, eds. *Sources and Methods in Indigenous Studies*. London: Routledge, 69–77.

Morrison, Toni, 2019. *Mouthful of Blood: Essays, Speeches, Meditations*. London: Chatto & Windus.

Raynes, Cameron. 2009. *The Last Protector: The Illegal Removal of Aboriginal Children from their Parents in South Australia*. Adelaide: Wakefield Press.

Sharpe, Christina, 2016. *In the Wake: On Blackness and Being*. Durham: Duke University Press.

Shellam, Tiffany, and Cruickshank, Joanna, 2019. Critical Archives: An Introduction. *Journal of Colonialism and Colonial History*, 20 (2), 1–8.

Simpson, Leanne Betasamosake, 2016. Indigenous Resurgence and Co-Resistance. *Critical Ethnic Studies*, 2 (2), 19–34.

Simpson, Leanne Betasamosake, 2017. *As We Have Always Done: Indigenous Freedom Through Radical Resistance*. Minneapolis, MN: University of Minnesota.

Simpson, Leanne Betasamosake, and Brand, Dionne, 2018. Temporary Spaces of Joy and Freedom. *Literary Review of Canada*, July 2018. Available from: https://reviewcanada.ca/magazine/2018/06/temporary-spaces-of-joy-and-freedom/ [Accessed 26 November 2020].

Stoler, Ann Laura, 2002. Colonial Archives and the Arts of Governance. *Archival Science*, 2, 87–109.

Stoler, Ann Laura, 2006a. Tense and Tender Ties: The Politics of Comparison in North American History and (Post) Colonial Studies. *In:* Ann Laura Stoler, ed. *Haunted by Empire: Geographies of Intimacy in North American History*. Durham: Duke University Press, 23–67.

Stoler, Ann Laura, 2006b. Intimidations of Empire: Predicaments of the Tactile and Unseen. *In:* Ann Laura Stoler, ed. *Haunted by Empire: Geographies of Intimacy in North American History*. Durham: Duke University Press, 1–22.

Stoler, Ann Laura, 2009. *Along the Archival Grain: Epistemic Anxieties and Colonial Common Sense*. Princeton, NJ: Princeton University Press.

Stoler, Ann Laura, ed., 2013. *Imperial Debris: On Ruins and Ruination*. Durham: Duke University Press.

Stoler, Ann Laura, 2016. *Duress: Imperial Durabilities in Our Times*. Durham: Duke University Press.

Suzack, Cheryl, Hundorf, Shari M., Perreault, Jeanne, and Barman, Jean, eds., 2010. *Indigenous Women and Feminism: Politic, Activism, Culture*. Vancouver: University of British Columbia.

Watson, Irene, and Venne, Sharon, 2010. Sex, Race and Questions of Aboriginality. *In:* Margaret Thornton, ed. *Sex Discrimination in Uncertain Times*. Canberra: ANU Epress, 347–67.

Watson, Judy, and Martin-Chew, Louise, 2009. *Blood Language*. Melbourne: The Miegunyah Press.

Wright, Alexis, 2002. Politics of Writing. *Southerly*, 62 (2), 10–20.

Chapter 4

Passport struggles

Lawful documents and the politics of recognition and refusal

Sara Dehm

Introduction

The passport is a jurisdictional document. This means that the passport is not only a document that has a particular legal status or that is instrumental to and created by legal regimes of state surveillance and migration control. Rather, as a jurisdictional document, the passport gives shape to legal relations, lawful subjects and practices of authority and recognition. In making this argument, I understand jurisdiction (literally meaning the power to speak the law) to be a site and practice of law's enunciation.[1] Understanding the passport *jurisdictionally* reveals how the changing forms of the passport affect relations and practices of law. It also allows for paying attention to distinct struggles over the recognition and significance of passports as legal documents that take place at these sites of law's enunciation.

This chapter traces two legal struggles over the changing forms and authority of passports: what I shall refer to as 'passport struggles'. The first passport struggle concerns recent campaigns to 'de-gender'—or gender otherwise—the contemporary state-issued passport. Here, I focus on two current legal cases in the United Kingdom and the United States that turn on legal concepts of veracity and privacy in order to limit or transform the power of the state to exclusively prescribe gender in binary (female/male) terms within contemporary passport systems. The second passport struggle, in contrast, centres on the use and recognition of passports issued by First Nations political authorities, using the case of the Haudenosaunee passport as an illustrative example.

As we shall see, the first struggle seeks to use the passport as an official document through which to challenge state practices of gender binarism, thereby expanding the modes of inclusion within state systems and transforming state practices concerning the identification and inscription of individuals as legal persons within such systems. In contrast, at stake in the second struggle is the lawful encounter between Indigenous nations and settler colonial states (Dorsett and McVeigh 2012, 98). This is a struggle for the instituting of legal relations that recognise Indigenous nations as sovereign authorities with the lawful capacity to use passports as official documents to both determine

DOI: 10.4324/9781003247593-6

membership within their nations and conduct their external affairs with other political authorities, including settler states. Ultimately, though, both passport struggles are animated by a particular politics of recognition, a politics that, in the context of contemporary liberal pluralism and settler colonialism, Glen Coulthard (2014, 3) has described as risking 'reproduc[ing] the very configurations of colonialist, racist, patriarchal state power that Indigenous peoples' demand for recognition has historically sought to transcend'.

This chapter thus seeks to trace and interrogate the legal histories and contemporary reception of the modern passport as a legal document. There is a rich body of migration studies scholarship showing how state documents such as the passport are used to solidify and police the stark legal distinction between people deemed to be citizens or non-citizens. This includes analysing how migrants 'on the ground experience, accept and reject state bureaucratic practices in a time of increasing securitization' (Horton 2020, 6). The two passport struggles that I explore in this chapter, however, play out either at the margins of state citizenship such that they seek to expand ideas and practices of inclusive citizenship and identity inscription, or reject state-bestowed citizenship outright in favour of other modes of identification, nationhood and political belonging. For this reason, state regimes of documentation and their embedded politics of recognition also need to be read alongside differingly situated and embodied politics of refusal articulated within collective struggles for different legal arrangements or legal categories. In the context of passport struggles, such politics of recognition and refusal have been heightened, as a result of an ever-increasing state trend towards biometrics that has given increased visibility or new significance to particular struggles over the passport form that may not have otherwise had the same meaning or significance.

This chapter proceeds as follows: first, I unpack the jurisdictional work of the passport as a particular legal document of identification created and standardised by nation-states over the course of the twentieth century, tracing both its changing material form and political effects. I then turn to consider two distinct passport struggles at the start of the twenty-first century, situating both within the longer intersecting gendered and racial histories of the passport. Finally, I conclude by considering the significance of practices of recognition and refusal in relation to present-day state bureaucratic practices of inscription and mechanisms of surveillance at the heart of contemporary state borders.

Passports, biometrics and the law

In recent years, critical migration scholarship has analysed how passports constitute a specific form of state documentation that function to enrol mobile people within transnational regimes of migration control, identity surveillance and racial exclusion. As a specific act of 'bureaucratic inscription', the passport as an official document symbolises the efforts of modern bureaucratic states to monopolise control over the 'legitimate means of movement' (Torpey 2000,

6). Yet, the document's materiality has also allowed for migrant acts of resistance to and subversion of such transnational forms of migration control and bureaucratic inscription, through, for example, practices of forged identities and counterfeit documents (Keshavarz 2019; Vogl this volume). As a result, as Sarah Horton (2020, 3, 6) has written, state documents like the passport become 'important sites' for both individual and collective action that have the capacity to 'transform migrant subjectivities and conceptualizations of their place in the nation'. This chapter, likewise, pays attention to struggles over the terms and recognition of passports in order to grasp the document's symbolic importance and transformative power in terms of recognition of identities and legal personhood. This section briefly introduces the passport as an historical creature of international law and domestic state practices, with a focus on the present-day passport's ever-increasing entanglement in what has been termed the 'biometric border' (Amoore 2006).

While contemporary international law treats passports as prima facie proof of a person's nationality, the document per se has no universal definition in nor formal status under international law.[2] This lack of exhaustive definition is also true in the domestic laws of many states. For example, Australian law does not define the term 'passport' in legislation or case law,[3] despite the fact that passports been mandatory travel documents since 1916 (or at least, mandated for persons over the age of 15 years leaving and entering the Commonwealth, with some notable racialised exceptions, as discussed below). As a matter of legal technicality, the passport constitutes a form of state-issued diplomatic communication that has the purpose of verifying an individual's identity and notifying other states that the passport-holder is entitled to the issuing state's protection while travelling abroad (Dehm 2018). For this reason, the passport is an official document that is state property and 'addressed to a global audience' (McKeown 2011, 1).[4] Yet, the act of possessing a passport does have substantive legal implications for mobile people. Adam Muchmore (2004, 317–318) has argued that the 'acquisition of a valid passport fundamentally changes the international legal status of an individual in relation to the passport-issuing state' such that the passport-holder's nationality now 'becomes a proper concern for international law'. In other words, the state act of issuing a passport not only transforms the relationship between the individual passport-holder and the passport-issuing state, it is also one that has jurisdictional consequences. For individuals, to cross a state border with or without a state-issued passport, or with or without state authorisation via such a passport, also can fundamentally transform their legal status and embodied experiences. Without a passport or state authorisation, a person's very presence in a state's territory is too readily deemed an infraction and potentially subject to state criminalisation, physical deportation and eventual exclusion. This attests to the power of the passport as a legal document: it facilitates, or at least has become instrumental within, state bureaucratic regimes that enact a kind of 'ontological policing' that makes people 'illegal' and creates 'humans who can be hunted' (Chamayou 2010, 2–3).

Beyond formal status, the material form that contemporary state-issued passports have come to take has been deeply influenced by standardisation efforts within international institutions since the early twentieth century. While this history is beyond the scope of this chapter, it is worth noting that, since 1980, the International Civil Aviation Organization (ICAO) has published recommended guidelines, entitled Doc 9303, for the promotion and standardisation of 'machine readable travel documents' (or MRTD). Now in its seventh edition, Doc 9303 consists of an elaborate 12-part manual that forensically details the recommended physical and technical specifications of MRTDs in order to, in ICAO's language, 'strengthen' the 'security and integrity of travel documents' (ICAO 2015; see also Dehm 2018, 346). These specifications cover, for example, the requirements of biometric ePassports to incorporate data on the unique physical properties of the passport holder (such as fingerprints and iris patterns), stored on a chipset located in the passport's cover. Through such initiatives, the contemporary passport has become, in the words of Mahmoud Keshavarz (2019, 10), a particular 'designed artifact' that not only serves state purposes for differentially controlling and restricting human movement in the service of capital and nationalism but also 'actively directs, frames, and articulates our understanding of contemporary politics in general and of mobility regimes in particular'. In particular, Keshavarz (2019, 75) draws attention to the design of the passport as a 'specific device enmeshed with bodies, relations and interactions' with state systems of identification and control.

In light of the rapid transformation of contemporary state border infrastructures, the passport as a legal document has become a 'gateway' to systems of migration management and practices of identification that exceed the document itself (Amoore 2008, 21). Amoore uses the concept of the biometric border to illuminate a 'dual-faced phenomenon' in how states in the Global North have come to control and securitise entry into their territories, especially at airports. For Amoore (2006, 336), the biometric border is constituted by, on one hand, the deployment of 'scientific technologies and managerial expertise' in border management and, on the other hand, a move to treat the physical bodies of travellers as 'sites of multiple encoded boundaries'. Biometric border systems thus produce 'particular visual knowledge of the body and subject' (Amoore and Hall 2009, 448) that is deployed within, what Joseph Pugliese (2010; 2013) has called, 'regimes of statist visuality': that is, bureaucratic regimes of truth that 'produce bodies that are either biometrically legible or not, bodies that are either precluded or enabled to cross the border' (Pugliese 2010, 159). In particular, biometric cameras that scan travellers at airports mean that the individual traveller's physical body and outward appearance (including how the traveller's body manifests certain social, religious or cultural practice such as through their hairstyle, attire or religious dress) becomes a 'site of observation, calculation, prediction, and action' (Adey 2009). As a result, the body of the individual traveller has at times come to stand in for the document of the passport itself.

The increased sophistication and proliferation of biometric identification systems at state borders have led to claims of and efforts for the 'disappearance' or 'abolition' of the state-issued passport as a physical document. In 2018, Sydney Airport, for example, implemented what was claimed to be the world's first 'passport-free' trial (Coyne 2019). This involved trialling the use of facial recognition software throughout the airport departure terminal, and specifically for all pre-boarding activities. Passengers who signed up to the trial were required to have their faces scanned at different points in the terminal, in lieu of presenting their passports, enabling what was heralded as a more efficient and faster 'contactless' boarding experience. Yet, while there remain legitimate concerns around privacy and the fallibility of technology systems, the designation of the pilot program as 'passport-free' was in itself somewhat misleading. Program participants were still required to possess—and indeed travel with—a physical passport, although they were not required to produce it as often as other travellers to immigration or airline officials.

While biometric borders purport to create a more 'seamless' travel experience (Broeders and Hampshire 2013), in practice, a wealth of scholarship documents how the use of such biometric technologies discriminates against specific groups of people, in particular exposing people who are racialised as non-white or gender-diverse individuals to heightened scrutiny from airport security personnel and state border officials (see for example, Pugliese 2010; Magnet 2011; Browne 2015). Much like the passport as a physical document, biometric borders continue to do racialising work, making particular bodies more 'suspect' than others, even when physical passports are no longer required to be produced by individual travellers. Importantly, scholars have shown how contemporary biometric technology mobilises and relies upon forms of knowledge and practices of surveillance that have their origins in antiblack racism and ideologies of biological essentialism, including through policing racial stereotypes and thereby creating 'different phenotypic others' (M'charek, Schramm and Skinner 2014, 468; Browne 2015, 10). Reminiscent of earlier 1990s rhetoric of a 'border-free' world under neoliberal globalisation, then, this promise of increased mobility in a 'passport-free' world is actualised for some privileged (dominantly, white, rich) people only. Instead, what is brought into being is a world that, in the words of Wendy Brown (2010, 7), 'harbours fundamental tensions between opening and barricading, fusion and partition, erasure and reinscription'. Put simply, it is a world that is animated by a liberal ideology of freedom of movement (that is in practice available only for a select few elite) while also simultaneously materialising ever-more-concrete technologies of border fortification (that are used to police and selectively exclude the majority of the world's poor) (Bauman 2000; Kotef 2015, 10). Biometric borders then have the potential to rearticulate and intensify the gendered and racial logics of exclusion of earlier state immigration bureaucratic regimes, of which the passport is a foundational official document, albeit in new ways.

Struggle #1: anti-discrimination and (de)gendering passports

In order to understand contemporary struggles for recognition in and through the passport, it is necessary to appreciate the gendered histories of the modern state-issued passport. As a document, it has long simultaneously reflected and articulated gendered social relations, often reproducing patriarchal, colonial regimes of mobility structured by class hierarchies and racialised subordination that differentially impact upon women depending on their particular social positions. While global gendered histories of the passport are yet to be written and exceed the scope of this chapter, a couple of situated examples from the early twentieth century and interwar period—a constitutive period in efforts to standardise the modern state-issued passport—illuminate this history. This gendered history is also marked by silences and exclusions on official passport documents, with, for example, other documents like marriage certificates also acting to restrict women's mobility at the turn of the twentieth century (Mongia 2018), and the designation of sex/gender only becoming a required universal marker on state-issued passports well into the twentieth century.

Gender has long been a central factor in determining who is able to be a bearer of a state-issued passport as a legal document. While in the US, like elsewhere, unmarried women could be issued a state passport in their own name, the US State Department, for example, up until World War I, had a practice of routinely issuing 'joint' passports to married couples. This means that the document bore the full name of the husband only, with the name of the married woman and any of her physical descriptions being entirely absent. Rather, the document only designated her presence through the phrase 'accompanied by his wife' or 'and wife'. As Craig Robertson (2010, 49) has written, this practice of recognising married women merely through a 'literal notation', rather than in their own legal personhood, largely 'reinforced [dominantly] accepted gender roles that clearly located the husband as the head of the household and apparently relegated his wife to a public life that ideally required his presence as a preferred chaperone'. Other states similarly opted to issue 'family' passports that assumed a male head of the family as the passport holder, a practice also endorsed by the League of Nations in its passport standardisation efforts in the interwar period.

This gendered social ordering through the passport form has, of course, not gone unchallenged. In 1924, suffragette campaigner and trailblazing barrister Helena Normanton made headlines across the British Empire as the first married woman to be issued a British passport in her maiden name. A similar attempt by New York journalist Ruth Hale to obtain a US passport in her maiden name was less successful. Hale and her supporters argued that to not recognise a woman's maiden name in her passport would be to require the woman to travel under a 'fictitious name', thereby also denying 'her identity, her personality, her capacities and her achievements' (quoted in Robertson

2010, 51). In response, the US State Department argued that issuing passports in a woman's married name only was necessary to accurately verify her identity and to do otherwise would create undue confusion, potential diplomatic miscommunications and additional work for immigration officials. As we shall see, such arguments based on a politics of veracity or bureaucratic legibility and convenience continue to resonate within contemporary struggle around gendered identification markers in state passports.

Yet, the practice of issuing passports to women in their own right did not necessarily guarantee freedom from discrimination, and, at times actually enabled states to enforce gender-specific travel restrictions. For example, in February 1917, the Australian government adopted war emergency measures that included refusing to grant passports to women and children to travel through 'danger zones' to Europe, with an exception for female nurses travelling in aid of the war effort (*Sydney Morning Herald* 1917). This discriminatory policy included refusing to issue passports to well-known Australian suffragettes to travel to and speak in Russia in the late stages of the war (*The Argus* 1917). Similarly, the British Home Office initially refused to issue passports to 180 English delegates to the International Congress of Women in the Hague in April 1915 on the basis that such political meetings were 'undesirable … so close to the seat of war' (*Daily Telegraph* 1915). Following the introduction of the *Passport Act 1920* (Cth) in Australia, the Minister's discretionary power to issue passports was repeatedly used to police women's mobility and sexual freedoms, with, for example, the Minister refusing passports to single women wanting to accompany men abroad and to women wanting to travel abroad to marry against their parents' wishes (Dolman and Lee 2008, 88). In addition, white Australian women who married Chinese men frequently faced difficulties obtaining passports, with the Department of Interior in the interwar period mandating custom officials to scrutinise such passport applications more closely (Bellino 2020). Inversely, Australian-born women of Chinese descent who married non-British subjects were deemed to lose their British nationality, and thus their entitlement to an Australian passport (Bellino 2020). While Australian married women did come to be issued with their own passports from 1949 onwards alongside legislative changes that introduced the formal category of 'Australian citizenship', it was not until 1983 that an Australian married woman no longer required her husband's permission in order to be issued a passport.

More recently, struggles around the gender politics and gendering of passports have been initiated by transgender, nonbinary and gender diverse people. In response to trans woman Estelle Asmodelle's pioneering campaign for the official recognition of her proper gender, in 1986 the Australian Department of Foreign Affairs (DFAT) issued her with a new passport that conformed with the sex designation on her amended birth certificate. Almost two decades later, in 2003, the Department would issue a passport with an 'X' gender category to Alex MacFarlane (officially now signalling 'non-binary/indeterminate/inter sex/unspecified/other'), a move that was then reported to be a 'global precedent' (Butler 2003). However, it was only in 2011, with the adoption of new DFAT guidelines (that removed the requirement for surgery in order to have the 'sex' indicator on an individual's passport changed to reflect their gender identity and that officially provided for a third gender option) that access to such passports for Australian citizens who are transgender, intersex or gender diverse has become considerably easier.[5] To date, at least another ten states globally including Argentina, Germany, India, Pakistan, Nepal and New Zealand now allow for the use of a 'X' gender marker in their passports.

Yet, so far, recognition in other jurisdictions has been slow or not forthcoming, resulting in the courts becoming a significant site of passport struggles. Two notable cases have been initiated in recent years in the UK and US in the hope of compelling reform to state passport policies and practices around sex/gender designation. In the UK, this litigation has valorised the legal concept of privacy, while in the US, the litigation has instead focused on legal arguments around veracity and equality before the law. Located within a gendered history of the state-issued passport, both cases represent contemporary instances within much longer anti-discrimination struggles over the passport as an 'accurate' official document of identity verification. There is much to be said about both these contemporary passport legal actions and their associated court decisions, including for example the extent to which legal arguments based on the paradigm of privacy may or may not be able to fully account for, challenge or transform public forms of homophobic, transphobic or anti-intersex violence and associated legal discourses and practices (Kendall 1992).[6] In this section, however, I read both these court cases as acts of individual refusals to be wrongly inscribed within state systems of identification as well as jurisdictional demands for state official documentation to acknowledge gender diversity by ensuring that official documents like the passport more accurately record the gender of individual passport holders.[7]

The UK litigation was initiated by Christie Elan-Cane, a long-time non-gendered activist. Although Elan-Cane first unsuccessfully inquired about the possibility of a gender-neutral UK passport in 1995, it was not until June 2017, following increased public campaigns and a series of governmental reviews, that Elan-Cane initiated judicial review of the 'continuing policy' of Her Majesty's Passport Office to require applicants for a British passport to declare their gender as either 'male' or 'female'.[8] In per witness statement to the court, Elan-Cane described this policy as requiring a 'degrading and humiliating application process' that forces non-gendered people to 'deny our identities and make what we feel to be a false declaration' (quoted in *R (on the application of Christie Elan-Cane) v Secretary of State for the Home Department* [2018] EWHC 1530, para. 6). In June 2018, the primary judge held that the UK authorities' refusal to issue Elan-Cane a passport with an 'X' gender marker engaged per right to privacy under article 8 of the *European Convention on Human Rights* (ECHR); however, the judge found that the UK had not acted unlawfully as they had no positive obligation to issue gender-neutral passports (*Elan-Cane* [2018] EWHC 1530).

Notably, the judicial reasoning in the case demonstrated a privileging of the desire for a 'coherent and consistent policy' over the rights of individuals to have their gender identity recognised and reflected in official documents like the passport. Ironically, this judicial choice to prioritise policy considerations, and in particular the government's recognised entitlement to assess the 'wider implications' of any policy change 'across government as a whole' (*Elan-Cane* [2018] EWHC 1530, para. 114) strangely negates one of the core contemporary functions of the passport: to be an 'accurate' official document of identification. While the primary judge acknowledged that Elan-Cane had a 'justifiably strong personal interest in gaining full legal recognition as being a non-gendered individual' (*Elan-Cane* [2018] EWHC 1530, para. 113), a denial of which 'may well cause the claimant … strong negative emotions', he nonetheless somewhat incongruously found that 'such strong emotions', in his opinion, were not necessarily justified in relation the UK passport policy given that the claimant did not strictly need to make a 'false' declaration of per gender on per passport application form and that the UK authorities, in the absence of any declaration, would simply 'transpose' one of two gender options from Elan-Cane's identification documents such as a birth certificate into the passport system (*Elan-Cane* [2018] EWHC 1530, para. 115). Indeed, the judge placed particular emphasis on the fact that the UK government had a review of its binary gender passport policy afoot,[9] and that there was no 'broad' international state consensus on how to recognise diverse gender identities in passports, particular for intersex or non-gendered people. Subsequently, the Court of Appeal upheld the decision, with Lady Justice King's leading judgment placing weight on the importance of a coherent government review process so that 'the passport issue' is not 'considered in isolation' (*R (on the application of Christie Elan-Cane) v Secretary of State for the Home Department* [2020] EWCA Civ 363, para. 70). As of early 2021, a further appeal is afoot, with Elan-Cane commenting that the continued legal struggle confronts a state bureaucratic system that 'refuses to acknowledge our disenfranchisement' and renders 'us socially invisible' (Wareham 2020).

In contrast, the US litigation has been more successful in its efforts to promote official recognition of diverse gender identities and advance political and legal reform of US passport law and policy. Unlike the English law's focus on the right to privacy via the ECHR, US law instead has allowed for advocates to mobilise arguments based on legal equality and the veracity of official documents. The US case was brought by Dana Zzyym, an American nonbinary intersex advocate and an associate director for the Intersex Campaign for Equality. In 2014, when applying for a passport, Zzyym refused to select either a 'male' or 'female' sex marker option, as required by the US federal form, and instead wrote 'intersex' below the 'sex' category on the application form. Like the UK Passport Office, the US State Department decided to deny the request.

This was despite the fact that, prior to 1976, US passports did not include any sex/gender marker. In 2015, Zzyym initiated a discrimination lawsuit against the State Department, arguing that the Department's refusal to issue them with a gender-neutral passport violated the guarantee of equality protection under the US Constitution, among other laws.

Initially, the US District Court found in favour of Zzyym on administrative grounds, holding that the Department's decision was 'arbitrary and capricious' as it had not followed a 'rational decision-making process in deciding to implement the binary-only gender policy' and ordered the Department to reconsider their decision (*Zzyym v Kerry* (D Col, Civ No 15-cv-02362-RBJ, 22 November 2016) 6). However, the Department refused to do so, prompting a further 2018 district court order, and eventually a US Court of Appeals judgment in 2020, both largely in Zzyym's favour (*Zzyym v Pompeo* (D Col, Civ No 15-cv-02362-RBJ, 19 September 2018); *Zzyym v Pompeo* (10th Cir, No 18-1453, 12 May 2020)). Importantly, the Court of Appeals found that the Department's binary sex policy would result in 'inevitable inaccuracies' and thus 'sunders' the reliability of passports as official identification documents (*Zzyym* (10th Cir, No 18-1453, 12 May 2020), 18–19). That said, the Court stopped short of ordering the Department to issue Zzyym an accurate passport, merely mandating that the Department review Zzyym's application once more. While, in Zzyym's words, the 'long battle' for the recognition of diverse gender identities continues, future legal and policy reform appears likely in light of a proposed Gender Inclusive Passport Act being currently before the US Congress and the new Biden administration's campaign commitment to introducing the option of an 'X' gender marker on government documents, including passports (Safronova 2021).

The initiation of both court actions represents a public political, legal and ethical challenge to present-day practices of gendered inscription in law's documents and seeks to offer some form of redress for such enduring bureaucratic forms of violence, mis-identification and exclusion. In contesting law's binary categories for inscribing humans, these challenges signal an important attempted reconfiguration of law's power and the jurisdiction of state authorities to fully determine identity categories. As Lee Godden (2007, 181) has argued, law 'through the assertion of jurisdiction, acts on and through bodies to "identify" and ascribe legal status to the subject/individual'. This means that jurisdiction

> is not simply the assertion of bare control over bodies in a territorial compass but also comprehends the manner and form by which law insinuates itself as the indispensable means of control by establishing a necessary nexus between body and 'law'.
>
> (Godden 2007, 181–182)

Both the Elan-Cane and Zzyym cases then represent a refusal on the part of nonbinary and gender diverse people to be 'wrongly' inscribed within state bureaucratic systems, even if such gestures are not refusing the act of bureaucratic inscription per se. Although these struggles still leave in place the state as the proper authority for authorising movement and for verifying the identities of individual travellers, they nonetheless promise to potentially 'queer' some of the basic categories for officially classifying individuals that have become foundational to state regimes of mobility (on 'queering' law's categories in an international human rights context, see Otto 2015; McNeilly 2019). In making visible present-day state bureaucratic practices that deny people their proper identities or even full legal personhood, these passport struggles not only insist on the recognition and legibility of more diverse gender identities within state border regimes of visuality and visibility, but also challenge the power of the passport as an official document to uphold restrictive regimes of gender binarism and discrimination.

Struggle #2: lawful encounters and First Nations passports

The passport as a gendered document, of course, intimately intersects with its history as a document of racial exclusion. In her compelling genealogy of the modern state vis-à-vis Indian intra-imperial migration, Radhika Mongia (2018, 113) argued that the passport was and remains a concrete technology that 'nationalise[s] bodies along racial lines', and that its attempted universalisation was, in part, borne out of efforts to restrict the entry of 'free' Indian migrants as British subjects to settler colonial states within the British Empire, like Canada, in the early twentieth century. In an Australian context, while Australian federated states from 1901 largely relied upon official mechanisms such as the passenger landing permit systems and the notorious dictation test to restrict and enforce racial entry quotas, a 1904 immigration amendment did exempt certain Indian and Japanese (but not Chinese) 'merchants, students and tourist travellers' from the dictation test provided that they possessed a passport issued by their government (Lake and Reynolds 2008, 161). Following the institution of a near-universal compulsory passport regime during World War I, the Australian government additionally negotiated arrangements with certain Southern European states such as Malta to restrict their issuing of passports to their nationals to travel to Australia (*Weekly Times* 1925).

Moreover, interwar state legislation providing for passports as compulsory travel documents also contained explicit racial exceptions. In Australia, while the adoption of the *Passport Act 1920* (Cth) made it a criminal offense to depart Australia without a passport, it explicitly excluded specific racialised categories of people from requiring a passport in order to leave Australia including, for instance, 'any aboriginal native of Asia, or any island in the East Indies, or in the Indian or Pacific Oceans' (section 3(2)(m)).[10] This provision functioned to advance an agenda of hegemonic white nationalism, making it not only easier for racialised non-white people to depart Australia but also acting as a 'surreptitious encouragement' (Chesterman and Galligan 1997, 99).

Despite this, racialised people were still able at times to defy border regimes and to travel in spite of such exclusions. In the late nineteenth and early twentieth centuries, Indigenous peoples across the British Empire were at times able to travel under different identity documents. For example, in the late nineteenth century, Indigenous seamen such as Native American whalers could travel on certificates of protection that were issued by port authorities and functioned as identity documents (Shoemaker 2015). Later, during the First World War, Australian Aboriginal soldiers largely used army-issued metal identity discs as a form of official identification that authorised war-related travel. Some Indigenous soldiers were subsequently issued British passports towards the end of the war to facilitate their repatriation back to Australia. This practice allowed, for instance, Aboriginal campaigner A.M. Fernando to use his British passport to remain in Europe, making a permanent home for himself in England and subsequently travelling extensively across Europe to draw public attention to the abuse of Aboriginal people in Australia (Paisley 2012).[11]

In Australia, the subsequent *Passport Act 1938* (Cth) formally recognised the power of the Minister to issue Australian passports to 'an aboriginal native' of Australia or 'of any country under the protection of His Majesty' as British subjects. However, in practice, Aboriginal peoples' access to Australian passports was still highly constrained by draconian state-based 'native' administration regimes that gave state officials extensive control over intimate facets of Aboriginal peoples' lives as well as their authorised movement. In the state of Western Australia, for example, Aboriginal people could in theory apply for a Certificate of Citizenship that would exempt them from the native administration regime and that looked and functioned 'in the manner of a passport' (*Natives (Citizenship Rights) Act 1944* (WA), section 5(4)). As a result, John Chesterman and Brian Galligan (1997, 133) have argued that Aboriginal people in Western Australia in the mid-twentieth century, as a matter of law, did not have citizenship rights but rather 'an ability to be exempted from the citizenship exclusion that otherwise affected' all Aboriginal peoples.

Not only have regimes of entitlements and access to the passport been highly racialised, but the question of what passports ought to be recognised and on what terms has long been a racialised one too (see for example, Singha 2013; Mongia 2018). Take but one example in the Australian context. Writing in *Australian Worker* union newspaper in 1923, acclaimed socialist writer Mary Gilmore raised alarm about British passports being issued to Indians residing in London, a practice that she saw as being a direct affront to Australia's then legal regime of white supremacy. 'It seems curious' she wrote, 'to think that the lives of the white races in the Empire should hinge on the meaning of a piece of paper issued to an individual in London' (Gilmore 1923). She went on to suggest that the 'question of the passport' was not a 'trifling matter', but rather one in which 'the colour of Australian democracy' and the survival of the White Australia policy was at stake. In this way, the passport as a modern state document was seen as central to and intimately entangled in transnational projects of whiteness that sought to 'draw the global colour line' within and beyond the British Empire (Lake and Reynolds 2008).

Yet, rather than focusing only on the racialising work of state-issued passports, this chapter now turns to passports issued by Indigenous First Nations political authorities in order to understand certain passports as legal documents of Indigenous sovereignty and self-determination. The use and recognition of First Nations passports have a long history, including for instance by Cayuga statesman Chief Deskaheh to travel to London and Geneva in the early 1920s to advocate for the recognition of Indigenous sovereignty and territorial rights (Franz 2020). More recently, First Nations passports have been used by delegates of the Aboriginal Provisional Government to leave and re-enter Australia when travelling to Libya in the 1980s and Canada in the 2010s (Robertson 2015). Since then, in February 2020, the Australian Border Force (2020) has issued an operational directive in relation to the border clearance of any non-citizens who asserts a right to enter Australia on the basis of 'claiming to be Aboriginal Australian or Torres Strait Islander'. While the directive does not recognise such a right of non-citizens, it does make clear that it does not apply to any person 'reasonably suspect[ed]' of being an Australian citizen.

Significantly, in July 2010, an international controversy arose when the Iroquois Nationals, the national men's lacrosse team of the Haudenosaunee Confederacy, were grounded at New York's JFK Airport en route to England to compete in the World Lacrosse Championships. The team, consistent with their practice for previous international tournaments since 1980, were travelling on their Haudenosaunee passports, issued by the Onondaga Nation.[12] To their frustration, new state biometric passport requirements adopted post-9/11 under the so-called Western Hemisphere Travel Initiative meant that both the US and UK authorities decided to no longer recognise their Haudenosaunee passports. This decision was based on deeming the team's Haudenosaunee passports not compliant with the new biometric requirements as they did not contain the mandated electronic chips, digital photographs or numerical barcodes in them (Mick 2010). Although the team's representatives were able to successfully lobby then-US Secretary of State Hillary Clinton for a 'one-time' exemption in the form of a letter of authorisation to allow them to leave and re-enter the US on their Haudenosaunee passports, this letter came too late to allow for re-application for UK visas. As a result, the team was prevented from participating in the lacrosse competition and forced to return home.

During their time in New York, the team's efforts to travel on their Haudenosaunee passports attracted significant international media attention, including interviews with the team's then-executive director, Percy Abrams. In one particular interview, Abrams (2010) explained at length why the team members had refused to apply for US or Canadian passports, despite their eligibility, stating that 'it was a matter of nationality … our nation is the Iroquois nation, or as we call ourselves the Haudenosaunee [and] the passport I carry is the Haudenosaunee passport'. It is worth quoting an extended excerpt from the interview transcript (Abrams 2010) to get a sense of how Abrams frames the significance of the Haudenosaunee passport as a legal document:

Abrams: We have the right of self-determination. We have the right to present our own passport.

Interviewer: But isn't this a situation where you would be able to hold on to your passport from the Iroquois confederacy to get a new [state-issued] one, or would you have to turn it in?

Abrams: Why would I turn it in?

Interviewer: If you decided to get a US passport, for example. Wouldn't you be able to have both?

Abrams: Well technically I suppose you could have both. But in this case we are representing the Iroquois nation in this tournament. When we go to the games, we present our passport … This is our nationality and our identity. That's the stance we're taking. [We are] asking the US to accept our nationality, our right to self-determination …

Interviewer: I guess I'm just wondering how getting this document would be any strike against your identity. You would still be exactly who you are, coming from where you came from ...

Abrams: [sighs] It's a matter of a national pride … This is the document that we wish to carry for this game. This is our choice and our right to carry this and we should be able to carry this and travel abroad. Let me just tell you we have been travelling for over 30 years with this document.

The above exchange is noteworthy, not simply for the interviewer's inability to recognise the foundational issue as one of Indigenous nationhood, identity and self-determination. Indeed, Abrams repeatedly framed the issuing and use of First Nations passports as a legal practice of Indigenous nationhood; that is, practices that constitute and reflect what Glen Coulthard (2014) has called a 'resurgent politics of recognition'. Coulthard describes such practices are:

> less oriented around attaining legal and political recognition by the state, and more about Indigenous peoples empowering themselves through cultural practices of individual and collective self-fashioning that seek to prefigure radical alternatives to the structural and subjective dimensions of colonial power.
>
> (2014, 18)

This struggle draws attention to the work of documents in shaping lawful encounters, or encounters between different forms of law: one emanating from the asserted authority of the state, the other grounded in Indigenous jurisprudence and sociality. Focusing on the encounter between these forms of law reveals how Indigenous uses of passports mark the failure of settler colonial states to fully monopolise the 'legitimate means of movement' (Torpey 2000, 6) in the face of Indigenous nations that refuse to stop being and acting sovereign (Simpson 2014; Dehm 2021). Since 2010, as a result of much political effort on the part of Haudenosaunee diplomats, the Iroquois Nationals have been able to travel on their Haudenosaunee passports to some foreign states, such as the Czech Republic in 2011 and Israel in 2018.

Conclusion: re-documenting the forms and ends of the passport

Law is of course only one site in which struggles around the power and significance of the modern passport play out. In 2017, at the National Gallery of Victoria's Triennial exhibition, I had the pleasure of encountering acclaimed Angolan photographer Edson Chagas' series, *Tipo Passe* (2014) (literally, 'passport photo' in Portuguese). *Tipo Passe* consists of a series of photographs that play on the genre of the official passport photo, with each photograph titled after and depicting a portrait of a different individual (see Figures 4.1 and 4.2). Yet in place of an official passport photo's biometric realism, in Chagas' creations, each person wears a distinct Bantu mask, a head adornment from pre-colonial times of cultural and religious significance, to conceal their face from view. Chagas' photographs thus invoke intertwined motifs of culture and identity in order to raise questions about the authenticity of official documents, the limits of bureaucratic

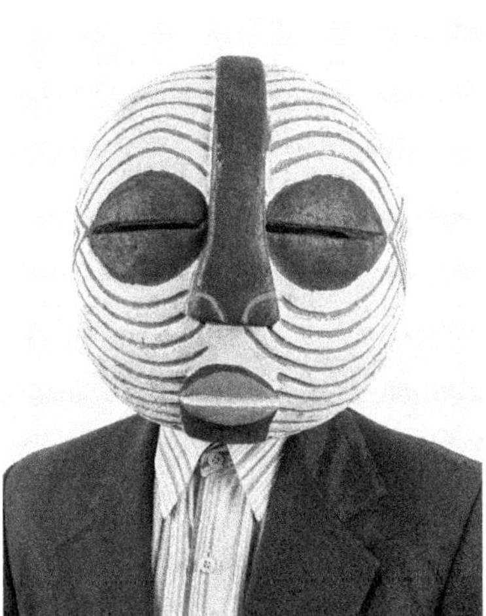

Figure 4.1 *Emmanuel C. Bofala* from the *Tipo Passe* series by Edson Chagas © Edson Chagas. Courtesy of Stevenson, Amsterdam/Cape Town/Johannesburg and A Palazzo, Italy.

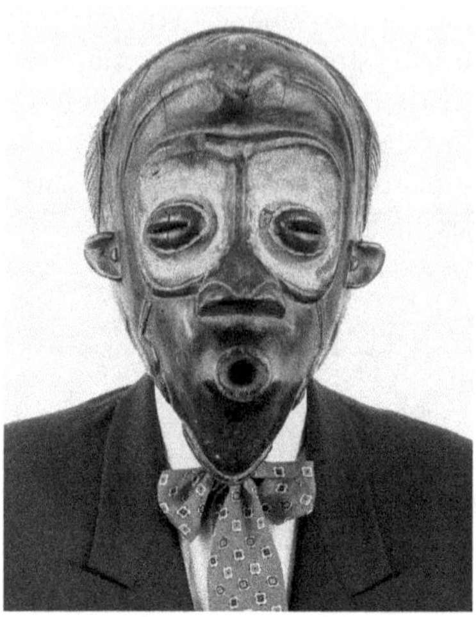

Figure 4.2 *Marcel D. Traoré* from the *Tipo Passe* series by Edson Chagas © Edson Chagas. Courtesy of Stevenson, Amsterdam/Cape Town/Johannesburg and A Palazzo, Italy.

knowability and even the constructed notions of legal personhood. The use of the Bantu masks, now considered valuable commodities on the global art market, draws attention to the commodification of African cultures and identities and the grossly uneven circulation of goods and people between the Global North and Global South, in an analogous way to the modern passport itself. Put differently, Chagas' artwork interrogates how African artwork may be highly valued and travel freely to states in the Global North but the majority of African people may not, discriminated against by reason of their nationality and respective passports.

In this sense, the series can be read as a critique of how modern passports purport to identify unique individuals for the purpose of facilitating movement, but can in fact do the opposite through 'classifying them into a collectivity' that may be 'restricted by its cross border mobility' (Jensen 2009, 817), thereby alluding to the racial violence underpinning contemporary state border regimes. Yet, read in another light, the photographs in *Tipo Passe* in and of themselves also perform a certain politics of refusal, with the individual subjects refusing to appear as the biometric rendering of human faces demanded by state authorities in seemingly benign bureaucratic documents like the passport. To re-document in this way is to draw into question the form and ends of the modern passport as an authentic and indeed desirable document of bureaucratic identification and inscription, as well as the uneven mobility regimes that it enables and sustains.

The future of passport struggles is by no means settled. Concerning passport struggles over gender recognition, in March 2017, Australian and

Aotearoa/New Zealand intersex organisations and advocates jointly issued the Darlington Statement (2017) that named and challenged acts of sex/gender classification as state 'structural violence'. While the Statement recognised that individuals should be 'free to choose' their gender markers, it also named the 'larger goal' to be 'not to seek new classifications but to end legal classification systems and the hierarchies that lie behind them'. Since then, in Australia, there have been legislative efforts to remove the designation of gender altogether from official documents like the passport (Kelly and Robert, 2018). Yet, even with such new initiatives, much more is needed to ensure that the long histories of discrimination, interrogation, harassment and even stasis do not continue to inform the experiences of transgender, nonbinary or gender diverse travellers at state borders (McNabb 2017, 34; Quinan and Bresser 2020).

Likewise, the very emergence of biometric borders and their entrenched racial logics has become the object of civil society and activist campaigns. Recently, the UN Special Rapporteur on Racism expressed concern at the 'prevalence of biometric data systems, racialized surveillance and racialized predictive analytics' in maintaining racially discriminatory state structures and urged that states needed to provide effective remedies, including compensation, for any such violations (*Racial Discrimination and Emerging Digital Technologies* 2020, para. 38). In the US context, for example, Mijente (2020), a Latinx and Chicanx social organisation for racial, economic and gender justice, continues to actively mount their #NoTechForICE campaign that puts public condemnation and scrutiny on multinational corporations that provide technology systems to state immigration enforcement. And, further, in September 2019, the Beyond Border Caucus of the Red Nation (a coalition of Indigenous and non-Indigenous activists advocating for Native liberation) issued a Manifesto acknowledging that the 'liberation of undocumented [people] is tied to the liberation of Indigenous people' and calling for the abolition of the immigration-prison-industrial complex. While such struggles present concrete challenges to the mechanisms of surveillance and 'ontology of exclusion' (Mountz 2011) at the heart of contemporary state borders, for now, these borders and their associated documentary practices continue to relentlessly and pervasively expand, including through using the material bodies of individual travellers as their targets and ends. The changing forms and functions of the modern passport show how physical documents are becoming ever-more entangled in, and even at times eclipsed by their digitised versions within, technological systems of surveillance and control themselves.

Notes

1 This follows Peter Rush's theorising of jurisdiction referring 'first and foremost to the power and authority to speak in the name of the law and only subsequently to the fact that law is stated—and stated to be someone or something' (Rush 1997, 150; see also Dorsett and McVeigh 2012).

2 The closest international definition of the modern passport is the fairly circular one provided by ICAO concerning a 'machine readable passport' (MRP) as a 'passport conforming with the specifications contained in Doc 9303-4'. MRP are a sub-set of the machine-readable travel documents (MRTD), defined as 'Official document[s], conforming with the specifications contained in Doc 9303, issued by a State or organization which is used by the holder for international travel (e.g. MRP)' (ICAO 2015, 15).
3 The *Australian Passports Act 2005* (Cth) does not define the term 'passport', and, like ICAO, only defines the term 'Australian passport' under section 6 in circular fashion as meaning 'a passport issued under this Act'. The Explanatory Memorandum (2004) does, however, note that a 'passport is a document', with 'document' being a defined term under the Act. For Australian case law concerning passports as legal documents, including an interesting reference to the idea of a destroyed passport as being a 'dead document' in the first-mentioned case, see *In the Marriage Of: Samir Saad Appellant/ Husband And: Hiam Saad Respondent/Wife* [1992] FamCA 44 (4 August 1992) and *1001288* [2010] RRTA 912 (22 October 2010).
4 For instance, an Australian passport is the property of the Australian state: *Australian Passports Act 2005* (Cth) section 54.
5 Under s 21 of the Australian Passport Determination 2015, it is 'preferable', but not essential, that the sex/gender in a person's Australian passport matches their cardinal documents, i.e. a birth certificate or a citizenship certificate.
6 Legal arguments that rest upon an asserted 'right to privacy' conceive of public authority as external to the 'private realm' and thus seek to arrange state jurisdiction in particular ways. As Kendall Thomas has demonstrated in the context of US sodomy laws criminalising certain forms of gay sex, the 'conceptual grid of the privacy paradigm' is unable to fully account for public forms of homophobic, transphobic or anti-intersex violence and associated legal discourses and practices. Thomas powerfully argues that while this need not mean abandoning legal claims based on the right to privacy, it does necessitate a more comprehensive analysis that 'force[s] privacy to go public' by advocating instead for a constitutional protection based on 'the physical security of the embodied individual' (Thomas 1992, 1443).
7 On gendered and queer practices of refusal as a mode of resistance to patriarchal cultures, see van Marle (2006).
8 In the UK, passports are issued by the Home Secretary in exercise of the Royal Prerogative. This means there is no specific law requiring inclusion of a gender category or status in UK passports, but rather the bureaucratic practice of requiring a gender category and using only male/female designations has developed over time and become entrenched in technological systems.
9 The primary judge held that this review would need to 'consider to what extent if any, in an age of increasing social and legal awareness and acceptance of the importance of issues relating to diversity and equality, the recording of an individual's sex and/ or gender in official and other documentation is justified. The range and nature of the documentation which may be affected will be required to be understood, including whether its purpose is to record historical or current information. It will also be necessary to consider the extent to which other identities both within and beyond the binary concept of gender are to be recognised, and if so, whether they are to be self determined or are to be objectively evidenced' (at para. 151).
10 Such provisions reflected earlier colonial legislation across the British Empire that treated indenture Indian and South Asian labour an 'an exception to the overarching principle of freedom of movement' and subject to specific mechanisms of control and coercion (Mongia 2018, 115).
11 Fiona Paisley notes how Fernando was likely to have been issued several British passports, including one that was issued to him in 1921 (likely for the purpose of repatriation

following wartime internment), stamped with an entry visa for Constantinople in 1923 and used (even though it had by then lapsed) by Fernando when travelling to several cities in Italy in 1925 until he was apprehended by the Milan police (Paisley 2012, 89).

12 The Haudenosaunee is a political confederacy that includes the Mohawk, Oneida, Onondaga, Cayuga, Seneca and Tuscarora First Nations.

References

Abrams, Percy, 2010. Interview with RT America: Iroquois Denied Sovereignty. Available from: https://www.youtube.com/watch?v=hbVs-oIGewo [Accessed 1 March 2021].

Achiume, Tendayi, 2020. *Racial Discrimination and Emerging Digital Technologies: A Human Rights Analysis: Report of the Special Rapporteur on Contemporary Forms of Racism, Racial Discrimination, Xenophobia and Related Intolerance* 2020, UN Doc A/HRC/44/57, UN Human Rights Council, 18 June.

Adey, Peter, 2009. Facing Airport Security: Affect, Biopolitics, and the Prreemptive Securitisation of the Mobile Body. *Environment and Planning D: Society and Space*, 27 (2), 274–95.

Amoore, Louise, 2006. Biometric Borders: Governing Mobilities in the War on Terror. *Political Geography*, 25 (3), 336–51.

Amoore, Louise, 2008. Governing by Identity. *In*: Colin J. Bennett and David Lyon, eds. *Playing the Identity Card: Surveillance, Security and Identification in Global Perspective*, Abington: Routledge, 21–36.

Amoore, Louise, and Hall, Alexandra, 2009. Taking People Apart: Digitised Dissection and the Body at the Border. *Environment and Planning D: Society and Space*, 27 (3), 444–64.

Australian Border Force, 2020. *Clearance at the Border of Non-citizens Claiming to be an Aboriginal Australian or Torres Strait Islander.* Operational Directive. 21 February. FOI Reference No FA 20/02/01156.

Bauman, Zygmunt, 2000. *Globalization: The Human Consequences.* New York: Columbia University Press.

Bellino, Emma, 2020. Married Women's Nationality and the White Australia Policy, 1920–1948. *Law and History*, 7 (1), 166–92.

Beyond Borders Caucus, 2019. Manifesto. The Red Nation. 6 September. Available from: http://therednation.org/caucuses/beyond-borders-caucus [Accessed 1 March 2021].

Broeders, Dennis, and Hampshire, James, 2013. Dreaming of Seamless Borders: ICTs and the Pre-Emptive Governance of Mobility in Europe. *Journal of Ethnic and Migration Studies*, 39 (8), 1201–18.

Brown, Wendy, 2010. *Walled States, Waning Sovereignty*. New York: Zone Books.

Browne, Simone, 2015. *Dark Matters: On the Surveillance of Blackness.* Durham: Duke University Press.

Butler, Julie, 2003. X Marks the Spot for Intersex Alex. *The West Australian*, 11 January, p. 3.

Chamayou, Gregorie, 2010. *Manhunts: A Philosophical History*. Princeton, NJ: Princeton University Press.

Chesterman, John, and Galligan, Brian, 1997. *Citizens Without Rights: Aborigines and Australian Citizenship.* Cambridge: Cambridge University Press.

Convention for the Protection of Human Rights and Fundamental Freedoms, Opened for Signature 4 November 1950, 213 UNTS 221 (entered into force 3 September 1953) (*European Convention on Human Rights/ECHR*).

Coulthard, Glen, 2014. *Red Skin, White Masks: Rejecting the Colonial Politics of Recognition.* Minneapolis: University of Minnesota.

Coyle, John, 2019. Soon You Won't Need a Passport—But the Delays Will Be Diabolical If Something Goes Wrong. *ABC News.* Available from: https://www.abc.net.au/news/2019-04-29/passports-airport-delays-future-of-travel/11054472 [Accessed 1 March 2021].

Daily Telegraph, 1915. Women's Congress: Limitation of Passports. *Daily Telegraph*, 22 April, p. 5.

Darlington Statement, 2017. *Joint Consensus Statement from the Intersex Community Retreat in Darlington*, 10 March. Available from: https://darlington.org.au/statement [Accessed 1 March 2021].

Dehm, Sara, 2018. Passport. *In*. Jessie Hohmann and Daniel Joyce, eds. *International Law's Objects.* Oxford: Oxford University Press, 342–56.

Dehm, Sara, 2021. Transnational Migration Law: Authority, Contestation, Decolonization. *In*: Peer Zumbansen, ed. *Oxford Handbook of Transnational Law.* Oxford: Oxford University Press, 683–705.

Dolman, Jane, and Lee, David, 2008. *Every Assistance and Protection: A History of the Australian Passport.* Sydney: Federation Press.

Dorsett, Shaunagh, and McVeigh, Shaun, 2012. *Jurisdiction.* Abington: Routledge.

Explanatory Memorandum, 2004. *Australian Passport Bill* (Cth).

Gilmore, Mary, 1923. The Passport and a White Australia. *Australian Worker.* 30 May, p. 5.

Godden, Lee, 2007. A Jurisdiction of Body and Desire: Exploring the Boundaries of Bodily Control in Prostitution Law. *In*: Shaun McVeigh, ed. *Jurisprudence of Jurisdiction.* London: Routledge-Cavendish, 181–201.

Franz, Margaret, 2020. Usurping the Contract: The Geneva Campaign (1923–1924) and the Refusal of Settler Sovereignty. *Communication and Critical/Cultural Studies*, 16 (4), 287–307.

Horton, Sarah B., 2020. Introduction. *In*: Sarah Horton and Josiah Heyman, eds. *Paper Trails: Migrants, Documents, and Legal Insecurity.* Durham: Duke University Press, 1–26.

ICAO, 2015. *Doc 9303: Machine Readable Travel Documents* (7th ed.). Montréal: ICAO. Available from: https://www.icao.int/publications/pages/publication.aspx?docnum=9303 [Accessed 1 March 2021].

Jansen, Stef, 2009. After the Red Passport: Towards an Anthropology of the Everyday Geopolitics of Entrapment in the EU's 'Immediate Outside'. *Journal of the Royal Anthropological Institute.* 15 (4), 815–32.

Kelly, Fiona, and Robert, Hannah, 2018. Explainer: Why Removing Sex from Birth Certificates Matters to Gender Diverse People. *The Conversation*, 25 October. Available from: https://theconversation.com/explainer-why-removing-sex-from-birth-certificates-matters-to-gender-diverse-people-105571 [Accessed 1 March 2021].

Keshavarz, Mahmoud, 2019. *The Design Politics of the Passport: Materiality, Immobility, and Dissent.* London: Bloomsbury.

Kotef, Hagar, 2015. *Movement and the Ordering of Freedom: On Liberal Governances of Mobility.* Durham: Duke University Press.

Lake, Marilyn, and Reynolds, Henry, 2008. *Drawing the Global Colour Line: White Men's Countries and the Question of Racial Equality.* Melbourne: Melbourne University Press.

Magnet, Shoshana A., 2011. *When Biometrics Fail: Gender, Race and the Technology of Identity.* Durham: Duke University Press.

M'charek, Amade, Schramm, Katharina, and Skinner, David, 2014. Topologies of Race: Doing Territory, Population and Identity in Europe. *Science, Technology & Human Values*, 39 (4), 468–87.

McKeown, Adam, 2011. *Melancholy Order: Asian Migration and the Globalization of Borders*. New York: Columbia University Press.

McNabb, Charlie, 2017. *Nonbinary Gender Identities: History, Culture, Resources*. Lanham: Rowman & Littlefield.

McNeilly, Kathryn, 2019. Sex/Gender is Fluid, What Now for Feminism and International Human Rights Law? A Call to Queer the Foundations. *In*: Susan Harris Rimmer and Kate Ogg, eds. *Research Handbook on Feminist Engagement with International Law*. Cheltenham: Edward Elgar, 430–44.

Mick, Hayley, 2010. Low-Tech Passports Ground Iroquois Lacrosse Team. *The Globe and Mail*, 14 July. Available from: https://www.theglobeandmail.com/news/world/low-tech-passports-ground-iroquois-lacrosse-team/article1387213 [Accessed 1 March 2021].

Mijente, 2020, #NoTechForICE. Available from: https://notechforice.com [Accessed 1 March 2021].

Mongia, Radhika, 2018. *Indian Migration and Empire: A Colonial Genealogy of the Modern State*. Durham: Duke University Press.

Mountz, Alison, 2011. Specters at the Port of Entry: Understanding State Mobilities Through an Ontology of Exclusion. *Mobilities*, 6 (3), 317–34.

Muchmore, Adam, 2004. Passports and Nationality in International Law. *UC Davis Journal of International Law and Policy*, 10, 301–55.

Otto, Dianne, 2015. Queering Gender [Identity] in International Law. *Nordic Journal of Human Rights*, 33 (4), 299–318.

Paisley, Fiona, 2012. *The Lone Protestor: AM Fernando in Australia and Europe*. Canberra: Aboriginal Studies Press.

Pugliese, Joseph, 2010. *Biometrics: Bodies, Technologies, Biopolitics*. New York: Routledge.

Pugliese, Joseph, 2013. Technologies of Extraterritorialisation, Statist Visuality and Irregular Migrants and Refugees. *Griffith Law Review*, 22 (3), 571–97.

Quinan, C. L., and Bresser, Nina, 2020. Gender at the Border: Global Responses to Gender-Diverse Subjectivities and Nonbinary Registration Practices. *Global Perspectives*, 1 (1). Available from: https://doi.org/10.1525/gp.2020.12553 [Accessed 1 March 2021].

Robertson, Craig, 2010. *The Passport in America: The History of a Document*. Oxford: Oxford University Press.

Robertson, Joshua, 2015. Tolerance of Travellers with Aboriginal Passports Amounts to Recognition, Says Activist. *The Guardian*, 20 April. Available from: https://www.theguardian.com/australia-news/2015/apr/20/tolerance-of-travellers-with-aboriginal-passports-amounts-to-recognition-says-activist [Accessed 1 March 2021].

Rush, Peter, 1997. An Altered Jurisdiction: Corporeal Traces of Law. *Griffith Law Review*, 6, 144–68.

Safronova, Valeriya, 2021. Passports May Soon Include a New Option for Gender Identity. *The New York Times*, 24 February. Available from: https://www.nytimes.com/2021/02/24/style/gender-neutral-x-passport-ids.html [Accessed 1 March 2021].

Shoemaker, Nancy, 2015. *Native American Whalemen and the World: Indigenous Encounters and the Contingency of Race*. Chapel Hill, NC: University of North Carolina Press.

Simpson, Audra, 2014. *Mohawk Interruptus: Political Life Across the Borders of Settler States*. Durham: Duke University Press.

Singha, Radhika, 2013. The Great War and a 'Proper' Passport for the Colony: Border-Crossing in British India, c.1882–1922. *Indian Economic and Social History Review*, 50 (3), 289–315.

Sydney Morning Herald, 1917. Passports to Europe: Women and Children Barred. *Sydney Morning Herald*, 7 February, p. 10.

Torpey, John, 2000. *The Invention of the Passport: Surveillance, Citizneship and the State*. Cambridge: Cambridge University Press.

The Argus, 1917. Women Refused Passports. *The Argus*, 28 July, p. 19.

Thomas, Kendall, 1992. Beyond the Privacy Principle. *Columbia Law Review*, 92 (6), 1431–516.

van Marle, Karin, ed., 2006. *Sex, Gender, Becoming: Post-Apartheid Reflections*. Pretoria: Pretoria University Law Press.

Wareham, Jamie, 2020. U.K. Supreme Court to Hear Major LGBTQ Rights Case on 'X' Passports. *Forbes*, 12 November. Available from: https://www.forbes.com/sites/jamiewareham/2020/11/12/uk-supreme-court-to-hear-major-lgbtq-rights-case-on-x-passports [Accessed 1 March 2021].

Weekly Times, 1925. Reply to Protest: British Encouraged. *Weekly Times*, 10 January, p. 9.

Legislation

Australia

Australian Passports Act 2005 (Cth)
Australian Passports Determination 2015 (Cth)
Natives (Citizenship Rights) Act 1944 (WA)
Passport Act 1920 (Cth)
Passport Act 1938 (Cth)

United States

U.S. Constitution (US)

Cases

Australia

1001288 [2010] RRTA 912 (22 October 2010).

In the Marriage Of: Samir Saad Appellant/Husband And: Hiam Saad Respondent/Wife [1992] FamCA 44 (4 August 1992).

United Kingdom

R (on the application of Christie Elan-Cane) v Secretary of State for the Home Department [2018] EWHC 1530 (22 June 2018).

R (on the application of Christie Elan-Cane) v Secretary of State for the Home Department [2020] EWCA Civ 363 (10 March 2020).

United States

Zzyym v Kerry (D Col, Civ No 15-cv-02362-RBJ, 22 November 2016).
Zzyym v Pompeo (D Col, Civ No 15-cv-02362-RBJ, 19 September 2018).
Zzyym v Pompeo (10th Cir, No 18-1453, 12 May 2020).

Artworks

Chagas, Edson, 2014. *Tipo Passe* [series]. Type C Photographs. 100 x 80 cm. National Gallery of Victoria (NGV).010237470Information Classification: General00Information Classification: General

Chapter 5

What is a bogus document?

Refugees, race and identity documents in Australian migration law

Anthea Vogl

Introduction

In 2020 an Iraqi refugee applicant—assigned the 'identifier' of DVH16 by the Australian Federal Circuit Court—challenged a finding that he had provided 'bogus documents' as evidence of his identity, nationality or citizenship in breach of the Australian *Migration Act 1958* (ss 5, 91WA). The original decision-maker in DVH16's case found his Iraqi Certificate of Nationality and National Identity Card to be bogus and that DVH16 had not given a reasonable explanation for providing these bogus items. The opportunity to provide a reasonable explanation clearly presented a challenge for DVH16, since in his view his documents were genuine (*DVH16 v Minister for Immigration* 2020).

As required by the *Migration Act 1958*, he was nonetheless given the opportunity to respond to the Department of Home Affairs Document Examination Unit (DEU) findings that his documents were bogus. In his response by email to a Departmental delegate, DVH16 wrote:

> hello Mr.Adam you send me email that you say my documents are (bogus document) i don't understand my documents are real what kind of prove you want me to give you for that because i don't understand please let me know thanks [sic].
>
> (*DVH16 v Minister for Immigration 2020* [34])

On appeal, DVH16's legal representation argued that, amongst other things, the above email indicated that the Department had not given DVH16 sufficient particulars as to why his documents were bogus to allow him to answer the claims. In the Federal Circuit Court of Australia, Nicholls J disagreed. Nicholls J found that DVH16 was given an opportunity to provide a reasonable explanation as to why his documents were not bogus; in making this finding he rejected the argument that the methods used by the Department to find the documents were bogus needed to be disclosed to DVH16 under the Act. DVH16's appeal failed, and his overall application for refugee protection was refused.

DOI: 10.4324/9781003247593-7

Under Australian law, a refugee who provides a 'bogus document' as evidence of 'identity, nationality or citizenship' without a reasonable explanation cannot be granted refugee status. The refusal of refugee status applies even if the person is otherwise found to be a refugee in need of protection (*Migration Act 1958* ss 91W, 91WA). The reforms were introduced under the *Migration Amendment (Protection and Other Measures) Act 2014* (Cth), which simultaneously established that the Minister must refuse to grant a visa where an applicant has 'destroyed or disposed of documentary evidence' of their identity without a reasonable excuse (*Migration Act 1958* ss 91W, 91WA). The Australian federal government presented the new provisions as another means to realise the never-finished task of securing the national border against the 'fake refugee immigrant', the 'welfare-fraud immigrant' and the 'criminal immigrant' (Razack 2000, 189; Parliament of Australia 2014b).

In relation to comparable requirements that refugees present 'proper' identity documents for entry into Canada, Sherene Razack has identified what she calls the 'rhetoric of betrayal'. She argues the differential treatment of refugees without acceptable identity documents is structured by a concealed racist logic that:

> [r]elies for its coherence on a national story of a Canada besieged and betrayed by bodies of colour. 'Proper' identity documents become defensible … as a way of separating the deserving from the undeserving and as a way of dealing with the inevitable duplicity of people of colour.
>
> (2000, 186)

In line with Razack, the Australian bogus document reforms also tell a story about deception, siege and race, even as the storyline is hard to pin down 'because its racist structure is not overt' (Razack 2000, 186). The same rhetoric of betrayal and deceit explicitly runs through the bogus document reforms, as well as the justifications provided in support of them. The reforms imagine and address the unidentified, raced body as actively deceiving the state, not in a general and unspecified manner, but through the use of a bogus identity document.

In this chapter I explore how the Australian reforms, with their focus trained on the deceit of the document rather than the document-holder, create another site for the assessment of deceit and duplicity. I read the bogus document reforms as a form of racial profiling where suspicion moves from the body and onto the document, and continues to shift between these sites. As the assessment of the fraud moves away from the person, away from speech and testimony and towards the object of the document, this brings into play new authoritative scientific and forensic discourses attached to the 'expert' assessment of documents. In the Australian context this has included the Department of Home Affairs ('the Department') DEU, which is deployed as yet another strategy to defend the state from the 'fake' and duplicitous refugee seeking entry.

I investigate the reforms and the demand for genuine refugee identity documents in three parts. Part One addresses the introduction of the bogus document reforms, their justification and content, demonstrating how the bogus document functions as a stand-in for the bogus refugee and the duplicitous person of colour seeking illegitimate entry into the state. Part Two places the reforms in the already-vexed context of refugee applicants' relationship with official identity documents. It reads the legislation as requiring refugees to present a 'stable self' as evidenced by particular kinds of documents in exchange for protection (Lyon 2001), even as the absence of documents is arguably intrinsic to, or at least extremely common for, people seeking refugee status. Part Three examines the small body of case law in relation to the reforms, focussing on what triggers a 'reasonable suspicion' that a document is bogus and addressing what the cases tell us about how the Department, and in particular the DEU, determines whether a document is bogus. Here, I draw on Simone Browne's notion of 'digital epidermalization' and Joseph Pugliese's idea of 'infrastructural whiteness' to think about how 'the body materializes with and against' identification technologies (Browne 2010; Pugliese 2012). I explore how analyses of raced surveillance and interpretative practices associated with identity documents and biometric technologies are productive in understanding the purpose of the reforms and how they operate.

Part One: how do you define bogus?

Razack's (2000, 187) analysis of the demand for proper identity documents within Canadian refugee law as deploying a rhetoric of betrayal emerges clearly in the reforms that established bogus documents as a barrier to refugee protection in Australia. In commending the reform bill to Parliament, then-Immigration Minister Scott Morrison invoked a familiar imagined asylum seeker: a bogus one. Here, though, the bogus refugee was not only lying in a general and unspecified manner. This imagined asylum seeker was specifically falsifying identity by submitting bogus documents to cheat a way into refugee protection. As this figure loomed in the background, the Minister justified the amendments on the basis that 'Australians need to be confident that those who are found to be refugees are in fact who they say they are'. He also stated that '[t]hese measures make it clear that Australians expect protection visa applications to be made in good faith, and with full disclosure of identity' (Parliament of Australia 2014b, 7278, Scott Morrison).

The Minister's speech gave the impression that 'Australians everywhere' were concerned with modes of identity verification in visa application processes. Other Liberal National Party MPs reported that people on the NSW Central Coast tell them 'everyday' how much they appreciate the government 'stopping the boats', and that people in the NSW electorate of Robertson want to have 'even more confidence' in the integrity of the government's management of refugee status determination processes (Parliament of Australia 2014b,

10027, Lucy Wickes). Numerous government speakers in support of the Bill paraphrased the same justification, stating that the reforms were required so we can be 'confident that those who are found to be refugees are, in fact, who they say they are' (Parliament of Australia 2014b, 7278, Scott Morrison).

Alongside the justification that 'we need to know they are who they say they are', the amendments were justified on the basis of concerns about an unmanageable backlog of asylum claims and delays in the processing of refugee claims (Parliament of Australia 2014b, 7278, Scott Morrison). Here, non-nationals, with bogus documents and purporting to be refugees, are not only threats to national security, criminals hiding in plain sight or duplicitous brown people seeking entry, but more prosaically, are responsible for clogging up refugee status determination processes and compromising the 'integrity of decision making' in order to 'extend their time in Australia' (Parliament of Australia 2014b, 7278, Scott Morrison). Even though the problem of extended delays may appear to be a benign procedural matter, the 'huge backlog' caused by unidentified or mis-identified asylum seekers also conjures up Razack's (2000, 191) notion of a 'nation besieged' by countless and unmanageable immigrants and refugees seeking to enter.

The Australian reforms are not unique insofar as they punish or seek to banish non-citizens who provide false or misleading information when seeking permanent or temporary entry into the state.[1] The use of the term 'bogus', though, is unique to the Australian legislation. While the *Migration Act* does not provide a definition of the word 'bogus' nor define what is and is not a 'document', it does provide a definition of a 'bogus document'. Section 5 of the Act tells us a bogus document 'in relation to a person' means 'a document that the Minister reasonably suspects is a document that'

- 'purports to have been, but was not, issued in respect of the person'; or
- 'is counterfeit or has been altered by a person who does not have authority to do so'; or
- 'was obtained because of a false or misleading statement, whether or not made knowingly' (*Migration Act 1958*)

The definition centres on various acts of deception and fraud. The second arm of the statutory definition, that a bogus document 'is a document that is counterfeit', is perfectly circular. It provides the basis for a broad discretion in determining whether a document meets the statutory definition of bogus (*Migration Act 1958* s 5).

The adjective bogus stands out in comparison to the generally sparse and restrained nature of legislative language. The word and its etymology are worth considering further, given the prevalence of rhetoric regarding 'bogus' refugees in Australian political discourse (Pickering 2001). Bogus, Anatoly Liberman (2017) notes, 'has the reputation of a word of unknown etymology'. The words *tantrabobus* and *tantrabogus* were recorded in the late eighteenth century as a Vermont colloquialism for an ill or odd-looking object (Liberman 2017). However, the word bogus is generally traced back to the period of the 1820s when it was used to refer to 'an apparatus for counterfeit coining' and then in the 1840s, also in reference to the coins themselves ('no luggage, no nor nothing, but a roll of bogus'). By the mid-century, it was used as an adjective whose meaning had shifted to signify something that was spurious, falsified or counterfeit in a general sense, similar to contemporary usage ('the whole thing was bogus'). A 'bogus caller' was one of the 2011 additions to the *Oxford English Dictionary*'s bogus entry, defined as a 'person who visits or telephones someone under false pretences' (*Oxford English Dictionary* 2021). A 'bogus refugee' is not listed. However, the extremely common trope of the 'bogus refugee' in political discourse means that the statutory use of the term, albeit in relation to the document, immediately extends to and implicates the document holder. The implication is that a bogus document belongs to the bogus refugee, despite the fact that the reforms permit the refugee applicant to provide a reasonable excuse for the transgression.

Alongside Razack's analysis of the threat of false papers, the obvious problem with the bogus document is that it disrupts the state's capacity to 'identify and enumerate its population and separate it by legal status' (Scott 1998; Horton 2020, 4). As noted, the vision of Australians 'everywhere' concerned with the stable identities of asylum seekers and non-citizens was at the centre of the rhetoric explaining the reforms. This rhetoric was explicit in connecting the absence of identity papers—and other forms of identification—with both security and risk. Lyon (2001, 291) traces the return to the body as a means of identification, and the shift in documenting individual identity away from 'predominantly print based information' to biometrics and electronically stored data. He highlights how the body itself is 'scrutinised and interrogated' as a source of surveillance data, noting that '[i]nformation for identification may now be extracted from the body that can override the person's own claims to a particular identity'. While he is careful to acknowledge that there is nothing entirely new about this, he does trace the way in which certain identity documents and forms of identification both create a 'stable self' in the eyes of the state *as well as* bring the 'stable' or identified body into an extended and increasingly networked system of surveillance (Lyon 2001). Thus, the refugee without documents, or worse still, with an undetected bogus document, is not only potentially unidentifiable but also un-surveilled or unseen—representing a real and present threat to the state 'forced to defend itself from bodies bent on betraying its trust' (Razack 2000, 187).

Part Two: refugees and authentic identity documents go together like...

Although the Australian reforms indicate otherwise, there is nothing simple or straightforward about refugees' relationships with identity documents, real or fake. Critically, prior to the Australian amendments, the regulation of bogus documents was not specifically directed towards those seeking refugee protection (*Migration Act 1958* s 103). Bogus documents were and are addressed elsewhere in the Act as grounds upon which any visa 'based on incorrect information' may be cancelled. The Act also sets out that in general any bogus document that is 'given, presented, produced or provided' is forfeited to the Commonwealth (*Migration Act 1958* ss 487ZI, 487ZJ). Bogus documents, and false and misleading information more generally, are also regulated by Public Interest Criterion (PIC) 4020, which attaches to the grant of most other non-protection visas. Under the PIC, the Minister must be satisfied of the applicant's identity and that the applicant has not provided a bogus document or false or misleading information. It also establishes that an applicant may be barred from making a further visa application for up to ten years for failing to establish identity, or up to three years for providing bogus documents or false information (Migration Regulations 1994, Schedule 4).

Notably, prior to 2014, the provisions governing evidence of identity for refugee applicants did not mention 'bogus documents'. The relevant section only addressed circumstances where the Department directly requested a protection visa applicant to 'produce … documentary evidence of the applicant's identity, nationality or citizenship', and an applicant refused or failed to comply with the request without a reasonable excuse. Such a failure allowed the Minster to 'draw any reasonable inference unfavourable to the applicant's identity' and nothing further (*Migration Act 1958* s 91W, No. 62 of 2013).

The reforms' specific focus on refugee applicants, and in particular the introduction of mandatory cancellation based on identity documentation is significant. The process of determining refugee status has been theorised as 'one of the most complex adjudication functions in industrialized societies' (Rousseau, Crépeau, Foxen and Houle 2002, 43). The complexity of the task is due to the unique elements of the decision-making process, which not only involves the applicant's first-person testimony as a central source of evidence, but frequently includes the translation of evidence across at least two languages; communication across a significant cultural divide; the requirement that the decision-maker have knowledge of the cultural, social and political environment in the applicant's country of origin; and the need for both the applicant and decision-maker to have the 'capacity to bear the psychological weight' of potentially distressing evidence of an applicant's experiences of persecution (Rousseau, Crépeau, Foxen and Houle 2002, 44). To determine the authenticity of documents, decision-makers must also have administrative knowledge of a country, to understand if and how official identity documents are issued, by whom and what (if any) factors determine their validity.

The process is especially difficult because of the regular absence of any kind of documentary evidence, let alone documentary sources that are reliable, probative and verifiable (Vogl 2013). This absence of documentary evidence includes identity documents, but extends beyond them. Documentary evidence going to the occurrence of particular events, travel routes, employment and education history and places of residence is also rare. The problem with the reforms is that the possession of, and need for, counterfeit identity documents to leave one's country of origin—alongside the difficulty of accessing identity documents—is intrinsic to, or at the very least, common to many refugees' experiences. Indeed, by virtue of seeking refugee status, an applicant is claiming that the government or local state authority (the same government or local authority that *issues* documents) is an agent of persecution, or is unwilling to provide protection from persecution. As Macklin (1998, 136) notes,

> it would be fundamentally unfair to impose on claimants an unreasonable burden to produce evidence, given the conditions under which they flee their countries of origin and the difficulty of obtaining documents from home once they have arrived in the country of asylum.

This is, however, exactly what the legislation does. Even though it also encompasses the possibility that an applicant might have a reasonable explanation for producing a bogus document or failing to establish identity, the starting point is that a refugee applicant will be able to provide documentation to allow the Australian government to establish who they are. And while providing bogus documents or destroying documents operate as grounds to deny refugee status under the reforms, having authentic documents certainly does not mean that a claimed identity will be found to be authentic, or necessarily strengthen a claim to refugee status. Since a dangerous relationship with a home state government is an element of the refugee definition, having *authentic* documents (which one is compelled to produce) can be taken as evidence of the inauthenticity of the claim. For example, the possession or use of a genuine passport to leave one's country of origin is regularly interrogated as evidence that the refugee applicant is not a person of interest to his or her government. The 'damned if you do, damned if you don't' situation facing refugees in relation to identity documents is captured in detail by Macklin in reflections on her experience as a refugee decision-maker in Canada. She notes that the following 'pattern of reasoning' is not uncommon:

> Claimants are rejected because they are unable to furnish sufficient identity documents or documents proving residence in a refugee camp etc. Some claimants protest that they are unable to obtain documents and are met with the reply that other claimants manage to do so ... Soon, all claimants show up with the requisite documents, having learned through the grapevine that the failure to produce documents will lead to rejection. Predictably, decision makers become suspicious of the authenticity of documents, and may even send them for forensic testing where (not

> surprisingly) a number will turn up as fake. This, in turn, is used to impugn the credibility of claimants, and can lead directly to rejection.
>
> (1998, 136)

Macklin (1998, 136) also notes that when decision-makers discover that it is possible to illicitly purchase documents which cannot be identified via forensic testing, the result is that the probative value of documents begins to be undermined altogether.

What Bibler Coutin (2020) has described as the 'double bind' of possessing legal documentation for migration to the United States applies to refugees seeking protection in Australia. Punishing refugees for knowingly or unknowingly holding particular documents, which may be necessary for departure from their country of origin, challenges the idea that having identity documents is normatively better or more secure for non-citizens (Yngvesson and Coutin 2006). Horton (2020, 8) notes the way documents can operate to constrict migrants' possibilities, as well as the potentially 'disqualifying, right-limiting character of the passport as a marker of nationality' (citing Torpey 2018, 155). Documents may, as Lyon notes, operate to increase the power and control of the state over migrants' lives and be used to undermine or dismiss one's own self-narrated identity. Documentation and biometric records leave migrants open to 'bureaucratic inscription' and surveillance at various and overlapping levels of government (Dehm 2018; Horton 2020, 4). Bibler Coutin (2020, 133) has extended this analysis, noting in her ethnographic work that the precise effect of certain documents for non-citizens can be so arbitrary and opaque that it is hard to predict. She describes 'the quasi-magical power of papers and records to transform persons by regularizing or criminalizing their presence' whereby documents 'create opportunities and double binds: they are key to obtaining legal status, but they also can make legalization impossible'.

Part Three: forming 'reasonable suspicions' and finding bogus documents in the case law

To date, only a small number of cases raise the two key provisions in the Act dealing with bogus documents for refugee applicants, and fewer still directly address these provisions. It is rare that the Department's finding that a document is 'bogus' is a contested fact before the courts, and so the document-as-object hangs in the background or is brushed aside, after an applicant concedes that they provided a bogus document and the case turns on another aspect of the reforms. This means a minority of cases raise the question of how precisely to identify a potentially bogus document and fewer still detail the proof-making processes used to show a document is or is not bogus. In cases where a document's inauthenticity is conceded by the applicant, the cases instead turn on questions such as whether the applicant was given sufficient notice of the Department's adverse inferences about a document in order to respond, or whether an applicant's explanation for providing a bogus document was 'reasonable' under the Act.

The first Full Federal Court decision in relation to the Act's proscription against bogus documents addresses whether the section is limited to the provision of bogus documents only as part of, or in connection with, protection visa applications or extends to the provision of bogus documents as proof of identity in any circumstance, including those unrelated to a protection visa application (*BGM16 v Minister for Immigration and Border Protection* 2017). The Department's submissions would have it that a false drivers' license presented at a state registry or fake identification used to enter a bar should act as a barrier to accessing refugee protection from the federal government. Although the Court rejected the Department's submissions as an incorrect interpretation of the section, they demonstrate the expansion of the 'internal border' for non-citizens, which involves the policing of migration status by internal government agencies and private actors (Weber 2013). Policing at these sites, and the regulation of the border itself are enabled by 'administrative and bureaucratic techniques', which operate around a range of documents including 'passports, visas, identification cards and their application procedures' (Browne 2010, 138).

In the cases addressing whether a document is bogus, the inaccessible and opaque nature of document examination 'expertise' relied on by the Department (and relevant review bodies) is a common theme. Like the assessment of the refugee claim itself, interpretation and evaluation of the document occur across jurisdictions, languages, translations and cultures, based on limited and incomplete insights about identity documents in the applicant's home state available from the Department's own 'country of origin information' databases (Gibb and Good 2013). Moreover, based on the text of available judgments, it is extremely difficult to ascertain what gives rise to a suspicion that a document may be bogus in the first instance.

The statutory definition sets out that the Minister must hold a 'reasonable suspicion' that a document is bogus on the basis of one or more of the three grounds outlined in Part Two (*Migration Act 1958* s 5). A number of the cases provide a glimpse as to what kinds of non-expert things raise such a suspicion. In *ASF17 v Minister for Immigration and Border Protection*, the applicant's claim was made on the basis that he was a stateless Faili Kurd. His 'Identity Card for Foreign Nationals' was deemed to be bogus on the basis that he also held an Iranian driver's licence, which country information 'suggested' only citizens may acquire (*ASF17 v Minister for Immigration and Border Protection* 2018). On appeal, the question of whether the decision-maker's suspicion was reasonable was raised. Although the assessment under s91WA appears to turn on the authenticity of *documents*, the decision also recorded that the applicant, in his first oral interview, had stated that he was an Iranian national but later explained he had mistakenly said this on account of bad advice to pretend he was a citizen of Iran. The decision-maker's overall assessment of the applicant's case was based on this original inconsistency in his testimony, and on an assumption that he was an Iranian citizen falsely presenting himself as a stateless Kurd.

The applicant was invited to provide an explanation for what the delegate suspected was a false Foreign Nationals Identity Card. The applicant provided a written response through a migration agent, claiming:

> his father had obtained the document in 1998 or 1999 and handed over his family's 'green cards' in exchange for the [foreign] National ID card(s). [He] claimed he was provided with the [Foreign] National ID card by his father and always believed it to be a genuine document.
>
> (*ASF17 v Minister for Immigration and Border Protection 2018* [12])

The documents in this case formed both the legal basis rejecting the claim for refugee status as well as the basis for doubting the applicant's oral evidence and credibility. The delegate's ultimate rejection of the authenticity of the document, which was upheld on appeal, was not primarily based on the document but rather on the finding that the applicant was not a 'credible, truthful or reliable witness' and that he was not a Faili Kurd as claimed but an Iranian citizen. The slippage here between disbelieving the applicant and doubting the authenticity of the document resulted in a finding that the document itself breached the relevant provision.

In another case, an Afghan identity document, commonly known as a *taskera*, was considered to be bogus on the basis of country information that such a document could only be issued in Afghanistan, and not in the Afghan Consulate in Pakistan (*AYZ18 v Minister for Immigration, Citizenship, Migrant Services and Multicultural Affairs* 2020). The finding was overturned on appeal. The delegate had overlooked clear evidence provided by the Department of Foreign Affairs and Trade that Afghan Consulates can and frequently do provide identity documents outside of Afghanistan. In that case, a further basis for finding that the document was bogus was discrepancies between the form of the applicant's *taskera* and the applicant's father's identity document, provided as further proof of the applicant's identity. On appeal, it became clear that the delegate had compared two entirely different forms of identity document, namely a birth certificate with a general identity document (*taskera*). As such, it was not open to the delegate to make a finding based upon the inconsistencies identified. The ability to clarify the ostensibly obvious error was complicated by the fact that the applicant himself was illiterate.

Surprisingly, in the above case, the document held to be bogus was in fact a photocopied version of the original document. Moreover, uncertified *copies* of original documents were assessed as bogus documents in a number of cases. Items forensically assessed for their authenticity included photocopies of identity documents (*AYZ18 v Minister for Immigration, Citizenship, Migrant Services and Multicultural Affairs* 2020), a photograph of a government identity document (*FLD18 v Minister for Home Affairs* 2020) and scanned photographs of an applicant wearing a military uniform (as evidence of national identity) (*DSM16 v Minister for Immigration* 2018). Copies of documents were nonetheless found to be bogus and to meet the definition of a bogus document under the Act. The fact that assessment of the copied documents took place as if they were assessments of the original documents—that were never in possession of the Department or accessed by forensic document experts—raises the extremely difficult question of what precisely is being assessed for imitation or authenticity?

In addressing identification verification processes and biometrics, Browne (2010, 133) draws on Frantz Fanon's notion of epidermalization, explained as the racialised body experiencing 'its being through others' whereby the 'dissociation between the self and the world' is experienced through the skin. That is, it is through skin or epidermalization that one is marked as other and as a 'contact moment of fracture of the body from its humaneness' (Browne 2010; citing Fanon 1967). This takes place, amongst other things, via an interpellating gaze, which might exclaim '"Look, a Negro!" or an "illegal alien", or some other negatively racialized subject position' (Browne 2010, 134).

Browne describes biometrics as a 'technology of measuring the living body' put to use in identification practices 'that enable the body to function as evidence'. However, she insists that identities 'in these digitizing discourses, must also be thought through their construction within discourse' (Browne 2010, 134). What is so useful in Browne's work for analysis of the bogus document cases and reforms is the way in which she casts both the object of identification (biometrics, passport and identity documents) and the practices of interpretation (the 'science' of interpreting biometric data, or the 'scientific' practices to determine if a document is bogus) as already informed and structured both by whiteness and an othering of the racialized body.

Pugliese (2012, 1) puts this in another way in his argument that biometrics, as a technology of authentication, only achieves its signifying status by 'being situated within relations of power and disciplinary techniques', which identify, classify and distribute 'templates of biometrically enrolled subjects across complex political, social and legal networks'. He demonstrates the ways in which biometric technologies are inscribed with normative categories such as race, gender, disability and sexuality at the same time as these infrastructural aspects are 'invisibilised' to enable 'ongoing pronouncements about the technology's neutral and non-discriminatory capability' (2012, 2). Precisely because such technologies are 'infrastructurally calibrated to whiteness' and designed with whiteness as a template, non-white subjects are often 'precluded from biometric enrolment due to the fact the technologies fail to "read" their biometric characteristics' (Pugliese 2012, 57). For the purposes of identification, the 'failure to enrol' or be recognised by a particular form of biotechnology confirms a non-white subject's failure to fit into predetermined 'white standards' or universal whiteness. Although the identity document is not necessarily also a biometric record, it is similarly represented as an 'ideologically neutral "conduit" of data, rather than ideologically inflected' and interpreted through networks of knowledge and power (Pugliese 2012, 58).

Similarly, Browne considers biometrics as involving moments of observation, calibration and application, and argues that the ideas of a body made other and out of place, and of epidermalization, are:

> useful when thinking through the moments of contact enacted at the 'institutional sites' of international border crossings and spaces of the internal borders of the state ... where identification, and increasingly biometric identification, is required to speak the 'truth' of and for muted bodies.
>
> (Browne 2010, 134–135)

Biometric technologies and methods of identification verification are not 'neutral, objective systems' but rather 'their seemingly pure geometry, their transcendental algorithms and apparently unmotivated digital formulae are all inflected with the dense sociocultural and historical significations of their designers' (Pugliese 2012, 78). The (bogus) identity document at the centre of the reforms is read alongside, and together with, the raced body already out of place, just as refugee testimony is heard—and disbelieved—in the same manner (Bohmer and Shuman 2018; Vogl 2018).

The Document Examination Unit

A number of the cases make reference to the Department's DEU or to reports provided to decision-makers by the DEU. Most references to DEU reports are perfunctory and remarkably short on detail. In all of the cases I read, there was no reference to scientific evidence or to the forensic methods the DEU adopts to reach its conclusions.[2] As with the following example, findings are generally declaratory, applied by the delegate and material factors in the final decision.

In *BYE17 v Minister for Immigration and Anor*, the applicant was an unaccompanied minor whose national identity card and birth certificate were referred to and assessed by the DEU in the first instance. The DEU findings were set out and applied by the delegate and referred to in the appeal judgment as follows:

> [The DEU] found that the birth certificate was fraudulently altered with entries for birth date, location and issue date removed and replacement entries added. The national identity card was found to be entirely counterfeit. Following forensic examination by the Department, I find that the birth certificate and national identity card are bogus documents in accordance with s5(1)(b).
>
> (*BYE17 v Minister for Immigration and Anor* 2018 [19])

The appeal, which did not turn on the DEU report or its findings, provides a sense of the opaque nature of references to the DEU, its methods and findings. It sets out that on review of the delegate's decision, the Tribunal also accepted the DEU report:

> The Tribunal said that it accepted that the DEU had expertise in document examination and that it had placed significant weight on the findings of the DEU as reported in the delegate's decision record ... *The Tribunal said that whilst the information provided in the delegate's decision record did not include the nature of the forensic examination undertaken by the DEU*, the delegate's decision record does report that the DEU found the birth certificate provided by the appellant was fraudulently altered.
>
> (*BYE17 v Minister for Immigration and Anor* 2018 [28] (my emphasis))[3]

The case of *DVH16 v Minister for Immigration*, referred to in the Introduction, deals directly with the content, methods and findings of a DEU report. In that case, the applicant argued that while the delegate referenced the conclusion reached in a DEU report and gave the applicant an opportunity to respond to this, the delegate 'did not give any detail as to how the conclusion was reached ... so as to make the giving of information to the applicant relevantly meaningful' (*DVH16 v Minister for Immigration* 2020). The applicant argued that the delegate 'failed to give the applicant particulars, or relevant details, of the DEU report which the delegate otherwise considered to be the reason or a part of the reason for his decision'. The alleged bogus documents were an Iraqi National Identity Card and an Iraqi Nationality Certificate. The applicant's argument was not accepted by the Federal Circuit Court. The case again confirms the minimal detail provided to the applicant about how his documents were found to be bogus, and highlights how this absence of information affects the 'opportunity' to provide a reasonable explanation for a bogus document, particularly where an applicant asserts a document's authenticity, as he did in this case.

It is worth noting that in cases where the DEU report is not directly contested, it is difficult to ascertain if further details about the DEU's methods were included in the original or review decision, given the limited number of cases that are on the public record. Judicial review decisions often include direct excerpts from Departmental or AAT decisions, but these are only fragments of the original decision. However, references to the DEU generally conform with the above insofar as its finding are declared (rather than explained) and then applied.

Reading the decisions raises rather than resolves questions as to what the DEU's precise expertise is, the methods it employs and its mandate within the Department. There is no direct mention of the DEU on the Department of Home Affairs website. A general internet search reveals a number of public references to the DEU to be in current and former employees' LinkedIn profiles or other online biographies. In terms of the Department's own reporting, the existence of the DEU is mentioned in some but not all annual reports. The Department's 2018–19 annual report makes no mention of the unit itself, and only references 'document examination' in relation to training provided by the Department to 'Australia's international partners' in order 'to enhance [their] border management and security capacity' (Department of Home Affairs 2019, 33, 66).[4] One of the more colourful references to the DEU is made in a case study in the 2010–2011 *Annual Report*. The case study begins:

> Torn, soaked and seemingly illegible; this was the state of a bundle of passports and other documents provided to the department's Document Examination Unit in late 2010. The discarded papers were found in a plastic bag hidden in the wheelhouse of SIEV [Suspected Illegal Entry Vessel] 201, a boat intercepted north-east of Christmas Island … Two weeks later, the Document Examination Unit in Canberra was given the arduous task of putting the scraps of paper back together.
>
> (Department of Immigration and Citizenship 2011, 148)

The case study then quotes a 'forensic document examiner' who said that the initial step was to separate the 'damp and smelly' documents without destroying them further: '[i]t was like a puzzle', Roslind said. 'We then had to dry the pieces, flatten them, and then start the time-consuming process of document reconstruction'. The case study gives little detail of the methods used by the DEU (beyond 'drying' and 'flattening') but does note that the documents helped confirm the identities of six 'irregular maritime arrivals', including three people who 'falsely claimed' to be minors during entry interviews.

A slightly clearer sense of what the DEU is, and what it does, is provided in the National Audit Office's report on the Department's identity verification arrangements for citizenship applications. The report does not address the specific challenges faced by refugee applicants in either accessing or verifying their documents, though it does list the 'resources' available within the Department to verify identity, of which the DEU is just one part (Australian National Audit Office 2015 [2.31]). The DEU is also referenced in an Ombudsman report on enhanced identity checking for applicants for citizenship by conferral. Again, though, no mention is made of the DEU's actual work, methods or the nature of its expertise. It is discussed as part of the Department's various 'strategic plans' for improving identity verification (Commonwealth Ombudsman 2017).

These reports make clear that the DEU sits within a network of identity verification strategies and databases. The mandate, scope and methods of the Departmental identity verification 'resources' listed in the National Audit Office report warrant further investigation. The DEU's expertise and methodologies in particular are certainly not clear in the decisions addressing the bogus document provisions, or in other information available from the Department. At a bare minimum, details about how this unit operates, and the forms of forensic expertise and methods it relies upon, should be made available so that those subject to its findings, including refugee applicants whose matters are *not* appealed, are able to test and respond to conclusions that their documents are bogus.

Conclusion

In 2015, the UNHCR completed the development of its Biometric Identity Management System (BIMS). Noting that 'biometrics provides an accurate way to verify identities using unique physiological characteristics, such as fingerprints, iris and facial features', the promotional brochure explains the UNHCR's Policy on Biometrics in Refugee Registration. It states that biometrics 'should be used as a routine part of identity management to ensure that refugees' personal identities cannot be lost, registered multiple times or subject to fraud or identity theft' (UNHCR n.d.). The BIMS promotional material also presents the system as complete and problem-solving:

> Identifying a person using BIMS is quick and simple. After enrolment, refugees and others of concern need only to present two or more biometric elements (e.g., two fingers, two eyes, or a combination thereof) for BIMS to be able to ascertain their identity within seconds. The matching time for identity checks during the roll out … was on average five seconds. (UNHCR n.d.)

The odd aspect of the material on BIMS is that it so assuredly bypasses the prior issue that the Australian reforms and identity document provisions attempt to address, namely refugee applicants' frequent lack of identity documents to begin with. While the BIMS may be able to register 'two eyes' or 'two fingers' it cannot in fact determine to whom the biometric data belongs. These questions are not the focus of the BIMS, which instead aims to achieve the goal of future identification once it has captured and stored as much biometric data as possible. This is confirmed by one of the promotional grab quotes from 43-year-old Congolese refugee Oliver, who states 'I can be someone now. I am registered globally with the UN and you'll always know who I am' (UNHCR n.d.).

In an understated formulation, the Explanatory Memorandum addressing the Australian bogus document reforms explained that 'the purpose of the new section 91WA is to encourage an applicant to comply and assist with authenticating their identity by providing a reasonable explanation for providing a bogus document' (Parliament of Australia 2014a, [55]). The section does not merely encourage applicants to assist. It functions via the threat of the outright refusal of a protection visa where a bogus document is provided without reasonable explanation. The Memorandum also states '[i]t would not be acceptable for the applicant to produce any document as documentary evidence of their identity … that is a bogus document' and that 'the purpose of the amendment is to ensure a protection visa applicant provides documentary evidence of their identity, nationality or citizenship wherever possible to do so' (Parliament of Australia 2014a, [57]).

In the frequent absence of stable documentary or biometric data to establish refugee applicants' identities, the Australian legislative reforms transfer the discretionary judgment of who is a bogus refugee—and the attendant racialised fear of duplicitous brown bodies at the border—onto a new question, of what is a bogus document. The relocation of the question of who is a fake refugee onto a document (or documents) is accompanied in the cases by an opaque scientific discourse about document examination and verification. Just as refugee oral testimony is generally assessed against the deeply subjective criteria of coherence, consistency and plausibility, 'document examination' techniques and biometrics function as another proxy for subjective judgments directed to the simultaneous and entwined questions of what is a bogus document and who is a bogus refugee.

Notes

1 For example, the relevant Canadian legislation uses the term 'misrepresentation' to capture different forms of immigration fraud, including the provision of fraudulent documents or making oral misrepresentations as part of a visa application (Macklin 2014).
2 For an excellent examination of the extent to which experts in the criminal courts are required, or rather not required, to explain their methods or demonstrate their expertise under the relevant rules see (Edmond, Martire and San Roque 2017, 624).
3 Note in this case the applicant did not concede that he had provided bogus documents.
4 Similar mention of 'document examination' training is made in previous reports, though with no reference to the unit itself, see e.g. (Department of Immigration and Border Protection 2017, 106)

References

Australian National Audit Office, 2015. Verifying Identity in the Citizenship Program. *Australian National Audit Office*. Available from: https://www.anao.gov.au/work/performance-audit/verifying-identity-citizenship-program [Accessed 10 December 2020].

Bibler Coutin, Susan, 2020. Opportunities and Double Binds: Legal Craft in an Era of Uncertainty. *In*: Sarah B. Horton and Josiah Josiah Heyman, eds. *Paper Trails: Migrants, Documents, and Legal Insecurity*. Durham: Duke University Press, 130–52.

Bohmer, Carol, and Shuman, Amy, 2018. *Political Asylum Deceptions: The Culture of Suspicion*. Cham, Switzerland: Palgrave Macmillan.

Browne, Simone, 2010. Digital Epidermalization: Race, Identity and Biometrics. *Critical Sociology*, 36 (1), 131–50.

Commonwealth Ombudsman, 2017. Delays in Processing of Applications for Australian Citizenship by Conferral. Available from: https://www.ombudsman.gov.au/_

_data/assets/pdf_file/0032/78980/Citizenship-own-motion-investigation-report.pdf [Accessed 10 December 2020].

Dehm, Sara, 2018. Passport. *In*: Jessie Hohmann and Daniel Joyce, eds. *International Law's Objects*. Oxford: Oxford University Press.

Department of Home Affairs, 2019. Annual Report 2018–2019. Available from: https://www.homeaffairs.gov.au/reports-and-pubs/Annualreports/diac-annual-report-2010-11.pdf; https://www.ombudsman.gov.au/__data/assets/pdf_file/0032/78980/Citizenship-own-motion-investigation-report.pdf [Accessed 10 December 2020].

Department of Immigration and Border Protection, 2017. Annual Report 2016–17. Available from: https://www.homeaffairs.gov.au/reports-and-pubs/Annualreports/2016-17/Complete.pdf [Accessed 10 December 2020].

Department of Immigration and Citizenship, 2011. Annual Report 2010–2011. Available from: https://www.homeaffairs.gov.au/reports-and-pubs/Annualreports/diac-annual-report-2010-11.pdf [Accessed 10 December 2020].

Edmond, Gary, Martire, Kristy and San Roque, Mehera, 2017. Expert Reports and the Forensic Sciences. *University of New South Wales Law Journal*, 40 (2), 590–637.

Fanon, Frantz, 1967. *Black Skin, White Masks*. New York: Grove Press.

Gibb, Robert, and Good, Anthony, 2013. Do the Facts Speak for Themselves? Country of Origin Information in French and British Refugee Status Determination Procedures. *International Journal of Refugee Law*, 25 (2), 291–322.

Horton, Sarah B., 2020. Introduction. *In*: Sarah B. Horton and Josiah Heyman, Josiah, eds. *Paper Trails: Migrants, Documents, and Legal Insecurity*. Durham: Duke University Press, 1–30.

Liberman, Anatoly, 2017. A Few Bogus Etymologies: "Tantrum," "Dander," "Dandruff," and "Dunderhead," along with "Getting One's Goat". *Oxford University Press Blog*. Available from: https://blog.oup.com/2017/09/tantrum-dandruff-dander-etymology/ [Accessed 10 December 2020].

Lyon, David, 2001. Under My Skin: From Identification Papers to Body Surveillance. *In*: Jane Caplan and John Torpey, eds. *Documenting Individual Identity: The Development of State Practices in the Modern World*. Princeton, NJ: Princeton University Press, 291–310.

Macklin, Audrey, 1998. Truth and Consequences: Credibility Determination in the Refugee Context. *In*: International Association of Refugee Law Judges ed. *The Realities of Refugee Determination on the Eve of a New Millennium: The Role of the Judiciary*. Haarlem: International Association of Refugee Law Judges, 134–40.

Macklin, Audrey, 2014. Citizenship Revocation, the Privilege to Have Rights and the Production of the Alien. *Queen's Law Journal*, 40 (1), 31–55.

Oxford English Dictionary, 2021. bogus, n.1 and adj. *Oxford University Press*. Available from https://www-oed-com.ezproxy.sl.nsw.gov.au/view/Entry/20990 [Accessed 4 March 2021].

Parliament of Australia, 2014a. Migration Amendment (Protection and Other Measures) Bill 2014 - Explanatory Memorandum. Available from: https://parlinfo.aph.gov.au/parlInfo/search/display/display.w3p;query=Id%3A%22legislation%2Fems%2Fr5303_ems_6ab8fffb-a1dd-4ffa-b95a-2f5852a17590%22 [Accessed 10 December 2020].

Parliament of Australia, 2014b. Migration Amendment (Protection and Other Measures) Bill 2014 - Second Reading. *House of Representatives*. Available from: https://parlinfo.aph.gov.au/parlInfo/search/display/display.w3p;query=Id%3A%22chamber%2Fhansardr%2Fcf028b00-427a-488c-8c92-2792de44c147%2F0191%22 [Accessed 10 December 2020].

Pickering, Sharon, 2001. Common Sense and Original Deviancy: News Discourses and Asylum Seekers in Australia. *Journal of Refugee Studies*, 14 (2), 169–86.
Pugliese, Joseph, 2012. *Biometrics: Bodies, Technologies, Biopolitics*. London: Taylor and Francis.
Razack, Sherene, 2000. Simple Logic: Race, the Identity Documents Rule and the Story of a Nation Besieged and Betrayed. *Journal of Law and Social Policy*, 15, 181–210.
Rousseau, Cécile, Crépeau, François, Foxen, Patricia and Houle, France, 2002. The Complexity of Determining Refugeehood: A Multidisciplinary Analysis of the Decision-making Process of the Canadian Immigration and Refugee Board. *Journal of Refugee Studies*, 15 (1), 43–70.
Scott, James C., 1998. *Seeing Like a State: How Certain Schemes to Improve the Human Condition Have Failed*. New Haven: Yale University Press.
Torpey, John C., 2018. *The Invention of the Passport: Surveillance, Citizenship and the State* (2nd ed.). Cambridge: Cambridge University Press.
UNHCR, n.d., Biometric Identity Management System Enhancing Registration and Data Management. Available from: https://www.unhcr.org/550c304c9.pdf [Accessed 10 December 2020].
Vogl, Anthea, 2013. Telling Stories from Start to Finish. *Griffith Law Review*, 22 (1), 63–86.
Vogl, Anthea, 2018. The Genres and Politics of Refugee Testimony. *Law and Literature*, 30 (1), 81–104.
Weber, Leanne, 2013. *Policing Non-Citizens*. Oxford, NY: Routledge.
Yngvesson, Barbara, and Coutin, Susan Bibler, 2006. Backed by Papers: Undoing Persons, Histories, and Return. *American Ethnologist*, 33 (2), 177–90.

Legislation

Migration Act 1958 (Cth).
Migration Regulations 1994 (Cth)
Migration Amendment (Protection and Other Measures) Act 2014 (Cth)

Cases

ASF17 v Minister for Immigration and Border Protection [2018] FCA 1149
AYZ18 v Minister for Immigration, Citizenship, Migrant Services and Multicultural Affairs [2020] FCA 429
BGM16 v Minister for Immigration and Border Protection [2017] FCAFC 72
BYE17 v Minister for Immigration & Anor [2018] FCCA 1625
DSM16 v Minister for Immigration [2018] FCCA 1615
DVH16 v Minister for Immigration [2020] FCCA 131
FLD18 v Minister for Home Affairs [2020] FCCA 87

Chapter 6

The historian as document producer

A candid reflection on the production of oral history timed summaries

Jesse Adams Stein

Introduction

This chapter draws attention to a seemingly innocuous document that is often produced in the oral history process. It considers the inevitable subjectivity, and the labour, that goes into the production of this kind of document. All this may sound like I am about to discuss interview transcripts, which is not my intention. Rather, the humble 'timed summary' is the focus of analysis here, a type of document that is rarely subject to scrutiny. Generally produced by oral historians (or assistants), timed summaries are documents that provide time-logged summary statements describing every two to five minutes of an interview, alongside selected keywords (Bradley 2014). These documents are primarily intended as 'finding aids' to accompany catalogue records in oral history collections.

Given their supplemental status, timed summaries can be understood as a form of 'paratext' that accompanies a 'main text' (in the form of an oral history interview recording). Here I am borrowing from Gérard Genette's concept of paratext (1982/1997), as well from expansions of his theory that have been undertaken since the emergence of digital forms of media (e.g. Benzon 2013; Birke and Christ 2013; McCracken 2013). Now a well-established analytical concept applied to documents, literature and narrative, paratext is usefully understood as the textual and visual framing devices employed in relation to a text (Birke and Christ 2013). Timed summaries are paratextual documents that supplement, accompany and frame oral history interviews. In the context of my analysis here, I am specifically considering the paratextual quality of timed summaries in relation to online and digitised oral history interviews. As noted by Dorothee Birke and Birte Christ (2013, 66), the concept of paratext has become 'a highly productive tool for the analysis of medial difference and medial change'. As oral history interviews are increasingly digitised and uploaded online, and made available through library databases and other online sources, the paratextual material that frames these interview recordings shifts markedly. Digital library catalogues, library metadata, links, supplemental images, online media players, transcripts and timed summaries; these (and other

DOI: 10.4324/9781003247593-8

elements) are what make up the paratextual layering surrounding the digital audio recording. None of these layers are entirely neutral, inevitable or natural; each of them has been designed, written and organised in some way, by a variety of authors (and/or designers).

In undertaking an examination of an apparently mundane or near-invisible document (such as a timed summary), the approach taken by ethnographer Annelise Riles is instructive. Riles (2006, 1) examines documents as ethnographic artefacts, and considers 'how ethnographers conceive, grasp, appreciate, see patterns' through the documents they use and produce. She notes, 'documents are special ethnographic subjects', in part because ethnographers document the world by producing their own documents (2006, 6). In this way documents both *record* 'modern knowledge practices', and they also *constitute* what is understood to be knowledge itself (Riles 2006, 7). This observation helps make the document 'strange', a form of distancing that allows an analysis to emerge, no matter how apparently straightforward or unproblematic a document may seem to be. This was also an approach taken by Don Brenneis (2006), who looked to his own 'enrollment in the projects of producing and evaluating bureaucratic documents' (in Riles 2006, 15). Brenneis found even the most mundane documents—*especially* the most mundane documents—to be particularly revealing vectors of cultural and social knowledge and power. Likewise, it is my intent to reflect upon my own position as producer of ordinary, unquestioned documents. Accordingly, this chapter addresses the role of the timed summary—as an historian-produced document—in the production of what we call history. I consider how historians, and those working in history-related labour, develop and understand the timed summary as part of the process of history-making, and how the production of this paratextual document operates in relation to the primary source (or the 'main text'), which in this case is the digital audio recording of an oral history interview.

Like indexes, timed summaries are designed for efficiency. They expedite access to the interview audio, allowing a researcher to identify particular time segments, so that they may play only the sections of an interview that pertain to particular topics or keywords. Timed summaries do the detailed work of a library cataloguer or archivist, but rarely are they authored by a librarian. Rather, timed summaries are often produced as an afterthought, for instance by a harried interviewer trying to finish off a project, or by a casual worker on relatively low pay. As with the graduate evaluation forms examined by Brenneis (2006), there is an assumed impartiality to timed summaries. Their function is not questioned, they are generally overlooked as *mere* summaries, banal statements of apparent facts. Timed summaries are invisible and naturalised in the catalogue record. Of course, library catalogue materials are neither neutral nor objective, although they are often assumed to be so (Lewis 2008). This is even more the case for timed summaries, which must in some way map a narrative that a person constructs about their own life.

Much has been said about the subjective nature of oral history interviewing. It is now a widely accepted view that oral histories are a constantly evolving process of historical meaning-making, where new interpretations are made at every stage. This occurs in the process of recording, in transcription, through historical interpretation and quote selection and through dissemination in all its forms. We now understand that the oral history interview is a co-production of meaning between the interviewer and interviewee; it is an exploration of the way memory operates in relation to a person's experience of the past, telling us how someone sees themselves 'in history' (Shopes 2011; Hamilton 2019).

Unlike the interview itself, timed summaries are not a co-production of meaning, but a forum in which the timed summary author exercises a small degree of power over a narrative, and must use their judgment and caution in relation to people's life stories. Oral historian Alessandro Portelli's more general comments about oral history are useful here:

> The control of the historical discourse remains firmly in the hands of the historian ... Instead of finding sources, the historian at least partly 'makes' them; though other people's words may be used it is still his or her discourse.
>
> (1981, 104–105)

Here, Portelli centres the historian in oral historical practice, describing how the historian does not sit to the side of the source material, but 'is pulled inside and becomes part of it' (1981, 105). My approach, therefore, is an effort to reveal some of what happens 'inside' the production of public history documents.

This chapter now moves to provide the background context to existing critiques of the oral history transcript, exploring flow-on implications for timed summaries in practice. From there, I focus on the specific use of oral history timed summaries as they exist within the National Library of Australia's oral history collection, particularly as they are made available online in tandem with digital audio. This brings me to openly reflect upon my own practice as an oral historian and writer of timed summaries, and to consider the labour and decision-making processes involved in the production of these documents. The chapter then engages with two particular oral history projects held with the National Library of Australia: *Bringing Them Home* and the *Reshaping Australian Manufacturing* oral history projects. While vastly different in terms of scale, content and political implications, both projects are examples of the online use of timed summaries as a research finding aid, and as an added layer of historical meaning available for public use. Finally, I reflect upon the dual role of timed summaries for current and future research uses. With the future in mind, the looming ubiquity of artificial intelligence is discussed in reference to the future production of such documents.

Existing critiques of oral history's written documents

We have come a long way since mid- to late twentieth-century critiques of oral history as being 'unreliable' because it is based on spoken, not written sources (Thomson 1998). Oral histories are evidently not about asserting 'facts', but about the subjective experience of history as felt by individuals and groups who are often left out of conventional text-based records. Oral history evidences information not so much about 'what happened' but about how people felt about what happened, or what should have happened, or what they wished happened. In this way, oral histories help us understand historical intentions, affect, rumour, cultural conventions and human responses to change. Insights such as these—about oral history's value—are now well established. Largely as a result of social history and feminist critiques of conventional historical methods, oral sources are no longer the 'underdog' in a false dichotomy between written sources and the spoken-word. In fact, the pendulum of oral history methodological discourse has shifted in another direction. Those who use oral histories are now strongly persuaded to avoid relying solely on interview transcriptions, and encouraged to attend closely to the aural source; to listen, so as to account for pauses, laughter, accents, sarcasm, awkwardness, tone and the sonic background of the interview (Samuel 1998; Gluck 2014; Bradley and Puri 2016; Hamilton 2019; Stein and Rowden 2019; Good 2000). The intimacy of hearing the voice—as opposed to the flattened and regulated nature of reading printed text—can change the listeners' relationship to the interviewee, allowing a deeper and more empathic engagement with the subject (Foster 1991; see also Bradley and Puri 2016). Digital technologies now mean that the cumbersome nature of audio tapes—the problem of fast-forwarding and rewinding, for instance—is no longer an issue, and digital audio files are increasingly accessible in online collections.

All this should mean that there is more *listening* and less *reading* going on in relation to digitised oral history interviews. However transcripts are *still* favoured by historians for reasons of practicality. Transcripts remain the easiest way to search interview content and access potential quotations. Oral historian Michael Frisch (2006, 102) has described the vast swathes of audio and video interview materials in public collections globally as 'notoriously underutilised' and 'largely untapped'. Although it is rarely admitted publicly, even oral historians themselves struggle to listen to their own interviews in their entirety, to say nothing of historians and other researchers who may wish to use the content later on (Frisch and Lambert 2012; Boyd 2014; Hamilton 2019). While this is regrettable, it is an understandable problem: oral histories are often very lengthy. Listening to an entire interview is not always feasible in today's fast-paced, time-poor and often precarious scholarly environment. Added to this, many collections do not catalogue oral histories in great detail, meaning that much of the content is buried, and therefore missed by researchers (Frisch 2006).

To address this problem, librarians and oral historians have increasingly encouraged the production of timed summaries—among other paratextual elements such as searchable metadata—to accompany oral history audio sources (Bradley 2014). This returns us to the point made earlier in this chapter: timed summaries are an exercise in efficiency. They enable faster location of relevant content, allowing a researcher to quickly locate only the part of an interview they wish to listen to. In this way, it could be said that timed summaries are 'centripetal' forms of paratext, to borrow Ellen McCracken's (2013) term, in that they (attempt to) draw the reader's attention back to the main text of the interview recording. This is unusual for a digital form of paratext; many paratextual layers on digital documents link us beyond the central content, moving out 'centrifugally' in McCracken's terms (2013).

While sections of the oral history community have been slow to catch on to the possibilities of digital content, the range of available technologies for creating, editing and sharing oral histories has expanded vastly over the past two decades (Frisch and Lambert 2012). This means that there is now a wealth of possibilities for digital audio or video to be paired with metadata and time-coded text content, enabling customised access to interviews online. There are possibilities for mapping interview data in new ways that are not chronological or linear, for instance, to map themes or keywords in interactive visual interfaces (Hibberd 2018). The main hindrance to this, however, has been a lack of funding in these areas to dedicate human working hours to summarising, coding and communicating interview content in innovative ways. Generally, collecting institutions have continued with established methods (e.g. using standard paratextual features such as transcripts, timed summaries or just simple catalogue records), because experimenting with newer forms is not financially feasible. There are moments, however, where an injection of funding can result in a boost to online oral history material, as we shall see further on with the *Bringing Them Home* oral history project.

There are inherent risks and challenges that emerge when making information available online in different forms, including issues with copyright, privacy and technical challenges such as file corruption and ongoing digital maintenance. Further, the use of timed summaries with an online player—where the listener can simply play the relevant parts of an interview, not its entire duration—could potentially enable an out-of-context engagement with an historical source. This may mean the listener misses vital contextual information or background detail before a particular keyword comes into play. However, the benefit of including timed summaries alongside online audio is that they are designed to lead researchers back to the primary source: to facilitate listening, rather than just reading a transcript (Ritchie 2015). All this means that the timed summary, as with all forms of metadata and cataloguing, is endowed with a particular responsibility to 'carry the interview'. A timed summary must communicate just enough so that a researcher will find the available material, but not so much information that the researcher might ignore the audio completely in favour of the summary alone. I am not convinced that I have hit this balance in my own work, as we shall see further on.

Oral history timed summaries at the National Library of Australia

The National Library of Australia's (NLA) 'Audio Management and Delivery System' (AMAD) is globally recognised as a leading system for delivering digital oral history and folklore audio through an open, free and relatively user-friendly online platform (Bradley 2014; Bradley and Puri 2016). This scheme is based on privileging the primary source, that is, bringing library users the audio content rather than principally offering transcripts. As noted by former NLA Oral History Curator, Kevin Bradley, this audio 'would need to be usable and discoverable in the existing and expanding infrastructure … to put these unstructured sound recordings on an even footing with more traditional sources of information' (2014, 188).

The hallmark of the AMAD system is that it produces a package of data involving an Extensible Markup Language (XML) system, and a Text Encoding Initiative (TEI) (Bradley and Puri 2016). Put in lay terms, this enables the transcript and the timed summary (where they exist) to be aligned with the digital audio, and delivered together (Bradley 2014). This system enables timed summaries to be entered through a back-end content management system (CMS), which pairs the summarised descriptions with the relevant time section in the interview. The CMS allows the timed summary writer to summarise sections of the interview (usually every two to five minutes, breaking the sections wherever it seems logical), and to add searchable keywords in an adjacent column. The keywords are a mix of proper nouns, themes and key topics. As I will explore further on, the timed summaries provide a more analytical framework than a verbatim transcript: the addition of keywords and the use of summaries mean that the timed summary writer must *interpret* the content and reframe it in terms that may be useful for someone potentially searching the material. Rather than repeating the voice of the speaker, the timed summary writer is another step removed: an interpreter.

When the text encoding on the timed summaries and transcripts is connected to the correct time in the interview's digital audio file, this enables users to simultaneously access audio and text materials that pertain to the same section of the interview. In practice, this means users can search for keywords and terms in the interview content, and then listen only to the identified passages. This also means researchers can cite a particular part of an interview, not just the interview in its entirety, which has theoretical benefits for citation transparency. The resultant layering of the 'main text' and paratextual elements—digital audio, timed summary, transcript, digital interface, etc.—produces an oral history experience that is altogether different from older forms of oral history exposure (which often involved a catalogue request, and a researcher being handed a tape and a set of headphones in a library setting). In some ways this layering makes the interview more than the sum of its parts. It becomes a primary source that is already interpreted and organised in particular ways. In the process, existing hierarchies—between 'primary' and 'secondary' sources, for instance—may seem to blur. But these layers of paratextual text and audio also open up new avenues for exposure to interview content, encouraging more listening and allowing easier access to recordings that were previously 'buried' deep in library collections.

The labour of oral history summary writing

I started writing timed summaries in 2010, as a form of casual work while undertaking my PhD. The interviews I summarised were existing National Library of Australia collection items prioritised for digital upload onto the aforementioned AMAD system. Since that time, I have written almost 50 oral history timed summaries, including of interviews dating back to the 1960s by Australian oral history pioneer Hazel de Berg (1913–1984), and a number of interviews from the *Bringing Them Home* oral history project (a significant national project in Australia, explained in detail further on). More recently, as a researcher and oral history interviewer, I have written timed summaries of my own interviews, as part of the *Reshaping Australian Manufacturing* oral history project. When an oral history interviewer or a research team agrees to undertake a new oral history project with the National Library of Australia, they are also expected to create timed summaries of the interviews they produce, which are to be entered via the online content management system. I now hire research assistants to write timed summaries for me, and it is quickly apparent how different everyone's summary 'style' is, and how this might impact a researcher's interpretation of an interview.

The experience of writing and contracting timed summaries has meant I have been able to develop a perspective that sees the summary's construction, and sees the condition in which they have been produced. Somewhere behind the scenes is a casual worker, often sitting in a café, wearing headphones, hoping their laptop computer battery will last another two hours. Sometimes these summary writers come to the interview with very little background knowledge about the interviewee (or the interviewer's project, for that matter). They must work with what they have—the audio in their ears. This means the summary writer may miss an obvious context or theme that was never explicitly stated in that particular interview. It can also mean that, like a transcriber, the summary writer sometimes has to replay the mumbled parts of an interview ten times until a place name crystallises. My experience as a writer and commissioner of timed summaries means I now see them fundamentally as a finding aid, which entails thinking closely about the experience of a future researcher. For instance, very generalised keywords such as 'feelings' or 'family' are of little use in a catalogue search. But more specific terms such as 'letterpress', '3D printing' or 'apprenticeship' have more potential value as searchable keywords.

As a casual worker in 2010, the pay for summary writing was modest. Payment was calculated by the 'recorded hour', not by the hours actually spent working, which gave me some impetus to work fast. In all of this I was also my own worst enemy. While other timed summaries tend to be quite brief, often eschewing full sentences and providing mostly keywords and general themes, my summaries often contain a lot of detail. Certainly, they do not transcribe the text, but they work hard (perhaps too hard) to convey all of what was said. My instincts were that the detail mattered, and that this is where the interviewee's humanity lay. In this, perhaps my judgment was off. In any case, the National Library of Australia did not seem to mind. Later, in 2017, I attended an Interviewer Training Session at the National Library and was bemused (and embarrassed) to discover that my timed summary for the *Interview with Alan Villiers by Hazel de Berg* was being used as the 'exemplar' summary for other interviewers and timed summary writers (Villiers 1970). Villiers' interview, as I recollect, was challenging because it contained a great deal of now-obscure sea-faring terminology, and Villiers himself had an unusual accent (the National Library subsequently promoted this interview on *Talk Like a Pirate Day*).

More than just making judgments about how much to include or leave out, the timed summary writer has to exercise judgment about the terminology they might use. For example, if an interviewee refers to abusive behaviour or sexual harassment in the workplace, without actually using that terminology, the timed summary writer has a choice whether to include the term 'sexual harassment', 'abuse' or 'bullying' (among other options) in the keyword section, even if the interviewees themselves might not have described their experience in that manner. In this, there is a delicate balance between not wanting to misrepresent the interviewee as a passive 'victim', but also a progressive desire to call out violence and prejudice where one sees it. Oral historian Katherine Borland (1998) has described a similar problem. Borland's feminist perspective shaped her interpretation of interview content, causing some tension with the interviewee, in this case her grandmother. Borland notes (1998, 324), 'as a feminist I am particularly sensitive to identifying gender dynamics in verbal art', and this influenced her framing and interpretation of her grandmother's experience. Borland's grandmother, however, objected that 'the story is no longer MY story at all' (1998, 327, caps in original). As Borland notes (1998, 327), this disagreement brings up a 'crucial issue in oral narrative scholarship—who controls the text'.

Like Borland, I regularly have to make judgment calls about gender, terminology, power dynamics and patriarchy in my interpretations of oral history content. In the context of the oral histories of manufacturing workers who undertook trade apprenticeships, this issue came up often (although I never encountered objections in the manner that Borland did). When a number of interviewees described routine (and sometimes sexualised) 'apprentice initiations' in factory contexts, I described such events as 'arguably a form of institutionally condoned child sex abuse' (Stein 2016, 46, see also 88). It was a deliberate choice to describe apprentice initiations in this manner, even though the interviewees never used this phrasing. This is particularly tricky interpretive territory: most interviewees did not describe the abuse in any detail, and conveyed more through dramatic pauses, gestures and other non-verbal cues. However, my background knowledge, accrued through undertaking many interviews with tradespeople, played a role here. I had a fairly clear sense of the suffering that some apprentices suffered at the hands of their 'masters' or older apprentices, in the name of 'initiation' and acceptance into the hegemonic masculine culture of factory trades. But in terms of clear, verbal 'evidence', not a lot is explicitly said by most of the men I interviewed, especially as they were addressing a relatively young, female interviewer (see Stein 2016, 88). I expand further on the ethical implications of interview interpretation and terminology choices in the following two sections.

Bringing Them Home oral history project

The ethical implications of timed summary writing were made particularly stark when I commenced work summarising interviews for the *Bringing Them Home* oral history project. In response to the *Bringing Them Home* (Human Rights and Equal Opportunity Commission 1997) report resulting from the *National Inquiry into the Separation of Aboriginal and Torres Strait Islander Children from Their Families* (1997), the Australian Commonwealth Government agreed to fund a large-scale national oral history project to record people's stories, under the auspices of the NLA. From 1998 to 2002, the *Bringing Them Home* oral history project collected the stories of Aboriginal and Torres Strait Islanders, as well as others, such as missionaries, nurses, administrators, police, all of whom were impacted by, or involved in, the process of child removal. Follow-up interviews with some of the original interviewees were also conducted in 2010. Uploading the oral history material online became a priority for the NLA (where interviewees' access permissions allowed) (National Library of Australia n.d.). It was clear that the scale of the project was such that it would take years for all the material to be transcribed and summarised. Unlike most oral history projects, however, generous funding was available for transcription and timed summary writing, and this is how I came to be sent this material for summarising in 2010 and 2011. Given the funding provided to the *Bringing Them Home* oral history project, most audio recordings of interviews in this collection are now available online, presented with full transcripts *and* timed summaries, where rights permissions allow. This means that someone accessing the interviews online is now able to have three experiences of the source simultaneously: the digital audio, the transcript and the summary, delivered in tandem. This means that, potentially, library users are more easily able to draw their own conclusions about the interview content, by comparing the different mediums.

Bringing Them Home was an unusually significant and sensitive oral history project. It had major ramifications for Australia's understanding of its history, and brought to light the catastrophic consequences of years of systematic racism embedded within government policy and social organisations throughout the twentieth century. The after-effects of the removal of Aboriginal and Torres Strait Islander children from their families will continue to be felt for many generations to come. The *Bringing Them Home* interviews provide important and detailed evidence to counter the claims made by critics of the so-called 'Black Arm Band' view of Australian history: historians and politicians who claimed that the focus on harm done to Indigenous people was too negative (Blainey 1993; see also discussion on John Howard's interview with John Laws in McKenna 1997).

As a casual worker assigned to summarise some of the *Bringing Them Home* interviews, I was not entirely prepared for what I might hear, although I had enough background knowledge to anticipate the (often heartbreaking) content. To many Australians, this history is not widely understood: the impacts of legislation pertaining to Aboriginal people's 'welfare' and 'protection' are not widely taught in lower secondary high school education. Put simply, a variety of state and Commonwealth legislation gave the power to the Aborigines Protection Board and the Aboriginal Welfare Board in Australia to forcibly remove Aboriginal and Torres Strait Islander children from their families and place them in institutions, in domestic service or in manual labour. I had the benefit of studying this history, but there is a significant difference between 'knowing the history' and hearing personal experiences told by those directly affected. The NLA required me to report any defamatory remarks, any full street addresses and make note of anything that might refer to Aboriginal 'Secret Men's Business' or 'Secret Women's Business' that should not be published. Other than this requirement, I was left to my own devices to summarise these interviews as best I could.

Interestingly, about half of the interviews I was given to summarise were with non-Indigenous people who had been involved, in some way, in the process of child removal. This included missionaries, teachers, nurses and administrators. For some, the interviews were a process of defending their role in this history, while for others it was a chance to atone and explain how their views may have changed over time. Writing the summaries of interviews with non-Indigenous Australians involved in child removal meant that I occasionally struggled when encountering what I felt were racist remarks, unfair statements or a certain kind of 'whitewashing' of uncomfortable histories. Generally, my strategy in those parts was to keep my descriptions very brief, but not entirely shy away from what was being said. I did not want to appear to promote the statements, but I also did not want to conceal them, revealing as they are of the way in which systemic racism functions socially.

John Bannister's 2001 interview with Kathleen Mack (1906–2004) is one such example (Mack 2001). From the 1930s to the mid-1950s, Mack was a nurse involved in caring for Aboriginal children who had been removed from their families and placed into children's homes and missions. Towards the end of the interview Mack was asked about her views on whether Australians should say 'sorry' for child removals, which was a particularly potent political debate in Australia in 2001. The transcript reads:

Bannister: What do you think about the whole current sorry issue debate that has gone on recently?

Mack: Most uncalled for. The Aboriginals that went through it did it because they wanted to and realised that they were the better off for it.

(Mack 2001)

My accompanying timed summary statement is brief, but makes some effort at distancing myself from the comment. I wrote: 'The "sorry" issue is uncalled for, in Kathleen's opinion' (Timed summary for Mack 2001). A few minutes later Bannister probed again:

Bannister: So in finishing up, where do you think we are in relation to the discussion that we've been having about children that have been separated from their parents?

Mack: Well, I believe that the best was done and that there was a very happy relationship between the children themselves, the parents and ourselves. I myself haven't known any difficulties through it all and the children or their parents can call on me at any time and we have a happy time together discussing old times and new times.

(Mack 2001)

My timed summary statement again put in place a sense of distance from this position. I wrote: 'Kathleen's view is that it was all for the best, and what she witnessed was positive' (Timed summary for Mack 2001). I made sure to use the term 'stolen generations' in the accompanying keywords for this section.

None of these timed-summary-writing decisions were particularly strategic, but rather made on gut instinct, back in 2010 and 2011. To some degree there was a practical imperative to my decision-making: using keyword terms such as 'stolen generations' or 'sexual harassment' serves an ongoing functional use for future researchers, which I felt would be more useful than less specific terminology. Further, my actions were an attempt at a performed kind of neutrality about a topic that I knew full well that no one could be 'neutral' about. This example again demonstrates how a timed summary is never simply a 'finding aid', but is a paratextual document with complexities of its own, and with a role in shaping the interpretation of another document (in this case the interview with Mack). The choices made by the authors of timed summaries are never solely based on a response to the content in the main document (the interview), but are always informed by existing knowledge (or lack thereof), experiences, biases and political positions. A timed summary writer must walk a tightrope between a responsibility to present the content as neutrally as possible, and a responsibility to those who may be victims of violence or bigotry, no matter how historical.

At a certain point the layering of meaning becomes almost overwhelming: one must remember that oral history interviews themselves are not a 'direct' encounter with the mind of another person, but are a mere sample, a conversation between two people which could have gone one way, and somehow went another. Oral history interviewers (and journalists) regularly lament that the best statements by interviewees always happen when the recorder is off. In this sense the interview recording—and its paratextual material—are only ever partial insights, and should always be analysed with this in mind. Moreover, like all documents, timed summaries will age over time: their research salience may increase or lessen over time, and their terminology may become dated. Any sense of control over an interview's interpretation remains illusory, and we must learn to be comfortable with that.

Reshaping Australian Manufacturing oral history project

Almost a decade later, I again found myself writing timed summaries. But this time it was as an interviewer managing my own (much smaller scale) oral history project: the *Reshaping Australian Manufacturing* oral history project undertaken with the NLA (2017–2019). As an individually run oral history project (conducted in addition to other forms of research), the number of interviewees was relatively small: 12. But the interviews were lengthy 'whole of life' accounts, where the interviewees narrate their life's journey loosely chronologically, from their birth and family background, to their contemporary experience. The interviewees were current and former manufacturing tradespeople with experience of dramatic economic, social and technological changes in Australia from the 1960s to the present. Leading the project meant that I had more vested interest in the thoroughness of the summaries, as *I* would be using them for my own research, in addition to their potential public use through the NLA catalogue. This changed the level of detail I was willing to include. The further complication was that, given time limitations, I was not able to write all the summaries myself, and I paid research assistants for (some of) this work. (This time I made sure they were fairly paid by the hour for their work, not by the 'recorded hour'.)

A great deal of the summarising process in *Reshaping Australian Manufacturing* involved putting a name to something, to describe, using keywords, the dynamic being discussed by the interviewee. For example, engineering patternmaker Debra Schuckar suggested a number of instances during her apprenticeship where she was treated differently because of her gender (Schuckar 2018). Being the only known female patternmaker in Australia, this was an ingrained part of her daily working experience. Despite describing times where people were verbally abusive, for example being addressed as 'you smart arse slut', Schuckar never once used the terms 'sexism' or 'sexual harassment' in the interview (2018). Nonetheless, I made the decision in several parts of the timed summary to include those terms in the keyword column. This was balanced, however, with my descriptions of Schuckar's testimony that also pointed to her sense of being respected by the great majority of her peers. Schuckar was proud of her ability to quietly and confidently manage the prejudiced men and boys she encountered:

> I just felt that quite demeaning like it didn't need to … I remember saying to him,
>
> 'Don't you ever talk to me like that ever again.'
>
> I said it very quietly and he apologised on the spot, and never ever … said one derogatory comment to me. I didn't handle it by being vocal. I handled it by being, what's the word … diplomatic and just teaching people to hold their tongue.
>
> (2018)

The timed summary for this section reads: 'Recalled a moment in trade school when she was sexually harassed and stood up for herself, diplomatically and not dramatically', alongside keywords including *sexism*, *sexual harassment*, *female apprentice*, *female tradesperson* (Timed summary for Schuckar 2018). Like Borland, I am 'concerned about the continued emotional effect alternative readings of personal narratives may have on our living subjects' (1998, 327–328). In this, a balance must be struck between the public interest and the welfare of the interviewee.

Recognising gender-power relations is a common part of interpreting manufacturing workers' interviews. It is rarely acknowledged by the interviewees themselves that gendered identities and roles are constructed in any way, however it occasionally emerges as a form of realisation for the interviewees as they are speaking. For example, former engineering patternmaker (now a teacher) Peter Williams said:

> it occurs to me that as, I'm not quite sure what it's like in other parts of the world, I haven't traveled overseas much at all, but I know in Australia, as Australian men, we identify personally very very strongly with what we do. For example if I go to a BBQ, and I'll meet somebody, meet a bloke, the conversation'll probably go along the lines of,
>
> 'G'day Jim, I'm Peter.'
>
> 'Oh g'day Peter how are you? Yeah …'
>
> 'Oh I'm pretty good yeah yeah, oh what do you do Jim?'
>
> (2018)

My timed summary text for Williams' reflection certainly strays into the territory of analysis, not mere summary. I wrote:

> Describes how Australian masculine identity is closely tied to work: men's socialisation is bound up with employment identity. Peter was confronted by the question of what it is to be a patternmaker who is no longer making patterns. Peter decided he had to be something else.
>
> Keywords: *Masculinity, Australian culture, employment, Australian masculinity, patternmaking, masculine identity, self-esteem.*
>
> (Williams 2017)

This sort of content would not appear in a verbatim transcript, and it demonstrates how a timed summary does active interpretive work. In this case, the Williams summary achieves added analytical content; however it also shows the potential for diverse interpretations, if the summaries are to be written from particular perspectives. While I might seek to make the Australian masculinity seem 'strange' and constructed, other authors might see masculinity as 'natural' or pre-given. Likewise, there are bound to be cultural and social elements of Williams' story that I am blind to. Once we take the time to examine timed summaries in detail, it is easy to see how far we have stepped from a 'mere summary' that abbreviates the interviewee's story.

Conclusion

The creation of timed summary documents places the historian or researcher in an unusual dual role. Not only is the interviewer the *producer* of an historical source, but they must also work in the service of potential future histories; this involves thinking carefully about how others might use the material later on. As noted earlier, the summariser must take on something of a librarian's mindset, and, to the extent that it is possible, project oneself into the future. This may mean guessing which topics and keywords might continue to be interpretable for future researchers. Of course, mistakes are inevitable, and some timed summaries may miss the mark completely for future use. Nonetheless, it is important to realise that the production of this form of document presents a distinct way of thinking about public history. It changes a dynamic in terms of who public history is 'in the service of'. Timed summaries necessitate a focus on detail, sometimes painstaking detail – and this level of detail is not always interesting to the interviewer, nor to the writer of the timed summary. This is detail produced for perpetuity, for potential future research, rather than for immediate gain. In that sense, the activity of writing timed summaries requires a dogged commitment to thoroughness that is increasingly rare in today's highly mediatised realm of short attention spans and social media scrolling. Timed summaries are a slow form of historical production. They are intrinsically inefficient in terms of labour time, despite existing for the purposes of research efficiency. The very value of timed summaries comes from this slowness and depth of engagement with content that might otherwise be archived and promptly forgotten.

Evidently, digital technologies are making incursions into the world of library cataloguing, image collation and audio transcription. There are now innumerable artificial intelligence (AI) services for transcribing interviews, image recognition and coding, indexing and other automatic metadata tools. While presently some of these tools are in the 'clunky' stages of beta development, we can be fairly confident that over time they will become more sharply honed and widely adopted by collecting institutions and online search services. Analysis is beginning to emerge about the benefits and problematic ethics of such systems (see for example, Hibberd 2018; Plosker 2018; Cohn 2019; Coleman 2020). In this context, one must ask whether timed summaries could be produced through AI, or, more to the point, how timed summaries might *not* be easily achieved through AI. As this chapter has demonstrated, timed summaries require an analytical framework for interpreting interview material, far more than verbatim transcription does. Without human judgment (flawed as it is), such documents would exist without an ethical framework and narrative clarity. Most importantly, they would lack a sense of responsibility towards those who share their life stories with the public in oral history form.

References

Benzon, Paul, 2013. Bootleg Paratextuality and Digital Temporality: Towards an Alternate Present of the DVD. *Narrative*, 21 (1), 88–104.

Birke, Dorothee, and Christ, Birte, 2013. Paratext and Digitised Narrative: Mapping the Field. *Narrative*, 21 (1), 65–87.

Blainey, Geoffrey A., 1993. Balance Sheet on our History. *Quadrant*, 37, 10–5.

Borland, Katherine, 1998. "That's Not What I Said": Interpretive Conflict in Oral Narrative Research. *In*: Robert Perks and Alistair Thomson, eds. *The Oral History Reader* (1st ed.). London: Routledge, 320–32.

Boyd, Douglas A., 2014. "I Just Want to Click on It to Listen": Oral History Archives, Orality and Usability. *In*: Douglas A. Boyd and Mary A. Larson, eds. *Oral History and the Digital Humanities: Voice, Access and Engagement*. New York: Palgrave Macmillan, 77–96.

Bradley, Kevin, 2014. Built on Sound Principles: Audio Management and Delivery at the National Library of Australia. *International Federation of Library Associations and Institutions*, 40 (3), 186–94.

Bradley, Kevin, and Puri, Anisa, 2016. Creating an Oral History Archive: Digital Opportunities and Ethical Issues. *Australian Historical Studies*, 47 (4), 75–91.

Brenneis, Donald, 2006. Reforming Promise. *In*: Annalise Riles, ed. *Documents: Artifacts of Modern Knowledge*. Ann Arbour, MI: University of Michigan Press, 41–70.

Cohn, Jonathan, 2019. Google's Algorithms Discriminate against Women and People of Colour. *The Conversation*. Available from: https://theconversation.com/googles

-algorithms-discriminate-against-women-and-people-of-colour-112516 [Accessed 12 February 2020].

Coleman, Catherine Nicole, 2020. Technology Should Reflect the Ethos of the Library. *Stanford Libraries Blog*. Available from: https://library.stanford.edu/blogs/stanford-libraries-blog/2020/03/technology-should-reflect-ethos-library [Accessed 17 March 2020].

Foster, David, 1991. *Self Portraits: Selected and Introduced by David Foster*. Canberra: National Library of Australia.

Frisch, Michael, 2006. Oral History and the Digital Revolution: Toward a Post-documentary Sensibility. *In*: Robert Perks and Alistair Thomson, eds. *The Oral History Reader* (1st ed.). London: Routledge, 102–14.

Frisch, Michael, and Lambert, Douglas, 2012. Mapping Approaches to Oral History Content Management in the Digital Age. *In*: Douglas Boyd, Steve Cohen, Brad Rakerd, and Dean Rehberger, eds. *Oral History in the Digital Age*. Washington, DC: Institute of Museum and Library Services. Available from: http://ohda.matrix.msu.edu/2012/07/mapping/ [Accessed 9 March 2020].

Genette, Gérard, 1982/1997. *Palimpsests: Literature in the Second Degree*. Translated by Channa Newman and Claude Dobrinsky. Lincoln: University of Nebraska Press.

Gluck, Sherna Berger, 2014. Why Do We Call It Oral History? Refocusing on Orality/Aurality in the Digital Age. *In*: M. Larson, ed. *Oral History and the Digital Humanities: Voice, Access and Engagement*. New York: Palgrave Macmillan, 35–52.

Good, Francis, 2000. Voice, Ear and Text: Words and Meaning. *Oral History Association of Australia Journal*, 22, 102–9.

Hamilton, Paula, 2019. "Speak, Memory": Current Issues in Oral and Public History. *In*: Paul Ashton and Alex Trapeznik, eds. *What is Public History Globally? Working with the Past in the Present*. London and New York: Bloomsbury Academic, 213–24.

Hibberd, Georgina, 2018. *Speculative Metaphors: A Design-led Approach to the Visualisation of Library Collections*. Thesis (PhD). University of Technology Sydney.

Lewis, Alison M., ed., 2008. *Questioning Library Neutrality: Essays from Progressive Librarian*. Duluth, MI: Library Juice Press.

McCracken, Ellen, 2013. Expanding Genette's Epitext/Peritext Model for Transitional Electronic Literature: Centrifugal and Centripetal Vectors on Kindles and iPads. *Narrative*, 21 (1), 105–24.

McKenna, Mark, 1997. *Different Perspectives on Black Armband History*. Politics and Public Administration Group Research Paper 5. Canberra: Parliament of Australia. Available from: www.aph.gov.au/About_Parliament/Parliamentary_Departments/Parliamentary_Library/pubs/rp/RP9798/98RP05#BLACK [Accessed 1 March 2020].

Mack, Kathleen, 2001. *Kathleen Mack interviewed by John Bannister in the Bringing them home oral history project*. Canberra: National Library of Australia. Available from: https://catalogue.nla.gov.au/Record/2258809 [Accessed 17 March 2020]. To access the specific parts of the interview discussed in this chapter, visit: https://nla.gov.au/nla.obj-218367374/listen/4-1204

National Library of Australia, nd. *Bringing Them Home Oral History Project: Project Introduction*. Canberra: National Library of Australia. Available from: www.nla.gov.au/oral-history/bringing-them-home-oral-history-project [Accessed 10 March 2020].

Portelli, Alessandro, 1981. The Peculiarities of Oral History. *History Workshop Journal*, 12 (1), 96–107.

Plosker, George, 2018. Artificial Intelligence Tools for Information Discovery. *Medford*, 42 (3), 31–5.

Riles, Annelise, ed., 2006. *Documents: Artifacts of Modern Knowledge*. Ann Arbour, MI: University of Michigan Press.

Ritchie, Donald A., 2015. *Doing Oral History: A Practical Guide*. Oxford and New York: Oxford University Press.

Samuel, Raphael, 1998. Perils of the Transcript. *In*: Robert Perks and Alistair Thomson, eds. *The Oral History Reader* (1st ed.). London: Routledge, 389–92.

Schuckar, Debra, 2018. *Debra Schuckar interviewed by Jesse Adams Stein in the Reshaping Australian manufacturing oral history project*. Canberra: National Library of Australia. Not yet available online. Catalogue record: https://nla.gov.au/nla.cat-vn7580622 [Accessed 20 March 2020].

Shopes, Linda, 2011. Editing Oral History for Publication. *Oral History Forum/d'histoire orale*, 31, 1–24.

Stein, Jesse Adams, 2016. *Hot Metal: Material Culture & Tangible Labour*. Manchester: Manchester University Press.

Stein, Jesse Adams, and Rowden, Emma, 2019. Speaking from the Inside: Challenging the Myths of Architectural History through the Oral Histories of Maitland Gaol. *In*: Janina Gosseye, Naomi Stead, and Deborah van der Plaat, eds. *Speaking of Buildings: Oral History in Architectural Research*. Princeton, NJ: Princeton Architectural Press, 28–49.

Thomson, Alistair, 1998. Fifty Years On: An International Perspective on Oral History. *Journal of American History*, 85 (2), 581–95.

Villiers, Alan, 1970. *Alan Villiers interviewed by Hazel de Berg for the Hazel de Berg collection*. Canberra: National Library of Australia. Available from https://catalogue.nla.gov.au/Record/1993818 [Accessed 10 March 2020].

Williams, Peter, 2017. *Peter Williams interviewed by Jesse Adams Stein in the Reshaping Australian Manufacturing Oral History Project*. Canberra: National Library of Australia. Available from: https://catalogue.nla.gov.au/Record/7540153 [Accessed 28 February 2020]. To access the specific part of the interview discussed in this chapter, visit: https://nla.gov.au/nla.obj-584861891/listen/2-4075.010238740

Chapter 7

Forty-nine most common phrases

Alison Whittaker

of the
Trevorrow v State of South Australia (No. 5) [2007] SASC 285
The forty-nine most common three-word phrases in the judgment of Justice Gray, ranked.

Secretary of the—
the secretary of
the plaintiff is

of the CWPRB
(of the Aborigines)

The Aborigines Act
from their parents.

Aborigines Act 1934
children from their
of the plaintiff.

That the APB
(The Maintenance Act
Act 1934 1939)
the Aborigines Department—

Aboriginal children from
of exemplary damages;
of Aboriginal children;
of the maintenance.

Power to remove.

DOI: 10.4324/9781003247593-9

Maintenance Act 1926.
Of the state,
the Crown Solicitor.

Remove Aboriginal children
to remove Aboriginal,
an Aboriginal child

The minister of
the plaintiff was,
and the CWPRB.

Award of exemplary
of the child
Minister of works
that the plaintiff
Chairman of the
and the child.

Neglected Aboriginal children,
the legal guardian:
Officers of the;
the chairman of;
control of the;
the removal of;
the power to;
legal guardian of.

To the minister,
his natural family.

Section 38 of
The children's,
the plaintiff and—

Conduct of the
Act 1926 1937.

exhibit tab

Inquest into the death of Ms Dhu (11020-14) [2016]

The forty-nine most common three-word phrases in the Western Australia Coroner's findings on the death of Ms Dhu, ranked.

First Class Constable
█████ █████ Dhu
The death of
Of █████ █████
Into the death
Death of █████
Dhu 11020 14

Inquest into the
11020 14 page
█████ Dhu 11020
Class Constable Matier

4 August 2014
Senior Constable Burgess
Exhibit 1 tab
3 August 2014

At the inquest
2 August 2014
Exhibit 3 tab

The emergency department
That she was
Am satisfied that
I am satisfied

Lock up keeper
To the effect
The police officers
Exhibit 4 tab

The effect that
's evidence was
Fitness to hold
Evidence was that
Of the police

The fact that
To hold form
Would have been
That she had
The Western Australia

There was no
Emergency department notes

Exhibit 2 tab
The custody system
█████ Dhu's temperature
The police vehicle
Lock up procedure

Ought to have
Western Australia police
Class Constable George
Through his counsel

Was feigning her
Lock up procedures.

the skeleton of the common law

'This Court is not free to adopt rules that accord with contemporary notions of justice and human rights if their adoption would fracture the skeleton of principle which gives the body of our law its shape and internal consistency.'

Mabo v Queensland (No 2) (1992) 175 CLR 1

The forty-nine most common three-word phrases in the Mabo decision, ranked.

The Murray Island—
The Murray Islands.

The common law
(By the Crown
Of the Crown).

New South Wales,
The Meriam people
(Of the Colony
Of the Murray)

Rights and interests
Law—native title

Common law native

Of New South
(In the Crown)

The Privy Council
(Of the Island)

The Land Act
(Of the Meriam)

Governor in council
(The Governor in
The Aboriginal inhabitants)

The colony of
The Crown in
that. The Crown
Act of State.

Lands of the
Inhabitants of the—
—to the Crown.

Interests in land
(Of the Aboriginal
Of the Islands)
Consistent with the—
—the Common wealth
Title of the–
—the Crown to
The rights of—

V Attorney General
For the purpose
Of native title.

Vested in the
The indigenous inhabitants
The native inhabitants

In relation to—
With respect to—
The Crown, the—

Of the native

Racial Discrimination Act
By the common—
The Racial Discrimination

An Act

Long Title

An Act for the regulation of visiting feet on Country.

1. Name of Act

This Act is the *Binaal Bunma-li, Warra-y Act 2018.*

2. Commencement

This Act is taken to have commenced *yilaalu.*

3. Definitions

Binaal Bunma-li: to soothe or settle down

Warra-y: to get up or swell

Accepted documentary items: such as determined by Elders through Country and prescribed by the regulations.

Regulations: such as determined by Elders through Country.

Feet: gumadhina.

Gumadhina: someone with hardened feet from lots of visiting.

Part III

Materiality

Chapter 8

Law's signature acts

Trish Luker

Introduction

In the lead up to the 2020 US Presidential election, the Supreme Court of Pennsylvania issued a unanimous ruling that, contrary to President Trump's claim, mailed-in and absentee ballots could not be declared invalid on the basis of signature comparison.[1] Postal voting has long been possible in a number of US states; however, in this election, the danger presented by the COVID-19 pandemic meant that an unprecedented number of voters chose this method, providing scope for Trump to contest the election on the grounds of voter fraud, and resulting in judicial scrutiny. In some states, signature matching is performed manually by comparing the voter's signature on the mailed-in ballot envelope with the signature on file; other states require that a witness attest that the ballot was completed by the intended voter; and still others use signature matching software (Stanford-MIT Healthy Elections Project 2020). In the battleground state of Pennsylvania, Department of State guidelines specify that mailed-in ballots should be counted, without the need for comparison with the signature on the file, as long as they contain a signature and voters provide valid identification during their ballot application process. In the 2020 election, Democrat nominee Joe Biden won control of the state by a narrow margin strongly supported by mail-in ballots. Donald Trump's election campaign challenged the validity of the signature matching rules, resulting in Pennsylvania's Secretary of the Commonwealth, Kathy Boockvar, successfully filing a motion to the Supreme Court to issue a declaratory ruling on the Department of State's guidelines on signature matching.[2] As these disputes illustrate, even in the digital age, signatures continue to perform an important role in giving effect to legal and political rights, such as voting. In this chapter, I will argue that rather than thinking of the signature as a handwritten inscription, we should consider it as an act or performance, such as the act of voting.

In other contexts, too, the pandemic has accelerated moves towards employing digital signatures on legal documents. For some years, electronic signatures have been validly used in a range of transactions, but particular legal documents have statutory requirements, including that the signature be witnessed,

DOI: 10.4324/9781003247593-11

or that it be in a specified form, such as being handwritten. However, in many countries, including Australia, social distancing requirements brought on by the pandemic pre-empted the introduction of legislation to facilitate electronic signatures and audio-visual witnessing of signatures on a range of legal documents, including wills, powers of attorney, deeds, affidavits and statutory declarations.[3] In some jurisdictions, even the common law rule dating back to the sixteenth century that deeds must be written on paper, parchment or vellum, signed, sealed and delivered, has now been superseded by the use of electronic documents and witnessing via audio visual link.[4]

Such changes are challenging the conventional understanding of a signature as a person's own name, written by hand on a paper document. In the twenty-first century, the use of digital devices has largely replaced writing by hand and, for some at least, the ability to write cursively, including signing one's own name, is diminishing (Brown 2013). Furthermore, paper documents as media of inscription are being replaced by digital media. The use of electronic formats for signatures may take a range of forms, such as the insertion of a digital image of a signature into a digital file; the use of a personal identification number, digital fingerprint or a stylus on an electronic pad; or, increasingly, technologies involving encryption, including digital signatures, cryptography, biometrics or voice recognition.

This chapter investigates the signature as a material artefact of legal documentary practices, in order to better understand the impact of changes that are occurring in the digital age. It begins by investigating the history of the signature, tracing how it emerged from previous symbolic rituals, identity signs and notarial practices that were connected with the emergence of distinctive legally binding documents. In law, the requirement that certain actions be in writing and signed serves to link an individual to a document: it identifies the signatory, indicates the signatory's intention to be bound to the contents of the document and provides a written record in the event that a dispute arises. As a unique sign of an individual, the originality of the manuscript signature is read as a sign of authenticity and functions to indicate the presence and intention of the signatory. However, while the signature generally performs the function of verification of the signatory or authentication of information, its specific role is determined by the nature and context of the document in question (Mason 2016).

In one form or another, signatures have been components of legal documents in Western European traditions since at least the fifteenth century. Common transactions, including conveyancing, wills and contracts, generally require the signatures of the parties and witnesses for effective execution. Adopting the Statute of Frauds (Imp) (1677), most common law jurisdictions require contracts for the sale of land to be in writing and signed by the party to be charged (Christensen and Low 2003). The signature of the testator, or another person in their presence and at their direction, is usually a formal requirement in making a valid will. Formation of contract requires that all the material and the essential terms agreed to by the parties be in writing and must be signed by the parties, or by another lawfully authorised person. It is a mandatory requirement for execution that a deed is signed. A party becomes liable to a bill of exchange by signing the document.

Given the ubiquity of the requirement that legal documents include signatures, there has been surprising little attention to signatures in jurisprudence or legal scholarship (see, however, Hancher 1992; Harris 2005; Reed 2000; Mason 2016). Chris Reed suggests that this is due to its self-evident nature—'the paradigm case of signature is the signatory's name, written in his or her own hand, on a paper document ("manuscript signature") and this is so universally understood by lawyers and non-lawyers alike that it requires no special treatment' (2000, 2). However, as an artefact distinctly of literate cultures, the suggestion that the signature is 'universally understood' is far too simplistic; for example, Western legal documentary practices have commonly been employed in settler-colonial contexts to rationalise oppressive decision-making, disenfranchise Indigenous peoples and subject them to colonial regulation (Luker 2009, 2016).

In the digital age, disputes have arisen from technologies which generate surrogates for the handwritten signature. These disruptions of law's paradigm case arise where digital technologies depart from the production of a physical document, instead producing 'an intangible electronic series of bits which convey no meaning without a computer and software to interpret' (Christensen and Low 2003) and have tested conventional understandings of the signature as a mark on a written document. If, however, we accept that writing is itself a technology (Ong 2002), and that handwriting is an identification technology, then it is possible to recognise continuity between the analogue and digital forms of the signature. While the technological apparatus and the nature of the performance have changed, digital media function through the use of new technology that substitutes for the traditional technology of the handwritten signature.

Tracing the development of English law relating to the signature from earliest records until the end of the twentieth century, Reed (2000) argues that a change has occurred in judicial and legislative understanding which can be characterised as a shift from form to function: in earlier times, attention was paid to the characteristics of the mark itself; however, more recently, the signature is assessed in terms of its function. While the line of cases applying a functional approach dates back over 150 years, Reed argues that this approach more readily reflects electronic signatures. This transition is also reflected in Australian cases, as I will go on to discuss. I will argue that rather than thinking of the signature in terms of its physical properties, it is more productive to consider it in terms of its function, where the context of the performance of the signature act determines if it can be read as a sign indicating meaning, such as authorship, consent or intention.

This approach has been taken up by French anthropologist of writing, Béatrice Fraenkel, author of the only book-length cultural history of the signature, *La Signature: Genèse d'un Signe* (*The Signature: Genesis of a Sign*) (1992).

In this wide-ranging text, available only in French, Fraenkel demonstrates how the signature emerged in Europe as an identity sign that best responds to the demands of modern identity, including the individuated or singular self, the capacity to make moral judgments, to act within the law and to consent to actions.[5] This was accompanied by increased literacy, the spread of written law and the establishment of bureaucratic government. Importantly, as Fraenkel argues, the signature became a validation sign that transformed a written document into legal action (1992, 7).

Fraenkel (2012) has since developed her work in relation to a theory of 'writing acts', arguing that in some situations, when writing, we are doing something beyond the obvious activity of writing. Extending J.L. Austin's (1975) framework for speech acts and their performative force, Fraenkel argues that writing also can have distinctive effects that exceed the meaning of what is written, giving it 'graphic force' (2012, 35). As a case study, she has investigated writing acts found in urban spaces, such as political graffiti and 'catastrophe writings' that emerged on the streets of New York in the wake of 9/11, as having graphic force, such as incitement to collective commemoration. Fraenkel refers to acts that result in the making of graffiti as a 'family' of writing acts, joined together by their location in 'the city', because they are simultaneously enunciations and actions 'where the mere fact of writing is recognised as a meaningful act in itself' (2012, 34–35).

Fraenkel suggests that the verb 'to sign' is a paradigm for a distinct family of writing acts which can be performed by certain subjects, such as 'the legal person' (2012, 41). Notwithstanding her earlier important contribution to understanding the signature, to date, she does not appear to have developed this theorisation of signatures as writing acts. However, I will argue that Fraenkel's framework for writing acts can be productively drawn upon to interrogate the function of the signature in law, including into the digital age. The signature is an identity sign that communicates the presence of the signatory at a particular time. When performed for legal purposes, the meaning of the signature cannot be reduced to *what* is written, but rather, must be understood within the context of the act of writing.

Social ontologist, Barry Smith (2012, 2014), has also used Austin's work as the departure point for a theory of 'document acts' to explain the way that documents, further to their role in recording of information, have the capacity to bring about other effects. His theory includes an account of the different things that we can do to a document, such as signing it, the performance of which has potential to create further effects, including legal obligations. As he points out, a signature on a document may play a variety of roles: as a record of the performance of the signature, as evidence of the signatory's agreement to the validity of the document and potentially as initiator of further documents acts (2012, 21). Smith's theorisation of document acts is valuable because it provides a comprehensive framework for an investigation of the signature as a writing act with legal effects.

This chapter includes analysis of Australian legal disputes where the existence of a legally valid signature has been contested or where it is of evidentiary significance. While few in number, these cases demonstrate that Australian courts have struggled to establish a coherent approach. When presented with the requirement to make decisions about the validity of a signature, legal decision-makers clearly do understand its graphic force. However, in some important cases, courts have failed to pay sufficient attention to the context of the production of the signature, to its essential performative characteristics that give it signification or graphic force and to its power to transform a written document into a legal action.

What is a signature?

The word 'signature' comes from the Latin *signare*, meaning to sign or mark, deriving from *signum*, in reference to the impression made by a seal, from which signatures emerged. Many of the earliest documented references to signatures are to those that were intended to have legal effect (*Oxford English Dictionary*). Tracing the history of the development of literacy in England, medieval historian M.T. Clanchy (1979) argues that writing and documents emerged from record keeping based in memory, and did not, at first, command trust. Prior to written records, symbolic objects, such as knives or swords, served to symbolise a legal act, such as the conveyance of property. He illustrates the performative character of the act of signing through its legacy in oral ceremonies such as the placing of hands on a bible, uttering oaths, the breaking of objects, the signing of the cross or the exchange of a lock of hair. As Clanchy (1979, 203) elaborates, 'before conveyances were made with documents, the witnesses "heard" the donor utter the words of the grant and "saw" him make the transfer by a symbolic object, such as a knife or a turf from the land'.

As Fraenkel (1992) demonstrates, the manuscript signature emerged during the sixteenth century from earlier systems of symbolic identity signs that utilised images, such as coats of arms and seals, to represent the characteristics of an individual. In France, a 1554 ordinance made it a compulsory addition to notarised acts, even if the signatory was illiterate (Fraenkel 1992, 12). Similarly, in her important genealogy of the law through the history of the file, German legal historian and media theorist, Cornelia Vismann (2008, 71–72), argued that during the medieval period in Europe, a shift occurred in governance practices, from records, such as Roman codicils that were used as official texts or recording devices, to documents, such as certificates, whose function it was 'to preserve, not to transmit'. She suggests that the visual appearance of documents, including the use of ornamental writing, specific layout and formats, 'turned into formalities endowed with legal force' (2008, 72). It is during this time, Vismann argues, that handwritten signatures emerged, 'as one of the most important operatives attesting to the binding force of documented law' (2008, 73).

The handwritten signature paralleled increased standardisation in systems of identification and recognition through the stabilisation of nomenclature that was characteristic of European societies as they increased in size and individuals became more mobile. The concept of individualised identity and subjectivity is itself tied to the emergence of the modern bureaucratic state and the development of documentary practices which made citizens visible and 'open to the scrutiny of officialdom' (Caplan and Torpey 2001, 1). It was associated with the increasingly widespread use of inherited patronymic names. One of the key functions of the emergence of written forms of individualised identification in Western Europe was as a means to record real property ownership, inheritance and exchange through contracts, wills and estates. These are legal documents on which the signatures of parties and testators function as signs of agreement, obligation or receipt; the signatories' authentic identity is subsequently verified by a witness through another signature or mark. In the United Kingdom, the Statute of Frauds 1677 required written agreement and signatures for certain contracts, especially transfer of land, and many contemporary legislative requirements inherit these provisions (Weber 2015, 103).

As these accounts demonstrate, the meaning of the signature in Western European traditions is closely aligned with the history of writing and of documents, particularly legal documents. Since at least the sixteenth century, the signature has been epitomised by the action of an individual hand-writing their name onto physical material, such as paper, parchment or vellum, on which is written other information. In order for a manuscript signature to have legal effect, it must meet certain requirements: it must be attached to a document and be recognisable as that of the author to whom it is attributed (witnessed). While many documents are commonplace, the presence of an individual's signature elevates the status of a document from something that may be valued only for its informational content to one that performs a function, such as recording an agreement between parties (as in a contract), recording the wishes of the signatory (as on a will) or being tendered as evidence in legal proceedings (as on an affidavit or witness statement). Each of these contexts is a writing act, where, in the correct circumstances, the inscription of the signature has the potential to transform the document from something that is valued only for its informational content to an object with legal force. In this way, the signature is a graphic mark that changes the world around it.

Writing acts

While there has been little scholarly interest in the signature in legal theory, there has been some attention within semiotics, linguistics, cultural theory and the visual arts. These accounts frequently refer to J.L. Austin's (1975) influential philosophy of language as speech acts and his reference to the signature as a non-verbal form of performative utterance. Austin was concerned with the production of speech, rather than writing. However, he uses the signature to make a point: while in a verbal utterance, the origin of the utterance is made explicit through the identification of the speaker who performs the speech act, in a written utterance (or transcription), this is most often performed by appending the speaker's signature (1975, 60). Austin's inclusion of the signature as a sign that indicates individual identity was later roundly critiqued by Jacques Derrida (1982) in one of the pieces that contributed to the development of his account of the primacy of writing over speech. Derrida argued that signatures cannot function as unique signs of identity because they are inherently variable, can be imitated and must be repeatable ('iterable') (229).[6] It is possible to characterise the distinction between the approaches to the signature taken by Austin and Derrida in terms of function versus form. Austin was concerned with the performative effects of speech (such as a request, a promise, a demand) which he referred to as illocutionary force. Derrida, on the other hand, focussed on the form of the signature, how it is penned and whether it is readable ('iterable', 315) in the absence of the signer. However, Derrida was concerned less with the significance of the signature as a linguistic sign and more with deconstructing the primacy attributed to speech and the individual speaker as the origin of thought. In linguistic theory, up until the second half of the twentieth century, the influential work of key theorists, particularly Emile Benveniste and Austin, has resulted in privileged attention to speech as a medium of communication. The contribution of Derrida, and others, was regarded as an important correction to this.

The foundational work of Austin and Derrida has been influential in analyses of the signature in the humanities. Linguist Roy Harris, for example, uses the signature as a test case in his book-length argument for a renewed appreciation of writing as a form of communication separate to speech. He identifies the signature as the 'reflexive sign *par excellence*; it signified by reference to its own making and the identity of its maker' (2005, 162). The signature, Harris argues, is essentially a phenomenon of writing that does not have a counterpart in speech (2005,182). Harris highlights the paradoxical nature of the signature: while it is commonly written as the name of the signatory, this is not a requirement; any written mark made by a particular individual may be a signature, as long as she or he has the authority to perform the act (2005, 182). Furthermore, as Harris points out, there appears to be a contradiction in the expectation that, as a precaution against forgery, a signature be both distinctive (belonging to one person alone) but also recognisably uniform (always the same), the point also made by Derrida.

In other disciplines, there are diverse approaches to analyses of the signature. Within cultural theory, Josh Lauer, for example, focuses on the 'autographmania' that developed in the United States during the nineteenth century, when the signatures of important people were seen to hold an authentic trace of the past, enabling a viewer or collector to establish a direct connection with a specific past (2007, 145). Historian David Luebke (2004) uses signatures affixed to a petition as a framework to analyse the social conditions in East Fresia in the 1700s. In the Australian context, literary scholar Penny van Toorn (2006) recounted how Aboriginal ceremonial signs were appropriated by colonist John Batman to function as signatures in an attempt to legitimise deeds that were created to procure the land now encompassing the city of Melbourne.

Theoretical attention to the signature in semiotics and linguistics has been influential in law. Legal theorist Michael Hancher, for example, finds Austin's approach valuable, arguing that the contention that the signature represents the 'personal agency' of the signer is supported in English and American law (1992, 227). This, he argues, is demonstrated in the law's accommodation of variability in an individual's signature, where '[o]ften the law requires nothing of a signature other than that it be a documentary mark intended by the signer to be (and to be accepted as) a signature' (1992, 230). Hancher concludes that there is a difference between the legal history of signatures in the French and Anglophone traditions reflected in the different approaches taken by Derrida and Austin; in the common law Anglophone tradition, the signature need not conform to an iterable form but rather depends upon judicial assessment of intention (1992, 235).

Fraenkel (2006; 2007) also engages with Austin's account of communication but argues that he did not provide an adequate account of the act of writing.[7] For Austin, the problem is the attachment of utterances to their author. However, he pays no attention to the specific temporal and spatial dimensions of written acts, nor to their materiality (2006, [12]). Fraenkel argues that writing also has distinctive illocutionary force, which she refers to as 'graphic force', that is, effects that are not reducible to the transmission of the written message but are the result of the way the message is presented to the reader (2012, 34). She also argues that, in writing, we are producing written objects that are embedded within a situation or environment which gives the object meaning (2012, 39).

Fraenkel makes the important point that where Austin refers to written (as opposed to speech) acts, these are almost always legal or regulatory documents, such as contracts, wills or decrees (2006, [6]). Indeed, she argues that Austin's theory of performativity is dependent on a legal matrix (2006, [31]). While Austin treats these acts as if it is not important that they are written (2006, [29]), Fraenkel argues that it is precisely the materiality of writing that establishes legal performativity. Unlike speech, writing can be detached from its origin and 'inserted into a system of writing chains' (2006, [56]). Fraenkel draws on the common law in her account of writing chains, pointing out that when writing decisions, judges draw on and contribute to the writing of other authors of the law (2006, [59–60]). Like Vismann (2008), Fraenkel points out that to ensure validity, legal documents are often required to carry not only the signature of the author, but also other signs of authority, such as seals and stamps, and to conform to certain graphic standards, such as formatting, layout and typography, each of which carries meaning and contributes to the performative force of the statement (2006, [74]). In this way, the written object is a 'mixture of modalities—enunciative, textual, graphic and material' (2006, [77]). As Fraenkel states: 'The law draws from the specifics of the written utterance a whole formalism and in turn makes written language the place of legal action' (2006, [76]). In the following section, I will draw on Fraenkel's framework to investigate the performative function of the signature as a writing act that gives effect to law.

Law's signature acts

In Anglophone law, the signature functions to authenticate the signatory and in this way to verify the validity or accuracy or the signatory's agreement to documentary information. Conventionally, the signature takes the form of a graphic representation of the name of the signatory, but this is not a requirement in law. Where disputes have occurred, these have often concerned the authenticity and/or validity of the signature. In attempting to determine whether a valid signature exists, courts have generally looked for two elements: firstly, evidence of a written or visual form and whether it meets the documentary requirement, and, secondly, evidence of the signatory's intention to authenticate and adopt the contents of a document on which the signature is inscribed. As a writing act, the signature functions as evidence of the presence and intention of the signatory.

Over centuries, in addition to the traditional manuscript signature, courts have accepted a wide variety of lexical or orthographic forms for signatures, including marks of any shape, such as the sign of the cross or an 'X', initials, a partial signature, illegible writing, writing made with the assistance of another person, the wrong name, only part of the name, words other than a name, abbreviations of a name or no writing at all.[8]

Courts have also considered a range of media for signatures, including seal imprints, fingerprints, rubber stamps, printed or lithographed names or the use of a stencil-pen. Signatures that are in some way not 'original' but have been produced by technology, including signature machines or typewriters, telegrams or telex machines, as well as those that are photocopied, faxed, electronically scanned, emails, produced digitally or cryptographically have all been accepted (see Mason 2016, for a thoroughgoing account). These cases have appeared in courts as new media and technologies have developed, presenting challenges to conventional understandings of the signature as the mark of an individual written in their own hand.

In each of these cases, courts have accepted these forms by analogy with a written manuscript signature, as long as the person making the mark indicates that they have approved the contents of the document, thereby authenticating the signature. Christensen et al. (2003, [7]) point out that the fact that a signature is not the result of signing is not important; the crucial element is that the person who made the mark adopts the document or approves the content.

In a defining case for the signature in Australian law, *R v Moore; Ex Parte Myers* (1884), a pawnbroker in Victoria, Australia, was convicted for neglecting to attach his own signature to a pledge ticket containing his printed name, 'Lewis M. Myers, per', which was followed by the written signature not of Myers but of an employee, 'F. O'Farrell'. This conviction was quashed on appeal. The Supreme Court of Victoria held that where a statute merely requires that a document be signed, this is satisfied by proof of the making of a mark on the document by, or by the authority of, the signatory. Citing a number of cases of English authority where documents were found to be validly signed not with a manuscript signature, but with a cross, initials or a part only of a name, Justice Higinbotham stated that

> A signature is only a mark and where a statute merely requires that a document shall be signed, the statute is satisfied by proof of the making of a mark upon the document by or by the authority of the signatory.
>
> (at 324)

This case is the authority in Australian law for acceptance of marks that are not manuscript signatures, such as crosses, initials, printed names and rubber stamps. It also functions as acknowledgement by an Australian court that it is not necessary for a person to sign a document by putting pen to paper; a signature can be made by an agent or by alternative means, such as a stamp of the person's signature (McCullagh, Little and Caelli 1998). However, the decision does not provide clear guidance as to which elements of the written message function to authenticate the document: the printed name of the pawnbroker, the written signature of the employee, perhaps the combination of the two—or indeed, if other factors have been taken into account, such as whether the pawnbroker's pledge ticket was in a standardised form lending it authenticity and legitimacy, whether the employee's signature functioned as the witness to the signature of the pawnbroker or indeed, whether other evidence, such as testimony from the pawnbroker, indicated intention to be bound by the agreement. Using Fraenkel's framework, we can think of each of these characteristics represented in the document as elements of different 'writing chains', the combined effect of which serves as the performance of the lawful outcome.

In a number of cases, courts have been faced with questions about the necessity of 'original' signatures, particularly where the signatory acts as the agent of an authority, such as a government department. These cases demonstrate a shift in judicial understanding of the signature, with increasing acceptance of a range of electronic media, less attention to form and more attention to the range of factors contributing to the function of the signature. For example, in *Re Deleso* (1978), the Supreme Court of South Australia upheld the application of a debtor who requested the court set aside a bankruptcy notice that was a 'photocopy' of a document (referred to as an 'electronic xerographic copy'), on the grounds that it did not contain an original signature of the Registrar of Taxation. The debtor had been shown the original document by the bailiff but had been left with a photocopy, which Justice Rogerson determined had not been duly served. Rule 15(a) of the Bankruptcy Rules 1968 specified that multiple copies of the document should each personally be signed by the Registrar and that 'service of a bankruptcy notice shall be effected by delivering to the debtor personally a copy of the bankruptcy notice signed by the Registrar', stating that bankruptcy notices must be 'clearly authentic, official documents' (at 704). The court engaged with the concept of a 'copy' of a document in light of new technology, but attributed importance to the form of the signature, in particular, the authenticity of an 'original' mark penned by the signatory 'personally' (at 702). In this way, the court sought to identify a direct line of attribution emanating from the signatory's own hand to the document. Further, the judge clearly identified the writing act necessary to give the document legal effect when he stated that the 'form of notice furnished to the Registrar does not become an actual bankruptcy notice until it has been signed, and issued as such, by the Registrar' (at 703). The court highlighted the significance to the genuineness of legal procedure of documentality, particularly the signature, stating:

> Now, bankruptcy notices are no longer sealed, nor even stamped, when they are issued. There are no official printed forms. All that authenticates a notice and at the same time proves to the debtor that the steps necessary for the issue of a bankruptcy notice have been taken by the creditor, is the signature of the Registrar.
>
> (at 704)

He added that 'in spite of the fact that the reproduction of handwriting by machines has become more efficient and more widespread ... it is still desirable that bankruptcy notices bear the original signature of the Registrar' (at 702). In this case, the judge attributed significance to form: to the originality of a signature as a way of authenticating a legal document, in order to give effect to the legal process. An original signature has additional value in law because it guarantees the presence of the signatory in order to perform the act of signing.

Ten years later, in *Deputy Commissioner of Taxation (Vic) v Boxshall* (1988), the Federal Court upheld an appeal by the Victorian Taxation Department that had issued a bankruptcy notice signed in the name of the Deputy Commissioner of Taxation by one of his authorised officers. The action raised questions about whether a signature must be signed by the signatory or whether it may be signed in his or her name by someone else. There were also questions as to the proper form of attestation of the signature to the petition. As in *Deleso*, the court paid careful attention to the Rules for the required form for a bankruptcy notice. Recognising that the *Bankruptcy Act 1966* (Cth) provided authority for a petition to be signed by an agent of the Deputy Commissioner, the court turned its attention to whether the signature of the witness was properly attested, concluding that it was not because the pro forma document inaccurately stated that the petition was 'signed by the petitioner in my presence'. The Court concluded that:

> It is true, on the facts of this case, that the duly authorised agent of the Deputy Commissioner signed the Deputy Commissioner's name in the presence of the attesting witness; but it is misleading to say that the petition was signed by the petitioner in the presence of that witness. The Deputy Commissioner is the petitioner and he did not sign the petition.
>
> (at 180)

In this case, the court allowed for a signatory's agent to sign on his or her behalf. However, it distinguished the performative requirements of the different writing chains of signatory and witness and the inter-dependency of them on the document in order to give effect to the legal act.

Over 20 years later, in *Deputy Commissioner of Taxation v Brilliant Homes Management Pty Ltd* [2011], the Federal Court held that a computer-printed or typed name of the Deputy Commissioner is an acceptable substitute for a handwritten signature. Justice Rares stated that: 'It is not necessary that a physical or handwritten signature or a facsimile of a handwritten signature be placed on a document for it to be "signed"' (par. 11). In this case, the judge pointed to the history of seals and wax as support for the argument that handwritten signatures are not necessary on official documents (par. 12), particularly where it is possible for a court to take judicial notice of the signatory's official role. He determined that the name of the signatory appearing in print on the statement above her official title amounted to a 'printed name' in the place of her signature (par. 13) and that a facsimile signature is not additionally necessary. In this case, the judge regarded a 'written, printed or stamped name' as a signature. This case reflects a departure from the approach taken in *Deleso* over 30 years earlier when a photocopy of a signature was found to make a bankruptcy notice ineffectual.

These cases reveal that, at various times, there has been legal uncertainty about the validity of a signature which does not provide evidence of the presence of the signatory at the moment of the signing, the scene of production of the legal object, in the way outlined by Fraenkel. While a stamped facsimile of a signature attempts to reproduce the manuscript form, it does not indicate the action of an individual hand-writing their name, but rather points to the absence of the subject whose handwriting it replicates. This appears to have given rise to judicial concern about inauthenticity and raised questions about the potential for fraud, one of the key rationales for the use of signatures on legal documents. Photocopied, scanned and PDF formats as signatures are actually images, not writing, and in this way, they reference the history of identity signs including coats of arms and seals. While they resemble signatures, they are not made using signature performances, but rather are reproduced in the absence of the signatory. This suggests that Fraenkel's framework for understanding the signature as an authenticating performance does not take sufficient account of digital technologies and does not accord with the current legal position. Alternatively, it may suggest that understanding the performance of the signature should now take account of the act of appending an image as an authenticating performance.

At other times, Australian courts have been faced with disputes about the location of a signature. Signatures usually appear in designated spaces, commonly at the end of documents, after preceding text, to indicate agreement or adherence to the text above. This is considered significant in legal documents, such as wills, and is important where a testator wishes to explain, modify or revoke provisions, resulting in the need for a codicil that is signed and witnessed in the same way as the original legal document. In *Druin Pty Ltd ATF the Druin (No 3)* [2014], the guarantor to a credit agreement had signed his name and included other details on a document, not in the correct space, but in the space where the witness to the execution of a guarantee should have signed, even though a guarantor was not a requirement of the transaction. The question presented to the court was whether this error was sufficient to make the defendant liable as a guarantor. Justice Robb concluded that 'the signature, albeit not in the correct place, manifested an intention, objectively ascertained, that the defendant would be bound by the terms of the guarantee' and that this intention could be ascertained as long as the signature was contained 'within the four corners of the document' (par. 25). This case offers support for Harris' (2005, 180) argument that 'in the case of a signature, its distinctive position in the graphic space available is usually sufficient to identify it *as a signature*'.

The location of a signature was also considered in *Campbell v Director of Prosecutions for the Commonwealth of Australia* [1995], where the Supreme Court of Victoria devoted unusually detailed and careful consideration to the statutory definition of the word 'signature'. In this case, it was alleged that a Commissioner of the Supreme Court had signed as a witness to an affidavit, knowing that the statement was in fact untrue, and in breach of section 142(d) of the *Evidence Act 1958* (Victoria). The question that the court had to address was whether a signature authentication of a legal declaration needs to agree to the truth of the contents of the document or whether it functions only to verify the signature of the declarant. Providing a careful and contextualised interpretation of the provision, as well as previous judicial attention to the meaning of the signature, Justice Ormiston identified two purposes served by the signature when inscribed on a document: firstly, to indicate that the signatory affirms the authenticity of the document (such as in a contract, where the signature of a party indicates that the text should be treated as a true exposition of the contract); and secondly, by being placed on a document outside the text, the signature functions to make the whole document binding on the person whose name or mark it contains (at 658). Considering the signature as outside the text is consistent with Fraenkel's argument that the signature is a writing act, an authenticating performance that gives effect to law. However, in this case, the court highlighted the interrelationship of the two parts of the document: 'neither the declaration nor the clause had a life of its own' (at 654). Where a signature is performed for the purpose of authenticating another person's signature, the writing acts are multiplied and layered: the witness's signature functions to authenticate the presence of the signatory, whose signature functions to indicate the validity or accuracy of the information.

While law characteristically demands a high level of formalism, in more recent times, when disputes concerning signatures have appeared before courts, decision-makers have often been less concerned with the form of a signature or the media of its inscription, but rather, have sought ways to determine whether its purpose, such as authentication or verification of identity, can be supported. This suggests that legal decision-makers have recognised that the performative force of the signature cannot be represented in a single orthographic mark, but rather draws on a 'mixture of modalities' (Fraenkel 2006, [77]) to determine if a legal act has occurred. These cases demonstrate that when presented with disputes, legal decision-makers recognise that the function of the signature in law is not reflected in *what* it says, its informational content, but rather in the way it functions as an inscription linking a document to the signatory. Maurizio Ferraris (2013, 300) describes it as an example of an 'idiom', 'a unique and idiomatic trait of an individual' that plays a decisive role in validating social objects (2013, 298), such as legal documents, and binding them to the subject. Indeed, the presence of a signature may be decisive in determining whether an object is a document. For example, in *The Estate of Robin Michael (deceased)* [2016], a case concerning an informal will, the court found that a computer file containing a document entitled 'last will and testament' was a 'document' for the purposes of s 12(2) of the *Wills Act 1936* (SA) because the facsimile signature found on the computer file document and its printout closely resembles the signature of the deceased. In this case, the justices paid close attention to the clear expression of testamentary intentions of the deceased. This demonstrates how, in the performance of a signature act, a 'document' with legal effect is created, supporting Fraenkel's argument that the signature participates in the production of legal objects.

Perhaps the most infamous judicial interpretation of a signature in Australian law occurred in the Federal Court decision in *Cubillo v Commonwealth* [2000], the landmark legal action taken by members of the Stolen Generations, Lorna Cubillo and Peter Gunner, against the Commonwealth government. Cubillo and Gunner sought compensation for the harm caused to them as a result of being removed from their families and communities in the Northern Territory of Australia during the 1940s and 1950s under policies of assimilation implemented with respect to Aboriginal people. In this case, over 2000 pages of archival documents were tendered as evidence by the applicants. In his decision, Justice O'Loughlin identified one particular document, a 'Form of Consent by a Parent' (Exhibit A21), as evidence that Gunner's mother, Topsy Kundrilba, had given her consent to his removal and institutionalisation. The document is a simple, typed, pro forma on a piece of A4 paper that had been located among many other relevant documents in the National Archives of Australia. The wording is like a statutory declaration, where names are inserted into a narrative statement that is phrased in the form of a request. At the bottom of the document is a thumbprint or fingerprint, around which is the statement 'signed of my own free will this _ day of 1956 in the presence of _', but the gaps have not been filled in. The typed words 'her' and 'mark' appear on either side of the print, and 'TOPSY' and 'KUNDRILBA' above and below.[9] The document is undated, unwitnessed and bears no official letterhead, seal or insignia (see Figure 8.1).

Kundrilba had passed away by the time of the litigation and was therefore unable to give evidence. However, the document with her purported thumbprint was crucial to Justice O'Loughlin's decision that she had given her consent to her child's removal. In this case, an unverified physical mark on a document was interpreted as evidence of a writing act with important legal consequences, despite the absence of evidence that the person who made the mark approved or even understood the contents of the document.

While the document was itself unwitnessed, in the trial, evidence was taken from a witness who Justice O'Loughlin considered likely to have been responsible for obtaining the signature. Harry Kitching, a patrol officer in the region at the time, gave evidence that while he recognised the form, he could not recall anything about Peter Gunner's situation, nor why he recommended that Gunner be taken away. In his affidavit, he said 'I had no recollection of being present when Topsy marked the form'. Importantly, Kitching also said: 'I note that it was not signed or dated' (Kitching's affidavit, paras 82–83, cited in transcript 7 August 1998, 95), underlining his knowledge of the performative characteristics of signature acts. This case clearly calls attention to the graphic force of the signature and its power to transform a written document into a legal action. In elaborating on legal writing acts, Fraenkel (2008, 19) states that 'the traces found on legal acts, those of the author of the action, the scribe, the officer responsible for validation, possibly witnesses of the act, only form the front of the stage'. Where legal writing acts occur in colonial contexts, such as in this case, the documents produced carry traces of violence and dispossession, surveillance and control. In this case, the document containing the thumbprint raises crucial questions about power and control on the frontier of settler colonial states, Indigenous sovereignty and autonomy, and cross-cultural understanding.

As Fraenkel points out, legal writing acts are part of a vast network of material culture encompassing documentary creation, duplication and circulation; preservation, archiving and destruction; organisation, management and storage; as well as attention to the paper, digital or other material form. When applied to legal documents, all of these factors contribute to the validation process of legal acts that may have evidentiary value (Fraenkel 2008, 20). Within this network of writing chains, the signature is part of a larger action, presuming

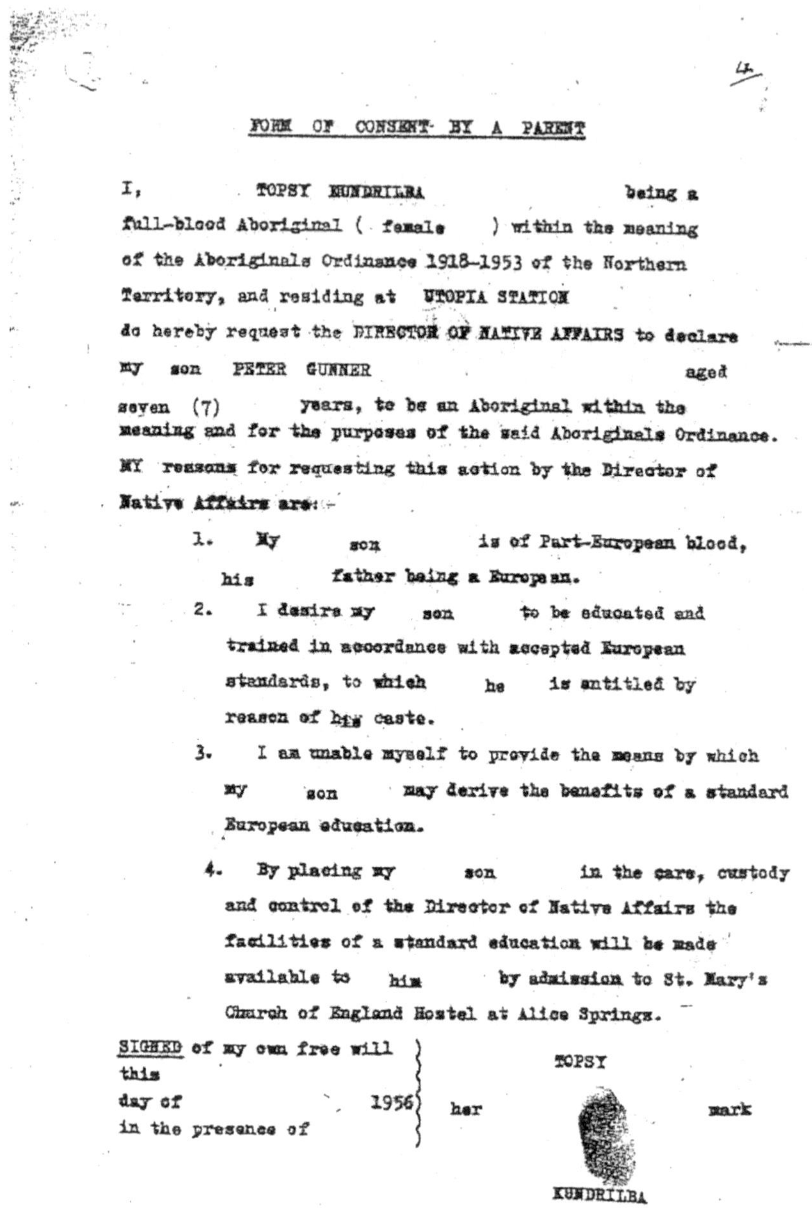

4

FORM OF CONSENT BY A PARENT

I, TOPSY KUNDRILBA being a full-blood Aboriginal (female) within the meaning of the Aboriginals Ordinance 1918–1953 of the Northern Territory, and residing at UTOPIA STATION do hereby request the DIRECTOR OF NATIVE AFFAIRS to declare my son PETER GUNNER aged seven (7) years, to be an Aboriginal within the meaning and for the purposes of the said Aboriginals Ordinance.

MY reasons for requesting this action by the Director of Native Affairs are:-

1. My son is of Part-European blood, his father being a European.
2. I desire my son to be educated and trained in accordance with accepted European standards, to which he is entitled by reason of his caste.
3. I am unable myself to provide the means by which my son may derive the benefits of a standard European education.
4. By placing my son in the care, custody and control of the Director of Native Affairs the facilities of a standard education will be made available to him by admission to St. Mary's Church of England Hostel at Alice Springs.

SIGNED of my own free will
this
day of 1956
in the presence of

TOPSY
her mark
KUNDRILBA

Figure 8.1 National Archives of Australia: Welfare Branch; F1, Correspondence files, annual single number series, 1956–1957, 1956/2077, 'Welfare Branch Declaration to be a Ward Peter Gunner'. Tendered as evidence by the respondent in relation to Peter Gunner in *Cubillo v Commonwealth* (2000) 174 ALR 97 as 'Form of Consent by a Parent'. Reproduced with the permission of the Federal Court of Australia.

'several actants, several authors, several hands', involving 'a tangle of "micro acts"—acts of reading ... and acts of verification' (2008, 22).

Digital signatures

In the digital age, signatures have departed widely from the traditional handwritten manuscript form. A signature may take the form of a typed line in an email or a scanned image of a manuscript signature. Digital technology has provided further options, such as typing the signatory's name into an electronic document or a biodynamic version of a manuscript signature involving the use of a special pen on a screen or digital pad. There are also specific signature technologies that in no way resemble handwriting, such as digital signatures, cryptographic systems that send data with a message to confirm the integrity and authenticity of the signature, public key cryptography (with third party verification of identity), fingerprints, biometrics or voice recognition. These technologies not only perform the function of 'signing' the document, but also verify the authenticity of the signatory (Weber 2015, 107).

Distinguishing digital signatures from those that are handwritten, the Australian Law Dictionary defines them as 'authenticating the sender of a document electronically'. As with the earlier technological forms of printing machines, signatures on telexes and facsimiles, Australian law has developed to take account of new digital technologies—by pursuing a media-neutral approach, with an objective standard that provides for flexibility in technological development. A digital signature is not defined by a specific technology, but rather requires that the technology produce certain elements: a method to identify the signatory, a method to indicate the signatory's intention or approval of the information and a method that is as reliable as appropriate for the circumstances, with or without further evidence (Weber 2015, 110). Attention to these elements suggests a decisive shift in the type of acts required for the performance of the signature in law. In the digital age, signatures are no longer defined or appraised by their form, but rather, by their function. Indeed, in some instances, the required acts do not result in a signature at all, but rather, perform functions that emulate the identificatory effects of the signature, and in this way, they act as alternatives to the signature. As with many other digital media that have replaced paper-based media—such as digital libraries, digital archives, e-documents, e-books, tablets, digital files, e-pages, digital pens—the various methods and formats of digital signatures function by emulating the characteristics of paper-based media and in this way appear as substitutes for manuscript forms.

For example, in *Harding v Brisbane City Council* [2009], the Queensland Planning and Environment Court considered the validity of an electronic signature that was made by digitally inserting a driver's license details into an online site, in view of the fact that the information provided was slightly incorrect. Under the *Electronic Transactions (Queensland) Act 2001*, a range of documentary acts, including providing a signature, can be performed electronically. Under this framework, an identification document, such as a birth certificate, Medicare card, citizenship certificate, rates notice, passport or driver's licence, functions in place of the signature. The 'signatory' must also perform an act that indicates agreement to the recipient's acceptance of the document electronically, with 'the same status as if I had signed it' (par. 15). District Court Judge Robin pointed out that a driver's licence contains details 'truly personal to the holder', including name, address and physical details, as well as a signature (par. 23). Rather than a witness to the signature act, digital signatures use other methods for verification of the signatory's presence and agreement, such as identification documents.

In another case heard in Queensland, the same approach was taken to apply to a contract for the sale of property. In *Stellard Pty Ltd v North Queensland Fuel Pty Ltd* (BC201503878) [2015], the Supreme Court of Queensland was required to consider whether a contract for the sale of property was properly executed through an email exchange. One party said that there was no intention to be legally bound by the exchange. The *Property Law Act 1974* (Queensland) specifies that the contract for sale of land must be in writing and signed. As in the previous case, the court referred to the provisions of the *Electronic Transactions (Queensland) Act 2001*. In this case, the defendant argued that the email, sent by a legal representative, did not identify anyone as the acceptor of the offer and therefore did not meet the requirement of a signature. However, the court concluded that the requirement of the signatory's intention could be established by further evidence made up of conversations and other emails. In this case, rather than one moment of inscription, the performance of the signature act was taken to have occurred over time and across different writing acts.

As in the United States, signatures also have been in dispute in Australian electoral law, where the *Commonwealth Electoral Act 1918* requires that a person must personally sign the prescribed form in order to be registered to vote. In *Getup Ltd v Electoral Commissioner* [2010], the Federal Court of Australia was faced with the question of whether a signature digitally signed using an electronic signature tool was valid for the purposes of registration. When, in 2010, a federal election was called with a particularly brief period allowed for voter enrolment, the political advocacy group, Getup, encouraged young people who were not enrolled to vote to do so and provided a website to facilitate this. The site allowed people to use a digital pen, finger or mouse to draw a signature, with the capacity to make fine adjustments to the image (to make it more recognisable as the person's handwritten signature), including changing the thickness of strokes, editing, erasing, modifying and reconstructing the image. The signature tool allowed a person to hand write their signature and produces an image that closely imitated the handwritten form, although, as a digital image, it was actually made up of dots and spaces or dashes. A young woman, Sophie Trevitt, who had recently become eligible to vote in

Australian elections, attempted to enrol using the website and a digital pen. Her signature was witnessed by another person who was enrolled. Once all the details, including evidence of her identity in the form of a driver's licence or passport, had been entered, the website generated a document in PDF format which was emailed to an online fax service and faxed to the Australian Electoral Commission. Section 336 of the Electoral Act specifies that any signature on 'electoral paper' must be signed by a person with 'his or her personal signature'. However, as in the Queensland cases, the *Electronic Transactions Act 1999* (Cth) allows electronic signatures to substitute for manuscript signatures, if two criteria are met: firstly, a method is used to identify the person and indicate the person's approval of the information communicated; and secondly, having regard to all the relevant circumstances at the time the method was used, the method was as reliable as was appropriate for the purposes for which the information was communicated.

The Commissioner rejected the electoral application on the grounds that the signature was made up of 'broken lines (or dots and dashes)', that it was highly pixelated, suggesting that this rendered it unreliable, and expressed concern that these features could, if ever necessary, compromise comparison between a handwritten signature on a postal vote and the digital signature on record (par. 16). In providing digital technology that attempts to imitate an analogue form of the signature, Getup had attempted to bridge the legislative requirements, resulting in a legal test case for its application in electoral law, a defining jurisdiction of citizenship. However, the Commissioner's concern about the graphic characteristics of the signature suggests residue attachment to understanding the signature through its manuscript form. In its decision, the court upheld the voter registration, pointing out that it was consistent with previous acceptance of registration on faxes, as scanned PDFs and scanned JPEP files sent by email. In this way, the court recognised the evolution of digital media, whilst also applying the principle of media neutrality. The court clearly recognised the importance of the issue at stake in this case, the democratic right to vote in a federal election, and rejected the perfunctory basis on which it had been denied.

Conclusion

In Western European legal traditions, the signature functions as an identity sign, which, when attached to a legal document, links an individual to the document and may be read to indicate certain conditions, such as understanding, agreement or intention, with potential legal effects. Taking a wide variety of forms, the signature has a longstanding history as a material artefact of Western legal documentary practices. Commonly taken for granted as a necessary feature of legal processes and transactions, the signature has been a ubiquitous presence on legal documents. During the analogue age, legal disputes over signatures often resulted in attention to the form of the signature as the basis for assessing validity and authenticity. However, the shift to the digital age has resulted in new media and modes for the production of signatures that do not result in a traditional handwritten analogue form. As a technology, handwriting is directly performed on the specific medium of paper and is characterised by uniqueness and originality, whereas digital technology functions through repetition and imitation, is not tied to specific media, nor to a particular material presence. To the chagrin of ex-President Trump and his supporters, no evidence of significant election fraud could be established on the basis of voter signatures in the 2020 US election. As the cases in the US and Australia demonstrate, it is not the formal properties of the signature that determine its legal validity, but rather, whether it functionally satisfies the requirements of the given circumstances. When applied to law's documents, the signature is not an inscription, but an act.

Notes

1 *In Re: November 3, 2020 General Election Petition of Kathy Boockvar, Secretary of the Commonwealth of Pennsylvania* No 149 MM 2020 (Saylor, C J, Baer, Todd, Donohue, Dougherty, Wecht, Mundy JJ) 16 October 2020. Litigation occurred in several states, including other swing states Arizona, Florida, Michigan, North Carolina and Wisconsin: see Stanford-MIT Healthy Elections Project, 2020.
2 Pennsylvania Department of State, *Guidance Concerning Examination of Absentee and Mail-In Ballot Return Envelopes* (11 September 2020): https://www.dos.pa.gov/VotingElections/OtherServicesEvents/Documents/Examination%20of%20Absentee%20and%20Mail-In%20Ballot%20Return%20Envelopes.pdf [accessed 28 March 2021].
3 For example, the Corporations (Coronavirus Economic Response) Determination (No 1) 2020 (Cth) (Determination) introduced temporary legislation that expanded the capacity of Australian companies to electronically execute documents using electronic signatures. In some Australian states and Territories, temporary legislation was introduced allowing electronic execution with witnessing by audio visual link of wills, powers of attorney, deeds or agreements, enduring guardianship appointments, affidavits and statutory declarations (e.g. *Stronger Communities Legislation Amendment (Courts and Civil) Act 2020* (NSW)).
4 The Electronic Transactions Amendment (COVID-19 Witnessing of Documents) Regulation 2020 (NSW) amends the *Conveyancing Act 1919* (NSW) permitting a deed to be created in electronic form and electronically signed and attested.
5 I am grateful to Paul Macovaz for research assistance in reading and understanding this text.
6 I have used this framework myself in a previous publication: Luker 2009.
7 Most of Fraenkel's work is published in French only.
8 For an account of these and many other decisions, see Mason 2016.
9 I have discussed this exhibit taking different approaches in previous published work: Luker 2016. See also the podcast *Reading the Signs* [online], History Lab Podcast.

References

Austin, J. L., 1975. *How to do Things with Words* (2nd ed.). Harvard: Harvard University Press.

Brown, Louise, 2013. Why Johnny Can't Sign His Name: Cursive Writing Goes the Way of the Quill. *Toronto Star*, 23 June. Available from: https://www.thestar.com/yourtoronto/education/2013/06/23/why_johnny_cant_sign_his_name_cursive_writing_goes_the_way_of_the_quill.html [Accessed 28 March 2021].

Caplan, Jane, and Torpey, John, 2001. Introduction. *In*: Jane Caplan and John Torpey, eds. *Documenting Individual Identity: State Practices in the Modern World* Princeton, NJ: Princeton University Press, 1–12.

Christensen, Sharon, Duncan, William, and Low, Rouhshi, 2003. The Statue of Frauds in the Digital Age – Maintaining the Integrity of Signatures. *E LAW: Murdoch University Electronic Journal of Law*, 10 (4). Available from: http://classic.austlii.edu.au/au/journals/MurUEJL/2003/ [Accessed 28 March 2021].

Christensen, Sharon, and Low, Rouhshi, 2003. Moving the Statute of Frauds to the Digital Age. *Australian Law Journal*, 77 (7), 416–9.

Clanchy, Michael, 1979. *From Memory to Written Record in England, 1066–1307*. London: Edward Arnold.

Derrida, Jacques, 1982. *Margins of Philosophy*. Translated and with additional notes by Alan Bass. Chicago, IL: The University of Chicago Press.

Ferraris, Maurizio, 2013. *Documentality: Why it is Necessary to Leave Traces*. Translated by Richard Davies. New York: Fordham University Press.

Fraenkel, Béatrice, 1992. *La Signature: Genèse d'un Signe*. Paris: Gallimard.

Fraenkel, Béatrice, 2006. Actes écrits, actes oraux: la performativité à l'épreuve de l'écriture (Written Acts and Speech Acts: performativity and writing practices). *Études de communication langages, information, mediations (Communication Studies: Languages, Information, Mediations)*, 29. Available from: journals.openedition.org/edc/369 [Accessed 28 March 2021].

Fraenkel, Béatrice, 2007. Actes d'écriture: quand écrire c'est faire (Writing Acts: How to Do Things with Writing). *Langage et société*, 121–122 (3), 101–12.

Fraenkel, Béatrice, 2008. La signature: du signe à l'acte ('The Signature: From the Sign to the Act). *Societies & Representations*, 1 (25), 15–23.

Fraenkel, Béatrice, 2012. Writing Acts: When Writing is Doing. *In*: David Barton and Uta Papen, eds. *The Anthropology of Writing: Understanding Textually Mediated Worlds*. London: Bloomsbury Publishing, 33–43.

Hancher, Michael, 1992. The Law of Signatures. *In*: Roberta Kevelson, ed. *Law and Aesthetics*. New York: Peter Lang Publishing.

Harris, Roy, 2005. *Rethinking Writing*. London: Bloomsbury Publishing PLC. Available from: http://ebookcentral.proquest.com/lib/uts/detail.action?docID=436544 [Accessed 28 March 2021].

History Lab Podcast, *Reading the Signs*, season 3, episode 3, released 18 February 2020. Available from: https://historylab.net/s3e3-reading-the-signs/ [Accessed 19 May 2021].

Lauer, Josh, 2007. Traces of the Real: Autographomania and the Cult of the Signers in Nineteenth-Century America. *Text and Performance Quarterly*, 27 (2), 143–63.

Luebke, David, 2004. Signatures and Political Culture in Eighteenth-Century Germany. *The Journal of Modern History*, 76 (3), 497–530.

Luker, Trish, 2009. Reading the Evidentiary Void: The Body at the Scene of Writing. *Griffith Law Review*, 18 (2), 298–312.

Luker, Trish, 2016. Animating the Archive: Artefacts of Law. *In*: Stewart Motha and Honni van Rijswijk, eds. *Law, Memory, Violence: Uncovering the Counter-Archive*. London: Routledge, 70–96.

Mason, Stephen, 2016. *Electronic Signatures in Law* (4th ed.). Cambridge: Cambridge University Press.

McCullagh, Adrian, Little, Peter, and Caelli, William, 1998. Electronic Signatures: Understand the Past to Develop the Future. *University of New South Wales Law Journal*, 21 (2), 452–65.

Ong, Walter, 2002. *Orality and Literacy: The Technologizing of the Word* (2nd ed.) London: Routledge.

Reed, Chris, 2000. What is a Signature? *The Journal of Information, Law and Technology*, 3. Available from: www.elj.warwick.ac.uk/jilt/00-3/reed.html/ [Accessed 28 March 2021].

Smith, Barry, 2012. How to Do Things with Documents. *Rivisti di Estetica*, 50, 179–98.

Smith, Barry, 2014. Document Acts. *In*: Anita Konzelmann-Ziv and Hans Bernard Schmid, eds. *Institutions, Emotions, and Group Agents. Contributions to Social Ontology*. Dordrecht: Springer, 19–31.

Stanford-MIT Healthy Elections Project, 2020. Behind the Scenes of Mail Voting: The Rules and Procedures for Signature Verification in the 2020 General Election. Available from: https://healthyelections.org/sites/default/files/2020-10/Signature_Verification_0.pdf [Accessed 28 March 2021].

Van Troon, Penny, 2006. *Writing Never Arrives Naked: Early Aboriginal cultures of writing in Australia*. Canberra: Aboriginal Studies Press.

Vismann, Cornelia, 2008. *Files: Law and media technology*. Stanford: Stanford University Press.

Weber, Dane, 2015. Tech Neutrality in Australian Signature Law. *Griffith Law School Research Paper*, No. 17-10, 24 (1). Available from: www.ssrn.com/abstract=2929147 [Accessed 28 March 2021].

Cases

Australia

Campbell v Director of Prosecutions for the Commonwealth of Australia [1995] 2 VR 654

Cubillo v Commonwealth [2000] FCA 1084

Deputy Commissioner of Taxation (Vic) v Boxshall (1988) 83 ALR 175

Deputy Commissioner of Taxation v Brilliant Homes Management Pty Ltd [2011] FCA 1539

Druin Pty Ltd ATF the Druin (No. 3) Trust (t/as Harvey Norman Commercial Division) v Corbin BC201403296 [2014] NSWSC 510

Getup Ltd v Electoral Commissioner (2010) 268 ALR 797

Harding v Brisbane City Council [2009] QPELR 207

R v Moore; Ex Parte Myers (1884) 10 VLR 322

Re Deleso (1978) 24 ALR 701

Stellard Pty Ltd v North Queensland Fuel Pty Ltd (BC201503878) [2015] QSC 119

The Estate of Robin Michael (deceased) [2016] SASC 164

United States

In Re: November 3, 2020 General Election Petition of Kathy Boockvar, Secretary of the Commonwealth of Pennsylvania No. 149 MM 2020

Chapter 9

Treaty documents

Materialising international legal agreement

Jessie Hohmann

Introduction

In May 2019, the Vienna Convention on the Law of Treaties (VCLT) was feted at a 50th birthday celebration at the United Nations in New York. Amid the speeches and other official proceedings, the treaty was exhibited in a glass cabinet: a thick stack of papers, loosely bound within a dark cover, four sets of holes punched at the left, with muted blue cord running through two of them. It was prominently and reverently displayed where the representatives of states, treaty law experts and the pilgrims of international law could come to see the original text—typewritten in a font and format familiar to any reader of United Nations (UN) documents (the UN strictly controlling font use (United Nations n.d. a; United Nations Editorial Manual 1983)). Attendees pronounced the treaty the guest of honour, and described 'folks literally lining up to get a photo taken with the VCLT' (Hollis 2019a, 2019b). The Vienna Convention codifies the international law on treaties, in a treaty. It thus occupies a special and preeminent place among the 70,000 or so treaties currently registered with the United Nations (United Nations n.d. b). As the treaty on treaties, the VCLT carries layers of symbolism, as treaties themselves are already preeminent artefacts in international law; 'associated with history-changing moments', treaties epitomise 'progress, peace, history, prosperity, human dignity, order, unity, systematicity, and disciplinary identity' (d'Aspremont 2020, 46; see also Hollis 2006, 3).

According to international law, however, the essence of a treaty consists not in any record, document or other tangible form; rather, the treaty rests in the *agreement* between parties. The celebrity of the VCLT as a material artefact sits oddly against this doctrine. Yet the attention lavished on the document signals the important role of the material in the law. These material objects—treaty documents—manifest and embody law, and legal relations and intentions precede their creation, as well as infusing their forms. They have not only legal but political functions, and their forms reflect struggles between the parties for hierarchy, control and power at the time of their negotiation and conclusion. In addition, the material forms of treaties serve both symbolic and very

DOI: 10.4324/9781003247593-12

practical functions—whether evidentiary or doctrinal—in ongoing disputes about rights, status and sovereignty for their signatories or those made subject to them.

This chapter reflects on the relationship between treaties and their documented form, across a range of their manifestations. After setting out some thoughts on the interplay of form and intention, I then turn to focus on three examples of treaty forms. First, colonial treaties in the 'scramble for Africa', where European powers purported to 'carve up' Africa between them, with treaties as important proof of their claims. Second, treaties recorded in Wampum, the diplomatic technology of Indigenous Peoples on the east coast of North America. Third, the modern multilateral treaty. In doing so, the chapter shines a light on what these material forms of law show us within the frame of international law.

The interplay of form and intention

A treaty is an agreement between international entities that binds their conduct towards each other, governed by international law. Treaties have an important status: they are 'the founding documents of most of the regimes and institutions which constitute the international legal order' and as such, as d'Aspremont (2020, 46) notes, occupy a special space in that order, as well 'as in the consciousness and imagination of international lawyers'. Their negotiation may stretch over years, and their final conclusion be marked by 'elaborate protocol and the heaviest symbolism' (Keene 2012, 475). For instance, in the negotiations leading to the signing of the Treaty of Versailles, which codified the terms of the peace between the winners and losers after World War I, the representatives of the defeated powers were not permitted to sit at the negotiating table. At the signing of the terms of the peace itself, the German delegate caused affront by declining to rise to his feet during his speech (Frazer 1919, 111). More recently, when the Paris Climate Agreement was concluded in 2015, the moment was marked by the banging of a small, green, climate-friendly and leaf-shaped gavel, emblazoned with the logo of the conference of the parties (Goldenberg et al. 2015). Despite d'Aspremont's reference to documents, however, according to international law the essence of a treaty consists not in any record, document or other tangible form; rather, the treaty rests in the *agreement* between parties. And agreement can be expressed in many ways, some of which are immaterial or ephemeral, for example, the spoken word, the handshake, the exchange of ritual gifts which are consumed or used up in the ceremony (see further Calloway 2013, Chapter 3; see more generally Welch, 2017).

When a treaty is recorded in a written document, the question of whether or not the text encapsulates intention is the subject of much debate in international legal practice and scholarship (Fitzmaurice 2006, 198–204). In disputes over a treaty, the argument will turn on what the parties intended (VCLT Art

31–33).[1] While words written on a treaty document will no doubt be mobilised to support a party's position, the document itself is not the treaty, since the treaty lies in the agreement, and the written words are only evidence of it (United Nations International Law Commission 1950, para 30; Fitzmaurice 1958, 158). It is clear, though, that for those concluding treaties, the material document is generally not an afterthought or merely a convenient way to record the agreement for posterity. Many treaties have a distinctive material manifestation. They appear made for presentation, with striking calligraphy, ribbons or tape and colourful seals. In the past, thought was given to the quality of the paper or vellum, not only on which the treaty's articles were recorded, but also for letters of ratification (Sowerby 2019, 204). Many are bound into large volumes, such as the Vienna Convention on the Law of Treaties. Often, they are stored carefully in their own special boxes, like the 1918 peace Treaty of Brest-Litovsk, between the Bolshevik government of Russia and the Central Powers (the German Empire, Austria-Hungary, Bulgaria and the Ottoman Empire), that ended Russia's participation in the First World War (see Figure 9.1). While even recent treaties often look old-fashioned, given the sovereign paraphernalia attached, some treaty documents deliberately signal modernity in their forms. This is the case for the typewritten text of Western Treaty 8, concluded in 1899 between the Crown and the Indigenous Peoples

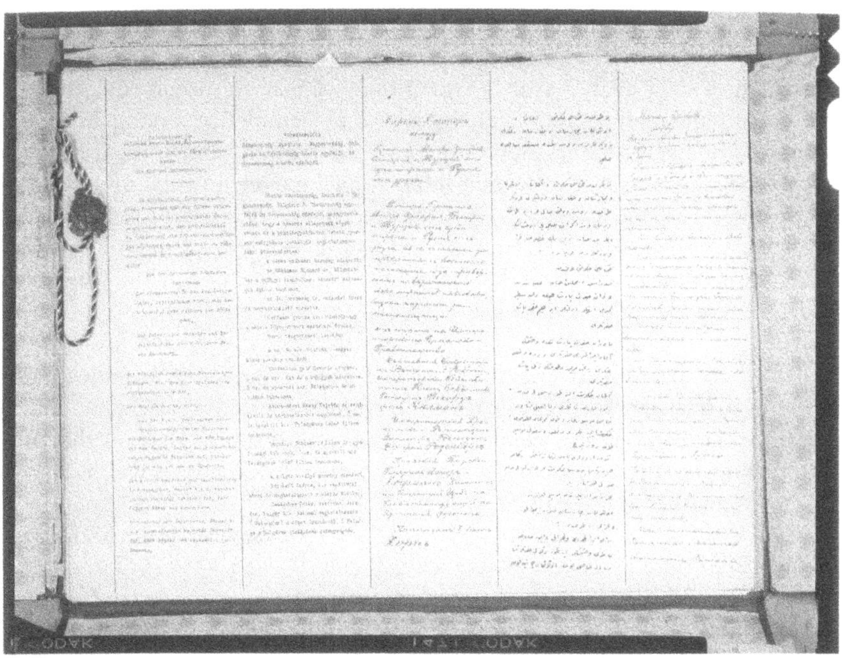

Figure 9.1 Treaty of Brest-Litovsk.

of what is now Northern Alberta, British Columbia and Canada's Northwest Territories (Hohmann 2018). Similarly, the pre-printed treaties used by the British in the 'scramble for Africa': these were not just instruments to acquire and implement rights. The 'civilizing mission' was arguably 'accomplished on the face of these documents' which self-consciously embodied modernity and bureaucratic technology (Harris 2020, 3).

Although lawyers seldom remark upon it, much care and attention are given to treaties' materiality. A treaty may, as a matter of law, *require* a material form. For example, when the United Kingdom ratifies a treaty, it must be 'signed by the Sovereign and sealed with the Great Seal' (Roberts 2019, 630): the seal must find a material surface on which to be embossed. Each country has a specific ratification practice, often highly dependent on documents of certain forms, deposited with certain agencies, in certain specific ways (see for example, Republic of South Africa n.d., detailing the process in South Africa). In modern practice, instruments of ratification, that is, documents, must be lodged with the repository state or international organisation (United Nations Charter Art. 102; United Nations 2012, 3). Moreover, treaties are important historical artefacts, and carry symbolic weight: at its 50th anniversary celebrations, the VCLT was described as 'a cornerstone of multilateralism'; as 'an essential framework for international relations, and for the rules-based international order'; and as a symbol 'of the universality of international law' (Espinosa Garces 2019). And indeed, much symbolism arguably rests in the material form which records the agreement. States have certainly felt this to be the case: writing in 1897, Francois Stewart Jones described the delicate matter of precedence of signatures on a treaty—that is, which state's signature should come first on the document, in recognition of the state's pre-eminence among European polities. This issue was 'a source of much contention, and sometimes even placed the adjustment of important international matters in jeopardy' (Stewart Jones 1897, 424; see Welch 2017, 3 on precedence of states in early modern Europe more generally). To 'put an end to this element of discord' Stewart Jones tells us, 'the principle of the *alternat* was finally introduced' (Stewart Jones 1897, 424). The use of *alternat* was

> the right of each sovereign or head of a government to have his name appear first in the counterpart of the treaty which he is to retain, and to have the name of his plenipotentiary occupy the first place in the enumeration of the negotiators at the head of that document, as well as among the signatures at the end.
>
> (Stewart Jones 1897, 424)

Nevertheless, the actual application of *alternat* still left plenty of room for states to assert their supposed superiority. As Stewart Jones notes, within Europe, the Holy Roman Empire was long 'recognized as first in dignity' and signed even over the *French* princes, but Great Britain held out longest of all European states against the United States, finally acceding to the *alternat* in an 1815 treaty to regulate commerce and navigation (Stewart Jones 1897, 425).

The value of treaties as historical documents is illustrated by the care taken to preserve them—and the originals are handled metaphorically, and sometimes literally—with gloves. While the Tartu Peace Treaty of 1920, through which the state of Estonia was birthed, is shown with the museum gloves with which it would be handled (Varrak 2017), the Canadian government jealously guards the fragile historical treaties with Canada's Indigenous Peoples, which form an important foundation for the Canadian state. Now, only the digital documents can be studied, in order to preserve the brittle originals. Who can now touch the document, to feel the thin paper, or smell the last traces of ink? Digitisation may protect the historical record, and make these treaty documents accessible to all with an internet connection, but it also asserts the state's control over these artefacts, and thus over the still contested historical record of treaty making in Canada (see Treaty 7 Elders et al. 1996; Hohmann 2018; see more generally Campos 2014). In the face of the significance of these treaties' material forms, the question of agreement and intention is very much alive. With respect to Western Treaty 8, the Indigenous signatories continue to resist the state's interpretation of the agreement, and the reduction of its terms to the documented, type-written, text (Hohmann 2018). The Tartu Peace Treaty, which is referred to as Estonia's 'birth certificate', is also mobilised to contest current legal and political developments, a symbolic as well as legal document that speaks to the founding of the nation, and can be used to question or bolster present governments' care of and commitment to the Estonian state (Medijainen 2010, 202; Varrak 2017). These examples serve to introduce the complex interplay of materiality and intention at play in the conclusion of treaties, in their subsequent political and legal lives and in their symbolic status.

I turn now to concentrate more fully on the material forms of three particular treaty types. The first are colonial treaties concluded in the European 'scramble for Africa' which sought to gain control of land, resources or rights of access, often in the barest of articles, or using standard form templates. The second are treaties which are recorded in other material forms—forms that Eurocentric eyes would not easily recognise as documents (even if the present volume significantly complicates our understanding of documents): here I will concentrate on treaties recorded in Wampum—strings or belts of beads, which were an important diplomatic technology of the East Coast First Nations in what is now North America. Finally, I will turn to modern multilateral treaties, such as the VCLT discussed above. The chapter considers the often-ignored interplay between intention and the material in treaty making, and foregrounds the way treaty forms embody and make law manifest.

Treaties and their materiality—three examples

Colonial treaties: standard forms and ad-hoc scrawls, which 'in a couple of articles must grant us everything'

During the late 1800s, European states engaged in a period of imperial expansion in Africa. This 'scramble for Africa', when European powers purported to claim and 'carve up' the continent amongst themselves, was accompanied by a notable spike in treaty making (Keene 2012, 481). Although it is clear that African peoples had long engaged in treaty making practices both with European states and amongst themselves (Smith 1973; Sahli and El Ouazzani 2012, 398–404), treaties in the 'scramble for Africa' were different in that they purported to extinguish the sovereignty over territory of the African signatory. Sir Fredrick Lugard, British explorer, mercenary, treaty maker (and in later life, international legal figure),[2] described the treaties being 'produced in cartloads' (Lugard 1926, 15). Discussing these treaty making practices, Lugard wrote in the pages of the *Geographical Journal* that 'I have known a valuable concession purchased by the present of an old pair of boots' (Lugard 1893, 53).

The most well-known of the European treaty making parties adventuring in Africa at the time was headed by Henry Morton Stanley, who followed instructions to conclude treaties that must 'in a couple of articles … grant us everything' (Maurice 1957, 161). Stanley was in the employ of the infamous King Leopold II of Belgium, whose personal rule of the Congo Free State from 1884 to 1908 was an 'unprecedented system of wealth extraction and servitude' based on the forced labour of the population (Martineau 2018, 185; see also Ascherson 1964). Beheadings, floggings and the severing of hands were widespread and applied so ruthlessly as to prompt other contemporary European powers to investigate and press for the removal of Leopold's personal control (Casement 1904; Ascherson 1964), though, as Martineau (2018, 186) notes 'the colonizing enterprise of the Congo Basin was, in and of itself, never questioned'.

The surge in treaty making in the scramble for Africa prompted quick, standard-form treaties: fill-in-the blank documents, with spaces left to write the names of the parties, the boundaries of the territories claimed and the place of the treaty's conclusion; but with standard articles already drafted.[3] These were used by British trading companies, at times by Stanley and by other European treaty parties (Surun 2014, 191). Standard form treaties suited situations where junior agents (who had neither experience nor the confidence of their foreign ministries to negotiate further) were sent far from colonial outposts, in haste and in potential competition with the agents of other European powers or trading companies, to claim territory (Harris 2020, 5). As Harris (2020, 3) writes, 'the very act of using a pre-printed treaty meant that terms were unilaterally drafted by Europeans and presented by them to their counterparties in a physical form that spoke of pre-determination, regularity, and rationality'. These implications were understood at the time, and standard forms were spurned by some, such as Lugard, on the basis that they were inadequate to constitute an actual agreement (Surun 2014, 209). Accordingly, some treaties were simply ad-hoc documents prepared on the spot, a few scrawled articles setting sweeping terms. (Surun 2014, 209; see also Aalberts 2018a, 454, figure 33.1).

Whether or not these instruments constituted agreements in any sense—that is, whether the two parties could have had a shared understanding of what was transpiring, or have freely consented—continues to be debated, with some in favour (see Mugambwa 1987; Hebie 2015, 27-29). Others, however, reject the possibility of real consent to alienate land or sovereignty in the colonial treaty making process (see Watson 2014, 155). The question of whether any such understanding could amount to a valid treaty under European understandings of international law also remains a live one, with continuing impacts including very real loss of sovereign and territorial rights (see for example, Mugambwa 1987; United Nations Commission on Human Rights 1992, 1995, 1999; Hebie 2015).

European states referred to these documents as treaties at the time of their conclusion, and treated them as having full legal effect (see for example, Keene 2012, 484) particularly to found claims against other European powers (Hebie 2015, 27–28). African signatories at times strongly contested the treaties, including their individual terms, and prepared written translations of the texts in Arabic and local languages, which were duly signed by both parties (Touval 1966; Hebie 2015, 27–28; Shumway 2015). Nevertheless, it is generally conceded that in many cases, the primary audience for the document—those scraps of paper marked by the confident scrawls of Stanley and his ilk and the unpractised crosses of the African signatories—was not the African peoples, but other European powers (Mugambwa 1987, 82–84). These treaties arguably operated not as records of agreement between the two parties, but as evidence of the control of territory, trade and goods, to *other* European powers, to exclude their competing claims. 'From this perspective', as Surun (2014, 209) writes, 'the treaties constitute so many performative utterances, whose accumulation established a kind of empire of paper' for the European signatories.[4]

The proper paper form was insisted upon.[5] Harris (2020, 18), for example, notes an instance where the failure to use the standard form prompted the British Foreign Office to send instructions that the treaty must be redone. But these papers operated with hard effects on the ground. Harris (2020, 18) writes that, meanwhile,

> the British claim to this territory was resolved (at least vis-à-vis the other European powers) by typically negotiated chancery-chancery treaties with the Germans and Leopold's Congo Free State. But in the meantime, Africans had been required to ratify what they had already agreed to in order to meet the requirements of the British legal machine.

Subsequently, the contemporary legal order has accepted even the most patently exploitative treaties, such as those where African peoples exchanged their sovereignty for 20 bolts of cloth. Most of Africa was deemed under international law as *terra nullius*—no one's land—inhabited only by people so primitive that they did not count: they had no sovereignty to cede, no laws, no legal personality in international law, and could not be seen as having the capacity to enter into international treaties. The 'standard of civilisation' in nineteenth-century international law drew the boundary 'between European states as the Family of Nations on the one hand, and barbarian nations and savage entities, on the other [who] ... lacked any status, rights, and duties within the international legal order' (Aalberts 2018a, 456). Even though international law has since recognised, at least in some instances, that Africa was not a *terra nullius*, it has nonetheless confirmed the legal validity of African treaties—notably in the still contested Western Sahara—as between the European signatories (Western Sahara Ad. Op ICJ Rep 80 [1975]). Yet the material forms of these treaties trouble the confident dismissal of the African signatories, and the consequent attempt to erase African sovereignty. As Aalberts (2018a, 455) has argued, the treaties, and particularly the African 'signatures—or rather marks or crosses' appear at first sight to embody the standard of civilization, with the flamboyant European signature juxtaposed with the wobbly, unpractised cross. But they 'embody at the same time the condition of possibility of the nineteenth-century international legal order, and undermine its defining framework and thus constitute its condition of impossibility'. She goes on to argue that:

> While the treaties provided proper legal title to the colonial enterprise, in line with legal positivist doctrine, they also implied a status of the chiefs that – according to the same doctrine – these savage rulers could not have. The very 'cross' by which they at once officially ceded their sovereignty to the colonial powers also implied they had the legal status as sovereigns to do so. After all, the right to enter into international treaties – including ones that restrict sovereign power – is an attribute of state sovereignty.
>
> (Aalberts 2018a, 459)

The signature, as Aalberts (2018b, 878) notes, showed the Indigenous party as a 'subject and an object through the same strike of the pen' (see also Surun 2014, 190), thus both insider and outsider, always present at the foundational moment of the European claim, and always there materialised on the treaty document—to this day—to trouble the claims of European states, their role in colonisation and international law's ongoing failures in meaningful decolonisation.

Treaties without documents: wampum and Indigenous treaties in North America

With the essence of a treaty existing in the agreement between the parties, a treaty with no document is just as much a treaty as one recorded on the most sumptuous of vellums. Yet treaty records in forms other than words on paper (or similar media such as parchment) also inform our understanding of what a document is. This is notably the case for treaties recorded in wampum, a communication technology of the First Nations in the eastern parts of what are now Canada and the United States. Wampum belts are a longstanding and important element of North American Indigenous Peoples' diplomacy, both between Indigenous Peoples and western nations, and among Indigenous Peoples themselves (Two Row Wampum Renewal Campaign n.d.; Jacobs 1949; Jennings et al. 1995). Wampum itself refers to small white and purple beads, fashioned laboriously from shell, which have been used by Indigenous Peoples on the east coast of Turtle Island (now North America) for over a thousand years (Jacobs 1949, 597; Haas 2007, 78). The beads are threaded onto skins, which are made into collars and girdles, as well as belts. The belts were used in ceremonies and to record important events, not only treaties but marriages, for example (Haas 2007, 78).

The exchange of wampum was an important, often essential, condition of any treaty agreement. Wampum signified the undertaking of obligation and the wampum belt formed the record of agreement (Borrows 2005, 161–162; Calloway 2013, 27).[6] The British Crown unquestionably understood wampum as treaty making: for example, the 1764 Treaty of Niagara, which brought the Crown within the already existing web of treaty relationships among the First Nations of Turtle Island, was not given written form, though it gave effect to the written text of the Royal Proclamation of 1763. It was solemnified with the giving and receiving of wampum on both sides but no written treaty text was concluded at the time (Hewitt 2021; Coyle 2007, n14).[7] When asserting their treaty rights against the state, Indigenous Peoples who produced wampum belts often relied on them, presenting them to Crown or legal officials and explaining the terms as expressed in the belt (Renard Painter 2017; Hale 1897). Indeed, Indigenous Peoples continue to do so today (The Two Row Wampum Renewal Campaign n.d.). But how do the material records—the treaty objects—add to our understanding of the law they purport to create and govern? From the perspective of the European law of nations, the wampum belt is a non-legal artefact. No matter how important on the ground, and how central to treaty negotiations, once the treaty was concluded (where it was, at least, recognised that wampum was a necessary accoutrement of negotiations), the wampum belt ceased to have any objectivity in law. This is perhaps not surprising, given that the nations who had created the wampum belt were themselves to become mere objects of law, not regarded as sovereign subjects (see Figure 9.2).

In the 1990s, Miguel Alfonso Martínez, the then-United Nations Special Rapporteur on Treaties, Agreements and Other Constructive Arrangements between States and Indigenous Populations, submitted a series of reports to the United Nations in which he noted that many agreements between European states and Indigenous polities should be considered valid treaties (United

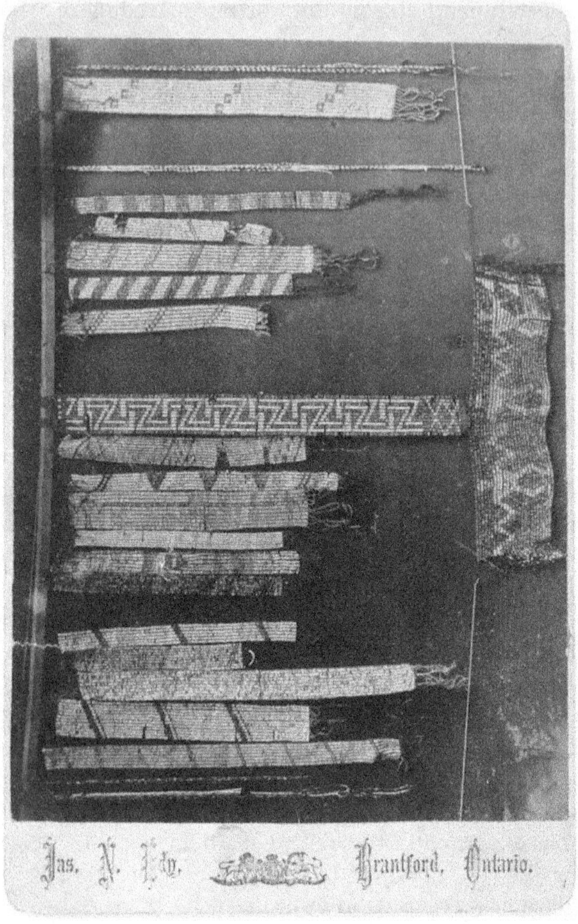

Figure 9.2 Wampum belts and strings preserved by the Six Nations in the 1870s (Library and Archives Canada MIKAN 3367331).

Nations Commission on Human Rights 1992; 1995; 1999). He wrote, nevertheless, of the problem of

> the absence of an 'indigenous version' of these instruments, or the fact that, if such a version exists, it is not deposited with the competent official agencies of the nation-State concerned in the appropriate historical archives, nor does it appear in the treaty series published by the non-indigenous academy.
>
> (United Nations Commission on Human Rights 1995, [149])

Identifying this problem illustrates the centrality that written forms have taken: such that they can be deposited in the 'appropriate' historical archives and published in the relevant books. Yet, as objects, wampum belts exist independently and continue to trouble the state's assertions to sovereign control, and the smooth presentation of Euro-Canadian law's wholeness. In 1923, the Royal Canadian Mounted Police invaded and occupied the Six Nations' Grand River Reserve. The police forcibly removed the wampum belts cataloguing and recording the history of the Haudenosaunee confederation and its diplomatic relations were confiscated (Renard Painter 2017).[8] The authorities' unease with the existence of these Indigenous records of governance and diplomacy points to their latent animate power—their ability to recall and communicate their own history and to make claims on the future (Bruchac 2018, 69–70)—even as they were denied any relevance as legal or historical records, and reduced to art objects and anthropological curios (Hale 1897; Bruchac 2018, 69–70; Hewitt 2021). The anxiety evident in the police raids, and the wider outlawing of rituals and ceremonies such as, on the West Coast, the Potlatch (Mathias and Yabsley 1991), show how such objects can undermine the state's legal foundations, at the same time as they can be used to support them, existing in uneasy relationship with state understandings—or assertions—of treaty agreements.

Interestingly, where European historians have concentrated on the place of wampum belts in treaty negotiations, they have often equated First Nations' reliance on them to the reading of a text. For example, at a treaty council in 1753, Calloway writes, the Indigenous nation explained a delay in beginning the proceedings because the Indigenous nation had mislaid some wampum strings. Calloway (2013, 27) writes that it 'was almost as if the Indians had misplaced the notes for a speech'. Other accounts recall that a speaker would often turn to consult the wampum belt while giving a speech (Calloway 2013, 27). In 1897, the anthropologist Horatio Hale (1897, 247), writing in the *Journal of the Anthropological Institute of Great Britain and Ireland*, characterised wampum as 'a literature of aboriginal diplomatic records'. At the same time, historians have noted that scribes recording the treaty negotiations in North America took little notice of the details of wampum belts exchanged, concentrating instead on the oratory between the parties, and in particular on the rhetorical skills of Indigenous negotiators (Muller 2007, 136). In doing so, they concentrated on and helped to create a picture of Indigenous Peoples as oral cultures in the European historical record.

Yet wampum is a sophisticated information communication technology, of 'economic, social, political, and ideational complexity' (Ceci 1982, 99). It is significant that wampum can be understood as an information storage and retrieval technology similar to that undergirding the digitisation of information. Angela Haas (2007, 77) has noted that the wampum belt is a hypertextual technology which, as such, has 'extended human memories of inherited knowledges through interconnected, nonlinear designs and associative storage and retrieval methods'. She argues that wampum approximates the binary technology used in computer programming, and is a no less sophisticated form of communication.

International and Euro-Canadian law has consistently excluded the relevance of any wampum belt to an interpretation of the Royal Proclamation, relying only on the European text of the Royal Proclamation to found legal authority.[9] Obviously, as Martínez noted in respect of Indigenous versions of treaties, things not written down cannot be filed away in the states' archives or official record-keeping repositories (United Nations Commission on Human Rights, 1995, [149]). Accordingly, these objects have been, quite literally, written out of the historical record. The paper records crowd the imagined and real spaces of the archive, leaving no space for the physical presence of other treaty forms. Yet it is significant that the digitisation of images of objects makes new space in these archives for objects, rendered into two dimensions, and new technologies can then also remake these objects into 3D projections or 3D printed artefacts, on our personal computer screens or in our homes.

The binary language of the wampum record opens up the role that the digital plays in troubling our understanding of (legal) documents more broadly. Wampum as hypertext—with its binaries of purple and white; the zeros and ones—and European (here specifically Canadian) law's difficulty with understanding it as legal text, prefigure the difficulty of rendering the concept of the document forward into the digital age.[10] Thus wampum is a binary information technology, one that predates the current debates over the digitisation of documents, and what impact this has on their status as legal documents. But the failure of courts to be able to acknowledge wampum as a legal document might have lessons for broader struggles in the legal understanding of digitised documents.

Modern multilateral treaties: symbols of a rule-based multilateral international order

Multilateral treaties are an ancient tool of international diplomacy, but it was only in 1815 that multilateral treaties as we now understand them—a single legal instrument that binds all parties under the same terms—emerged into international law (Reuter, Law of Treaties 5 (cited in Keene 2012)). In fact, despite their centrality to post-1945 international law under the United Nations, multilateral treaties are still an exceptional way for states to make agreements, as opposed to the ordinary daily business of bilateral activity (Hollis 2006). They carry heavy symbolism in a contemporary international law based, in theory, on the sovereign equality of states: they represent participation as equals in the rules of the international order. For instance, at its 50th anniversary celebrations, the VCLT was described as 'a cornerstone of multilateralism'; as 'an essential framework for international relations, and for the rules-based international order' and as a symbol 'of the universality of international law' (Espinosa Garces 2019).

The material forms of modern multilateral treaties bear the traits of this universality, as well as calling it into question by pointing to the dominance of European forms and processes. As a legal requirement under Article 102 of the United Nations Charter, a treaty must be registered, at least if the parties will seek to invoke it before any organ of the UN (United Nations Charter Art 102(1) and (2)). This requirement has, alongside its aims of transparency in international relations (Donaldson 2017), pushed states further toward documenting treaties in written form. Donaldson (2017, 616) notes that the *form* of agreements between governments has had an impact on their legal character, noting 'the ubiquity of legal forms', where, 'even where parties considered themselves to be making, at best, a "non-binding agreement," they drifted by habit and training into forms characteristic of a treaty'.

All treaties registered with the UN are collected into the UN Treaty Series—bound volumes strongly resembling court reports. An interested reader can now find the digitised version of certified true copies of each treaty registered under the UN, arranged by subject matter under 29 chapter headings, including 'Pacific Settlement of International Disputes' (Chapter II), 'Narcotic Drugs and Psychotropic Substances' (Chapter VI), 'Navigation' (Chapter XII) and 'Fiscal Matters' (Chapter XXVIII) in the United Nations Treaty Collection (United Nations n.d. b). The documents are not completely standard in their online presentation. Some include a cover page with a bar code and file name before the scanned treaty text. They must, in the case of multilateral treaties, include the treaty text in all official UN languages (Chinese, Spanish, English, Russian, Arabic and French), and the depositing parties must supply both a hard copy and electronic version of the treaty (United Nations 2012, 35). Some of the older records are inexpertly scanned in their digital lives—some slightly wonky, or with traces of characters having bled through from the other side of the original. A treaty will not be registered if it is not complete, thus parties must also provide 'a copy of all enclosures, such as protocols, exchanges of notes, authentic texts, annexes, etc.' (United Nations 2012, 35). The treaty, the UN Handbook reminds us, may not be reproduced in any single document but made up of a collection of adhesions, accessions, letters of ratification or even unilateral declarations (United Nations 2012, 35). If 'important "political" clauses would be in the principal text, and signed by more senior figures or with greater solemnity' as Donaldson (2017, 580–581) writes, 'more trivial or detailed clauses could be relegated to an ancillary text, sometimes signed separately by lesser figures (without necessarily implying any lesser degree of legal force)'. The language of 'enclosures' and 'adhesions' also points to the materiality of the treaties, as well as to their existence as bounded entities: they are held together into one legal object, rather than existing as a dispersed set of objects that refer or gesture to each other. At the same time, the legal character of the relations undertaken in multilateral treaty making pulls against any coherent understanding of the treaty document as one thing. As states can enter reservations to a treaty (see VCLT Art 2, 19–21; Swaine 2020, 285), the actual obligations existing between them in fact may render the treaty a honeycomb of different obligations, rather than a solid mass of law. The parties' undertakings *vis à vis* each other will only be evident with reference to the specific reservations and interpretive statements made between them (VCLT Art 2, 19–21; Swaine 2020, 285).

If no particular form determines the existence of a treaty, why do modern multilateral treaties look so alike? For there is a striking similarity to the treaties' presentation, from the black-bordered, UN-logoed title page, to the use of a standard font. The first, and most obvious, reason for this uniformity is that the UN Treaty Handbook itself provides standard forms—or model instruments—for treaty making. These fill-in-the-blank documents are included in annexes to the handbook for the convenience of any diplomat or treaty technocrat, and uncannily recall the standard form treaties concluded in the European 'scramble for Africa' discussed above. These forms must also be read in light of the UN's deeper obsessions with *form*, which encompass strict conventions and explicit rules governing font, grammar and use of italics, and use of the UN Logo (see United Nations n. d. b; United Nations 1983; Roele, 2015).

But there are other factors at play: as Vaughan Lowe (2007, 22), a previous Chichele Chair of Public International Law at the University of Oxford, wrote, those who make treaties set about this activity 'according to a style so homogenous as to delight the drafter of a medieval book of court forms'. After all, he notes, they

> are trained in the lawyer's and diplomat's arts, often in one of a handful of universities in Europe or North America; dispatched to international conferences and organizations, where they meet others who have read the same books, the same law reports and treaties and are perhaps alumni of the same university
>
> (Lowe 2007, 22)

Despite the six official languages of the UN, and the principle of the sovereign equality of states, the form of multilateral treaties carries the echoes of European international law, in its dominance by western institutions, forms and education. The 'diplomatic craft of drafting' (Donaldson 2017, 580) bears the marks of its guild.

Conclusion

The relationship between a treaty and its record in a document is multifaceted and far from straightforward. Although no material form is required to constitute a treaty, the material forms of treaties are highly illuminating. They illustrate the importance of moments of agreement in international law; they symbolise multilateralism and the peaceful ordering of international relations.

Yet at the same time they materialise struggles for power and pre-eminence amongst states. Tensions are revealed as treaties, and the law underpinning them, attempt to assimilate or knit-up international legal entities within the conventions and norms of European-dominated international law. As the example of wampum demonstrates, this is sometimes unsuccessful, with other treaty forms remaining to underpin other understandings of the treaty relationship, and to serve as material nodes of resistance. The material forms of treaties also illustrate the influence of European legal processes, ideas and forms on international law—from the dominance of a small club of similarly educated and experienced statesmen (and now sometimes women) to the very fact of treaty documents as words on paper (or parchment and vellum). And yet other treaty forms—such as treaties recorded in wampum—point to the challenges, as well as the opportunities, that digital technologies bring for reimagining our understanding of the document itself.

Legal arguments will disavow the treaty document's status as law, but the material forms of treaties cannot be dismissed entirely: they are preeminent legal artefacts, potent symbols of power, and resistance, in the international order. International lawyers might dismiss the form of a treaty as irrelevant to legal argument. Yet we can still find them clustered around a glass box, displayed in a room at the United Nations. Like reverent pilgrims or excited fans, they come to see, to almost touch, to bask in the aura of the law made manifest before them.

Notes

1 Note that, according to Article 1(a) the VCLT governs only written treaties, although, as its principles reflect customary international law for treaty interpretation, they can apply also to disputes over unwritten treaties.

2 Between 1922 and 1936, Lugard was the British representative on the League of Nations' Permanent Mandates Commission. His publications on international law include *The Dual Mandate in British Tropical Africa* (1926).

3 See for example, the treaty between the 'Jakri' and the British in 1884, reproduced in Harris (2020, 13).

4 For further discussion of the signature see Luker, this volume.

5 For a further discussion of the form of documents, see Biber, this volume.

6 For further discussion of the wampum and their use in Haudenosaunee diplomacy see Jennings et al. (1995); Borrows (1997); Tidridge (2015). For further discussion of the materiality of treaties and their ability to prompt new understandings and conversations about international law through art, law and object, see Buchanan and Hewitt (2018).

7 Notably, the commitments undertaken in the treaty of Niagara were given domestic legal recognition in Chippewas of Sarnia Band v. Canada (A.G.) (2000), 51 O.R. (3d) 641 at paras. 19–21.

8 These forced confiscations can be contrasted with the designation (albeit problematic and subsequently abused), south of the border, of the State of New York as the *Ho-sen-na-ge-tah* (official wampum keeper) by the Onondaga Chiefs, in order to prevent further thefts and losses of their diplomatic records. See New York State Indian Law § 27, NY L.1899, c. 150; amended L.1971, c. 960, eff. June 25, 1971; repealed 1992) and the discussion in Burchac 2018.

9 See St Catherines Milling and Lumber Co v the Queen (1888) 14 AC 46 (PC); R v Tennisco (1986).
10 See Biber, this volume.

References

Aalberts, Tanja, 2018a. Sovereign Marks. *In*: Jessie Hohmann and Joyce Daniel, eds. *International Law's Objects*. Oxford: Oxford University Press, 453–62.

Aalberts, Tanja, 2018b. Misrecognition in Legal Practice: The Aporia of the Family of Nations. *Review of International Studies*, 44 (5), 863–81.

Ascherson, Neal, 1964. *The King Incorporated: Leopold II in the Age of Trusts*. Belgium: Doubleday.

Borrows, John, 2005. Creating an Indigenous Legal Community: 5th Annual John Tait Memorial Lecture. *McGill Law Journal*, 50 (3), 153–79.

Borrows, John, 1997. Wampum at Niagara: The Royal Proclamation, Canadian Legal History, and Self-Government. *In*: Michael Asch, ed. *Aboriginal and Treaty Rights in Canada: Essays on Law, Equity and Respect for Difference*. Vancouver: UBC Press.

Bruchac, Margaret M., 2018. Broken Chains of Custody: Possessing, Dispossessing, and Repossessing Lost Wampum Belts. *Proceedings of the American Philosophical Society*, 162 (1), 56–105.

Buchanan, Ruth, and Hewitt, Jeffery, 2018. Treaty Canoe. *In*: Jessie Hohmann and Daniel Joyce, eds. *International Law's Objects*. Oxford: Oxford University Press, 491–503.

Calloway, Colin G., 2013. *Pen and Ink Witchcraft: Treaties and Treaty Making in American Indian History*. New York: Oxford University Press.

Campos, Luis Roberto, 2014. *Archiving Memory: Explorer and Trader Accounts as Evidence in Aboriginal Rights and Title Litigation*. Thesis (SJD). University of Toronto. Available from: https://tspace.library.utoronto.ca/bitstream/1807/68197/1/Campos_Luis_R_201411_SJD_thesis.pdf [Accessed 20 June 2020].

Casement, Roger, 1904. *Correspondence and Report from His Majesty's Consul at Boma Respecting the Administration of the Independent State of the Congo: Presented to both Houses of Parliament by Command of His Majesty, February 1904*. London: Harrison and Sons.

Ceci, Lynn, 1982. The Value of Wampum among the New York Iroquois: A Case Study in Artifact Analysis. *Journal of Anthropological Research*, 38 (1), 97–107.

Coyle, Michael, 2007. Respect for Treaty Rights in Ontario: The Law of the Land? *Ottawa Law Review*, 39 (2), 405–39.

d'Aspremont, Jean, 2020. Current Theorizations about the Treaty in International Law. *In*: Duncan B. Hollis, ed. *The Oxford Guide to Treaties* (2nd ed.). Oxford: Oxford University Press, 46–58.

Donaldson, Megan, 2017. The Survival of the Secret Treaty: Publicity, Secrecy, and Legality in the International Order. *The American Journal of International Law*, 111 (3), 575–627.

Espinosa Garces, Maria Fernanda, 2019. *Statement by H.E. Mrs. Maria Fernanda Espinosa Garces, President of the 73rd Session of the UN General Assembly (23 May 2019)*. Available from: https://www.un.org/pga/73/2019/05/23/the-vienna-convention-on-the-law-of-treaties-at-fifty-an-anniversary-celebration/ [Accessed 19 March 2020].

Fitzmaurice, Gerald, 1958. Some Problems Regarding the Formal Sources of International Law. *In*: F. M. van Asbeck, ed. *Symbolae Verzijl*. The Hague: Martinus Nijhoff, 153–76.

Fitzmaurice, Malgosia, 2006. The Practical Working of the Law of Treaties. *In*: Malcolm Evans, ed. *International Law* Oxford. Oxford: Oxford University Press.

Frazer, Elizabeth, 1919. The Signature. *The Saturday Evening Post*, 30 August. Available from: https://www.saturdayeveningpost.com/flipbooks/reprints/The_Signature/ [Accessed 20 June 2020].

Goldenberd, Suzanne, Vidal, John, Taylor, Lenore, Vaughan, Adam, and Harvey, Fiona, 2015. Paris Climate Deal: Nearly 200 Nations Sign in End of Fossil Fuel Era. *The Guardian*, 13 December. Available from: https://www.theguardian.com/environment/2015/dec/12/paris-climate-deal-200-nations-sign-finish-fossil-fuel-era [Accessed 19 June 2020].

Harris Steven, M., 2020. Manufacturing International Law: Pre-Printed Treaties in the 'Scramble for Africa'. *Journal of the History of International Law / Revue d'histoire du droit international*, 22 (1), 1–27.

Haas, Angela M., 2007. Wampum as Hypertext: An American Indian Intellectual Tradition of Multimedia Theory and Practice. *Studies in American Indian Literatures*, 19 (4), 77–100.

Hale, Horatio, 1897. Four Huron Wampum Records: A Study of Aboriginal American History and Mnemonic Symbols. *The Journal of the Anthropological Institute of Great Britain and Ireland*, 26, 221–47.

Hewitt, Jeffery, 2021. Certain (mis)Conceptions: Westphalian Origins, Portraiture and Wampum. *In*: Shane Chalmers and Sundhya Pahuja, eds. *Routledge Handbook of International Law and the Humanities*. Abingdon: Routledge.

Hohmann, Jessie, 2018. The Treaty 8 Typewriter: Tracing the Roles of Material Things in Imagining, Realising and Resisting Colonial Worlds. *London Review of International Law*, 5 (3), 371–96.

Hollis, Duncan, 2006. Introduction. *In*: Duncan B. Hollis, Merritt R. Blakeslee, and L. Benjamin Ederington, eds. *National Treaty Law and Practice: Studies on the Law of Treaties*, vol. 1. Netherlands: Martinus Nijhoff.

Hollis, Duncan, 2019a. The Guest of Honor. @UN with the Original #VCLT 50 Years on. Looking fwd to Assessing Its Legacy & Its Future. *Twitter Post*, 24 May 2019. Available from: https://twitter.com/DuncanHollis/status/1131571145638121472 [Accessed 22 June 2020].

Hollis, Duncan, 2019b. There Were Many Birthday Wishes But No Singing. Still Folks Literally Lining Up to Get a Photo Taken with the #VCLT. *Twitter Post*, 24 May 2019. Available from: https://twitter.com/DuncanHollis/status/1131656208409141252 [Accessed 22 June 2020].

Hébié, Mamadou, 2015. The Role of the Agreements Concluded with Local Political Entities in the Course of French Colonial Expansion in West Africa. *British Yearbook of International Law*, 85 (1), 21–89.

Jacobs, Wilbur R., 1949. The Protocol of Indian Diplomacy. *The William and Mary Quarterly*, 6 (4), 596.

Jennings, Francis, Fenton, William N., Druke, Mary A., and Miller, David R., eds., 1995. *The History and Culture of Iroquois Diplomacy*. Syracuse: Syracuse University Press.

Keene, Edward, 2012. The Treaty-Making Revolution of the Nineteenth Century. *The International History Review*, 33 (4), 475–500.

Lowe, Vaughan, 2007. *International Law*. Oxford: Oxford/Clarendon.

Lugard, Frederick J. D., 1893. Treaty-Making in Africa. *The Geographical Journal*, 1(1), 53–5.

Lugard, Frederick J. D., 1926. *The Dual Mandate in British Tropical Africa*. Edinburgh and London: William Blackwood & Son.

Martineau, Anne-Charlotte, 2018. Chicotte. *In*: Jessie Hohmann and Daniel Joyce, eds. *International Law's Objects*. Oxford: Oxford University Press, 182–190.

Mathias, J., and Yabsley, G. R., 1991. Conspiracy of Legislation: The Suppression of Indian Rights in Canada. *BC Studies*, 89 (Spring), 34–47.

Maurice, Albert, 1957. *H.M. Stanley Unpublished Letters*. London: W & R Chambers.

Medijainen, Eero, 2010. Article 5: Permanent Neutrality in The Tartu Peace Treaty, 1920. *Journal of Baltic Studies*, 41 (2), 201–14.

Mugambwa, John, 1987. Treaties or Scraps of Paper? A Second Look at the Legal Character of the Nineteenth Century British/African Colonial Agreements. *The Comparative and International Law Journal of Southern Africa*, 20 (1), 79–93.

Muller, Kathryn V., 2007. The Two 'Mystery Belts' of Grand River: A Biography of the Two Row Wampum and the Friendship Belt. *The American Indian Quarterly*, 31 (1), 129–64.

Renard Painter, Genevieve, 2017. A Letter from the Huadenosaunee Confederacy to King George V: Writing and Reading Jurisdictions in International Legal History. *London Review of International Law*, 5 (1), 7–48.

Republic of South Africa, n.d. *Ratification/Accession Procedure*. Department of International Relations and Cooperation, Office of the Chief State Law Advisor. Available from: http://www.dirco.gov.za/chiefstatelawadvicer/ratification.html [Accessed 19 June 2020].

Reuter, Paul, 1995. *Introduction to the Law of Treaties*. Translated by Jose Mico and Peter Haggenmacher (2nd ed.). London: Kegan Paul.

Roberts, Ivor, ed., 2019. *Satow's Diplomatic Practice* (7th ed.). Oxford: Oxford University Press.

Roele, Isobel, 2015. Reading UN Security Council Resolutions through Valverde's Chronotopes. *Feminist Legal Studies*, 23, 369–74.

Sahli, Fatiha, and El Ouazzani, Abdelmalek, 2012. Africa North of the Sahara and Arab Countries. *In*: Bardo Fassbender and Anne Peters, eds. *The Oxford Handbook of the History of International Law*. Oxford: Oxford University Press.

Shumway, Rebecca, 2015. Palavers and Treaty Making in the British Acquisition of the Gold Coast Colony (West Africa). *In*: Saliha Belmessous, ed. *Empire by Treaty: Negotiating European Expansion, 1600–1900*. Oxford: Oxford University Press.

Smith, Robert, 1973. Peace and Palaver: International Relations in Pre-Colonial West-Africa. *Journal of African History*, 14 (4), 599–621.

Sowerby, Tracey A., 2019. Negotiating with Material Text: Royal Correspondence Between England and the Wider World. *In*: Tracey A. Sowerby and Joanna Craigwood, eds. *Cultures of Diplomacy and Literary Writing in the Early Modern World*. Oxford: Oxford University Press.

Stewart Jones, Francois, 1897. Treaties and Treaty-Making. *Political Science Quarterly*, 12 (3), 420–49.

Surun, Isabelle, 2014. Writing Sovereignty in Invisible Ink? Autochthonous Sovereignty and Territorial Appropriations in Nineteenth-Century Franco-African Treaties. Translated by Arby Gharibian. *Annales*, 69 (2), 313–48.

Swaine, Edward T., 2020, Treaty Reservations. *In*: Daniel Hollis, ed. *The Oxford Handbook of Treaties* (2nd ed.). Oxford: Oxford University Press, 285–308.

Tidridge, Nathan, 2015. *The Queen at the Council Fire: The Treaty of Niagara, Reconciliation and the Dignified Crown in Canada*. Toronto: Dundurn.

Touval, Saadia, 1966. Treaties, Borders, and the Partition of Africa. *Journal of African History*, 7 (2), 279–93.

Treaty 7 Elders and Tribal Council with Hildebrant, Walter, First Rider, Dorothy, and Carter, Sarah, 1996. *The True Spirit and Original Intent of Treaty 7*. Montreal and Kingston, London, Buffalo: McGill Queen's University Press.

Two Row Wampum Renewal Campaign, n.d. Two Row Wampum Renewal Campaign. Available from: https://honorthetworow.org/ [Accessed 22 June 2020].
United Nations, Charter of the United Nations, 24 October 1945, 1 UNTS XVI.
United Nations, Commission on Human Rights, 1999. *Study on Treaties, Agreements and Other Constructive Arrangements between States and Indigenous Populations: Final Report by Miguel Alfonso Martínez, Special Rapporteur.* UN Doc E/CN.4/Sub.2/1999/20.
United Nations, Commission on Human Rights, 1995. *Study on Treaties, Agreements and Other Constructive Arrangements between States and Indigenous Populations: Second Progress Report by Miguel Alfonso Martínez, Special Rapporteur.* UN Doc E/CN.4/Sub.2/1995/27.
United Nations, Commission on Human Rights, 1992. *Study on Treaties, Agreements and Other Constructive Arrangements between States and Indigenous Populations: First Progress Report by Miguel Alfonso Martínez, Special Rapporteur.* UN Doc E/CN.4/Sub.2/1992/32.
United Nations International Law Commission, 1951. *Yearbook of the International Law Commission, 1951 Volume 2: Documents of the Third Session Including the Report of the Committee to the General Assembly, Report by Mr. J.L. Brierly, Special Rapporteur.* UNDOC A/CN.4/32, 1–16.
United Nations, 1983. *United Nations Editorial Manual* United Nations, New York.
United Nations, 2012. *Treaty Handbook* (revised edition). Available from: https://treaties.un.org/doc/source/publications/THB/English.pdf [Accessed 22 June 2020].
United Nations, n.d.a. *United Nations Web Style Guide.* Available from: https://www.un.org/styleguide/ [Accessed 20 June 2020].
United Nations, n.d.b. *Treaties.* Available from: https://treaties.un.org/ [Accessed 20 June 2020].
Varrak, Toomas, 2017. The Tartu Peace Treaty, The New Border Treaty and Relations with Russia. *Diplomatica 161/162,* 10 February 2017. Available from: https://icds.ee/the-tartu-peace-treaty-the-new-border-treaty-and-relations-with-russia/ [Accessed 22 June 2020].
Vienna Convention on the Law of Treaties, 1969. UNTS, vol. 1155, 331, opened for signature 23 May 1969, entered into force 27 January 1980.
Watson, Irene, 2014. *Aboriginal Peoples, Colonialism and International Law: Raw Law.* London, UK: Routledge.
Welch, Ellen R., 2017. *Theatre of Diplomacy: International Relations and the Performing Arts in Early Modern France.* Philadelphia, PA: University of Pennsylvania Press.

Chapter 10

Conjuring documents

Informal wills

Katherine Biber

In June 1948, Cecil George Harris died following an accident on his Saskatchewan wheat farm, on the flat, isolated and usually dry prairie lands. He had been trapped underneath his tractor for 12 hours in a torrential summer downpour. His wife and neighbours eventually found him during a lightning storm. Despite their best efforts, he died of his injuries.

Two of his curious neighbours went to examine Harris' stricken tractor. Doing so, they found that Harris had scratched a message into the paint on the fender. It read:

> *In case I die in this mess I leave all to the wife. Cecil Geo. Harris*

The neighbours removed the fender after his funeral and conveyed it to a local lawyer. The fender message was later held to be Harris' valid will (*Estate of Harris* [1948] Can. Bar Rev. Vol XXVI, 1242–1244). Because this case is now a quirky landmark of Saskatchewan succession law, the fender, and the knife Harris used to carve his message, are now on display in the library of the University of Saskatchewan law school. When Cecil Harris scratched a message into his tractor fender, he created an artefact that had never been previously thought of as either a will or a document. Nevertheless, the fender was admitted to probate: it was held to be his last will and testament.

This chapter examines informal wills—including that inscribed on Harris' fender—and the ways that courts have been challenged by the documentary nature of the will. It explores instances where people created documents that were not wills, or wills that were not documents, and where the courts interpreted them *as documents* and *as wills* regardless.

What is a document?

In Western legal traditions, documents—more than witnesses or physical objects—have become the most important form of evidence. But in the digital age, the distinction between a document, a witness and real evidence is becoming more difficult to perceive, and pointless to sustain. What we understand

DOI: 10.4324/9781003247593-13

as a 'document' has expanded to include a potentially limitless range of digital forms and technological devices for the capture and storage of data, compounding the challenges posed by matters of proof and use. These emerging understandings, however, also enable us to see more clearly that the history of documentation has always presented challenges to what a document *is*. In 1951, French librarian and documentary theorist Suzanne Briet asked 'What is a document?', and distinguished an antelope in the wild (fauna) from an antelope confined in a zoo, or taxidermal in a museum, or captured audiovisually, or described in an encyclopaedia (a document) (2006 [1951], 10–11). Briet's approach was groundbreaking for tethering documentation to information, and detaching it from the material constraints of writing implement and surface. Following Briet, this chapter traces the longer history of materiality, immateriality and ephemerality in documentation.

For documents, the entanglement of form and function conflates what a document *is* and what a document *does*. The philosopher Barry Smith (2014) offers a theory of 'document acts' to expand upon John Searle's work on 'speech acts', which itself draws upon J.L. Austin's (1975) theory of performative utterances. For Smith, document acts are performed at two levels. In the first, humans do things with documents to signal that they regard them *as documents* (instead of, for instance, mere paper). Here, Smith includes acts such as signing or stamping documents, depositing them in registries, using them to grant permission, prove identity or publish rules (2014, 20). In the second, Smith draws upon the work of economist Hernando de Soto, in which documents function within economies and bureaucracies, and in which *documents inaugurate* new states of affairs (2014, 19). By doing things with documents, Smith writes, we can change the world (2012, [5]–[6]). This is both social reality and ontological magic (Smith 2012, [7]).

Documents are crucial to the construction of systems in which they function: the registries and agencies whose work is propelled by documents, the staff and officials who perform document acts, the channels and processes by which documents move and ultimately their storage and perhaps their destruction. For Smith, whereas speech acts are 'events', documents are 'objects', and they endure through time, and have the capability to 'float free' from their creators, with the capacity to 'live lives of their own' (2014, 24). Furthermore, documents can have multiple creators, and they—and their meaning—are transformed whenever they are stamped, or when somebody adds an entry, or signs it, or appends an annexure (Smith 2014, 24).

What is a will?

For Smith, wills are part of the category of documents needed by a society which has outgrown what was previously achieved through human memory and face-to-face interactions. Wills, and other documents in this cohort, 'create and sustain the sorts of enduring and re-usable deontic powers', necessary for 'new and more complex forms of social order which are characteristic of modern civilization' (Smith 2012, [26]).

Whereas wills are powerful documents because of what they can do, in law, a will is not ordinarily recognisable as a will until it fulfils the requirements of the documentary form. That is, it needs to be a documentary object in order for it to enact a documentary performance which can have a legal effect. Documents need to *be* in order to *do*. This chapter reveals that, in certain circumstances, courts have conjured documents from performances; document acts sometimes give rise to documentary objects that otherwise did not exist.

A will is a legal instrument which distributes a person's assets, and administers their affairs, after their death. Except in very limited exceptional circumstances, a will is a document. To be a valid will, it must have certain formal requirements: it must be in writing, on paper, signed by the testator, witnessed by other people and formally executed. Specific formal language is encouraged, to ensure that the testator's wishes can be accurately followed. The best way for testators to ensure their will is valid is to follow the form: formalities distinguish a formal will from an informal one. Informal wills are not necessarily invalid, but they require the court to examine them for evidence that draws analogies between the form and the facts, so that they might be recognised as wills and interpreted as valid.

Succession law gives rise to the full spectrum of human conduct: all of the human emotions are revealed in people's last wills and testaments, and in the conduct of their beneficiaries and descendants after death. Grief, generosity, love and consideration; prudence and planning; regret, remorse and missed opportunities; hate, spite, retribution; sometimes eccentricity. Probate courts are required to walk into this emotional minefield, and they do so when the person whose wishes are being enforced has already died. What would they have wanted? The primary evidence of a deceased person's wishes is their last will and testament. And when they have not left one, or when the one they left is deficient, the court looks for clues, inferences and other tools enabling it to turn artefacts into documents, and documents into wills.

One aim of this chapter is to debunk the perception that the law clings to archaic formalities about documents. In the digital age, serious and careful consideration has been given to reforming the laws relating to wills, so that formal requirements are relaxed where possible, without diminishing the function of wills, and whilst also preserving the principle of testamentary freedom. However, as this chapter will reveal, despite enduring perceptions that the law is rigid and traditional, there is a longer history of courts validating—as documents and as wills—artefacts that are neither, and doing so with considerable tact, creativity and sensitivity.

The United States scholar of law and literature, Cathrine O. Frank (2006; 2010), traces the statutory changes brought about by the 1837 Wills Act in the United Kingdom, and how these were reflected in Victorian fiction. Now a written instrument, the will inaugurated new documentary forms for creating socio-legal entities. Frank writes, 'Like the birth and marriage certificate, the written will is a legal register of identity' (2006, 325–326; 2010, 1). Here is a document that gives birth to a new class of legal subjects: testators—crucial operators in the flourishing of capitalism. Strange and hidden wills were a key device in Victorian fiction. Frank writes, 'the Victorian novel is littered with wills, tucked away in its bedsteads, cupboards, and chests but always emerging' (2010, 14). Epic narratives of inheritance charted how 'the will—that legalistic fetish expressing its testator's state of mind—also served as a legal technology for textualizing people and making them legible' (Frank 2006, 327). Legislative change brought about a transformation in the individual; whereas customary laws constrained property holders through primogeniture, law reform permitted greater freedom in the distribution of wealth. For Frank, this marked a change from the expression of individual, or private, 'character' to the creation of social, or public, 'identity' (2006, 326; 2010, 3–4). More broadly, of course, it had the effect of transforming people into testators, and their legal advisors into conduits of the state's control of private property rights. Lawyers, by drafting uniform instruments to transmit assets, aided in building ever-larger bureaucracies for the public regulation of private wealth. This is David Graeber's (2015, 15–16) 'utopia of rules', in which 'paperwork' functions to provide state oversight of private profit and interests.

Formal and informal wills

The twenty-first century has witnessed moves seeking to relax the formal requirements needed in order for private property to be bequeathed. In the United Kingdom, for instance, a long-running process has sought to modernise the law relating to wills (UK Law Commission, 2017). It responds to the convergence of an aging population, new medical understandings about the cognitive capacity of people with certain conditions, the rapid transition to digital technologies, acceptance of diverse types of family formation and increasing rates of property ownership. The reforms aim to dispense with the formalities of will-making wherever possible, ensuring that it is a simple and accessible process for people to make a valid will. Whilst certain measures are needed to protect testators from fraud and undue influence, the broad objective is to support testamentary freedom and to prioritise testator intentions (UK Law Commission 2017, 13).

In the United States, the legal scholar Stephen Clowney (2008) has demonstrated that testators have, for a very long time, created informal wills and that, most of the time, no legal dispute has arisen. His focus is the holograph, or holographic, will. These are wholly handwritten, usually unwitnessed, and are valid in many jurisdictions, in some circumstances (Ellwand 2014, 2–3). Holograph wills are conceptually considered to be 'home-made wills'; collectively these arise where a person has made their will without the assistance of a lawyer.

Home-made wills have been said to give rise to 'difficulties', 'inelegancies', 'ambiguities', 'colloquialisms', they 'may use words improperly' or 'use the vernacular' (Haines 2007, [1.44]). In the words of one commentator, they are reserved for 'times of crisis, isolation, or poverty' (Ellwand 2014, 22); that is, occasions where a testator does not have the opportunity to make a valid formal will. Authors of succession law texts repeat apocryphal lawyer jokes: in these jokes, people who refuse to use a lawyer when making their will, after their death inadvertently contribute to the enrichment of the lawyers who will litigate their drafting errors. In David Haines' text, makers of home-made wills 'may have led to the cliché which is the toast of the Chancery bar: "Here's to the man who makes his own will"' (2007, [1.44]).

For Clowney (2008), who undertook a large-scale study of home-made wills in the United States, the 'patchwork of humorous anecdotes and appellate level court decisions' provides a distorted account; his research points to the 'rich diversity' of testators in his study, and notes that home-made wills are made by people across the entire socio-economic spectrum, and most are made by women (2008, 46). He argues that to characterise home-made will-makers as foolish, ignorant or hellbent on squandering their possessions is offensive and usually wrong. He shows that most of their wills are held to be valid and give rise to no dispute.

Despite the method used in its making, Cecil George Harris' tractor fender message was held to be an exemplar of a holograph will. Celebrated for his enactment of 'Prairie practicality', Harris took an important step when he 'unwittingly' or 'perhaps intuitively' placed his signature at the end of his message (Ellwand 2014, 14–15). The inclusion and placement of a signature, and also the mark made when signing, have attracted considerable judicial attention (Halsbury's, 2nd ed, 1940, Vol. XXXIV, Sect. 2, [67–77]). In another Saskatchewan case, Cornelia Cleveland Smith left a wholly handwritten document which she signed, 'Mother' (*In re Smith Estate* [1948] 2 WWR 55). In a dispute between her children, the court was asked whether 'Mother' was a sufficient signature for a will (at 56). The court reviewed *Halsbury's Laws of England*, 2nd ed, which stated:

> A mark or initials are sufficient if intended to represent a signature, even though the testator's hand is guided in making it, and whether the testator can write or not. A stamped signature may be sufficient. A signature however must have been made with the purpose of authenticating the instrument.
>
> (at 56)

Halsbury's also stated that 'Signature in an erroneous or assumed name, if intended as the name of the testator, is enough'. Following this authority, the court in *Smith* found that 'Mother' was a sufficient signature, and that hers was a valid holograph will (at 57).

Reflecting his frustrations about the strict interpretation of rules relating to signatures in Australian succession law, Paul de Jersey, speaking extra-judicially, observed the formal arrangement of the will document. He celebrated the removal of the long-standing requirement that a signature be applied at the 'foot or end' of the will (2010, 239). His remarks acknowledge that the will is a material artefact, and that its legal force has long been bound to the architecture of the page. In *How the Page Matters* (2011), Bonnie Mak points to the 'dynamic relationship between material and meaning' which is enacted and embodied by the page (2011, 3). Mak investigates the page as both 'material platform' and 'cognitive space' (2011, 3). For Mak, the 'strategies of the page may be simultaneous, overlapping, mutually responsive, complementary, and even contradictory' (2011, 4). She writes, the 'architecture of the page is thus a complex and responsive entanglement of platform, text, image, graphic markings, and blank space' (2011, 5). By logging his frustrations about the legal significance of signature placement, de Jersey is implicitly acknowledging the history of the page as, in Mak's words, 'a favoured space and metaphor for the graphic communication of ideas' (2011, 8). For Mak, the page is not only a 'vehicle or container' for ideas, but itself implicated in the creation and interpretation of those ideas (2011, 9). It is situated at the centre of the 'complicated dynamic of intention and reception' (2011, 21). Connecting this with the concept of 'document acts', the arrangement of the page can play a crucial role in the inauguration of new and lawful states of affairs. In pausing over the placement of the signature on a will document, and in acknowledging that there has long been a right and wrong place for the signature to appear, de Jersey is reminding himself—and us—that the page is there, and its physicality is tethered to its legality. That the placement of the signature can suddenly cease to matter, however, tells us that this entanglement is neither natural nor necessary, and that the page—materially and legally—is reimaginable.

Formalism and functionalism

Informal, holographic, home-made or otherwise strange wills give rise to two strands of jurisprudence. One of these might be termed 'formalist' and the other 'functionalist'. The former is dominant; as the legal scholars Collins and Skover (1992, 509) state, 'Law is bound by its form'. They observe that even law's metaphors embody a commitment to form: 'put it in writing', 'signed and sealed', 'the letter of the law', 'black letter law', 'by the book' (1992, 514).

Formalists are concerned with the *form* of legal documents and lawful conduct. They argue that there is an important rationale in applying legal formalities strictly: formalities sort sincere legal instruments from those which are gratuitous, impulsive or which otherwise do not expect to be enforced. Formalities will, for example, prevent people from giving away their property accidentally or recklessly.

The United States legal philosopher Lon Fuller, in his landmark 1941 essay, 'Consideration and Form', undertook an inquiry into the 'rationale of legal formalities' in document-making (1941, 799; see also Kennedy 1973; 1976; 2000). Fuller, a scholar of contracts, was seeking to distinguish enforceable contracts from what he called 'gratuitous promises', because the latter might be made 'impulsively and without proper deliberation' (1941, 799). For Fuller, what distinguishes these is not their content or effect, but rather the manner in which they have been made: their form (1941, 799). To draw upon Fuller's work here is not to conflate the promises made in contract law with the gifts given in wills. Instead, it is to draw upon his analysis of 'form' as a significant component of legal document-making. For Fuller, the formality of legal documentation has three primary functions: the first of these is evidentiary; the formalities are evidence of the intention to create a legal effect. The second is cautionary, or deterrent, because the formalities serve as a warning to the document-maker of the potential legal effects of their promise. The third is channelling, by which Fuller means that the formality creates a legal framework that channels the actions of a party towards a better understanding of their intentions. Form is a device for the 'channeling of expression' (1941, 803).

The formalities are deliberate devices, wilfully deployed by people signalling their intentions. They serve as a convenience and a short cut, saving future recipients the effort of having to look beneath the surface of the document, searching for context, intention or other modes for interpretation. The formalities testify to their own agreed meaning, and foreclose the need to look deeper. Fuller is interested in the formality of the 'seal', but we might equally consider the signature, or the use of prescribed words, or other agreed devices.

Fuller makes the point that strict formality increases individual autonomy. People are more likely to have their personal wishes enforced, even eccentric or unconventional wishes, where those wishes are articulated through agreed, traditional forms (1941, 814). The United States legal scholar Melanie Leslie disputes this reasoning, arguing that the documentary formalities intended to bolster testamentary freedom end up constraining it (1996, 235–236).

Fuller cautions that formalities are valuable legal institutions, but also obstacles to innovation (1941, 803). For this reason, form is not always necessary nor appropriate. Form, he writes, should be reserved for 'relatively important transactions' (1941, 805). Law should know its place, and it has no place where, in his words, 'life has already organized itself effectively' (1941, 806).

The other jurisprudential strand—an alternative to formalism—is 'functionalism'. Advanced by most contemporary Anglophone scholars, and most closely associated with United States legal scholar and historian John Langbein, functionalism allows courts to look at the context, intention or purpose of a document, rather than its form, and give expression to those objectives. Functionalism is said to advance testamentary freedom, liberating testators from the strict formalities of will-making. Some functionalist scholars and practitioners advocate for 'testamentary rescue', where informal documents are rescued from the consequences of their errors through fancy jurisprudential footwork (e.g. du Toit 2014).

A key figure in anti-formalism, Langbein (1975; 1987; 1993–1994; 2017) argues that where harmless execution errors occur in the making of wills, judges must have authority to overlook the errors and give effect to the testator's intentions, where the document nevertheless embodies those intentions. Known as the 'dispensing power', it empowers judges to, in effect, correct drafting errors in order to advance a testator's wishes. Other scholars, including James Lindgren (1992), argue that the dispensing power is inadequate, that most of the formalities in wills are historical anachronisms, and that most formalities ought to be eliminated in favour of other methods of passing property after death (1992, 1033; see also Clowney 2008, 66–68). Lindgren believes that succession law has unfairly assumed that laypeople are ignorant; he wrote, 'sure, they don't know the law, but they usually know what they want. The fear that they might improvidently give away their property at death has left a legacy of formalism unmatched in American Law' (1992, 1009). This argument is bolstered by changes in other areas—including insurance, banking and trusts—where lesser requirements are sufficient to pass property after death (see Clowney 2008, 68).

In support of her critique of testamentary freedom, Leslie finds that the case law shows—'quietly but fervently'—courts will impose normative or moral views about how estates should be distributed, and will overlook testamentary intent in order to prioritise those they regard as having 'a superior moral claim to the testator's assets', primarily dependant spouses or blood relatives (1996, 236). For Leslie, a concern with the satisfaction of documentary formalities disguises a concern to enforce moral norms arising from familial duty (1996, 237).

Paper, objects and documents

For Clowney (2008), most of the contemporary legal criticisms of informal wills lack proper foundation, by conflating informality and ignorance. These criticisms overstate the occurrence of forgery and fraud, he writes, or they assume that informality arises from poor estate planning (giving rise to class-based pejoratives such as 'trailer park' estate planning), or they inaccurately argue that potential heirs will attempt to probate documents which were never intended to function as wills (2008, 35–36). He observes, 'commentators worry that any casual or offhand writing—a greeting card, a love letter, a few sentences scribbled on hotel stationary—can be construed inappropriately as a will'; proponents of formality argue, Clowney writes, that these are necessary 'to separate the legal wheat from the chaff and keep testators from accidentally giving away their property' (2008, 35–36). The fear that certain papers (cards, notes, love letters) might be mistaken for legal papers (say, wills) is not borne out by the case law. More commonly, what arises is that some will documents (draft wills, unsigned wills, revoked wills) give rise to a dispute, particularly where multiple will documents have been created by a single testator during their lifetime. An artefact's status *as* a document is less frequently disputed than the status *of* a document as being a last will and testament.

For Clowney, the only requirements for a valid will ought to be writing and a signature: 'Signature indicates a decision, final unless later revoked, and supplies evidence of genuineness' (2008, 69). The court assessing Cecil Harris' tractor fender took a similar view. When he carved his final message into the fender, Harris placed his signature at the end of it, and this was found to be a formal component in an otherwise informal will. Evidence was taken from his bank manager and also from his friend and former business partner that the handwriting and signature on the fender matched Harris'. His wife and his lawyer also swore affidavits that the handwriting on the fender was authentic. That this evidence required the deponents to compare his usual handwriting *on paper* against a large message *scratched into metal with a knife* seems to represent a blurring of form and function that could have—but here did not—represented an insurmountable leap between evidentiary forms. Here, Harris' fender slid smoothly from being an object to a document.

On the day he received it, Harris' lawyer took the step of calling a professional photographer to photograph the fender, with the expectation that this image would be required in court (Ellwand 2014, 9–10). The idea that one document—a photograph—can prove the contents of another—a scratched fender—is something that the law of evidence provides tools for achieving. But Harris' lawyer had not anticipated that the fender *itself* would need to be brought into the courtroom. Nor was it expected that the court would order the message to be cut from the remainder of the fender, with the message portion physically appended to the court file. The fender stayed in the court registry until 1996, when the court handed it to the University of Saskatchewan law school. In displaying it behind glass in a vitrine, the law library transformed this document back into an object.

The history of succession law is filled with instances of people leaving strange, surprising, eccentric or cruel artefacts behind for their loved ones to wrestle with, conjuring enforceable wills from, amongst other things, an eggshell, a nurse's petticoat, scratchings on a wall or suicide notes. As Cathrine O. Frank (2006) observed, the legal narratives in which 'curious wills' are litigated run parallel with the literary narratives in Victorian novels in which they function as devices—of plot, character, place and context. One of Frank's texts is H. Rider Haggard's 1888 novel *Mr Meeson's Will*, in which the protagonist, Augusta Smithers, encourages Mr Meeson to have his will tattooed onto her back. This later gives rise to a legal dispute about the will's validity. It also gives rise to a fundamental evidentiary dispute: is Augusta a witness or a document? Her solicitor wonders whether, if her skin were flayed, it would satisfy the requirement of paper: 'if carefully removed and dried, [it] would make excellent parchment'; by leaving it upon her body, it might be regarded as 'parchment in its green state' (Frank 2006, 334). The

Defence argues that, if Augusta is a document, she is not entitled to speak: 'there is no precedent for a document giving evidence' (Frank 2006, 334). For Frank, the novel's satire arises from the conflict between the rule-bound law, on one hand, and common sense and humanity, on the other (2006, 334). It is a tension which emerges as a clear theme in the case law arising from informal wills.

In 1925 in England, a ship pilot named James Barnes died. On top of his wardrobe, his wife Margaret, known as 'Mag', found an empty eggshell resting on cotton wool in a small wooden box (*Hodson v Barnes* [1926] Times LR, Friday 3 December 1926, 71; at 72). On the eggshell, in indelible ink, in Barnes' handwriting, was this message:

> *17-1925. Mag. Everything i possess. – J.B.*
>
> (at 71)

In court, Margaret asserted that this eggshell represented her husband's last will and testament; she said it revoked his earlier—formal—will, in which she was to share his estate with his children from a prior marriage, and all of his grandchildren.

The eggshell was tendered into evidence. The President of the Court, Lord Merrivale, announced: 'It is a fragile thing. It is here' (at 71).

The facts in this case are complex and rather sad, and in the end the Court ruled that the eggshell—and all of the evidence received about it, and about Barnes' special egg-rich diet, and about his other will—was not sufficient to revoke his earlier will, and to convey the entirety of his estate to his current wife. Instead, the court described the eggshell artefact as 'one of the most grotesque proceedings conceivable'; 'one of the most incredible things of which [the Court] had ever heard', and which was also 'inconsistent with the character of the testator' (at 72).

The following year, 1926, George Hazeltine, described as a rich and eccentric recluse, wrote on his nurse's petticoat what purported to be his last will and testament. By this device, the court was told, he revoked his earlier will, which divided his large estate amongst various charitable and educational institutions. Instead, according to the petticoat will, his estate would go to his grandniece, with considerable gifts to the nurse and the hospital matron who attended to him in his final days. Against a complicated factual background, most of the court's attention was paid not to the form of the document, but to whether it was made freely, and without undue influence. A judge ruled that, because the nurses who witnessed the will were also its beneficiaries, it was null and void. On appeal to a jury, the jury held that the will was valid, albeit the matter had meanwhile settled out of court. *The Los Angeles Times* described the case—with its raunchy exhibit—as 'more like Exhibit A in a divorce action than a will' (1926, A1), but since six firms of attorneys litigated the matter, it seemed that—as the old jokes affirm—the real winners were the lawyers.

In a 1988 case in South Australia, Pantelej Slavinskyj, born in the USSR, left a message shortly before he died (*In the Estate of Slavinskyj* (1988) 53 SASR 221). On a plasterboard wall in his house, in poorly spelled Ukrainian, he wrote [here translated into English by the court]:

> *To all my nieces*
> *USSR. Ukrainian Socialist Republic 324047*
> *Krivoy Rog*
> *R – K Keina*
> *Karbyshova Street*
> *No. 10 Flat 69 N.G. Kartvova* (at 229).

Into a crack in the wall, he placed an envelope on which he had written the name and address of one niece. He had two of his neighbours witness these acts, and one of them—the one who could read Ukrainian—signed the wall. Mr Slavinskyj died shortly after; his neighbour who signed the wall died before the court hearing. The court judgment, written by Justice Legoe, is filled with irresistible references to the story of Pyramus and Thisbe, two lovers separated by a wall, but who nevertheless whisper to each other through a small crack in it. Re-told in Shakespeare's *A Midsummer Night's Dream*, Legoe J reproduces dialogue from the play-within-a-play performed in Act V, Scene 1. In the play Snout the Tinker, playing the Wall, explains the function of the wall in transacting human affairs.

> WALL: In this same interlude it doth befall
> That I, one Snout by name, present a wall;
> And such a wall, as I would have you think,
> That had in it a crannied hole or chink,
> Through which the lovers, Pyramus and Thisby,
> Did whisper often very secretly.
> This loam, this rough-cast and this stone doth show
> That I am that same wall; the truth is so:
> And this the cranny is, right and sinister,
> Through which the fearful lovers are to whisper.
> (*A Midsummer Night's Dream*, Act V, Scene I)

Whilst it is not convention for legal judgments to cite Shakespeare, nor is it rare, as the Bard is known for capturing the enduring themes of humanity. Christopher Legoe, reflecting in his retirement, explained: 'I felt that sometimes poetry, and particularly Shakespeare, had a wonderful ability to describe human feelings, human intentions, human understandings, and human meanings. And I did quote Shakespeare on more than one occasion, I'm afraid' (History Lab, at 13:36).

The court was told that it would be possible to cut out that portion of the wall—the documentary portion—and bring it to court, but the registrar had said that a photograph would do. As Snout the Tinker had observed: 'You can never bring in a wall' (Act III, Scene 1). Legoe, speaking in his retirement, explained why he did not require the wall to be brought before the court: 'Well, because it was somewhat impractical and it might destroy the wording, whereas the photograph would of course give the complete wording and be undestroyed' (History Lab, at 18:20). The photograph formed part of the judgment, but its poor quality meant that it could not be reproduced in the reported judgment.

The Supreme Court of South Australia was clear: the wall was a document. Legoe J ruled, 'The document in this case is the wall, and like Snout the Tinker, represents the division between neighbours, namely, the deceased and his universal devisees and legatees in the USSR' (at 233). But the court was hesitant: the wall was signed by one witness, not two. In his writing on the wall, Slavinskyj did not appoint an executor. But on the other hand, the court was confident: the deceased's intentions were clear: he wanted the writing on the wall, together with the envelope stuck in the wall, to constitute his last will and testament. He had done something ceremonial and solemn when he invited the neighbours to witness his writing on the wall and his placing of the envelope into the crack. Legoe J, again drawing upon Shakespeare, wrote:

> The circumstances and the words actually used by the testator leave me in no doubt whatsoever that what the testator was doing was attempting to express his final disposition of his estate to his nieces in Russia by publishing this fact in a way which can have had no other intention. As two members of the audience to the Pyramus and Thisbe drama remarked: 'Would you desire lime and hair to speak better?' and 'It is the wittiest partition that ever I heard discourse.'
>
> (at 233, citing Act V, Scene I)

For all of these documentary insufficiencies, the court found solutions; 18 George Street, Semaphore Park is a small weatherboard and tin cottage with a carport and a mature *Ficus carica* tree behind a picket fence in Adelaide's western beachfront suburbs (Google Street View, captured Jan 2008). Upon a wall inside that house, in March 1984, Slavinskyj and his neighbours, the Skoryks from number 14, performed a series of document acts, conjuring the ontological magic that would convey this modest property to three women he had never met, in the USSR.

Suicide notes as wills

Within the jurisprudence of informal wills is a large body of suicide notes, or other communications made concurrently with the event of suicide. Some of these communications contain testamentary intentions. That is, amongst the other messages that the person is communicating—their regrets, anger, pain, their apologies for their suicide—there are also expressions about how they want their property and assets to be distributed after their death. In some cases, the courts find these writings to have testamentary force; sometimes they don't. In one case, a man died by suicide after a long history of mental illness. He had made a valid will many years earlier, but left an unsigned note shortly before his death:

> MUM AND
> DAD I THINK
> I M DYING
> PLEASE
> LOOK
> AFTER
> ALL
> MY
> GOOD
> WRITING.
> THERE
> MIGHT
> BE
> SOME
> MORE
> IN
> THE DRAWER
> TAKE CARE OF 'EM
> I WANT YOU
> TO HAVE MY HOUSE.
> (*Alexander Costa and anor v The Public Trustee in the Estate of Robert Costa* [2007] NSWSC 1271 at [7])

The first time it came before a court, the court was clear that this was a document, that it embodied the deceased's wishes and that he deliberately left it in a prominent place. However, it was not signed; the manner in which it was written down the page, the court said, was 'expressing emotions and not legal intentions' (*Alexander Costa and anor v The Public Trustee in the Estate of Robert Costa* [2007] NSWSC 1271 at [15]). He did not entrust it to anyone, and there was no other evidence to support that these really were his wishes for the distribution of his property after death. Because the deceased knew how to make a valid will —having made one before—the court reasoned that he must have known that in creating this document, he was not creating an enforceable will. The court concluded that 'its form and wording' meant that the document was not a testamentary instrument; rather it expressed wishes and requests

(*Alexander Costa and anor v The Public Trustee in the Estate of Robert Costa* [2007] NSWSC 1271 at [19]).

However, this decision was appealed and the appellate court, with identical facts before it, made the opposite decision. On appeal, the court decided to give less weight to matters of form, and more weight to the fact that 'the document was written on a solemn unique occasion, as a last message to his parents, the persons apparently closest to him' (*Costa and Another v The Public Trustee of NSW* [2008] NSWCA 223 at [28]). It was held to be his last will and testament. The decision illustrates that the same piece of paper might be recognised as mere paper or a legal instrument, and that it travels between these categories at varying speeds, and depending upon one's point of view, the transition from mere paper to legal will turns upon either jurisprudence or magic.

Wills in the digital age

More recently, courts have been challenged by the presentation of testamentary messages prepared or contained on, for instance, DVDs (*Wilden (Deceased)* [2015] SASC 9 (30 January 2015)) and digital videos (*Re Estate of Wai Fun CHAN, Deceased* [2015] NSWSC 1107 (7 August 2015)), iPhone notes (*Re Yu* [2013] QSC 322 (6 November 2013)), Microsoft Word documents (*Yazbek v Yazbek & Anor* [2012] NSWSC 594 (1 June 2012)), encrypted computer files (*The Estate of Roger Christopher Currie, late of Balmain* [2015] NSWSC 1098 (5 August 2015)) and other digital artefacts. The law is prepared to accept that these artefacts are all 'documents', but some of them are found to be valid wills, and some are not.

The functionalist scholar, Lindgren, writes critically of the 'print paradigm' that he regards as having dominated succession law. For Lindgren, paper is administratively convenient, and its abstraction, and its preparation by legal professionals, effectively serve a channelling function (1992, 1021). He argues that visual technologies—his example is the videotape—provide superior means for assessing the validity of wills, the manner in which they were executed and the cognitive state of the testator (1992, 1021). Lindgren draws upon Collins and Skover (1992), who describe visual documents as 'paratexts', 'new and context-rich' and superior to pre-electronic forms of communication, which they identify as 'oral, scribal, print' (in Lindgren 1992, 1021). For Collins and Skover (1992, 510), the paratext goes 'beyond' the text, and encompasses technologies for capturing images and sounds. For Collins and Skover, pre-electronic forms are characterised by 'closure, systematization, control, abstraction', and are at odds with forms which are 'open ended, uncategorized, uncontrolled, and particular' (1992, 535). Broadly, they argue for the law to take a more tolerant view of emerging technologies. Paratext is more commonly associated with Gérard Genette, the structuralist literary theorist who deployed the term alongside peritext, epitext, hypotext; all terms which help to elucidate how the form of the text is bound together with its function (see Tomlins 2014). Expanding its application to new digital technologies offers a promising way forward.

An example of this arose following a man's death by suicide in 2016. A friend found an unsent text message on his mobile phone. It read:

> *Dave Nic you and Jack keep all that I have house and superannuation, put my ashes in the back garden with Trish Julie will take her stuff only she's ok gone back to her ex AGAIN I'm beaten. A bit of cash behind TV and a bit in the bank Cash card pin 3636*
> *MRN190162Q*
> *10/10/2016*
> *My will*
> (*Re Nichol; Nichol v Nichol* [2017] QSC 220 (9 October 2017))

After a bitter dispute between the man's widow and his brother and nephew, the Supreme Court of Queensland decided that this was a valid will (*Re Nichol; Nichol v Nichol* [2017] QSC 220 (9 October 2017)).

The Supreme Court of Queensland had no difficulty in finding that the unsent text message was a 'document'. However, it was not a formal will. The court noted that the unsent message was identified as a will—'*my will*'—dated—*10/10/2016*—and contained the deceased's initials and date of birth—'*MRN190162*'. It included clear wishes about the distribution of his assets, identified most of his assets, provided a pin code and gave instructions about the placement of his ashes. The court also heard evidence about his state of mind at the time of his death and determined that he had sufficient capacity to make a will. Consideration was given to the fact that he did not send the text message: did it mean that his will was still in 'draft' form and did not reflect his final wishes? The court accepted evidence that he did not send the message so that his family would not interrupt his suicide. Despite lacking nearly all of the formalities of a will, it was found to be his valid last will and testament.

Conclusion

For centuries, across the jurisdictions of the civil law and common law worlds, the last will and testament has been a powerful technical document. Its formal elements enable it to communicate beyond the grave, to give voice to the dead and to devise strategies by which a person's memory might survive them, by distributing their property in accordance with their wishes. The law is committed to honouring the wishes of the dead, and to giving people the freedom to do what they like with their possessions. But where people depart from the agreed form of the legal document, the law has left a long history of conjuring meaning from the material, immaterial and ephemeral artefacts left behind. Entangling form and function, object and performance, paper and digital, law enacts its ontological magic in attempting to do justice to the dead.

References

Austin, J. L., 1975. *How to do Things with Words* (2nd ed.). Harvard: Harvard University Press.

Briet, Suzanne, 2006 [1951]. *What is Documentation?* Translated and edited by Ronald E. Day and Laurent Martinet, with Hermina G.B. Anghelescu. Lanham, MD: Scarecrow Press.

Clowney, Stephen, 2008. In Their Own Hand: An Analysis of Holographic Wills and Homemade Willmaking. *Real Property, Trust and Estate Law Journal*, 43, 27–71.

Collins, Ronald K. L., and Skover, David M., 1992. Paratexts. *Stanford Law Review*, 44 (3), 509–52.

De Jersey, Paul A. C., 2010. Court Intrusion into Testamentary Disposition: A Beneficial Jurisdiction? *Queensland University of Technology Law and Justice Journal*, 10 (2), 233–45.

Du Toit, Francois, 2014. Testamentary Rescue: An Analysis of the Intention Requirement in Australia and South Africa. *Australian Property Law Journal*, 23, 56–82.

Ellwand, Geoff, 2014. An Analysis of Canada's Most Famous Holograph Will: How a Saskatchewan Farmer Scratched His Way Into Legal History. *Saskatchewan Law Review*, 77, 1–25.

Frank, Cathrine O., 2006. Of Testaments and Tattoos: The Wills Act of 1837 and Rider Haggard's *Mr Meeson's Will* (1888). *Law & Literature*, 18 (3), 323–41.

Frank, Cathrine O., 2010. *Law, Literature and the Transmission of Culture in England, 1837–1925*. Abingdon: Routledge.

Fuller, Lon L., 1941. Consideration and Form. *Columbia Law Review*, 41, 799–824.

Google Street View, 2008. *Google Maps*. Available from: https://maps.google.com [Accessed 25 November 2020].

Graeber, David, 2015. *The Utopia of Rules: On technology, stupidity and the secret joys of bureaucracy*. Brooklyn/London: Melville House Publishing.

Haines, David M. Q. C., 2007. *Construction of Wills in Australia*. Sydney: LexisNexis Butterworths.

Halsbury's Laws of England (2nd ed.) 1940. London: Butterworth and Co.

History Lab, 2019. *In Case I Die in This Mess*. History Lab Podcast, season 3, episode 1, released 12 December 2019. Available from: https://historylab.net/s3ep1-in-case-i-die-in-this-mess/ [Accessed 25 November 2020].

Kennedy, Duncan, 1973. Legal Formality. *The Journal of Legal Studies*, 2 (2), 351–98.

Kennedy, Duncan, 1976. Form and Substance in Private Law Adjudication. *Harvard Law Review*, 89 (8), 1685–778.

Kennedy, Duncan, 2000. From the Will Theory to the Principle of Private Autonomy: Lon Fuller's 'Consideration and Form'. *Columbia Law Review*, 100 (1), 94–175.

Langbein, John H., 1975. Substantial Compliance with the Wills Act. *Harvard Law Review*, 88 (3), 489–531.

Langbein, John H., 1987. Excusing Harmless Errors in the Execution of Wills: A report on Australia's tranquil revolution in probate law. *Columbia Law Review*, 87 (1), 1–54.

Langbein, John H., 1993–1994. Will Contests (book review). *The Yale Law Journal*, 103, 2039–48.

Langbein, John H., 2017. Absorbing South Australia's Wills Act Dispensing Power in the United States: Emulation, Resistance, Expansion. *Adelaide Law Review*, 38, 1–11.

Law Commission (United Kingdom), 2017. *Making A Will*. Consultation Paper, CP231.

Leslie, Melanie B., 1996. The Myth of Testamentary Freedom. *Arizona Law Review*, 38, 235–90.

Lindgren, James, 1992. The Fall of Formalism. *Albany Law Review*, 55, 1009–33.
Los Angeles Times, 1926. Will On Petticoat May Dispose of Large Estate. *Los Angeles Times*, 1 February, A1.
Mak, Bonnie, 2011. *How the Page Matters*. Toronto: University of Toronto Press.
Shakespeare, William, 2014 [1595]. *A Midsummer Night's Dream*. Minneapolis, MN: Lerner Publishing Group.
Smith, Barry, 2012. How to do Things with Documents. *Rivista di Estetica*, 50, 179–98.
Smith, Barry, 2014. Document acts. *In*: Anita Konzelmann Ziv and Hans Bernhard Schmid, eds. *Institutions, Emotions, and Group Agents*. Dordrecht: Springer, 19–31.
Tomlins, Christopher, 2014. The Confessions of Nat Turner: A Paratextual Analysis. *Law & History*, 1, 1–28.

Cases

Alan Yazbek v Ghosn Yazbek & Anor [2012] NSWSC 594 (1 June 2012)
Alexander Costa and anor v The Public Trustee in the Estate of Robert Costa [2007] NSWSC 1271
Costa and Another v The Public Trustee of NSW [2008] NSWCA 223
Estate of Harris [1948] Can. Bar Rev. Vol XXVI, 1242–1244
Estate of Roger Christopher Currie, late of Balmain [2015] NSWSC 1098 (5 August 2015)
Hodson v Barnes [1926] Times LR, Friday 3 December 1926, 71
In re Smith Estate [1948] 2 Western Weekly Reports (Saskatchewan) 55
In the Estate of Slavinskyj (1988) 53 SASR 221
Re Estate of Wai Fun Chan, Deceased [2015] NSWSC 1107 (7 August 2015)
Re Nichol; Nichol v Nichol [2017] QSC 220 (9 October 2017)
Re Yu [2013] QSC 322 (6 November 2013)
Wilden (Deceased) [2015] SASC 9 (30 January 2015)

Chapter 11

Powerful documents from the archive

Nyungar letters and the Ancestors' Words project

Anna Haebich, Darryl Kickett, Marion Kickett, Anthony Kickett and Jeannie Morrison

> This project can help to heal the broken spirits of Noongar people. It can help to fix the broken relationships between black and white Australians. Taking the letters of the Ancestors back to the families brings together all the stories of courage and activism in the letters and in family memories. Working together with creative people the families can present the letters and stories in ways that will engage everyone. This can create a ripple effect of healing for us all.
>
> (Darryl Kickett, Nyungar Nation Elder 2018)

Introduction

State and national archives and libraries in Australia hold vast collections of historical documents written *about* Aboriginal people that come from a wide range of colonial public and private 'sites of writing' (van Toorn 2006, 1). Until recent years these documents dominated Australia's celebratory foundational histories. Aboriginal voices are dimmed in the collections but not absent from their pages. The orality of Aboriginal cultures is there in English-language records of oratory such as the translation of the first deputation to a colonial governor in the Swan River Colony in 1833, spoken in Nyungar language and printed in the local newspaper, the *Perth Gazette* (Haebich 2018, 42–47). There are also documents written *by* Aboriginal people. These include letters where they speak directly from the page to government officials, seeking to negotiate or to protest their conditions, using their own words in a mode recognisable to colonial authorities. In Australia in the nineteenth and twentieth centuries, Indigenous letter and petition writing became an important means for Aboriginal people to communicate their claims and concerns to authorities (van Toorn 2006; Curthoys and Mitchell 2011). This was the case in Western Australia from the early 1900s when a rush of Nyungar people, 'literally writing for survival', wrote letters to the new Aborigines Department challenging its regime of legislation and administration curtailing their rights

DOI: 10.4324/9781003247593-14

and independence (Davis et al. 1990, 3). Like the documents written by Van Diemen's Land First Nations people in the 1840s, they are a potent force for decolonising histories and archives, 'mark[ing] the point' where the people 'step out from the shadows of apparent hegemonic control' (Stevens 2017, xl).

Of the documents held by the Department of Aboriginal Affairs (DAA) archive in the State Records Office of Western Australia, these letters written by Ancestors of today's Nyungar families are the most treasured of all, being their words and thoughts transported into the present. For their families, these letters are far more than paper documents. They are their Ancestors' precious words, voices, thoughts and traces of their touch connecting with their own skin. They evoke emotions of grief, joy, sorrow and anger. Released to their families from the archive, their stories of courage and activism are restored to their status as living knowledge and heritage. They provide solace from the pain and trauma that fill the archives. They are also powerful gifts of truth-telling of Nyungar survival against the odds. In a settler-colonial society, the letters have continuing relevance for repeated cycles of injustice and denial of Aboriginal political, cultural and legal rights. They speak directly to a key element of the 2017 Uluru Statement from the Heart to the Australian government calling for the 'truth-telling' of Australia's history and colonisation; the letters 'tell plainly the structural nature of our problem … the *torment of our powerlessness*'.[1]

Nyungar Elder and leader, Dean Collard, described the Ancestors letters as 'foundational documents of the Nyungar nation' (personal communication, 2018). The Nyungar nation of over 40,000 people is now the largest Aboriginal nation in Australia, with growing political and economic status following the Nyungar native title decision and negotiated government settlement of money, land and services in the pipeline. The Ancestors' epistolary activism can inspire new narratives to bridge the past catastrophic destruction of land, culture and people by settler colonists and this new hopeful future. Their words can unite and restore the resilience of Nyungar family lineages and connections with Country and heal the gaps to reconnect the Stolen Generations with their families. The letters can unleash creativity to engage everyone in new reflective studies reimagining the past. This is the unique significance and power of the Ancestors' words.

Ancestors' Words project

This chapter introduces *Ancestors' Words: Nyungar Letter Writing in the Archive*, an Australia Research Council-funded project established at Curtin University in Perth in 2015, the first comprehensive study to recover and analyse Nyungar letter writing in the DAA archives over the period 1860 to 1960, working directly with Elders and families of the letter writers using innovative collaborative action research methodologies. Research into Indigenous epistolary is not new, and there are various published histories and analyses of letter writing in Australian colonial archives (Nelson, Smith and Grimshaw 2002; Van Toorn 2006; Stevens 2017), but the approach of this project is new.

We sought to develop an innovative process for working with the letters and families that would bring out the special power of the Ancestors' words. Working from the premise that 'no one size fits all', we envisaged a Nyungar-driven methodology built on four pillars of Nyungar law and culture: Elders' authority to maintain family history, *kartijin* (knowledge), working together through relationships and values of respect and generosity. Nyungar people led and participated at all levels of the project. A working group of Elders led by Dean Collard provided cultural guidance on ethical practice and protocols for community engagement and impact and sustainable outcomes. The project team[2] included six Nyungar members who contributed their cultural knowledge and understanding and creative outcomes with four *Wedjella* (non-Indigenous) members, including project leader Anna Haebich, all experienced in working with Nyungar people and Indigenous methodologies. Also vital is Ernie Stringer's concept of action research as:

> a pedagogy of possibility … a process of learning … from assisting other people in exploring their own experience in their own terms, and understanding their own situation better as they do it … possibilities emerge when the pedagogy helps to frame the issue in terms that resonate with their own understanding and experience of that same issue.
>
> (2014, 435)

We also heeded Stringer's advice about starting small: 'I've seen over and over again people that start off small and just build stuff that becomes momentous' (2014, 434). With this in mind, we shifted our strategy from presentations about the project and readings of letters to groups of Elders not directly connected to the letters and began the process of returning letters directly to the Elder descendants of the letter writers who shared them with their families at their own pace. We called this very gradual process 'slow research': the focus is on culture, family, relationships and creating and sharing good outcomes and hospitality.

The project gathered over 180 letters from the DAA archive. Identifying letters in the general administrative files (the other major category of personal files is restricted for family access only) was not easy. The vital stage of returning letters to the family was led by Nyungar Elder Darryl Kickett. He began with the task of identifying the appropriate Elders, drawing mainly on his and other Elders' genealogical knowledge. It was the case that the letter writers were known of and remembered by the Elders and families. Great care was taken in preparing for the returns, beginning with meeting to explain to the Elders the project and permissions required and organising a formal meeting at a safe place and time. Material to be returned included photocopies and digital USB copies of the letters and transcripts, a brief genealogy and 'cheat sheets' with historical context and a copy of the *Aborigines Act 1905*. The original letters are permanently archived in the State Records Office of Western Australia and can only be viewed by families on request. The returns followed Nyungar protocols, being respectful of the deeply felt emotions for families seeing the treasured Ancestors' words for the first time. Discussion of the family relationships ensured Elders' cultural safety and freedom to share thoughts and emotions and stories recalled. Special caution was followed for Elders reading the words of the police and department officers. Yarning with Elders and families reunited the Ancestors' words and feelings hidden in the letters with the families' epic journeys of survival and brought understanding of what happened to the generations before. Elders were informed of the limits of copyright law and principles of Indigenous Cultural and Intellectual Property Rights to protect their heritage of the letters. Each situation required an attentive 'ethics of listening to the past, the present and future—an ethics of paying attention' (Swain 2014, 111). Project team member and Nyungar Elder Jeannie Morrison commented after attending meetings with Darryl Kickett:

> The meetings with descendants were unique in that there was a lot of trust with the project team in the delivery and respectful discussion and connections with the descendants which I feel makes this project very unique in its execution and reporting … each situation is unique and requires the utmost sensitivity as each letter and descendant has some degree of emotional involvement in the receiving and the giving.

In 2017, to accommodate the many Elders descended from the Gnowangerup deputation signatories, we held a group workshop at the mission site in Gnowangerup. Elders gathered for two days and nights of storytelling and reminiscing. A copy of the deputation letter was added to the Gnowangerup Aboriginal Cultural Heritage Centre. Our youngest Nyungar team member, Kamsani bin Salleh, was inspired by

> how this letter from Gnowangerup was able to bring all these Elders back to the same mission, to see that there was still some hurt residing but their resilience showed the power that the words written on this paper had.
>
> (bin Salleh, 2017)

The project is committed to decolonising archived collections of Indigenous epistolary activism with reference to issues of access, copyright, reproduction, ethical use and respect for privacy. Verne Harris, archivist for Nelson Mandela, told an Ancestors' Words workshop of Elders, archivists and researchers in Perth in 2018 of his pessimism about achieving recognition of Nyungar rights over the archive, despite the many recommendations made over 20 years ago by the *Bringing Them Home Report* for archives to be returned to communities in line with human rights principles of self-determination, non-discrimination and cultural renewal (Human Rights and Equal Opportunity Commission 1996). The Ancestors' Words project held a special workshop at the State Records Office in Perth for Gnowangerup Elders who had requested to see the original deputation letter and the archives. The power of the original letters was on show as families shed tears of sorrow and joy and exclaimed over snippets of new family information. In discussion with the archivists they called for Nyungar families to assist in managing their family archives to ensure access for them and protocols for other researchers. Discussion shifted to consolidating regional strategies for local Nyungar keeping places that could hold copies of the letters along with genealogies and histories of local families. A subsequent survey for the project showed the lack of resource capacity to achieve this goal.

A vital ongoing discussion led by the Nyungar Working Group addresses the future location and custodianship of the central data base of documents, currently held at Curtin University. The documents include copies and complete transcripts of the 180 Ancestors' letters and government responses in the original files. The data base is designed to provide culturally appropriate storage and access. The Nyungar Working Group considered several options including a central Nyungar Digital Keeping Place raised with the South West Land and Sea Council. However, the Elders' preference remains for local keeping places where families can add information and interviews and photographs and hold workshops for youth and non-Indigenous visitors.

Creative activism by families working directly with their letters through visual arts, performance, literature and story-telling could also unsettle 'Anglo-European approaches to archiving the past' and create 'a double movement towards decolonising history and decolonising the stage' (Neumeier and Schaffer 2014). The rich creativity sparked by the potent fit between activism expressed in the Ancestors' letters and family stories of resistance and resilience is discussed further in the final section of this chapter, with examples of creative writing based on the letters by Nyungar Elders Darryl Kickett and Jeannie Morrison.

Archive, letters, documents

The following critical overview of the DAA archive's complex provenance is a further vital decolonising strategy. Drawing on research by Marsh and Kinnane (2003) and Haebich (2017; 2008), the overview reveals the histories and contexts of the original operational working documents produced by the department, then in the 1970s their transfer to the archival repository for conservation, preservation and public research. The analysis exposes the conditions the Ancestors protested in their letters and the punishments and denigration they risked in reply, as well as the controversies once the archive became public and the new purposes it continues to fulfil.

The DAA archive is a tangible artifact of the settler colonial hegemony in Western Australia from 1897 to 1972 with a significant afterlife extending into the present. It has been likened to the relic instrument of 'a repressive regime' in the manner of Stasi records of former East Germany (Marsh and Kinnane 2003, 113). Like most settler colonial archives it is difficult to work with, being multilayered, and constituted by 'active, generative substances' with complex histories recorded within their documents (Stoler 2009, 1). The DAA archive covers several consecutive administrations: Aborigines Department (1897–1908), Department of Aborigines and Fisheries (1909–1920), Department of the North West (1920–1926), Aborigines Department (1926–1936), Department of Native Affairs (1936–1954) and Department of Native Welfare (1954–1972). They shared foundational policies and laws and also had practices unique to their times. A grid of uniformity was imposed over the diversity of Aboriginal lives, cultures and country. English language took precedence over Aboriginal languages, still widely spoken; even individual's names and homelands were Anglicised.

The documents tell histories in which colonial stakeholders win over Aboriginal rights. They 'speak from the voice of a European' (Marsh and Kinnane 2003, 311). Western ontologies dominate and denigrate: Indigenous people are 'the object (and subject) of the gaze of colonial authorities and experts' (Russell 2004, 161). New approaches to archival practice involving reading against the grain have ignited decades of fierce debate over contested politics, truths, ontologies and historiographies.

The distress for Aboriginal people can be profound: the pervading racism, bureaucratic language, disparaging comments, cruel decisions, the errors and disclosure of private information. The voices of desperation calling from the files to please bring a child back home, help the sick ones, grant rations, give clothes, tents and blankets broke the hearts of our archive researchers. Recalling the painful feelings of working intensively with projects in the NSW archives, Koorie archivists Kirsten Thorpe and Cassandra Willis (2019) wrote: 'Despite all our efforts to be resilient, we realize that we still carry the feelings of distress … of trying to navigate these projects with sensitivity and respect whilst being the face of an archive of trauma'.

The *Aborigines Act 1905* was Western Australia's principal colonising instrument. Expanding on legislation passed in Queensland in 1897, it granted unprecedented powers to control virtually every aspect of the lives of men, women and children deemed to be 'Aboriginal' or 'half-caste', from birth to death (Haebich 1992). Although they were officially deemed to be British subjects, the Act made Aboriginal people 'citizens minus' stripped of all their rights (Mercer 2010). The department in Perth, together with local police officers, controlled employment, marriages, sexual contacts, movements, residences, town curfews, access to land, guns and alcohol and measures to discipline and punish. There were provisions for the responsible Minister to approve exemptions from the Act for persons 'of a suitable degree of civilisation' but, as we will see, they were rarely granted and the privilege could be cancelled at any time for minor infringements. The Act legalised institutional racism and discrimination at all levels of government and society. Policies shifted between protection, civilising, dispossession, segregation, absorption and assimilation; the Act accommodated them all. Families were the target of appalling neglect and constant interference. The Chief Protector of Aborigines' powers of guardianship over Aboriginal children instituted a state-wide system of forced removals that broke families' spirits. The department was responsible for the negligent, segregated services—medical, schooling, rations, shelter and other welfare—provided begrudgingly at a minimum cost. This culminated in an enduring legacy of poverty and neglect.

All was recorded in numbing detail in the department's accumulating operational documents. Administrative files were busy sites of writing headed with file numbers, dates, and filled with names of Aboriginal people, staff, local agents for the department—police, resident magistrates, pastoralists, doctors, missionaries, citizens from all backgrounds most with complaints and requests to remove Aboriginal families. The files listed sites of surveillance and control—town reserves, camps, institutions, prohibited areas and work places—and routine local police duties—rationing, removing children, supervising Aboriginal institutions and enforcing controls generally. Like other colonial archives, the DAA archive reveals the department to have been an 'unruly, piecemeal venture' responding haphazardly to 'events on the ground, laws and duties, bureaucratic need and pressures' (Stoler 2009, 21).

The Chief Protector of Aborigines held the reins of power; combined with limited accountability, this created the potential for a personal fiefdom. Appointed Chief Protector in 1915, Auber Octavius Neville ruled for the next 25 years and left an indelible stamp on Aboriginal affairs to this day. To meet citizen's demands to remove Nyungar families and culture from southwest farming regions, Neville created Carrolup and Moore River native settlements in 1915 and 1918, to act as 'clearing houses': Elders and their cultural knowledge would pass away, and children trained there as domestic servants and farm labourers would marry and merge into the rural working poor (Haebich 1992, 157). Services were now centralised at the settlements, leaving needy families with no safety net but lifelong detention in the settlements or minimal rations outside. Nyungar poverty escalated, and separated families and children were devastated (Haebich 2004).

Neville's weapon to extend his management and control across the state was his record system. Under his watch, he transformed the departmental records into well-oiled machines and the principles he established endured. All decisions, actions, interventions, surveillance, family and personal details and data for planning and reports were to be concentrated in the Perth office. He introduced the first centralised card systems and registers for ready access to vital statistics: issue of rations, blankets, tents and clothing; work permits, agreements and recognisances, gun licenses and exemptions; Aboriginal convictions generally and breaches of the 1905 Act; and registration of marriages and deaths (but rarely births). Neville also standardised forms and procedures for staff in head office and the local police (Haebich 1992, 160–161). His actions increased the vulnerability of families to the removal of their children. They survived by closely monitoring the police and making themselves invisible to them.

Neville sought to cut through such resistance using his pioneering system of personal files containing information about individuals and families collated in documents and card indexes to provide an apparatus for their surveillance and invasive micro-management. This information was his weapon to break up Aboriginal families as the 'fulcrum and the map of Indigenous law and power', thereby denying them the universal human right to live according to their culture and transmit that culture to their children and in this way to eradicate the colonists' so-called Aboriginal problem (Dodson 1994, 36). Particular targets were girls forcibly removed from their families to the settlements to train as domestic servants and sent out to work under his authority, to control their personal and sexual behaviour. Some files held hundreds of documents, including department and personal correspondence, details of employment and wages, requests for earnings to be forwarded, personal spending, medical problems, friendships, boyfriends, courtship and marriage. These personal files became Neville's principal record category, comprising 54 percent of all new records counted at over 27,000 new files between 1926 and 1959, many created before Neville's retirement in 1940. With an estimated state Aboriginal population of only 15,000 people this indicates the level of surveillance operating (Marsh and Kinnane 2003, 120–121).

Worried by statistics showing a dramatic increase in the Nyungar population from the 1920s, Neville began populating working records with fractional calculations of racial descent and race mixing which soon resembled an alarming 'racial archive' in the department (Fritsch 2005, 200). Ann Stoler (2009, 4) reminds us that racial categories are 'mutating ontologies' that can be reformulated 'again and again' according to historical exigencies. In the 1930s, when National Socialist Germany was recasting its definitions of Aryan and Jew, Neville proposed to extend existing racial definitions under the 1905 Act to include 'quadroons' and 'lighter castes'. In 1936, he achieved the amendment of legislation to implement the policy of biological absorption and remove Aboriginal physical *and* cultural characteristics by encouraging young people to marry 'white' (Haebich 2000, 271–275). Neville's retirement in 1940 and the outbreak of war prevented this ultimate solution, but documents record children classified as 'nearly white' being sent to Sister Kate's Quarter Caste Children's Home in Perth to be groomed for their 'ultimate absorption' (Haebich 2000, 280–287).

In 1948 a challenging new era of reform began. It promised a clean slate: a state policy of Aboriginal assimilation, a new Commissioner of Native Affairs—Stanley G. Middleton—new field staff, mainstreaming of all services, federal social service benefits becoming available, planned speedy reform for Aboriginal citizenship and the repeal of laws described by Middleton as 'repugnant to basic humanitarian and welfare principles' and 'unparalleled in the legislative treatment of any other people in the Commonwealth or Pacific territories' (Haebich 2008, 218). Middleton was shocked by Neville's legacy: the personal files and 'caste cards' with fractions 'obsessively mapped and meticulously recorded' as far as '21/23rds' (WASRO 993 1945-0803); conditions at Moore River settlement where 'inmates' sat 'absolutely silent and just stared' (Middleton 1986, n.p.); and evidence in the records of past 'illegal and unsatisfactory procedures' when the department 'seldom, if ever' obtained ministerial warrants to commit children to institutions (WASRO 993 1950-0052). In 1962 the national policy of assimilation was announced, but progress in Western Australia had stalled. Legal equality was not achieved until 1972. Government promises for better conditions were frustrated by lack of political will and funding, and many families remained in dire poverty.

Middleton's concerns may have accelerated the destruction of files that began in 1938 and escalated during the 1950s with 55 percent of administrative files, 21 percent of personal files and 71 percent of staff files destroyed (Marsh and Kinnane 2003, 121 and 125). The value of archival records was also in the ascendant, with a State Archivist appointed in 1945, archiving of state records in the J.S. Battye Library of West Australian History and State Archives from 1956 and a Records Committee in 1958 to oversee disposal schedules for departments. It was not until the 1990s that calls for a moratorium on the destruction of invaluable Aboriginal records began (Marsh and Kinnane 2003, 116–120).

1972 saw the big shift of the department's closely guarded records to the archival repository for storage, conservation, preservation and public research. In that year, the Aboriginal Affairs Planning Authority Act (AAPA) dismantled the department and repealed the last discriminatory laws. Remaining operational records went to the AAPA or Department of Community Welfare which took over child and family matters. Most archived government records slid into oblivion, but the DAA archive began a new life of research and controversy. The documents exposed, for the first time, the full extent of the government's despotic powers to a more sympathetic public following the successful 1967 citizenship referendum. In 1979, while the state prepared to celebrate 150 years of colonial settlement, Nyungar playwright Jack Davis and local historians were constructing very different critical accounts from the DAA archive. The conservative government was caught off guard but acted quickly to staunch the flow of information. In 1981, the Minister responsible, Bill Hassell, embargoed all use of the DAA archive and threatened prosecutions. Police archives were already quarantined. Censorship continued as DAA files were designated permanently 'restricted' or 'open' for access to *bona fide* researchers (Haebich 2017). Many files remain restricted and unassessed to this day.

Use of the DAA archive only increased over time. Aboriginal families searched for their histories and the Stolen Generations found lifelines back to their families, and this escalated in the 1990s with the Aboriginal Legal Service assisting with testimonies for the *Bringing Them Home Report*. Many felt aggrieved by what they read and the terse bureaucratic language used. Information in Neville's many personal files was often so private and contentious that the Department of Community Welfare introduced an embargo to protect privacy by restricting access to the individual concerned or, if deceased, their immediate descendants, and began returning files to families. The department also developed a one-stop-service with support for family history research and counselling services and to return files, since disbanded. Some families have drawn on them to record their Ancestors' lives. Steve Kinnane (2003, 138–139) wrote his grandmother's biography, *Shadow Lines*, from her hefty 300-page file, but he called the documents 'double-edged': they enabled him to write her story but said that it would have been preferable if the files and culture that created them also did not exist.

For Aboriginal people, the DAA archives have proved an intensely emotionally conflicted site of irresolvable tensions, being the repositories of priceless family history and of tragic family loss and injustice. At the same time, this knowledge stolen from families has become a vital source of healing for Aboriginal families, researchers and organisations. The National Report of the Royal Commission into Aboriginal Deaths in Custody cited Senator Patrick Dodson's list of ways the information was being put to use:

> [to] reinstate pride in family experiences; enhance a stronger sense of identity; re-establish contacts with family members; reaffirm interaction with broad family networks; revive and maintain Aboriginal traditions … understand the historical background of contemporary personal issues … re-claim ownership of material pertaining to family life.
>
> (1991, 78)

The documents continue to inspire Aboriginal writers' critical works across history, biography, family memoir, fiction, theatre and film to achieve national and international success. These too contribute to decolonising the archive. Kim Scott's multi-award winning novel *Benang* (1999) is a serious exposé of Neville's distorted vision of race that permeates the archive and the eugenic manipulations he proposes for racial elimination as the ultimate solution. Jack Davis's play *No Sugar* is unsettling: tragic and humorous in the manner of Nyungar story-telling with facts of political sedition, corruption and racial abuse taken directly from the DAA archive. Neville is lampooned as a comical beleaguered despot directing Aboriginal people to wait their turn at the back of his office, waving files and shouting into the phone to the police while dictating missives to his secretary pounding away on her typewriter. Variations of this scene have been reconstructed in the feature film *Rabbit Proof Fence* (1996) and the documentaries *Black Magic* (1988), *Coolbaroo Club* (1996) and *Case 452: A Son's Journey to Find His Mother* (2005). *No Sugar* (1986) became the first Aboriginal play to be performed at the Perth Festival and toured around Australia and to Vancouver and London.

Ancestors' words recovered

Many of the Ancestors' letters recovered in our research were sent from towns across Nyungar country between 1900 and 1920. They addressed broad themes of asserting rights, resisting segregation, staying alive, surviving poverty, keeping families together and more mundane matters like food rations, rail passes and sickness. Most were handwritten by the Ancestors or family members, literacy being a legacy of mission schooling at New Norcia and in Perth and country towns, and from 1914 at Carrolup and Moore River government settlements. Writers usually adopted a formal and direct style that may have followed conventions of the day, but could have come from traditions of Nyungar diplomacy for addressing strangers (Haebich 2018, 17–18). The letters are visually and emotionally striking. Words made in haste and anger are scored into the paper. Others are scribed in perfect cursive script, wary of the recipients' authority. In some you can hear the writer's voice. To see and touch these traces made by the Ancestors, long deceased but known and remembered, is a profound experience for the families.

A distressing presence in the Ancestors' letters files is the official correspondence that the letters provoked in reply. The correspondence reveals closed circuits of shared racist preconceptions and preordained discriminatory decisions with little or no effort to get to the facts of a case. They passed between officers of the Aborigines and police departments, sometimes to the Chief Protector, Commissioner of Police or even responsible Minister of the Crown. Police reports on the person's character, usually negative, were often attached. The often cruel and derogatory wording of decisions sent in reply can be devastating for families to read and requires careful preparation for the returns and follow-up. The coupling of the letters and replies allows for new critical analysis of police communications then and their legacy today. For doubting critics, the official documents filed unedited without thought that they could be read today add credibility to Nyungar historical accounts.

The early decades witnessed a rush of letter writing. There was much to protest about with the 1905 Aborigines Act, the grab-bag of other laws for Aboriginal people and those for the wider community. The stability of families with small farms and reliable work who had survived against all odds was in the balance. Then the rush declined by 1920, perhaps due to the greater risks of Neville's regime of law enforcement and child removals. Also, children were barred from the state schools and literacy. Neville engineered a scenario of spiralling poverty that rippled out across the families and down the generations. Elder Cliff Humphries explained 'We were a bunch of cast-offs in our own country' (Haebich 1985, n.p.).

It seems that Aboriginal people were not informed directly about the 1905 Act, but they bumped unwittingly into its local manifestation, the town police constable, who ordered them out of hotels, confiscated their guns, shot their dogs, kept them out of town and removed their children. Early letters of barely concealed outrage and alarm suggest encounters of this nature. These were letters of protest but also ways for the Ancestors to learn about their rights and how their protests would be handled and by whom. One indignant letter writer challenged why he was barred from the visiting doctor's consulting rooms in the town hotel (WASRO 652 1918-0049). A brief telegram sent in haste by an elderly man, Chucky, in 1907, demanded to know whether the local constable had 'any right to take away my Rifle cannot kill kangaroo refuse to give it to me' (WASRO 255 1907-0286). One man wrote asking why he should have to pay rates and taxes on his farm when he was not entitled to vote or enter hotels (Haebich 1992, 126). Other letters were more measured, like this letter from a distraught unnamed young father in the most perfect script:

> I am afraid that [my wife] will cimmit sueside if the boy is not back soon for she is good for nothing only cry day and night … pleas send the boy back as quick as you can it did not take long for him to go but it takes a long time for him to come back.

The Chief Protector authorised the return with a quick scribble in indelible blue pencil (WASRO 255 1903-0012).

Once caught in this labyrinthine world, the only avenue of escape was to apply for an exemption from the 1905 Act. That letters requesting exemption constituted over half those recovered by the project is evidence of the level of protest and anguish felt by the writers to regain their human rights. Exemptions were rarely granted. Applications were dealt with in correspondence between the department and local police. The applicants were rarely if ever interviewed or asked to provide supporting evidence to demonstrate they were of a 'suitable degree of civilisation'. Instead, officers routinely recommended against exemptions, calling them 'permits to obtain liquor' and applicants 'alcoholics' who would supply alcohol to others (WASRO 652 1913-0498). This was also the opinion at head office: exemptions were a ploy to obtain alcohol, prohibited to Aboriginal people under the 1905 Act. Responding to an application from a young man in Bridgetown, Chief Protector Gale instructed the local police officer:

> Unless you can give some very strong reasons why [he] should be exempted from the Aborigines Act I shall not for one moment entertain his application, as most of the trouble in connection with the full-blooded Aborigines being supplied with liquor comes through the half-castes.
>
> (Kickett and Haebich 2018, 153)

In 1918, Chief Protector Neville advised the Minister against approving exemption for an upstanding senior Nyungar man because 'he was addicted to drink, and does not bear a good character. I recommend that the application be refused'. His advice was accepted (WASRO 652 1918-0827).

Indignation at such treatment of the Ancestors is still palpable today. One hundred and ten years after Chucky's protest against police confiscating his rifle, a reading of his telegram to a group of Elders at an information workshop in Albany led to an hour of yarning and storytelling about how the rifle was his livelihood; how there was no work for him to support his family; how this undermined men's authority; reminiscence about hunting in the old days; police abuse of their powers, then and now; and climaxing in condemnation of the recent Northern Territory intervention. The subject of exemptions and rights was also a hot topic at the project workshop for families at the State Records Office in 2017. In this context, public controversy raging in the media over politicians with dual citizenship holding seats in federal parliament prompted fiery discussion about workshop participants' rights as citizens and First Peoples and the unfinished business of a negotiated treaty that would uphold their rights.

Creative writing

A special achievement of the Ancestors' Words project has been the creative writing and theatre written by descendants of the letter writers. The project working group began the discussion that the letters could be used to create theatre, and this remained an ongoing proposition. In 2017 Yirra Yaakin Theatre Company director, Kyle Morrison, workshopped the possibility of a protest document, like the Gnowangerup letter, being used to celebrate the 50th anniversary of the 1967 referendum for Aboriginal citizenship. In 2019 we held a project symposium with Deakin University to share our ideas with local Indigenous researchers and researchers in Indigenous studies. A highlight was the performance by project team member Carolyn Lewis of her play based on letters written by her grandmother to her family from Moore River settlement. We also watched Sharon Huebner and Ezzard Flowers' video *No Longer a Wandering Spirit, Parts 1 and 2* that links letters of Bessy Flowers, who was sent from Albany in Western Australia to a Victorian mission to marry in 1867, to the recent reunions of her descendants in Victoria and relatives in the west (Huebner and Flowers 2016). Then, in 2019, *Westerly* magazine invited the project to collaborate on a collection of stories by descendants of the letter writers for a special online issue of *Westerly* in print and podcast form. Kim Scott and Elfie Shiosaki led three creative writing workshops and were guest editors. Two of the participants, Nyungar Elders Jeannie Morrison and Darryl Kickett, present stories here. The *eWesterly* issue and podcast are free to download from their website.[3]

Darryl wrote of his ancestor Billie Kickett who, as a young man in 1870, helped lead the John Forrest expedition through treacherous country from Perth to Adelaide, leading to the laying of a telegraph line along the coastline. Here he reflects on a matter of family injustice in a letter written by his ancestor James Yombich Kickett, how words he wrote in good faith to an imagined protector prompted words from a distant authority returned to the family in letters that offered no help or restitution. Jeannie conjured up a scenario for her ancestor Jack Starr after reading his letters requesting the Chief Protector's permission to marry and for an exemption. The story, told with a twist, is about Jack Starr and a young female friend setting out to escape the controls of their work bosses and the government.

"It wasn't my dogs"
James Yombich Kickett

Darryl Kickett, Marion Kickett and Anthony Kickett

Koora, yey, kalyakoorl (past, present, forever): James Yombich Kickett's letter

The Nyungar words above are from the publication *Koompkanying the Pumphrey Bridge Story Book.* This Pumphrey Bridge story is full of photos, with family gatherings of the past and present, the images telling happy stories to the readers. The photos bring the koora, yey, kalyakoorl into clear focus. The koora is also created in the present and then past and present continue on in stories that help new generations to understand their own lives, reassuring them and preparing them for the future. The old stories seem to have a way of resurfacing in the future in different ways and this phenomenon is certainly illustrated

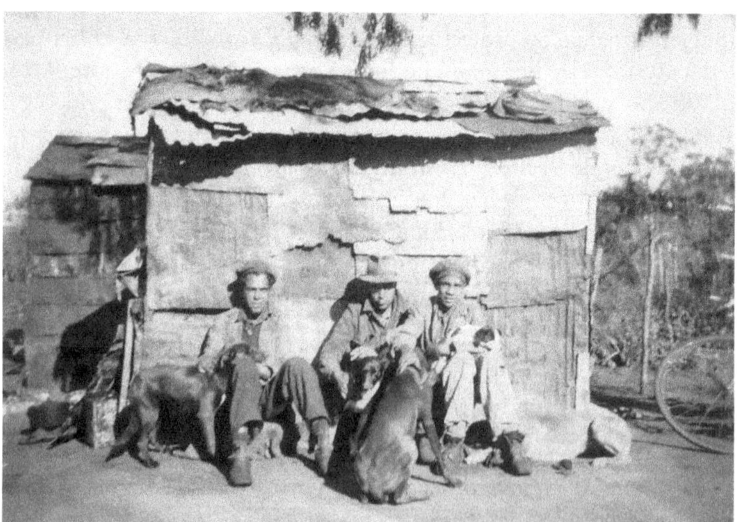

Figure 11.1 George Kickett, Walter Kickett (grandson of James Yombuch), Scott Blurton with family dogs, c. 1936, image courtesy of Professor Marion Kickett.

in this story generously given here by Marion Kickett, great-grand daughter of James Yombich Kickett.

> As a child I remember my father telling me about the shooting of his grandfather's dogs. Dogs were always an important commodity of our family.
>
> I was thinking about this photo of my sister Jan and I. In the background is Dad's Kangaroo dog Boo-ma. Dad and his brother trained Boo-ma to bring down the big male kangaroos, obviously Dad had a great deal of faith in this dog and named him accordingly. In the photo I am about 8 or 9 months old and Jan is approximately 4 years old.
>
> Boo-ma was shot by the police who came whilst my Dad was at work. Apparently the dog had killed sheep. I was 5 years old at the time in year one at school when the dog was shot. I clearly remember Mum saying to us when we got home from school 'wait until your father gets home he will bury Boo-ma'. The school photo was taken around the same time the dog was shot.
>
> The photo of Jan holding Donna shows one of our other dogs called Monty. Uncle Andy Kickett used to tease us and say we had a Whydjella and a Noongar Dog. He would get angry because Monty (black in colour) our Noongar dog was the dog who wanted to bite uncle and of course it wasn't right Monty being black. We had these two dogs before I was born one for hunting and the other for protection when Dad worked away. After both our dogs were shot we found out that sheep were still being killed by a dog. So our two dogs were wrongly shot. I remember my father's words as he was burying our dogs 'they still killing our dogs'. Being only 5 years old I asked who else's dogs were shot. It was then the story of Grandfather Yombich was told to me. As I grew older I remember hearing different versions of the story many more times.

Setting the scene for disadvantage

During the period from 1829 (the year the colonial government began in Western Australia) to when James Yombich Kickett's (Yombich) dogs were shot in 1907, a series of events had combined to impact the wellbeing of Nyungar families. From these events Lois Tilbrook (1983) argues that the economy of the Aborigines had been irreversibly disrupted from the time the first boatload of British colonists landed at Fremantle (Tilbrook 1983).

Looking back on diseases, massacres and stealing Nyungar children all seemed to be attempts to smash the Nyungar Bibbulmen family and break their spirit. The British colonial experiment left a catastrophic impact on Nyungar people in the south west of Western Australia. The once thriving population of thousands was reduced to a mere 1200 in the census count of 1901.

Remnants of families were left in positions of powerlessness and at the mercy of new authorities who seemed indifferent to the needs of the original people. It seemed new governments were only concerned about their own growth and prosperity.

One essential need for Nyungar families was to be able to access their tribal lands to hunt. The hunting lands were blocked by the new laws, interfering with Yombich's ability to feed his family. Fences interfered with the spear hunting including tracking and stalking kangaroos and other animals. In less than a century dingoes were replaced by the kangaroo dogs specially bred to assist with a family meat supply. Yombich's people embraced these new dog breeds from Britain.

Bush meat in 1907 became more and more scarce as competition for the game meat grew with colonists equipped with their guns and dogs efficiently decimating local bush supplies. New fences created barriers that cut across ancient hunting trails, blocking out hunters like Yombich. All this was changing forever the old lifestyles that were scripted directly from the dreaming.

Ironically, the new colonial laws placed guns out of reach for Yombich's people as police strictly regulated the use of guns under the provisions of the 1905 Aborigines Act. Hunting dogs on camp sites were culled, impacting negatively on families. Jobs introduced by the settler colonists and offered to the Nyungar were intermittent and not always available due to the seasonal nature of work and, at times, there was preference to hire new immigrant workers from the 1890s gold rushes. Social benefits like invalid and old age pensions and maternity allowances were introduced by the federal government in 1908 and 1912 respectively. Such benefits could not be accessed by the families subjected to the laws of the Aborigines Act 1905. Many turned to the Aborigines Department for 'rations' provided for in the Act—flour, tea and sugar.

Yombich's letter from the koora

The scene was set by the events described above to create the circumstances within which James Kickett wrote his letter dated 5 May 1907 about police shooting his valuable dogs.

A copy of the original letter is set out in Figure 11.2. The following is a transcription of the letter:

Beverley

May 5th 1907

To Mr Prinsep

Aboriginal Protector

Perth

Dear Sir

I am taking the liberty of writing to you re Police shooting dogs. A certain Gentleman laid information to the Police to the effect that my dogs were killing his sheep. The Police

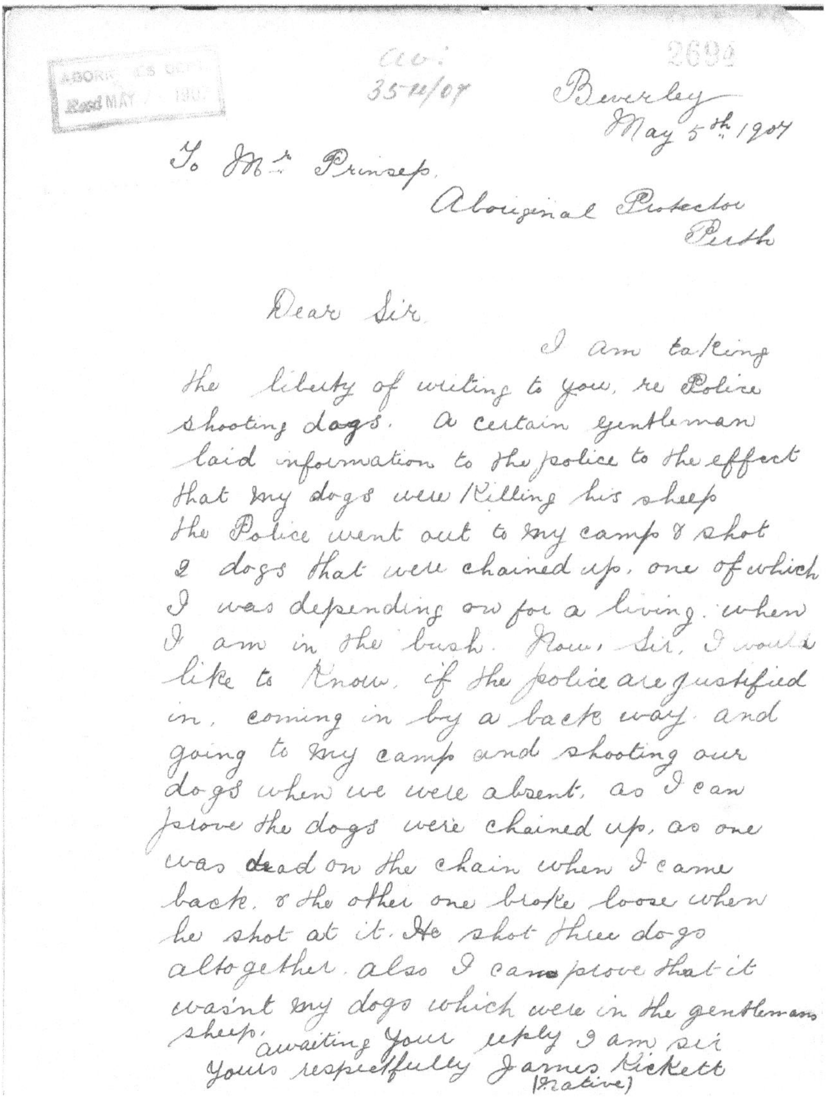

Beverley
May 5th 1907

To Mr Prinsep,
Aboriginal Protector
Perth

Dear Sir,

I am taking the liberty of writing to you, re Police shooting dogs. a certain gentleman laid information to the police to the effect that my dogs were Killing his sheep the Police went out to my camp & shot 2 dogs that were chained up, one of which I was depending on for a living. when I am in the bush. Now, Sir, I would like to Know, if the police are justified in, coming in by a back way. and going to my camp and shooting our dogs when we were absent, as I can prove the dogs were chained up, as one was dead on the chain when I came back, & the other one broke loose when he shot at it. He shot three dogs altogether. also I can prove that it wasn't my dogs which were in the gentlemans sheep, awaiting your reply I am sir

Yours respectfully James Kickett (Native)

Figure 11.2 James Kickett letter, courtesy of Darryl Kickett, Marion Kickett and Anthony Kickett and State Records Office of Western Australia 255 1907-0357.

went out to my camp and shot 2 dogs that were chained up, one of which I was depending on for living, when I am in the bush. Now Sir I would like to know if the Police are justified in coming in by a back way and going to our camp and shooting our dogs when we're absent, as I can prove the dogs were chained up, as one was dead on the chain when I came back & the other one broke loose when he shot at it. He shot three dogs all together. Also I can prove that it wasn't my dogs that were in the Gentleman's sheep.

Awaiting your reply
I am Sir
yours respectfully
James Kickett
Native

The original letter was located in the DAA archives of the Western Australian State Records Office in Perth (WASRO 255 1907-0357 James Kickett). The contents of this file included the Kickett letter, a note from the Chief Protector of Aborigines, Charles Prinsep, to Edmund Pechelle and a request from Pechelle to the Commissioner of Police requesting a police report on the complaint by Kickett, a police report in reply dated 11 June 1907 and an internal note from Pechelle to Prinsep that the police report was 'satisfactory'.

Transcript of report of Constable Cotty to Sub-Inspector Duncan in 354/1907:

Sub Insp Duncan

I respectfully report re the attached. That in May inst. Mr Robin Farmer reported to me that the natives dogs had been killing his sheep and on the 1st May he caught two of them in the act. He stated the natives were camped near his home stead and requested the police to destroy these dogs in consequence of Mr Robins report. P C Wood approached to the Natives camp to make inquiries and on his arrival found four dogs in the camp belonging to a native named Yombich and his woman. P C Wood shot two dogs the two that had killed the sheep and left the native Yombich and his woman a dog each one kangaroo and one ordinary dog.

Yombich came to me and complained about the police shooting his dogs and when I explained to him that these two dogs had been killing Mr Robins sheep and also that they were only allowed one dog each unless licensed he seemed quite satisfied. This is the first intimation I have heard of any dogs belonging to James Kickett having been shot by police.

J H Cotty

Constable 218

11.6.07.

The Kickett letter is exceptionally well written, laying out the facts from Yombich's viewpoint and issuing a strong rebuttal with confidence to the accusation that his dogs had killed the sheep. He even asserts that he could prove it was not his dogs. However, Yombich does not give any details on the evidence that proves his dogs were not in with sheep.

In support of his claim, Yombich lists specific facts in his letter. He claims that both dogs were 'chained up' when police shot at them. One died still

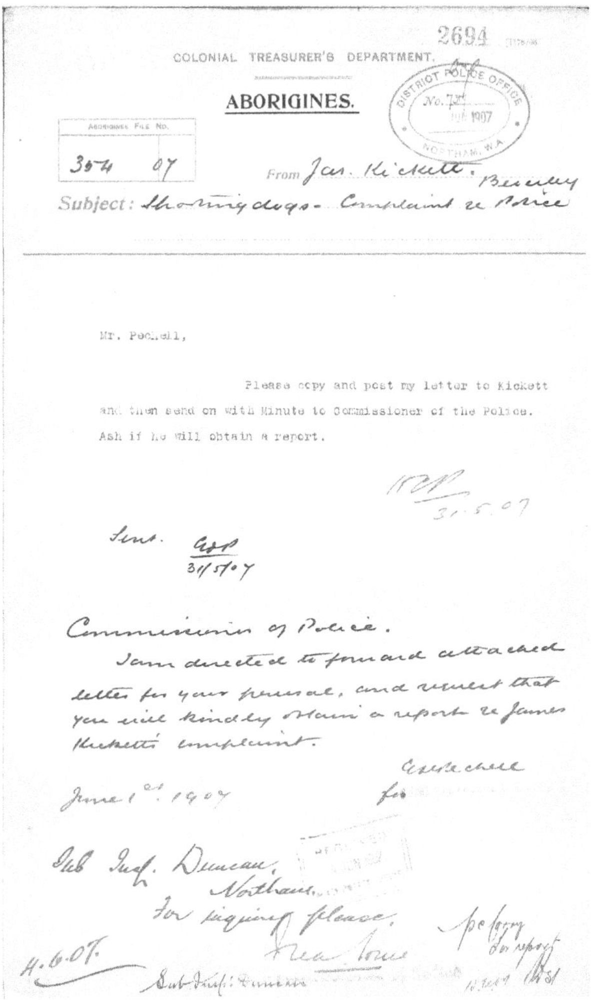

2694

COLONIAL TREASURER'S DEPARTMENT.

ABORIGINES.

DISTRICT POLICE OFFICE No. 72 1907 NORTHAM, W.A.

Aborigines File No. 354 07

From Jas. Kickett. Beverley

Subject: Shooting dogs - Complaint re Police

Mr. Pochell,

Please copy and post my letter to Kickett and then send on with Minute to Commissioner of the Police. Ask if he will obtain a report.

31.5.07

Sent. 31/5/07

Commissioner of Police.

I am directed to forward attached letter for your perusal, and request that you will kindly obtain a report re James Kickett's complaint.

for

June 1st 1907

Sub Insp. Duncan, Northam,

For enquiry please,

4.6.07.

Figure 11.3 Chief Protector of Aborigines, Charles Prinsep, to Commissioner of Police, courtesy of State Records Office of Western Australia 255 1907-0357.

constrained by a chain. The second dog had 'broke loose' from a restraint when shot at. The letter points to a third dog killed by police. Clearly Yombich was offended by police shooting the valuable hunting dog that he, at the age of 42, 'depended on' to hunt down the game when he was in the bush. A dog may be a good hunter for kangaroo or goanna as a source of food. Dogs are also highly valued as companions and are, in some places, kinship-connected through dreamtime and law. Importantly, they can offer protection from physical and spiritual threats, and on cold nights dogs provided warmth (see news article

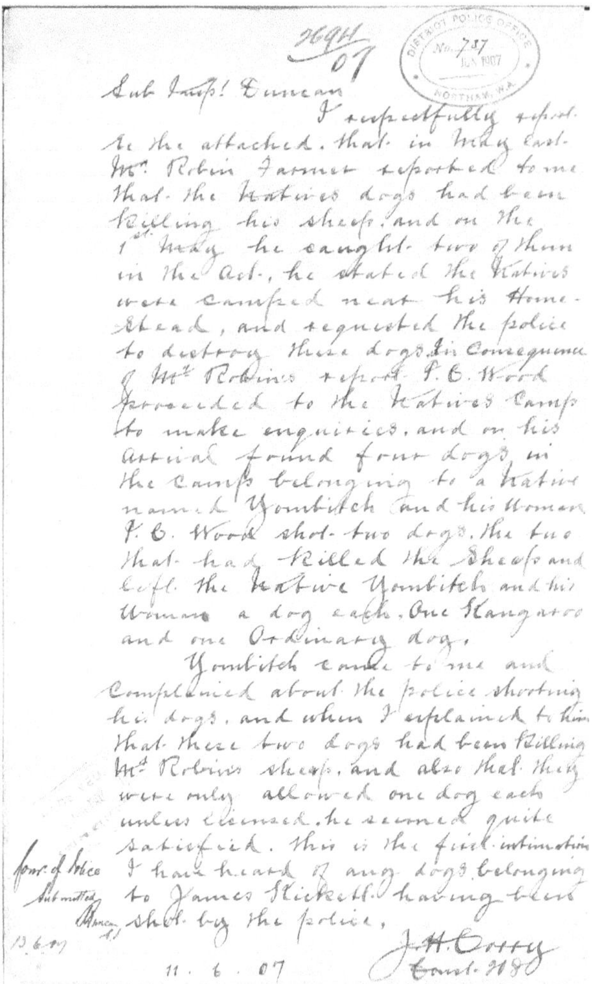

2694/07

DISTRICT POLICE OFFICE No. 737 JUN 1907 NORTHAM W.A.

Sub Insp! Duncan

I respectfully report re the attached. that in May last Mr Robin Farmer reported to me that the Natives dogs had been killing his sheep. and on the 1st May he caught two of them in the Act, he stated the Natives were camped near his Homestead, and requested the police to destroy these dogs. In Consequence of Mr Robins report P.C. Wood proceeded to the Natives Camp to make enquiries. and on his arrival found four dogs in the Camp belonging to a Native named Yombitch and his Woman P.C. Wood shot two dogs. the two that had Killed the Sheep and left the Native Yombitch and his Woman a dog each. One Kangaroo and one Ordinary dog.

Yombitch came to me and Complained about the police shooting his dogs. and when I explained to him that these two dogs had been Killing Mr Robins sheep. and also that they were only allowed one dog each unless licensed. he seemed quite satisfied. this is the first intimation I have heard of any dogs belonging to James Stickett having been shot by the police,

J.H. Cotty
Const. 2180

11 . 6 . 07

Comr. of Police
Submitted
Duncan S.I.
13.6.07

Figure 11.4 Constable Cotty to Sub-Inspector Duncan in WASRO 255 1907-0357.

dated 28 February 2013 at the website of the *Animal Management in Rural and Remote Indigenous Communities*).

Yombich was further offended by the policeman, Constable Wood, coming in by 'the back way' to his home as well as shooting the dogs when he and his family were not home. One can imagine how the unapologetic desecration of the Yombich home (with scenes of treasured family dogs lying dead in pools of blood) impacted traumatically on his wife and three young children.

We note that Prinsep asked the Commissioner of Police for a report on the incident described in the Kickett letter. The PC Cotty report dated 11 June 1907 stated that a local farmer Mr Robin witnessed two dogs killing his sheep on the 1 May 1907, specifically pointing to two native dogs from a native camp. The report further confirmed that police had met with Yombich and explained two dogs had killed the sheep and that they (meaning Yombich and his wife May) were only allowed one dog each. The extra dogs in his home would require the payment of a licence fee. Cotty stated that he believed Yombich to be satisfied with the explanation.

When Cotty said in his report that he explained to Yombich that he and his 'woman' were only allowed one dog each unless the additional dogs on site were licensed, Cotty was referring to the Dog Act 1903 in Western Australia. The Act had a special section for the dogs belonging to Aboriginal people. Section 29 directed that Aboriginal males were not allowed to keep more than one unregistered dog. This one dog had to be a male and free from mange or any other contagious disease.

Section 29 also described circumstances where police were authorised by the Act to destroy the dogs belonging to Aboriginal families, without first obtaining a court order. When the number of unregistered dogs kept in Aboriginal homes exceeded the number of adult males, police were authorised to execute any surplus dogs.

Tracking through evidence

One obvious reason Yombich claims his dogs were innocent was because they were tied to chains at the Kickett home. One could imagine that after hearing the accusations made about his dogs, Yombich, being an experienced hunter, would have carried out two urgent actions. Firstly, he would have checked for signs of sheep blood and wool on the dogs, and secondly, he would have searched for dog tracks near the sheep and checked the direction the tracks went to see if the tracks belonged to his dogs. PC Wood, without conducting a proper investigation to establish the facts, took it upon himself to kill the innocent dogs. Cotty then had to rely on the 1903 Dog Act as the reason for shooting the dogs, that any excess dogs could be destroyed without a court order. It is certain that a search for blood and wool traces on the accused dogs would be included in any proper police investigation. The details are not on file. We assume that Yombich would have raised this with Cotty as well as the absence of tracks and sheep blood. This would explain why Yombich was confident he could provide proof that it was not his dogs.

Unfortunately, the official reply from Chief Protector Prinsep to the James Kickett letter is missing from the file. However, document 354/07 titled *Colonial Secretary's Department Police 2694/07* has this note written on it:

> '*Seen – Explanation satisfactory 20/6/07*'.

The copy of the police page dated 20 June 1907 shows police authorities are satisfied with the explanation given by the Cotty report of 11 June 1907.

Thus, any reply from Prinsep to Kickett would have supported the Cotty report finding on the two points that the Kickett dogs had killed the sheep and that excess dogs were living at the Kickett home.

Conclusion

The family of Yombich, his wife May and his three children, Herbert (ten years), Douglas (eight) and Thomas (six) would have arrived home to find the slain dogs. They were left to clean up the tragic mess left behind by an insensitive police officer. The desecration of the family home would have been permanently etched in the memory of the family. One can plainly deduce that the sheer lack of respect shown by police for his family would have driven Yombich to take the matter further and write the letter of complaint.

The sequence of events is interesting with Robin, the farmer, complaining to police on 1 May 1907 then, soon after, Yombich meets the police for an explanation of the dog shooting, and on the 5 May 1907, not satisfied with the Cotty meeting, he sends a letter to Prinsep. The Cotty reply to Sub Inspector Duncan of the Northam office was dated 11 June 1907. This was six weeks after the shooting incident, long after any evidence of an attack by Yombich's dogs could be gathered, long enough to cobble together a 'reasonable' excuse and certainly long enough to demonstrate their disrespect for Yombich's urgent complaint.

Simply put, the factual evidence that might have been uncovered by the police during their investigation to support any guilty verdict and dispel any suspicions today is missing. The thought of police acting from a base of discrimination towards Aboriginal people is not unusual given the history of Aboriginal police relationships.

The flimsy police evidence described above could have been tested in a court of law if Yombich had access to legal counsel. Any reader of this paper could be confident that the dogs would have been given a stay of execution until the dogs were deemed guilty beyond reasonable doubt. One option that seems to have been excluded by PC Cotty is that Yombich could have been asked to license his extra dogs thus avoiding all of the nasty performance.

A surprising point to the story is that when Cotty met Yombich, he did not realise the person standing in front of him named Yombich was also James Kickett, the man who was responsible for the writing of the letter of complaint.

Kalyakoorl (forever)

We didn't have any guns in our home. We had dogs. Sometimes we went out with our yonga dogs. We kept away from the roads making a path through

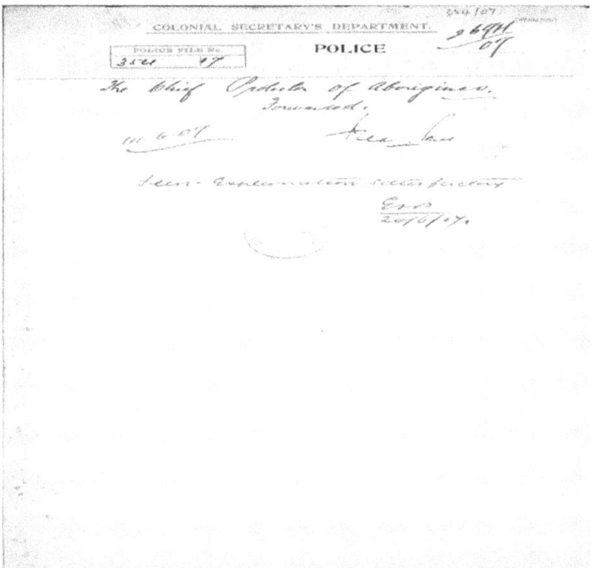
COLONIAL SECRETARY'S DEPARTMENT.

POLICE

POLICE FILE No.

The Chief Protector of Aborigines,
Forwarded.

Figure 11.5 Pechelle to Chief Protector Prinsep 'Seems explanation satisfactory', courtesy of State Records Office of Western Australia 255 1907-0357.

fences and back lanes to the remnant bush lands. To take our dogs hunting because we had no meat.

We had a greyhound-like dog who'd grab a rabbit and throw it in the air and catch it in his jaws and kill it with a shake or two of its head. And sometimes if we were lucky the dogs would corner a kangaroo in the bush. Dogs would rush in and grab it by the throat before it could strike the dogs. Sometimes we had to go in with a big stick to put it down.

A young dog needed to be trained with support of an older dog with us urging the dog to chase a kangaroo or rabbit that may have jumped out in our path. In this way by watching the older dog the younger dog learned to kill without damaging the meat. Then we came along. Then we would bleed the kangaroo by cutting its throat.

So when Yombich's dog was shot he didn't have an experienced dog to coach the younger dog, which might have caused difficulty. Added to his anger ...

With our dogs, we felt safe with them sitting outside the house at night to warn us if anyone was coming near our place. They could even detect bad spirits.

All this is still carried on today, right now.

These words from the past speak today directly to the Uluru Statement: they 'tell plainly the structural nature of our problem ... the *torment of our powerlessness*' (Uluru Statement 2017).

Boordawon (soon or later)

Jack and Ruby
State Records Office of Western Australia 653 1924-0488
Written by Jeannie Morrison

I don't know Jack. I've never met him, but I've been reading his letters to Mr Neville, the Chief Protector of Aborigines. He wants to get married and he's asked permission from the department. It was the way things were done those days, having to ask Government for things that you want in life. Under the 1905 Act, Aboriginal people, like my mother, were sent to work on farms as domestics when they were in their teens. Any wages earned were redirected back to the department and recorded and held in an account. The process was to write to the department to access their pay to purchase items. Mr Neville would decide whether permission was granted according to individual circumstances.

Jack

Jack was a real character who was determined to find a wife to take back to Currawagh Station. He stated his position to Mr Neville that he worked carting rams and cattle to different towns justifying his eligibility and responsibilities to marry. The answer was always no.

Jack wakes slowly and looks across through half closed eyes to the clock sitting on his bedside table. Shit, its 4:00 am he sighs, time to get up. He rolls out of bed and dresses in his worn jeans, check shirt and battered hat. He puts the kettle on for a quick cuppa before he heads off to load up the truck.

He's had a busy morning and finished what he needed to do by two thirty. He thinks about Ruby. He smiles to himself and decides to turn the truck towards Doorawah Station. It will only take a couple of hours to get to Ruby then we can head off to Carnarvon before it gets too late.

Ruby

I've been working at Doorawarah Station for three years now doing all kinds of domestic jobs. I'm here under the 1905 Act which my people whisper about. I was living at the mission with my mother and sisters and as soon as I turned 14 years old I was taken to 2 other farms which I ran away from. Now I'm here at Doorawarah working for old Mrs Carter. She alright to me though.

It's a beautiful early spring day, the sun is warm, I can smell the moisture of the ground and trees and plants around the garden Mrs painfully planted in the hard ground. She made a vegie garden too and she asks me to get vegies from the garden and help to prepare them for the evening meal. Mr Carter is out bush droving the cattle, so only me and Mrs is here with her two children that I help to look after.

I was washing the clothes in the laundry out the back of the house. I've lit the fire under the big copper and washing the clothes from the dirty laundry bag Mrs gave me. There's an old electric washing machine with rollers over the cement twin sink where you put the clothes through the wringer squeezing soapy water from them and they drop into a trough of cold water to rinse, then they are put back through the roller to wring them out again, then into the basket then pegged onto the clothes line.

In the distance I see a large dust cloud which usually means someone is coming down the road into the farm. As it gets closer I see it's a truck. Then I see Jack. He comes into the yard and waits, engine purring, a wide grin on his face. I walk the short distance to the truck.

'What do you want Jack?' I ask.

'I've come for *you* Ruby. Come with me to Carnarvon, we can get married' he says enthusiastically. 'I've got something for you' he says with a cheeky look on his face.

Jack pulls out three flash looking dresses, waving them from the window as if it were a prize.

I felt a sense of excitement. This is the perfect opportunity. I thought to myself. 'Come on Ruby, jump in' says Jack, getting slightly agitated. 'Wait a minute' I said, 'Just gotta grab a couple of things while the Mrs is busy'.

I run quickly into the house and throw what little possessions I have into a pillow case and quietly make my way to the truck. Can't see Mrs anywhere. I climb into the truck and Jack pulls away from the farm, my prison, this hell hole.

A few minutes later, hearing the sound of the engine, Mrs comes running from the back door in time to see Jack's truck heading towards the main road.

'Bloody girl' she says angrily. 'Takin' off like that without a word'.

'So Jack, what's the plan?' I ask as he settles in the rhythmic motions of changing gears and the loud throttle of the engine.

'We get to Carnarvon tonight, we can probably get married tomorrow or the day after, then I'll take you to Currawagh Station as my wife'.

I give him a slow smile of assurance.

We drive in silence, sometimes some small talk about news of people we know and have seen lately. After a few hours, the sun has set, we see the lights of Carnarvon approaching. My mind is racing. Soon we enter the long main street. Jack pulls into the closest garage to refuel.

'Just gunna fuel up' says Jack as he climbs down from his seat and walks to the back of the truck. I hear him unscrewing the metal cap of the fuel tank and then the crank of the bowser spewing out fuel into the truck's tank.

I wait a few moments, then pick up the pillow case and the dresses Jack bought, I quietly open the door, and slip away into the night.

Western Australia State Records Office

File numbers only, names of individuals and places withheld.

WASRO 255 1907-0286
WASRO 255 1907-0357
WASRO 652 1912-0095
WASRO 652 1913-0498
WASRO 652 1918-0049
WASRO 653 1924-0488
WASRO 993 1939-0087
WASRO 993 1945-0803
WASRO 993 1950-0052

Notes

1 The 2017 National Aboriginal and Torres Strait Islander Uluru Statement from the Heart sets out three key elements of reform for the Australian government: constitutional change, legislative change and truth-telling (National Constitutional Convention 2017).

2 Team members are Anna Haebich, Darryl Kickett, Elfie Shiosaki, Carolyn Lewis, Jeannie Morrison, Kamsani Bin Saleh, Irma Woods, Gabriel Maddock, Tiffany Shellam, Ellen Kraly.

3 The *eWesterly* issue and podcast *Ancestors' Words* are free to download from the website. https://westerlymag.com.au/issues/ancestors-words/

References

bin Salleh, Kamsani, 2017. *Albany/Gnowangerup Report 7–12/8/17 for Ancestors Words project*. Bentley: Curtin University.

Centre for Aboriginal Studies, 2020. CAS500 Indigenous Research Methodologies. Bentley: Curtin University. Available from: https://study.curtin.edu.au/offering/unit-pg-cas500-indigenous-research-methodologies--inds5004/ [Accessed 23 October 2020].

Curthoys, Ann, and Mitchell, Jessie, 2011. 'Bring this good paper to the Governor': Aboriginal petitions in Britain's Australian colonies. *In*: Saliha Bellmessous, ed. *Native Claims: indigenous Law against Empire 1500–1921*. Oxford and New York: Oxford University Press, 182–203.

Davis, Jack, 1982. *Kullark/The Dreamers*. Sydney: Currency Press.

Davis, Jack, 1986. *No Sugar*. Sydney: Currency Press.

Davis, Jack, Muecke, Stephen, Narogin, Mudrooroo, and Shoemaker, Adam, eds., 1990. *Paperbark a Collection of Black Australian Writings*. St Lucia: University of Queensland Press.

Dodson, Mick, 1994. The Rights of Indigenous People in the International Year of the Family. *Family Matters*, 37, 34–41.

Dodson, Patrick, 1991. *National Report of The Royal Commission into Aboriginal Deaths in Custody*, vol. 2. Canberra: Government Printer.

Dustman, Eric L., Kohan, Mark B., and Stringer, Ernie T., 2014. Starting Out and Building Small with Ernie Stringer: Personal Insights into Action Research and Educational Change. *Action Research*, 124, 426–43.

Fritzsche, Peter, 2005. The Archive and the Case of the German Nation. *In*: Antoinette Burton, ed. *Archive Stories: Facts, Fictions, and the Writing of History*. Durham, NC: Duke University Press, 184–208.

Haebich, Anna, 1985. *Interview with Cliff Humphries, A Bunch of Caste-Offs Trends in Aboriginal History of Western Australia 1900–1936*, vol. 2. Thesis (PhD). Western Australia: Murdoch University.

Haebich, Anna, 1992. *For Their Own Good Aborigines and Government in the South West of Western Australia 1900–1940* (2nd ed.). Nedlands, WA: University of Western Australia Press.

Haebich, Anna, 2000, *Broken Circles: Fragmenting Indigenous Families 1800–2000*. Fremantle, WA: Fremantle Arts Centre Press.

Haebich, Anna, 2004. "Clearing the Wheat Belt": Erasing the Indigenous Presence in the Southwest of Western Australia. *In*: A. Dirk Moses, ed. *Genocide and Settler Society*. Oxford: Berhahn Books, 267–89.

Haebich, Anna, 2008. *Spinning the Dream: Assimilation in Australia 1950–1970*. Fremantle, WA: Fremantle Arts Centre Press.

Haebich, Anna, 2014. Fever in the archive. *Humanities Australia*, 5, 23–35.

Haebich, Anna, 2017. Aboriginal Lives Trapped in the Archives. *In*: Paul Longley Arthur, ed. *Migrant Nation: Australian Culture, Society and Identity*. London: Anthem Press, 37–56.

Haebich, Anna, 2018. *Dancing in Shadows Histories of Nyungar Performance*. Crawley, WA: University of Western Australia Press.

Haebich, Anna, Shellam, Tiffany, and Kickett, Darryl, 2019. Ancestors' Words: Nyungar Letter Writing in the Archive (1860–1960). *Ancestors words new Aboriginal writing from Western Australia Westerly*, Special Issue 8, 30–34. Available from: https://www.westerlymag.com.au/wp-content/uploads/edd/2019/12/Ancestors-Words.pdf [Accessed 23 October 2020].

Huebner, Sharon, and Flowers, Ezzard, 2016. *No Longer a Wandering Spirit, Parts 1 and 2*. Melbourne: State Library of Victoria. Available from: https://www.slv.vic.gov.au/view-discuss/no-longer-wandering-spirit-part-one; https://www.slv.vic.gov.au/view-discuss/no-longer-wandering-spirit-part-two [Accessed 23 October 2020].

Human Rights and Equal Opportunity Commission, 1997. *Bringing Them Home: Report of the National Inquiry into the Separation of Aboriginal and Torres Strait Islander Children from their Families*. Sydney: Human Rights and Equal Opportunity Commission.

Humphreys, Cathy, McCarthy, Gavan, and Swain, Shurlee, n.d. *Find & Connect, History About Australian Orphanages, Children's Homes & Other Institutions*. University of Melbourne, Australian Catholic University. Available from: https://www.findandconnect.gov.au/guide/wa/WE00788 [Accessed 23 October 2020].

Kickett, Darryl 2018. 'Through Eyes of an Elder', Ancestors' Words project report, Curtin University [typescript].

Kickett, Darryl, and Haebich, Anna, 2018. Ancestors Words: The Power of Nyungar Letter Writing. *First things first: Griffith Review*, 60, 146–56.

Kickett, Darryl, 2019. Billie and Forrest. *Ancestors Words New Aboriginal Writing from Western Australia Westerly*, Special Issue 8, 18–27. Available from: https://www.westerlymag.com.au/wp-content/uploads/edd/2019/12/Ancestors-Words.pdf [Accessed 23 October 2020].

Kinnane, Stephen, 2003. *Shadow Lines*. Fremantle: Fremantle Arts Centre Press.

Marsh, Lauren, and Kinnane, Stephen, 2003. Ghost Files: The Missing Files of the Department of Indigenous Affairs Archives. *Journal of Studies in Western Australian History*, 23, 111–27.

Mercer, David, 2010. 'Citizen Minus'?: Indigenous Australians and the citizenship question. *Citizenship Studies*, 7, 421–45.

Middleton, Stanley G., 1986. *Interview by Bill Bunbury* [transcript]. Perth: Library Board of Western Australia.

Morrison, Jeannie, 2019. Jack and Ruby. *Ancestors Words new Aboriginal Writing from Western Australia Westerly*, Special Issue 8, 13–15. Available from: https://www.westerlymag.com.au/wp-content/uploads/edd/2019/12/Ancestors-Words.pdf [Accessed 23 October 2020].

Morrison, Jeannie, 2020. *Team Member Report: Ancestors Words Project*. Bentley: Curtin University.

National Constitutional Convention, 2017. *Uluru Statement from the Heart*. Available from: https://ulurustatement.org/ [Accessed 23 October 2020].

Nelson, Elizabeth, Smith, Sandra, and Grimshaw, Patricia, eds., 2002. *Letters from Aboriginal Women of Victoria, 1867–1926*. Melbourne: History Department, The University of Melbourne.

Neumeier, Beate, and Shaffer, Kay, eds., 2014. *Decolonizing the Landscape: Indigenous Cultures in Australia*. Amsterdam: Rudopi.

Russell, Lynette, 2004. Indigenous Knowledge and Archives: Accessing Hidden History and Understandings. *Australian Academic & Research Libraries*, 36 (2), 161–71.

Scott, Kim, 1999. *Benang: From the Heart*. Fremantle: Fremantle Arts Centre Press.

Scott, Kim, and Shiosaki, Elfie, guest eds., 2019. *Ancestors Words new Aboriginal Writing from Western Australia Westerly*, Special Issue 8. Available from: https://www.westerlymag.com.au/wp-content/uploads/edd/2019/12/Ancestors-Words.pdf [Accessed 23 October 2020].

Seaman, Paul, 1984. *The Aboriginal Land Inquiry: Report*. Perth: West Australian Government.

South West Land and Sea Council, Host, John, and Owen, Chris, 2009. *'It's Still in My Heart, This is My Country' the Single Noongar Claim History*. Crawley, WA: UWA Publishing.

South West Land and Sea Council, n.d. Settlement Agreement. Available from: http://www.noongar.org.au/settlement-agreement [Accessed 23 October 2020].

Stevens, Leonie, 2017. *'Me write myself' The free Aboriginal inhabitants of Van Dieman's Land at Wybalenna*. Clayton, Victoria: Monash University Publishing.

Stoler, Ann, 2009. *Along the Archival Grain: Epistemic Anxieties and Colonial Common Sense*. Princeton, NJ: Princeton University Press.

Swain, Rachel, 2014. Burning Daylight: Contemporary Indigenous Dance, Loss and Cultural Intuition. *In*: Paul Macneill, ed. *Ethics and the Arts*. London: Springer, 99–112.

van Toorn, Penny, 2006. *Writing Never Arrives Naked: Early Cultures of Writing in Australia*. Canberra: Aboriginal Studies Press.

Thorpe, Kirsten, and Willis, Cassandra, 2019. Aboriginal Histories in Australian Government Archives: Working with Records of Trauma. *Roots*, 10. Available from: https://www.laacollective.org/work/aboriginal-histories-in-australia-government-archives [Accessed 23 October 2020].

Tilbrook, Lois, 1983. *Nyungar Tradition: Glimpses of Aborigines of South-Western Australia 1829–1914*. Nedlands, Australia: University of Western Australian Press.

Chapter 12

Material violence

Destruction, mishaps and redaction of Stasi photographs

Donna West Brett

The records of the German Democratic Republic's (GDR) Ministry for State Security (Ministerium für Staatssicherheit, MfS), commonly known as the Stasi, are held in extensive archives over multiple locations. Known for the insidious mass surveillance of citizens during the period of the Cold War and the Berlin Wall, the Stasi recorded and documented the lives of East and West Germans and foreign nationals. The resulting records include a reported 180 kilometres of files, 35.6 million card indexes, tape recordings, videos, ephemera such as human odours and nearly 2 million photographs documenting the everyday lives of GDR and foreign citizens (Childs 1999, 104; Springer 2020). Photographs in the Stasi archive were largely taken for the purposes of surveillance and were sometimes later used as evidence in criminal prosecutions; as such they were made with a specific sanctioned audience in mind. These include observational photographs taken of individuals or dissident groups over a long period of time, and those that document traces of successful or failed escapes from the GDR, which I have written about elsewhere (Brett 2017; 2019b). Their worth was determined by the power they exercised—to intimidate, humiliate, prosecute or punish—and once deemed to have served their purpose, they were filed and largely forgotten. Many of these photographs also implicitly record the mass surveillance activities of the regime that illuminate the Stasi's observation methods of control and subjugation. The photographs were subsequently stored in files, in envelopes, in negative holders, pasted onto pages with rudimentary notations or at times accompanied by extensive case records and documents.

A large number of records and photographs were damaged in the efforts by the Stasi to destroy evidence of their surveillance regime in late 1989 to early 1990. Over 15,500 bags of torn or shredded files are in the process of recovery by archive personnel and volunteers by hand, or by digital scanning, with many more irretrievably damaged (Childs 1999, 103; Der Spiegel 2020; Jedlitschka 2012, 86). Evidence, as embodied in the photographs discussed here is manifold; it is both the evidentiary qualities of the photograph as a product of surveillance, and evidence of the surveillance machine made manifest in the ministry records. Many photographs are also physically marred,

DOI: 10.4324/9781003247593-15

with the blemishes, scratches, blurs and other flaws occurring during the act of taking and developing the photograph, or in the documentation and archiving process (Orbán 2014). On supply of these materials to researchers they are digitised and censored; for example, files are redacted, and images are pixilated. During the censoring process meaning itself becomes obscured and the remedial possibility of public dissemination is impeded. This has real implications in terms of textual and visual readings of Stasi surveillance documents, in that redaction and digitisation both enable and complicate interpretation in the present (Ring 2014, 389).

This chapter considers select photographs that have been subject to material violence by way of destruction, photographic mishaps and redaction. Material violence is made complex through myriad layers of action, trace and interpretation drawn from the initial violating act of mass-surveillance that consisted of both real and perceived acts of observation (Miller 2004, 95). This initial violation of public trust is complicated and reinforced by the attempted violent destruction of the Stasi files to destroy evidence of unlawful citizen surveillance. This chapter further considers these violating actions in terms of the motivation and methods of Stasi surveillance practices, the physical reality of covert operations and ensuing photographic material traces, and lastly, the ways in which meaning is obfuscated via archival interventions.

Operationally meaningful photographs

The function of the Stasi surveillance machine was established by the GDR constitution as an organ of the state and as an investigative arm of law enforcement. In accordance with the Ministry's mission, it was charged with securing material that could be used as official evidence and bear witness in legal cases against the perceived enemy, often dissident citizens. A training manual written in the late 1980s for Stasi operatives, titled *On Requirements and Ways of Developing Operationally Meaningful Photos in the Observation Process*, sets out imperatives for mass observation and the management of relevant materials in preparation for criminal proceedings and lawful examination. The central goal of this report was to clearly demonstrate

> the importance of photographic documentation as a means of assessing a context, that is to say a means of gaining true and objective information, and not just as an illustrative addendum to observational reports. In other words, photographic documentation serves the purposes of ascertaining the truth.
>
> (BStU MfS HA VIII 5824, 186)

The requirements for surveillance photography were to acquire 'operatively meaningful information and evidence' set against the background of related enemy activity and attacks such as the intensification of political-ideological activities, political tourism, underground activities, or economic interference (BStU MfS HA VIII 5824, 187). Given the significance of the undertaking, it is not surprising that the report gave specific importance to the photographic record in providing an indelible record of suspect activities. The Ministry declared that an advantage of the photographic medium, as a meaningful, permanent, verifiable and precisely fixed rendition of evidence, was as 'an objective and always reproducible pictorial reproduction' (Suckut 1985, 128f; Hartewig 2004, 29). An operative photograph, as noted in the training guidelines, is only meaningful and useful if an operative agent captures the observed activity in a way that can be used as evidence in the investigation process (BStU MfS HA VIII 5824, 189).

To this end the guidelines specify various methods such as capturing a subject at 'exactly the moment in which there can be no doubt about the documented action … If this is not the case, the photograph can no longer serve as indisputable evidence for this action' (BStU MfS HA VIII 5824, 190). Along with attaining what the Ministry determined as 'indisputable' evidential photographs, operatives were required to supply standard information such as the duration and conditions of the operation, establish relevant activities and irrelevant information, observe subject habits, patterns, idiosyncratic behaviour and to ascertain whether the subject may be familiar with the means and methods of espionage (BStU MfS HA VIII 5824, 192). As the German historian Karin Hartewig observes, photography became a medium for the procurement of evidence and an all-purpose weapon for the secret police. As Hartewig put it,

> The thoughts on the unlimited availability of pictorial information bear witness to the omnipotence fantasy of a surveillance bureaucracy in the information age. Talking about photography was now part of a bureaucratic discourse. The medium of photography had become an integral part of a political secret police whose development was inspired by the guiding idea of 'scientific socialism'. The photograph promised complete foresight, prognosis and prevention.
>
> (2004, 29)

By 1952 the Stasi employed photography for security operations and developed its own Technical Operation Centre where agents were trained at the observation and photography school (Hartewig 2004; Macrakis 2008, 128–129; Betts 2010, 194–196). Furthermore, the Legal University was established in Potsdam where, in the 1980s, Stasi officers could attend seminars on the identification of subjects, another on 'Operative Psychology' for the analysis of subject behaviour or a year-long module on working with unofficial collaborators (Ring 2014, 392). Despite these training programmes and accompanying guidelines set out to distinguish desirable and non-desirable photographs (BStU MfS HA VIII 5824), the records contain a wide range of images that vary distinctly in both technical and aesthetic accomplishments. As we will see, the aims of covert operations for the mass-surveillance of citizens were subject to both state imperatives and to individual operational methods and capabilities, which resulted in a wide range of photographic outcomes.

The material violence of destruction

On 16 January 1990, GDR citizens stormed the office of the Ministry for State Security (commonly known as the Stasi) on Normannenstraße, Berlin. Their goal was twofold. First, they aimed to force the dissolution of the Ministry, and second, to prevent further reported destruction of files by staff officials under orders to erase traces of its unlawful state surveillance actions (Morgenstern and Richter 1990, 1; Jarausch and Gransow 1994, 101–102). In addition to the violent destruction of documents relating to the regime itself, or files on individuals and groups, a substantial number of photographs were damaged, ripped, burned or disposed of using a wet shredder or *feuchtschredder* (BStU website; Jedlitschka 2012, 97; Gieseke 2014, 198; Biber 2018, 296). While some of these photographs now reside in relation to their written documentation such as extensive observation reports, interviews or ephemeral material, many others are orphaned from any context, or have scant recorded details. Any accompanying documentation was either non-existent, destroyed or is in the process of reparative remediation, making it often particularly difficult to understand the context of the photographic observation.

Included in the archive is a file that features photographs of apartment buildings and shops in West Berlin taken from differing perspectives with the streets evacuated of people (BStU MfS HA I Fo 1429). Whereas surveillance photographs operate on the presumed basis of the infallible truth-telling capacity of the camera, like many others in the archive these photographs are unilluminating as to the reason for their existence. Rather, their evidentiary power for the purposes of the Stasi surveillance machine, is drawn from and reinforced by other forms of record keeping no longer extant. One example features an apartment building on a street corner taken by a small camera such as the 'Ammer' that would have been hidden by a Stasi agent in the confines of a jacket. This is indicated by the format of the negative and the tell-tale vignette (the distinct circular shading) caused when the lens is obstructed by the outline of a buttonhole. Hence, the photograph was shot from the angle of the observer's torso. The other, rather blurred photograph printed from a 35 mm film is of a street corner that features a four-story apartment building with businesses at ground-level including a funeral parlour, a fashion store, and a florist (Figure 12.1). This photograph, taken in the early 1980s, features a digital stamp that defines the negative sequence number 12 followed by the time of 11:37 a.m.[1] Shot from eye height the photograph also shows a disruptive, blurred finger in the top left-hand corner that partially obstructs the image, which together with the odd angle alludes to some sense of urgency in taking the photograph. Each image has been methodically torn into roughly

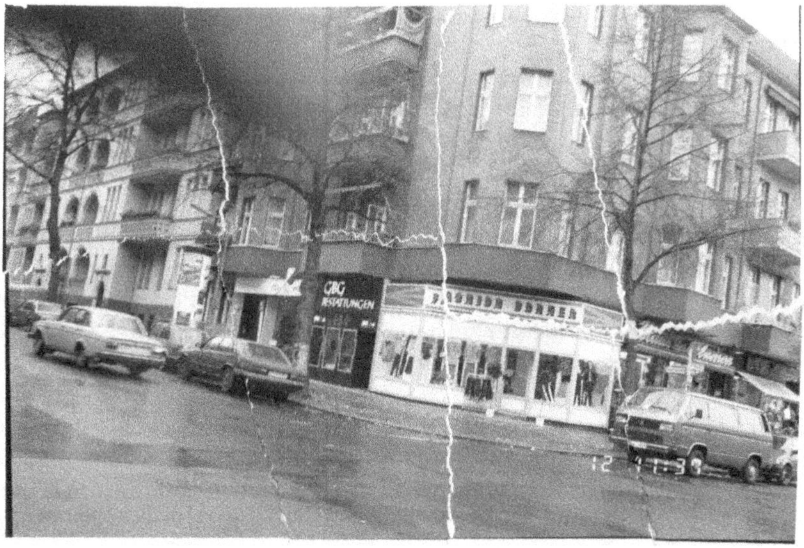

Figure 12.1 Apartments and shops in West Berlin, Stasi Records Agency, Berlin, BStU MfS HA I Fo 1429 Bild 0007.

even-sized pieces, both vertically and horizontally, by the actions of determined hands as they ripped the photographic paper and created jagged lines that mar the surface. As such, these images hold the trace of destruction in their very materiality as the plastic surface of the image resisted the tearing movement of hurried hands.

Efforts of rudimentary archival repair in the application of sticky tape on the reverse side, leave the uneven and broken photographic surfaces unhindered as they flop and slump, their flimsy physicality made evident on handling. This unexpected fragility transforms these objects into corporeal ruins with a tactility that reinforces the original violence of destruction as the image's instability is disturbingly experienced with each touch. This destructive act can be seen as an embedded secondary violation that reinforces the intrusion and control of the regime as embodied in the original incarnation of the image. Why these photographs were designated and prioritised for destruction is unknown, and it is likely that any accompanying material is no longer extant. The reason is most assuredly related to Erich Mielke's orders to Stasi employees to remove specific files from storage, or to destroy them, particularly those that revealed the extent of surveillance such as that of West Berlin (Gieseke 2014, 198).

While the reason for the destruction of this case file seems obscure, others appear more apparent including surveillance records of individuals and groups, or photographic documentation of escape attempts. I have written elsewhere about these photographic records whose haunting subjects and material characteristics continue to compel and disturb (Brett 2017; 2019b). The first relates to a file on an East German suspect titled 'Delegat' that contains black and white 35 mm prints in between tissue paper and Polaroid photographs mounted onto card. We know his code name not from any accompanying documentation, because there is none, but rather from scant notations written in pencil on the objects' verso. Of the 103 photographs taken in 1984 of Delegat's apartment, or those taken of him in public, only a few extant records were damaged, with perhaps many others burned or shredded. While some pages have been torn vertically and horizontally in line with the mounted photographs, one has been violently torn into multiple pieces. Here, the material qualities of the Polaroid temper the efforts of destruction. The torn backing mount reveals the violence enacted on the record, with much of the card and one image missing, leaving behind jagged edges that align with the plastic-based Polaroid images (Figure 12.2). The remedial efforts to repair these records, like those discussed earlier, amount to what seems to be hastily applied sticking tape. The Polaroid surface is also damaged, marred by visceral scratches and scrapes from fingernails, or from the momentary bending of the images in the act of destruction causing the plastic-based surface to fracture like impacted glass. Lastly, several of these photographs bear traces of their making that have left their mark in the top left-hand corner of the image field, torn as the photographer hastily removed the developing layer. These visceral traces of corporeal intervention, to what would normally be objects held in a state of stasis in the archive, bring home the urgency and sporadic nature of the task to destroy the State Security's files.

The haptic qualities of photographs often unsettle our seeing and bring us beyond the mere visual to the physical, such as the dog-eared photograph in a wallet, the discarded portrait in a junk shop or the long-forgotten yet much-handled photograph in an archive. The trace of a photograph is more than just a trace of the subject captured as an indexical relation to a referent; it is also a trace of its existence as an object. Over the life of a photograph from its formation as a negative or a print, or as something that is looked at, handled, mishandled, stored and recovered, each encounter leaves traces of its history in the material substrate of the photograph (Edwards and Hart 2004; Domanska 2006; Smith 2014, 29–46; Campany 2015, 32–34). As David Campany, Shawn Michelle Smith and others have noted, Barthes' concern with the material status of photographs as objects was as mediators of desire. For the violently torn photographs discussed here this sense of touch was one of destruction fuelled by an imperative to destroy records of evidence (both the subjects and the surveillance machine), but we may assume also driven by frustration, anger, and fear as agents urgently responded to the task at hand. One last example is that of a set of photographs mounted on paper board (Figure 12.3) which feature a family and their *Schleuser* (people smugglers Kay Mierendorff and Karl-Heinz Hetzschold) who were intercepted by the secret police and border guards on 21 September 1973, as they attempted to escape the GDR (BStU HA IX Fo

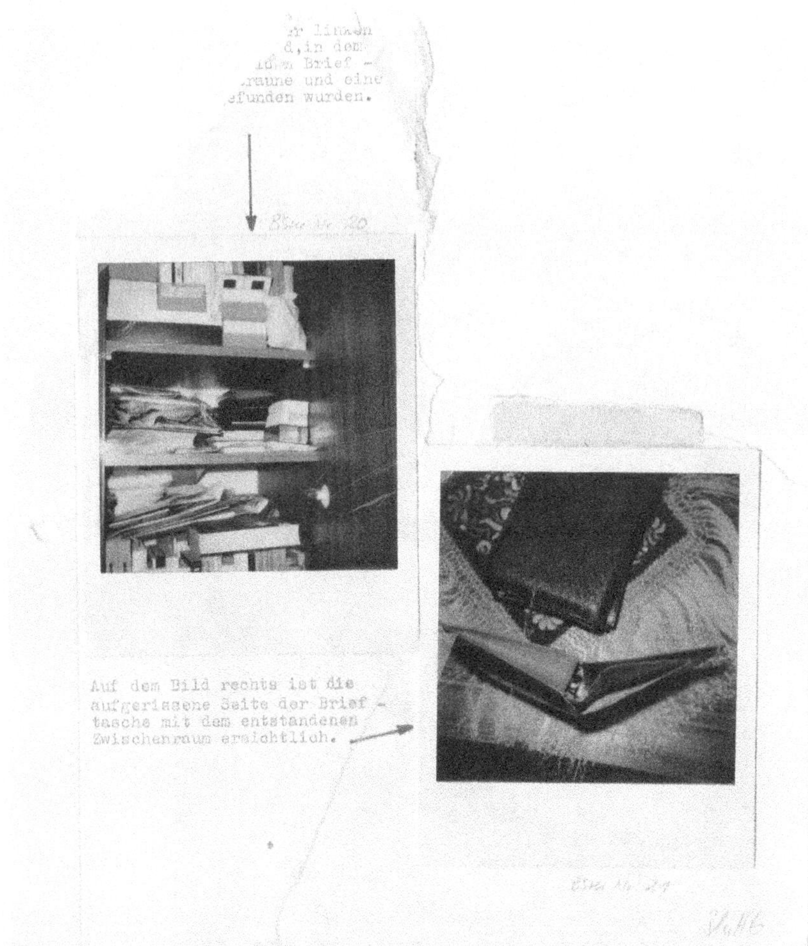

Figure 12.2 **Apartment search and observation of 'Delegat', 1984, Stasi Records Agency, Berlin, BstU MfS HA II Fo 69 Bl. 0006.**

2180). Rather than focusing on the content of the photographs, which I have written about elsewhere, I will emphasise here their material qualities (Brett 2017; 2019b).

In the effort to destroy these records a Stasi officer has forcibly ripped the pages from the file and in so doing, the left-hand edge has an enduring ragged contour. The pages were subsequently torn horizontally with this bodily action meeting the resistance of the photograph itself and forcing the motion along the border of the image. One tear mark, however, bridges the substrate

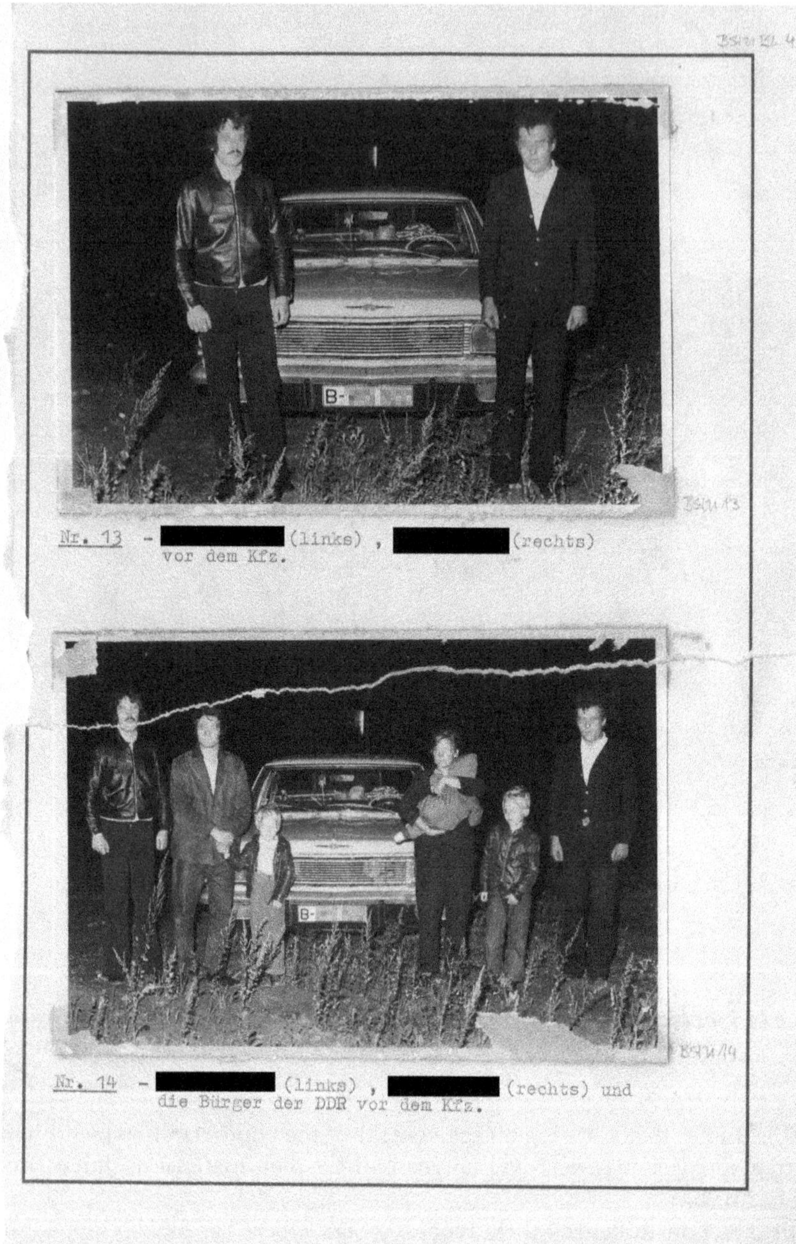

Figure 12.3 East German family and their helpers after a failed escape attempt on 21 September 1973. Stasi Records Agency, Berlin, BStU HA IX Fo 2180 Bl. 0004.

of the mount to traverse across the upper quarter of one photograph to visually decapitate the head of a *Schleuser* standing on the left of the family group, which leaves a permanent scar across the surface. This wound-like lacuna further violates the unsettling scene before us of the family and their people smugglers as they are photographed by the Stasi in the moments after the re-enaction of their failed escape attempt. Here, the initial violating act of image making in recording the family at a juncture of extreme vulnerability, is reinforced by the attempted undoing of the record by a destructive and violent act. On handling these records that total four pages and eight photographs, the destructive traces are made poignantly evident as the torn pages separate in the viewer's hands as a visceral reminder of the earlier violating act. On closer inspection further traces of use are made evident as one becomes aware of the buffed edges of the photographs. It seems these photographs were removed from an earlier substrate and re-mounted in their current form, with traces of the former mount appearing at the edges. These pictures are also scuffed and worn with the image layer missing in several sections, the corners marred by tears in the paper and a persistent stain that runs across the top and bottom of each image. There seems no doubt that the stains were caused by the glue applied to the verso of the photographs to adhere them to the paper mount. Lastly, although the names of the people smugglers are a matter of public record, their identity and names have been redacted for the purposes of supply and publication. The censoring pixilation applied to the figures to obscure their identities, in addition to the poorly typed labels add a further layer of mark-making to the supplied digital file, hence emphasising the desire to see that which is hidden. Destroyed photographs such as these are objects that as Elizabeth Edwards (2009, 130) argues 'constitute material performances of a complex range of historiographical desires in the negotiation of the relations among past, present and future'. Whereas Edwards applied this consideration to survey photographs of England in the nineteenth century, it can also be applied to documents and photographs from the Stasi archive in that the entire archive is in constant negotiation and transformation (Brenneis 2006, 43) between the pastness of such material objects, their power and agency today and into the future.

Scratches, stains and tears

During my research in the Stasi archive I received odd looks directed at my undue attention to particular photographs as I carefully and speedily rummaged through prints held between tissue or viewed 4 × 5 mm and 35 mm negatives on a light-table, the glare of the surface burning my retina. While I was indeed looking for aesthetically interesting photographs, the startling number of failed images also caught my attention with their surface damage, chemical accidents, and ripped or torn ends of films that indicate either a lack of photographic ability or an urgency of process. Their materiality as negatives or prints is comprised of elements such as film, paper, inscriptions and components of making including exposure times, chemicals, development, printing or archiving, each of which, as Edwards (2009, 136) argues, mediates experiences and articulates desires. These unruly photographs render not just the intended target but also the frustration, the boredom, the hurried pace and the mis-aimed shot. These photographs are inadequate, and in their illegibility, they become what Hito Steyerl calls a poor image, wrecked by the violence and history of their making. 'A poor image', Steyerl claims, 'is an image that remains unresolved—puzzling and inconclusive … It cannot give a comprehensive account of the situation it is supposed to represent … they are poor images of the conditions that brought them into being' (2012, 156). The retention of these photographs by the Ministry indicates the presence of evidential material within the image that often remains indiscernible to the present-day viewer and a belief in the truth-telling capability of photographs despite their quality. Furthermore, the retention of such images and their associated records indicates the meticulous attention to detail and bureaucratic ideological approach to record-keeping demonstrated by the regime.

The concept of a poor image is made poignantly evident by one of the Polaroid photographs held in the 'Delegat' file. This photograph of the subject's wallet has a tell-tale tear in the top left-hand corner indicating it was taken by the same camera as those discussed earlier (Figure 12.2). Across the surface of the photograph are numerous fractures that form a rhythmical pattern of both regular and irregular lines. Caused by the rapid removal of the film from the camera body, these marks indicate both a hurried and urgent action, but also possibly that of frustration and carelessness (Brett 2019a). The Polaroid is unmoored from its context having been torn from its file and mount during its attempted destruction by a Stasi employee. That the image was retained along with many others damaged in the process of observation is substantiated by the bureaucratic ideology of the regime and the strict control of film and exposures by the MfS. As the Cold War continued into the 1980s and the GDR slowly moved toward financial and social decline, the German Unified Party (SED) 'focused on economic strategy and stipulated a demand for a better relation between the investment of basic funds and the results yielded by these investments'. One possibility to take account of changing economic conditions was to 'use resources more sparingly' (BStU MfS HA VIII 6022, 10; Lichter, Löffler & Siegloch 2015). For the Stasi this meant finding ways to cut operative surveillance costs because 'operative image documentation directly contributes to the quality of our political operative work' (BStU MfS HA VIII 6022, 10). Strategies outlined in a report from 1982 included using fewer frames to capture covert operations and the use of a rewinding device to prevent the waste of unused film. The report implies that every photographic frame is accounted for in the observation process.

A further set of photographs numbering 671 in total is included in the archive as 35 mm negatives held in plastic sleeves, and when reproduced for researchers, they are framed to exclude the surrounding film edge and sprockets

(BStU MfS HA XX Fo 177; Menner 2014). A majority of these small, seemingly insignificant, badly exposed and poorly developed negatives feature a view from a high point across from a mailbox located in front of Robert Zywitz & Co. Herren und Damen Maßschneiderei (a gentlemen and ladies' tailor). Mailboxes were of particular interest to the surveillance of the population as they were often used for dead letter drops, a classic espionage technique and a way by which spies or informers could transfer information (Maddrell 2011, 29; Childs and Popplewell 1996, 160). The secret police also intercepted letters from mailboxes in the street or from homes and steamed them open to read or check the contents including a reported 90,000 letters and 4,000 packages daily (Sperling 2013, 212).

In studying these negatives, one observes a level of repetition, of banality, of one press of the shutter after another, the observer's eye constantly on its target yet on occasion wavering. While the general view and position do not change, a sense of boredom is made palpable in these endless images, and we can imagine the observer's body as it shifts periodically to ease the intense ache of sitting for long periods. Visually scanning these negatives in a short-allotted time, they meld together, figure after figure posting a letter, entering a building, chatting in groups, stopping for one reason or another. What stand out from this morass of rather average and dull images are several negatives that are poorly shot, badly exposed or marked by processing chemicals and water stains. These various visual aberrations seem to indicate either an urgent task or a half-hearted approach to the job at hand. One such example bears alternating streaks of light and dark across the face of the emulsion, formed by hasty development of the film, which seem to mimic the movement of the subject, the pulsing breath of the photographer or the action of the shutter.

Toward the end of a film roll is a negative that is dramatically marked by developing chemicals and wrecked by the very means of its own creation (Figure 12.4). The photograph as evidence, as index, as a record of the world is here undone in its very making, and as such it rips a hole in the effort to record the truth of the event. Chemicals embedded in the layers of emulsion, and which bring the image into formation, tear the image apart and form ectoplasmic stains of failure. Coupled with a violent tear and hole in the negative—most likely formed when the film was caught in the process of ejection from the developing tank—these marks obliterate any evidence that may have been held in this picture. This physical hole is a visual disturbance that impacts on the image's wholeness (Karmo 1977), but it is equally a shadow and a negative space that is empty of any signifying sign other than itself. But the hole is not just a hole, rather it is a sign of the photographic process, and the making of the image (Casati and Varzi 2019). This void is equally a trace of movement; as the film was torn from the developing tank the formation of the hole caused ripples and echoes of its own making across the centre of the negative. In turn, this sense of violence and the hole's qualities of absence emphasise the

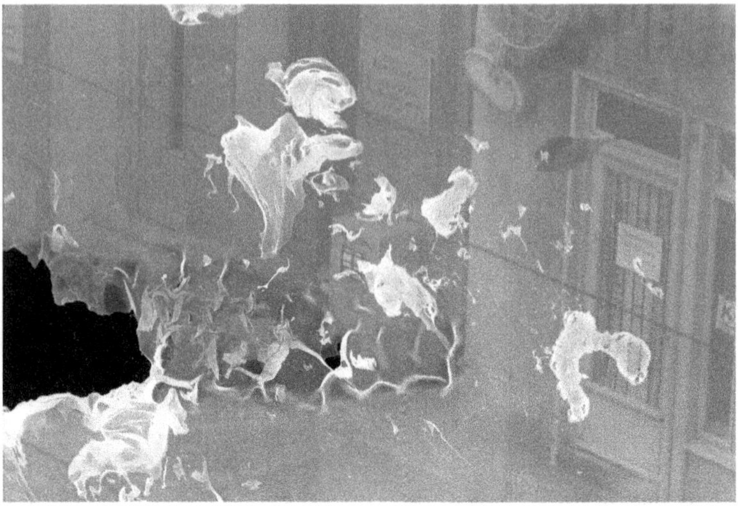

Figure 12.4 Observation of people putting mail into public mailboxes and emptying the mail. Stasi Records Agency, BStU MfS HA XX Fo 177 Bild 0567.

presence of the chemical stains that obliterate visual information. As a veiling mechanism, the stain here is both a trace of failure in action and an 'ambivalent space of fluidity' (Baker 2001, 8), in which the image transmutes in and out of legibility. The space of the stain is the space of the picture; in other words it is 'inscribed in the picture' (Lacan 1978, 99; Baker 2001, 13) and as such it brings to bear figurative associations of damage and mishaps (Black and Shera 2014, 136).

Such marks allude to the intensity of surveillance and observation strategies that are hurried, tense or indeed enacted under pressure over hours or days. Twelve photographs in the archive (Figure 12.5) taken in 1965 record the action of an operative following unknown subjects through a park over the course of a day (BStU MfS HA VII Fo 79 1–12). Rather than rendering the subject of their surveillance activity with clarity, as one would expect of surveillance-based records, these photographs are blurred to some extent; some are shot on angles that make the subject illegible, other have visual intrusions, or poor exposure due to slow shutter speeds in low light conditions. And yet, these photographs, despite their seemingly profound uselessness are carefully kept between sheets of tissue paper, assiduously numbered and ordered. This tension between an operational objective and its dismal failure shifts our focus away from the photograph as index, where the study of the subject matter is paramount, to the photograph's signification, its mode of production, dissemination and material properties. These images testify to the success of the regime's archiving practices, and regardless of their probative value, the

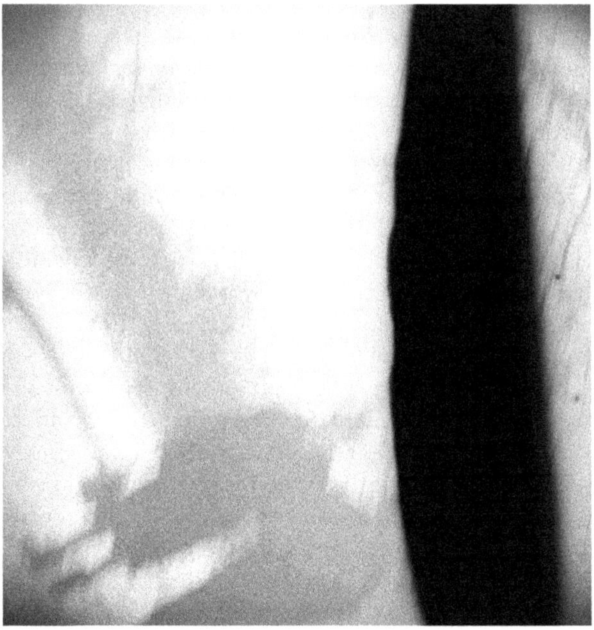

Figure 12.5 Hidden camera observation of walkers in a park in winter, 1965. Stasi Records Agency, BStU MfS HA VII Fo 79 Bild 0001.

surveillance operation may have achieved the desired objective of fear, docility and self-monitoring known as the Focusing Principle (Miller 2004, 95). This principle is based on creating the perception that one was always being looked at and assisted the regime in keeping the East German population in check.

Here, these perceivably failed surveillance photographs, rather than mediating experience and meaning, obscure it. Reminiscent of evidence tampering these photographs fail to tell us much at all about the subjects, nor do they give us a specific reason for their existence. Instead these illegible objects reveal modes of production. As such these photographs indicate an urgency of action by the observer attempting to keep up with moving subjects and to remain unobserved. As the operative follows the subjects down a path in an unknown park in the middle of winter, with their body swathed in heavy winter gear, moving up and down as motion dictates, the camera—hidden somewhere in their coat or bag—is triggered by the shutter release held in a pocket. As with many of these photographs, the attempt at rendering the subject before them onto the film emulsion is subject to luck and happenstance, for while the photographer sees the goal of their photographic endeavour, the camera is often looking elsewhere.

Redaction and pixilation

On viewing photographs and files in the archive, a researcher has access to the full contents of a supplied record. After perusing the content, a researcher then determines what pages, sections or images they wish to have copied and completes an order form specifying file names, page numbers or image numbers. While one can take written or typed notes in the reading room, photographs are not permitted. On receipt of the ordered records some months later, one receives either image files on discs through the post, or more recently, access to an agency website for download of the records as digital files. Somewhere along this process of digitisation, files and images are formally assessed by an archivist for confidential information, or for privacy concerns. The resultant files received by the researcher are inevitably altered by an official redaction and pixilation process, which tends to obscure part if not all information and meaning. Redaction is a long-practised method of concealing data in official records that has been deemed secret or sensitive and requires some level of censorship (Biber 2018, 288). The point of redaction is to make sections of a document or image unreadable or unrecognisable such as an individual's name, age, occupation or address, or indeed a person's face. This approach is understandable given that many individuals whose details appear in the files are still alive or the information may reveal the identity of an unofficial informer. The redaction itself draws attention to that which has been erased and yet may remain recorded in research notes or in visual recall, from which other inferences can be made. What is of interest here is the ways in which this process alters the readability of an image and potentially changes its meaning, and in what ways it physically changes the image in material form.

The first example is from a set of images initially reproduced in an essay on escape photographs focussing on the emotive experiences of loss and humiliation (Brett 2017, 278–279). After two years of developing a plan to escape East Germany for the West, Family M paid 30,000 Deutschmarks per person to people smugglers working out of West Germany to take them across the border in the trunk of a Ford Granada in April 1982 (BStU MfS HA IX 1310). Herr and Frau M and their young child met their *Schleuser* (people smugglers) one evening and drove toward the Drewitz border crossing in the Berlin district of Zehlendorf.[2] At some stage the car stopped and the trunk was opened at which time Family M realised their journey had been intercepted by border guards. At the time of this attempted escape Stasi operatives often required photographic documentation for the purposes of arresting and prosecuting the would-be escapees, which was attained either at the point of interception or shortly after the fact.

On this occasion, and with many others, the Stasi enacted the heinous undertaking of forcing the family to re-enact their attempted escape for the camera. Among a small number of photographs taken, one is particularly poignant (Figure 12.6). In this image Frau M is seen in a heightened state

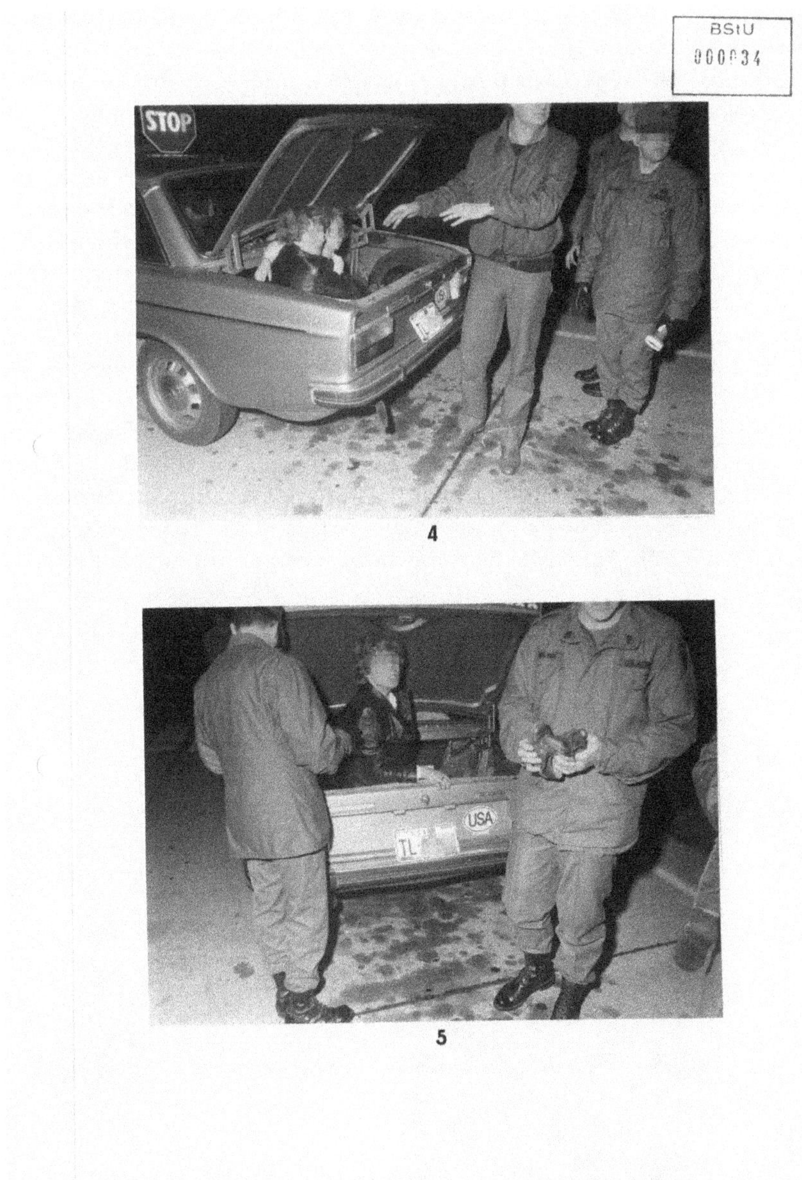

Figure 12.6 Family M intercepted at the border, 25 April 1982. Stasi Records Agency, Berlin, BStU MfS HA IX 1310 S. 0034.

of anxiety looking in the direction of her son whose foot can be seen at the edge of the photograph as he is taken away. In between them an officer in an American Army jacket, and likely one of the smugglers, holds the boy's shoes in his hands. The tension in this photograph is made clear by the position and conjunction of the three central figures and the two partial figures at the picture's edge. In the original photograph, the anxiety of the mother is clearly apparent, most particularly in her eyes, which from memory of seeing the photograph in the archive, held a sense of intense loss and emotional shock. The applied pixilation over Frau M's eyes obliterates any suggestion of her emotional response and, as it draws our focal attention, it equally enhances our desire to see beyond this wound-like mark.

The processes around redaction and pixilation are reviewed from time to time by the archive, and this is made evident in the range of methodologies used. Methods for the occlusion of an individual's identity seem to have adapted along with technological advancements from the use of tape or cut paper placed over the subject's eyes as the photograph was copied, the digital application of black rectangles or pixilation of the eyes, to most recently in 2018, the complete obliteration of a subject's face in the process of digitisation (Figure 12.7). Although there had been mention of new regulations, I

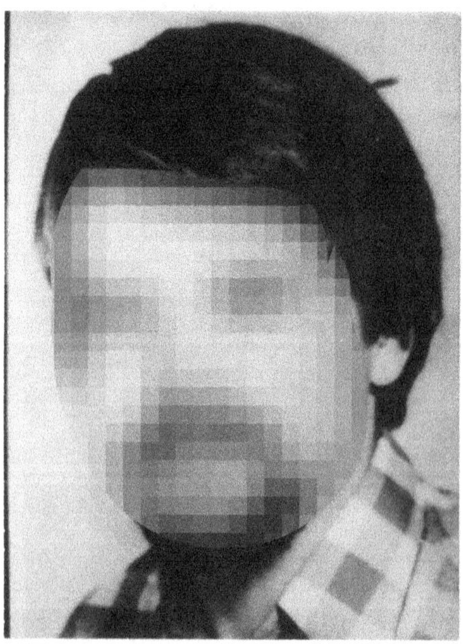

Figure 12.7 Harald Hauswald, photographer. Passport photos and portraits of members of the opposition movement. Stasi Records Agency, BStU MfS HA XX Fo 107 Bild 0008.

was assured by an archivist that the level of such occlusion is dependent on who processes the request (18 April 2018). This observation resonates with that of Katherine Biber (2018, 303), who observed that individual bureaucrats use recognisable techniques in redacting documents that result in identifiable mark-making. This can also be said of the photographers themselves whose aesthetic approach and idiosyncratic methods make visible their ways of seeing and recording during the surveillance process.

By rendering the image completely unreadable, the obliteration of an individual's identity has stark and painful parallels to the Stasi's surveillance regime of covert operations, victim persecution and imprisonment. Over the course of the regime several East German documentary photographers came under the watchful eye of the Stasi including Sibylle Bergemann, Ute Mahler, Gundula Schulze-Eldowy, Thomas Höpker and Harald Hauswald (Shaul 2010; Vowinckel 2018, 143–144 and 2019). Like many other so-called dissidents, in 1983 Hauswald's apartment and darkroom were searched and a selection of photographs confiscated (Vowinckel 2018, 143; BStU MfS HA XV AOP 17395/91–1, 165). As Vowinckel notes, Hauswald was arrested in 1983 for unauthorised publication outside the GDR and again in 1986 as he took photographs of security forces at a rally but was released the following day (2018, 144; 2019, 122; BStU MfS HA XV AOP 17386/91–2, 312).

Hauswald's photobook (1987) produced with Lutz Rathenow titled *Ostberlin: Die Andere Seite einer Stadt* (East Berlin: The Other Side of a City) also drew the ire of the regime with an extensive analysis and critique of various photographs (Vowinckel 2019, 124). This critique centred on photographs that showed the city in an undesirable light including those of run-down streets and houses, passport control points and 'grumpy looking' people on public transportation (Colberg 2009). As early as 1983, documents in Hauswald's Stasi file noted that his photographs conveyed anti-socialist messages in West German newspapers (Vowinckel 2019, 122; BStU MfS HA XV AOP 17395/91–1, 2). Located in a file, along with other passport photographs and portraits of so-called members of the opposition, is a photograph of Harald Hauswald. Sporting a dark beret and a checked shirt, this formal portrait may have been used to identify the photographer, whereas many other operative photographs taken by Stasi officers would be included in his person file to substantiate surveillance operations. This photograph of Hauswald is startling in the complete pixilation of his face and beard, despite the well-known fact that he was closely monitored by the Stasi for 12 years. After the opening of the archive he was granted access to his own personal file (Colberg 2009), which contains a reported 1500 documents under the code name *Radfahrer* or cyclist (Schmidt 2019).

Digitising these images erases more than just the identity of the subject. The materiality of the photographs is transformed from paper and chemicals to pixels and code, touch is eliminated, and the object is transmuted into ephemeral immaterial data unmoored from its origin (Doane 2007; Seppänen 2017, 115; Henning 2018). Inscriptions on the verso of the photographs are often not transcribed nor kept with the image metadata and negative reproductions are cropped to the image frame with the film-type details and film sprockets erased. In fact, any distinction of the object as a negative is eliminated in the making of a positive, enacting a physical loss of materiality. Joanna Sassoon (2004) argues that what she calls a digital shadow (after Walter Benjamin's echo of the original) obscures the balance between materiality and context that determines photographic meaning. For Sassoon, the digital process translates a material object and empties it of visual clues, and 'where once materiality and meaning were bound up in a complex, synergistic and symbiotic relationship, the resultant digital object is an ephemeral ghost whose materiality is at best intangible' (2004, 199). Increasingly images are displaced from their original setting by their display on a screen leading the researcher to question whether the original image was a print or a negative, did it have an inscription, or other related information? The digital images reproduced here cannot convey the physical effect of handling a photograph held together with sticky tape as it warps and flops in one's hand, or the shock of realising that the torn images remain so, their detached parts constantly reiterating the trauma and destruction as they are handled and separated over and over.

Whereas the processes of redaction and pixilation are grounded in policies of national security, archival policy or privacy, they have unintended consequences of interest to those who work with archival material. As Lars Rutz, a former GDR citizen who was arrested and deported to the West, has noted about his own Stasi file, there is an inherent tension between the right to privacy and the right to information for victims of state persecution. As vehicles for 'collective memory building' the archive's responsibility to promote, interpret or indeed preserve memory is inevitably one of constant evaluation and of legal and ethical frameworks (Rutz 2019, 133). While the pixilation of the subjects may represent a double loss in terms of the remedial possibilities of such archival endeavours, the digitisation of these images represents a further loss and deterioration of meaning when the images are edited from their original context, or key data is erased from documents. As the director of the Berlin-Hohenschönhausen Memorial (a former Stasi prison) Hubertus Knabe found, 'you often get copies of files that you can't understand'. When the museum was opened in 1994, it requested a list of former prisoners; however the files were forwarded to the institution with all the prisoners' names redacted. 'It was useless for us', as Knabe put it (Matthews 2017).

Conclusion

In researching this extensive archive, it becomes apparent that observations of perceived unlawful activity are always subject to varying levels of obfuscation such as that of visual clues by image blur, poor camera sightlines and in the very processes of surveillance and documentation. In 1962, a major surveillance operation code-named 'Operation Biscaya' took place over several months in

East Berlin and demonstrates the complexity of observational activities and file retention. The target of the operation was the reported digging of an escape tunnel from West Berlin under the Berlin Wall to a former restaurant called Grenzquell in Kreuzberg, located on the corner of Köpenicker Straße and Bethaniendamm. In the file are extensive reports including pages of precise observational notations that take place between July and August 1962, listing all persons of interest who came and went from the former restaurant, or were in the vicinity. These notes include descriptions of the suspects' height, hair colour, clothing, what time they arrived and left and the number plates of any vehicles. In addition, the file includes reports by informers, interviews with neighbours and 12 extant photographs from an original 19.

On the verso of these photographs are various inscriptions noting the time and actions of those observed. Although these specific photographs were taken over a period of a few hours, and hence one imagines that there was some importance placed both on the activities and on the photographic record, none of the images correspond with the written notations in the file (Brett 2019b, 36–37). Indeed, it seems as if these photographs, in their lack of corresponding textual recording, were expected to stand in for the written descriptions (Figure 12.8). Yet, neither the photographs, nor the inscriptions provide us with much concrete information, and we are left to make assumptions about what may have occurred on this day and why the Stasi were so intensely focused

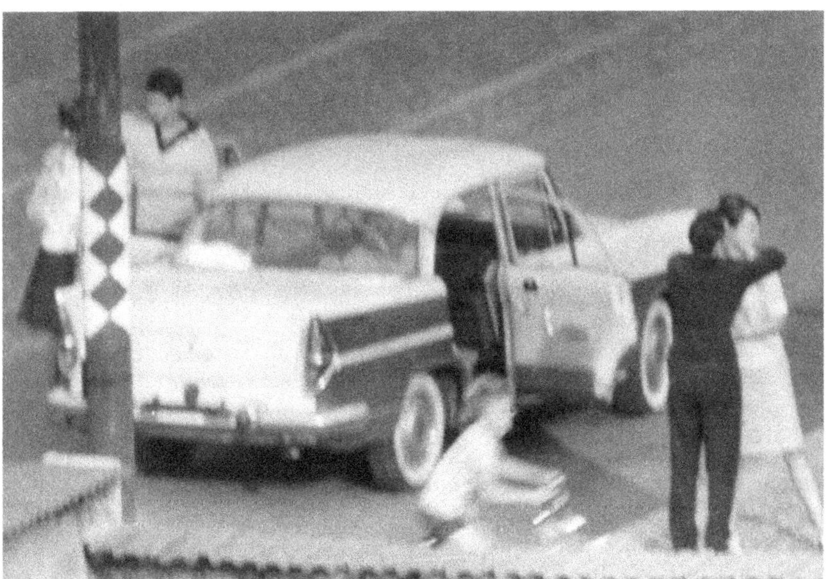

Figure 12.8 Observation of a possible escape incident near a checkpoint in Berlin, 26 August 1962. Stasi Records Agency, Berlin. BStU MfS HA I 13255, Bild 0123 7.

on the activities in the street. The urgency of the agent's task is inscribed into the photographs by the very nature of movement itself forming an unruly motion blur across the picture field. By distorting perception in this way, the photographic blur implies both a space that is made real by the suggestion of action and brings an uncertainty to the space inhabited by the perception of factuality. Whereas Jennifer Good (2019, 415) argues, in her analysis of domestic abuse photographs, that the photographic blur is both the violating act of surveillance and a disruption in the visual field caused by the urgent physical response of the agent in recording the subjects in motion. Photographic blur may obscure the visible, yet it is also an indicator of time passing, or duration, in a way that an in-focus image is not. The blurred image also draws attention to the subject in flight, the motion indicating they are moving in a direction that lies outside the picture frame. As yet another type of material violence, the visual blur signifies more than itself and is, in effect, an index of the violating actions of state surveillance.

While every mark and material trace contributes to the archive's material and visual history, they also raise difficult questions about the evidentiary aspects of such documents and their role as 'Meaningful Photos in the Observation Process'. Furthermore, archival material interventions such as destruction or redaction inevitably present a tension between the desire for transparency of state-controlled surveillance and the need to protect identities of victims and perpetrators. While the camera makes visible the subjects of observation, the photographs and associated records intended for surveillance or prosecution purposes, were hidden from the public eye by bureaucratic means and even now are occluded by the archive.

Abbreviations

BStU Der Bundesbeauftragte für die Unterlagen des Staatssicherheitsdienstes der ehemaligen Deutschen Demokratischen Republik/The Federal Commissioner for the Records of the State Security Service of the former German Democratic Republic

HA Hauptabteilung/Main Department

MfS Ministerium für Staatssicherheit/Ministry for State Security

Acknowledgements

I extend sincere thanks to Mareike Notarp at the BStU/Stasi Records Agency. The translation of Stasi archive files is by Dr Niklas Fischer, unless otherwise indicated. Research for this chapter was presented at the 'Material Practices of Visual History' conference, Photographic History Research Centre, De Montfort University, Leicester, 18–19 June 2018, and 'What is a Document? A Workshop on Documentation, Records and Evidence, University of Technology Sydney, 8–9 November 2018'.

Funding

Research for this essay was funded by the University of Sydney, FASS Research Support Scheme, 2016, the School of Literature, Art and Media Research Support Scheme, 2018 and the Ernst and Rosemarie Keller Award, the Australian Academy of the Humanities, 2017.

Images and Archival Sources

All images and archives courtesy Der Bundesbeauftragte für die Unterlagen des Staatssicherheitsdienstes der ehemaligen Deutschen Demokratischen Republik (BStU Berlin).

BStU MfS HA IX 1310
BStU MfS HA VIII 5824
BStU MfS HA VIII 6022
BStU MfS HA XV AOP 17386
BStU MfS HA XV AOP 17395

Notes

1 I extend sincere thanks to those who assisted in identifying the digital stamp including Michael Parry, Simm Steel, Stephen Whiteman, Fiona Gill, Eric Riddler, Bob Jansen, Tom Loveday and Bernd Heer.
2 *Schleuser* defines people smugglers who are generally paid to facilitate illegal migration and considered as terrorists, as opposed to *Fluchthelfer*, who assist for family, social or moral reasons.

References

Baker, George, 2001. The Space of the Stain. *Grey Room*, 5, 5–37.

Betts, Paul, 2010. *Within Walls: Private Life in the German Democratic Republic*. Oxford: Oxford University Press.

Biber, Katherine, 2018. The Art of Bureaucracy: Redacted Ready-Mades. *In*: Desmond Manderson, ed. *Law and the Visual: Representations, Technologies, Critique*. Toronto: University of Toronto Press, 286–309.

Black, Prudence and Shera, Peta Allen, 2014. Stained Evidence: Blood, Semen and Matter on the Clothes of Kennedy, Lewinsky, and Margiela., *Australian Feminist Law Journal*, 40 (1), 135–146.

Brenneis, Don, 2006. Reforming Promise. *In*: Annelise Riles, eds. *Documents: Artifacts of Modern Knowledge*. Ann Arbor: The University of Michigan Press, 41–70.

Brett, Donna West, 2017. Looking and Feeling: Photographing Escape from East Germany. *In*: Burcu Dogramaci and Elizabeth Otto, eds. *Passages of Exile*. Munich: Text + Kritik, 268–85.

Brett, Donna West, 2019a. Stasi Surveillance Photographs and Extra-Archival Legacy. *Photography and Culture*, 12 (2), 227–48.

Brett, Donna West, 2019b. Witnessing the Archive: The Stasi, Photography and Escape from the GDR. *In*: Donna West Brett and Natalya Lusty, eds. *Photography and Ontology: Unsettling Images*. New York: Routledge, 24–40.

Campany, David, 2015. *A Handful of Dust: From the Cosmic to the Domestic.* London: Mack.

Casati, Roberto, and Varzi, Achille, 2019. Holes. *In*: Edward N. Zalta, ed. *The Stanford Encyclopedia of Philosophy*, Summer ed. Available from: https://plato.stanford.edu/archives/sum2019/entries/holes/ [Accessed 20 April 2020].

Childs, David, and Popplewell, Richard, 1996. *The Stasi: The East German Intelligence and Security Service.* Basingstoke: Palgrave.

Childs, David, 1999. The Shadow of the Stasi. *In*: Patricia Smith, ed. *After the Wall: Eastern Germany Since 1989.* Boulder and Oxford: Westview Press, 93–108.

Colberg, Joerg, 2009. Spotlight: Harald Hauswald, the images of Others, and the Stasi. Available from: http://jmcolberg.com/weblog/2009/04/spotlight_harald_hauswald_the_images_of_others_and_the_stasi/ [Accessed: 20 April 2020].

Der Spiegel, 2007. New Computer Program to Reassemble Shredded Stasi Files. *Der Spiegel*, 5 October. Available from: https://www.spiegel.de/international/germany/puzzling-together-the-past-new-computer-program-to-reassemble-shredded-stasi-files-a-482136.html [Accessed: viewed 29 April 2020].

Doane, Mary Ann, 2007. The Indexical and the Concept of Medium Specificity. *Differences: A Journal of Feminist Cultural Studies*, 18, 128–52.

Domanska, Ewa, 2006. The Material Presence of the Past. *History and Theory*, 45, 337–48.

Edwards, Elizabeth, 2009. Photography and the Material Evidence of the Past. *History and Theory*, 48, 130–50.

Edwards, Elizabeth, and Hart, Janice, eds., 2004. *Photographs, Objects, Histories: On the Materiality of Images.* London: Routledge.

Gieseke, Jens, 2014. *The History of the Stasi: East Germany's Secret Police, 1945–1990.* Munich: Berghahn.

Good, Jennifer, 2019. The Impossible Photograph: Blur and Domestic Violence. *Photography and Culture*, 12 (4), 415–27.

Hartewig, Karin, 2004. *Das Auge Der Partei: Fotografie und Staatsicherheit.* Berlin: Ch. Links Verlag.

Henning, Michelle, 2018. *Photography: The Unfettered Image.* London: Routledge.

Jarausch, Konrad, and Gransow, Volker, 1994. *Uniting Germany: Documents and Debates 1944–1993.* Translated by Brown, Allison, and Cooper, Belinda. Providence: Berghahn.

Jedlitschka, Karsten, 2012. The Lives of Others: East German State Security Service's Archival Legacy. *The American Archivist*, 75, 81–108.

Karmo, Toomas, 1977. Disturbances. *Analysis*, 37, 147–8.

Lacan, Jacques, 1978. *The Four Fundamental Concepts of Psycho-Analysis.* Translated by Sheridan, Alan. New York: W.W. Norton.

Lichter, Andreas, Löffler, Max, and Siegloch, Sebastian, 2015. *The Economic Costs of Mass Surveillance: Insights from Stasi Spying in East Germany.* Discussion paper No. 9245. Bonn: Institute for the Study of Labor (IZA).

Macrakis, Kristie, 2008. *Seduced by Secrets: Inside the Stasi's Spy-Tech World.* Cambridge: Cambridge University Press.

Maddrell, Paul, 2011. Western Espionage and Stasi Counterespionage in East Germany, 1953–61. *In*: Kristie Macrakis, Thomas Wegener Friis, and Helmut Müller–Enbergs, eds. *East German Foreign Intelligence: Myth, Reality and Controversy.* London: Routledge, 19–33.

Matthews, David. 2017. How the Stasi Archive Handles Potentially Incriminating Information. *Times Higher Education*, 2329, 26 October. Available from: https://www.tim

eshighereducation.com/features/how-stasi-archive-handles-potentially-incriminating-information [Accessed 18 April 2020].

Menner, Simon, 2014. *Top Secret: Images from the Stasi Archives*. Ostfildern: Hatje Cantz Verlag.

Miller, Barbara, 2004. *The Stasi Files Unveiled: Guilt and Compliance in a Unified Germany*. New Brunswick: Transaction Publishers.

Morgenstern, Klaus, and Richter, Wolfgang, 1990. Erst gestürmt, dann verwüstet. Aufrufe zur Besonnenheit gingen unter: Hans Modrow appellierte an Vernunft. [First Stormed, then Ravaged. Calls to Remain Calm Go Unheeded: Hans Modrow Appeals to Reason]. *Neues Deutschland*, 16 January.

Orbán, Katalin, 2014. A Language of Scratches and Stitches: The Graphic Novel between Hyperreading and Print. *Critical Inquiry*, 40 (3), 169–81.

Rathenow, Lutz, and Hauswald, Harald, 1987. *Ostberlin: Die Andere Seite einer Stadt in Texten und Bildern*. Munich: Piper Verlag.

Ring, Annie, 2014. The (W)hole in the Archive. *Paragraph*, 37 (3), 387–402.

Rutz, Lars, 2019. The Stasi Archive: My Life in a Surveillance File. *Law & History*, 6 (2), 133–58.

Sassoon, Joanna, 2004. Photographic Materiality in the Age of Digital Reproduction. *In*: Elizabeth Edwards and Janice Hart, eds. *Photographs, Objects, Histories: On the Materiality of Images*. London: Routledge, 186–202.

Schmidt, Kristi, 2019. Beyond Stasi Control: Harald Hauswald. *Exberliner*, 4 November. Available from: https://www.exberliner.com/features/people/harald-hauswald [Accessed 22 April 2020].

Seppänen, Janne, 2017. Unruly Representation: Materiality, Indexicality and Agency of the Photographic Trace. *Photographies*, 10 (1), 113–28.

Shaul, Matthew, 2010. The Impossibility of Socialist Realism: Photographer Gundula Schulze-Eldowy and the East German Stasi. *In*: Outi Remes and Pam Skelton, eds. *Conspiracy Dwellings: Surveillance in Contemporary Art*. Newcastle upon Tyne: Cambridge Scholars Publishing, 19–34.

Smith, Shawn Michelle, 2014. Photography between Desire and Grief: Roland Barthes and F. Holland Day. *In*: Elspeth H. Brown and Thy Phu, eds. *Feeling Photography*. Durham: Duke University Press, 29–46.

Sperling, Stefan, 2013. *Reasons of Conscience: The Bioethics Debate in Germany*. Chicago, IL: University of Chicago Press.

Springer, Philipp, 2020. *Der Blick der Staatssicherheit: Fotografien aus dem Archiv des MfS*. Dresden: Sandstein Verlag.

Steyerl, Hito, 2012. *The Wretched of the Screen*. Berlin: Sternberg Press.

Suckut, Siegfried, ed., 1985/1996. *Das Wörterbuch der Staatsshicherheit. Definitionen zur politisch-operativen Arbeit*. Berlin: Ch Links Verlag.

Vowinckel, Annette, 2018. Photographic Nuisance. Stern Photographers Thomas Höpker and Harald Schmitt in the GDR. *Journal of Modern European History*, 16 (1), 126–45.

Vowinckel, Annette, 2019. Photojournalism East/West: The Cold War, the Iron Curtain, and the Trade of Photographs. *In*: Henrik G. Bastiansen, Martin Klimke, and Rolf Werenskjold, eds. *Media and the Cold War in the 1980s*. Cham: Palgrave Macmillan, 115–35.

Part IV

Aesthetics

Chapter 13

Artists and legal documents

Aesthetic, witnessing and affective power

Priya Vaughan

Introduction: the creative allure of legal documents

Contemporary artists have long mined institutional cultures and archives, folding their documents, bureaucratic systems, aesthetic norms and histories of operation into creative processes and products. A growing number of artists have turned their attention to the sphere of law, creating works by reproducing, replicating or appropriating law's archives and documents. Indeed, the appropriation of legal documents by creative practitioners is a burgeoning field. Artists, curators, filmmakers, television producers, podcasters, playwrights and others have been drawn to real legal records, and deployed them in various creative enterprises. Although sometimes criticised for sensationalism, voyeurism or exploitation, creative works made from legal documents take advantage of the qualities that give these documents their power: factual and historical heft, attachment to sincere emotional events and the ability to elucidate legal systems and processes. As a result, legal documents provide a rich resource for artists. In some instances, these materials are available because the principles of open justice require it (see for example, Biber 2011). In other instances, artists gain access to such materials due to their personal, professional, cultural or familial connection to particular legal, judicial or forensic events or activities. There are multiple instances in which artists are also legal or forensic professionals, and they draw upon materials encountered as part of this work.[1] Artists making works in the law's archive are magnifying, subverting, redirecting, revelling in or examining the latent power of legal documents to creative and evocative ends. This chapter focuses on the engagements of contemporary visual artists with documents of the law and considers what it is about these documents—that witness, record and archive the legal event—that makes them so compelling for the artists who engage with them. It reflects upon these creative products and considers three dimensions, or facets, of legal documents which are exploited or amplified by artists: the *aesthetic of the form*, the *witnessing potential* of documents and the legal document's *affective power*. These three dimensions are loosely constituted, with porous borders, but they present a useful means through which to account for the impact and power of artworks created with legal documents.[2]

DOI: 10.4324/9781003247593-17

In researching this field, the work of 40 artists, working globally, was surveyed. These visual artists use legal documents as part of their practice, either occasionally or regularly.[3] Artists were identified via a systematic survey of relevant literature, and other materials from the visual arts, museum studies and humanities. Alongside this research, this chapter draws on interviews undertaken with Shevaun Wright and Bindi Cole Chocka: two artists drawing on the law and its documents in their practice.[4] Since the initial identification of the 40 artists, other relevant practitioners who qualify to join this list have been encountered. This gives an indication of the level of creative interest in legal documents and suggests that artistic engagement with the law and its processes is ongoing. In undertaking this survey, it became clear that artists work with legal documents in various ways. As will be described below, artists may include, in their artworks, unaltered original documents (or copies of these); they may focus on particular fragments or sections of documents; remix or deface documents; or fabricate legal documents and their tropes. The visual effect of artworks using documents varies, as does conceptual focus. Some artists work with documents that are personal and relate to their own experiences; others use documents relating to strangers. Sometimes artists draw on materials relating to events that are well-known (or notorious), while others utilise those which are old, obscure or incomplete.

This chapter will focus in particular on the work of four Australian artists: Vernon Ah Kee, Shevaun Wright, Judy Watson and Bindi Cole Chocka. It is not a coincidence that these artists are Indigenous Australians. In Australia, and other settler-colonial contexts, First Nations peoples have been at the forefront of counter-archival scholarly, creative and political work engaging with colonial, legal and other documents and archives (see, for example, the work of Fiona Foley (2020), Julie Gough (2001), Natalie Harkin (2014, 2019), Jeanine Leane (2017, 2018), Aileen Moreton-Robinson (2004), Kirsten Thorpe (2014) and Judy Watson (2009)). It should be noted, however, that this use of legal documents is a global phenomenon which reflects broader engagement, within and beyond the humanities, with archives and their materials. As outlined in the introduction to this collection, legal scholarship has undertaken an 'archival turn' which has influenced the way documents are analysed and interpreted within the discipline. Similarly, visual art has experienced its own archival turn, with the result that documents, documentary practices and archival collections play a role in both artmaking, and in the study, analysis and sale of artworks. Indeed, Sven Spieker shows that although this archival turn occurred late in the twentieth century, the 'bureaucratic archive' has influenced and engaged artists, in varying ways, since early in that century (Spieker 2008, 1–12; see also Jolly 2014). This archival turn has manifested in various ways including as a creative interrogation, by artists, of 'the historical legacy of archival production' (Enwezor 2007, 21), the creation of documents and archives *as art* (Breakell 2015, 1; Vaughan 2016), and the use of documentary practices to create a record of ephemeral and performance-based works and the art creation process (Berger and Santone 2016, 201). As will be explored across this chapter, the legal archive has been amongst those institutional archives plumbed by artists influenced by this archival turn (Carbone 2017, 101). This creative interrogation of the legal archive can be seen as part of a longer history of diverse interactions and interconnections between the spheres of art and law (see Ben-Dor 2011; Young 2013; Manderson 2018; Kee 2019).

Artistic use of legal documents and legal archives can also be connected to contemporary art engagements, beginning in the 1970s and continuing into the present, with Barthes' *The Death of the Author* (Eklund 2004), concepts of simulacra and simulation (Baudrillard 1994), text-based art (Selenitsch 2013) and the forensic-aesthetic (Bray 2014). These engagements reflect broader art-world interrogation of ideologies, arguably enshrined in the Romantic era, which position artists, and their works, as virtuosic, original, authentic and aesthetically transcendent. Here, legal documents are akin to ready-mades (Biber 2018): items of textual, material and visual culture that have become acceptable art-materials as a result of contemporary art's embrace of pastiche, appropriation and engagement with experiences of the everyday (Danto 2014).

Aesthetics of form: Shevaun Wright's contracts

It has been observed that systems of law have their own aesthetic tenets and visual qualities which confer and communicate authority and legitimacy (Dahlberg 2012, 4). These aesthetic regimes—as embodied by material and visual elements such as architecture, clothing and iconography, as well as other performative, textual and cultural legal qualities (Dahlberg 2012, 1–6)—have been the subject of artistic interest.[5] The aesthetic qualities of legal textual documents have also been investigated and exploited by artists. Here, the unremarkable visual trope of black text on white paper has proved a fertile space for artistic expression. This engagement with the institutional and textual domain of the law can be connected to broader artistic use, critique and replication of institutional administrative and bureaucratic aesthetics emerging in the 1960s with the rise of conceptual art (Buchloh 1990, 119). The visual and material properties of legal textual documents can be seen to embody what Don Handelman (2010, 75–76) identifies as the bureaucratic aesthetic: a material and visual embodiment of the logic of the modern state which operates to divide, classify and designate intellectual, geographic and social space. In using such documents, artists highlight a tension implicit in the aesthetic qualities of the bureaucratic textual document; these are forms that are both valuable and ubiquitous, singular and multiple, and powerful and workaday.[6] Artists often exploit these seeming contradictions to present a critique of the law, government or the social dynamics of power. For example, Jenny Holzer has critiqued government mechanisms and incursions of civil liberties via an extensive body of work using government and other documents which exploit the quintessential aesthetic trope of government secrecy: redaction (Fracsina 2016).[7]

Shevaun Wright's oeuvre embodies artistic interrogation and exploration of the aesthetics of legal documents (see Wright, this volume).[8] Wright is a trained lawyer, and a practicing artist (Wright 2015, 68). As such, her art making is intensely interdisciplinary; Wright utilises diverse artistic modes to create artworks which conceptually and aesthetically operate between and across the disciplines of art and law. Seeking to make legal theories, concepts and practices visible, *and* visual, for art audiences, the artist likens her creative practice to that of a translator. She works directly with legal materials, such as judicial decisions and submissions made to courts by lawyers, and appropriates modes of legal writing to create artworks intended to facilitate audience engagement with legal and social complexities. Drawing on postcolonial and feminist scholarship, as well as her own Aboriginal heritage (Wright 2015, 68), Wright explores the artistic and aesthetic qualities of the law, the socio-cultural norms embedded in, and masked by, legal systems, and identifies points of convergence between legal and art spheres. As the artist explains:

> I'm interested in the role of aesthetics in the law. So I'm looking at … [the] poetry in legal language … [the] very visual language of legal theory, and … [using this] to drill down into deeper structures in the law … I see a lot of similarities, unfortunately, between the art world and the legal world. In terms of the bodies that are represented and who gets to speak, who is spoken for. I try and … mine those similarities to bring them out. (personal communication 2018)

In directly reproducing legal materials, or mimicking legal documents, Wright literally brings the language and visual culture of the law into the space of the art gallery. Wright's goal is to create artworks which communicate ideas with clarity, in order to facilitate engagement, and encourage thinking and discussion. As a result, her works can be characterised as direct, in terms of their material, aesthetic and conceptual qualities. The authentic legal documents Wright reproduces in her artworks remain recognisable legal documents. While the artist may intervene in their content, or present them across different media, she never obfuscates their origin.

For example, in her work *Apologies* (Figure 13.1), Wright reproduced legal documents generated by the Federal Court case *Eatock v Bolt (No 2)* (2011), an appeal by Andrew Bolt and the Herald and Weekly Times Pty Ltd in the wake of Pat Eatock's successful complaint against them for race discrimination (MARS 2018). In creating *Apologies*, Wright reproduced Justice Bromberg's judgment, and other documents from the case. Portions of these documents are engraved on four Perspex sheets; some opaque, some transparent. These sheets are suspended from the ceiling of the exhibition space so that a viewer can look both across and through them. Approached as individual sheets, the texts on each panel are legible, with conventional legal formatting and language retained. Considered together, due to the transparent quality of some

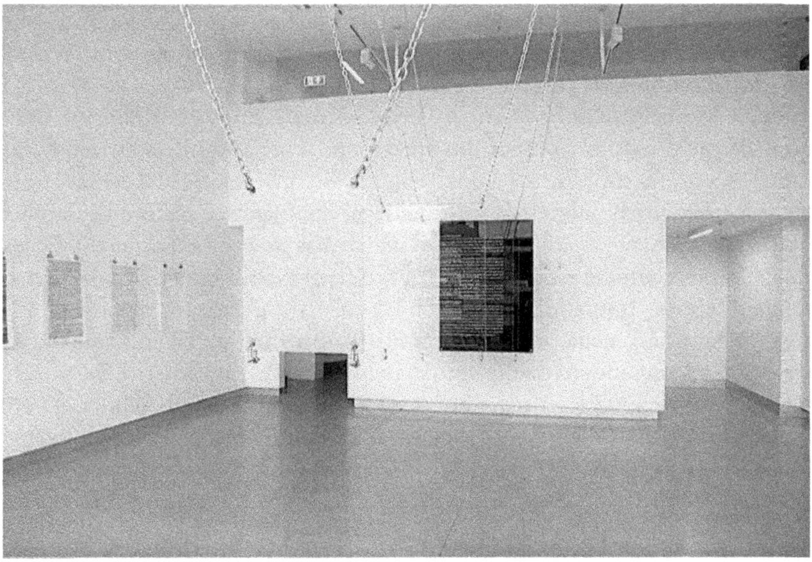

Figure 13.1 Shevaun Wright, *Apologies*, 2018. Paper, Perspex, metal chains, hooks and clips, dimensions variable. Courtesy of the artist and MARS. © Shevaun Wright.

of the Perspex, the sheets—and their texts—become indistinct and difficult to discern. Here textual documents, produced in the course of a costs appeal, are reproduced and manipulated by Wright, but they are not radically altered; textual documents they were, and so they remain. When Wright presents legal documents of her own creation as artworks, this ethos of faithful replication is also invoked, with the fictional documents adhering to legal requisites and formats. The veracity of documents, or the appearance of veracity, is important because, as Wright observes, 'it can add weight to a work' (personal communication 2018). For audiences, the presence of real legal materials can highlight the reality of the social situation that Wright is exploring. However, as will be considered further, Wright also likes to transgress, and play at, the intersection between reality and fiction, in order to engage her audience.

Due to her engagement with legal materials, text inevitably stands as the defining aesthetic feature of Wright's works. Typically, it is legible, typed text, produced in the law's preferred fonts of *Arial*, *Verdana* or *Times New Roman* (Federal Court of Australia n.d.a). The aesthetic effect is immediate—the works evoke not only the court room, but also the archive, the office and bureaucratic systems broadly. The centrality of text also dovetails with Wright's artistic agenda, as she reflects, 'I am finding it difficult to get away from text, just because there's a lot I want to say. Law is all about words so … if I want to interrogate that, I have to do it through text' (personal communication 2018).

As a legal practitioner, Shevaun Wright started out doing litigation, and later worked reviewing contracts. In her art practice, the concept and form of the contract are also a fertile starting point for creative action, with Wright producing a number of contract-based artworks.[9] For a lawyer, a contract is a document formalising an agreement between parties and specifying the obligations of these parties to meet the agreement. For Wright, as an artist, the contract is a useful tool for engaging with important subjects and social ideals. Wright is particularly interested in using legal contracts to explore the notion of the *social contract*—a political theory which has its roots in Ancient Greek philosophy, but which entered modern scholarship as a result of work from Thomas Hobbes, Immanuel Kant, John Locke, Jean-Jacques Rousseau and others (D'Agostino, Gaus and Thrasher 2019). Broadly, social contract theory envisions civil societies as being founded on an agreement between citizens and their state or sovereign regarding moral and ethical norms which govern their society. Critics of the theory argue that the notion of the social contract—predicated on the presumption that a society is made up of equal individuals capable of exercising their free will—fails to acknowledge social inequities embedded in so-called liberal societies, as experienced by women and ethnic, racial, cultural and sexual minorities (see for example Pateman 1988; Mills 1997). For Wright, the social contract remains a 'powerful metaphor' (personal communication 2018) despite this longstanding scholarly critique.

The Rape Contract is one of Wright's most affecting contract-based works.[10] The work is constituted by 14 sheets of A4 paper, presented in white wooden frames. At first glance these sheets of paper seem unremarkable; simple typed sheets from some kind of legal document. Closer engagement reveals that this is, as baldly stated on page one, a 'Rape Contract' which spells out the terms of agreement between a cis-gendered woman and the state for restitution after rape. The contract outlines the conditions to be met by both parties in order for the women to receive *Victim Services*, namely *Social Payments* 'in the form of legal redress, compensation and acknowledgement' (Wright, this volume). These social payments will only be delivered if the woman meets 'community and legal expectations around victimhood' (Wright, this volume) including, adhering to 'strict dress codes (not wearing revealing clothing) … [and abiding to] limitations on … [their] social behaviours, such as not drinking excessively or acting in a sexually promiscuous way' (Heffernan 2018, 28). Modelled on a manned security services contract, the Rape Contract utilises the formal language of commercial law to outline the '"Key Performance Indicators", indemnities, limitations of liability, behavioural specifications and dispute mechanisms' imposed by the state onto the women to whom reparations are to be made (Wright, this volume). The woman's identity, experiences, requirements and motivations for engaging with this contract are not accommodated in the typed text, making the inequity between the two signing parties clear. Despite this exclusion, the nameless woman has been given a right of reply in the artwork, albeit one which is shielded from immediate view. Audience members approaching the framed contract are directed to examine each sheet under the light of an LED torch. When cast over a document, the light reveals small, white, handwritten text penned in 'invisible UV ink' (personal communication 2018). Hand-written around the margins and between the lines of typed text, are 'excerpts from notes, personal writings, psychiatric reports and a police report taken from a victim of a violent rape' (Wright, this volume). The contrast is striking, with the extremely personal, sometimes graphic handwritten annotations responding to, or challenging, the impersonal contractual conditions laid out in the typed text.

The Rape Contract stands as both a highly personal representation of an individual woman's experience of rape and its legal aftermath, as well as a critique of social contract theory and the legal form the theory privileges: the *contract*.

The work was inspired by Wright's personal experience assisting a survivor through the Australian legal system. Wright describes the process as 'traumatising' and notes that it gave her an insight into the brutal reality of legal practice. In response, she set about penning a rape contract, envisioning it as a 'fragment' of the social contract operating between citizens and their states (personal communication 2018). Penning this fragment was a means of rendering visible the inequities of power and moral expectations to which women are subject in law and society. Drawing on Carine M. Mardorossian's, *Framing the Rape Victim: Gender and Agency Reconsidered* (2014), Wright sought to articulate social and legal expectations regarding the actions, appearance and behaviours of the "ideal" rape victim, in order to challenge the idea of the law's rational impartiality regarding gender and sexual violence. The artwork also explores notions of consent, equity and neutrality as they relate to the legal contract, with a particular focus on the way fundamental social and monetary inequities can be enshrined in commercial and other contracts. The artist hoped to get her audience thinking about the concept of consent in the law and in society. Wright notes, 'if consent is a fiction at law in all these important contracts that surround us every day … [then] how is that related to the problem of consent in interpersonal situations?' (personal communication 2018). Further, Wright used a commercial contract as the basis for the work in order to draw attention to continuities between the legal and art worlds in terms of experiences of exclusion and alienation. As an Aboriginal woman artist, Wright felt deeply 'frustrated by the continued marginalisation and distortion of Indigenous and female voices within the legal and art spheres' (Wright, this volume). The contract, an important legal tool at the core of commercial art operations, is deployed by the artist to reflect the shared culture of discrimination in evidence in both spheres.

Wright utilised heavily redacted documents detailing a rape—including police and psychiatric reports—to transcribe onto the contract. Wright also annotated the survivor's personal feelings and responses to the contract, and to the process of bringing the civil claim, thus giving dimension and depth to the woman reduced to the stereotype of *victim* by the terms of the contract. These personal interjections express pain, frustration and anger, but there are also moments of levity. As Wright notes, 'there were jokes in there too. And also acknowledgement that she's not supposed to joke about it, as the "ideal" rape victim' (personal communication 2018). These annotations inject the voice of the survivor into the work, electrifying the banal legalese of the contract and making acute all that is omitted from its clauses. As a result, the text inscribed in invisible ink both documents the experiences of the survivor, and makes space for her humanity.

The process of making the rape contract required careful legal consideration. Redactions had to be made in any documents quoted in the work so they conformed with the law. As a result, the work became, for Wright, 'an expression of the limits of expression' (personal communication 2018).

The aesthetic dimensions of the artwork direct audience engagements and responses to it. Wright sought to keep the contract 'very formal, in black and white [as] with other contracts so it gives the sensation that it's … a real legal document' (personal communication 2018). The use of the invisible ink shapes the way the audience interacts with the work, as Wright reflects, 'I try and make it like an act of discovery' (personal communication 2018). In order to see the handwritten annotations with a torch, the viewer must be physically close to the contract, resulting in a sense of uncomfortable proximity to the dynamics of power and exclusion embodied by it. *The Rape Contract* is literally activated by the viewer; without the torch light, the work tells only one side of the story. In discerning the hidden annotations littering the work, the viewer becomes embroiled in a kind of forensic work which uncovers an alternative narrative—obscured by the terms of the rape contract—regarding sexual violence, and the law's mechanisms relating to such acts. As such, audience members become entangled and implicated in the work, and in the cultural mores and legal tenets which it seeks to demystify and critique.

Material witnesses: Judy Watson and Bindi Cole Chocka

In law, a witness is an individual who provides the court with information that pertains to the case under consideration. The information furnished by this individual is a type of evidence (Federal Court of Australia, n.d.b). In archaeology, anthropology, museology and elsewhere, the capacity to witness has also been attributed to non-human entities. For example, material culture, particularly so-called heritage items, have been acknowledged as witnessing-objects; tangible survivors of events of the past that, by their very existence and persistence, testify to the histories which produced or were endured by them (see for example Friedman 1992; Barkan 2002; Phillips 2005; Farrell-Racette 2009). As art historian and curator Ruth Phillips observes, 'historical objects are witnesses, things that were *there, then*. They bear their makers' marks … and have a compelling agency to cause people living in the present to enunciate their relationships to the past' (Phillips 2005, 108 italics in original). A parallel might be drawn between the witnessing power of material culture and the function of contemporaneous records in law. These are notes made during or following an event under consideration and are utilised to 'strengthen the accuracy and trustworthiness of … evidence in court' (Paterson et al. 2018, 275).

Artists often draw upon legal documents to exploit this witnessing power. In many instances these documents are incorporated into artworks in ways which position them as evidence: providing testimony (rather than representations, as in legal contexts) about the validity of the artist's position, or anchoring artworks in reality. Here the concept of evidence operates beyond the legal definition of the term, to denote something that is implicated in a social web of meaning that can be referred to, and considered, to make inferences about that social web and the world it reflects (Caswell and Gilliland 2015, 623–624).

In this context, legal documents may be utilised by artists because they have an aura of authenticity. As Rebecca Scott Bray (2014, 76) has observed, these are artefacts that are imbued with 'historical authenticity … [and] are considered representational in their connection to [law's events] … It is their indexicality that matters'. It is this connection to, and embodiment of, reality that electrifies such documents, and which operates to distinguish, and sometimes elevate, the works of art in which they appear. Pablo Picasso once quipped that art 'is a lie that makes us realise the truth' (Klein 2004). Artworks made from legal documents may be creative, subjective and fictional, but they are constituted by and built on materials which record (versions) of reality. In Picasso's formulation these artworks are *truths which communicate truths*. However, despite this association with truth, reality and evidence, artists rarely use such legal documents uncritically, and often an interrogation of the validity, fallibility or witnessing capacity of documents is the central aim of artworks produced. As Trish Luker (2017, 114) has observed, sometimes legal documents, such as those produced by colonial governments, are 'an inadequate source of information about what happened in the past' and must be augmented with the voices, views and accounts of those recorded in them. Artwork using legal documents can contribute to this augmentation.[11]

Judy Watson's artist's books *a preponderance of aboriginal blood* and *under the Act* stand as two aesthetically and emotionally compelling works which rely upon, and unsettle, the testimonial authenticity of legal documents.[12] Directly reproducing material archived in the State Library of Queensland, Watson's works are made up of a series of *chin-collé* etchings. In *a preponderance of aboriginal blood*, Watson has directly reproduced correspondence and other archival records regarding the rights of Aboriginal people to vote in the Australian state of Queensland. Watson's 'Aboriginal matrilineal family is from *Waanyi* country in North-west Queensland' (Watson 2019, 43); thus her focus on the archives of the Queensland state is both personal and political. Before Aboriginal people were given the right to vote in federal and state elections in the 1960s 'eligibility to vote was based on the specious issue of the percentage of Aboriginal blood' (Best 2018, 99). Watson presents archival texts in black and white or sepia, augmenting them with etched plumes of rust-red ink which overlay document texts like splatters or seepages of blood. The same technique is deployed in *under the Act* in which blood-like sprays and spatters are inked across government and family documents relating to the operation of the *Aboriginals Protection and Restriction of the Sale of Opium Act 1897*. This was draconian protectionist legislation which controlled the lives of Aboriginal peoples in Queensland (see discussion in Cadet-James, James, McGinty and McGregor 2017).

In each of these works, Watson's augmentation of government documents is striking but not dramatically interventionist. Speaking about *a preponderance of aboriginal blood*, Watson notes 'because the material from the archives

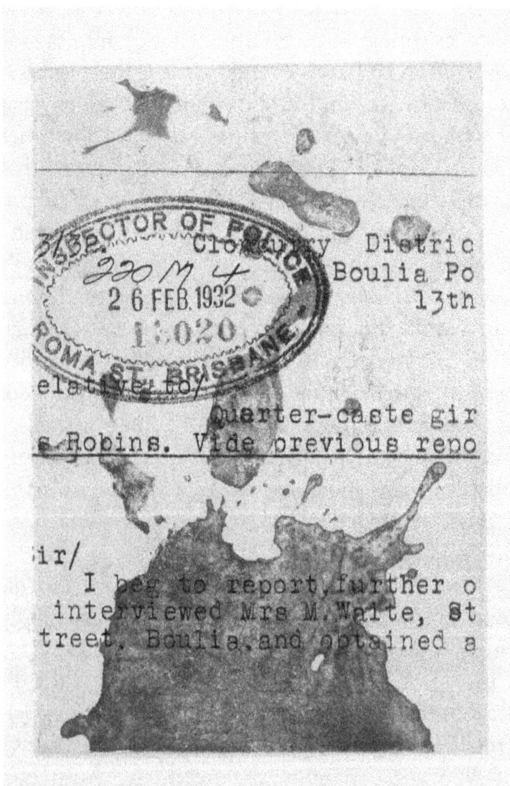

Figure 13.2 Judy Watson, page 2 from artist's book *a preponderance of aboriginal blood*, 2005. Courtesy of Judy Watson and grahame galleries + editions. Photographer Carl Warner. © Judy Watson.

already has a latent power, I didn't want to change this very much' (UTS Art, n.d.). The latent power that Watson identifies perhaps derives from the aura of authenticity described above. As records which testify to the lived experience of Aboriginal people subject to oppressive legislation, Watson's bloody splatters heighten the instrumentality of these documents, their role in classifying, dividing and policing Indigenous Australians in Queensland. As Lena Fritsch has observed, Watson's 'red drops and stains symbolise the blood of Aboriginal people and the percentage of blood that classified them, while the archival texts are inextricably intertwined with their devastating social, physical and emotional impact' (2018, n.p.). The application of blood has a striking visual effect, creating a dramatic moment of contrast, and even contradiction. These documents, articulated in an impersonal language and shrouded with the authority of government, have a ubiquitous quality that might lead the viewer to believe that they are inoffensive artefacts of bureaucracy. Watson contradicts this, heightening their horror—these documents literally have blood *on their hands*. Further, as Luker has shown, though Watson does not dramatically rework these documents, her application of blood does make portions of text illegible. Thus, Watson 'obscures the details of the archival documents, and … engages in a counter-archival practice to undermine' the legislative authority embodied and reflected within them (Luker 2016, 91). Here, legal documents are directly reproduced and offered, by the artist, as witnesses. But due to Watson's intervention, the events they address are not those they were originally intended to attest to. Rather than supporting the government policy and legislation under which they were created, these documents testify to the lived reality of life under these legal mechanisms, rather than to the validity of the colonial ideologies that created them.

Watson's work articulates a broad social commentary about Australian colonial legal systems and histories; however, elsewhere the testamentary power of legal documents is drawn upon for more personal, and cathartic ends. Bindi Cole Chocka's *EH5452* is an immersive installation featuring carceral and other prison-related documents. The work recreates the cell in which Chocka was housed while incarcerated at HM Prison Holloway (UK) due to 'drug charges' (Andrew 2012, 83). Seeking to come to terms with a past that had caused her shame, and to recount her conversion to Christianity, Chocka described the work as a *coming out* to the art world. As she recalls:

> I had been volunteering in the local women's prison … I would go in every week for four years and spend time with women in there, building relationships with them … I would go in and mostly encourage the women that despite their circumstances it didn't have to define their lives. When they got out of prison they didn't have to be ashamed because there was plenty of opportunity for them if they wanted to turn their lives around. Look at me, I was in fact them. But … I hadn't really told anybody in my world, apart from people very close to me, that I had been

> in prison. I was achieving acclaim as an artist; I was developing a national profile. I had these kind of fragmented worlds going on … So, this particular work … was kind of my coming out … It enabled me to come out to the art world about the truth of the situation. But more than that, it allowed me to be exactly who I am in every sphere of my world. It didn't have to be one thing here and another thing there. It kind of brought all the fragmented pieces together.
>
> (personal communication 2018)

As well as coming out as an 'ex-con', Chocka also used the work to come out as a Christian, something that was—perhaps ironically—'equally, if not more, scary' (personal communication 2018). A former atheist, Chocka recalled how 'people outside of Christianity can think [negatively] about Christians' and so felt nervous about outing herself (personal communication 2018). Alongside furniture adorned with biblical quotations relating to spiritual freedom and rebirth, *EH5452* includes a video of Chocka, adorned in black and white prison stripes, reading with great feeling from her prison diary (another type of informal legal document) about the lows and highs of incarceration, including her revelation about the importance of Christ in her life. Contributing to the surreal aura of the video, Chocka reads her diary as if it is a bedtime story, sitting in a baby-blue room, surrounded by fluffy white clouds and taxidermal black crows, while melancholic piano music plays. Chocka's cell also features a display of photographs, documents, videos, audiotapes, notebooks and prison paraphernalia amassed by the artist while incarcerated. Chocka's

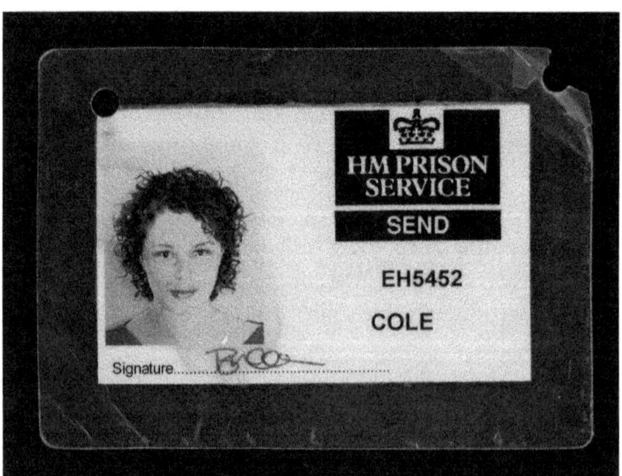

Figure 13.3 Bindi Cole Chocka, *EH5452* (detail), 2012. Re-created prison cell: documents and objects from prison, furniture, fabric, single-channel projection, single-channel video, audio, dimensions variable. Courtesy of the artist © Bindi Cole Chocka.

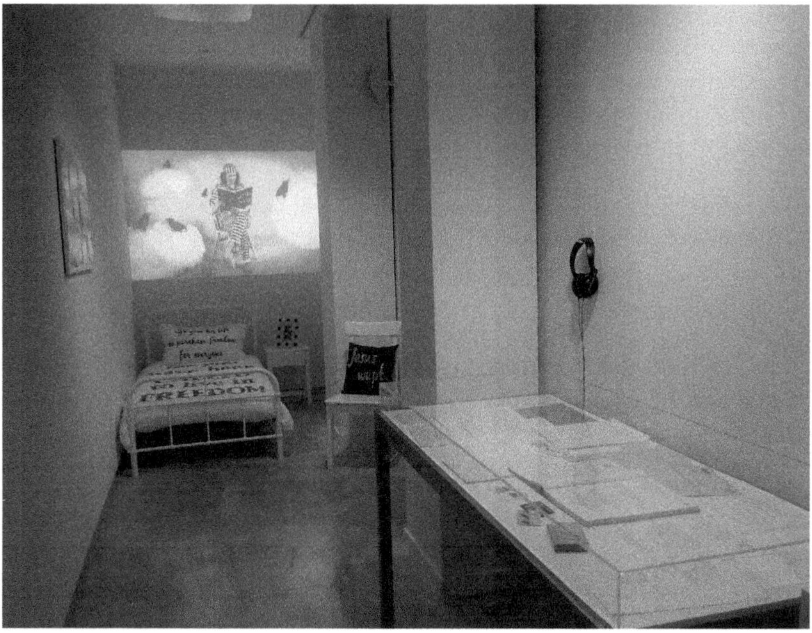

Figure 13.4 Bindi Cole Chocka, *EH5452* (installation view), 2012. Re-created prison cell: documents and objects from prison, furniture, fabric, single-channel projection, single-channel video, audio, dimensions variable. Courtesy of the artist © Bindi Cole Chocka.

video recitation is also interspersed with images of these items. These relics of Chocka's time in Holloway operate as a kind of evidence which anchors the surreal, atmospheric space of the cell to the real world. These objects operate as proof that the fiction of the art-cell is anchored in fact and offer testimony about Chocka's experience of prison and her embrace of Christianity.

Affective powers: Vernon Ah Kee's *tall man*

Affect is a slippery concept which is typically used to suggest 'a force that creates a relationship (conscious or otherwise) between a body (individual or collective) and the world' (Cifor 2016, 10). Affect denotes a relationship or exchange between agents, or between agents and things, which alters, or produces a response in, one or both of these entities (Seigworth and Gregg 2010, 1). In this chapter, I consider affect as the power (latent or manifest) of *things* to emotionally and intellectually move, or create feeling in, a person. Documents, alongside other forms of material culture, have been identified as having an affective potential (see for example White 2014). As Yael

Navaro-Yashin (2007, 81) has observed, 'it is not that documents maintain autonomous or self-contained affectivities, but that they are perceived or experienced as affectively charged phenomena when produced and transacted in specific contexts of social relation'. The affective power and potential of documents are explored and enhanced by artists creating pieces that draw on the legal archive. In many instances the affective power of these artworks cannot be divorced from the aesthetic qualities and witnessing properties of legal documents discussed above. To explore this, I will consider Vernon Ah Kee's video installation work *tall man*. Ah Kee belongs to the *Kuku Yalandji, Waanji, Yidinji and Gugu Yimithirr* peoples (McDowell 2016).

tall man uses mobile phone and other video footage—the bulk of which was filmed by police on Palm Island—to present an affective insight into the 2004 Palm Island riot. Palm Island or *Bwgcolman* is a tropical island that sits in the Coral Sea, 65 kilometres off the Queensland coast, Australia (Palm Island Aboriginal Shire Council, n.d.). Palm Island's traditional custodians are the *Manbarra* and *Buluguban* people (Watson 2018). In 1918 the island, which had previously been gazetted as an Aboriginal reserve, was established as a site where Aboriginal and Torres Strait Islander peoples, who had been forcibly removed from their Countries across Queensland, were exiled (Watson 2018). So began Palm Island's bleak history as 'a kind of tropical gulag' (Hooper 2009, 12) in which Aboriginal and Torres Strait Islander inmates were subject to punitive violence, rationed supplies, slave-like labour conditions and extreme control over their daily lives (Watson 2018). Despite the dire conditions, the community on Palm Island resisted and protested their treatment, including by organising strikes and later by taking legal action over industrial relations and racial discrimination (Watson 2018). Strict controls over the Palm Island community did not cease until the late 1970s, and in 1985 the 'autonomous Palm Island Aboriginal Council [was] established under the *Community Services (Aborigines) Act 1984* (Qld)' (Queensland Government 2018). In 2004, Palm Island resident Mulrunji was arrested for allegedly swearing at police officers, including arresting officer Senior Sergeant Christopher Hurley. Bystanders reported they did not hear this swearing, but instead heard Mulrunji singing *Who Let the Dogs Out* by the Baha Men (Hooper 2009, 23–24; Watson 2018). Less than 60 minutes after these events, Mulrunji was found dead in his cell at the local police station. His liver had been ruptured, causing his death, and he was found to have broken ribs and a lung puncture (Watson 2018). The death in custody, and the attribution of this death to accident, caused great distress and anger in the Palm Island Community and prompted protest and, later, what has been labelled both civil disobedience and rioting (Watson 2018). In the wake of these events, Lex Wotton, former Palm Islander Councillor, was charged with and ultimately convicted of inciting a riot (Robertson 2016). Although Deputy State Coroner Christine Clements found that Senior Sergeant Christopher Hurley fatally assaulted Mulrunji, he was ultimately acquitted of assault and manslaughter charges (SBS News 2016).

Ah Kee's *tall man* is presented across four large screens. At times the viewer sees the same images replicated; at other times each screen plays distinct footage, offering different perspectives on the same events. The restlessly moving footage narrates the story of the Palm Island riot and its aftermath in a series of vignettes: the community waiting to hear the cause of Mulrunji's death in police custody; Palm Island's then-mayor, Erykah Kyle, delivering the pathologist's findings about the death over a microphone to a crowd; community disbelief and shock as Kyle relays that the death is being classified as an accident, the result of 'a fall … [causing] compressive force on his body';[13] Lex Wotton, tall, muscular and shirtless, taking the microphone and imploring the crowd, 'come on people, we all wanted this, we wanted to know. Will we accept this?' (Duff 2011, 5); Wotton walking with 'determined purpose into the police station yard, wielding a large garden spade' (Allas 2012, 22); the police, in a state of barely disguised agitation, equipping themselves with weapons to face rioters, as Senior Sergeant Roger Whyte moots firing 'a few rounds in the air to scare the shit out of these cunts' (Watson 2018); aerial and ground shots of the police station and police accommodation on fire, smoke rising into the sapphire blue sky; and finally, the Palm Island community holding banners of protest outside the Townsville Court during Lex Wotton's trial for inciting the riot (Duff 2011, 5). Here, Lex Wotton's mother addresses the media directly (Gertrude Contemporary 2011), calling for around the clock security for men in custody on Palm Island as they need to be protected from

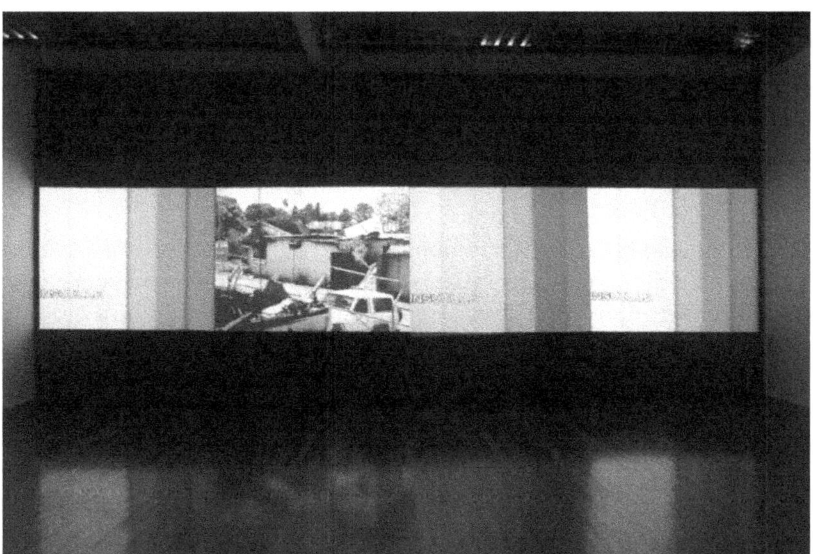

Figure 13.5 Vernon Ah Kee, *tall man*, 2010. Four channel video installation, 11:10 min. Image courtesy the artist and Milani Gallery, Brisbane. ©Vernon Ah Kee.

the 'prison system'. As she speaks her anguish becomes increasingly evident until she cries out, 'people are distressed, please! We are oppressed people!'

Artfully knitted together, the work presents a tense, multi-perspectival, participant's-eye-view narrative in which a community—who have suffered decades of prejudice and injustice (Hooper 2009, 10–13)— respond to Mulrunji's death in grief and anger. The intrinsically multi-perspectival quality of *tall man* at first evokes feelings of confusion, even anxiety. The composition of the work acts to embroil the viewer, who is forced to almost constantly scan the screens trying to catch the thread of the narrative. The film often also requires repeat viewing, as it is rare to enter the exhibition space at the start of Ah Kee's film. This frenetic, uncertain viewing experience evokes something of the confusion and unease of Palm Islanders in the wake of Mulrunji's death. Unpolished (and possibly never intended for wider consumption), the footage Ah Kee presents is often uncomfortable to watch, capturing unguarded and ugly moments of anger, fear and confusion. The end of *tall man*'s film sequence is marked by a coloured test screen pattern and the blaring of a sine wave tone adding a feeling of chaos and suggesting a breakdown in communication. The story comes to an abrupt halt, rather than a resolved ending. After a brief lull, the film plays again.

The impact of Ah Kee's installation is made particularly acute by recognition that some of the footage that Ah Kee used to construct *tall man* is the product of a criminal investigation; evidence that was presented at Lex Wotton's trial and intended to prove him guilty of inciting the riot (Duff 2011, 5). Ah Kee has not revealed how he came to possess this evidentiary material stating, 'I can't really say where all the footage came from … but I can say that it didn't come from Lex [Wotton] and that it was the footage used to convict him' (Don 2011). The affective power of this work comes from both its aesthetic form (one inextricably linked to the visual traits of the legal material on which it is based), the witnessing capacity of the documents used *and* Ah Kee's manipulation of these qualities. Ah Kee's skilful presentation of this material creates an immersive and emotional experience for the viewer—one replete with interest, anxiety, dread, confusion, sorrow and excitement. *tall man* does not present a clear narrative to viewers, nor does it furnish an audience with any background information about Palm Island's history, Mulrunji's death in custody, Wotton's arrest or Hurley's acquittal. In a sense, *tall man* starts in the middle of the story, well after the death of Mulrunji in custody, and in the long wake of Palm Island's grim colonial history. Without this backstory the onus is on the audience to educate themselves, an action which could be framed as part of the work's ongoing affect. Knowing something of this history gives the artwork further meaning and significance. At the centre of the artwork are two *tall men*; Lex Wotton (whose actions are documented, and play in an endless loop, across the installation) and Senior Sergeant Christopher Hurley (who is never pictured in the film, but whose presence is inescapably evoked). The respective fates of these two men in the wake of the riot—one Aboriginal, one non-Aboriginal, one convicted, one acquitted—shapes the viewers' interpretation of *tall man*, rendering the events on Palm Island a symptomatic legacy of Australia's colonisation. The installation speaks to a legacy which still impacts Indigenous peoples across the nation, and, in ways both overt and subtle, shapes the social, legal and government response to their lives and their deaths.

As discussed above, the legal documents used in *tall man* were furnished as evidence in a legal proceeding. As such, they achieved the status of evidence when they were adduced to attest to the validity of narratives articulated about Lex Wotton in court. As a result, they have become a special category of material culture imbued with significance because of their connection to notions of proof and truth. In Ah Kee's artwork, this status and function are inevitably evoked, but in the work, these legal materials become evidentiary in new ways. In *tall man* the video evidence both articulates the story of the Palm Island riot, and acts as a signifier for the legal proceeding, and its outcome, for which it was compiled and presented. Constructed from video of 'real events', *tall man* has an aura of authenticity, and the narrative it builds feels compelling because it is the stuff of reality; shaky mobile camera footage of the mayor, fearful profanities uttered by police just off screen, the palpable indignation and frustration of Wotton. All are captured without artifice or intervention, enhancing the viewer's engagement, making them feel present at the moment the footage was shot. Ah Kee's editing of this material is not didactic—but it does present, by foregrounding the events which drove the community to boiling point, Wotton and the Palm Island community in a sympathetic light. By casting these events in this light using legal evidence, Ah Kee unsettles the notion that the footage that constitutes his work leads naturally to the lawful conclusion that was reached against Wotton. Here, a document of evidence, accepted by the court for its probative value, is re-presented by Ah Kee to challenge the justness of Wotton's conviction. If the viewer has knowledge of the history of Palm Island, the work also inevitably draws our attention to decades of injustice endured by those living on the island. These images do not speak for themselves; Ah Kee speaks through them. Through his skilful adversarialism, he presents the evidence in a manner that makes Wotton's actions both understandable and even heroic. Ah Kee shows us that documentary evidence must be verified, authenticated and interpreted by a qualified witness. Meeting none of the formal legal conventions required for the production of evidence, Ah Kee nevertheless testifies to the audience about the riot, the evidence which documents it, Wotton's culpability and the rightness of the case brought before the court.

Affect is central to the experience, and the aims, of *tall man*. As Ah Kee has stated, the artwork poses 'questions that compel. What of Lex Wotton? And why don't we talk about Palm Island? When we say "Palm Island", there are connotations that fix us, that give us pause, and send our emotions racing toward tipping points' (Gittins 2014, 22). In affectively materialising and visualising these questions through *tall man*, the artist purposefully pushes the audience headlong into these *tipping points*. His use and reinterpretation of legal evidence also evoke other unsettling questions regarding the morality, transparency and fairness of the legal processes (and documents that were furnished at them) that led to Wotton's conviction.

Conclusion: documents put to work

As the above discussion illustrates, artists engage with the aesthetic qualities, witnessing capacity and affective power of legal documents to various thematic and intellectual ends. Although the creative intentions of artists are diverse, certain thematic trends emerge when considering these works. For example, artworks featuring legal documents are often—though not exclusively—socially engaged and outward-looking in terms of their conceptual concerns (e.g. the legacies of colonisation, systemic racism, social inequality and manifestations of prejudice and privilege). In these works, legal documents act as avatars for the legal institutions—and indeed the states, nations or cultures—in which they were produced, embodying and reflecting the ideologies which direct their operation. Another broad thematic focus across these works is the analysis of concepts core to ideologies of justice namely *proof, truth* and *evidence*. Here, legal documents act as sites of interrogation, where such concepts can be examined and stress-tested. In this way, when legal documents are put to work in, and as, artworks, their original function or status shifts and is often expanded. Unlike legal actors (police, lawyers, judges, juries, etc.) who must handle and interpret legal documents in particular ways, artists have creative freedom to interpret and represent documents and the histories, cases or individuals they represent, in ways that don't have currency or meaning inside legal institutions. The artist, and their audience, can be reflexive, speculative, imaginative and playful with legal documents when they are used in artworks. In this way, when redeployed as art objects, legal documents have the power to express experiences, emotions and ideas beyond the scope of the law or the mechanisms or motivations that originally prompted the creation of such documents (White 2014, 87). This interrogation, disruption and expansion of the significance of legal documents connects directly to the motivations characterising the archival turn in the visual arts (Enwezor 2007, 22; Vaughan 2016, 229).

While the portent of a legal document might shift or expand in the space of the artwork, it is important to acknowledge that their 'earlier status and identity' *as a document* are never entirely shrugged off or discarded (Berrebi 2007, 113). Indeed, in the works of Ah Kee, Wright, Watson, Chocka and other artists drawing on legal documents, this document-status is purposefully retained and even celebrated. The artistic exploration of a document's aesthetic qualities, witnessing capacity or affective power is often dependent on the dimensions, connotations and visual and emotive powers intrinsic to these documents. It is the documentary-quality of these artworks which operates to deliver the *punctum* (Barthes, 1921) and the punch, to a viewer, and which is at the crux of the narratives they articulate.

Acknowledgements

Thank you to Shevaun Wright and Bindi Cole Chocka for generously sharing your experiences, insights (and images of your artworks) and for allowing me to reproduce these here. Thank you to Judy Watson and Vernon Ah Kee for kindly allowing me to include images of your works. My respect and thanks go to the anonymous survivor whose feelings and responses add great power and humanity to *The Rape Contract.* My gratitude to Katherine Biber and Trish Luker, for enabling me to write this chapter, and for mentorship, thoughtful feedback and encouragement as it took shape.

Notes

1 These include artists such as Teresa Margolles (Bray 2013), Jason File (Biber 2019, 178–179) and Jan Rosseel (Peeters 2015).

2 In her examination of the 'cultural use of legal archives' Scott Bray asserts that artists engage with the artefacts of law by working in and across three types of archives: the legal archive (materials directly produced by law enforcement, etc.), the quasi-legal archive (true crime novels, news and social media about crime, etc.) and the extra-legal archive (materials produced as part of forensic or other legal procedures that are ultimately not included in the legal archive) (Bray 2014, 76–93). In Scott Bray's schema, the artworks explored here can be seen as belonging to the legal archive.

3 Some of these artists, including Shevaun Wright, Carey Young and Carolyn McKay, have contributed chapters to this volume.

4 These interviews were undertaken between the artists and Priya Vaughan at the University of Technology, Sydney (UTS), between July and August 2018 as part of 'What Is a Document? Evidentiary Challenges in the Digital Age Project' (ARC DP160100414).

5 See for example works by Carey Young including *Palais de Justice* (2017), *Before the Law* (2017), *We the People* (2013). For more on Young's practice see Young and Kee's chapter in this volume.

6 For discussion on the 'mundane' and 'ordinary' qualities of legal files see discussion in Barrera 2008, 6.

7 Indeed redaction, and other destroyed or censored official documents, have proved appealing for a number of artists such as Joshua Craze, William E. Jones, Jason File, Mari Bastashevski, Edmund Clark, Mariam Ghani, Chitra Ganesh, Tim Sherratt, Laura Poitras and Jill Magid. Further, redacted documents leaked by Nauru detention staff, and published in *The Guardian*, were the focus of artworks produced for the *All We Can't See* exhibition in 2018 (All We Can't See 2018).

8 Other artist's exploring similar terrain include Carolyn McKay, Sadie Barnette, SUPERFLEX, Carey Young, Milo Rau, Amala Groom and Susan Schuppli.

9 Wright has created numerous contract-based artworks including *The (Foreign Investment) Scam* (2014) and *The Amended Artist's Reserved Rights Transfer and Sale Agreement* (2019). To view these and other works by the artist see: https://www.shevaunwright.com/. Wright is one of a number of contemporary artists who create, subvert, enact and test the legal limits of legal contracts in their art practice. Artists who have produced

contracts as artworks include SUPERFLEX, Carey Young, Jill Magid, Andrea Fraser, Jason File, Etienne Chambaud and Adrian Piper.

10 See Wright's artist statement, and images of this work, in this volume.

11 Kee's *tall man* can be understood as one such augmentation, as can Judy Watson's artworks which are discussed below. Indeed, in Australia there has been a flourishing of creative engagements with law's archive by Indigenous artists, poets, authors, scholars, community members and others. For more see Harkin and Leane, and Haebich et al. (both this volume).

12 Artists also working in this space include Susan Schuppli, Josh Begel and Šejla Kamerić.

13 For a detailed retelling of events depicted in this work, see Hooper (2009) and Watson (2018).

References

All We Can't See, 2018. *All We Can't See*. Available from: https://allwecantsee.com/ [Accessed 15 December 2019].

Allas, Tess, 2012. Vernon Ah Kee. *In*: Carly Lane and Francesca Cubillo, eds. *Undisclosed: 2nd Indigenous Art Triennial*. Canberra: National Gallery of Australia.

Andrew, Brooke, 2012. Taboo: Dirty and Pretty at the Same Time. *In*: Brook Andrew, ed. *Taboo*. Sydney: Museum of Contemporary Art.

Barkan, Elazar, 2002. Amending Historical Injustices: The Restitution of Cultural Property—An Overview. *In*: Elazar Barkan and Ronald Bush, eds. *Claiming the Stones, Naming the Bones: Cultural property and the negotiation of national and ethnic identity*. Los Angeles, CA: Getty, 16–46.

Barthes, Roland, 1921. *Camera Lucida: Reflections on Photography*. London: Fontana Paperbacks.

Barrera, Leticia, 2008. Files Circulation and the Forms of Legal Experts: Agency and Personhood in the Argentine Supreme Court. *Journal of Legal Anthropology*, 1 (1), 3–24.

Baudrillard, Jean, 1994. *Simulacra and Simulation*. Ann Arbor, MI: University of Michigan Press.

Ben-Dor, Oren, ed., 2011. *Law and Art Justice, Ethics and Aesthetics*. Oxon, USA and Canada: Routledge.

Berger, Christian, and Santone, Jessica, 2016. Introduction: Documentation as Art Practice in the 1960s. *Visual Resources*, 32, 201–9.

Berrebi, Sophie, 2007. Documentary and the Dialectical Document in Contemporary Art. *In*: Margriet Schavemarker and Mischa Rakier, eds. *Right About Now: Art & Theory Since the 1990s*. Amsterdam: Valiz.

Best, Susan, 2018. Anger and Repair. *Third Text*, 32, 79–100.

Biber, Katherine, 2011. Evidence from the Archive: Implementing the Court Information Act in NSW. *Sydney Law Review*, 33, 575–98.

Biber, Katherine, 2018. The Art of Bureaucracy: Redacted Ready-mades. *In*: Desmond Manderson, ed. *Law and the Visual: Representations, Technologies, Critique*. Toronto, Buffalo and London: University of Toronto Press, 286–309.

Biber, Katherine, 2019. *In Crime's Archive: The Cultural Afterlife of Evidence*. Oxon and New York: Routledge.

Biber, Katherine, and Dalton, Derek, 2009. Making Art from Evidence: Secret Sex and Police Surveillance in the Tearoom. *Crime Media Culture*, 5, 243–67.

Bray, Rebecca Scott, 2013. Uneasy Evidence: The Medico-Legal Portraits of Teresa Margolles and Libia Posada. *Griffith Law Review*, 22, 28–62.

Bray, Rebecca Scott, 2014. Rotten Prettiness? The Forensic Aesthetic and Crime as Art. *Australian Feminist Law Journal*, 40, 69–95.

Breakell, Sue, 2015. Archival Practices and the Practice of Archives in the Visual Arts. *Archives and Records*, 36, 1–5.

Buchloh, Benjamin H. D., 1990. Conceptual Art 1962–1969: From the Aesthetic of Administration to the Critique of Institutions. *October*, 55, 105–43.

Cadet-James, Yvonne, James, Robert Andrew, McGinty, Sue, and McGregor, Russell, 2017. Protection. *In*: Yvonne Cadet-James, Robert Andrew James, Sue McGinty, and Russell McGregor, eds. *Gugu Badhun: People of the Valley of Lagoons*. Canberra, ACT: Aboriginal Studies Press, 37–44.

Carbone, Kathy Michelle, 2017. Artists and Records: Moving History and Memory. *Archives and Records*, 38 (1), 100–18.

Caswell, Michelle, and Gilliland, Anne, 2015. False Promise and New Hope: Dead Perpetrators, Imagined Documents and Emergent Archival Evidence. *The International Journal of Human Rights*, 19, 615–27.

Chocka, Bindi Cole, 2018. Personal Communication. *Telephone Interview with Priya Vaughan*, 17th August.

Cifor, Markia, 2016. Affecting Relations: Introducing Affect Theory to Archival Discourse. *Archival Science*, 16, 7–31.

D'Agostino, Fred, Gaus, Gerald, and Thrasher, John, 2019. Contemporary Approaches to the Social Contract. *The Stanford Encyclopedia of Philosophy*. Available from: https://plato.stanford.edu/archives/fall2019/entries/contractarianism-contemporary [Accessed 15 December 2020].

Dahlberg, Lief, 2012. Introduction. Visualising Law and Authority. *In*: Lief Dahlberg, ed. *Visualizing Law and Authority: Essays on Legal Aesthetics*. Germany: De Gruyter.

Danto, Arthur C., 2014. *After the End of Art: Contemporary Art and the Pale of History*. Princeton, NJ: Princeton University Press.

Don, Sallie. 2011. Tragedy of Palm Island in the frame. *The Australian*, 7 October, p. 15.

Duff, Alisa, 2011. Tall Man by Vernon Ah Kee. *Art Monthly*, 239, 5–6.

Eklund, Douglas, 2004. The Pictures Generation. *Heilbrunn Timeline of Art History*. Available from: https://www.metmuseum.org/toah/hd/pcgn/hd_pcgn.htm [Accessed 3 December 2020].

Enwezor, Okwui, 2007. *Archive Fever: Photography Between History and the Monument*. New York: Steidl.

Farrell-Racette, Sherry, 2009. Looking for Stories and Unbroken Threads: Museum Artifacts as Women's History and Cultural Legacy. *In*: Gail Guthrie Valaskakis, Madeleine Dion Stout, and Eric Guimond eds., *Restoring the balance: First Nations women, community, and culture*. Winnipeg: University of Manitoba Press, 283–312.

Federal Court of Australia, n.d.a. Preparing Documents for Court. *Federal Court of Australia*. Available from: https://www.fedcourt.gov.au/online-services/preparing-documents-for-the-court [Accessed 25 February 2020].

Federal Court of Australia, n.d.b. *Being a Witness*. Available from: https://www.fedcourt.gov.au/going-to-court/i-am-a-witness/being-a-witness#:~:text=A%20witness%20is%20a%20person,evidence%20is%20sometimes%20called%20testifying [Accessed 25 February 2020].

Foley, Fiona, 2020. *Biting the Clouds: A Badtjala perspective on the Aboriginals Protection and Restriction of the Sale of Opium Act*. Queensland: UQP.

Frascina, Francis, 2016. Redaction. *Art Monthly*, 393, 1–4.

Friedman, Jonathan, 1992. The Past in the Future: History and the Politics of Identity. *American Anthropologist*, 94, 837–59.

Fritsch, Lena, 2018. Judy Watson. *Museum of Contemporary Art*. Available from: https://www.mca.com.au/artists-works/artists/judy-watson/ [Accessed 2nd May 2019].

Gallagher, Katie. 2018. Irish Director Vincent Lambe Defends Controversial Short Film Detainment about Killing of Jamie Bulger. *Irish Mirror*. Available from: https://www.irishmirror.ie/whats-on/film-news/irish-director-vincent-lambe-defends-13439809 [Accessed 12 July 2020].

Gertrude Contemporary, 2011. Vernon Ah Kee: Tall Man. Available from: http://gertrude.org.au/docs/vernon-ah-kee.pdf [Accessed 7 June 2020].

Gittins, Paulette, 2014. *Art + Soul Series Two [video]*. Australia: ATOM.

Gough, Julie, 2001. *Julie Gough, Transforming histories: The Visual Disclosure of Contentious Pasts*. Thesis (PhD). University of Tasmania.

Handelman, Don, 2010. Folding and Enfolding Walls: Statist Imperatives and Bureaucratic Aesthetics in DIVIDED JERUSALEM. *Social Analysis*, 54, 60–79.

Harkin, Natalie, 2014. The Poetics of (Re)Mapping Archives: Memory in the Blood. *Journal of the Association for the Study of Australian Literature*, 14 (3), 1–14.

Harkin, Natalie, 2019. *Archival Poetics*. Australia: Vagabond Press.

Heffernan, Tara, 2018. (Very) unfinished business: Perspectives on curating feminism in the age of Tumblr politics. *Eyeline*, 89, 26–34.

Hooper, Chloe, 2009. *The Tall Man: Death and Life on Palm Island*. Australia: Penguin.

Jolly, Martyn, 2014. Big Archives and Small Collections: Remarks on the Archival mode in contemporary Australian Art and Visual Culture. *Public History Review*, 21, 60–80.

Kee, Joan, 2019. *Models of Integrity: Art and Law in Post-Sixties America*. Oakland, CA: University of California.

Klein, Jeremy, 2004. ABSTRACTIONS. *Et Centera*, 61, 140–41.

Leane, Jeanine, 2017. Gathering: The Politics of Memory and Contemporary Aboriginal Women's Writing. *Antipodes*, 31 (2), 242–51.

Leane, Jeanine, 2018. *Walk Back Over*. Carlton South, Victoria, Australia: Cordite Books.

Luker, Trish, 2016. Animating the Archive: Artefacts of Law. *In*: Stewart Motha and Honni van Rijswijk, eds. *Law, Memory, Violence: Uncovering the Counter-Archive*. Oxon and New York: Routledge.

Luker, Trish, 2017. Decolonising Archives: Indigenous Challenges to Record Keeping in 'Reconciling' Settler Colonial States. *Australian Feminist Studies*, 32, 108–25.

McDowell, Tara, 2016. Vernon Ah Kee. *Museum of Contemporary Art*. Available from: https://www.mca.com.au/artists-works/artists/vernon-ah-kee/ [Accessed 2 February 2021].

Manderson, Desmond, ed., 2018. *Law and the Visual: Representations, Technologies, Critique*. Toronto, Buffalo and London: University of Toronto Press.

Mardorossian, Carine M., 2014. *Framing the Rape Victim: Gender and Agency Reconsidered*. New Brunswick, NJ and London: Rutgers University Press.

MARS, 2018. *Shevaun Wright | Apologies*. Windsor, Victoria: MARS.

Mills, Charles W., 1997. *The Racial Contract*. Ithaca, NY: Cornell University Press.

Moreton-Robinson, Aileen, 2004. Whiteness, Epistemology and Indigenous Representation. *In*: Aileen Moreton-Robinson, ed. *Whitening Race: Essays in Social and Cultural Criticism*. Australia: Aboriginal Studies Press, 75–88.

Navaro-Yashin, Yael, 2007. Make-Believe Papers, Legal Forms and the Counterfeit: Affective Interactions between Documents and People in Britain and Cyprus. *Anthropological Theory*, 7, 79–98.

Palm Island Shire Council, n.d. *About Palm Island*. Available from: http://www.palmcouncil.qld.gov.au/about-palm-island [Accessed 2 February 2021].

Pateman, Carol, 1988. *The Sexual Contract*. California: Stanford University Press.

Paterson, Helen M, Golde, Celine van, Devery, Chris, Cowdery, Nicholas, and Kemp, Richard, 2018. iWitnessed: Capturing Contemporaneous Accounts to Enhance Witness Evidence. *Current Issues in Criminal Justice*, 29 (3), 273–81.

Peeters, Tom, 2015. Photographer Jan Rosseel evokes the most traumatic case in Belgian crime history. *Flanders Today*. Available from: http://www.flanderstoday.eu/arts/photographer-jan-rosseel-evokes-most-traumatic-case-in-Belgian-crime-history/ [Accessed 13 March 2018].

Phillips, Ruth, 2005. Re-placing Objects: Historical Practices for the Second Museum Age. *Canadian Historical Review*, 86, 83–110.

Queensland Government, 2018. *Palm Island*. Available from: https://www.qld.gov.au/atsi/cultural-awareness-heritage-arts/community-histories/community-histories-n-p/community-histories-palm-island [Accessed 6 February 2021].

Robertson, Joshua, 2016. 'You're My Warrior': Lex Wotton and the Fight for Justice after the Palm Island Riots. *The Guardian*, 7 December. Available from: https://www.theguardian.com/australia-news/2016/dec/07/youre-my-warrior-lex-wotton-and-the-fight-for-justice-after-the-palm-island-uprising [Accessed 10 October 2020].

SBS News, 2016. Palm Island Verdict: 12 Years in the Making. *SBS News*. Available from: https://www.sbs.com.au/news/palm-island-verdict-12-years-in-the-making [Accessed 10 October 2020].

Seigworth, Gregory J., and Gregg, Melissa, 2010. An Inventory of Shimmers. *In*: Gregory J. Seigworth and Melissa Gregg, eds. *The Affect Theory Reader*. USA: Duke University Press.

Selenitsch, Alex, 2013. As It Was, As It Is. *In*: Anne Kirker, Katarina Paseta, Alex Selenitsch, and Linda Short, eds. *Born to Concrete: Visual Poetry from the Collections of Heide Museum of Modern Art and the University of Queensland*. Bulleen, Victoria: Heide Museum of Modern Art and the University of Queensland.

Spieker, Sven, 2008. *The Big Archive: Art from Bureaucracy*. Cambridge, MA and London, England: MIT Press.

Thorpe, Kirsten, 2014. Indigenous Records: Connecting, Critiquing and Diversifying Collections. *Archives and Manuscripts*, 42 (2), 211–4.

UTS Art, n.d. *Judy Watson 'A Preponderance of Aboriginal Blood'*. Available from: http://art.uts.edu.au/index.php/judy-watson-a-preponderance-of-aboriginal-blood/ [Accessed 2 May 2019].

Vaughan, Sian, 2016. Reflecting on Practice: Artists' Experiences in the Archives. *In*: Fiorella Foscarini, Heather MacNeil, Bonnie Mak, and Gillian Oliver, eds. *Engaging with Records and Archives: Histories and Theories*. Great Britain: Facet Publishing.

Watson, Joanne, 2018. A Century of Activism and Heartache: The Troubled History of Palm Island. *Griffith Review*, 60. Available from: https://www.griffithreview.com/articles/century-activism-heartache-troubled-history-palm-island/ [Accessed 5 January 2021].

Watson, Judy, and Martin-Chew, Louise, 2009. *Judy Watson: Blood Language*. Carlton, Victoria: Miegunyah Press.

Waton, Judy, 2019. A Preponderance *of Aboriginal Blood*. Queensland: Grahame Galleries + Editions | Numero Uno Publications.

White, Melissa Autumn, 2014. Archives of Intimacy and Trauma: Queer Migration Documents as Technologies of Affect. *Radical History Review*, 120, 75–93.

Wright, Shevaun, 2015. Shevaun Wright. *In*: Campbelltown Art Gallery, ed. *Parliament of New South Wales Aboriginal Art Prize 2015*. Campbelltown: Campbelltown Art Gallery.

Wright, Shevaun, 2018. Personal Communication. *Interview with Priya Vaughan*, 6 July. Sydney: University of Technology, Sydney.

Wright, Shevaun, 2019. *Shevaun Wright*. Available from: https://www.shevaunwright.com/ [Accessed 5 December 2020].

Young, Alison, 2013. *Judging the Image: Art, Value, Law: Representations, Technologies, Critique*. London and New York: Taylor and Francis.

Artworks

Ah Kee, Vernon, 2010. *tall man*. Four channel video installation, 11:10 min.

Chocka, Bindi Cole, 2012. *EH5452*. Re-created prison cell: documents and objects from prison, furniture, fabric, single-channel projection, single-channel video, audio, dimensions variable.

Watson, Judy, 2005. *a preponderance of aboriginal blood*. Etching with chine collé, framed. 14 portrait etchings: frame 49 x 37.5 x 3cm, 2 landscape etchings: frame 37.5 x 49 x 3cm. Museum of Contemporary Art Australia and Tate, Accession number: 2016.18A-P.

Watson, Judy, 2007. Under *the act*. Etchings on chine collé paper, illustrated book.

Wright, Shevaun, 2014. *The (Foreign Investment) Scam*. Prints, 42 × 32 cm.

Wright, Shevaun, 2016. *The Rape Contract*. 14 sheets of paper, wooden boxes, UV ink, torches, 36 × 27 cm (each frame).

Wright, Shevaun, 2018. *Apologies*. Paper, Perspex, metal chains, hooks and clips, dimensions variable.

Wright, Shevaun, 2019. *The Amended Artist's Reserved Rights Transfer and Sale Agreement*. Digital print on paper. 8 panels, each 29.5 × 29.5 inches (framed).

Young, Carey, 2013. *We the People*. C-type photograph, 190 × 124 cm.

Young, Carey, 2017. *Before the Law*. Series of digital C-type photographs. Each 127 × 84.6 cm.

Young, Carey, 2017. *Palais de Justice*. Single-channel HD video (from 4K), 16:9, colour, quadraphonic sound. 17 min 58 secs.

Chapter 14

The Rape Contract

Shevaun Wright

Frustrated by the continued marginalisation and distortion of Indigenous and female voices within the legal and art spheres, I seek to subvert systemic discrimination by cannibalising what is one of the most privileged forms of Western discourse: the legal contract.

Fundamental to Western legal scholarship is the problematic metaphor of the social contract: the idea that a person's moral and political obligations are dependent upon a shared social contract or agreement to form the society in which they live.

Whilst sustaining significant critique, contractualism and contractarianism continue to permeate the praxis of law as an instrument for organising human relations. Carole Pateman's foundational work *The Sexual Contract* (1988) and Charles W. Mills' *The Racial Contract* (1997) have significantly eroded the premise of the liberal individual in Hobbesian and Rawlsian theories of social contract. The inadequacy of contract as a means of attempting to undercut relations of social classes and market forces has also been observed by art scholar Alexander Alberro (2003) with his assertion that Seth Siegelaub and Bob Projansky's *The Artist's Contract* unwittingly contributed to the commodification of conceptual art. *The Artist's Contract* was a document drafted in 1971 by attorney Projansky at the request of Siegelaub. It sought to protect artists' rights to resale royalties, moral rights and rights to exhibit work. It was rarely used as it only served artists who were established, selling well and who had the power to negotiate contracts for sale. Indeed, the reception of *The Artist's Contract* by artists, collectors and gallerists has served as a microcosm for the limited utility of social contract theory. Aimed at securing liberal values of freedom and self-will via individualised, adversarial negotiations, social contract theory has instead whitewashed the subjugation of the 'feminine', the 'racial other' and the 'sexually deviant' within this competitive contractual framework.

The Rape Contract (Figures 14.1 and 14.2) is a visual and literal manifestation of a part of my social contract. It formalises the agreement struck by persons (particularly cisgender women) with the state for their membership of society and entitlement to reparation for rape. Created in response to the

DOI: 10.4324/9781003247593-18

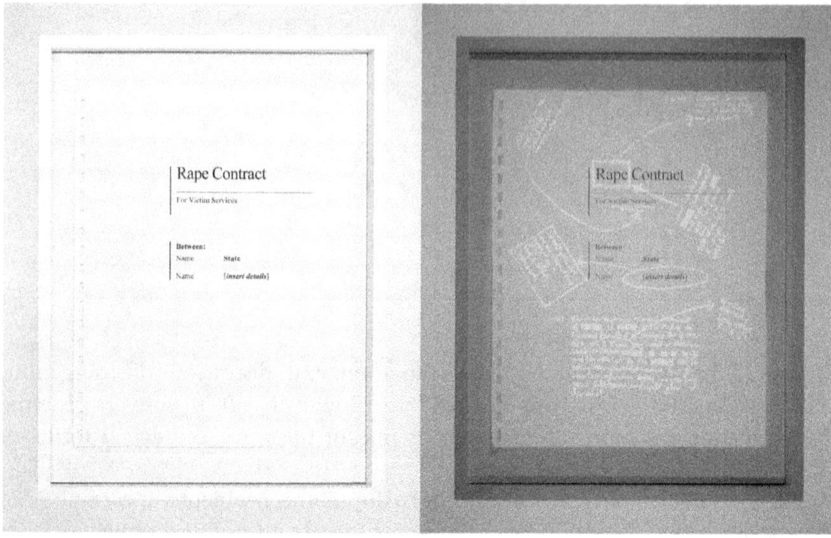

Figure 14.1 Shevaun Wright, *Title Page* detail from *The Rape Contract*, 2016. Fourteen sheets of paper, wooden box, UVB ink, torches. 36 × 27 cm (each frame). Courtesy of the artist © Shevaun Wright.

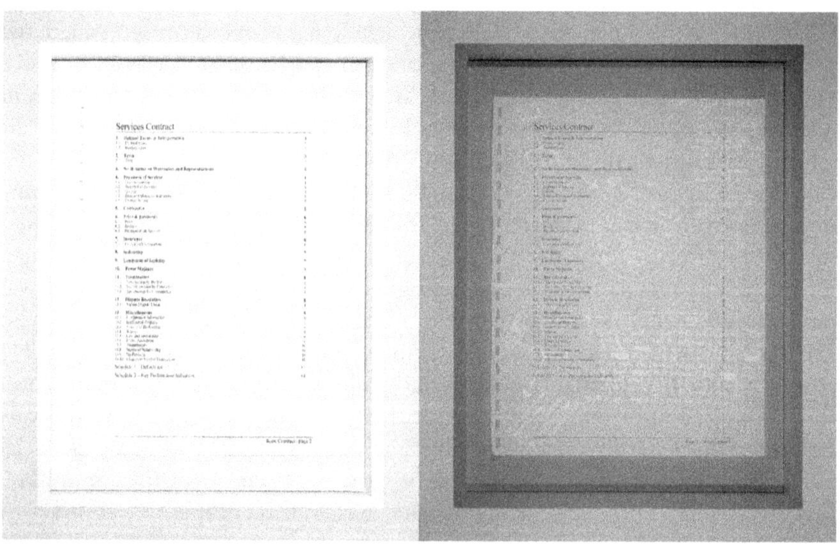

Figure 14.2 Shevaun Wright, *Page Two* detail from *The Rape Contract*, 2016. Fourteen sheets of paper, wooden box, UVB ink, torches. 36 × 27 cm (each frame). Courtesy of the artist © Shevaun Wright.

disempowering experience of assisting my close friend negotiate the Australian legal system as a victim of rape, the document is presented as a commercial services contract for 'Victim Services'. It provides capped 'Social Payments' in the form of legal redress, compensation and acknowledgement in exchange for the achievement of community and legal expectations of victimhood. Informed by Carine M. Mardorossian's groundbreaking work *Framing the Rape Victim: Gender and Agency Reconsidered* (2014), it articulates the 'Key Performance Indicators', indemnities, limitations of liability, behavioural specifications and dispute mechanisms enforced against victims.

Overlaid upon the formal legal document are excerpts from notes, personal writings, psychiatric reports and a police report taken from a victim of a violent rape. They have been transcribed by me in invisible UV ink. Names, locations and identifying factors were redacted, and certain restricted documents left out altogether. Not only were we writing in invisible ink; her voice, as with the voices of many victims, was being doubly erased in this process.

The completed work is displayed with a 'trigger warning'. Visitors are invited to pick up mini forensic LED flashlights as part of the installation in order to see the victim's speech. It is a choice, and it comes with a warning. Indeed, speaking of the experience of victims, one survivor has said: 'such is the insidious nature of sexual assault, and, by association, PTSD. Just when you think you're okay, a trigger will catch you completely off-guard, and make you realise you're anything but, or ever will be'.

Abjuring outright protest, this artwork aims to open a space in which to engage in a meaningful dialogue about the absurdities of ascribing neutrality to legalese, by bringing into relief the anachronistic expectations and standards of the law regarding the feminised body to, as one survivor put it, 'gain a sense of normality in the depravity'. Thus, by translating the emotionally charged topic of rape into commercial terms, the project traverses the theoretical divide between art and law, integrating cross-disciplinary feminist critiques to collapse axiomatic assertions of an impenetrable, rational and impartial legal framework, in favour of an aesthetics of ambiguity and dispersed perspective.

The Rape Contract is part of a larger project that investigates the relationship between art and law, part of the growing field of legal aesthetics. The field of legal aesthetics can be divided into theorists who identify with the term and those who engage with it in less direct ways. The term 'legal aesthetics' has been invoked to denote a broad range of studies into the relationship between aesthetics and law. Legal theorist Pierre Schlag (2002, 1050) criticises prior understandings of the relationship between aesthetics and law as a search for beauty, and adopts a broader definition of aesthetics as 'the forms, images, tropes, perceptions, and sensibilities that help shape the creation, apprehension, and even identity of human endeavors, including, most topically, law'.

While Schlag is primarily concerned with abstract conceptions of the law, feminist legal scholars and critical race scholars have been preoccupied with giving a human form to the purportedly abstract, disembodied operations of the law. An aesthetics of law can be found in this legal scholarship. Essays are rich with metaphor and visual language as tools with which to demonstrate the biased operation of the Anglo-American legal system. Key examples include Jennifer Nedelsky's (1990) idea of boundedness and the body, Cheryl I Harris' (1993) whiteness as property and Ngaire Naffine's (1997) hole in the body bag. Reviewing this literature gives rise to a desire for translation into art, and the collapse of what is impersonal into real human experiences.

Loss is central to my work. In the context of legal aesthetics, loss is more than the potential to lose a case or litigation. It is also what is left behind or forgotten, covered over and unheard within the structures of the law. Loss in this sense can be understood in terms of the *différend*, a neologism coined by Jean François Lyotard (1988) as a short-hand for what is lost in language games; what damage is caused when a single universal standard or criterion is imposed upon another discourse. A *différend* occurs in the case of conflict between two parties where the issues cannot be equitably resolved for lack of a rule of judgment that can be applicable to both. The parties cannot agree on a rule or criterion by which to determine their dispute.

Litigation stands in opposition to a *différend* in that it presupposes a system by which the dispute can be resolved within the law. Lyotard also distinguishes between a plaintiff and victim. The former is a wronged party to a litigation; the latter a wronged party to a *différend*. A victim's wrong cannot be heard for many reasons; they may have been threatened and silenced or they may be able to speak but the system itself is not constructed to facilitate the hearing of this speech or translate it into terms that can be heard. *The Rape Contract* sets out to display this through the negation of the victim survivor's voice. Not only are facts and names redacted, hidden forever, their voice is also subordinated to the law, to the black and white text. It sits around it and alongside it, squeezing into the spaces. It waits for someone to hear it, to see it, with the light of 'otherness'. Not the clear light of day, where it is lost in bureaucracy, stigma and institutional speak, but in the forensic light of a black light torch, picked up by a curious and sympathetic viewer who wants to see this *différend* in operation.

References

Alberro, Alexandra, 2003. *Conceptual Art and the Politics of Publicity*. Cambridge, MA: MIT Press.

Harris, Cheryl I, 1993. Whiteness as Property. *Harvard Law Review*, 106 (8), 1707–91.

Lyotard, Jean-François, 1988. *The Différend: Phrases in Dispute*. Manchester: Manchester University Press.

Mardorossian, Carine M, 2014. *Framing the Rape Victim: Gender and Agency Reconsidered*. New Brunswick, NJ and London: Rutgers University Press.

Mills, Charles W, 1997. *The Racial Contract*. Ithaca, NY: Cornell University Press.

Naffine, Ngaire, 1997. The Body Bag. *In*: Ngaire Naffine and Rosemary Owens, eds. *Sexing the Subject of Law*. North Ryde, NSW: LBC Information Services, 79–93.

Nedelsky, Jennifer, 1990. Law, Boundaries, and the Bounded Self. *Representations*, 30 (Special Issue: Law and the Order of Culture), 162–89.

Pateman, Carole, 1988. *The Sexual Contract*. Stanford, CA: Stanford University Press.

Schlag, Pierre, 2002. The Aesthetics of American Law. *Harvard Law Review*, 115, 1047–2364.

Chapter 15

The aesthetic archive

Appropriating legal documents in visual art

Carolyn McKay

Introduction

Can visual artists transform the legal archive into a critique of justice? This chapter examines the *justiceINjustice* exhibition as an exercise in the artistic appropriation of law's documents and their metamorphoses into visual art objects. I argue that although exhibiting artists appropriated legal documents reporting on profoundly difficult events—moments of violence, trauma and injustice—the artworks they created evinced material and sensorial aspects of injustice not immediately apparent on the face of the lifeless documents they drew upon. Key to the success of these artworks was the process through which they were created. Artists engaged with law's documents through consultation, the building of trust and with the utmost respect. In this analysis, I apply a theoretical framework of visual criminology and aim to establish a relationship between criminal law archives and visual art practices about those documents.

The 2018 exhibition *justiceINjustice* at The Lock-Up Contemporary Art Space in Newcastle, New South Wales (NSW), Australia, aimed to scrutinise public interest cases of injustice in a multi-layered manner that would transcend official police, judicial or coronial narratives, immerse viewers in a forensic aesthetic and amplify the inadequacies of the criminal justice system. Given my interdisciplinary practice in criminology and visual art, I was invited to curate the exhibition—to select and work with the artists alongside The Lock-Up's Jessi England and Courtney Novak, and collate relevant legal and coronial materials for public display. *justiceINjustice* drew together seven visual artists—Corinne Brittain, Rob Cleworth, Blak Douglas, Bianca Willoughby (formerly John A Douglas), Leah Emery, Richard Lewer and Lezlie Tilley—and three criminal lawyers—Karen Wells, Ray Watterson and Robert Cavanagh—to respond to high-profile Australian cases of injustice: deaths in custody, inadequate police investigation, excessive police force, wrongful convictions and wrongful detention.

Conflating art and crime

I commence with a brief overview of my own visual arts practice that, since 2008, has had as its modus operandi the appropriation of archival material.

DOI: 10.4324/9781003247593-19

While I hold legal qualifications and currently work as a legal academic, for over 20 years I've had a career as a visual artist that has gradually come to intersect with my interest in criminal justice. This evolving conflation of art and criminal law started to take shape during *Word of Mouth* 2008–2009, my project for a masters by research at Sydney College of the Arts, focusing on *viva voce* eyewitness testimony in the site of courtroom murder trials. During several trials, I sat in the public gallery and noted fragments of testimony produced during the epistemic process that is evidence-in-chief and cross-examination (Roberts and Zuckerman 2010). The vivid testimonial phrases inspired a body of digital work.[1] The works examine how the past violence remains unseen and ob/scene, or off-stage, from the criminal courtroom, somewhat akin to an ancient Greek tragedy, yet the live human voice is tasked with resuscitating the past crime scene (McKay 2010).

Notable in the development of my visual arts practice has been one particular site: The Lock-Up in Newcastle, an historic nineteenth-century police station, complete with exercise yard, cells, a leather upholstered padded cell, anti-graffiti surfaces covered in graffiti and an abundance of ambience and atmosphere. The space has been repurposed as a contemporary art site. During the *Word of Mouth* project, I was selected to undertake an artist's residency at The Lock-Up, staying for three weeks in the upstairs converted detective offices. I was provided with access to The Lock-Up's archive of mugshots with accompanying textual biographical data records from the late 1800s. This led me to research historical records at the Newcastle Region Library where I came across the textually rich 'New South Wales Reports of Crime, etc., etc., for police information' from 1862, on 35 mm microfilm reels. From these archives, the two-channel video work *Reports of Crime, Etc., Etc.,* was born, later exhibited in solo shows.[2] Since then, I've found The Lock-Up to be an evocative site for creation and exhibition. It has influenced my artistic and academic engagement with a range of historical and contemporary criminal justice issues from medieval suicide to futuristic imprisonment,[3] to taking text from a police archive of criminal monikers and re-casting the names as an alphabetical, tongue-twisting prison muster in an audio video installation.[4] These projects have all involved a form of the excavation (Guiney 2020) of overlooked documents and a milking of various archival resources to generate a reimagining and a 'cultural afterlife' (Biber 2019, 1) of that dusty material. A level of treasure hunting is implicit in my processes; there is always a search for rich and resonant or surprising text that stimulates my imagination.

Overview of *justiceINjustice*

The premise of the exhibition was devised in 2017 by solicitor Karen Wells and her legal colleagues. They were inspired by the potency of The Lock-Up's 2016 exhibition *The Most Gaoled Race on Earth* by Blak Douglas and Adam Geczy, an exhibition that spoke directly about racism and the oppressive nature of colonisation and legal procedure. This exhibition got the lawyers thinking about a potential collaboration, between themselves and artists, to unpack a number of high-profile cases in which they had been involved through the University of Newcastle Legal Centre. I was later invited to act as curator, and I devised the title *justiceINjustice*. In collaboration with Jessi England (then director of The Lock-Up), we recruited artists to take part.

Six contemporary visual artists (Corinne Brittain, Rob Cleworth, Blak Douglas, Bianca Willoughby, Leah Emery and Lezlie Tilley) were commissioned to revisit official legal archives and respond to public interest cases of injustice. The project embedded the artists in cases of wrongful detention, deaths in custody, deaths during police operations, investigative failures and unsolved homicides and possible wrongful conviction. Their immersion in these cases was driven and facilitated by discussions with the three criminal lawyers who had been involved in related court hearings, coronial inquests and public interest advocacy. In some instances, the artists also liaised with grieving families and, prior to the exhibition's public opening, a private and very emotional viewing was held for those families. One artwork involved communication with a convicted person. The extant work of the seventh artist, Richard Lewer, was included in the exhibition as his work so clearly spoke to the theme.

While there have been many domestic and international exhibitions that have explored the crime genre, *justiceINjustice* was unique in its complex, collaborative research process that occurred between the three lawyers, the artists and many of the victims' families, and ultimately informed the commissioned six new artworks. *justiceINjustice* was also significant in its investigation of contemporary (as distinct from historical) criminal justice issues, for instance, current unsolved disappearances, a (then) live issue of potential wrongful conviction, the continuing outrage of Aboriginal deaths in custody, as well as police fatal shootings of people with mental illness. The confluence of all such factors meant that the project was, at times, an emotionally challenging and taxing process for everyone involved.

Like all curators, I worked as a go-between for the artists and The Lock-Up, and supported the artists, as required, during their research, creative practices and in finalising their installation concepts (Legacies Now 2010). This project was complex, given the number of disparate participants from both within, and outside, the art world, the cross-cultural issues (see Onciul 2019) and the consultative processes with affected family members and the three lawyers. It was made all the more sensitive given the difficult and tragic nature of the cases to which the artists had been tasked with response. A terrible sadness haunted each case and each artist's creative process. Within such a mix, the role of the curator can be an invisible and thankless one, a backstage liaison officer who must deal with competing concerns while facilitating the project's aesthetic aspirations and ensuring that progress remains on track for the all-important opening night. In addition to the go-between role, I was commissioned to write a curatorial essay as part of the exhibition catalogue (McKay 2018a) and was involved in the public programmes that presented the miscarriage of justice issues to broad audiences. I was also tasked with collating relevant legal archives of each case for display. The cases had all generated mountains of text: judgments from criminal courts and civil administrative tribunals, as well as submissions to inquiries, findings from inquests and royal commissions, reports to parliament and police integrity commissions (see endnotes for details). The publicly available documentation was compiled into separate folders for each case and laid out flat on a table: bound slabs of script from accumulated legal procedures, numb and inert compared with the sensorial richness of the nearby artworks. The folders nevertheless had a role to play in providing context and were well-thumbed by the exhibition's close.

In thinking about my curatorial role, I started with a consideration of British colonisation that imported and imposed its criminal justice system. I contemplated how our contemporary criminal justice system is a mechanism of institutions of enforcement, prosecution and punishment that operate to maintain social control and impose penalty on the guilty, pursuant to the rule of law. Although the ideals of the rule of law convey aspirations to legitimacy, fairness and transparency, scratching the surface reveals acts of injustice (McKay 2018a). This was the context for *justiceINjustice*, and it was through dialogue with the three lawyers and their clients—the impacted families and one convicted person—that the artists explored situations where the criminal justice system had failed.

In addition to the exhibition, the *justiceINjustice* project had an extensive public programme. At the 2018 Newcastle Writers' Festival I chaired a session with artist Rob Cleworth in discussion with Melinda Dundas, widow of Roni Levi, a man who had been shot dead by police on Bondi Beach in 1997, and solicitor Karen Wells. There was an associated 'Songs for Justice' event featuring musicians, and an eight-hour Art + Law symposium at The Lock-Up presented as part of Law Week 2018. Poignantly, a number of families who were connected with the cases explored in the exhibition made long journeys to attend and participate. For instance, Ted and Helen Russell, parents of Eddie Russell, the young Aboriginal man who died in prison custody and whose case Bianca Willoughby responded to, drove almost 600 kilometres from Walgett to Newcastle. Also in attendance was Melinda Dundas, widow of Roni Levi, who travelled from Melbourne to contribute to a panel, while Chris Rau, sister of Cornelia Rau who was wrongfully detained in immigration detention, addressed the event. The day was one of high emotion and compelling discussion regarding public interest advocacy, social justice and a range of unjust and tragic instances. It was a powerful example of engagement with a very broad audience. *justiceINjustice* had a pedagogical aspect too: 200 law students at the University of Newcastle Law School completed a reflective assessment task responding to the exhibition and symposium (Campbell 2020).

justiceINjustice: the methodologies

The curatorial directive for *justiceINjustice* involved the artistic appropriation of the legal document and its transformation into visual art object. Following individual consultation, the artists were allocated particular cases and were then faced with the overwhelming task of synthesising legal narratives, arcane text and pieces of evidence to develop their creative response, conscious of the need for sensitivity and empathy in these contemporary cases of human tragedy. Each of the artists involved in *justiceINjustice* undertook a significant amount of research in the production of their work, and it is instructive to unpack this process. The artists made use of a range of law documents from coronial inquests, police integrity commissions, corrective services records and royal commissions to research and shape aesthetic responses. The resulting exhibited artworks recast the original textual legal sources, tangibly immersing viewers in unforgiving, experiential installations, all within the carceral and historic site of The Lock-Up. Below I examine each artist's methodology and how they sought to represent the cases anew and highlight the structural inequalities that framed the events.

The over-representation of Aboriginal people is evident at every level of the Australian criminal justice system, and two installations responded to the deaths in custody of young Aboriginal men. The first, Melbourne-based Richard Lewer's *Never Shall be Forgotten—A Mother's Story* 2017, was an extant work that had been commissioned for *The National: New Australian Art* held at Sydney's Carriageworks in 2017. Even though this artwork related to a case outside the involvement of the three lawyers, it so clearly spoke to the curatorial directive that it was included in the exhibition. This hand-drawn animation responded to the 1983 death in Roebourne, Western Australia, of 16-year-old John Pat (Grabosky 1988; Purdy 1994; Cunneen 2006). Seriously injured during a fight with off-duty police officers, young John Pat later died in the police lock-up. The police officers involved were acquitted of his manslaughter, but John Pat's death, as a juvenile in police custody, was a catalyst for the Royal Commission into Aboriginal Deaths in Custody, conducted between 1987 and 1991 (RCIADIC 1991), to investigate the deaths of 99 Aboriginal and Torres Strait Islander people. How poignant, I thought, to have Lewer's video work exhibited in a former police lock-up throughout *justiceINjustice*. Lewer's animation guides us through the story from the perspective of John Pat's mother, Mavis Pat. Lewer is a self-described 'social realist' (Gallo 2015, n.p.) and, according to Slade (2017, n.p.), his creative process involves a 'reluctant ethnography': travelling to Roebourne to meet Mavis and other family members as a way to be immersed in their grief. The artist himself is visible in the video, clearly manipulating the images. He is 'ever-present in the unfolding horror—he assumes the role of narrator and, in doing so, makes himself, and by extension all of us, complicit in this history' (Slade 2017, n.p.).

Shamefully, deaths in custody of Aboriginal people have continued, despite the Royal Commission's recommendations targeted at the practices of law enforcement and correctional facilities (Doherty and Bricknell 2020a; *The Guardian* 2020). The site-specific multi-channel work *No System to Fail* 2018 by Bianca Willoughby (formerly John A. Douglas) was installed in two contiguous cells at The Lock-Up. In Cell F was a two-channel synchronised video projection including footage evoking long road trips in prison trucks. Cell G contained a single-channel video installation with audio and text, and a galvanised iron bucket with a mop. The bucket was filled with pungent disinfectant, the same regulation brand used in NSW correctional facilities, its stench permeating the space. The pre-existing detention-grade toilet in Cell G was uncovered to form an explicit element of the installation.

This installation responds to the death in custody of a young, partially deaf and vulnerable Aboriginal man with intellectual impairments, Edward (Eddie) Russell. Following conviction for several offences, Russell had been transferred from one correctional facility to another, shunted from cell to cell, and he was ultimately incarcerated in Long Bay Gaol where he took his own life in 1999, alone in a single cell (McGowan 2018).[5] This installation, founded on the artist's distillation of hundreds of pages of medical reports and legal resources, is forthright in its execution. It immerses viewers in a very candid experience of carceral space, the 'aesthetics of authority' (Ferrell 1999, 403), and provokes a perspective of the criminal justice 'system' as punitive and futile. Remarkably, on the opening night, Eddie Russell's father, Ted Russell, drove all the way from Walgett to Newcastle, a distance of approximately 600

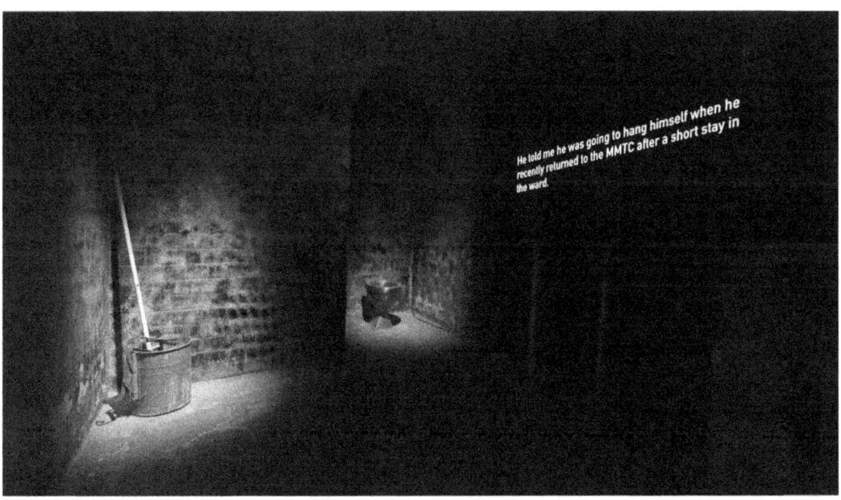

Figure 15.1 Bianca Willoughby (formerly John A. Douglas) *No System to Fail* (view 1) 2018 site-specific multi-channel synchronised video installation with sound, text and objects. Image courtesy of the artist, John A. Douglas.

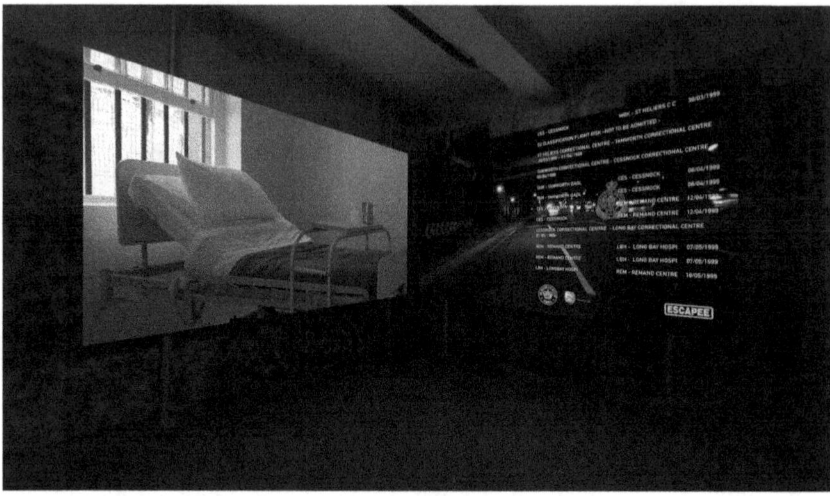

Figure 15.2 Bianca Willoughby (formerly John A. Douglas) *No System to Fail* (view 2) 2018 site-specific multi-channel synchronised video installation with sound, text and objects. Image courtesy of the artist, John A. Douglas.

kilometres, to attend the opening and also to present a family photograph of his son, Eddie, that was added to the exhibition. Bianca Willoughby (formerly John A. Douglas) is a Sydney-based, interdisciplinary artist and, through strange coincidence, it was during the *justiceINjustice* project that she discovered that she is descendant of the Walbunja people of the Yuin Nation. This went some way, I understand, in alleviating her initial reticence of being a white person creating work and commentary about an Aboriginal man's experience.

Systemic failures in detention facilities have continued, and Corinne Brittain's installation, *STRANDED (I have done nothing wrong)* 2018 critiques the treatment of Cornelia Rau during 2004–2005. Brittain is a Sydney-based interdisciplinary artist, and her research focuses on human interactions with lived environments. Cornelia Rau, a permanent Australian resident, was wrongfully detained in a Queensland prison and then at the notorious Baxter Detention Centre, an immigration detention facility in South Australia, while experiencing mental illness. Brittain researched judicial decisions, legal documents and the media and consulted with Cornelia Rau's sister, Chris.[6] She found that, during her wrongful detention and long periods of solitary confinement, Cornelia Rau's recurring mantra was *I have done nothing wrong*. In a claustrophobic cell, Brittain's installation of rusted wire bedsprings and cascade of red tape dangling from metal mesh simultaneously evokes beauty and violence. McGowan (2018, n.p.) reviewed this installation in *The Guardian* as 'subtly disturbing'. It presents a potent critique of harsh bureaucracy, cruelty and the dereliction of the state's duty to care for vulnerable people. It certainly invites viewers to interrogate the role of immigration detention, and the experiences of those detained in those facilities.

Blak Douglas, a contemporary Sydney-based artist with Dhungatti Aboriginal origins, responded to the flawed criminal investigations into the disappearance of baby Azaria Chamberlain. Lindy and Michael Chamberlain had reported that Azaria had been taken by a dingo from their campsite at Uluru in 1980. Her body was never found. At the scene, the dingo theory was supported by Aboriginal trackers who had found fresh dingo paw prints in the vicinity, and this evidence was initially accepted in the first inquest into Azaria's disappearance. However, the Aboriginal trackers' evidence had little traction in later proceedings, and the Chamberlains were convicted of murder/accessory after the fact to murder. After a protracted legal process, they were eventually exonerated (Biber 2019).[7] Blak Douglas consulted with the *justiceINjustice* lawyers who had worked on securing the final coronial inquest into the death of Azaria, and his painting, *A Dog's Breakfast* 2018, examines the non-recognition of Aboriginal knowledge. The painting appropriates and re-visions iconic imagery: the dingo road sign, 'baby change table' symbol and Uluru. Subtly placed in the painting—not immediately visible—are the five Anangu trackers in spirit form whose knowledge had been marginalised by the white criminal justice system.

Brisbane-based Leah Emery's installation *Vigil* 2018 continues the theme of investigative failure. This work responds to the unsolved disappearance of three young women: Leanne Goodall, 20, Robyn Hickie, 18, and Amanda Robinson,

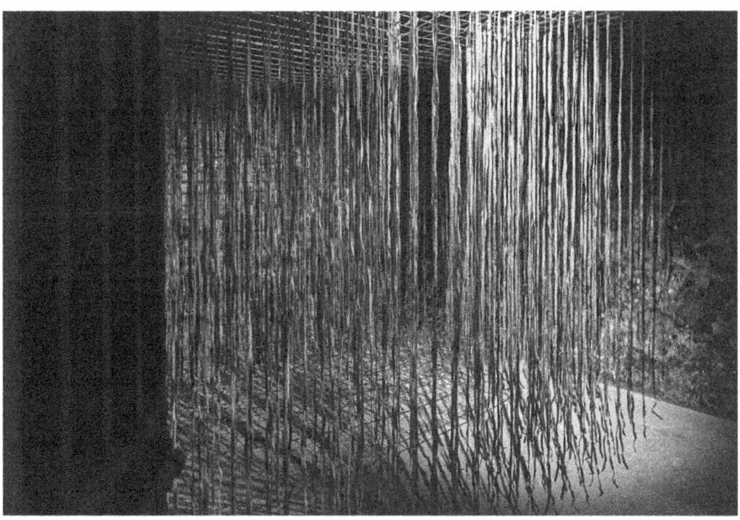

Figure 15.3 Corinne Brittain *STRANDED (I have done nothing wrong)* 2018 hand-dyed cotton tape, wax, steel grid, mattress spring. Image courtesy of Jess Henderson, Fourth Street Studio.

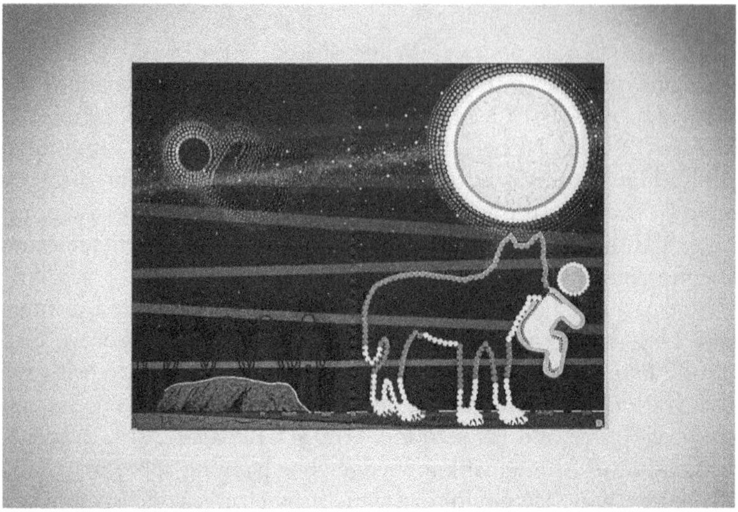

Figure 15.4 Blak Douglas *A Dog's Breakfast* 2018 synthetic polymer on canvas (Permaplastik Paints) 150 cm × 200 cm. Image courtesy of Jess Henderson, Fourth Street Studio.

14, from the Newcastle area during 1978–1979 and the ongoing frustrations felt by their family members regarding the police investigations. A special task force, Strike Force Fenwick, was formed in 1998, some 20 years too late, to investigate why police had not treated these cases as suspected homicides, and why evidence had not been pursued. Eventually, an inquest found that the three young women had been abducted and killed by people unknown. Emery appropriated text from the Strike Force Fenwick findings and printed this onto a Perspex screen in such a way as to spell out 'NEVER'. On close inspection, we can see that each letter of 'NEVER' is constituted by a list of investigative failures in smaller font. Placed behind the screen is a softly blowing curtain of 1970s fabric printed with the word 'DONE', the curtain conjuring a 'domestic metaphor', according to Emery's artist statement, of the houses that were never searched and the passage of time. When a viewer sits on the 1970s lounge chair facing the Perspex and the curtain, the two words form the message 'NEVER DONE' to evoke the suspects who were never questioned, the leads not followed and the lack of resolution. While the families have been holding vigil, a new Strike Force Arapairma was established in 2019 to reinvestigate the suspected murders of Robyn Hickie, Amanda Robinson and Gordana Kotevski (Partridge 2019).

Lezlie Tilley's 2018 works, *The Kathleen Folbigg Diaries* and *Memories Begun 8th January 1993* are also founded on text—in this instance, text appropriated from Kathleen Folbigg's personal diaries. These audio and video works were installed in The Lock-Up's historical, leather padded cell as well as a contiguous cell. In 2003, Kathleen Folbigg was convicted of three counts of murder and one count of manslaughter in relation to the deaths of her four babies.[8] Folbigg's convictions were secured on the basis of circumstantial and forensic evidence, as well as seemingly devastating admissions contained in her personal diaries. Questions remained about her convictions and a few months after *justiceINjustice* opened, it was announced that there would be an inquiry into Folbigg's convictions on the basis of fresh evidence relating to the children's causes of death and evidence regarding the diary entries (State of NSW 2019). However, the inquiry confirmed her guilt and convictions (State of NSW 2019). In Tilley's artworks, she reproduces text from Folbigg's diaries (with Folbigg's permission) to present a different context as the words scroll down the emotionally charged surface of the padded cell and the overlapping voices in the adjoining cell obscure a singular truth. Folbigg remains incarcerated and, during *justiceINjustice*, she wrote a letter to Newcastle-based Tilley from prison, a stream of consciousness description of being transported from one correctional facility to another and a brief glimpse of the world outside the prison walls. With her permission, this letter was also included in *justiceINjustice*, an unexpected addition to both the exhibition and the expanding Folbigg archive.

The final installation in *justiceINjustice* was Rob Cleworth's suite of works, *Taharah*, *True Blue* and *Dear Roni* 2018. Like Tilley, Cleworth is based in Newcastle, and he consulted closely on the development of his body of work with both Roni Levi's widow, Melinda Dundas, as well as the three *justiceINjustice*

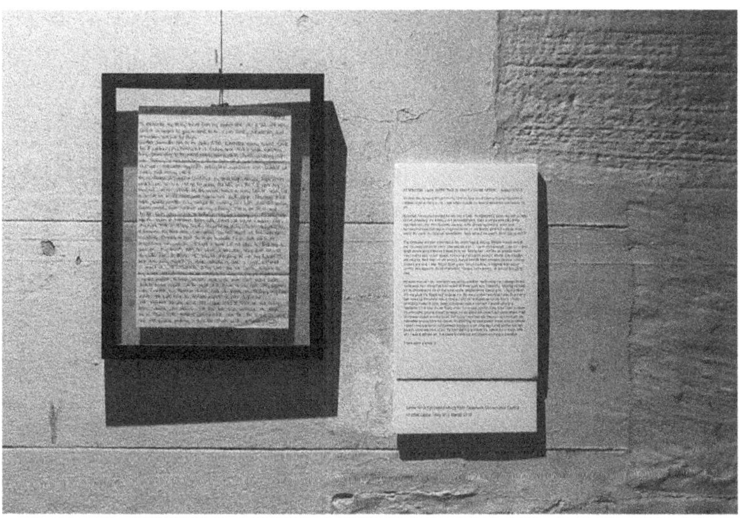

Figure 15.5 Lezlie Tilley *The Kathleen Folbigg Diaries* and *Memories Begun 8th January 1993* (view 1) 2018 video and audio installation. Image courtesy of Jess Henderson, Fourth Street Studio.

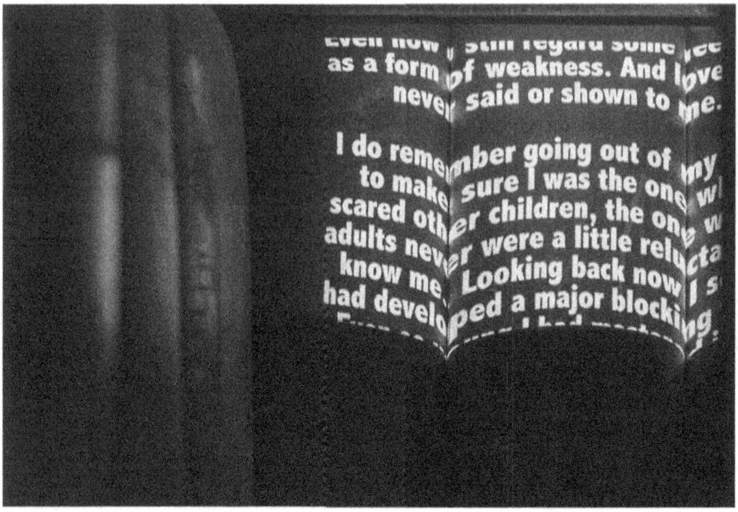

Figure 15.6 Lezlie Tilley *The Kathleen Folbigg Diaries* and *Memories Begun 8th January 1993* (view 2) 2018 video and audio installation. Image courtesy of Jess Henderson, Fourth Street Studio.

lawyers. Collectively, Cleworth's works respond to the 1997 death of Roni Levi who was experiencing mental illness at the time he was shot and killed by police officers on Bondi Beach. While this fatal incident occurred some time ago, it remains of contemporary significance given that shooting deaths in police custody or during police operations continue and often involve people with mental health issues (Doherty and Bricknell 2020b). The two police officers involved in shooting Roni Levi were later investigated by the Police Integrity Commission (2001) that found that they had not been subjected to blood, urine or breath tests following the fatal shooting despite the fact that they were already under investigation for drug allegations. Roni Levi was a French photographer and, in an odd coincidence, his death on Bondi Beach was captured by another French photographer, Jean-Pierre Bratanoff-Firgoff. The Bratanoff-Firgoff images, which were tendered as potent evidence in a coronial inquest into Levi's death and much reproduced in media reportage, contradicted police accounts of the fatal incident. Cleworth's work *True Blue* reproduces these images, with Bratanoff-Firgoff's permission, but re-purposes them by fracturing them with expressive paint and the jarring use of collage. *Dear Roni* includes a collection of personal family photographs while *Taharah* evokes moving water to reference the cleansing and preparation for Jewish burial. Hung on three adjoining walls, the suite of works provides an intense interplay of legal evidence, disturbing images from the moment of death, intermixed with a moving family portrait.

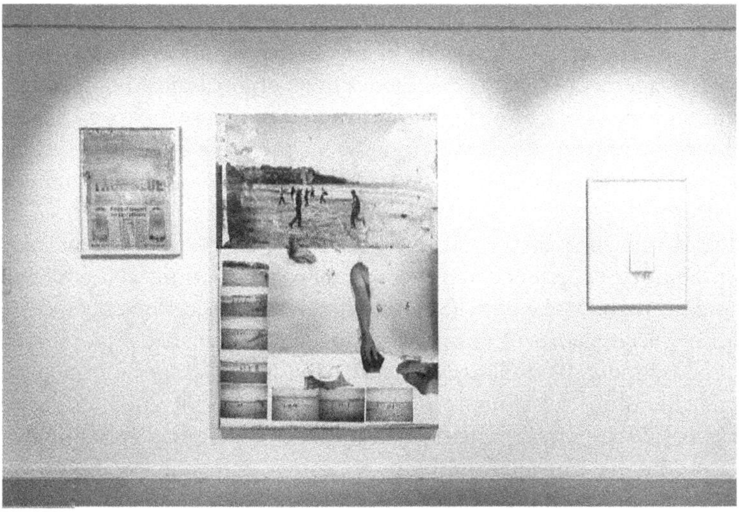

Figure 15.7 Rob Cleworth *Taharah, True Blue* and *Dear Roni* 2018 inkjet photograph and oil paint (photographs courtesy of Jean-Paul Bratanoff-Firgoff). Image courtesy of Jess Henderson, Fourth Street Studio.

Visual arts meets criminology

While the concept of creative practice as a research methodology or as research in and of itself is not new, within the realm of legal academia and practice, it is still novel and not well understood. Here I examine the visual, material and sensorial thinking implicit in the aesthetic practices of the *justiceINjustice* artists and fundamental to their re-purposing and translation of the legal documents. I argue that there are a number of ways to appreciate the use of visual art practice as a research methodology: as a potent artefact, as an innovative and aesthetic means of presenting research and as a legitimate tool for generating new knowledge. This is significant given the developing engagement of criminological research and scholarship with materiality, sensory experience, atmosphere and aesthetics.

Art practice and knowledge

There has been a growing appreciation of 'visual epistemology' (Klinke 2014, 2), that is, the concept that images (and I would add a range of other three-dimensional visual art forms such as installations) may contain more than just what is immediately visible; they may be the product of and embody high-level understanding or knowledge. Artworks that are the product of the artist's externalisation of such high-level understanding may operate as epistemic media (Klinke 2014), potentially enabling the visual communication of knowledge, while recognising that each viewer perceives the artwork through their own subjectivity. The knowledge-value of art can also be understood through the aesthetic engagement of artists: 'aesthetics in its original meaning is simply knowing through perception, or knowing through the senses' (Story, Brown and Carrabine 2017, 109). Aesthetic engagement therefore necessarily implicates the senses. To focus only on the visual as knowledge would be to indulge in ocularcentrism (Jay 1993; Levin 1993; McClanahan and South 2020) while ignoring the significance of the other senses and their place in knowledge production. Sensory experience activates complex connections across neural pathways and throughout the body (Sullivan 2010). Within arts practices, there has long been a recognition of sensorial engagements with spatiality, temporality and embodiment, as well as the haptic, tactile, olfactory and auditory elements, that is, more sensuous forms of intellect (Zardini 2005; McLeod 2006; Knueppel 2010). Perhaps, then, the concept of sensuous epistemology might be a productive concept and more consistent with phenomenological understandings of perception as multi-sensorial (Merleau-Ponty 1964; 1968). Sensorial experience is fundamental to cognitive process and the production of understanding and knowledge; disciplines including the visual arts, design, performance, music and architecture are necessarily already sensorial.

The unseen processes and resulting works of the *justiceINjustice* artists demonstrate the 'imaginative and intellectual work undertaken by artists' as a form of research (Sullivan 2010, xix). In the gallery space, viewers experience the final artworks, or research outputs, possibly unaware of the extensive research, experimentation, discarded failures and production processes that fed into that final object or installation (Sullivan 2006). In the combination of imagination with intellect, Sullivan (2006, 32, 2010) argues the creative, reflexive and critical inquiry of artists is a 'profound form of human engagement' that produces fresh ways of perceiving the world, new and inventive interpretations and reveals 'layers of subtleties that conventional methods would fail to perceive' (McKay 2013b, 95; see also Gray and Malins 2004). The artist's studio is a site of iterative experimentation, like a laboratory, where intellect, embodied gesture and the sensorial mesh. Gibson suggests that artist-researchers can entwine embodied, experiential, implicit and intuitive knowledge with analytical, discovery-based and critically distanced research: the different modes of cognition enrich and inform each other. Central to practice-led research, Bolt (2010, 29) suggests there is a 'double articulation between theory and practice, whereby theory emerges from a reflexive practice at the same time that practice is informed by theory' reiterating the generative and circular relationship between the different forms of engagement and cognition.

Creative practice necessarily involves the handling of materials and tools. Handleability underpins the process of experimentation and sensorial processes to generate a particular form of tacit knowledge or *material* thinking, the type of thinking that emerges when hand, eye, mind, ideas and tools combine (Carter

2004; Bolt 2010). An active and embodied engagement with problem solving and inquiry through tangible materials and tools—including digital manipulations—is a reflective and iterative process that not only brings into existence a new artefact, it can also transform research perspectives and critical analysis. Haseman (2006) suggests practice-based research can be a means to entwine quantitative, qualitative and performative aspects, a methodological triumvirate perhaps (McKay 2013a; 2013b). The outputs of creative practice research may express the research as well as 'in that expression [become] the research itself' (Haseman 2006, 3, 6). Of relevance to *justiceINjustice*, the process of making and exhibiting artwork provided a means to explore rich archival resources through material and sensorial methods to point to law's failures and law's limits. Having enriched the documents with tactile, sensory, affective and intuitive qualities, conceivably, the artists' inference was that law's documents lack these attributes. This enabled artists to challenge the political dimensions to 'draw attention to a matter, turn it into an experience, rewrite it' (Verbeek 2012, 26–27 cited in Bardzell et al. 2015, 2095). Their artworks enlivened, animated and amplified (Bray 2017) the otherwise dispassionate and numb archival texts. In this way, the artworks could reach diverse audiences beyond those who would typically engage with the legal documents.

Cultural/visual/sensory criminology

How might visual arts methods intersect with criminology? More specifically, how might the different 'knowledge practices' (Riles 1999, 806) of artists, made manifest in their translating of law's documents and archives, be examined through cultural, visual or sensory criminology? Can creative knowledge-making processes take these inert, abstract and passionless documents and make them tangible, perceptible and appreciable? I argue that while law's documents or 'textual ruins' (Vismann 2001, 198) might provide a means to access the past, the immersive artworks are palpably *present* expressions of injustice.

Practice-based research is still novel in the field of criminology where scholars traditionally focus on quantitative techniques and the gathering of empirical data. Since the 1990s, criminology has seen a shift to engagement with the cultural, visual and sensorial—subsets of critical criminology (Yar 2017). These smaller subsets often engage *textually* with the potency of images, visuality, representation and spectacle, but rarely produce critically engaged creative outputs themselves or in collaboration. On this basis, creative research methods address the perceived problem that there is 'too much talking and writing in criminology and not enough sensuous depiction … there is a lot of explaining and critiquing, but very little showing' (Redmon 2017, 357 referencing Rafter 2014 and Ferrell 2011, see also Ferrell 2008). Redmon (2017, 357) tackles the absence of criminologists actively *producing* or *crafting* knowledge using documentary films or other readily available audio-visual tools. There are exceptions to this alleged absence and, while the use of audio-visual tools in the hands of criminologists must be distinguished from the professional practice of artists who produce exhibition-worthy works, there have been provocative applications. For instance, Canadian carceral geographer Brett Story is also a filmmaker whose *The Prison in Twelve Landscapes* is an example of digging 'into other ways of "knowing"' through aesthetic and affective engagement (Story, Brown and Carrabine 2017, 109). Then there is the prurient photo-elicitation technique of Heith Copes and Jared Ragland that is presented as criminological research of the lived experiences of vulnerable and criminalised people (Copes et al. 2018).

Creating conceptually or politically engaged contemporary artwork involves traditional research and critical analysis. Apart from formal training, the process of studio experimentation entails delving and exploring (Doyle 2013); an immersion in formal aesthetics and composition but also gut instincts; investigation and interpretation; trial and error; creation and destruction. Nevertheless, it does seem that there is a developing place in criminology for artistic, aesthetic and political intervention particularly 'in sites of collective anguish' (Jeffries 2103, 315) and the depiction of human sensorial experience (Redmon 2017). This developing interest can be understood in the context of various forms of criminology including cultural, visual and sensory. The 'cultural turn' in criminological scholarship acknowledges the interrelationship between law, crime and cultural space (Ferrell and Sanders 1995). In an interplay of sociology, cultural studies and postmodernism, cultural criminology provides a compelling means to understand the convergence of politics, imagery and symbolism, cultural constructions of marginalisation, and entangled cultural relationships and shared meanings (Ferrell 1999). Of relevance to *justiceINjustice* is Ferrell's (1999, 399) assertion that cultural criminology can produce 'attentiveness to structures of power and nuances of meaning' as well as an attentiveness to marginality, authority and criminality. As 'a methodology of attentiveness' (Ferrell 1999, 400), cultural criminology values reflexivity and recognises the researcher's own subjectivity, a method that resonates with the process of a visual artist.

The theoretical focus can then be further narrowed to the 'visual turn' (Carrabine 2012), now expressed in 'visual criminology'. Visual criminology emerged from criminology's fixation on visual representations of criminality, originating in Cesare Lombroso's co-opting of photographic images as depicting typologies of deviance and through to the development of mug shots (Rafter 2014; West 2017). Photographs have long been persuasive and probative (Biber 2019), and visual criminology recognises that since the nineteenth century, visuality and visibility have been critical in crime prevention, law enforcement and criminal justice (Sekula 1986). In the contemporary setting, there has been much engagement with visibility, visuality, spectacle and representation enabling the interrogation of images and signs (Walby et al. 2016). An engagement with the visual unpacks ways of seeing (Benjamin 1968; Sontag 1977; Berger 1973; Biber 2006) and provides a means to understand how systems of representation function both 'honorifically and repressively' (Sekula 1986, 6) in the production and control of images, particularly those produced through state-operated agencies (McKay 2018c). Visibility and visual representations remain intimately connected with power relations, hierarchies, classification and judgment (Sontag 1977; Sekula 1986; Tagg 1988; Foucault 1977). Increasingly, criminological research can now be understood through the image as much as through text (Young 1996; Hayward 2009), and scholars are more ready to accept the visual as 'a constitutive part of knowledge' (West 2017, 274). With this greater appreciation of the visual, visual criminology is seen as a critically engaged means to draw attention to ethical questions regarding visual production and representation (Young 2010; Carrabine 2012, 463–465; see also Brown 2014, 181). It enables visual attentiveness to be entwined with 'politically-charged analysis' (Hayward 2009, 12), another methodology that relates closely to contemporary visual arts practice.

More recently, there has been a sensory turn in criminology that acknowledges subjective and embodied experience and pushes back against the hegemony of vision (Jay 1993; Levin 1993). McClanahan and South (2020) argue for a sensory criminology that recognises the multisensorial nature of perception, while Brown and Carrabine (2019) see the need to expand the sensory and phenomenological dimensions in sociology. Millie (2017) seeks to develop an aesthetic criminology that draws attention to sensory, affective and emotive experience and speaks to the relationship between politics, aesthetics and order. Young's (2019) examination of criminal justice atmospheres sees a confluence of spatial, affective and aesthetic elements with reflexive engagement and critique. Such concepts resonate with the practice-based research methodologies of the *justiceINjustice* artists and the resulting immersive and multisensorial installations within the re-purposed law enforcement space of the historical Lock-Up. The *justiceINjustice* project very much evidenced 'sensual integration of method, subject, and situation' (Ferrell 2011, 50).

justiceINjustice: outcomes

With this visual and sensorial criminological understanding, I examine the *justiceINjustice* outcomes of the artistic appropriations of archives and legal documents and their transformation into visual art objects. As mentioned earlier, the six commissioned artists found the project profoundly confronting and challenging, particularly given that the curatorial directive to work on criminal justice issues was unfamiliar to most of the artists. It was overwhelming to sift through volumes of legal and archival text, synthesise the materials and respond in a creative manner. I wrote in the catalogue essay:

> As he stepped into the unfamiliar territory of coronial inquests, police integrity investigations and criminal procedure, one artist described the project as one of the most engaging and rewarding … and simultaneously, the most difficult.
>
> (McKay 2018a, n.p.)

The six commissioned artists experienced varying levels of consultation or collaboration with the three lawyers, a novel experience for all involved:

> While the lawyers came to the project from a discursive world, the artists have focused on materiality, sensoriality and intuition to produce work that is both creative and critically engaged. Yet, as various artists stated, the first-hand experiences, illuminating backstories and moving insights of the three lawyers sparked creative concepts and metaphorical responses. (McKay 2018a, n.p.)

Additionally, there were the consultations with family members that required a great level of respect, sensitivity, empathy and developing trust when dealing with these incidents of raw emotion, tragedy, trauma and loss. It was profoundly sad. Yet, it was the factual bases and contemporary settings of the *justiceINjustice* cases that made the artworks really *matter* (Bray 2014), as well as the significance of the creative acts of justice in honour of the absent.

The *justiceINjustice* artists revisited official texts and archive material to represent them anew, to highlight some of the structural inequalities and injustices that framed the cases, to respect the victims as well as recognise the 'entire complement of damage' (Bray 2017, 147). The exhibition saw the legal documents and archives freed from the rules of evidence and legal procedure begging the question: what happens 'when evidence is cut loose and runs wild' (Biber 2019, 59)? What are the dangers of rebranding forensic evidence as 'art' (Bray 2017)? As the curator of *justiceINjustice*, I saw evidence and archives replaced with visible and 'unsettling perspectives' (Biber 2019, 4); I saw artworks that tangibly expressed implicit experience and made accessible 'the visible and invisible fabric of lived experience' (Redmon 2017, 358). Bray asks: 'can an artwork return us to evidence but corrupt its evidential surety and instead invite us to imagine?' (2017, 148). This is a pertinent question in relation to several of the *justiceINjustice* works, for example, Leah Emery's *Vigil* that explicitly returned us to a series of unsolved crimes. At its best, contemporary archive-based art should go beyond mere decoration, mere re-presentation; it should question, it should probe, it should be transformative of the source materials. In this transformation, the artworks could transcend the official police, coronial or judicial narratives. Instead, the artworks immersed viewers in wrongful detention through the violence of the rusty wire bedsprings of Brittain's installation; the phenomenological attributes, specifically, the olfactory and auditory sensorial elements of imprisonment in Bianca Willoughby's conjoined installations. These two works, in particular, speak to Millie's (2017, 16) conception of 'aesthetic criminology … concerned with all these "sights and sounds and smells", as well as with emotive and affective responses to sensory encounters'. They provide an unforgiving corporeal, experiential moment.

The *justiceINjustice* artworks embraced what Rugoff (1997, 17–18, 62) refers to as a 'forensic aesthetic' that make demands of the audience to scrutinise the art objects as evidence, to dissect the who, what, where and why of the incident, its melancholic aftermath, its post-mortem, and to contemplate the absence of each human subject (see also Bray 2017). Rugoff (1997, 75) notes that the forensic aesthetic does not necessarily generate 'explicitly political art' but it certainly does enable a means to explore 'matters of public concern' or, in the *justiceINjustice* context, public interest cases. However, Rugoff (1997, 99) posits that the forensic aesthetic parallels 'postmodern' experience in that it 'stresses the contingency of any given viewpoint'; that is, no absolute truth is necessarily revealed by its repurposing or translation into art object. While Bianca Willoughby's work does not declare an objective truth, it does strongly advocate for Eddie Russell and his family and points to the lack of a humane 'system' in the criminal justice 'system'. These difficult art objects may give rise to curiosity, voyeurism, horror or profound sadness and can provoke 'unforeseeable harms ... emotional effects' because there are 'facets of the afterlife of evidence' that forever stick (Biber 2019, 129–130; see also Rugoff 1997; Bray 2017). Apart from Cleworth's image of a police notebook and photographs of the fatal shooting of Roni Levi, there was little forensic evidence directly exhibited in *justiceINjustice*. Instead, the artists have re-purposed the evidence, translated and transformed it aesthetically to, perhaps, generate a form of secondary data (Bray 2017). Such data, if the artworks can indeed be reduced to that term, have empathetic dimensions.

Conclusion

justiceINjustice was founded on a transformative engagement with law's documents to reveal epic failures of the criminal justice system. The creative outcomes evinced material and sensorial aspects of injustice not immediately apparent on the face of the remnant insensate legal documents. Through the individual efforts of the artists, *justiceINjustice* contributed a potent collective and visceral understanding of injustice and the impacts on victims, grieving families and society. The artists succeeded in tangibly immersing viewers in seven unforgiving, experiential installations, all within the grim, carceral site of The Lock-Up. The artists' engagement with material and sensorial methods allowed their creative research and installations to be presented to diverse audiences outside strict artistic or academic circles (McKay 2018b). In this way, the project contributed broadly to debate concerning how law enforcement and regimes of prosecution and punishment impact marginalised communities and vulnerable people. As artist Bianca Willoughby said in talking about the installation and Aboriginal deaths in custody:

> I really didn't want it to be about white guilt ... I wanted this to be about, look, this is what has happened; fuck guilt, we need to be angry about this. This must not be forgotten. It's what people have gone through and are still going through. White guilt is useless.
>
> (in McGowan 2018, n.p.)

This comment manifests the artist's commitment to social justice and art as advocacy, also important to artist Corinne Brittain who, in the same review, was quoted as saying:

> The subtext of this work is the relevance it has to our current cultural context in terms of refugees and asylum seekers … I agreed to do the work if I could reference that because I think historical injustice should be given voice, but it was also making it relevant to now, which was really important to me.
>
> (McGowan 2018, n.p.)

The project was a great success with high attendance rates, extensive public programming, pedagogical outcomes, national media attention and was ultimately recognised by a 2018 Museum and Galleries of NSW 'Inspiring Museums and Galleries in Excellence' award for Exhibition Projects, Galleries (organisations with two or less paid staff). *justiceINjustice* received national attention and was reviewed as 'groundbreaking' and a means to help 'change the way lawyers and the public understand the victim's experience of injustice' (Fairley 2018, n.p.). The exhibition was reviewed in *The Guardian* as 'eclectic' yet, with mention of my curation, that it was 'brought together by a clear-eyed focus and, ultimately, an underlying humanity' (McGowan 2018, n.p.). Importantly, the project foregrounded material and aesthetic engagement as a research methodology with epistemic value. As Bray (2017, 149) writes, sometimes 'we can wring more reflection from aesthetic processes'. The transformative acts of the artists in taking law's documents and creating new perspectives resulted in profound distillations of the essence of miscarriage of justice: multisensorial experiences of injustice and dark episodes. If the 'heart of art' is new knowledge (Sullivan 2006, 22), *justiceINjustice* succeeded in not only explaining the issues, but generating experiential encounters and deep awareness.

Acknowledgement

justiceINjustice was supported/funded by Create NSW, NSW Trade & Investment Crown Lands, Headjam, Hunter TAFE, *The Herald*, the City of Newcastle, the University of Newcastle, Sydney Institute of Criminology (University of Sydney Law School) and Merridy Elphick Lawyers.

Websites

Artists:

Corinne Brittain http://corinnebrittain.com/about/corinne-brittain.html

Rob Cleworth https://robcleworth.weebly.com/

Blak Douglas https://blakdouglas.com.au/

Bianca Willoughby (formerly John A. Douglas) https://www.johnadouglas.com.au/

Leah Emery https://www.leahemeryart.com/about
Richard Lewer https://richardlewer.com/
Lezlie Tilley https://www.mayspace.com.au/artists-works/lezlie-tilley
Gallery: The Lock-Up http://www.thelockup.org.au/whats-on/justiceinjustice
Photographer: Fourth Street Studio https://fourthstreetstudio.pixieset.com/justiceinjustice/
Curator: Carolyn McKay https://www.carolynmckay.com/

Notes

1 Digital works between 2008 and 2009 included *Fragments* (photomedia works on cotton rag), *I'm Talking about Truth and Lies* (digital video 20:45 min), *Utterance* (digital video 06:06 min) and *Oath* (digital video 02:04 min).
2 *Reports of Crime, Etc., Etc.,* was exhibited in solo shows at The Lock-Up (2010) and Mosman Art Gallery's The Cube (2011).
3 Digital works included *Felonia de se,* soundscape installed in the padded cell during *Bodies in Distress* event, The Lock-Up 2012 and *Model Prison*, installation, *Doing Time* group exhibition, Verge Gallery, University of Sydney 2015.
4 In 2015, I was commissioned by The Lock-Up to create *Moniker* for *Exhibit A*, curated by Carrie Miller. Criminal monikers were sourced with the assistance of Archivist, Gionni Di Gravio, from the University of Newcastle Auchmuty Library's cultural collection.
5 For related case law, see: *Russell v Commissioner of Police, New South Wales Police Service & ors* [2001] NSWADT 32; *Commissioner of Police, NSW Police Service v Estate Edward John Russell and ors.* [2001] NSWSC 745; *Russell v Commissioner of Police, New South Wales Police Service & Ors (No 2)* [2002] NSWADT 252.
6 For related case law, see: *Public Trustee, South Australia as tutor for Cornelia Rau v The Commonwealth of Australia; G4S Australia Pty Ltd & Falck Global Solutions Ltd - Cross Defendants* [2009] NSWSC 1008; *Public Trustee of South Australia as tutor for Cornelia Rau v Commonwealth of Australia* [2010] NSWSC 1224; Summary of the Submission of the Rau Family to the Inquiry into the Detention of Cornelia Rau.
7 For related case law and inquests see: *Chamberlain v R* [1982] FCA 235; (1982) 69 FLR 445; *Chamberlain v R (No 1)* [1983] HCA 13; (1983) 153 CLR 514; *Re Alice Lynne Chamberlain and Michael Leigh Chamberlain v R* [1983] FCA 78; (1983) 72 FLR 1; *Chamberlain v R (No 2) ("Chamberlain case")* [1984] HCA 7; (1984) 153 CLR 521; *Royal Commission of Inquiry into Chamberlain Convictions, Report*, Commonwealth Parliamentary Papers (1987), volume 15, paper 192; *Reference under s.433A of the Criminal Code by the Attorney-General for the Northern Territory of Australia of Convictions of Alice Lynne Chamberlain and Michael Leigh Chamberlain*, Court of Criminal Appeal, 19 February, 14 and 15 September 1988; *Inquest into the Death of Azaria Chamberlain* 13 December 1995; *Inquest into the Death of Azaria Chantel Loren Chamberlain* [2012] NTMC 020; https://lindychamberlain.com/legal-process-and-findings/findings-and-transcripts/
8 For related case law, see: *R v Folbigg* [2003] NSWSC 895; *R v Folbigg* [2005] NSWCCA 23; *Folbigg v The Queen* [2005] HCATrans 657; *Folbigg v R* [2007] NSWCCA 128; *Folbigg v R* [2007] NSWCCA 371.

References

Bardzell, Jeffrey, Bardzell, Shaowen, and Hansen, Lone Koefoed, 2015. Immodest Proposals: Research Through Design and Knowledge. *Proceedings of the 33rd Annual ACM Conference on Human Factors in Computing Systems*, 2093–102.

Benjamin, Walter, 1968. *Illuminations*, vol. 241, no. 2. New York: Schocken Books.

Berger, John, 1973. *Ways of Seeing*. London: BBC and Penguin Books.

Biber, Katherine, 2006. Photographs and Labels: Against a Criminology of Innocence. *Law Text Culture*, 10, 19.

Biber, Katherine, 2007. *Captive Images: Race, Crime, Photography*. Abingdon: Routledge.

Biber, Katherine, 2019. *In Crime's Archive: The Cultural Afterlife of Evidence*. Abington; Routledge.

Bolt, Barbara, 2010. The Magic is in Handling. *In*: Estelle Barrett and Barbara Bolt, eds. *Practice as Research: Approaches to Creative Arts Enquiry*. London, UK: I B Tauris.

Bray, Rebecca Scott, 2014. Rotten Prettiness? The Forensic Aesthetic and Crime As Art. *Australian Feminist Law Journal*, 40, 69–95.

Bray, Rebecca Scott, 2017. Images of Fatal Violence: Negotiating the Dark Heart of Death Research. *Mortality*, 22 (2), 136–54.

Brown, Michelle, 2014. Visual Criminology and Carceral Studies: Counter-Images in the Carceral Age. *Theoretical Criminology*, 18 (2), 176–97.

Brown, Michelle, and Carrabine, Eamonn, 2019. The Critical Foundations of Visual Criminology: The State, Crisis, and the Sensory, *Critical Criminology*, 27, 191–205.

Campbell, Sher, 2020. justiceINjustice: Identity and Reflection through Art and Law. *Professional Legal Education Conference*, 1–3 October. Queensland: Bond University.

Carrabine, Eamonn, 2012. Just Images: Aesthetics, Ethics and Visual Criminology. *British Journal of Criminology*, 52 (3), 463–89.

Carter, Paul, 2004. *Material Thinking: The Theory and Practice of Creative Research*. Melbourne: Melbourne University Press.

Copes, Heith, Tchoula, Whitney, Brookman, Fiona, and Ragland, Jared, 2018. Photo-Elicitation Interviews with Vulnerable Populations: Practical and Ethical Considerations. *Deviant Behavior*, 39 (4), 475–94.

Cunneen, Chris, 2006. Aboriginal Deaths in Custody: A Continuing Systematic Abuse. *Social Justice*, 33 (4 (106)), 37–51.

Doherty, Laura, and Bricknell, Samantha, 2020a. *Deaths in custody in Australia 2017–18*. Statistical Report no. 21. Canberra: Australian Institute of Criminology. Available from: https://aic.gov.au/publications/sr/sr21 [Accessed 18 January 2020].

Doherty, Laura, and Bricknell, Samantha, 2020b. *Shooting Deaths in Police Custody*. Statistical Bulletin no. 19. Canberra: Australian Institute of Criminology. Available from: https://aic.gov.au/publications/sb/sb19 [Accessed 18 January 2020].

Doyle, Peter, 2013. The kibitzing archive. *Text*, 18, 1–13.

Fairley, Gina, 2018. Lawyers and Artists Collaborate to Expose Injustice. *Artshub*, 23, March 2018. Available from: https://visual.artshub.com.au/news-article/sponsored-content/museums/gina-fairley/lawyers-and-artists-collaborate-to-expose-injustice-255416 [Accessed 18 January 2020].

Ferrell, Jeff, 1999. Cultural Criminology. *Annual Review of Sociology*, 25 (1), 395–418.

Ferrell, Jeff, 2008. Crime and Popular Culture: Theory and Method. *Crime and Popular Culture Conference*, 28 October. Warrensburg, MO, USA: University of Central Missouri, October.

Ferrell, Jeff, 2011. Disciplinarity and Drift. *In*: Mary Bosworth and Carolyn Hoyle, eds. *What is Criminology?* Oxford: Oxford University Press, 62–75.

Ferrell, Jeff, and Sanders, C. R., eds., 1995. *Cultural Criminology*. Boston, MA: Northeastern University Press.

Foucault, Michel, 1977. *Discipline and Punish: The Birth of the Prison*. New York: Vintage.

Gallo, Rebecca, 2015. Richard Lewer: You wouldn't make this stuff up. *Vault: Australasian Art & Culture*, April, 2015.

Gibson, Ross, 2010. The Known World. TEXT, special issue 8, website series. Available: http://www.textjournal.com.au/speciss/issue8/Gibson.pdf [Accessed 18 January 2020].

Gorrey, Megan, 2018. 'We Will Take This to Our Graves': Courtney Topic's Death Was Preventable, Coroner Finds. *Sydney Morning Herald*. July 30. Available from: https://www.smh.com.au/national/nsw/errors-were-made-shooting-death-of-courtney-topic-by-police-was-preventable-coroner-finds-20180727-p4ztzk.html [Accessed 18 January 2020].

Grabosky, Peter N., 1988. Aboriginal Deaths in Custody: The Case of John Pat. *Race & Class*, 29 (3), 87–95.

Gray, Carole, and Malins, Julian, 2004. *Visualizing Research: A Guide to the Research Process in Art and Design*. Aldershot, Hants, England and Burlington, VT: Ashgate.

Green, Lelia, 2007. Recognising Practice-Led Research... at Last! *Proceedings of the Hatched 07 Arts Research Symposium*.

Guiney, Thomas, 2020. Excavating the Archive: Reflections on a Historical Criminology of Government, Penal Policy and Criminal Justice Change. *Criminology & Criminal Justice*, 20 (1), 76–92.

Haseman, Bradley C., 2006. A Manifesto for Performative Research. *Media International Australia Incorporating Culture and Policy: Quarterly Journal of Media Research and Resources*, 118, 98–106.

Hayward, Keith, 2009. Visual Criminology: Cultural Criminology-Style: Keith Hayward makes the case for 'visual criminology'. *Criminal Justice Matters*, 78 (1), 12–4.

Jay, Martin, 1993. *Downcast Eyes: The Denigration of Vision in Twentieth-Century French Thought*. California: University of California Press.

Jay, Martin, 2002. That Visual Turn: The Advent of Visual Culture. *Journal of Visual Culture*, 1 (1), 87–92.

Jefferies, Fiona, 2013. Documentary Noir in the City of Fear: Feminicide, Impunity and Grassroots Communication in Ciudad Juarez. *Crime Media Culture*, 9 (3), 301–17.

Klinke, Harald, ed., 2014. *Art Theory as Visual Epistemology*. Newcastle upon Tyne, UK: Cambridge Scholars Publishing.

Knueppel, Gabriele, 2010. *Sensory Spatiality: Tangible and Intangible Dynamics in Interior Architectural Design*. Thesis (PhD). RMIT University.

Legacies Now, 2010. *Curatorial Toolkit. A Practical Guide for Curators*. Available from: https://visualarts.net.au/media/uploads/files/Curatorial_Toolkit.pdf [Accessed 18 January 2020].

Levin, David M., 1993. *Modernity and the Hegemony of Vision*. California: University of California Press.

McClanahan, Bill, and South, Nigel, 2020. "All Knowledge Begins with the Senses": Towards a Sensory Criminology. *British Journal of Criminology*, 60, 3–23.

McGowan, Michael, 2018. 'This Must Not Be Forgotten': The Artists Painting a Picture of Australian Injustice. *The Guardian*, 28 March 2018. Available from: https://www

.theguardian.com/artanddesign/2018/mar/28/system-failure-the-artists-exploring-miscarriages-of-justice-in-australia [Accessed 18 January 2020].

McKay, Carolyn, 2010. Murder Ob/Scene: The Seen, Unseen and Ob/Scene in Murder Trials. *Law Text Culture*, 14 (1), 79–93.

McKay, Carolyn, 2013a. Covert: The Artist as Voyeur. *Surveillance & Society*, 11 (3), 334–53.

McKay, Carolyn, 2013b. Art, Criminology and Research. *In*: Denise Thwaites, ed. *Critical Animalia: A Decade between Disciplines*. Newcastle: CLP, 93–6.

McKay, Carolyn, 2017. Model Prison. *The Annual Review of Interdisciplinary Justice Research*, 6, 230–5.

McKay, Carolyn, 2018a. *justiceINjustice* [exhibition catalogue]. Newcastle: The Lock-Up.

McKay, Carolyn, 2018b. justiceINjustice Collaboration, *PacifiCrim, Newsletter of the Australian and New Zealand Society of Criminology*, 15 (2), 4–5.

McKay, Carolyn, 2018c. *The Pixelated Prisoner: Prison video links, court 'appearance' and the justice matrix*. Abingdon, Oxon and New York: Routledge.

McKay, Carolyn, forthcoming. Who's Been Sleeping in My Bed? Cheap Motel Rooms and Transgression. *In*: Michael Fiddler, Travis Linnemann, and Theo Kindynis, eds. *Ghost Criminology*, NYUP.

McLeod, Ross, 2006. *The Sensuous Intellect*. Melbourne: RMIT University Press.

Merleau-Ponty, Maurice, 1964. *The Primacy of Perception: And Other Essays on Phenomenological Psychology, the Philosophy of Art, History and Politics*. Evanston, IL: Northwestern University Press.

Merleau-Ponty, Maurice, 1968. *The Visible and the Invisible: Followed By Working Notes* Evanston, IL: Northwestern University Press.

Millie, Andrew, 2017. Urban Interventionism as a Challenge to Aesthetic Order: Towards an Aesthetic Criminology. *Crime, Media, Culture*, 13 (1): 3–20.

Onciul, Bryony, 2019. Community engagement, Indigenous heritage and the complex figure of the curator: Foe, facilitator, friend or forsaken? *In*: Philpp Schorch and Conal McCarthy, eds. *Curatopia: Museums and the future of curatorship*. Manchester: Manchester University Press.

Parker, James E. K., 2015. *Acoustic Jurisprudence: Listening to the Trial of Simon Bikindi*. New York: Oxford University Press.

Parker, James E. K., 2019. Sonic Lawfare: On the Jurisprudence of Weaponised Sound. *Sound Studies*, February, 1–25.

Partridge, Emma, 2019. 'I Hope to God They Get Answers': Strike Force Set Up Into Missing Girls. *Sydney Morning Herald*, June 6, 2019. Available from: https://www.smh.com.au/national/nsw/i-hope-to-god-they-get-answers-strike-force-set-up-into-missing-girls-20190606-p51v28.html [Accessed 18 January 2020].

Police Integrity Commission, 2001. *Report to Parliament Operation Saigon*. Available from: https://media.opengov.nsw.gov.au/pairtree_root/8d/b8/10/3b/7f/37/4f/38/89/6f/08/04/b5/19/a1/8b/obj/Saigon_Report.pdf [Accessed 18 January 2020].

Purdy, Jeannine, 1994. Royal Commissions and Omissions: What Was Left out of the Report on the Death on John Pat. *Australian Journal of Law and Society*, 10, 37–66.

Rafter, Nicole, 2014. Introduction to Special Issue on Visual Culture and the Iconography of Crime and Punishment. *Theoretical Criminology*, 18 (2), 127–33.

Redmon, David, 2017. Documentary Criminology: Girl Model as Case Study. *Crime Media Culture: An International Journal*, 13 (3), 357–74.

Riles, Annelise, 1999. Models and Documents: Artifacts of International Legal Knowledge. *International and Comparative Law Quarterly*, 48 (4), 805–25.

Roberts, Paul, and Zuckerman, Adrian, 2010. *Criminal Evidence*. New York: Oxford University Press.

Royal Commission into Aboriginal Deaths in Custody (RCIADIC), 1991. *Report of the Inquiry into The Death of John Peter Pat*. Australia: Australian Parliament.

Rugoff, Ralph, 1997. *Scene of the Crime*. Los Angeles, CA: UCLA/Armand Hammer Museum of Art in association with MIT Press.

Sekula, Allan, 1986. The Body and the Archive. *October*, 39, 3–64.

Slade, Lisa, 2017. *Artist Text. The National New Australian Art*. Available from: https://the-national.com.au/artists/richard-lewer-1/never-shall-be-forgotten-a-mothers-story/ [Accessed 18 January 2020].

Sontag, Susan, 1977. *On Photography*. London: Penguin Books.

State Coroner (NSW), 2001. *Report By the NSW State Coroner Into the Deaths in Custody/Police Operations*. NSW: NSW State Coroner.

State of New South Wales, 2019. *Inquiry into the convictions of Kathleen Megan Folbigg*. Available from: https://www.folbigginquiry.justice.nsw.gov.au/Documents/Report%20of%20the%20Inquiry%20into%20the%20convictions%20of%20Kathleen%20Megan%20Folbigg.pdf [Accessed 18 January 2020].

Stolterman, Erik, and Wiberg, Mikael, 2010. Concept-Driven Interaction Design Research. *Human–Computer Interaction*, 25 (2), 95–118.

Story, Brett, Brown, Michelle, and Carrabine, Eemonn, 2017. The Prison in Twelve Landscapes: An Interview with Film Producer and Director Brett Story. *Crime, Media, Culture*, 13 (1), 107–13.

Sullivan, Graeme, 2006. Research Acts in Art Practice. *Studies in Art Education*, 48 (1), 19–35.

Sullivan, Graeme, 2010. *Art Practice as Research: Inquiry in Visual Arts*. Thousand Oaks, CA: Sage.

Tagg, John, 1988. *The Burden of Representation: Essays on Photographies and Histories*, vol. 80. Minneapolis: University of Minnesota Press.

The Guardian, 2020. Deaths Inside: Indigenous Australian Deaths in Custody. *The Guardian*, 28 August. Available from: https://www.theguardian.com/australia-news/ng-interactive/2018/aug/28/deaths-inside-indigenous-australian-deaths-in-custody [Accessed 18 January 2020].

Verbeek, Peter-Paul, 2012. Politics at Issue. On Art and the Democratization of Things. *In*: Jorinde Seijdel, ed. *Open 24: Politics of Things*. Rotterdam: Open!

Vismann, Cornelia, 2001. The Love of Ruins. *Perspectives on Science*, 9 (2), 196–209.

Walby, Kevin, Jochelson, Richard, Bertrand, Michelle, and Kohm, Steven, 2016. Visualizing Justice. *The Annual Review of Interdisciplinary Justice Research*, 5, 5–14.

West, Kate, 2017. Visual Criminology and Lombroso: In Memory of Nicole Rafter (1936–2016). *Theoretical Criminology*, 21 (3), 271–87.

Yar, Majid, 2017. Toward a Cultural Criminology of the Internet. *In*: Kevin Steinmetz and Matt Nobles, eds. *Technocrime and Criminological Theory*. Milton: Routledge, 132–48.

Young, Alison, 1996. *Imagining Crime: Textual Outlaws and Criminal Conversations*. London: Sage.

Young, Alison, 2010. *The Scene of Violence: Crime, Cinema, Affect*. Abingdon; New York: Routledge-Cavendish.

Young, Alison, 2019. Japanese Atmospheres of Criminal Justice. *British Journal of Criminology*, 59 (4), 765–79.

Zardini, Mirko, 2005. *Sense of the City: An Alternative Approach to Urbanism*. Montréal: Canadian Centre for Architecture.

Artworks

Brittain, Corinne, 2018. *STRANDED (I have done nothing wrong)*. Hand dyed cotton tape, wax, steel grid, mattress spring. 190cm × 320cm × 240cm.

Douglas, Blak, 2018. *A Dog's Breakfast*. Synthetic polymer on canvas (Permaplastik Paints). 150cm × 200cm.

Cleworth, Rob, 2017–2018. *True Blue – colour field painting*. Inkjet photograph and oil paint on canvas mounted on plywood panels. 3 parts: 61.5cm × 77.5cm; 195cm × 160cm.

Cleworth, Rob, 2018a. *Dear Roni*. Digitally re-printed photographs and text on paper provided by Roni Levi's family and his widow Melinda Dundas.

Cleworth, Rob, 2018b. *Taharah*. Oil paint on photo canvas on plywood panel.

Emery, Leah 2018. *Vigil*. Installation comprising of vintage curtain, fan and chair, velvet, metal stand, perspex, acrylic. Dimensions variable.

Lewer, Richard, 2017. *Never Shall Be Forgotten – A Mother's Story*. Single channel, hand drawn, digital animation, colour and black and white, sound. 05:04 mins, aspect ratio: 16:9, dimensions variable.

McKay, Carolyn, 2008–2009. *Fragments*. Photomedia works on cotton rag.

McKay, Carolyn, 2008–2009. *Utterance*. Digital video. 06:06 min.

McKay, Carolyn, 2008–2009. *Oath*. Digital video. 02:04 min.

McKay, Carolyn, 2009. *I'm Talking about Truth and Lies*. Digital video. 20:45 min.

McKay, Carolyn, 2010. *Reports of Crime, Etc., Etc.* 2-channel video installation.

McKay, Carolyn, 2012. *Felonia de se*. Soundscape.

McKay, Carolyn, 2015a. *Model Prison*. HD video installation. 07:25 mins.

McKay, Carolyn, 2015b. *Moniker*. Video installation with audio, with printed fabric and performance. 07:54 minutes, looped.

Tilley, Lezlie, 2018. *The Kathleen Folbigg Diaries*. 4 Channel sound installation. 15 minutes.

Tilley, Lezlie, 2018. *Memories started 8th January 1993*. Video installation.

Willoughby, Bianca (formerly John A Douglas), 2018. *No System to Fail*. Multi-channel video and sound installation, galvanised iron bucket, mop, disinfectant.

Chapter 16

OA_RR

Documenting sovereignty

Georgine Clarsen

Introduction

Indigenous voices and stories have become increasingly amplified in Australian national life. In the cultural production of academics, activists, filmmakers, songwriters and painters, as well as in radio programmes, memoirs, submissions to commissions of inquiry, social media and in the growing practice of 'welcome to country' ceremonies, Indigenous experiences and perspectives are forging spaces in the public domain. In this cultural resurgence, attending to Indigenous representation and providing opportunities to 'give voice to the voiceless' are central to settler movements for social justice, decolonisation and Indigenous recognition (Dreher and Mondal 2018a, 4). But precisely what should settler allies *do* with those voices, stories and testimonies; with all those welcomes; and with that listening, reading, empathising and witnessing? What responsibilities are entailed by hearing, beyond respectful reception? How, as one recent volume put it, can a progressive, decolonising politics move beyond a focus on speech and representation to an *active* reception, an attentiveness and ethical responsiveness to those voices and stories (Dreher and Mondal 2018b)? How can they (we) take the next steps and break their (our) complicity with ongoing colonial violence and the continuing dispossession of Indigenous lands and cultures in this present moment?

The Melbourne artist, Reko Rennie, offers one provocative response to those crucial questions. In his video installation *OA_RR*, part of the 3rd National Indigenous Art Triennial at the National Gallery of Australia in 2017 called *Defying Empire* (Baum 2017), Rennie refuses to voice a painful story of Indigenous loss, suffering or injustice. Nor does he provide an uplifting story of continuity, endurance or triumph, though both oppression and survival are central to the issues he addresses. He refuses to tell a story at all. Instead, Rennie offers his viewers documentation of the contemporary facticity of Indigenous sovereignty, manifested in the 'micro', intimate register of everyday familial love. This chapter analyses *OA_RR* as a performative attestation of ongoing Indigenous sovereignty. I read Rennie's installation as both a process (the documentation of a real-life journey) and a thing (a material document of that

DOI: 10.4324/9781003247593-20

journey) through which Rennie commands his viewers to live with and around the fact of Indigenous sovereignty. In the process of producing that installation/document, Rennie created and deployed a series of other documents, and together they archive a body of Indigenous knowledge about colonisation, particularly about the experiences of child removal. By closely attending to the personal, historical and cultural contexts of those documents, this chapter considers what Rennie's artwork demands from viewers who are moved by it. In particular, I ask: how should non-Indigenous viewers read and actively attend to this artwork and how should they (we) respond ethically to it?

Defying empire: exhibiting *OA_RR*

The enigmatically entitled *OA_RR* is a short road movie, less than nine minutes long, that documents a 2,000-kilometre car trip made by Reko Rennie, from his home in Melbourne to his Kamilaroi country in north-western NSW (National Gallery of Australia 2017). Exhibited as a three-channel video installation, *OA_RR* is projected onto large screens arranged in a U-shape in front of viewers. There is no dialogue, but a minimalist soundtrack by Nick Cave and the Bad Seeds echoes through the gallery, calling us to the work even before we see it. Slide guitar and percussion evokes the familiar filmic genre of lonely journeys along empty frontier roads. The car, however, is no rough frontier workhorse. Eye-popping and luxurious, it vibrates with a vitality that is freighted with meaning.

Rennie's road movie quickly becomes a 'no-road movie' (Probyn 2005) as the luxury car moves off the bitumen and onto Rennie's red-dirt Kamilaroi country. The absence of other traffic heightens the sense that we are watching a singular and very personal journey. The clues Rennie offers to help us read this installation are oblique and fleeting but the configuration of the screens creates the sense that we, too, are travelling in that classy car. Our bodies respond to the mesmerising sounds and images of smooth motion: a car moving through wooded grasslands, trees and sky reflected on the shiny paintwork, wheels rolling on bitumen and dirt, views through the windscreen, aerial shots of the vehicle trailing clouds of red dust and close-ups of the car's interior. We begin to observe details of the car. The camera lingers on the vehicle's insignia. We see the coveted bonnet mascot, the winged 'Spirit of Ecstasy' and the chrome radiator grill and headlights. This is a Rolls Royce Corniche sedan, one of the most expensive makes in the world, which has long symbolised British royalty, privilege and entitlement. Rennie's Corniche, which dates from the early 1970s when he was born, is now even more impressive than it ever was. He has repainted it in a flash metallic finish: a gold base overlaid with vibrant designs in black and hot pink. The impassive driver is shot in close-up, his eyes hidden behind sunglasses and his leather-gloved hands sliding smoothly along the steering wheel. This is emphatically not the kind of car usually associated with 'driving while black' (Gilroy 2001; Clarsen 2017a).

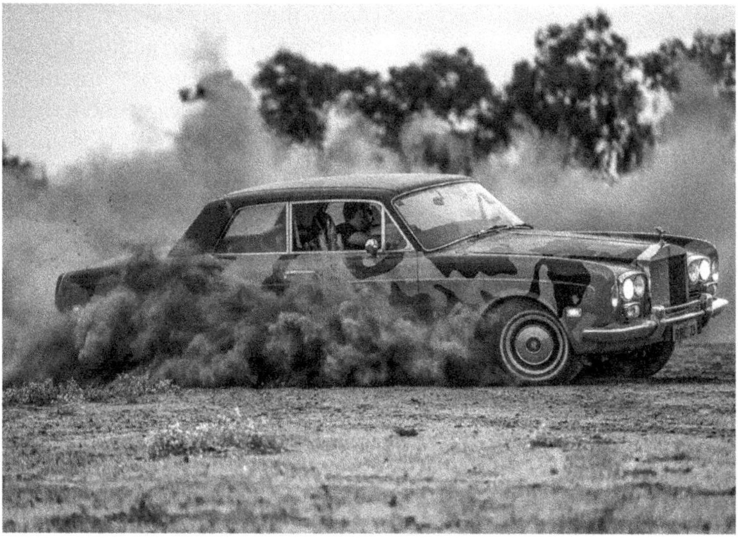

Figure 16.1 Reko Renie, *Rolls Royce*. Still image from three-channel video installation *OA_RR*, 2017. Courtesy of the artist © Reko Rennie.

A camera from a passenger point of view slowly pans to the lacquered mahogany dashboard, with its black and chrome instruments and leather trim. It comes to rest on a colour photograph stuck to the dashboard in front of the driver. A long close-up reveals a humble family snapshot set in a suburban back yard. A young boy sits in an old-fashioned pram with what must be his grandmother crouched close behind him, her arm lovingly encircling him. The woman and child smile happily at the photographer. We begin to wonder if this photograph is the key to the trip. Is this what is being so elaborately transported? As the camera moves up to the driver's face, framed in the rear-view mirror, and then shifts to his point of view through the windscreen onto the moving landscape, we are invited to make a story. Perhaps the boy, now a man, is driving. And perhaps the woman, possibly now dead, is being driven in style. With the realisation of a connection between the driver and the snapshot, the trip becomes infused with tenderness and immense dignity. We give ourselves over to the dreamy movement of the car as the day draws to a close. But without warning the journey takes a surprising and rather violent turn. Like a western-suburbs hoon thrashing his car, the driver swerves the Rolls Royce off-track to execute a series of overlaid donuts. The soundtrack swells and an extended sequence, some two and a half minutes long, shows the Corniche carving circular patterns into the red earth in balletic arcs, releasing clouds of dust. At the conclusion of these mesmerising spinouts, a camera inside the vehicle returns to the snapshot on the dashboard, the image bouncing with the movement of the car. If we look closely, however, we can see that something has happened. The footage, which is warmly lit in the red afternoon sunlight, is projected in mirror reverse, suggesting that the boy and his grandmother now are placed in a different relation. With the burnouts done, the earth inscribed, and a subtle change signalled in the relationship between the grandchild and grandmother, the driver smoothly points the car back the way it came. A luminous red sunset back-lights the car and for a lingering moment its headlights dazzle the viewer as it heads for home in darkness. For the first time, we no longer feel we might be a participant in the journey. Instead, we are 'spotlighted' as the soundtrack recedes and the images fade to black. We are put on the spot to respond. A final high aerial shot shows what has been left behind: a complex overlay of circular patterns in a massive geometric formation remains engraved into the red dirt. Rennie has inscribed an ephemeral document on his country, his mechanical 'mark'.

In the sections that follow, I tease out the careful layering of documents that constitute this artwork. At its centre, as it is in the car, is a photograph that registers a moment of family love some three and a half decades ago. That document stands in for a loved one who is sadly gone and the agency of the now-adult grandson who remains. The Rolls Royce itself is also a material document. In restoring it, not back to its pompous original condition but in his flamboyant signature style, Rennie has created an object that documents a cross-cultural history of settler-colonial relations in Australia. I show how that car/document is located within a long genealogy of artworks that archive a history of Indigenous knowledge of colonisation through the bodies of cars. The

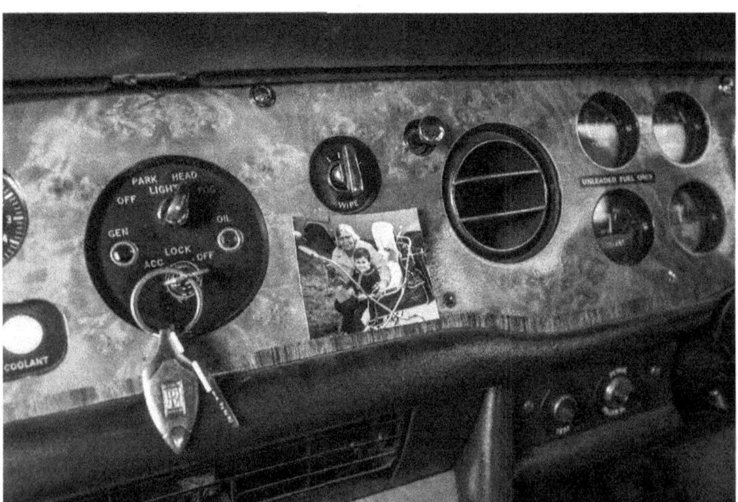

Figure 16.2 Reko Renie, *Family Snapshot, Reko Renie and His Nan*. Still image from three-channel video installation *OA_RR*, 2017. Courtesy of the artist © Reko Rennie.

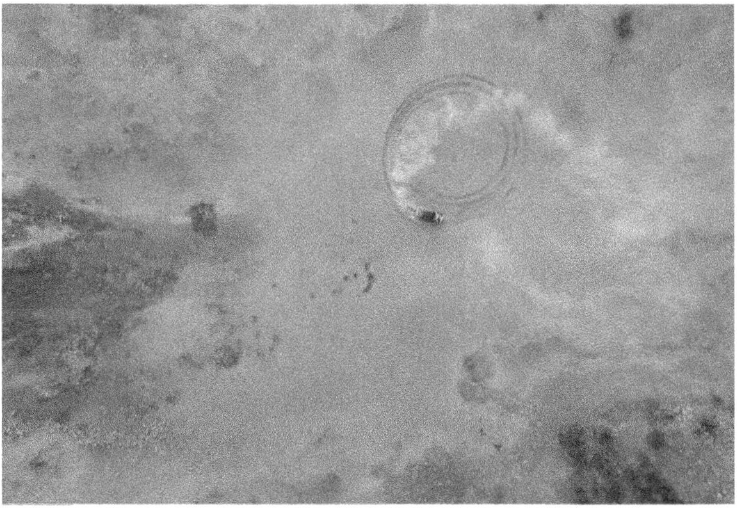

Figure 16.3 Reko Renie, *Carving a Mechanical Inscription on Kamillaroi Country*. Still image from three-channel video installation *OA_RR*, 2017. Courtesy of the artist © Reko Rennie.

sand engraving that Rennie inscribes on the earth, in a pattern that references Kamilaroi sacred practices, is also a powerful material document. It certifies the ongoing vibrancy of Kamilaroi culture in the contemporary idiom of a working-class, urban Aboriginal man. The final installation/document that is *OA_RR* animates those other documents in a medium that continues to be exhibited and archived long after Rennie's road trip was completed. Lastly, this response by one non-Indigenous viewer may be considered a secondary document of that installation, which attempts to think through, attend and respond to that primary documentation that Rennie has put in front of us.

OA_RR and Reko Rennie's visual language

OA_RR brings together Rennie's identity as an urban, working-class Aboriginal man: his 'westie' masculinity enamoured by prestige cars and his Kamilaroi pride expressed through traditional designs, reworked with a graffiti and pop-art sensibility. Rennie's career began early, tagging carriages and corrugated-iron hoardings in the streets and railway yards near his home in Footscray. As Rennie reflected, 'I didn't go to art school, so the majority of my work is informed through my identity and the history of Aboriginal affairs in this country' (Caisley 2018). Thirty years later, his voice is greatly amplified. Rennie's work is hung in galleries and arts festivals around the world, and his commissions include bronze sculptures, public memorials, murals and huge neon signs. His art, however, continues to evoke the rattle and hiss of an aerosol can, the squeal of a sign-writer's felt marker and the bling of a neon logo (Presley 2017). Like the late Howard Arkley, the Melbourne artist of suburbia, and the late New York artist of Cuban and Haitian descent Jean-Michel Basquiat, who were both early inspirations, Rennie draws on an array of international cultural references: from advertising, graphic design, graffiti, stencil work, pop art, hip hop, abstraction, neon signs, comics and political posters (National Gallery of Australia 2017).

Unlike Arkley and Basquiat, however, Rennie's work is always informed by the politics of settler colonialism and rooted in his Kamilaroi identity. He reassembles set-pieces of the British Empire, such as crowns, postage stamps, imperial regalia and aristocratic insignia, undercutting and compounding their meanings with stereotypical Australian iconography. Recurring themes are images of native animals like the 'Big Red' kangaroo, depictions of Aboriginal warriors wielding a spear or nulla-nulla, traditional weapons arranged into a coat of arms, as well as contemporary Indigenous political motifs, like an abstracted Aboriginal flag that is rendered in gold-plated aluminium as a dripping graffiti crown that calls to mind Basquiat's three-pointed proxy signature (Rennie 2013). Emblematic of Rennie's work are stylised Kamilaroi men's sacred motifs, which he likens to the European tradition of aristocratic family crests, in which unique visual designs symbolise membership of the nobility (Harvey 2013; Alessi 2014).

Dendroglyphs, or patterned designs that were carved into the trunks of living trees, marked Indigenous sacred sites throughout what is now western NSW, southern Queensland and northern Victoria. The carvings were associated with initiation ceremonies, burial mounds and bora grounds for Wiradjuri and Kamilaroi nations (State Library of NSW 2011). Rennie re-visions the diamond-shaped ceremonial incisions, rendering them in psychedelic colours and the hard-edge patterning of pop art. In a further re-working, Rennie sometimes overpaints the stylised dendroglyph pattern with a 'camouflage' of vibrant colours, in what he calls his 'Visible/Invisible' style (Lyon Housemuseum 2017). Camouflage is most often designed to disguise, but Rennie's pink and black 'camouflaged' gold Corniche shouts entitlement. It sings out, demanding attention:

> Rather than concealing your identity and hiding, which was a big part of my father's generation, my grandmother's and those before them … my use of camouflage aims to amplify rather than conceal … and to stake my claim to a luminous, commanding form of cultural visibility.
>
> (Cuthbertson 2017)

Similarly, the large circles his Corniche inscribes into the red dirt at the high point of his journey reference the ephemeral sand engravings that were a central element of Kamilaroi ceremonies. By driving curved lines into the surface of his country, the Corniche turned into a tool for carving, Rennie collapses the past and the present and invokes the continuing power and legibility of these sacred patterns.

Roadworks: Aboriginal art and cars

When motor vehicles were first imported into Australia at the turn of the twentieth century, settlers embraced them as a powerful colonising apparatus. Cars and trucks offered both a material and symbolic means of 'conquering' terrain. From the very earliest days of the 'horseless carriage', settlers invested a great deal in their ability to travel at accelerating speed over what they routinely called 'empty' landscapes. They obsessively documented their long motor journeys throughout the continent in every form of media available to them, especially in newspapers, trade magazines, radio and newsreels. Motoring interests financed long-distance car rallies, announced prizes for 'smashing' land-speed records or 'opening out' a new route, so elevating cars into powerful symbols of colonisers' domination over Aboriginal lands (Clarsen 2015). These celebratory stories of motor travel transformed what was ostensibly a practical mode of transportation into a medium of communication, producing an archive of settlers' status as mobile moderns, at home and legitimately in possession of the whole continent (Clarsen 2017b). Simultaneously in those early years, cars and trucks also came to operate as a medium of communication in Indigenous communities, though in very different terms. The centrality of cars in Indigenous lives and cultures is a recurring theme in contemporary Aboriginal art production.

In spite of Aboriginal people's material poverty and the heightened surveillance they were subjected to, trucks and cars quickly became prized objects. As early as the first decades of the twentieth century, a few Aboriginal families and communities found ways to own vehicles, no matter how battered or worn. After the 1950s, more were able to get their hands on the wheel, and they created tenacious and lively cultures of Indigenous automobility, whenever and however they were able (Clarsen 2015). Automobiles' flexibility made them particularly well adapted to negotiate the dangers, oppressions and indignities of life under colonialism, and motor vehicles were turned to every purpose. Cars were used to hunt and gather the bush foods that were becoming increasingly scarce, to continue connections to country and ceremonial life, to maintain family ties, to follow seasonal work, to stay one step ahead of the feared 'welfare', to avoid racism on public transport, to bring the dead back to country for dignified funerals, to organise politically, to move away from reserves and missions to establish smaller outstations on homelands and to produce the artwork now found in major collections around the world (Clarsen 2017b). In short, motor vehicles and the practices they afford became central to the new pleasures, practices, accommodations, refusals, resistances and collaborations with the colonial system. The importance of motor vehicles in Aboriginal lives has simultaneously constituted cars and driving offences as a focal point for the disciplinary power of the colonial state (Anthony and Blagg 2013; Anthony and Tranter 2019; Tranter and Anthony 2019).

Aboriginal art production has given expression to and amplified the long-standing importance of cars in daily life, in political struggles and in cultural practices. When read together, the countless automobilic artworks—including tee-shirts designs, ceramics, paintings, films and large sculptures—constitute an archive of colonisation that does not simply document Indigenous memories and knowledge, but is a site of knowledge production that works to structure the contemporary experience of living as an Indigenous person in Australia. Those artists' documents, or 'roadworks', as Ursula Frederick (2011) has called them, may be read as a genealogy of Rennie's installation, a genealogy that he had previously contributed to.

The late Ngarrindjeri artist Trevor Nickolls, one of the pioneers of the urban Aboriginal art movement during the 1970s, employed cars to explore the disjunction between Western and Aboriginal cultures. His *Family in Blue Holden* (1998) was painted during the 50th anniversary of the much-loved FJ Holden, the first car that Nickolls owned. It depicts the artist with his friend, the late Gija or East Kimberley master painter Rover Thomas, as passengers in the back seat of a vibrant blue Holden convertible, the car that symbolised the post-war suburban prosperity of white Australia. A family of Wandjina spirit beings from Thomas' home country drive the car through a surreal and cartoonish urban dreamscape. Their passengers are far from primitives heading for extinction, as settlers had tried to convince themselves, but mobile subjects who exude immense power and certainty about their place in a hybrid world, where there is no simple division between modernity and tradition. Other Aboriginal artists before and since Nickolls have employed automobiles in their art practice, according to their own cultural imperatives and the material circumstances of their lives. The urban artist and Waanyi man from northwest Queensland, Gordon Hookey, for example, has also used automobiles to represent contemporary Aboriginal perspectives in his *A Painting for the Underdawg* (2005), held by the National Gallery of Australia.

Motor vehicles played a central role in the development of the Papunya Tula painting movement of the Western Desert during the 1970s. Even before that, in the 1940s and 1950s, the founder of the Hermannsburg School and the first commercially successful Indigenous artist, Albert Namatjira, famously owned several cars, though he gained little benefit from them (Croft 2001). 'Car fever' or the 'indomitable will to car ownership', as curator Vivien Johnson (2007, n.p.) put it, fostered a close connection between paintings and motor cars in the formative years of the Papunya Tula movement. In their desire for automobility, Papunya artists increased the scale of their paintings. No longer satisfied with the small boards they had been using, they began to create large canvases that commanded the price of a used car. The artists dubbed those paintings 'mutukayi ones'. Famously, the motor cars they purchased were often in such terrible condition that they broke down before the artists could drive them from the Alice Springs car yard to their communities. A little over a decade later, a master Warlpiri artist of the Papunya school, Michael Nelson Tjakamarra, was commissioned to paint one of BMW's Art Cars, thereby turning a luxury motor car into a 'canvas'. Presaging Rennie's later use of Kamilaroi dendroglyph designs, Tjakamarra transformed a BMW M3 into a document of his Warlpiri identity, by inscribing its body with the title deeds to his country under the laws of Western Desert art and culture (Tjakamarra 1989; Johnson et al 2007). In a similar vein, the Melbourne-based artist, Biggibilla, who is Reko Rennie's father, painted a Porsche Carrera Coupe with songlines from his Yuwaalaraay country in 1999 and also on a BMW motorcycle (Biggibilla n.d.; Biggibilla 1999).

Most Central Australian car-themed art is much more modest in its expression than Tjakamarra's BMW, however, and is often executed with more than a touch of humour. Artists from the small community of Utopia in the Central Desert, for example, have used the free 'spare parts shop' (Boulter 1993) of car doors, engine bonnets and hubcaps that have been discarded around their community as surfaces for their paintings. Others, like the Western Arrernte, Yankunytjatjara and Pitjantjatjara digital artist, Robert Fielding, have also brought new life to the many cars abandoned in the desert. Fielding re-painted the rusting wrecks that were overgrown with scrub near his community of Mimili in the APY (Anangu Pitjantjatjara Yankunytjatjara) lands, in the north-west of South Australia. Using reflective paints, he illuminated the car bodies *in situ*, with candles placed inside crevices. His ghostly, long-exposure photographic images honour the vehicles' former lives, the epic journeys they had once taken and the memories of the people who had travelled in them. Fielding's art, which archives individual and community histories, is dedicated to 'salvaging what belongs to the elders of our communities' (Schubert 2017).

A clapped-out used car, or 'bomb', also provided a central metaphor for a collaborative exhibition by Blak Douglas and Adam Geczy (2013/2014) at the Museum of Contemporary Aboriginal Art in Utrecht, the Netherlands. Entitled *BOMB*, the exhibition was part of the city's commemoration of the 300th anniversary of the Treaty of Utrecht, which helped create the conditions that empowered Britain to colonise large parts of the globe, including Australia. The artists placed a used BMW, the same model that had been painted by Michael Nelson Tjakamarra for the BMW Art Car series, in the window of the shopfront gallery. Rather than Warlpiri deeds of sovereignty, however, they painted this bomb, now at the end of its useful life, with a large Union Jack, the symbol of settler sovereignty. With this reinterpretation of Tjakamarra's famous artwork, the artists created a material document of the dispossession of Aboriginal people and gave visual force to the great distance between impoverished Indigenous communities and the slick corporate world that the BMW Art Cars epitomise (Museum of Contemporary Aboriginal Art 2013/2014).[1]

The portrayal of automobiles as objects of desire, symbols of Indigenous identities and as documentation of post-invasion histories is not confined to male artists. The Utopia artist Lucky Kngwarreye's *Hunting Kangaroo* series (1996), held in NSW's Museum of Applied Arts and Sciences, depicts a joyous kangaroo hunt from the back of a red utility truck across spinifex country near her home at the Ngkaweneyerre camp in Central Australia. In this series, automobiles are incorporated into old practices, documenting the everyday entanglements between automobiles and the Indigenous geographies that have emerged under new circumstances. In a similar vein, the ceramic work of Western Arrente artist, Rona Rubjuntja Panangka (Hermannsburg Potters Aboriginal Corporation n.d.) of the Hermannsburg Potters Aboriginal Corporation, documents everyday automobilic pleasures and memories. Her pots are painted with exuberant images of Black families crammed into Toyota 'troopies', the vehicles of choice in the Central Desert. Further south, 20 Tjanpi Desert Weavers, from the Ngaanyatjarra Pitjantjatjara Yankunytjatjara Women's Council in Central Australia, won a prestigious national art prize with their almost full-size *Grass Toyota* in 2005. Constructed in local minyerri grass and incorporating elements from discarded cars, the work playfully documents the Toyota as a woman's object, used for gathering art materials, hunting for food, generating cash income, teaching culture to children and caring for country (NPY Women's Council n.d.; Watson 2012). As Jennifer Biddle (2012, 10) put it, Tjanpi fibre arts provides 'ritualised forms of caring for country. Concrete processes in which country is held in the mind as much as it is in the hand'. In a final example, four women artists from the small community of Irrunytju in the Gibson Desert—Roma Butler, Ivy Laidlaw, Tjawina Roberts and Jennifer Mitchell—sliced the side from a wrecked Toyota and painted it to document a new dreaming story about their survival in the desert after their car broke down during a trip to collect art materials. Their work, *The Toyota*, was exhibited at the University of South Australia in Adelaide as part of their group exhibition, *Kapi Ungkupayi/He Gave Us Water* (SASA Gallery 2015), which protested at governmental defunding of Indigenous communities.

Before exhibiting *OA_RR*, Rennie had also participated in this long genealogy of Indigenous 'roadworks', where vehicles provide a medium for documenting and archiving Aboriginal experiences and histories of colonisation. Rennie contributed a rusted 1950s International truck he found abandoned on a Pilbara pastoral station to *Marlbatharndu Wanggagu: Once Upon a Time in the West*, a group exhibition at Perth's FORM Gallery (Wood and Dowding 2014, 204–211). The exhibition marked the expiration of 99-year pastoral leases on the lands of Yinhawangka, Banyjima and Nyiyaparli peoples in the north of that state. It documented the oral memories of Aboriginal men and women pastoral workers, creating an archive of their historical experiences. For Rennie, the battered station truck, its hardworking life there for all to see, spoke to Aboriginal knowledge of the real pastoral history of Australia. He created a material document of that history by leaving the truck unrestored and painting its sun-bleached surface with heroic images of Aboriginal 'cowboys' on horseback. To the doors he added a coat of arms of crossed traditional implements, topped with a stylish cowboy hat. In a cursive script that echoed the Coca-Cola logo, he reproduced pointed quotes from the former workers' oral testimonies. 'Stolen Lands', 'We Worked for Rations', 'This Land Is Ours' and 'Pastoralists = Squatters' spoke to the dispossession and exploitation of those people whose unpaid labour had been the backbone of the industry (Rennie 2014).[2] In the course this collaboration, Rennie made a connection to his own family's experience on the other side of the continent. His paternal grandmother, Julia, and her younger brother, Rennie's great-uncle, had been stolen from their family in the early decades of the twentieth century and enslaved on a pastoral station in north-western NSW as young children.

Terror and the big black car

Children were stolen from Aboriginal families and communities from the earliest days of British invasion. Some children who survived frontier massacres were abducted and raised by settlers (Haebich and Delroy 1999, 6–19; Murray and Howes 2019, 7–10; Karskens 2020). Others were forced into institutions throughout the nineteenth century, such as Governor Macquarie's Paramatta Native Institution (Brook and Cohen 1991; Read 2006). By the turn of the twentieth century, each state and territory had established legal frameworks that enabled the removal of any Aboriginal child at the whim of Aboriginal 'protectors' (Read 2014). Of the 'vast, coercive powers' that white authorities bestowed on themselves, wrote Quentin Beresford (2006, 11) in his biography of the activist Robert Riley,

> the power to remove children from their families was the most feared … The sight of parents wailing as black police cars sped away down dusty roads carrying traumatised children bound for institutions was common throughout Australia in the 1930s and 1940s.

Painful first-person accounts of child removal, documented in private memoir and official inquiries, have frequently been structured around childhood memories of being helpless and imprisoned, locked into a 'big black car' that snatched them away from protesting family.

Margaret Tucker's harrowing memoir, *If Everyone Cared* (1977), is perhaps the earliest published first-person account of forced removal. She wrote, 'we were terrified of the thought of being separated from our parents', who were 'fighting to keep them together as a family' (1977, 82). Tucker was abducted in about 1916 when she was aged 12, from the Moonahculla settlement near Deniliquin in NSW. Most children at the 'black's camp' on the Australian Inland Mission reserve had already been removed when the police arrived at their schoolroom with a motor car to forcibly take her, her sister May and their friend Myrtle Taylor to the notorious Cootamundra Domestic Training School. She remembered the angry and tearful protests from the mothers of the settlement, as they were taken way. She wrote that the girls 'last memory of [their mother] for many years was her waving pathetically as we waved back and called goodbye to her, but we were too far away for her to hear us'. Tucker later learned that relatives found her mother the next day, 'half demented and ill' in the long grass at the side of the road, 25 miles distant from the mission. More than 60 years later, Margaret Tucker continued to ask herself, 'how many black children were taken like that?' (1977, 90–95).

Tucker's question was answered not long after, with the publication of historian Peter Read's pamphlet (1981), *The Stolen Generations: The Removal of Aboriginal Children in New South Wales, 1883 to 1969.* Commissioned by the NSW Department of Aboriginal Affairs and based on his research into the NSW State Archives and interviews with scores of Wiradjuri people, Read estimated that throughout Australia as many as 50,000 Aboriginal children had been removed by church and state agencies since British invasion. Fifteen years later, in 1995, the Human Rights and Equal Opportunity Commission began gathering oral testimony across Australia from those generations of stolen children. Published as *Bringing Them Home*, the Report of the National Inquiry into the Separation of Aboriginal and Torres Strait Islander Children from Their Families (Human Rights and Equal Opportunity Commission 1997) documented the lifelong and intergenerational effects of those systematic policies. An official motor car was prominent in many survivors' testimonies. For example, in confidential evidence, an unnamed NSW woman who was removed from her family in the 1960s and placed in the Parramatta Girl's Home testified:

> The biggest hurt, I think, was having my mum chase the welfare car – I'll always remember it – we were looking out the window and mum was running behind us and singing out for us. They locked us in the police cell up here and mum was walking up and down outside the police station and crying and screaming out for us.
>
> (Human Rights and Equal Opportunity Commission 1997, 40)[3]

In testimony to the Federal Court in Darwin in 1999, the late Lorna Cubillo remembered in searing detail the day in 1947 when she and 17 other children, from babies to just under 12 years old, were taken from the Australian Inland Mission School at Phillip Creek, near Tennant Creek in the Northern Territory. Just seven or eight years old herself, her experience on that day 'burned forever in her memory' (*Cubillo v The Commonwealth*, Transcript of Proceedings 1999, 136–137). She recalled that early in the morning they were loaded onto the back of a Bedford International truck, its open tray covered only with chicken wire and containing a 44-gallon drum of water, to be incarcerated in the Retta Dixon Home in Darwin. The journey of some 1,000 kilometres took two days and two nights. Cubillo testified to the 'screaming', the 'crying' and the 'panic' as the children were ordered onto the truck. She remembered that Auntie Rosie put a breast-feeding baby, Gwen, into her arms to care for on the long journey. And she remembered the mothers, 'beating their heads with sticks and rocks' and throwing dirt over themselves. The bleeding mothers 'chased the truck from Phillip Creek, screaming and crying', until the women disappeared from the view of the frightened children, hidden by the dust thrown up by the truck. 'We were in the back of the truck all the time, day and night, without cover'. Lorna recalled trying to help Gwen stay warm and drawing water in her mouth from the drum and passing it into the baby's mouth to feed her.

Such painful events, with the role of vehicles very often recalled in acute detail, are documented in a growing archive of poems, songs, paintings, films, local histories, fiction, podcasts and autobiographies that gives voice to devastating experiences of child removal. The late Ngarrindjeri singer, Ruby Hunter, spoke of being taken from her mother and father in the late 1950s at the age of eight. Hunter remembers that lollies, a brown paper parcel of new clothes and the promise of visiting the circus had enticed her and her brothers and sister into a big black car. They were taken to the Seaforth Children's home in South Australia and she never saw her mother again (Brady 1998). Further west, Nyoongar artist Sandra Hill, whose work was also included in the National Gallery of Australia's *Defying Empire* exhibition, has devoted much of her art practice to Aboriginal women's experiences of assimilation and forced domestic labour. Her mother's side of her family has four generations of stolen children taken by Western Australian welfare administrations, whose removal practices were particularly harsh. Hill was herself taken from her mother's care in 1958, along with her 3 siblings, and they were not reunited until 27 years later (Hylands 2003). In a radio documentary on Sister Kate's institution in suburban Perth, Hill put on record the story of her mother and aunt's abduction. She related how in 1933 the two young sisters were grabbed and thrown into the back of a black car. Locked in, they heard their mother, Mary, scream 'Give me back my babies! Give me back my babies! That was the last memory they had of their mother' (Huntley 2018, n.p.).

Senior Nyoongah woman Laurel Nannup, in her autobiographical book, *A Story to Tell* (2007), wrote in similar terms of the big black car that took her and her sister, when they were aged eight and six, from their family in the Aboriginal reserve at Pinjarra in the early 1950s. They were taken to the Pallotine Catholic Mission in Wandering, a cold section of the escarpment south of Perth. Her simple woodcut, *Leaving Home*, depicts two small girls viewed from behind and holding hands in front of a black car that looms above them. In the text, Nannup remembers 'a big black car pulling up and a white lady getting out. Then we were put into the car, sitting there crying for our mum ... We felt so alone and wanted to go home to Pinjarra' (Nannup

2007, 40–41). Brothers Lester and Paul Parfitt similarly recalled vivid memories of being stolen and brought to Wandering Mission when they were six and four years old. 'This big white truck pulled up and someone said, "Your parents don't want you anymore." … It's hard to describe the loneliness, the heartache' (Laurie 2017). Seventy years on, the brothers spoke of the abuse and cruelty of the nuns and priests towards the children, made public for the first time in testimony given at the Royal Commission into Institutional Responses to Child Sexual Abuse.[4] Historian Anna Haebich (2000, 342) summarised the ubiquity of such 'heart-wrenching moments' in stolen generation testimony when 'the children are suddenly torn away from their families. Bundled into an official black car, they were driven off in a cloud of dust, their anguished faces peering out helplessly as their wailing mothers disappeared from view'.

Documenting a sovereign return

Reko Rennie's beloved Nan, Julia Murray, was taken from her family in 1912, when she was about nine years of age. She had been born underneath a tree beside the Namoi river near Walgett in western NSW (Biggabilla n.d.). There had been fierce struggles over those north-western grasslands of NSW. By the 1830s, settlers had violently seized the floodplains along the northern rivers, and their sheep and cattle thrived on the rich grasslands that had been created by thousands of years of Indigenous land care. Mortality among Kamilaroi people was high, and survivors were reduced to living in reserves, surrounded by pastoral leases. The second half of the nineteenth century saw a system that Heather Goodall (2008, 34–38 and 66–85) characterised as 'dual occupancy', which allowed some 'fragile accommodation' for Aboriginal people to continue living on their own lands as essential workers for the pastoral industry and to maintain a degree of economic and cultural autonomy through their creative engagement with the new economy. The refuge afforded by those parcels of reserved land was brief, however. With closer settlement and the establishment of townships in the late nineteenth century, reserves were progressively revoked throughout the early decades of the twentieth century and the lands handed over to settlers. In 1915 and again in 1918, the NSW *Aborigines Act 1905* was amended to strengthen the Board's powers to remove children and control the movements of adults. Julia Murray was stolen by the NSW Aboriginal Protection Board's 'Kids' collectors' (Goodall 2008, 144) and placed in the nearby Angeldool Mission and Aboriginal School, which had been established in 1912, and never saw her parents again. At Angeldool, she was trained to be a domestic servant, 'enslaved' as her grandson termed it, to white families. Julia was subsequently apprenticed, as the Act euphemistically termed it, in several households under a scheme where she was to be paid sixpence per week, though, like most Aboriginal people at that time, she was unlikely to have ever seen her wages (Parliament of Australia 2006; Gray

2008; Thornton and Luker 2009; Haskins 2019). At 15, Julia was sent to the Dungalear pastoral station north-east of Walgett, where her younger brother also worked. The artist Biggibilla, Julia's son and Reko Rennie's father, stated that Julia and her brother worked on Dungalear station until 1954, when all the Indigenous workers walked off in protest (Biggibilla n.d.; Dowding and Wood 2014, 205).

Dungalear had been set up in the 1880s by the Campbell family who had themselves fled Scotland in the 1840s during the Highland clearances, when the clans were dispossessed by newcomers who brought large-scale sheep pastoralism to their lands (Carnegie 1979; Brady 1918, 973–976). By the twentieth century, the Campbells had become a leading pastoral family with their home in the wealthy Melbourne suburb of Toorak. A sale notice for Dungalear Station in 1924, when Julia and her brother worked there, recorded that the station was approximately 660 square kilometres and well-stocked with fine Merino sheep, cattle and horses. The station sold for 185,000 pounds or approximately 12 million Australian dollars in 2020 terms (Sydney Morning Herald 1924).[5] By the age of 42, then, Julia Murray had been forced to provide almost three decades of unfree labour to the pastoralists who had stolen her country and extracted huge profits from it. The many stories of immensely wealthy pastoralists who drove across their stations or attended church in luxury British cars while their Aboriginal workers were unpaid provoked Rennie to create his installation (National Gallery of Australia n.d.).

In documenting his drive from Melbourne to Walgett in a Rolls Royce that he had customised 'Blackfella way', his family snapshot fixed to the dashboard, Rennie has carefully inserted his Nan (and thereby himself) into an entirely re-visioned 'big black car' story. *OA_RR* documents a loving and tender reversal or re-visioning of the injustice, humiliation and trauma visited upon Julia in her capture and enslavement. The enigmatic title of his installation signals that public restitution. Based on his earlier work, the title may be variously interpreted as Original Aboriginal_Reko Rennie; or Original Aboriginal_Rolls Royce; or perhaps even, Order of Australia_Reko Rennie; or Original Aboriginal_Regina Rex. Whichever interpretation we choose, in all those possibilities Rennie asserts the originatory, First Nation, status of Aboriginal people, the Original Aboriginal Royalty of Australia (Australian Council for the Arts 2015). In an affirmation of Julia's humanity, indeed her regal rank, Rennie ceremonially returns her to their country. As a member of the grandchildren's generations, he returns *with* her (and, by extension, with *all* the children taken in those big black cars), retrospectively according to her the dignity that her sovereign status as a member of the Kamilaroi nation dictates. In *OA_RR*, this proudly auto-mobile Black man drives his beloved Nan, an Original Aboriginal monarch, in a resplendent Rolls Royce, the epitome of British aristocratic privilege, back to their country with pomp and style.

What does this document demand of its viewers?

At the conclusion of his journey, Rennie turns his car back to his Melbourne home leaving behind a newly created document, his giant sand inscription. That ephemeral document, rendered by contemporary mechanical means, references traditional Kamilaroi ceremonial ground designs created by hand. That final image of Rennie's installation might be productively viewed as a literal instantiation of what the Canadian First Nations (Dene) theorist, Glen Coulthard, terms 'grounded normativity' (2014, 13), or an ethical, land-connected practice based on the experiential knowledge of Indigenous law. In *Red Skin, White Masks: Rejecting the Cultural Politics of Recognition*, Coulthard drew on Frantz Fanon to theorise a 'resurgent politics of recognition' which, unlike Fanon's earlier formulation, is 'attentive to the subjective and structural composition of settler-colonial power' (2014, 24). A First Nations' politics of recognition, Coulthard insists, is radically different from the forms of recognition extended by settler institutions in that it rejects a unilinear vision of history as a succession of stages: it refuses to view Indigenous tradition as a relic that can be relegated to the past. Practices of grounded normativity constitute a radical response to the threat of annihilation in the face of settler-colonial power. They remake Indigenous identities and histories, and re-install Indigenous law through a cultural stance of self-recognition, which critically evaluates, reconstructs and creatively redeploys in the present, the traditional practices of particular peoples in specific places (2014, 48–49).

Considered in these terms, Rennie's artwork is much more than a moving family story told by a car-loving artist. *OA_RR* documents and archives a political and legal actuality of national import: that Julia Murray's sovereign status is founded in the past *and* obtains in the present. Julia's sovereign status is an abiding reality: performed, unceded and not a matter for debate or settler approval. Rennie's elaborate performance of self-recognition, which is simultaneously playful and deadly serious, exists in a different register from the affirmations of Aboriginal sovereignty now routine in setter institutions and social gatherings that declare their commitment to reconciliation or Indigenous recognition—in parliaments, arts festivals, political demonstrations, universities and galleries. Rennie is not simply making a familiar didactic point which, after years of repetition can all too often appear merely a matter of 'good form'. As Sarah Keenan (2014) and others have argued, actions such as the one that Rennie has performed are much more radical and unsettling in that they assert a contemporary Indigenous presence in opposition to and outside of colonial Australia. They arrest that familiarity and produce an 'elsewhere' to the settler-colonial state that serves to 'keep open the question of who and what constitutes "Australia" both now and in the future' (Keenan 2014, 180).

OA_RR is a material reality that directs a royal command to those who have viewed and been moved by it. We who have witnessed the process of documenting Julia Murray's sovereignty are left with that injunction in the final moments of the installation. As the car turns away from the sand sculpture, its headlights shine into the eyes of viewers, directly implicating us, who are now in the path of the car. We are asked to imagine Rennie's journey home. How do we look at, listen to, reflect on and understand this Indigenous documentation of contemporary political reality? Where do we stand in relation to it? What past does it archive? What future does it imagine and invite us to buy into? What is different now we have encountered this document? How might this reality shift the present, in which dominant conceptions of history, for all the goodwill expressed by settler allies, are unable to encompass Indigenous sovereignty as more than a symbolic gesture? Perhaps the power of *OA_RR* is that it leaves viewers uncertain of how to process the incommensurability of settler-colonial assumptions of sovereignty and this demonstration of the radical Indigenous 'elsewhere' of unceded sovereignty. This quandary may be, as Lisa Slater (2018, 183) suggests, a much-needed place of giving-over to the other, or the 'unguarded, respectful non-comprehension' that can provide the space for ethical encounters across difference. This grandson's loving enactment and documentation of Indigenous sovereignty, grounded in the terror, pain and injustice of stolen generations and the intergenerational trauma it continues to produce, has drawn on contemporary reconstructions of traditional practices to demand a re-thinking and re-doing of settler-colonial relations of power.

Notes

1 Cars have also been a central focus of numerous Indigenous film productions or joint collaborations, such as the acclaimed *Bush Mechanics* series of 1998 and 2001, set in Yuendumu, west of Alice Springs, and directed by David Batty and Francis Jupurrula Kelly (Paul and Bolognese 2018) and the *Black As* web series, also directed by David Batty and set around the Arnhem Land township of Ramingining (Clarsen 2018); or in road movies such as *Beneath Clouds* (2002), directed by Ivan Sen, *Backroads* (1977) directed by Phillip Noyce and *Wrong Side of the Road* (1981) directed by Ned Lander.

2 Alice Springs filmmaker Warwick Thornton used a battered Toyota HiAce in his 2012 immersive installation, *Mother Courage*, for dOCUMENTA (13) in Kassell, Germany, and at the Australian Centre for the Moving Image in Melbourne. The installation projects film footage into the van of a travelling artist, who has set up shop far from her home, where she may be able to make contact with buyers for her art. She is painting in the Western Desert style, while her rather bored grandson looks on, sipping on a can of Coke and listening to Central Australian Media Association's (CAAMA) Green Bush radio programme (Browning 2013). The work evokes the economic and social disaster that the Northern Territory Intervention has wreaked on Indigenous lives.

3 Since the National Inquiry, the National Library of Australia has continued to record stolen generation testimonies, which continues to expand the archive of harrowing memories of being abducted in cars. See: http://www.stolengenerationstestimonies.com/.

4 In Darlene Johnson's documentary *Stolen Generations* (2000), Cleonie Quayle remembers the terror of being enticed into the back seat of big black car at age five. And who can't bring to mind the dramatisation of Doris Pilkington's mother and her aunts—Molly, Gracie and Daisy's—violent abduction in Phillip Noyce's *Follow the Rabbit Proof*

Fence (2002). See also Veronica Brodie's testimony to Ngarrindjeri women's experiences (Bell 2008, 52–54).

5 This estimate is based on the Reserve Bank of Australia's Pre-Decimal Inflation Calculator. See: https://www.rba.gov.au/calculator/annualPreDecimal.html (accessed 20 October 2020).

References

Alessi, Vincent, 2014. Wearing His Own Crown: The Work of Reko Rennie. *Art and Australia*, 52 (1), 112–9.

Anthony, Thalia, and Blagg, Harry, 2013. STOP in the Name of Who's Law? Driving and the Regulation of Contested Space in Central Australia. *Social & Legal Studies*, 22 (1), 43–66.

Anthony, Thalia, and Tranter, Kieran, 2019. Travelling Our Way or No Way! The Collision of Automobilities in Australian Northern Territory Judicial Narratives. *Griffith Law Review*, 27 (3), 281–306.

Australia Council for the Arts, 2015. *The Personal Structures of Reko Rennie*. Available from: https://www.australiacouncil.gov.au/arts-in-daily-life/artist-stories/the-personal-structures-of-reko-rennie/ [Accessed 20 October 2020].

Baum, Tina, ed., 2017. *Defying Empire: 3rd National Indigenous Art Triennial*. Canberra: National Gallery of Australia.

Bell, Diane, ed., for the Ngarrindjeri Nation, 2008. *Listen to Ngarrindjeri Women Speaking: Kungun Ngarrindjeri miminar Yunnan*. Melbourne: Spinifex Press.

Beresford, Quentin, 2006. *Rob Riley: An Aboriginal Leader's Quest for Justice*. Canberra: Aboriginal Studies Press.

Biddle, Jennifer, 2012. A Politics of Proximity: Tjanpi and Other Experimental Western Desert Art. *Studies in Material Thinking*, 8 (10), 1–15.

Biggibilla, n.d. *Our Songs. Our Dreamtime*. Available from: https://biggibilla.net/biggibilla [accessed 20 October 2020].

Boulter, Michael, 1993. *The Art of Utopia: A New Direction in Contemporary Aboriginal Art*. Sydney: Craftsman House.

Brady, Edwin J., 1918. *Australia Unlimited*. Melbourne: George Robertson.

Brady, Nicole, 1998. Misery that's relived every day. *The Age*, 26 May, p. 3.

Brook, Jack, and Kohen, James L., 1991. *The Parramatta Native Institution and the Black Town: A History*. Sydney: UNSW Press.

Browning, Daniel, 2013. Warwick Thornton's Mother Courage. *AWAYE, ABC Radio National*. Available from: https://www.abc.net.au/radionational/programs/awaye/warwick-thornton27s-mother-courage/4489060 [Accessed 30 October 2020].

Caisley, Olivia, 2018. *Armed with History*. Australian, 15 September, Review section, p. 3.

Carnegie, Margaret, 1979. *Campbell, John Archibald (1854–1916). Australian Dictionary of Biography*, National Centre of Biography, Australian National University. Available From: http://adb.anu.edu.au/biography/campbell-john-archibald-195/text9341 [Accessed 9 November 2020].

Clarsen, Georgine, 2015. Mobile Encounters: Bicycles, Motor Cars and Australian Settler Colonialism. *History Australia*, 12 (1), 165–85.

Clarsen, Georgine, 2017a. Revisiting "Driving While Black": Racialized Automobilities in a Settler Colonial Context. *Mobility in History*, 8 (1), 47–55.

Clarsen, Georgine, 2017b. "Australia – Drive It Like You Stole It": Automobility as a Medium of Communication in Settler Colonial Australia. *Mobilities*, 12 (4), 520–33.

Clarsen, Georgine, 2018. Black As: Performing Indigenous difference. *In*: David Butz and Nancy Cook, eds. *Mobilities, Mobility Justice and Social Justice*. New York: Routledge, 159–72.

Coulthard, Glen, 2014. *Red Skin, White Masks: Rejecting the Cultural Politics of Recognition*. Minneapolis: University of Minnesota Press.

Croft, Brenda L., 2001. Albert's Gift. *In*: Brenda L. Croft, ed. *Indigenous Art: Art Gallery of Western Australia*. Perth: Art Gallery of Western Australia, 76–92.

Cuthbertson, Debbie, 2017. The Long Road Home. *The Age*, 20 May.

Douglas, Blak, and Geczy, Adam, 2013/14. *BOMB, Blak Douglas and Adam Geczy*. Utrecht, Netherlands: Museum of Contemporary Aboriginal Art (AAMU).

Dreher, Tanja, and Mondal, Anshuman A., 2018a. From Voice to Response: Ethical Responsiveness and the Politics of Difference. *In*: Tanja Dreher and Anshuman A. Mondal, eds. *Ethical Responsiveness and the Politics of Difference*. Cham, Switzerland: Palgrave Macmillan, 1–19.

Dreher, Tanja, and Mondal, Anshuman, eds., 2018b. *Ethical Responsiveness and the Politics of Difference*. Cham, Switzerland: Palgrave Macmillan.

Frederick, Ursula, 2011. Roadworks: Automobility and Belonging in Aboriginal Art. *Humanities Research*, XVII (2), 81–107.

Gilroy, Paul, 2001. Driving While Black. *In*: Daniel Miller, ed. *Car Cultures*. New York: Berg, 81–104.

Goodall, Heather, 2008. *Invasion to Embassy: Land in Aboriginal Politics in New South Wales, 1770–1972*. Sydney: Sydney University Press.

Gray, Stephen, 2008. Holding the Government to Account: The "Stolen Wages" Issue, Fiduciary Duty and Trust Law. *Melbourne University Law Review*, 32 (1), 115–40.

Haebich, Anna, 2000. *Broken Circles: Fragmenting Indigenous Families 1800–2000*. Perth: Fremantle Press, Perth.

Haebich, Anna, and Delroy, Ann, 1999. *The Stolen Generations: Separation of Aboriginal Children from their Families in Western Australia*. Perth: Western Australian Museum.

Harvey, Jirra Lulla, 2013. Rekospective. *Artlink*, 33 (2), 78–81.

Haskins, Victoria, 2019. Domesticating Colonizers: Domesticity, Indigenous Domestic Labor, and the Modern Settler Colonial Nation. *The American Historical Review*, 124 (4), 1290–301.

Hermannsburg Potters Aboriginal Corporation, n.d. *Rona Rubjuntja Panangka*. Available from: https://hermannsburgpotters.com.au/artist/rona-rubuntja-panangka [Accessed 21 October 2020].

Human Rights and Equal Opportunity Commission, 1997. *Bringing Them Home: report of the National Inquiry into the Separation of Aboriginal and Torres Strait Islander Children from their Families*. Sydney: Human Rights and Equal Opportunity Commission.

Huntley, Rebecca, 2018. Sister Kate's: Whitewashing the Children. *ABC Radio, The History Listen*. Available from: https://www.abc.net.au/radionational/programs/the-history-listen/sister-kates/10003902 [Accessed 20 October 2020].

Hylands, Peter, 2003. Interview with Sandra Hill. *Creative-I (Singapore)*, April 2003, 32–39. Available from: https://issuu.com/creativecowboy/docs/creative-i_2013_issue04?e=4180016/1968107 [Accessed 20 October 2020].

Johnson, Vivien, Kean, John, Long, Jeremy, and Thorley, Peter, 2007. *Mutukayi: public conversation on motor cars and Papunya painting*. Canberra: National Museum of Australia, 2 December. Available from: https://www.nma.gov.au/audio/uncategorised/mutukayi-motor-cars-and-papunya-painting/transcripts/mutukayi-motor-cars-and-papunya-painting [accessed 20 October 2020].

Karskens, Grace, 2020. *People of the River: Lost Worlds of Early Australia*. Sydney: Allen and Unwin.

Keenan, Sarah, 2014. Moments of Decolonization: Indigenous Australia in the Here and Now. *Canadian Journal of Law & Society*, 29 (2), 163–80.

Laurie, Victoria, 2017. Cries and Whispers from Wandering Mission Finally Heard a Half-Century on. *Australian*, 13 May.

Lyon, Housemuseum, 2017. Reko Rennie's colossal artwork for Lyon Housemuseum. *Art Almanac*, 1 (February 2017). Available from: https://www.art-almanac.com.au/reko-rennies-colossal-artwork-for-lyon-housemuseum/ [Accessed 20 October 2020].

Murray, Tom, and Howes, Hilary, 2019. Douglas Grant and Rudolf Marcuse: Wartime Encounters at the Edge of Art. *History and Anthropology*, DOI: 10.1080/02757206.2019.1607730.

Nannup, Laurel, 2007. *A Story to Tell*. Perth: UWA Publishing.

National Gallery of Australia, 2017. OA_RR Reko Rennie / Defying Empire. Tom Broadhurst (dir.), *Long Walk Films*. Available from: https://vimeo.com/223088699 [Accessed 20 October 2020].

National Gallery of Australia, n.d. *Reko Rennie: Defying Empire*. Available from: https://nga.gov.au/defyingempire/artists.cfm?artistirn=39617 [Accessed 20 October 2020].

Paul, Mandy, and Bolognese, Michelangelo, eds., 2018. *Bush Mechanics: From Yuendumu to the World*. Adelaide: Wakefield Press.

Presley, Ryan, 2017. Reko Rennie. *In*: Tina Baum, ed. *Defying Empire: 3rd National Indigenous Art Triennial*. Canberra: National Gallery of Australia, 106.

Probyn, Fiona. 2005, An Ethics of Following and the No Road Film: Trackers, Followers and Fanatics. *Australian Humanities Review*, 37 (December). Available from: http://australianhumanitiesreview.org/2005/12/01/an-ethics-of-following-and-the-no-road-film-trackers-followers-and-fanatics/ [Accessed 20 October 2020].

Read, Peter, 1981. *The Stolen Generations: The Removal of Aboriginal Children in New South Wales, 1883 to 1969*. Available from: https://www.aboriginalaffairs.nsw.gov.au/media/website_pages/new-knowledge/completed-research-and-evaluation/Stolen_Generations.pdf [Accessed 20 October 2020].

Read, Peter, 2006. Shelley's Mistake: The Parramatta Native Institution and the Stolen Generations. *In*: Martin Crotty and David Roberts, eds. *Great Mistakes in Australian History*. Sydney: UNSW Press, 32–47.

Read, Peter, 2014. Reflecting on the Stolen Generations. *Indigenous Law Bulletin*, 8 (13), 3–6.

SASA Gallery, 2015. *Kapi Ungkupayi/He Gave Us Water*. Available from: www.unisa.edu.au/Documents/EASS/SASA%20Gallery/PDF/Kapi%20catalogue.pdf [Accessed 29 October 2020].

Schubert, Steven, 2017. Abandoned Cars in Central Australian Desert Turned Into "Ghostly" Works of Illuminated Art. *ABC News*. Available from: https://www.abc.net.au/news/2017-11-06/abandoned-cars-central-australia-desert-illuminated-art/9053734 [Accessed 20 October 2020].

Slater, Lisa, 2018. The Anti-Festival: Kimberley Aboriginal Cultural Politics and the Artful Business of Creating Spaces for Kardiya to Hear and Feel Across Difference. *In*: Tanja Dreher and Anshuman A. Mondal, eds. *Ethical Responsiveness and the Politics of Difference*. Cham, Switzerland: Palgrave Macmillan, 169–86.

State Library of NSW, 2011. *Carved Trees: Aboriginal Cultures of Western NSW*. Available from: https://www2.sl.nsw.gov.au/archive/events/exhibitions/2011/carved_trees/docs/3449_carved_trees_guide.pdf [Accessed 30 October 2020].

Sydney Morning Herald, 1924. Dungalear Station. *Sydney Morning Herald*, 16 October, p. 7. Available from: https://trove.nla.gov.au/newspaper/article/16163955?searchTerm=dungalear%20station [Accessed 20 October 2020].

Thornton, Margaret, and Luker, Trish, 2009. The Wages of Sin: Compensation for Indigenous Workers. *The University of New South Wales Law Journal*, 32 (3), 647–73.

Transcript of Proceedings, *Cubillo v Commonwealth* (Federal Court of Australia, O'Loughlin J, 1 March 1999) 136–7 (Lorna Cubillo).

Tranter, Kieran, and Anthony, Thalia, 2019. Race, Australian Colonialism and Technologies of Mobility in Kalgoorlie. *University of Western Australia Law Review*, 45 (2), 99–135.

Tucker, Margaret, 1977. *If Everyone Cared*. Sydney: Ure Smith.

Watson, Penny, ed., 2012. *Tjanpi Desert Weavers*. South Yarra, Melbourne: Macmillan Art Publishing.

Wood, Sharmila, and Dowding, Andrew, 2014. Marlbatharndu Wanggagu: Once Upon a Time in the West. *Form Gallery, Perth*. Available from: https://issuu.com/form-wa/docs/once_upon_a_time_in_the_west_-_cata [Accessed 29 October 2020].

Artworks

Batty, David, 2016/2019 (dir.). *Black As*. Web docudrama series. Rebel Films. Melbourne, Australia.

Batty, David, and Francis Jupurrula Kelly, 2001 (dirs.). *Bush Mechanics*. Television docudrama series. Warlpiri Media Association (PAW Media), Yuendumu, Australia.

Biggibilla, 1999. *911 Porsche Carrera Coupe*. Painted motor car. Approx. 4300 x1730x1320 mm. Stuttgart, Germany: Porsche Museum.

Butler, Roma, Ivy Laidlaw, Tjawina Roberts, and Jennifer Mitchell, 2015. *The Toyota*. Painted side-section of motor car. Approx. 4000 × 300mm. Collection not known.

Douglas, Blak, and Adam Geczy, 2013/14. *BOMB*, Painted motor car. Approx. 4500 × 1800 × 1500 mm. Collection not known.

Fielding, Robert, 2017. *Graveyards in between*. Photographic series. C-type prints on lustre paper. 80 × 120 cm. Sydney, NSW: Art Gallery of NSW.

Hookey, Gordon, 2005. *A Painting for the Underdawg*. Oil on canvas. 133x250 cm. Canberra, Australia: National Gallery of Australia.

Johnson, Darlene, 2000 (dir.). *Stolen Generations*. Documentary. 52 mins. SBS Television.

Kngwarreye, Lucky, 1996. *Hunting kangaroo*. Acrylic paint on canvas. Museum of Applied Arts and Sciences, 306 × 15 mm. Sydney, Australia: Museum of Applied Arts and Sciences.

Lander, Ned, 1981 (dir.). *Wrong Side of the Road*. Drama/Music. 79 mins. Australian Film Commission.

Nannup, Laurel, 2001. *Crying for our Mum*. Woodcut printed on paper in black ink. 580.6 × 580 mm. Canberra, Australia: National Gallery of Australia.

Nickolls, Trevor, 1998. *Family in Blue Holden*. Synthetic polymer paint on canvas. 121.5 × 152.5 cm. Canberra, Australia: National Gallery of Australia.

Noyce, Phillip, 1977 (dir.). *Backroads*. Drama. 61 mins. Backroads Productions.

Noyce, Phillip, 2002 (dir.). *Follow the Rabbit-Proof Fence*. Drama. 93 mins. Rumbalara Films.

Rennie, Reko, 2013. *Royal Flag*. 24 carat gold on aluminium. 47x180 x4cm, weight 46 kg. National Gallery of Australia.

Rennie, Reko, 2014. *Pastoralists=Squatters*. Painted 1954 International truck. Approx. 4000 × 1800 × 1500 mm. Collection not known.

Rennie, Reko, 2017. *OA_RR*. Three-channel video installation. Approx 9 mins. Canberra: Australia: National Gallery of Australia.

Rubjuntja, Rona Panangka, 2019. *Kwatja (water) in the Fink River*. Terracotta and underglazes. 320 × 400 mm. Sydney, Australia: Art Gallery of NSW.

Sen, Ivan, 2002 (dir.). *Beneath Clouds*. Romance/Drama. 90 mins. NSW Film Commission and the Australian Film Finance Corporation.

Thornton, Warwick, 2012. *Mother Courage*. Two-channel video installation with Toyota Hi-Ace van. Dimensions not known. Collection not known.

Tjakamarra, Michael Nelson, 1989. *BMW M3 Group A*. Painted motor car. Approx. 4500 × 1800 × 1500 mm. Munich, Germany: Art Car Collection, BMW Museum.

Tjanpi Desert Weavers, 2005. *Grass Toyota*. Raffia, grass, jute string, chicken wire and steel. 4000 × 2000 mm. Darwin, Australia: Museum and Art Gallery of the Northern Territory.

Chapter 17

Historio-graphic

Knowledge design methods for interpreting documents

Anne Burdick, Jacqueline Lorber-Kasunic and Kate Sweetapple

To enact his unique form of cultural critique, the Austrian media critic Karl Kraus manipulated the graphical arrangement of texts in his journal *Die Fackel* (1899–1936). Kraus was editor and publisher of *Die Fackel*, whose media criticism tracked the rise of fascism in Europe. Kraus worked closely with his printer on the graphic details of each page, such as page- and line-breaks, cross-column juxtaposition or 'empty' white space where text once sat, in order to enact his distinctive 'art of critique' through wordplay, comparative analysis or visible censorship. It is this rationale that drives a pair of contemporary projects in which visual design strategies are used to interpret two very different historical works. *Writing Rights* is a set of diagrams that investigate the formulation of *The Declaration of Rights of Man and the Citizen* (1789). The *Fackel Schimpwörterbuch* is an unconventional corpus dictionary that uses visual compositions to examine the role of context in the meaning of pejorative terms in *Die Fackel*. Each project is centred on a set of primary documents that are graphically configured to generate new knowledge, an example of what Johanna Drucker (2014a) has called visual epistemology. Neither *Writing Rights* nor the *Fackel Schimpfwörterbuch* uses written narrative, verbal argument or exegesis to make its interpretive claims; the content consists solely of primary texts that are spatially arranged and graphically encoded to elicit alternative meanings.

Together, the projects serve as concrete examples of how graphic action can serve as textual interpretation, the primary argument that we make in this chapter. Through close examination of each project, we will show how spatial visual affordances, such as proximity and scale, can be used to envision relationships across time or between ideas, how typographic style can serve as both cultural and legal reference and analytic encoding and how graphic 'deformance', in which texts are taken out of their original contexts and re-ordered or re-situated, can be used to reveal aspects of textual materials that may not be apparent in their original form (Samuels and McGann 1999). More than simply visualisations meant to explain what exists, these works will demonstrate the generative capacity of visual forms of knowledge production and

DOI: 10.4324/9781003247593-21

the research claims that can be made through the specialised practice of knowledge design (Drucker 2014b; Schnapp 2013; Knowledge Design Lab n.d.).

What draws us as knowledge design researchers to textual analysis is an opportunity to develop visualisation practices that are aligned with interpretive humanities research. And equally, to create visual forms that reveal more wholly the human experiences held within historical literary and legal records: the paradoxes, conflicts, inconsistencies, inferences, contingencies and silences.

Visual interpretation

Legal, literary and historical interpretation is typically created and communicated through writing. In general, text-based arguments put original documents in dialogue with other texts—opinions, theories, histories, rulings and the like—within carefully sequenced linear compositions. While there are disciplinary-specific theories of interpretation, such as reader-response for literature, or, say, originalism for the law, interpretive practices tend to share a common form: written text that appears in media such as books, journals or court documents.

Scholarship in the digital humanities has expanded the range of forms that textual interpretation can take to include visualisations and multimedia presentations (Burdick et al. 2012). Scholars looking to take advantage of the capacities of computers to handle large quantities of data have turned to analytical tools drawn from the sciences to elicit new modes of understanding (Jessop 2008; Burdick et al. 2012; Staley 2014). Quantitative methods for examining the content of documents include text mining, network analysis and geospatial visualisation. These forms of 'distant reading' allow researchers to identify macro-scaled patterns derived from both the content and metadata of a corpus of documents (Moretti 2013). As the name implies, distant reading differentiates itself from the more traditional form of literary interpretation called 'close reading', in which a critic seeks to identify meanings latent within an individual text through careful examination of the internal structures and word choices that comprise a document. In more general terms, close reading is used to refer to the scholarly practice of interpretation applied to not only literature and legal documents but to culture writ large, wherein events, objects and images are treated as 'texts' to be 'read' by a subjective expert such as a literary critic, cultural historian or legal scholar. Interpretation is a contingent and situated process which occurs between the reader and the text, and where meaning is newly produced at every encounter and 'is necessarily grounded in embodied individuals whose historical and cultural identities factor into the work' (Drucker 2012a, [3]).

Visualisations tend to be the way in which distant reading strategies are manifest, as exemplified by the title of one of the field's foundational texts, *Graphs, Maps, and Trees* by Franco Moretti (2007). Whether it is a network diagram or a word cloud, such displays provide an abstract representation of a large quantity of documents in a single image generated through techniques, software and code generally derived from quantitative analysis in scientific contexts. This alignment with empiricism is approached with scepticism by many digital humanities (DH) scholars who advocate for a more qualitative approach (Drucker 2012b). A key criticism is the transformation of a text into ostensibly objective 'data', rather than *capta*, or information captured with intentionality. Data and its need for disambiguation are seen as anathema to the ambiguity and subjectivity of humanist interpretation found in close reading (Drucker 2011).

Others have argued that the visualisations may provide merely analysis or description rather than interpretation, which occurs after the fact, and elsewhere, specifically in written texts (Jockers 2013; Rockwell and Sinclair 2016; Weingart n.d.). For example, in Lauren F. Klein's lengthy paper, 'The Image of Absence: Archival Silence, Data Visualization, and James Hemings', an excellent work of DH scholarship, only two network diagrams are used to discuss the presence and absence of slaves in the archive of Thomas Jefferson's letters; the article is predominantly text (Klein 2013). In 'There's a Toy in My Essay', Stefan Sinclair and Geoffrey Rockwell (2016) introduce the notion of interactive data visualisations within an otherwise static essay as a way to provide a reader with the support information necessary to decipher its methodological foundations. Both of these examples show how DH visualisations tend to be used as evidence, even by those scholars who are proponents of their value. They operate in support of a text-based argument, rather than as the substance of the argument itself. As Stephen Ramsay explains, most visualisations that focus on texts:

> are there to demonstrate the facts of the case – to prove to the reader that things cluster this way or that, that there are indeed more instances of this feature than of that feature. Relatively few of them are there to offer the open possibilities of interpretative insight.
>
> (Ramsay 2011, 8)

This chapter argues for a kind of close reading through graphic action, rather than writing, what we have previously called 'graphic criticism' (Lorber-Kasunic and Sweetapple 2018). We include case studies that demonstrate how an interpretive visualisation can be the substance of an argument itself. Significantly, neither case study uses a quantitative, distant reading approach. Instead, the scale and methods are a form of close reading constructed through a careful reworking of original documents using the techniques of graphic deformance and interpretive diagramming. These methods rely heavily on processes in which researchers reassemble a text to create an alternate conceptual model, allowing previously unrecognised textual relationships to emerge. More than simply visualisations, we argue that these works demonstrate the generative capacity of visual forms of knowledge production where 'reading possibilities [are] potentiated by structuring the text through multiple lines and pathways, levels and hierarchies of relations, and by fragmenting text blocks into relations that alter the linear presentation conventionally assumed' (Drucker 2013, 86).

The page is what defines the terms for the graphic action of *Writing Rights* and the *Fackel Schimpfwörterbuch*. The page is the site where knowledge has been constructed and shared for centuries, spanning time periods and media, as Bonnie Mak (2012, 3) reminds us in *How the Page Matters*, 'to matter is not only to be of importance, to signify, to mean, but also to claim a certain physical space, to have a particular presence, to be uniquely embodied'. In each project, the page defines the context within which moves are made meaningful, establishing edges to align with or work against, creating the ground out of which figures emerge. Within the confines of the page, all moves are relative, and a composition is created incrementally as each change alters the dynamic of the whole. Unlike a software-created data visualisation, the page designs for each project are bespoke interpretations, the result of the expertise of designers. As we will demonstrate, graphic and spatial strategies that are interpretive rely on contextual cues such that placement, for example, can be understood as semantically encoded action that is value-laden within the territories of the page (Meirelles 2019).

To call attention to the page as both a physical and conceptual space is to redress the widely held perception that written texts are not visually embodied. The common presentation of text and image as binaries, as being one or the other, has meant that text is predominantly analysed from a linguistic perspective, with little attention paid to the semantic agency of the visual and material. As Kendall, Portela and White (2013, 1) write, 'it is a peculiarity of literary and textual studies that the vast majority of critical thought is devoted to engaging with the meaning of the text as if it were not delivered by visual means'. However, it is a text's embodiment—whether through the early scratchings of a draft manuscript, the template of a word processor, the column inches of a newspaper or an artfully crafted page of poetry—that enables it to be read. The mediation includes not only the mechanics of physical interaction, how a reader comes to hold or view a text, but also how a text is apprehended by the reader. A text's visible and tangible aspects offer an interdependent set of cues that perform two main functions. First, at the level of the text, punctuation and layout conventions structure the writing through visual signals that include typographic style, size, weight, page furniture (numbers, headers and the like) and spatial organisation, such as indentation for paragraphs or page breaks for chapters. These elements are described by structuralist literary theorist Gérard Genette as 'paratext', which 'function to point the text in a particular direction' (Tomlins 2014, 7). It is Genette's theory of paratext that enables historian Christopher Tomlins to engage with the largely overlooked semantic potential of visual forms in legal history.

In the English language, punctuation can be seen as an aspect of writing as a technology, distinct from speech. The punctuation in use today has a varied history informed by theories of grammar, semantics and the relationship between writing and speech (Lupton 1988). Though seldom considered a form of page design, punctuation is evidence that the visual form of the written text is fundamentally different from the spoken word; indeed, a text's composition and reading are impossible without visible structuring. Second, these visual cues combine with a text's material qualities to position a document culturally, allowing a reader to recognise, at a glance, its genre, authority and evidentiary status. For example, one can distinguish a passport from a newspaper, or perhaps less obviously, a tabloid newspaper from a broadsheet, without reading a word of text. Through experience, one is able to recognise the visual conventions associated with each: proportions, paper choices, ratio of words to images, graphic style, insignia and so on. And while these physical attributes situate the words of a text in the material world, they also conceptually frame the reader's expectations of the text as a document. These graphic elements, writes Drucker (2009, 162), 'make an important contribution to the production of semantic meaning … and can and should be understood as integral to textuality'.

Deforming the text, diagramming the page

The design-led research methods of the knowledge designer are built upon an understanding of how graphic, spatial and material qualities are integral to the semantics of any text. Working from this premise, we not only acknowledge how such factors inform the meaning of existing documents, we design new documents attentive to how this design gives shape to both written structure and cultural and legal meaning. In this chapter, we combine both actions through the (re-)design of historical materials using graphic deformance and interpretive diagramming, bringing together theoretical frameworks from literary studies and visual communication design.

Deformance, coined by literary scholar Jerome McGann and poet Lisa Samuels (1999), has its origins in the Latin word 'deformare', meaning to put out of shape or disfigure (*Oxford English Dictionary* n.d.). Deformance describes the 'process of altering, disrupting, or re-organising a text in order to bring to the surface previously inaccessible or obscured qualities of a work' (Lorber-Kasunic and Sweetapple 2018). Such interventions might include reading a poem backwards, or isolating all of the nouns, to bring us to 'a critical position in which we can imagine things about the text that we did not and perhaps could not otherwise know' (Samuels and McGann 1999, 36). Yet deformance is rare, Samuels and McGann (1999, 6) assert, likely due to the perceived futility of altering the artefact: 'interpreters—even radical ones—do not commonly locate hermeneutic vitality in the documentary features of literary works'. Yet it is precisely the interplay between a text and its signifiers—its graphical, spatial and linguistic features—that give deformance, particularly graphic deformance as we define it, its 'hermeneutic vitality'.

If graphic deformance is about reconfiguring a text, then diagramming is about how its rearrangement works in the space of the page. Diagrams, spatially organised graphic forms that structure semantic relations, have a long history. Their roots can be traced back to early surveying and record-keeping practices in ancient Egypt (Friendly 2008). However, it was not until the late sixteenth and early seventeenth centuries with the 'rise of analytic geometry and coordinate systems, theories of errors of measurement and estimation, the birth of probability theory, and the beginnings of demographic statistics' (Friendly 2008, 4) that diagrammatic forms became prevalent. The surge of diagrammatic representations in the late Renaissance/early Enlightenment, for example, was so widespread that it is difficult to imagine disciplines as diverse as anatomy, astronomy and medicine without them. Influential figures such as Galileo Galilei and Athanasius Kircher were quick to understand the value and capacity of diagrammatic representation for 'intellectual inquiry' (Drucker 2014a, 67–68). Nowadays, diagrams are commonplace in popular media, business communications and academic papers alike. Indeed, diagrammatic forms, such as bar charts, scatterplots or timelines, have become naturalised; the histories of their production and use are elided by the familiarity wrought by their prevalence.

Graphic criticism that exploits diagramming as a mode of inquiry, rather than as the replication of everyday forms, relies upon an understanding of how spatialisation and graphic signification—those 'documentary qualities'—structure how textual material is read sequentially, relationally and culturally. Designers are trained in such visual techniques, which can inform a practice of 'diagrammatic writing', in which 'spatial relationships, visual style, and organizational logic are equal in semantic significance to word choice and sentence structure' (Burdick 2003, 102–103). One of the best examples of diagrammatic writing is Drucker's 2013 chapbook (a small size book or pamphlet) of the same title. The book is written to make the reader conscious of the back-and-forth between graphical gestures and textual connotations. Each sentence is written as if it were speaking from its unique position on the page while discussing the characteristics of its own materialisation, a performance that calls attention to the 'architectures of the page' (Mak 2012) in the construction of meanings. As the book progresses, the reader is made aware of the shifting relations unfolding on each page and how each compositional move—adding or deleting text, changing size, style or position, delineating regions (such as columns or headers)—changes the dynamics of the page's relations and hence the semantics of its visual-verbal composite.

The words that sit in isolation on the opening page of *Diagrammatic Writing* succinctly capture the key takeaway of the book: 'The first words placed define the space' (Drucker 2013, 1). Words, place and space can be understood as the mutually defining components of the page. Communication designers manipulate aspects of each in order to create what they call a page's 'visual hierarchy', the graphically constructed relations between its parts. A visual hierarchy emphasises certain features and subjugates others to signify importance. Visual hierarchy can also provide a set of navigational cues about how a reader might sequence their reading, such as moving from a macrostructure to microcontent, from highlight to support text, from designated start to finish. To be understood, the graphic signalling relies upon the page conventions of different genres, communities and languages. But when the page is approached as a site of inquiry, words, place and space are recoded on new conceptual terms, made meaningful against such conventions.

Visible contrast can also be used to signify qualities that are categorical rather than hierarchical, distinctions of kind rather than degree. Alliance or opposition can be encoded through visual similarities and differences, and through positionality. Larkin and Simon (1987, 66) ascribe spatial relations between components as explicitly diagrammatic. Drucker (2014a, 106) notes that Larkin and Simon were the first to identify how 'spatial features of diagrams are directly related to a concept of location, and that location performs certain functions. Locations exercise constraints and express values through relations'. The topography of the page can similarly be understood in relation to established norms for the regions assigned to specific categories of text, such as titles, footers, pull-quotes, captions or body text. Yet there is no fixed formula for creating coded distinctions amongst textual elements. Metaphorical and material differences such as those between margin and centre, figure and ground, signal and noise, are all relative. Determining the size, colour, density, shape and position of graphic and textual elements is a contextually specific act. For example, a dark colour is not necessarily distinctive when it sits amongst other dark colours. Likewise, a single tiny shape is not necessarily diminutive if it sits alone in a landscape of large shapes. Such straightforward perceptual-semiotic concepts are considered foundational in communication design education where designers learn that the page, like the diagram, is a field of relations.

The case studies that follow make use of graphic deformance and interpretive diagramming to generate knowledge. The designed pages are 'objects to think with' rather than representations of events or data (Bender and Marrinan 2010, 9). They are what Daston and Galison (1992, 85) describe in their landmark work on objectivity in the visualisation of science, as 'materials from which concepts are formed and to which they are applied'. To read them, one must conceptually 'work' the material, that is, one must rely on a spatial logic in which the entire surface of the page, including the white space, is never devoid of meaning.

Seeing new relations in *Writing Rights*

Writing Rights studies the process by which the *French Declaration of the Rights of Man and of the Citizen* was written in the northern summer of 1789. *Writing Rights* was created when two of this chapter's authors, Jacqueline Lorber-Kasunic and Kate Sweetapple, were Visiting Fellows at the Humanities+Design lab at Stanford University in 2014. H+D Lab Director Nicole Coleman was acutely aware of the role design could play within DH research (Caviglia,

Coleman and Ciuccarelli 2012), as was Professor of History Dan Edelstein, for the team had previously developed the ground-breaking DH visualisation project *Mapping the Republic of Letters* (2009). In addition to Lorber-Kasunic and Sweetapple, the *Writing Rights* project brought in eighteenth-century Professor of Early Modern European History, Keith Baker. The team was interested in how design-led methods might provide alternate ways of looking at the historical and legal documents that led to the formulation of the Declaration. Primary materials were selected from the Archive Parlementaire (AP), a collection of letters, reports, speeches and first-hand accounts of the French Revolution that were initially gathered by government archivists in 1862. The AP is part of the *American and French Research on the Treasury of the French Language* or ARTFL project, a collaboration between the *Centre National de la Recherche Scientifique* and the University of Chicago. Established in 1981, it contains a broad range of French texts arranged chronologically.

The text of the Declaration contains a short Preamble and 17 Articles, the most well-known being Article 1: *Les hommes naissent et demeurent libres et égaux en droits. Les distinctions sociales ne peuvent être fondées que sur l'utilité commune.* ('Men are born and remain free and equal in rights. Social distinctions may be founded only upon the general good'). Considered a fundamental document of the French Revolution, the Declaration is widely referenced in the history of human and civil rights. However, as Baker (1994, 157) explains, it was 'an immensely complex document' to draft. It was 'drawn up with enormous difficulty and great urgency, at the cost of bitter argument, inevitable linguistic compromises, and dramatic theoretical tension, by an assembly profoundly divided over the nature and purpose of the text it was struggling to construct'. It was also the product of an enigmatic National Assembly. A disparate group of 1,200 men, whose composition consisted of

> deputies of the Third Estate who had declared themselves a National Assembly on 17 June, the liberal members of the privileged orders who voluntarily decided to join it before or after the date, and the more recalcitrant clerical and noble deputies who found themselves in this common assembly only on the King's orders.
>
> (Baker 1994, 171–172)

The 'radical uncertainty of its constitutional task' was further exacerbated by the National Assembly's general unpreparedness. It began with no agreed-upon organizational structure, procedural forms or established rules for deliberating or making decisions. The conditions were compounded by external pressures such as troops threatening to disperse the assembly and unrest in the provinces which added to the overall pandemonium (Baker 1994).

By mid-July 1789, there were as many as 48 drafts of the Declaration which varied in size and length. Some were single-authored such as those presented by Sieyés, Lafayette and Mournier while others were authored by a committee such as the one led by Mirabeau. With so much material, the *Writing Rights* team chose to focus their research on the debates that followed the selection of a draft by Assembly vote on 19 August. During this period, the Assembly went through the process of ratification with members proposing variations, from minor wordsmithing to the complete rewriting of articles. As Edelstein (2019, 183) explains, the Assembly 'chose the fairly undistinguished draft produced by a group of deputies from the Sixth Bureau (one of the thirty bureaus into which the Assembly had divided itself to facilitate discussion)'. However, its innocuous length did not prevent it from 'undergo[ing] drastic changes over the following week, with only the last five articles (20-24) finding their way into the Declaration (as articles 12-16)' (Edelstein 2019, 183).

To draw out the Declaration's chaotic process, the research project had two objectives. For the historians, the collaboration was an opportunity to re-examine the process of writing the Declaration using non-conventional methods. For the designers, it was an opportunity to test the capacity of graphic methods for generating new insights into well-known historical material. The project's focus was processual, meaning visualisation was used as an exploratory tool rather than an end point; experiments were more important than finished artefacts. It was unclear from the beginning as to what forms the experiments would take. The design research ultimately coalesced as two sets of 'Debate Diagrams' (DD), each of which explored a different aspect of the primary texts, both of which will be explored here. DD1 provides a descriptive visualisation of the way the text itself was transformed through the process of debate whereas DD2 makes qualitative assertions by diagramming the successes and failures of competing forces in shaping the Declaration.

Debate Diagram 1: descriptive visualisations

DD1 consisted of large format mappings, one for each article and the preamble, diagramming the discussion of many of the proposed alterations to the Sixth Bureau's draft. The visual system that structured the layout of each sheet was designed to identify individual 'speech acts', recorded assertions that were either spoken or written, as either a proposal, an amendment or a rebuttal. As shown in Figure 17.1, the components were arranged according to a consistent organisational logic: vertically, according to the sequence of the draft text, and horizontally from originals on the left moving toward the final text to the right. A vertical line divides the original texts from their alterations: *proposals*, *amendments* and *rebuttals*, placed from left to right in that order.

Figure 17.1 shows both details and the full-page image of Article VI. When seen as a whole, the page provides a sense of the rhythm and tone of the debate, which enabled the historians to see alignment (or not) between the original draft and the alterations, as well as their shared procedural qualities. In the detail, the speech acts identified as *proposals (1)*, which represented significant

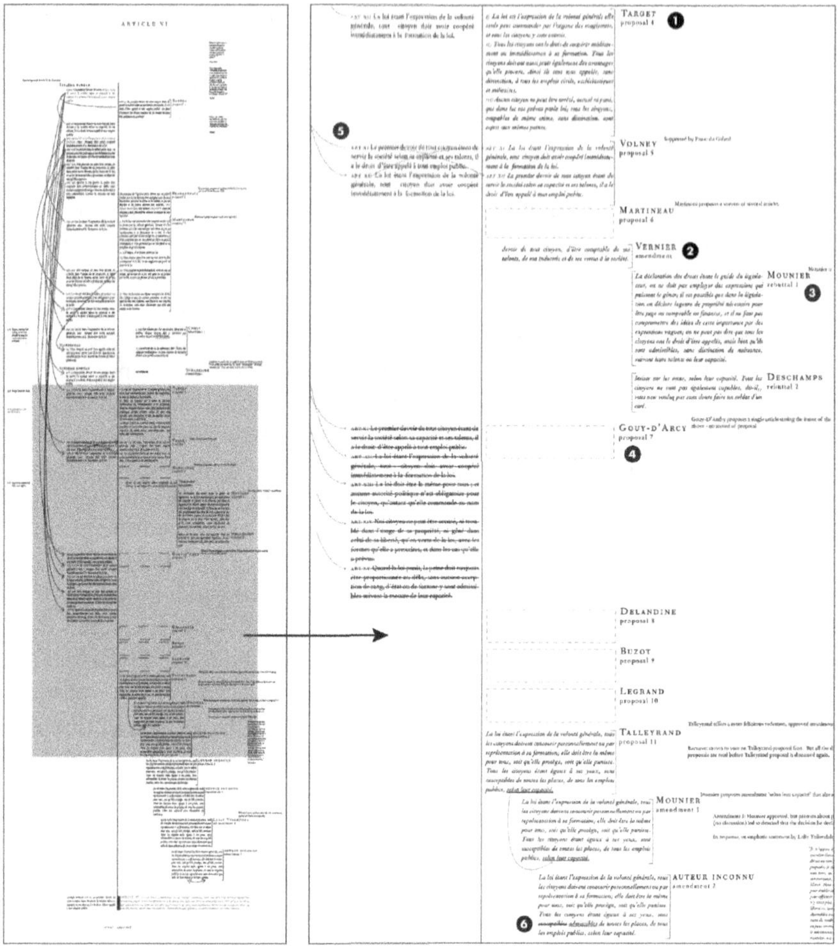

Figure 17.1 DDI Article VI full page plus detail. Jacqueline Lorber Kasunic and Kate Sweetapple (2018).

change, sit immediately to the right of the affiliated original text. *Amendments (2)*, which included revisions that alter how the idea was expressed, moved a short distance to the right. In keeping with the nature of a *rebuttal (3)*, such speech acts were represented by opposing brackets and the separation of the text from the main line of the debate, spatialising the ideological distance between the two speakers. The graphic encoding also included the use of empty boxes *(4)*, to signify source material whose presentation might have been recorded in the AP but whose actual text was missing. Elements such as arrows and lines *(5)* were used to connect alternative variations as a text was developed. Typographic style differentiated between speakers, speech acts and organisational texts, such as titles, while texts that were added were underlined and those that were deleted or replaced were struck out *(6)*.

Deforming the text, that is, graphically and spatially rearranging the debates, had four effects. First, it spatialised the debates, making apparent which articles were lengthy, or highly contested, and which were resolved quickly. Second, diagramming revealed the nature of the debate, whether it was focused on core ideas, say, or stylistic differences. Third, the arrows that track the lineage of the articles throughout the debate enabled the historians to keep track of where proposals came from. Very few articles were entirely new formulations. For instance, it became apparent that the political affiliations and court allegiances were not as clearly adhered to as originally thought. For example, Mounier, a member of the Third Estate, drew ideas or formulations originally proposed by a member of the Second Estate (clergy). Fourth, diagramming was able to graphically account for the absence of the data. That is, when there was a record of a member speaking to the assembly, but the content of the speech was no longer on record. Absences are often lost in the process of cleaning and modelling data in conventional visualisation processes. This is a significant concern for scholars whose source material is often incomplete (Klein 2013).

Isabel Meirelles (2019, 169) would label these diagrams 'descriptive visualisations', as they represent 'questions such as who, what, where and when?' She sees descriptive visualisations as valuable particularly in the early stages of research because of their capacity to reveal both the 'known and unknown features' of the source material. Meirelles points to the 'generative potential of descriptive representations' which enable us to arrive at 'new propositions and meanings' (2019, 170). This is certainly the case for the first set of diagrams which provided new ways of characterising the debates procedurally. In keeping with Meirelles' assertion, DD1 became the starting point for the interpretive work that followed.

Debate Diagram 2: argumentative visualisations

Using DD1, the historians were able to track the success or failure of the initial proposals, enabling new questions to arise such as: who were the originators of the key ideas evident in a ratified article? During the ratification process, what was the degree of contestation, or visible argumentation for each article? How close, or not, was each proposal to the version that was ratified? This last question drove the development of DD2, which showed only the proposals, organized in three columns—*close*, *successful* and *rejected*, from left to right—as an 'alternate conceptual model' for interpreting the events. As such, DD2 could be understood as what Meirelles would call an 'argumentative visualisation' in that it offers more than mere description (Meirelles 2019, 175). Indeed, the new configuration made it possible to compare the speech acts that went into each article according to the final outcome of the debates, revealing a set of relationships obscured by the chronology and conventional page structure of the parliamentary archive transcripts.

The tripartite categorisation of DD2 is the dominant structural feature of the page and performs the central task of this diagram: to visualise the composition of an article through the ultimate success or failure its proposals (Figure 17.2). Given that the highest value is accorded the texts that achieved ratification, the 'success' column sits, literally and metaphorically, in the centre column which is also wider than those for 'close' and 'rejected'. With larger type, the successful texts are given more space, while the smaller texts that reside on the margins are given secondary status, visually and conceptually. The speech acts are organized vertically in chronological order from top to bottom, making visible the sequence by which the final proposal was reached. A metaphorical relationship emerges between the material idea of alignment, which refers to physical arrangement of text on the page, and the concept of alliance, an example of how the spatial and graphic attributes of the page instantiate precisely constructed conceptual relationships, one of the key functions of an interpretive diagram.

Graphic coding adds further semantic detail to the diagrammatic structure of DD2. As with DD1, lines, strikeouts, typographic style, underlining and

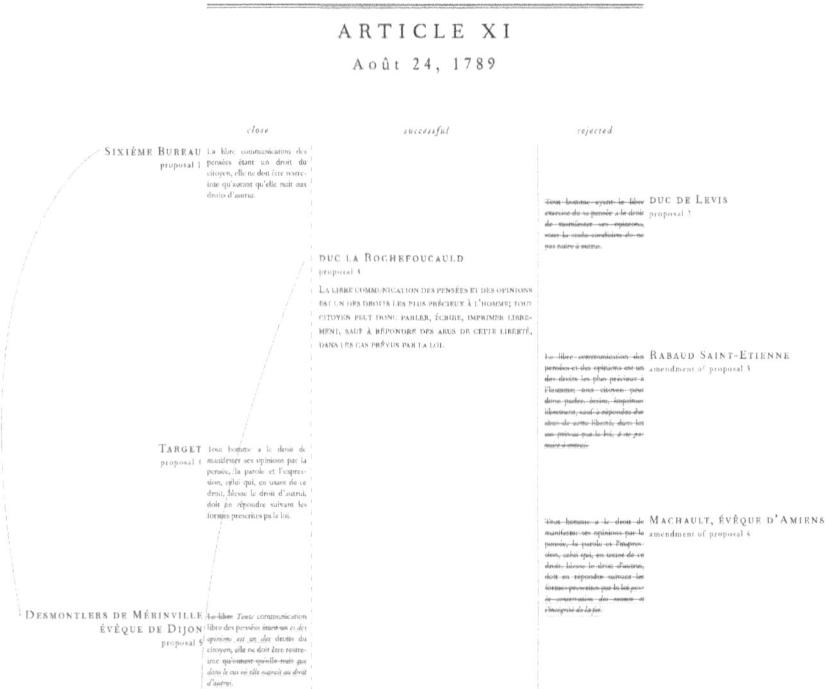

Figure 17.2 Detail of DD2 Article XI. Jacqueline Lorber Kasunic and Kate Sweetapple (2018).

the colour red are used to indicate the specific nature of the changes amongst the proposals. The graphic contrast between components is used to fine tune the visual hierarchy of the page's macrostructures, which has both operational and semantic effects. Distinguishing the textual alterations with graphic effects makes apparent how some articles were more vigorously contested at the level of single words and phrases. What Baker refers to as 'the wordsmithing' of the formulations may have done little to impact the intent of an article, and may be seen more as a desire to have the last word: in Article VI it was a reordering of words, from 'virtues and talents' to 'talents and virtues'. In other cases, the introduction of a phrase was more profound, such as the invocation of the 'supreme being' in the Preamble which did not appear at the beginning of the debate.

When viewed at a distance, each visualisation can be seen as a whole, the sum of a collection of discrete encoded moments, which allowed the researchers to step back and make comparisons between each article. For example, Article VI is the longest debate (spanning 2 full pages—with 11 proposals). Article XI, which refers to the right of any citizen to speak, write or publish freely within the bounds of the law, contains the highest number of rejected speech acts, whereas Article XIV, which foregrounds the need for a public tax, has just one rejection.

DD1 and DD2 offer an example of how the graphic and spatial reconfiguration of the primary materials created alternate interpretations and entry points into the debates. Through graphic deformance and interpretive diagramming, they created previously unseen qualitative relationships amongst the texts and provided non-linear and associative readings that opened new spaces of interpretation.

Making context visible in the *Fackel Schimpfwörterbuch*

Unlike *Writing Rights*, the *Fackel Schimpfwörterbuch* is a finished work, a text-dictionary that examines Kraus's use of disparaging language. The dictionary, whose corpus is *Die Fackel*, is part of a decades-long research initiative of the Commission for Non-Literary Text Types at the Austrian Academy of Sciences (OAW), a collaboration between one of this paper's authors, designer Anne Burdick, and literary scientists Evelyn Breiteneder and Hanno Biber, edited by Werner Welzig. Similar to *Writing Rights*, the *Fackel Schimpfwörterbuch* was the result of a small interdisciplinary research group. Where the Humanities + Design team's integration of design grew from the visualisations prominent in the digital humanities, the OAW team was ideologically aligned with Karl Kraus, who, as mentioned at the outset of this chapter, was highly attentive to the semantics of the printed page. The editors had concluded that conventional dictionary design was inadequate to address the typographic and spatial criticism of Kraus. They were keenly aware of the value of graphical manoeuvres as they adhered to what became known by the team as a 'Fackel' approach to the project; in other words, graphic and editorial gestures were always approached as being one-in-the-same.

Kraus was a key figure in Austrian intellectual history, and the research was built upon the digitisation of the complete collection of *Die Fackel* which was made publicly available in the early 2000s as the first instalment of the Austrian Academy Corpus (AAC), a database of nineteenth- and twentieth-century German language texts. The initiative also included the creation of a set of three text dictionaries, each of which examined the linguistic achievements of Kraus: a dictionary of idioms, a dictionary of pejorative terms and a dictionary of ideological themes. The first dictionary, the *Wörterbuch der Redensarten*, won numerous awards for both its design and lexicography, though its hybrid approach and visual-verbal interpretive strategies were quite controversial amongst linguistic and literary scholars. Similarly, the *Fackel Schimpfwörterbuch*, the second dictionary the team produced, took a highly unconventional form. In lieu of definitions and etymologies, entries were situated graphically in a range of distinct contexts as an interpretive strategy.

With the *Schimpfwörterbuch*, the editors concentrated on the way Kraus had manipulated language to achieve his derogatory effects, drawing upon thousands of examples from the complete publishing history of the journal. This was no small task: for Kraus, defamatory words were a means of satire and thus a way to deploy language in the service of political criticism. In 'Die neue Art des Schimpfens', roughly translated as 'the new art of criticism/disgrace/slamming', Kraus makes the distinction between words whose definition and tone are foul regardless of use or situation—words such as 'ass-face'—and those seemingly neutral words that, when placed precisely, offer scathing critique (Kraus 1911). The latter includes words such as artist, lawyer or historian, all three of which are included in the dictionary. This approach stands in contrast to standard lexicographic practice that attempts to clearly define all possible meanings of a dictionary entry.

The result of this exploration was the creation of a dictionary that uses the architectures of the page but also the web to provide 'concentric rings of context', enacted across a set of four distributed parts, three books and a website, as shown in Figure 17.3. The books include *Alpha*, which provides an alphabetical list of the dictionary's 2,367 words and phrases along with various indices. *Chrono* shows a chronologically sequenced subset of 555 entries provided with minimal context. Each entry in Alpha and Chrono includes a URL that points to a corresponding digital facsimile from *Die Fackel* within the AAC. *Explica* provides a demonstration of the editorial process through which the pejorative phrases were identified, cut out of their original context and re-situated within the dictionary's various sections.

The dictionary's organisation and displays operate as a form of visual-verbal, media-specific, linguistic analysis. The dictionary's 'content' is created entirely through highlighting, hiding, juxtaposing and re-contextualising the original

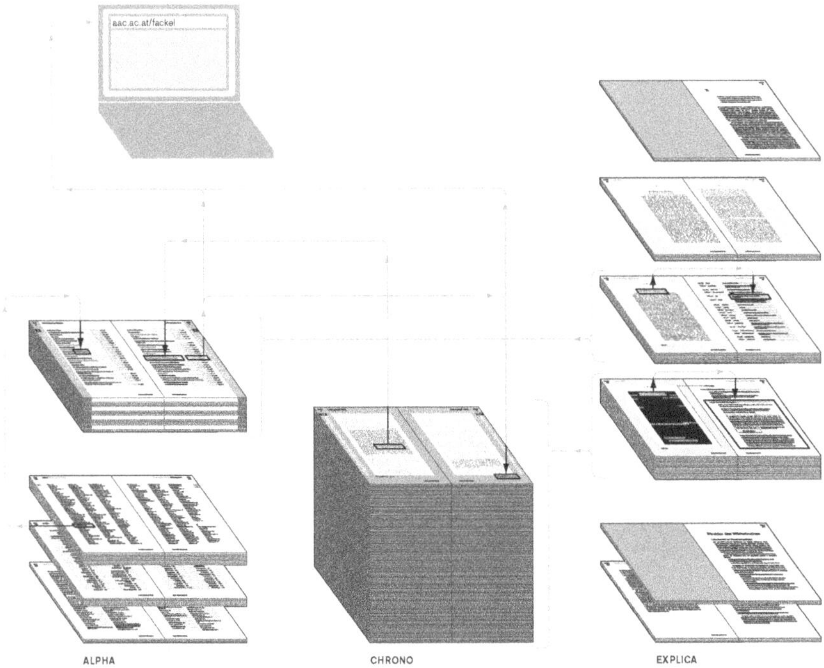

Figure 17.3 Diagram showing the connections between the book and web-based components of the *Fackel Schimpfwörterbuch*. Drawing by Anne Burdick (2003) made from pages of the *Fackel Schimpfwörterbuch*.

material in a variety of graphic-editorial compositions. The design makes visible the role of context in Kraus's 'art of disgrace' but also reveals the 'violence' inflicted on historical materials through the typically unseen processes of interpretation, an approach that allows for new linguistic, cultural and literary readings. The graphic deformance and interpretive diagramming rework the original material at the level of the word, the page, the journal and the discursive field, by placing its entries in different contexts, defined by the dictionary's design (Figure 17.4).

To demonstrate how a phrase is differently positioned across all components of the dictionary, we will examine a single entry, 'Zucht von Fortinbrassen', a reference to the triumph of Fortinbras (strong-in-arm) over Hamlet, that Kraus used pejoratively to allude to the rise of Nazism (Breitender 2020). On the full page of *Chrono* shown in the book on the left in Figure 17.4, the phrase appears in a printed facsimile of its original context—a page from *Die Fackel*. The phrase is printed in red, a graphic alert that calls attention to this first level in the visual hierarchy. Next, in black, is the entry's 'minimal context', a selection of text that the editors determined was the smallest portion of surrounding text

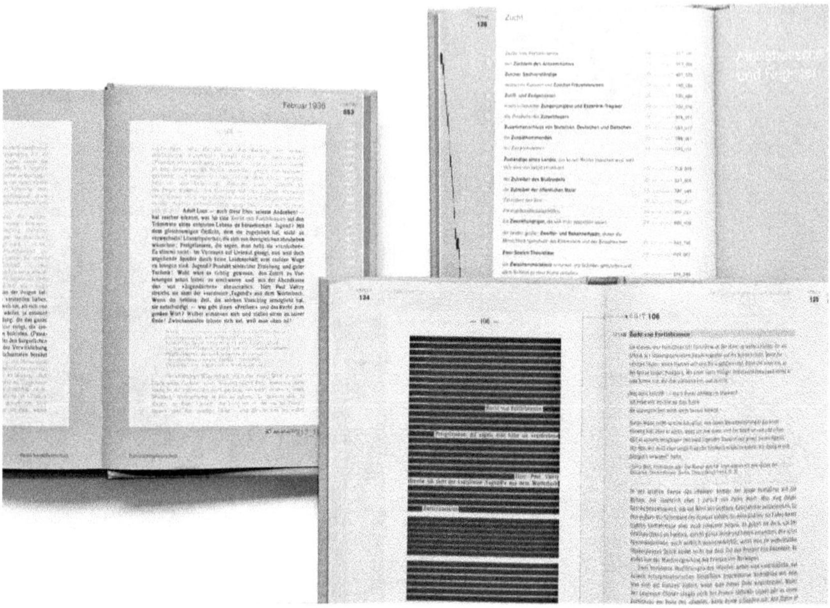

Figure 17.4 The entry 'Zucht von Fortinbrassen' as it appears in each of the three books that make up the *Fackel Schimpfwörterbuch*: (counter clockwise from upper right) *Alpha, Explica* and *Chrono.* Photography by Anne Burdick (2003).

required for a reader to make sense of Kraus's use of the term. The rest of the facsimile's page, including the remaining text and page number, is reprinted in beige so that it recedes. It is present and legible, but optional. The URL printed in the lower margin brings the reader to that specific page within the journal's digital archive. Once there, the reader can expand the context, moving from the page, to the complete article, to the contents of the issue, to all issues in that volume, all volumes in that year and finally, to the entire archive of *Die Fackel.*

All entries in *Chrono* similarly begin as page reprints, a form of 'visual-verbal quotation' used to 'maintain the materiality of the original source material' (Burdick 2003). The team first used this strategy in the *Fackel Worterbüch: Redensarten* to account for the fact that graphic treatment was integral to Kraus's media criticism. Kraus used diagrammatic writing techniques similar to those we saw in *Writing Rights*: spatialised texts in which positional relations have semantic impact, as well as empty space to represent erasure or silence. Such texts are inextricable from their material bodies. Thus, the 'content' that *Chrono* deforms is not simply text but entire pages of *Die Fackel.* Individual pages from the primary source material were captured, re-coloured and re-sequenced within the pages of a dictionary of pejorative terms. While the graphic-editorial gesture may appear to be a somewhat minimal intervention, it nonetheless offers an alternative conceptual model, an argumentative visualisation, a close reading of its selected texts.

Alpha's moves are more dramatic, and also more conventional. Figure 17.4 shows the last page of the alphabetical listing of entries within *Alpha* on the upper right. We see the entry, Zucht von Fortinbrassen, at the top of the page, a phrase amongst phrases that begin with the same letter and that have been identified as pejorative terms in *Die Fackel.* Most of the listings are printed in a black sans serif font, yet Zucht von Fortinbrassen and 554 others appear in a red serif typeface that matches the style in which they appear in *Chrono* in order to signify that they can be found there as well. *Alpha*'s list is not exhaustive, but it is representative of the depth and breadth of Kraus's satirical phrasings. The phrases are deformed as they are extracted and positioned within the context of the list.

Explica provides the supplementary texts that discuss how the dictionary works and the process of its creation. The entire book uses 'Wichtiges von Wichten', a significant essay from the final days of *Die Fackel*, as the source material for its demonstrations. In the first section, the essay appears intact, a sequence of facsimiles of each page of the entire essay. In the next section, the source material is reworked with graphic interventions that enact the editorial process of identifying pejorative terms. On left-hand pages, images of the original text are highlighted with beige bands that mark each word or phrase. On right-hand pages, the selected terms are placed within an alphabetical list. The juxtaposition represents the first interpretive steps: identifying texts *in situ*, then capturing and reordering them, *ex situ.* The section that follows, called 'Annotiertes Anmerkungen und Materialien' (roughly: 'annotated remarks and materials'), takes this one step further. As can be seen in the two-page spread on the bottom right of Figure 17.4, black bars strike out most of the text on the left, exposing only those words that made the final cut. Where redaction serves to protect privacy in legal contexts, here it can be seen as a kind of visual violence in which the fullness of the original source is denied to the reader—a single word or phrase is ripped from its context. On the right-hand page and beyond, each surviving phrase is put into a new, expanded, cultural context beyond *Die Fackel*: contemporaneous and historical texts in which the word or phrase has appeared. The editors do not include a written commentary, rather they simply present an arrangement of selected texts. The mix of texts illustrates how the phrase circulated within diverse contexts, from newspapers to literature, Goethe to the Bible, an evidentiary argument for the cultural significance of the selection and for Kraus's kaleidoscopic use of allusion in his writing.

The graphic lessons of *Explica* exemplify the critical awareness of context—graphically, culturally and linguistically—that Kraus brought to his satirical writing. It is this understanding of the power of positionality that similarly drives graphic deformance and interpretive diagramming as modes of inquiry and critique.

Conclusion

In this chapter, we have made a distinction between visualisations that serve as representations of information that is already known, and those that are performative, those that are 'knowledge generators capable of creating new information through their use' (Drucker 2014a, 65). As Drucker (2014a, 105) describes it, 'knowledge generators are graphical forms that operate relationally. They can be both static and dynamic but importantly, they support "combinatoric calculation" and allow components to be put together in multiple and often instructional ways'. In their use of word, place and space, this chapter's case studies make evident the capacity of the page as a site of interpretation through graphic action.

As such, the projects demonstrate the knowledge-generating capacity of showing, rather than telling. Each uses graphic deformance and interpretive diagramming to interrogate primary materials at very different stages in the research process. *Writing Rights* exemplified the use of visual methods in an exploratory phase in order to unpack and reconstruct, revealing previously unrecognised aspects of a collection of texts and an historical event, for scholars working within the archive. The *Fackel Schimpfwörterbuch*, on the other hand, demonstrates how critical graphic arrangement exploits the contingency of meaning as the editorial strategy for a reference work intended for an array of readers who are given what Ramsay (2011, 8) calls 'the intellectual latitude to see something new'. Although the methods have been put to use here in the context of historical and cultural interpretation, we assert that they are similarly applicable to 'law's documents' and invite further research in the context of legal scholarship and practice. Such work will demand an analogous collaborative process in which the selection and arrangement of texts are informed by diverse expertise to ensure that each graphic move generates nuanced understandings.

To this end, we conclude by drawing attention to how, in spite of growing interest in the scholarly potential of visualisation amongst humanities scholars (Jessop 2008), few have been attuned to the possible contributions of communication design to this area, with notable exceptions.[1] It is our hope that this chapter has made the case for the generative potential of graphic criticism, a form of close reading performed by knowledge design researchers with the capacity to surface the conflicts, inferences and silences—the human experiences—contained in our documents and archives.

Note

1 For more on the potential that design brings to the digital humanities, see (Burdick et al. 2012; McPherson 2018; Ruecker, Radzikowska and Sinclair 2016).

References

Baker, Keith M., 1994. The Idea of a Declaration of Rights. *In*: Dale Van Kley, ed. *The French Idea of Freedom: Origins of the Declaration of the Rights of Man and of the Citizen*. Stanford, CA: Stanford University Press, 154–96.

Bender, John, and Marrinan, Michael, 2010. *The Culture of Diagram*. Stanford, CA: Stanford University Press.

Breiteneder, Evelyn, 2020. *Email to Anne Burdick*. 3rd October.

Burdick, Anne, 2003. Design Writing. *In*: Brenda Laurel, ed. *Design Research: Methods and Perspectives*. Cambridge, MA: MIT Press, 101–8.

Burdick, Anne, Drucker, Johanna, Lunenfeld, Peter, Presner, Todd, and Schnapp, Jeffrey, 2012. *Digital_Humanities*. Cambridge, MA: MIT Press.

Caviglia, Giorgio, Ciuccarelli, Paolo, and Coleman, Nicole, 2012. Communication Design and Digital Humanities. Visualizations and Interfaces for Humanities Research. *Proceedings of the 4th International Forum of Design as a Process*.

Daston, Lorraine, and Galison, Peter, 1992. The Image of Objectivity. *Representations*, 40, 81–128.

Drucker, Johanna, 2009. *SpecLab: Digital Aesthetics and Projects in Speculative Computing*. Chicago, IL: University of Chicago Press.

Drucker, Johanna, 2011. Humanities Approaches to Graphical Display. *Digital Humanities Quarterly*, 005 (1).

Drucker, Johanna, 2012a. Representation and the Digital Environment: Essential Challenges for Humanists. *University of Minnesota Press Blog*. Available from: https://uminnpressblog.com/2012/05/16/representation-and-the-digital-environment-essential-challenges-for-humanists/ [Accessed: 27 August 2020].

Drucker, Johanna, 2012b. Humanistic Theory and Digital Scholarship. *In*: Matthew K. Gold, ed. *Debates in the Digital Humanities*. Minneapolis: University of Minnesota Press, 85–95.

Drucker, Johanna, 2013. *Diagrammatic writing*. Onomatopee, Eindhoven, Netherlands:Onomatopee Projects.

Drucker, Johanna, 2014a. *Graphesis: Visual Forms of Knowledge Production*. Cambridge, MA: Harvard University Press.

Drucker, Johanna, 2014b. Knowledge Design: A Conceptual and Curricular Challenge. *Design and Culture*, 6 (1), 65–83.

Edelstein, Dan, 2019. *On the Spirit of Rights*. Chicago, IL: The University of Chicago Press.

Friendly, Michael, 2008. A Brief History of Data Visualization. *In*: Chun-houh Chen, Wolfgang Härdle, and Antony Unwin, eds. *Handbook of Data Visualization*. Berlin, Heidelberg: Springer, 15–56.

Jessop, Martyn, 2008. Digital Visualization as a Scholarly Activity. *Literary and Linguistic Computing*, 23 (3), 281–93.

Jockers, Matthew L., 2013. *Macroanalysis: Digital Methods and Literary History*. Urbana, IL: University of Illinois Press.

Kendall, Judy, Portela, Manuel, and White, Glyn, 2013. Introducing Visual Text. *European Journal of English Studies*, 17 (1), 1–9.

Klein, Lauren F., 2013. The Image of Absence: Archival Silence, Data Visualization, and James Hemings. *American Literature*, 85 (4), 661–88.

Knowledge Design Lab, n.d. *What is Knowledge Design?*. Available from: http://knowledgedesignlab.com/?page_id=15 [Accessed 27 August 2020].

Kraus, Karl, 1911. Die neue Art des Schimpfens. *Die Fackel*, XIII (339/340), 51–6.

Larkin, Jill H., and Simon, Herbert A., 1987. Why a Diagram is (Sometimes) Worth Ten Thousand Words. *Cognitive Science*, 11 (1), 65–100.

Lorber-Kasunic, Jacqueline, and Sweetapple, Kate, 2018. Graphic Criticism and the Material Possibilities of Digital Texts. *Open Library of Humanities*, 4 (2), 1–33.

Lupton, Ellen, 1988. *Period Styles: A History of Punctuation*. New York: Cooper Union.

Mak, Bonnie, 2012. *How the Page Matters*. Toronto: University of Toronto Press.

McPherson, Tara, 2018. *Feminist in a Software Lab: Difference + Design*. Cambridge, MA and London, England: Harvard University Press.

Meirelles, Isabel, 2019: Visualizing Information. *In*: Julia Flanders and Fotis Jannidis, eds. *The Shape of Data in Digital Humanities Modeling Texts and Text-Based Resources*. Oxon and New York: Routledge.

Moretti, Franco, 2007. *Graphs, Maps, Trees: Abstract Models for Literary History*. London and New York: Verso.

Moretti, Franco, 2013. *Distant Reading*. London and New York: Verso.

Oxford English Dictionary, n.d. *Deform*, vol. 1. Available from: https://www-oed-com.ezproxy.lib.uts.edu.au/view/Entry/48971?rskey=QdeScB&result=3#eid#eid [Accessed: 5 October 2020].

Ramsay, Stephen, 2011. *Reading Machines: Toward an Algorithmic Criticism*. Urbana, IL: University of Illinois Press.

Rockwell, Geoffrey, and Sinclair, Stéfan, 2016. *Hermeneutica: Computer-Assisted Interpretation in the Humanities*. Cambridge, MA and London, England: MIT Press.

Ruecker, Stan, Radzikowska, Milena, and Sinclair, Stefan, 2016. *Visual Interface Design for Digital Cultural Heritage: A Guide to Rich-Prospect Browsing*. London and New York: Routledge.

Samuels, Lisa, and McGann, Jerome, 1999. Deformance and Interpretation. *New Literary History*, 30 (1), 25–56.

Schnapp, Jeffrey T., 2013. Knowledge Design. *Herrenhausen Lectures, Volkswagent Stiftung, Hannover, Germany*. Available from: http://jeffreyschnapp.com/wp-content/uploads/2011/06/HH_lectures_Schnapp_01.pdf [Accessed: 3 February 2019].

Staley, David J., 2014. *Computers, Visualization, and History: How New Technology Will Transform Our Understanding of the Past* (2nd ed.). Armonk, New York: M.E. Sharpe.

Tomlins, C., 2014. The Confessions of Nat Turner: A Paratextual Analysis. *Law and History*, 1 (1), 1–28.

Weingart, Scott B., n.d. Argument Clinic. *The Scottbot Irregular*. Available from: http://scottbot.net/argument-clinic/ [Accessed: 27 August 2020].

Chapter 18

Artistic license

Joan Kee interviews Carey Young

Since 2002, London-based visual artist Carey Young has developed a number of innovative, research-based bodies of artistic work which address law as subject and as artistic medium, and which have been exhibited in and collected by galleries and museums internationally. Joan Kee is a Detroit-based art historian and lawyer keenly interested in the insights artists bring to the theory, practice and envisioning of law through their works. For almost a decade, Young and Kee have been in regular dialogue, most recently concerning Young's 2017 work *Palais de Justice* for the journal *Law and Humanities*. On the occasion of the invitation to contribute to this publication, they conducted the interview via email.

Joan: Why law? Despite the extent to which contemporary art internalises some kind of law at almost every stage of creation, reception and circulation, artistic engagement with legal doctrines or approaches is not at all common. What keeps you interested in law as a subject?

Carey: In a broad sense, law intrigues me as a form of choreography relating to power. Law controls our movement, rights, autonomy and agency in the world, whilst also, in certain circumstances, preventing and removing those things. I imagine law in terms of lines, and that is a very visual thing, although law's linearity can be largely invisible, especially to those with privilege who are less constrained by these limits. As Catherine MacKinnon (2007, 39) said, 'The same people who have power in life have power in law'. So therefore, my interest is also to critique law as a form of power and violence, to try to work with our general desire for its protections even though it may oppress us, and to try and broaden the public understanding of law so that people may feel more able to critique it and engage with it themselves.

I started to work with law in 2001, having met a patent lawyer at Xerox's UK research centre, where I had set up an artist residency for myself. This piqued my interest in patents, which I saw as having an overlooked, if absurd, parallel with art and the commercial art gallery circuit, since patents can be

DOI: 10.4324/9781003247593-22

seen a framework for managing and commercialising creative output. Initially, it was IP that got me curious, but this soon expanded into an interest in contract law, then human rights, land law, outer space law, air law, law of the sea, advocacy skills and jurisprudence in general, all backed up by readings in critical legal theory. The more I discover about law the more deeply interested I get from an artistic perspective. I'd describe myself as somewhat feral in legal terms, since the legal fields that I've researched are particularly diverse. Unlike lawyers, I am the opposite of a specialist within one field, and not a jack of all trades either. I go deep into legal specialisms that interest me, but there is no pattern.

I spend considerable time in law libraries, especially in the early stages of developing a new artwork. I often approach the genesis of a project by starting with a theme in art which has been well worked by artists over a period of time. If we take landscape, for example, which has been a major artistic theme for hundreds of years, then that would naturally lead me to the land law section of a law library. I'd look at textbooks, legal theory on land law and its histories, reading examples of case law, looking at the language and learning methodologies, where appropriate, over a period of months. I might also try to speak with a specialist academic if I had specific questions or wanted research pointers. At some point, something from that legal research would connect with a specific artwork or artistic way of thinking about land, and this elision would create the

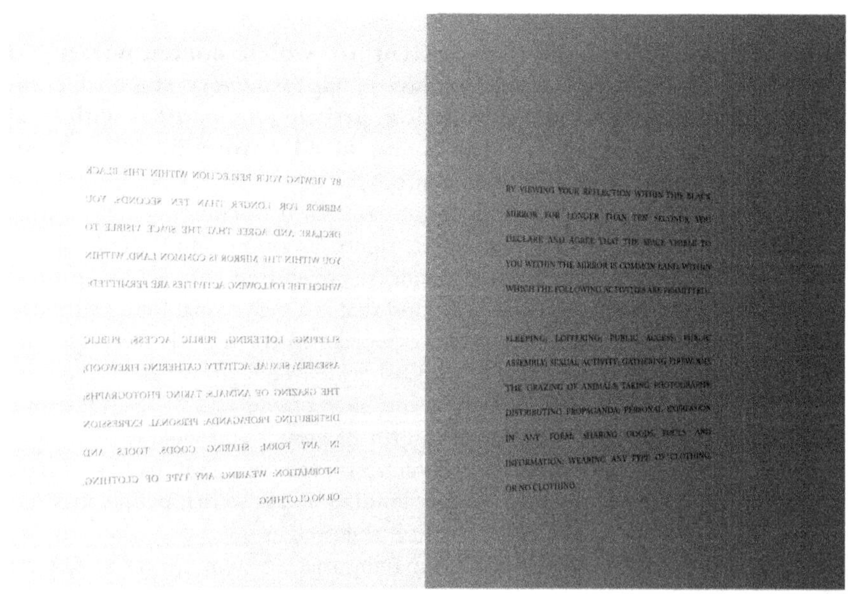

Figure 18.1 Carey Young *Obsidian Contract*, 2010 vinyl text and black mirror. Photo: Tim Bowditch. © Carey Young. Courtesy Copperfield Gallery, London, and Paula Cooper Gallery, New York.

spark of an idea for a piece. It is the fusion of art history and something specific from law—a case, an example, a document—that is the start. Often the aspects of art history I'm interested in have been ongoing concerns in my practice. With *Obsidian Contract* (2010), for example—a work which used a black mirror and a contract (written backwards, and only legible when read in the mirror)—I used a mix of contract law, research into the privatisation of land over the past 200 years, and art historical research into the use of black mirrors in art, from Claude Lorrain and the Romantic tradition onwards, which also had an origin in earlier Mesoamerican cultures, particularly pre-Columbian and Aztec, where they had been used within witchcraft and spiritual practices (Maillet 2004).

A further example is the exhibition *Consideration*, which was staged by the 2005 Performa Biennial of Visual Art Performance in New York, for which the starting point was an invitation to develop a performance-art based exhibition or project. I approached this by reading textbooks on contract law—a legal specialism which I imagined as a way of creating choreographic relationships, particularly those which concern choice. The task I set myself was to imagine ways in which I could develop contracts-as-artworks which could isolate particular moments of a visit to this particular art gallery. This included the experience of entering the show (the work *Artistic License*, 2005), the act of acquiring a work (*Donorcard*, 2005) or of considering a particular section of the gallery, and its prior history (*Declared Void*, 2005). This latter was an installation which made reference to an important sculptural work first exhibited in the same corner of the gallery, Sol LeWitt's *Incomplete Open Cubes* (1974) whilst also referring to human rights law, most specifically, contemporary examples of states of exception such as Guantánamo. It is usually a blend of legal theory, art theory and art history that create a kind of alchemical moment for me in terms of the generation of a work, as well as its resolution. Since then, I have created a whole body of work using contract law which comprises varied artistic media including video, photography, sculpture, installation and performance.

I've also spent years going into some depth with certain legal foci. For example, with space law (i.e. laws relating to outer space), a senior British lawyer—the UK expert in law relating to outer space—came on board as my advisor for a series of new works I was going to show at Paula Cooper Gallery in New York in 2010. Not only did she direct me to the key literature on outer space law (which I read, as well as educating myself about astrophysics via various degree-level textbooks) but she also shared various United Nations archival materials (the yearly meeting minutes of their Subcommittee on the Peaceful Uses of Outer Space, all of which I read), that ended up sparking an idea for a piece, *Report of the Legal Subcommittee* (2010). Beyond that, I became so fascinated by outer space law that I spent many weeks at the British Library going through obscure archival materials, as well as going deep into online, US-centric political material related to the commercialisation of outer space. In the end, after about 18 months or more of research, I was telling the lawyer things she didn't know. She ended up offering me a job at her law firm as a

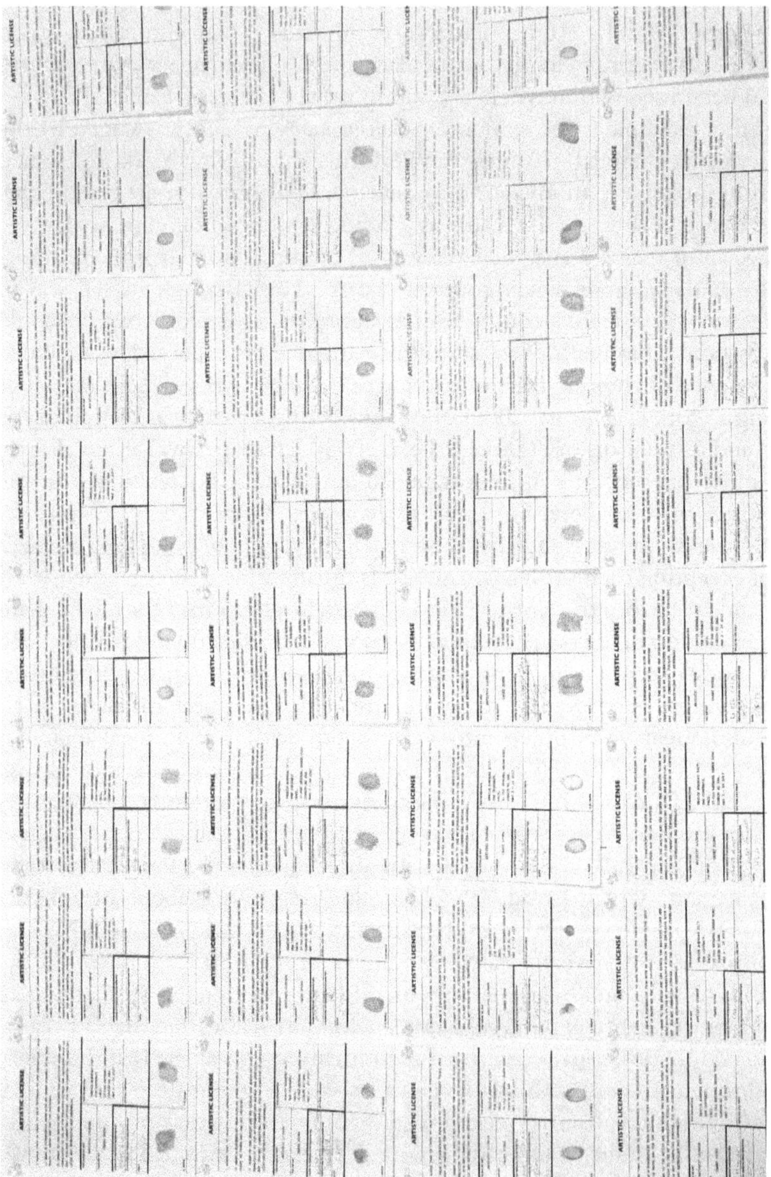

Figure 18.2 Carey Young *Artistic License* (detail), 2005 signed inkjet prints with fingerprinting ink, pins, table and chair, invigilator. Photo: Chelsey Browne. © Carey Young. Courtesy Paula Cooper Gallery, New York.

legal consultant on outer space law! I was flattered, but declined, as I needed to move on to other subject matter for another show—we artists can be such magpies—but it was an example that artists can develop deep expertise that has credibility in specialist fields. I'd like to underline that, as in my experience of conferences and other academic gatherings, legal and other academics tend to totally underestimate artists as researchers, let alone as thinkers.

Joan: You've observed how various forms of power are critiqued by artists, but not in a way that 'means anything to lawyers or those in power'. There have been artists, for example, who have used the language or form of the contract but without intending those agreements to have legal force. Yet you work closely with lawyers and do extensive research to ensure that your works adhere to the law. Do you think it is critical that your works be legally binding?

Carey: Yes, and this is hard to do. As bespoke legal instruments (which also take the form of a video, photograph, performance, etc.) the works are experimental and unusual. It's partly a kind of critical toughness with myself; in my view the work is better if it is credible to lawyers. This will give it a different kind of realism, a different engagement with 'the real'. Law is of course very abstract, and that abstraction interests me a great deal. The 'realism' of law, as I see it, is a connection with the body and with punishment, which often acts on

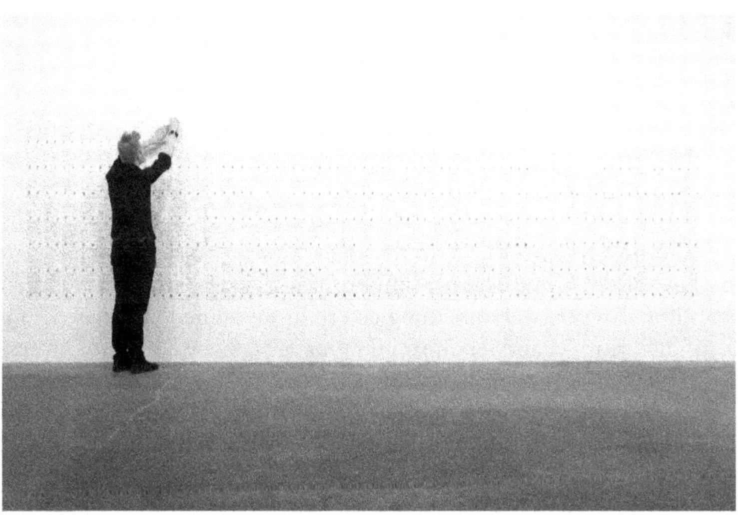

Figure 18.3 Carey Young *Artistic License* (detail), 2005 signed inkjet prints with fingerprinting ink, pins, table and chair, invigilator. Photo: Cameron Wittig. © Carey Young. Courtesy Midway Contemporary Art, Minneapolis, and Paula Cooper Gallery, New York.

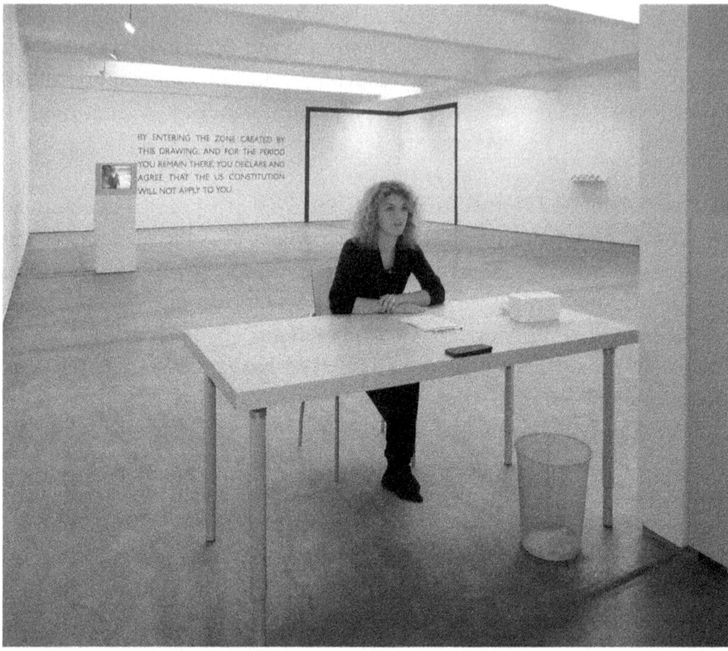

Figure 18.4 Carey Young *Artistic License* (detail), 2005 signed inkjet prints with fingerprinting ink, pins, table and chair, invigilator. © Carey Young. Courtesy Paula Cooper Gallery, New York.

the body, for example, to remove us from society (through incarceration), to remove our children, our finances, our property, our liberty—or to give access to those things. That kind of realism is about as real as things get for humanity, in terms of pain, or being able to operate in the world, or a sense of actually wishing to continue existing.

I like the idea of the work having a kind of uncanniness, that it may mean one thing to a non-lawyer, and something else to those trained in the law. This is not in terms of elitism, or hidden meanings, but in terms of a sense of professional subjectivity. Some lawyers have remarked that they could have worded my works differently. To me, this illustrates how law is often misinterpreted as being monolithic. Instead, as utterances of lawyers and judges, law is full of personal expression, and relies on all sorts of varied argumentation to take on its force. I don't care whether another lawyer would have worded my works differently, because it doesn't mean the wording I used is wrong (by definition, if a lawyer is prepared to use it in court then it is viable)—it means that law is often subjective. In essence, since many of my works are experimental in legal terms, they can be at the margins of what is legally acceptable or possible. Not

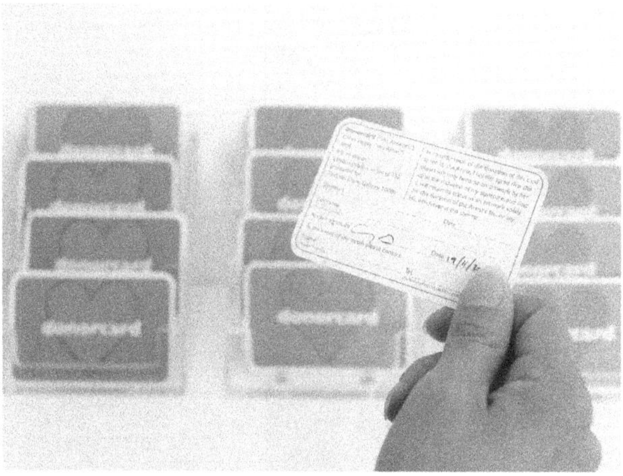

Figure 18.5 Carey Young *Donorcard* (detail 1), 2005 series of unique cards signed by the artist and to be signed by the viewer. © Carey Young. Courtesy Thomas Dane Gallery, London, and Paula Cooper Gallery, New York.

'following the rules' as such, but being at the edge of the rules. Or sometimes the performance or visual presentation of the legal text undercuts its seriousness, imbuing it with other meanings which open it out into other more emotional registers. I'm not interested in anarchy as such, but in the margins of law, the forgotten details, the rich strangeness of its language and bringing that into the public domain, for public examination and critique.

For example, in my photographic project *Redshift Series* (2010), a copyright clause was included within the title of the works, which will release copyright of the images in an innovative way, 'spreading' these rights across the world, 100 miles per year a certain date after my death, as if to slowly suggest the arc of a comet. In *Report of the Legal Subcommittee* (2010), a found text from the UN meeting minutes I mentioned above, documents the moment when a series of international UN delegations discuss the fact they have tried, and failed, over a period of 40 years, to come up with a legal definition of outer space. This is a very human moment, where humanity's attempts at managing, let alone understanding, outer space seems totally futile.

Joan: Along these lines, what has been the most challenging element of working with lawyers? Often histories of contemporary art or legal scholarship gloss over the process by which a work gets made. How do you begin to work with lawyers? Is it a lengthy process of conversation and exchange? Having been a lawyer, I know that working with a legal team is as much about managing personality fit as it is about precision—any

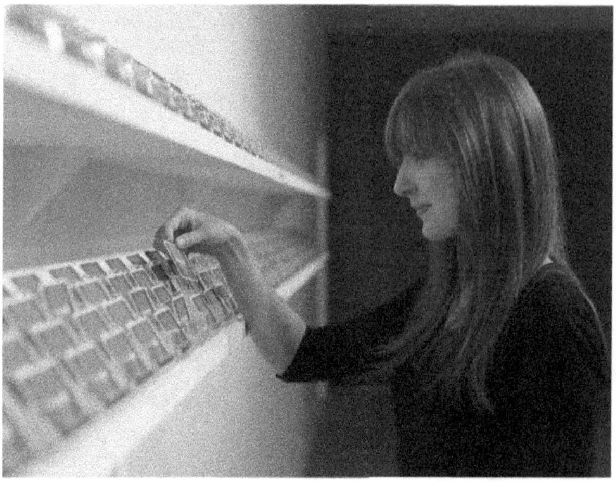

Figure 18.6 Carey Young *Donorcard*, 2005 series of unique cards signed by the artist and to be signed by the viewer. Photo: Rafael Goldchain. © Carey Young. Courtesy The Power Plant, Toronto, and Paula Cooper Gallery, New York.

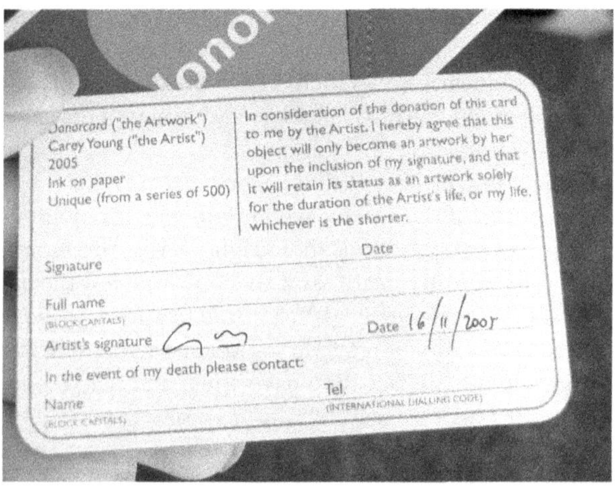

Figure 18.7 Carey Young *Donorcard* (detail 2), 2005 series of unique cards signed by the artist and to be signed by the viewer. © Carey Young. Courtesy Thomas Dane, London, and Paula Cooper Gallery, New York.

instances where personal subjectivity has shaped the working process?

Carey: It's exactly down to personality. Robert Lands, the lawyer I have worked with the most (since 2005) has stayed a long-term collaborator because he is creative, open-minded and informed about art. These are key qualities. Generosity is also important, as I will often do considerable work to hone the legal wording suggested by a lawyer-collaborator, and this needs time to discuss. Although working 'on the clock', they have to be willing to give extra time to get something right, and meeting in person has been essential, so things feel convivial—you can't really be playful over email. Repartee has been important. A clearness over roles too—Robert describes his input as 'drafting assistance' rather than anything artistic or conceptual: content, meaning, aesthetics and ideas is down to me. It should also be noted that 'drafting assistance' does not convey the considerable back and forth that goes in to agreeing on the legal wording for a work. I have also worked a lot with a legal researcher, an academic who has a background in legal, political and critical theory, philosophy and art history. He is a brilliant man and has been a key person acting as a further discussant. He knows so much about the histories of law. For example, he is an expert on artist commission contracts from the Renaissance period. I often need suggestions for my research—where to find examples, theory and cases that fit my ideas, so I can do further research. These collaborators have been perfect for giving me these leads.

Meeting my collaborators has taken time, and often serendipity is involved. In general, the right kind of lawyer will already be connected to art in some way. Perhaps they are an intellectual property advisor specialising in creative practice and/or advising artists and galleries. They might be on the board of an art gallery. They may have been recommended to me personally, or I have met them through a serendipitous crossing of professional paths, and sensed a possible shared set of interests. In general, my collaborators, of which there have been very few (I prefer to keep working with the same people) have playful, creative minds, are senior in their fields and are very open-minded. For example, working on something together will involve a lot of back and forth. I may ask for a particular draft legal text to accomplish a particular artistic task. The lawyer's initial draft may be very long—this was the case, for example, with *Declared Void*. I spend a lot of time wordsmithing edits to distil the text to a minimum, with each word having resonance and clarity. Since this is also a design task, because I need to make the text look good on the wall, for example, where every word will have impact on the way the piece manifests, the aim is to use concise, potent language. So much legal writing is extensively long and complex and I've discovered through this process that it is often possible to reduce it to a much briefer essence. Sometimes I have to cast aside my own favoured wordings because it doesn't have enough legal bearing, so the process of agreeing on a final wording—final also meaning that the lawyer involved would be prepared to defend it in court if necessary—has to be a joint one. Artists often don't like to have to cast aside their own ideas, so this can be difficult for me, although it's also interesting (one has to be very committed to the collaboration). I have always been very happy with the final result.

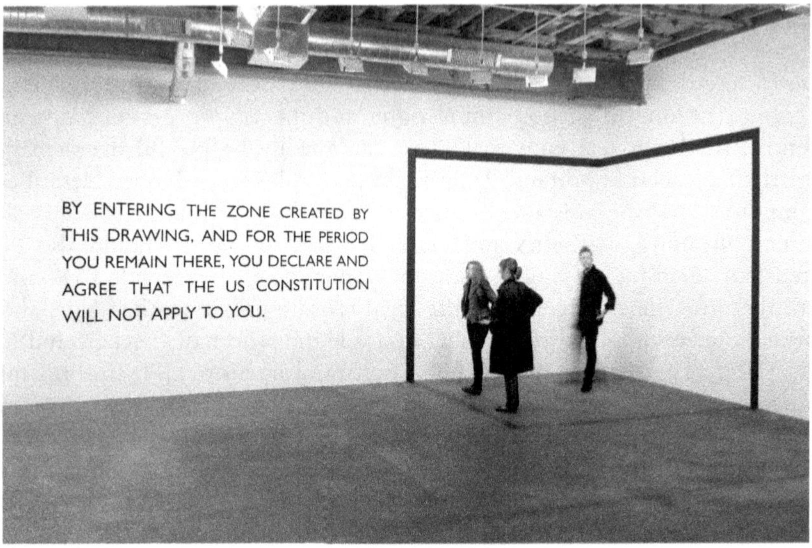

Figure 18.8 Carey Young *Declared Void*, 2005 vinyl drawing and text dimensions variable. Photo: Cameron Wittig. © Carey Young. Courtesy Midway Contemporary Art, Minneapolis, and Paula Cooper Gallery, New York.

Joan: There has been a small but growing body of legal scholarship discussing artworks as a lens for thinking differently about various branches of law. For example, artworks that problematise certain actions in ways that almost demand legal attention. Do you think art can or should affect how jurists approach cases?

Carey: The work of the group Forensic Architecture, based at Goldsmiths, University of London, and Lawrence Abu Hamdan, provide notable and innovative examples of the way artists can produce credible legal evidence through their artistic work. In the case of Forensic Architecture, their practice, which presents architectural evidence relating to buildings and urban environments, and investigates human rights violations, has been commissioned for, and used as advocacy and evidence in trials, tribunals, parliamentary inquiries, UN assemblies, citizens assemblies and truth commissions, as well as being exhibited at major art exhibitions such as Documenta (2017) or the Whitney Biennial (2019) (Forensic Architecture n.d.). Abu Hamdan, a sometime collaborator and former PhD student of Forensic Architecture's academic programme, works in a similar way. So here we have an example—admittedly unusual—of artists being approached before trial, to create forms of evidence through their own rigorous analytical, technological and artistic processes, with the resulting projects often exhibited as artistic works at the highest levels of the international art gallery circuit, as well as being used within a legal context. Moreover, according to Eyal Weizman, director of Forensic Architecture, the group's work seeks to point to 'longer histories of oppression and injustice'; working within the legal sphere allows them 'to show its intrinsic biases and the injustices contained in the law' (Strecker et al. 2019, 147).

Artists' capacity to understand, work with and challenge legal norms is radically underestimated within legal, and legal-academic spheres. Artists working with law—and I mean the ones who have a longstanding commitment to the field, including Jill Magid, Susan Schuppli and some notable others—have some deep understanding of law's problematics, even though they have not studied black letter law. This knowledge can be broad and about a whole field, but it's important input. I think there is a snobbery about this—as if anyone considering law has to have done the usual formal study. I don't think so. Or do they have to be a philosopher or a legal theorist? Look at their artistic work, and then tell me it isn't insightful. That is what legal academia has not yet done. They are missing a trick. Then this knowledge does not get brought into legal training in any way, even in the schools which have academics specifically devoted to law's intersections with aesthetics.

The field of criminology may be an interesting comparison, and the fact that photographers have done so many projects featuring prisons—this is a huge genre within documentary photography in particular. In my experience this work can be seen as useful and credible within the field of criminology, in that some of these photographic projects bring marginalised voices and experiences, as well as discussion of prison conditions, to the fore. Yet when we compare with legal academia, there is almost no knowledge of the growing number of important contemporary artists who are using law in their work. In my view, the gap is because with a few notable exceptions, such as Desmond Manderson—academics with a grounding or specialism in law tend not to know about or engage with contemporary art—their knowledge can be limited to pre-20th century Western art history. Contemporary art is then a form of 'unknown unknown'.

To answer your question from another perspective, we could consider Richard Sherwin's 'Visual Persuasion Project' at New York University Law School, an interdisciplinary course which helps law students develop their visual literacy in relation to law, in particular, how to 'think in images', how to produce visualisations of evidence and how to undertake what he terms 'visual advocacy'. In the digital era, when images and video evidence are increasingly used in court, it surprises me that these skills are not taught more widely. So here we are not talking about art as such, but more about developing a necessary understanding of how images can influence us, how they convey meaning, or issues of editing, authorship and a general critical ability to analyse visual meaning, which would profoundly affect—and benefit—how jurists approach cases.

Finally, from another standpoint, in certain courts, most particularly the Constitutional Court of South Africa, artwork has been commissioned and gifted to create an environment for court users in which art is a 'visual interface' for the law and for the judicial system. As such, visitors and court users are encouraged to reflect on the judicial process simply through being in the building and passing the artistic works, like a form of memory palace. Most of these works are not to my taste, but that's not the point I'm making. At this court, visitors and court users are encouraged by the court itself to think about the way jurists approach cases, because of the artworks on view. That's a forward-thinking approach to art's capacity to reflect on and address the judicial system.

Joan: Given that you teach at an art school, do you think law should be taught in art schools?

Carey: I think art students should be encouraged to have informed, omnivorous opinions about current affairs and to follow the news closely. To get outside their own field, and to expose themselves to wider issues. This should be supplemented by regular lectures from interdisciplinary academics and thinkers whose work abuts the art sphere. Art school is often much too hermetic, with visiting speakers often limited to other artists, art critics, art historians—thereby giving these young artists the feeling that art is a superior lens for viewing any subject—rather than that other disciplines have entirely different questions, histories, biases, motivations and uses. (In fact, I have noticed that academics from a surprising range of subjects seem to think their discipline is the privileged lens for viewing any other field, that any other field collapses into theirs—so perhaps the problem is a lack of cross-disciplinary teaching and thinking within the academy.) So, law should not be taught in art schools unless the students come to it in a curious way, as a source of power that is ripe for critique and analysis. Therefore, that probably means speeding quickly by the usual material on copyright and appropriation, which almost always kills artistic interest in the subject of law. That's been circulating around the work of artists such as Richard Prince (who is perhaps best known for using images created by others in his photographic works, without attribution) for far too long, mostly in US circles, and is much too hermetic.

I have started to offer a law-based seminar at the Slade School of Fine Art in London, where I teach fine art, and it's been striking to me that these sessions have consistently had many students attending. Indeed, it had started as a one-off event but due to student enthusiasm it became a series. These are students who are actively curious about law and who are already either working artistically with it in some way, or who are wanting to start. I also gave a week-long workshop at a Zurich art school recently which was similarly popular. I think there may be something in the air, a real hunger and curiosity about law amongst young artists. It's refreshing, and perhaps part of the activist, politically-motivated orientation of this exciting younger generation.

To answer your question in a different way, I think law should be taught in high schools and perhaps earlier than that. Kids know all about what's fair or unfair, and they know about power and its abuses. It would be very possible to teach some legal principles and skills in ways that feel relevant and engaging. For older kids, being taught to understand contracts and some basic legal terminology would be a very useful enabler for adult life. The art would just follow after that—art students would already realise how important and omnipresent the law is, and how engaged they need to be in order to speak back to power.

I also think that art should be taught in law schools in that the excellent contemporary art which uses and addresses law could be a wonderful springboard for pedagogical discussions around the ethics, political implications, limits and potential futures of law. But this step would mean that law schools need to hire academics who know some contemporary art history, better still if they follow contemporary art. This is a very, very rare occurrence at present.

Joan: If risk management is a recurring theme in contemporary art since at least the 1960s, have there been situations where you have faced actual or potential legal difficulty?

Carey: *Palais de Justice* (2017, 17 mins 58 secs) is a video artwork which I filmed at the eponymous Brussels courthouse, Belgium's main working court. My subject was the many female judges working in real trials, whom I filmed without permission, always shooting at a voyeuristic distance, through the circular windows in the courtroom doors, which I used as ocular or framing devices. The aim was, through careful shooting and editing, to evoke a functioning legal system in which the patriarchal order appears to have been reversed. I had sought permission to film from the President of the court, but this was denied to me, for reasons of 'terrorism'—a reason I could not take seriously, not least when there were usually many tourists in the building, with cameras not dissimilar to mine. The fact that this was one of the largest buildings in the world, and thus my minimal equipment was hardly likely to be in the way, gave me more of a 'brass neck'.

Nevertheless, there was always a risk that my subjects could bring suit against me: this was a judicial lion's den. Belgian law has tight privacy protections for individuals, and artists have no automatic right of free speech. I paid a local lawyer for advice, and she devised an argument that we could use in court, if the need arose, that anyone on the bench within a trial was revealing themselves in public, as a public figure, and therefore had no privacy right. This was a creative argument, not guaranteed to win, but it gave me confidence to continue, and since I did not include any defendants, or the faces of anyone not considered a 'public figure' according to the lawyer's rationale, I felt there was no ethical problem. Fortunately, there was not cause to test the argument within a trial situation, although it turned out to be very useful in terms of reassuring security guards and police in the Palais that I had an acceptable right to film, as otherwise, without filming permissions or a press pass, I would have been required to leave on almost every visit. This kind of accidental discovery totally enabled my project to take place and in the end, through using various 'guerilla film-making' strategies (minimal equipment and crew, shooting quickly in an inconspicuous way and making it look like I wasn't filming), I managed to film there over a period of two years, even without official permission.

When the piece was exhibited for the first time, the lawyer who advised me kindly worked out who all the judges and lawyers were, with a view to asking their permission for their footage to be used. This was no mean feat as over 7,000 lawyers and judges work at the Palais, and I had been unable to ask the judges for permission at the time of filming. Even then, this was a risk as the piece was already on show at the Dallas Museum of Art. The lawyer convinced me that it was worth seeking out the judges at this point, instead of them finding out via media coverage that had started to generate around the work. In the end, her careful handling led to all of them agreeing to support the project, and indeed some of them have come to meet me and have asked for prints and stills from the work as they were so pleased with the way I have represented them, as powerful female intellectuals at work.

Joan: How do you calculate risk? At what point does a potential work become too risky to undertake? It's a question many art students ask me in the U.S., which, as we both know, is litigation central.

Carey: I took a risk every time I went to Brussels, and every day that I shot. The project was self-funded, and I had no idea if each shooting day would be the last. But my strategy—of just winging it and dressing carefully downbeat, making it look like the camera wasn't rolling, or that I was waiting for someone—paid off. Being a woman helped, also; I don't think anybody expects a woman to be a film-maker, so it's good cover. My assistant made friends with the guards at the entrance, so that helped also. I chose my assistant because he had a background in parkour and had already climbed this vast building at night as a teenager. That was totally the right attitude for this project. In essence I knew this work had fantastic potential—there was always such wonderful material around so many corners, and at every visit I got great footage, so the risk/reward was absolutely worth it, even in the final stages where I was using paparazzi-length lenses to achieve extreme close-ups. This was high risk, as the lenses looked so intrusive. In general, it was a Werner Herzog-type approach. Earn the necessary money yourself, live and shoot on minimal means, be clever about how you gain access and feel no remorse, since your intention is to create poetic images. Ultimately, although creating a work full of criticality that is about the act of judging—including by the artist and viewer—my approach was incredibly positive towards the judges, and the Palais' indefinably enigmatic atmosphere.

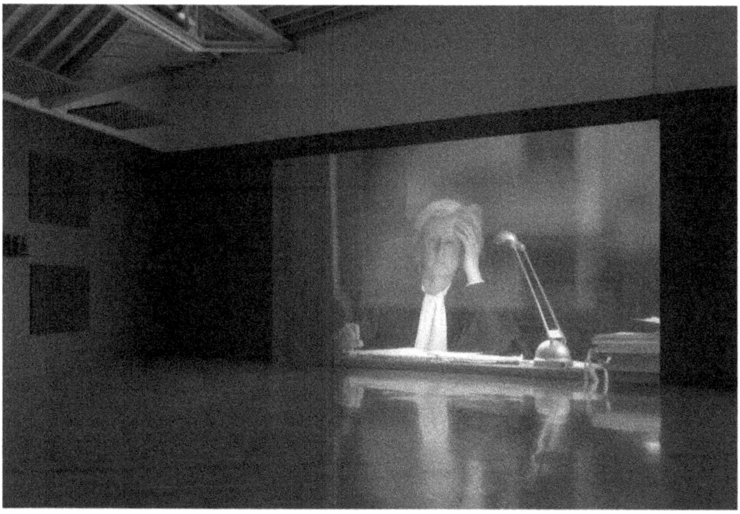

Figure 18.9 Carey Young *Palais de Justice*, 2017 single-channel HD video (from 4K); 16:9, colour, quadraphonic sound; 17 mins 58 secs. Photo: Steven Probert. © Carey Young. Courtesy Paula Cooper Gallery, New York.

Joan: While artists often regard the law as a codified body of regulation largely expressed through punishment or surveillance, I am struck by how your works emphasise non-institutionalised legal practices. An example is negotiation, which frequently surfaces in your work. How do interpersonal relationships figure in your work?

Carey: Negotiation skills featured in one piece, *Conflict Management* (2003), in which the services of a professional arbitrator are offered to the public for free for a period of one day, which they can use to solve disputes of any kind, including personal, professional and family-related issues. Arbitrators—also known as mediators—are conflict resolution specialists often used to avoid legal recourse, for example, in commercial situations in which conventional discussion processes have broken down, but in which agreement is considered vital. In the piece, the arbitrator offers their services from a stall in a city marketplace for the period of one day. I saw this as creating a 'temporary peace zone'—like a mirage. Signs next to the mediator's stall advertise the kinds of disputes they can assist with (personal, family and professional matters) and the piece is advertised in advance in local media, and sometimes on advertising hoardings (depending on the art institution's budget.) The piece has been commissioned by major art institutions in Budapest, Karlsruhe, Tirana, Taipei and San Francisco, and was so popular in Karlsruhe that the arbitrator told me she was considering renting a market stall in the future in order to continue to publicise her services.

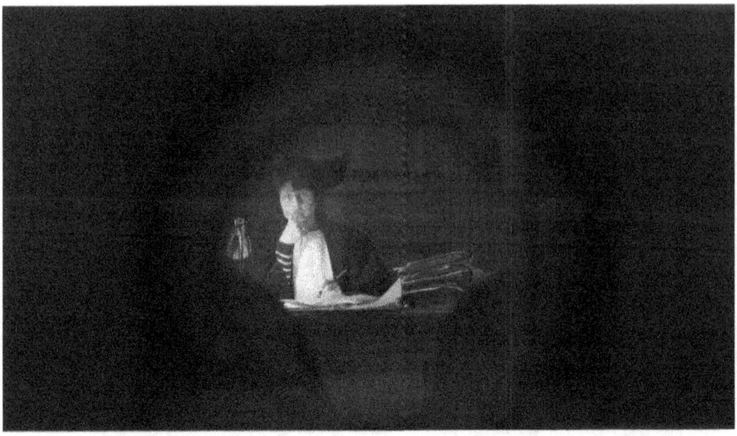

Figure 18.10 Carey Young *Palais de Justice* (still), 2017 single-channel HD video (from 4K); 16:9, colour, quadraphonic sound; 17 mins 58 secs. © Carey Young. Courtesy Paula Cooper Gallery, New York.

I did not choose conflict resolution as a theme and method due to its relation to law—I got interested in it whilst working for a political and economic think tank in London, where such methods must have arisen in conversation, sparking my interest. In terms of interpersonal relationships, the mediators all offered to continue to offer their services for free to people approaching them via the project. Thus, people could continue to use mediation until they had found resolution, so that the piece really could fully intervene to solve a problem.

My artistic interest was particularly in questions of dematerialised form—how could a piece come to operate and exist within human relationships? As such, the piece 'existed' in many ways, including within the lives and circumstances of those taking up the offer of mediation. A further example of this approach was my earlier work *Win-Win* (2002), which was an immense and highly-formal 'process piece' which took place at the Kunstverein in Munich—a gallery with a longstanding commitment to showing experimental art by young artists. The director and curator, Maria Lind, allowed me to stage this piece, which involved training the institution's staff in negotiation skills via a specialised trainer. The aim with negotiation skills is to create a mutually advantageous result, and therefore a balance, rather than giving more power to the institution. I specified that the piece then 'existed' whenever they used these skills in their professional work for the Kunstverein. Therefore, the piece was sited within the social architecture of the Kunstverein, including its relationships with artists, the media, the board, various political figures in Munich and beyond, as well as the public. The piece influenced the staging of shows by other artists, for example. Again, this work directly featured interpersonal relationships, although since then, my work has tended to use contracts to intervene in interpersonal relationships.

Joan: Another notable element of your work is your attention to form. I'm thinking here, for instance, of *Declared Void* or *Obsidian Contract*. Such attention seems intended to emphasise just how much law relies on aesthetics. What are some of your thoughts concerning the relationship of visual form to law?

Carey: I concur with the view that the field of law, including legal academia, has a tendency to see art and aesthetics, let alone images themselves, as frivolous or generally as something 'other'. I'm more interested in the idea that law was always already an aesthetic practice. As David Graeber (2015) puts it, law is a 'structure of the imagination'. If that isn't a provocation to artists working in any art form, what is? It's a surprising idea, and then it immediately sets law up as a series of aesthetic, sensory encounters within its domain of power. Once one thinks of it this way—and these aspects of law can be some of the most emotionally resonant and memorable, for good or bad reasons, whether we are in the dock, in prison, presiding over a trial, studying in law school or visiting a legal archive—then the doors are open for artistic methodologies. This is beyond the definition of 'art's law' as given by Costas Douzinas and Lynda Nead (1999, 11), as 'the representation of law, justice and other legal themes in art'—simply because the examples given within this genre—as developed by academics in the many law and aesthetics papers and conference streams that I have attended over the last 20 years—tend to stop in the late 19th century, whereas the art I am talking about is modern and contemporary.

When considering the overlaps between art and law, it is also important to put aside any notions that art pertains solely to 'images'. This is to remain uneducated to the fact that art takes so many forms, from the dematerialised practices familiar from the 1960s onwards, to video art, installation and many other media which address and utilise experiences and space, in galleries or beyond. One must also abandon any notion that contemporary artists seek beauty with their work. This very idea is an embarrassment within the field. Depending on their intent, artists may seek seduction, surprise, ambiguity, to make people laugh—and many combinations of these—I'd be doing artists a disservice by trying to sum up the many and varied intentions.

Artists can often feel alienated by law, not least as it regulates their access to and use of images and other materials they may otherwise wish to utilise freely. But when curious artists start to consider law's aesthetics, and therefore what there is to work with artistically in terms of referencing law within their work, they might think only of black fonts on a white page, the wood of courtroom walls or the appearance of judicial attire. Perhaps a statue of Justitia may make it on to that list, and some legal characters from TV or film. But that's a very thin set of options in terms of aesthetic starting points. But once one starts to engage and really think, the list gets far longer. In particular, in my experience it is essential to start visiting legal architecture or referencing the experience you or others may have had during such visits. The sounds, the smells, the legal documents one receives in advance of such a visit or finds on location; the architectural details and patinas. All these things are evidence of aesthetic decisions intended to convey a sense of law. Yet they vary so much. For example, Europe and America (but generally not the UK) has a broad spread of significant architectural commissions for recent, showcase court and penal architecture. There are few visual similarities across these designs, yet all of them are intended to convey ideas of modernity, access, openness, equality and progress in relation to legal process. Comparing these vocabularies is highly instructive in terms of gauging state commitment to and belief in the rule of law. The comparison can be done visually—and by determining what such architectural languages give in terms of expressing legal, political and ethical ideals. If law is a 'museum of order', as Foucault (1977) suggests, studying its architectures gives us some of its most potent aesthetic vocabularies. Law is 'etched in stone' as Pierre Schlag reminds us (2002, 1051).

Joan: Are there any legal scholars you read, or legal ideas that you're especially fascinated by?

Carey: There are many. Some of Peter Goodrich's texts have been important for my work, such as *Oedipus Lex*, which I first encountered early in my artistic engagement with law. That book was important in nourishing my curiosity in law and in helping me see wider links to the humanities, philosophy and history. His focus on the relations between law and psychoanalysis, images, law and the senses, law and love, has been consistently useful and inspiring. Equally important for my work has been Patricia J. Williams' *The Alchemy of Race and Rights*, which I first read in 2015 when filming *Palais de Justice*, which gives us so many examples of the ways in which law's structural biases interface with individual experience—something which reaches to the very core of my motivations to, and approach to shooting with this piece. The fact, for example, that law is taught using such dated examples, in which women are so stereotyped, just serves to reinforce societal and legal patriarchy at a wider level.

The language of both writers is exquisite, and that also inspires me. It's often phrases that are a starting point—I write them down and I have a long list from many authors including Foucault, Derrida, Judith Butler, Richard Sherwin, Des Manderson, Katherine Fischer Taylor. Catherine MacKinnon's feminist rage in relation to law has also helped articulate the power imbalances inherent to law and how they crush women's lives in many and varied ways. That also helped as background research for *Palais de Justice* and helps orient the piece when I give public talks about it.

Deleuze's *Masochism: Coldness and Cruelty and Venus in Furs* has been even more central to me. In particular, this quote: 'By scrupulously applying the law we are able to demonstrate its absurdity and provoke the very disorder that is intended to prevent or to conjure … By zealously embracing it, we may hope to partake of its pleasures' (1991, 88). Whilst Deleuze was writing of von Sacher Masoch's short story *Venus in Furs* in terms of the ways in which the protagonist uses legal contracts to derive pleasure, the quote feels resonant to my work, because throughout my artistic career, I have placed myself in what others may see as a complicit position, making work about that complicity, as an engaged, deeply informed insider rather than as someone fully outside an institution one seeks to criticise.

I would counter that criticism with the view that it is impossible to stand outside corporate networks and take a position as an outsider, so therefore why not go deeper inside in order to bring material out for public critique, such as within the realm of art galleries, and any ensuing discourse around such exhibitions, such as press coverage. From 1997–2002, I worked part time in an international IT management consultancy and made a large body of artistic work relating to corporate language and power using an insider's knowledge. I used my desk job as a research base for my artistic work, as well as giving me an identity which I played with within my work, as a way of discussing the ways in which art never seems free of the processes of commodification. With law, I took the same approach, first working in an IP advisory role for artists, then spending many years reading legal textbooks and archive material—therefore trying to give my work a richer research base, and more credibility within the legal sphere. The 'zealous embracing' is, quite probably, akin to masochism—there is a serious pleasure for me in finding source material deep within a legal archive or textbook, and in inhabiting legal language and working with and against its constraints. It's playful, inspiring and a lesser-trodden path.

Recently, I've been enjoying *Law is a White Dog* by Colin Dayan, *Material Witness* by Susan Schuppli and Bryonn Bain's *The Ugly Side of Beautiful: Rethinking Race and Prison in America.* I also often return to legal theory relating to legal fictions, which remains an animating idea in relation to my artistic practice.

Joan: The art and law intersection is heavily mediated by questions of visibility, e.g., how art makes law visible, or how law relies on text as opposed to visual art. I'm interested, however, in other sensory capacities—how does aurality and questions of sound factor into your thinking?

Carey: Aurality would not be the first quality one would think of in relation to my work, but for an example, I would suggest my video *Palais de Justice*. The soundtrack was composed from field recordings of the interior of the Palais de Justice—its marble-clad corridors and vast central hall atopped with a high cupola provide the kind of echo chamber which produces an intense sonic experience of legal process. Somehow, if one stands under the cupola, in the main *salle des pas perdus* (the giant 'hall of lost footsteps', as the French translation has it) one feels like one is hearing a choir of remote voices, discussing cases, whispering—with footsteps, jailers' keys jangling, the dull and distant thud of leather-panelled doors, carried over long distances by the endless stone-clad corridors. The resulting sonic effect, which is lofty and floating, but also has a terrible undertow of the effects of law on real lives, suggested to me an abstraction of law—so the soundtrack in this piece has an ethereal, floating character which matches the visuals, which are full of glassy reflections. Nevertheless, whilst we cannot hear specific dialogue or trial proceedings, the voices which carry most are male, which also seemed totally apt, given law's embedded patriarchal values. Whilst we see many female judges and lawyers on screen, the sound of the work is almost exclusively male. It has been described as like a 'remote male choir', a dialectic which seems to get to the heart of the work.

The work is installed with four speakers placed very high up, in what must already be a relatively cavernous gallery space, since the work is projected 7 metres wide. The effect of the speakers and the wide spread of these subtle and shifting layers of sound is to suggest the enormity of the Palais and its architecture, and the sense of the building as sublime (and thus of law as sublime)—which was in essence the original commission received by Joseph Polaert, the architect of the building.

I took a different approach to aurality with the video *Uncertain Contract* (2008), which features an actor performing select words from a commercial contract, as if he is undergoing an acting exercise to derive all possible interpretations of each term. Within an exhibition, which might be a solo or group show, the actor's voice occasionally rings out across the space, with his legal terminology—'contract', 'service' and 'parties' being a few examples—interrupting the experience of viewing other works, as if contractual language and thinking permeates every single moment and thread of meaning everywhere else.

Joan: Your works concern mostly laws in Anglo-American jurisdictions. Have you also considered engaging with laws outside this discursive landscape? Or, for that matter, with laws from earlier periods of time?

Carey: I've long wanted to do a work relating to Roman law, but this hasn't happened yet; it's brewing though. I'm quite interested in the artistic position that if one is going to make art about law, one should speak of jurisdictions that one is part of, as this is the one the artist knows and is part of, and to do otherwise might be unethical, superficial or offensive in other ways. My artwork *Palais de Justice* relates more to the Franco-Belgian than Anglo-American legal framework since there happen to be so many female judges working within Belgium. This is largely because the profession of judge in Belgium is more accessible to new and younger recruits; one can become a judge straight from college, and therefore access to the profession is considerably easier than, for example in the UK context, where various kinds of structural bias has meant many women left the profession before receiving the 'tap on the shoulder' at a later stage of their career.

Otherwise, I am always looking for other examples, including within the field of international law itself. Researching my work takes considerable time and I have other such examples at the research stage, although they have not been made yet. For example, to develop the themes in *Declared Void* into new works, I have researched the extra-legal for over ten years, and these examples often come through news coverage on an international basis. These might take me into more local legal frameworks, although I'd be wary of that for the aforementioned reasons. I'm always looking for lawyer collaborators though—and as such, if I was going to go down this path, I would need one based within the jurisdiction which I seek to engage with.

Joan: You have described law as an artistic medium. Could you elaborate on this? On one level, it suggests law as having its own materiality, something not generally discussed within the broad constellation of thinking known as legal scholarship. On another level, the idea of law as artistic medium reflects an intention to mediate between various strands of inquiry.

Carey: I devised the concept of law as an artistic medium in around 2003/4 and first wrote about this in 2005, as a kind of intellectual and art historical challenge which I set myself and others. What are its inherent properties as a medium for artists? And therefore: can it be moulded? The 'plasticity' of law—something to be shaped, smashed, formed—has a hopeful agenda in my eyes. If an artist such as myself, who has no formal legal training, can manipulate legal methods and reasoning in order to make it both more understandable to the public, and also something which can bend to her will, can it, by implication, be more accessible for everyone, less dominant, biased and alienating, and ultimately more fair?

To answer the question, what is law as an artistic medium, it is important to go beyond the aesthetic, material aspects—words on a page or whatever—and really deal with law as a set of immaterial agreements, offers, promises, relationships, etc. Therefore, I believe language has to be involved, whether performed or textual. The work needs to operate as a legal instrument, which is what I try to do, or legal tools, such as pieces of evidence for use in trials, which is what artists such as Forensic Architecture or Lawrence Abu Hamdan do. In my view, it is the credibility of these things as legal devices, and not the form which they take, which is important. The ultimate form of the work could be anything. In my case, artworks which are also legal instruments, and which use law as an artistic medium, have taken the form of installation, video, photographs, print and performance. To look at these pieces, you would not immediately know they are 'works of law' as such, they might look like pieces of performance art or whatever, but they also have this dual identity as 'works of law' that are credible to lawyers and have legal force.

Joan: Works like *Palais de Justice* and *Uncertain Contract* invoke the question of law and affect, something that hasn't been as extensively discussed as it should. I'm wondering if you might comment on this.

Carey: The study of emotions in relation to law is clearly important, since law undoubtedly deals with and in emotion. To ignore that may be yet another result of a sexist legal tradition that sees such concerns as 'feminine'. Art that deals with law inevitably also deals in the complex emotional territory around and of law in almost any form. Just to think about public alienation in response to law—this is a widespread emotional response to law. Art can help counteract such responses by reframing the debate and the subject of law into something more understandable, seductive, emotive or accessible, let alone profound or unforgettably poignant.

Joan: What kinds of legal research do you undertake?

Carey: It's varied. I visit legal libraries—most often, the law library at University College London. Internet research is vital, whether news stories from international newspapers, repositories of international law or legal journals. Conferences and events within law schools are often handy; my Honorary Fellowship in the Law School at Birkbeck has been consistently useful, as they have long been at the forefront of scholarship in Critical Legal Studies and London has had an active scene in terms of this field. Scholars such as Les Moran (Birkbeck) have been very kind in sending me papers they think I'd be interested in and hanging out with Birkbeck's law faculty has been a favourite activity. I often consult legal academic specialists in relation to specific projects, so in that case I would make specific approaches and invitations for that person to be an advisor on a project. I sometimes attend lectures at more conventional 'black letter' law schools such as University College London, or the University of Oxford. Twitter has proven useful for my research, since it's the social media tool of choice for law scholars, so it is often the way I find out about relevant events.

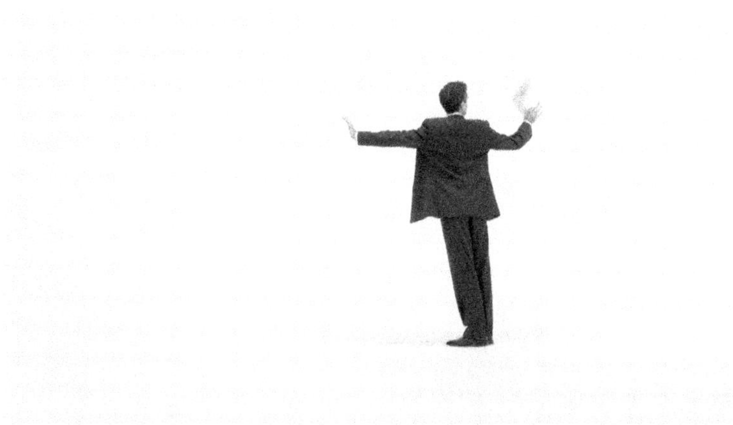

Figure 18.11 Carey Young *Uncertain Contract*, 2008 HD video, 14 minutes 57 seconds. © Carey Young. Courtesy Paula Cooper Gallery, New York.

References

Bain, Bryonn, 2012. *The Ugly Side of Beautiful: Rethinking Race and Prison in America*. Chicago: Third World Press.

Dayan, Colin, 2011. *The Law is a White Dog: How Legal Rituals Make and Unmake Persons*. Princeton, NJ: Princeton University Press.

Deleuze, Gilles, 1991. *Masochism: Coldness and Cruelty and Venus in Furs*. New York:Zone.

Douzinas, Costas, and Nead, Lynda, 1999. Introduction. *In*: Costas Douzinas and Lynda Nead, eds. *Law and the Image: The Authority of Art and the Aesthetics of Law*. London and Chicago, IL: University of Chicago Press.

Forensic Architecture, n.d. Forensic Architecture. Available from: https://forensic-architecture.org/ [Accessed 30 Jan 2021].

Foucault, Michel, 1977. *Discipline and Punish*. New York: Pantheon.

Graeber, David, 2015. *The Utopia of Rules: On Technology, Stupidity and the Secret Joys of Bureaucracy*. New York: Melville House.

Goodrich, Peter, 1995. *Oedipus Lex: Psychoanalysis, History, Law*. Berkeley and Los Angeles, CA: University of California Press.

MacKinnon, Catherine, 2007. *Women's Lives, Men's Laws*. Cambridge, MA: Belknap/Harvard University Press.

Maillet, Arnaud, 2004. *The Claude Glass: Use and Meaning of the Claude Glass in Western Art*. New York: Zone.

Schlag, Pierre, 2002. The Aesthetics of American Law. *Harvard Law Review*, 115, 1047–2364.

Strecker, Alexander, Weizman, Eyal, Varvia, Christina, Levidis, Stefanos, and Zembashi, Nicholas, 2019. Movement Towards the Light: Investigations in Athens – Interview with Forensic Architecture. *In*: Alexander Strecker, ed. *For Ever More Images?* Athens: Onassis Foundation.

Williams, Patricia J., 1992. *The Alchemy of Race and Rights*. Cambridge MA: Harvard University Press.

LeWitt, Sol, 1974. *Incomplete Open Cubes*. 122 Painted wooden structures and pencil on painted wooden base. Structures: 2 5/8 × 2 5/8 × 2 5/8 inches each. Base: 29 × 70 × 65 inches. The Met.

Young, Carey, 2002. *Win-Win*. Negotiation skills course, staff of the Kunstverein München, verbal interactions, ink on paper.

Young, Carey, 2003. *Conflict Management*. Professional arbitrator, table, chairs, two noticeboards, media advertising, members of the public. Commissioned by Museum Ludwig, Budapest.

Young, Carey, 2005a. *Artistic License*. Signed inkjet prints with fingerprinting ink, pins, table and chair, invigilator.

Young, Carey, 2005b. *Declared Void*. Vinyl drawing and text. Dimensions variable.

Young, Carey, 2005c. *Donorcard*. Ink on paper, signed with archival ink. 5.5 × 8.5 cm.

Young, Carey, 2008. *Uncertain Contract*. HD Video. 14 mins 57 secs (looped). Actor: Mark Oosterveen.

Young, Carey, 2010a. *Obsidian Contract*. Vinyl text and black mirror. Mirror: 69.9 × 54.6 cm; text: 24.8 × 19.1 cm; distance from text to wall: 7.5 cm.

Young, Carey, 2010b. *Redshift series*. Series of cameraless c-type photographs made using meteorite slices. 84.1 × 106.7 cm.

Young, Carey, 2010c. *Report of the Legal Subcommittee*. Inkjet print. 102.97 × 82.43 cm.

Young, Carey, 2017. *Palais de Justice*. Single-channel HD video (from 4K), 16:9, colour, quadraphonic sound. 17 min 58 secs, 17 mins 58 secs.

Index

www.ingramcontent.com/pod-product-compliance
Lightning Source LLC
LaVergne TN
LVHW021117300926
849160LV00010B/758
* 9 7 8 1 0 3 2 1 6 2 2 1 8 *